Lecture Notes in Computer Science 15751

Founding Editors

Gerhard Goos
Juris Hartmanis

Editorial Board Members

Elisa Bertino , *Purdue University, West Lafayette, IN, USA*
Wen Gao, *Peking University, Beijing, China*
Bernhard Steffen , *TU Dortmund University, Dortmund, Germany*
Moti Yung , *Columbia University, New York, NY, USA*

The series Lecture Notes in Computer Science (LNCS), including its subseries Lecture Notes in Artificial Intelligence (LNAI) and Lecture Notes in Bioinformatics (LNBI), has established itself as a medium for the publication of new developments in computer science and information technology research, teaching, and education.

LNCS enjoys close cooperation with the computer science R & D community, the series counts many renowned academics among its volume editors and paper authors, and collaborates with prestigious societies. Its mission is to serve this international community by providing an invaluable service, mainly focused on the publication of conference and workshop proceedings and postproceedings. LNCS commenced publication in 1973.

Christina Garman · Pedro Moreno-Sanchez
Editors

Financial Cryptography and Data Security

29th International Conference, FC 2025
Miyakojima, Japan, April 14–18, 2025
Revised Selected Papers, Part I

Editors
Christina Garman
Purdue University
West Lafayette, IN, USA

Pedro Moreno-Sanchez
IMDEA Software Institute
Pozuelo de Alarcón, Spain

ISSN 0302-9743   ISSN 1611-3349 (electronic)
Lecture Notes in Computer Science
ISBN 978-3-032-07023-4   ISBN 978-3-032-07024-1 (eBook)
https://doi.org/10.1007/978-3-032-07024-1

© International Financial Cryptography Association 2026

This work is subject to copyright. All rights are solely and exclusively licensed by the Publisher, whether the whole or part of the material is concerned, specifically the rights of translation, reprinting, reuse of illustrations, recitation, broadcasting, reproduction on microfilms or in any other physical way, and transmission or information storage and retrieval, electronic adaptation, computer software, or by similar or dissimilar methodology now known or hereafter developed.
The use of general descriptive names, registered names, trademarks, service marks, etc. in this publication does not imply, even in the absence of a specific statement, that such names are exempt from the relevant protective laws and regulations and therefore free for general use.
The publisher, the authors and the editors are safe to assume that the advice and information in this book are believed to be true and accurate at the date of publication. Neither the publisher nor the authors or the editors give a warranty, expressed or implied, with respect to the material contained herein or for any errors or omissions that may have been made. The publisher remains neutral with regard to jurisdictional claims in published maps and institutional affiliations.

This Springer imprint is published by the registered company Springer Nature Switzerland AG
The registered company address is: Gewerbestrasse 11, 6330 Cham, Switzerland

If disposing of this product, please recycle the paper.

Preface

The Twenty-Ninth International Conference on Financial Cryptography and Data Security (FC 2025) was held on 14–18 April 2025 at the Hotel Shigira Mirage in Miyakojima, Japan. The conference is organized annually by the International Financial Cryptography Association (IFCA).

The Program Committee used the HotCRP system to organize the reviewing process, with a special thanks to Christian Cachin for graciously setting up a server for these purposes. We received 300 submissions and accepted 46 papers (42 regular papers, 3 short papers and 1 Systematization of Knowledge (SoK) paper). The acceptance rate was 15%. Papers received 2 reviews in a first round of double-blind peer review, with some papers subjected to an early rejection if both reviews were negative. The papers that proceeded to a second round of reviews received an additional 2 reviews. Some papers received a fifth review in a third round of reviews at the discretion of the program chairs.

We provided an open call for the nomination of program committee members. We curated a committee of 126 experts in cryptography, blockchain technology, security, and privacy, with members spanning academia and industry, as well as senior and junior positions. The members also used external reviewers at their discretion. Most members received 7 or 8 submissions to review, which we appreciate is a considerable amount of work. We thank all reviewers for demonstrating their careful consideration of each assigned paper, for providing useful feedback to the authors, and for lively discussions of the merits of each paper. The success of the conference and the final program is in large part due to the efforts of the program committee.

For the conference itself, we visited for the first time the island of Miyakojima in Japan. The conference ran Monday to Thursday, with Friday reserved for 6 workshops. Papers were split into 12 sessions, which are only slightly adjusted for these proceedings. The paper presentations were augmented with one highly engaging keynote. For the keynote, we invited Ed Felten (Offchain Labs) who presented his thoughts on "Toward a Practical Theory of On-Chain Resource Pricing." The program also included a rump session hosted by Andrew Miller, and a general meeting that included an election for members of the steering committee.

The success of FC 2025 would not have been possible without the contributions of a large number of people and organizations. Our general chairs, Kazue Sako and Rafael Hirschfeld, did countless organizational and logistical tasks to secure a beautiful location, ensure the smooth operation of the conference, and provide attendees with a full schedule of fun social activities. We thank the steering committee (listed below) and previous FC 2024 chairs (Jeremy Clark and Elaine Shi) for helpful guidance. We thank our sponsors whose generous support made this event possible. Our platinum sponsors: a16z crypto research, Covenant Holdings, and Sui. Our gold sponsor: Ethereum Foundation. Our silver sponsors: Common Prefix, Flashbots, Input Output, and Silence Laboratories. Thank you to all the authors, presenters, and attendees of the conference. Financial

Cryptography continues to maintain a high academic standard because of your diverse interests and innovation. You are helping sustain a vibrant community through your participation and perspectives.

June 2025

Christina Garman
Pedro Moreno-Sanchez

Organization

General Chairs

Rafael Hirschfeld   Unipay Technologies, The Netherlands
Kazue Sako   Waseda University, Japan

Program Committee Chairs

Christina Garman   Purdue University, USA
Pedro Moreno-Sanchez   IMDEA Software Institute, Spain

Steering Committee

Joseph Bonneau   NYU & a16z crypto, USA
Sven Dietrich   City University of New York, USA
Rafael Hirschfeld   Unipay Technologies, The Netherlands
Andrew Miller   University of Illinois Urbana-Champaign, USA
Monica Quaintance   Zenia Systems, USA
Burton Rosenberg   University of Miami, USA
Kazue Sako   Waseda University, Japan

Program Committee

Hamza Abusalah   IMDEA Software Institute, Spain
Ghada Almashaqbeh   University of Connecticut, USA
Orestis Alpos   Common Prefix, Switzerland
Jayamine Alupotha   University of Bern, Switzerland
Lukas Aumayr   Common Prefix, Switzerland
Zeta Avarikioti   TU Wien & Common Prefix, Austria
Massimo Bartoletti   University of Cagliari, Italy
Soumya Basu   Nuveaux Trading, USA
Don Beaver   Fierce Logic, USA
Adithya Bhat   Visa Research, USA
Alexander R. Block   University of Illinois Chicago, USA
Joseph Bonneau   NYU & a16z crypto, USA
Rainer Böhme   University of Innsbruck, Austria
Stefanos Chaliasos   Imperial College London, UK

Panagiotis Chatzigiannis	Visa Research, USA
James Hsin-yu Chiang	Aarhus University, Denmark
Hao Chung	Carnegie Mellon University, USA
Michele Ciampi	University of Edinburgh, UK
Jeremy Clark	Concordia University, Canada
Bernardo David	IT University of Copenhagen & Common Prefix, Denmark
Rafael Dowsley	Monash University, Australia
Sisi Duan	Tsinghua University, China
Yue Duan	Singapore Management University, Singapore
Muhammed F. Esgin	Monash University, Australia
Aleksander Essex	Western University, Canada
Ittay Eyal	Technion, Israel
Hanwen Feng	University of Sydney, Australia
Christof Ferreira Torres	INESC-ID Instituto Superior Técnico (IST) & University of Lisbon, Portugal
Arthur Gervais	University College London, UK
Noemi Glaeser	University of Maryland, USA
Tiantian Gong	Purdue University, USA
Yue Guo	JP Morgan AI Research, USA
Suyash Gupta	University of Oregon, USA
Lucjan Hanzlik	CISPA Helmholtz Center for Information Security, Germany
Hannes Hartenstein	Karlsruhe Institute of Technology, Germany
Bernhard Haslhofer	Complexity Science Hub, Austria
Ningyu He	The Hong Kong Polytechnic University, China
Lioba Heimbach	ETH Zurich, Switzerland
Jaap-Henk Hoepman	Radboud University & Karlstad University, The Netherlands
Yan Ji	Chainlink Labs, USA
Xiangkun Jia	Institute of Software, Chinese Academy of Sciences, China
Yanxue Jia	Purdue University, USA
Chenglu Jin	CWI Amsterdam, The Netherlands
Tushar Jois	City College of New York, USA
Ari Juels	Cornell Tech, USA
Ghassan Karame	Ruhr-University Bochum, Germany
Harish Karthikeyan	JP Morgan AI Research, USA
Mahimna Kelkar	Cornell University, USA
Lucianna Kiffer	IMDEA Networks, Spain
Jason Kim	Georgia Institute of Technology, USA
Lefteris Kokoris Kogias	Mysten Labs, Greece

Yashvanth Kondi	Silence Laboratories (Deel), USA
Kari Kostiainen	ETH Zurich, Switzerland
Mario Larangeira	Tokyo Institute of Technology & IOG, Japan
Duc V. Le	Visa Research, USA
Eysa Lee	Brown University, USA
Stefanos Leonardos	King's College London, UK
Jacob Leshno	University of Chicago, USA
Jiasun Li	George Mason University, USA
Orfeas Stefanos Thyfronitis Litos	Imperial College London & Common Prefix, UK
Jing Liu	MPI-SP & UC Irvine, Germany
Xiangyu Liu	Purdue University & Georgia Institute of Technology, USA
Zeyan Liu	University of Louisville, USA
Chen-Da Liu-Zhang	Lucerne University of Applied Sciences and Arts & Web3 Foundation, Switzerland
Donghang Lu	TikTok, USA
Yuan Lu	Institute of Software Chinese Academy of Sciences, China
Varun Madathil	Yale University, USA
Akaki Mamageishvili	Offchain Labs, USA
Easwar Vivek Mangipudi	Supra Research, USA
Elisaweta Masserova	Carnegie Mellon University, USA
Shin'ichiro Matsuo	Virginia Tech & Georgetown University, USA
Roman Matzutt	Fraunhofer FIT, Germany
Patrick McCorry	Arbitrum Foundation, USA
Kelsey Melissaris	Aarhus University, Denmark
Johnnatan Messias	MPI-SWS, Germany
Jason Milionis	Columbia University, USA
Pratyush Mishra	University of Pennsylvania, USA
Ciamac Moallemi	Columbia University, USA
Malte Möser	Chainalysis, USA
Neha Narula	MIT, USA
Georgios Palaiokrassas	Yale University, USA
Georgios Panagiotakos	IOG, Greece
Dimitrios Papadopoulos	HKUST, China
Krzysztof Pietrzak	Institute of Science and Technology Austria (ISTA), Austria
Kaihua Qin	Yale University, USA
Alfredo Rial	Nym Technologies, Belgium
Pierre-Louis Roman	None, Switzerland
Tim Roughgarden	Columbia University & a16z crypto, USA
Reihaneh Safavi-Naini	University of Calgary, Canada

Giulia Scaffino	TU Wien & Common Prefix, Austria
Ignacio Amores Sesar	University of Bern, Switzerland
Nibesh Shrestha	Supra Research, USA
Pratik Soni	University of Utah, USA
Alberto Sonnino	Mysten Labs & University College London, UK
Alexander Spiegelman	Aptos Labs, USA
Srivatsan Sridhar	Stanford University, USA
Chrysoula Stathakopoulou	Chainlink Labs, USA
Erkan Tairi	ENS Paris, France
Wenpin Tang	Columbia University, USA
Sri AravindaKrishnan Thyagarajan	University of Sydney, Australia
Daniel Tschudi	Concordium, Switzerland
Taro Tsuchiya	Carnegie Mellon University, USA
Marie Vasek	UCL, UK
Friedhelm Victor	TRM Labs, USA
Yann Vonlanthen	ETH Zurich, Switzerland
Anh V. Vu	University of Cambridge, UK
Jun Wan	Five Rings LLC, USA
Ding Wang	Nankai University, China
Haoyu Wang	Huazhong University of Science and Technology, China
Kanye Ye Wang	University of Macau, China
Qin Wang	CSIRO Data61, Australia
Shouqiao Wang	Columbia University, USA
Xuechao Wang	HKUST (GZ), China
Zhipeng Wang	Imperial College London, UK
Ke Wu	University of Michigan, USA
Matheus Xavier Ferreira	University of Virginia, USA
Zhuolun Xiang	Aptos Labs, USA
Guowen Xu	University of Electronic Science and Technology of China, China
Jiahua Xu	University College London, UK
Yingjie Xue	The Hong Kong University of Science and Technology (Guangzhou), China
Aviv Yaish	Yale University, USA
Zheng Yang	Southwest University, China
Mengqian Zhang	Yale University, USA
Hong-Sheng Zhou	Virginia Commonwealth University, USA
Liyi Zhou	University of Sydney, Australia
Yajin Zhou	Zhejiang University & BlockSec, China

Additional Reviewers

Sharad Agarwal
Jannik Albrecht
Parwat Singh Anjana
Arasu Arun
Gennaro Avitabile
Akhil Bandarupalli
Kyle Beadle
Nidhish Bhimrajka
Hangcheng Cao
Yiyue Cao
Wonseok Choi
Lei Fan
Matthias Grundmann
Jia Hu
Florian Jacob
Yu Shen
Zhenghao Lu
Rujia Li
Enrico Lipparini
Zeyu Liu
Anna Piscitelli

Judith Senn
Yu Xia
Qianyu Yu
Tsz Hon Yuen
Zhelei Zhou
Jiajun Xin
Pengzhi Xing
Jianting Zhang
Mingfei Zhang
Rui Zhang
Bolin Zhang
Hongxiao Wang
Cong Wu
Sravya Yandamuri
Yuchen Ye
Nikhil Vanjani
Ioannis Tzannetos
Giannis Tzannetos
Andrei Tonkikh
Zhelei Zhou

Contents

Layer 2

A Formally Verified Lightning Network 3
   *Grzegorz Fabiański, Rafał Stefański,
and Orfeas Stefanos Thyfronitis Litos*

Strengthening Multi-hop Channels via Strategic Mesh Connections 21
   Shuyang Tang and Sherman S. M. Chow

IvyAPC: Auditable Generalized Payment Channels 39
   *Ming Li, Yuxian Li, Jian Weng, Yingjiu Li, Jiasi Weng, Junzuo Lai,
and Robert H. Deng*

A Framework for Combined Transaction Posting and Pricing for Layer 2
Blockchains 56
   Shouqiao Wang, Davide Crapis, and Ciamac C. Moallemi

X-Transfer: Enabling and Optimizing Cross-PCN Transactions 73
   *Lukas Aumayr, Zeta Avarikioti, Iosif Salem, Stefan Schmid,
and Michelle Yeo*

DeFi

am-AMM: An Auction-Managed Automated Market Maker 93
   Austin Adams, Ciamac C. Moallemi, Sara Reynolds, and Dan Robinson

The Case of FBA as a DEX Processing Model 109
   Tiantian Gong, Zeyu Liu, and Aniket Kate

Securely Computing One-Sided Matching Markets 126
   *James Hsin-Yu Chiang, Ivan Damgård, Claudio Orlandi,
Mahak Pancholi, and Mark Simkin*

Robust Double Auctions for Resource Allocation 144
   *Arthur Lazzaretti, Charalampos Papamanthou,
and Ismael Hishon-Rezaizadeh*

Zero-Knowledge and Its Applications

Verifying Jolt zkVM Lookup Semantics 163
    Carl Kwan, Quang Dao, and Justin Thaler

*Proo*φ: A ZKP Market Mechanism 180
    Wenhao Wang, Lulu Zhou, Aviv Yaish, Fan Zhang, Ben Fisch,
    and Benjamin Livshits

SoK: Trusted Setups for Powers-of-Tau Strings 197
    Faxing Wang, Shaanan Cohney, and Joseph Bonneau

Short Paper: Curve Forests: Transparent Zero-Knowledge Set Membership
with Batching and Strong Security 219
    Matteo Campanelli, Mathias Hall-Andersen,
    and Simon Holmgaard Kamp

Modeling Bitcoin and Incentives

A Composability Treatment of Bitcoin's Transaction Ledger with Variable
Difficulty 233
    Juan Garay, Yun Lu, Julien Prat, Brady Testa, and Vassilis Zikas

Rapidash: Atomic Swaps Secure Under User-Miner Collusion 249
    Hao Chung, Elisaweta Masserova, Elaine Shi,
    and Sri AravindaKrishnan Thyagarajan

Serial Monopoly on Blockchains with Quasi-patient Users 267
    Paolo Penna and Manvir Schneider

Efficient Blockchains

Pilotfish: Distributed Execution for Scalable Blockchains 287
    Quentin Kniep, Lefteris Kokoris-Kogias, Alberto Sonnino,
    Igor Zablotchi, and Nuda Zhang

ANTHEMIUS: Efficient and Modular Block Assembly for Concurrent
Execution 307
    Ray Neiheiser and Eleftherios Kokoris-Kogias

Broadcast

Communication and Round Efficient Parallel Broadcast Protocols 327
    Nibesh Shrestha, Ittai Abraham, and Kartik Nayak

Towards Optimal Parallel Broadcast Under a Dishonest Majority 345
   Daniel Collins, Sisi Duan, Julian Loss, Charalampos Papamanthou,
   Giorgos Tsimos, and Haochen Wang

Encryption and Its Applications

Overlapped Bootstrapping for FHEW/TFHE and Its Application to SHA3 367
   Deokhwa Hong, Youngjin Choi, Yongwoo Lee, and Young-Sik Kim

Lixom: Protecting Encryption Keys with Execute-Only Memory 385
   Tristan Hornetz, Lukas Gerlach, and Michael Schwarz

Leveraging Homomorphic Encryption for Maximal Extractable Value
(MEV) Mitigation: Blind Arbitrage on Decentralised Exchanges 402
   Jonathan Passerat-Palmbach

Author Index 419

Layer 2

A Formally Verified Lightning Network

Grzegorz Fabiański[1](✉) , Rafał Stefański[1] ,
and Orfeas Stefanos Thyfronitis Litos[2]

[1] University of Warsaw, Warsaw, Poland
grzegorz.fabianski@mimuw.edu.pl
[2] Imperial College London, London, England

Abstract. In this work we use formal verification to prove that the Lightning Network (LN), the most prominent scaling technique for Bitcoin, always safeguards the funds of honest users. We provide a custom implementation of (a simplification of) LN, express the desired security goals and, for the first time, we provide a machine checkable proof that they are upheld under every scenario, all in an integrated fashion. We build our system using the Why3 platform.

1 Introduction

Bitcoin [1] is the oldest and consistently the highest valued blockchain. However, despite its value and prominence, it faces severe scalability issues [2] both in terms of throughput and of latency: it natively supports only up to 7 transactions per second and requires 1 hour from transaction submission to its verification.

To alleviate this limitation, the *Lightning Network* (LN) [3] has been developed. It lifts payments *off-chain*, i.e., it enables parties to securely pay each other without interacting with the blockchain. LN users enjoy latency and throughput limited only by the communication network between the transacting parties, avoid the hefty per-payment on-chain fees, and relieve other blockchain users from having to reach consensus on every single payment.

As of this writing, over \$120M are contained in LN. This makes LN a security-critical application. Nevertheless, to the best of the authors' knowledge, its complex design[1] has never been formally verified for crucial properties such as safeguarding honest parties' funds. The current work aims to fill this gap. We employ the Why3 [4] formal verification platform to implement a subset of LN, formally specify the desired security properties and mechanically prove that our implementation adheres to them under all execution paths. Our system consists of 6060 lines of program code and 7420 lines of verification code.

1.1 Overview of LN

The central construct of LN is the *payment channel*. Each channel has exactly two parties, each of which has some coins in it. One party can pay the other via an

---

[1] https://github.com/lightning/bolts/blob/master/00-introduction.md

update of the channel state, which is done collaboratively with its counterparty. Each party is guaranteed that they can *unilaterally* close the channel on-chain and get their fair share of coins at any time. Channel updates are very cheap: the counterparties just need to exchange a few messages—no interaction with third parties or the blockchain is needed for paying within one's channel.

In slightly more detail, LN works as follows: To initially transfer coins from the blockchain to a new channel, the two parties collaboratively create a "joint account". This involves the two parties generating three Bitcoin transactions, with one submitted on-chain (the *funding transaction*) and the other two stored locally off-chain (the *commitment transactions*). The funding transaction transfers the initial coins to the joint account, whereas the commitment transactions safeguard each party's access to its coins: each party can publish on-chain one of the commitment transactions to move its coins back to the blockchain without needing the cooperation of its counterparty. This ensures that no trust between parties is needed. All in all, when published on-chain, the funding transaction opens the channel and the commitment transaction closes it.

On each payment, two things happen: Firstly a new pair of commitment transactions is generated, reflecting the balance of coins after the payment. Secondly, the previous pair of commitment transactions are *revoked*. A revoked commitment transaction corresponds to an old channel state and thus should never be published on-chain. A malicious party can nevertheless publish it—this could be beneficial if the older balance were in its favor. In such a case, the honest counterparty can publish the corresponding *revocation* transaction (which was generated when the offending commitment transaction was revoked) within a timeframe and punish its counterparty by confiscating all channel coins.

To sum up, a channel needs one on-chain transaction to open, one on-chain transaction to close and can support a practically unlimited number of off-chain payments. It offers low latency, high throughput, no fees and needs no extra trust requirements compared to the underlying blockchain.

The main focus of this work is the security of a single, two-party channel. Channel operations consist of funding a new channel, processing off-chain payments, and closing the channel in a way that the rightful funds are returned to the two parties on-chain. We do not model networks of multiple parties, nor the multi-hop payments supported by production implementations.

1.2 Why3

We implement and specify LN in Why3 [4], a framework for formally verifying high-level code. Why3 focuses on proof automation using SMT solvers. It is largely composed of two parts: Firstly, there is the WhyML language, used to express programs. It also supports expressing formal specifications in first-order logic in the form of inline assertions, separate lemmas, or function pre- and postconditions; this allows for natural code constructs. Secondly, there is the *driver* which translates the verification conditions of WhyML code into SMT queries. The novelty of Why3 lies in the relatively seamless integration of a variety of

SMT solvers. In the current work we have taken advantage of this feature by using both Alt-Ergo [5] and CVC4 [6].

Another important formal verification tool commonly used in the context of cryptographic protocols is EasyCrypt [7]. We note that we chose not to formalize LN using EasyCrypt because the latter is more geared towards low-level, probabilistic reasoning and computational assumptions—features that are used by most cryptographic protocols, but challenging for the general-purpose formal verification tools. In contrast, our approach assumes idealized low-level primitives (i.e., digital signatures) and proves security unconditionally (i.e., without a negligible probability of failure), therefore is largely incompatible with EasyCrypt. In fact, our approach of deterministically modeling signatures obviates the need for EasyCrypt, thereby simplifying our overall proof effort.

1.3 Preliminaries on Cryptography

LN relies on *digital signatures*, which consist of three algorithms: key generation, signing and verification. In our work, we adopt the *ideal functionality* defined in [8] to model these operations. Instead of running the algorithms, parties send queries to and receive outputs from the functionality, which internally keeps track of the signed messages and embodies the single source of truth, obviating the need for randomness and hard-to-model computational assumptions (see Subsect. 4.1). Since the functionality masks the need for such assumptions, we can strengthen our Why3 modeling of the adversary to an unbounded one. In fact, instead of modeling the adversary as a polynomially bounded Turing machine in the context of Why3, the security result proven by our code is against any sequence of choices made by the adversary, even non-computable ones. Although strengthening the adversary in this way might seem counterintuitive, it actually makes the verification effort simpler and clearer. The powers of such an adversary are directly expressed via *universal non-determinism*, which is readily available in Why3. We note that our high-level result (Definition 1) directly carries over to bounded adversaries. Therefore our definition also covers real-world systems which, due to their use of practical constructions of the digital signature algorithms, can only be secure against bounded adversaries.

1.4 Our Contributions

This work consists of the following contributions:

- We provide an implementation of the two-party LN interactions in Why3,
- We implement the subset of Bitcoin logic that is relevant to LN in Why3,
- We define *funds security* for an honest client in the presence of a Byzantine counterparty,
- We provide a machine-checkable proof of the funds security of LN channels,
- We demonstrate how to define *funds ownership* in the presence of multisig accounts and signed transactions stored off-chain,

– We identify crucial properties that any LN implementation should uphold to guarantee funds security and use them to modularize our proof. This provides a blueprint for proving the security of production LN implementations.

Limitations. The main simplifications in our implementation compared to the real Lightning Network (LN) is that it only supports direct payments between two parties. As such it does not support multi-hop payments or HTLCs. Furthermore, we use a simplified model of Bitcoin which, in particular, does not include on-chain fees (see Sect. 3 for more details).

1.5 Protocol Flow in Our Implementation

Our work focuses on a single, two-party LN channel over Bitcoin. We implement a fragment of the LN functionality, namely direct payments between two parties. We do not include HTLCs and multi-hop payments in our implementation.

The operation of our channel closely follows that of production LN implementations. When one of the two parties (a.k.a. the *funder*) is instructed to open a new channel, the funding process begins. The funder notifies its counterparty (a.k.a. the *fundee*) and the two parties engage in a series of messages, at the end of which the channel is established. All initial funds belong to the funder and they originate from the funder's on-chain bitcoins.

Once a channel has been established, a payment can be initiated by either side. The payer specifies the amount of in-channel funds to transfer, which is subtracted from the payer's channel balance. After a few messages, the payee's balance is increased by the payment sum. Channels support an arbitrary number of sequential payments.

At any moment, either party can initiate the closing procedure. An honest party also closes its channel if its counterparty misbehaves (e.g., stops responding). An honest closing party is guaranteed to receive its channel balance on-chain after bounded delay. Internally, channel closure is initiated by submitting a single transaction on-chain that reflects the channel balance. This starts a timer, during which the counterparty can dispute the claimed channel balance if the closing party submitted an outdated channel state. Honest client operation guarantees that the honest party loses no funds due to failed disputes.

1.6 Security Goals

We consider two standard properties of LN: The first one, which we call *funds security*, states that a party can always close the channel and transfer its rightful funds on-chain within a bounded time frame. For the sake of funds security, we assume that the honest party interacts with a malicious, byzantine party that also controls the environment. The second property called *liveness* states that channel funding and channel payments between two honest parties will always complete in a bounded amount of time. For the sake of liveness, we assume that two parties are honest, but the adversary controls the network and payment requests (see Subsect. 1.7 for more details).

In this work, we only prove funds security, not liveness. In fact, we are aware that in a scenario when the two honest parties try to initiate payments simultaneously in both directions, our implementation might deadlock. (This does not violate the guarantee of funds security, as the deadlock can be resolved by either party closing the channel). Nonetheless, we do test that a simple channel opening and payment scenario completes successfully (see twoHonestParties.mlw). As the violation of funds security is far more detrimental than the violation of liveness, we believe that such an approach strikes a reasonable balance between proof complexity and practical relevance.

1.7 Adversarial Model

In our model, funds security is formalized via a 1-player game, following established cryptographic practice. The game is played by the adversary. Different moves in the game correspond to different actions that the adversary can carry out in real life. For example, it can choose to deliver a message to the ledger, or to have the corrupted channel party send arbitrary messages to its honest counterparty. These two moves correspond to the power to control the network and to corrupt one channel party respectively. Its control over the corrupted party is complete: it can send and sign arbitrary messages on its behalf at any point in time. On the other hand, its control over the network is encumbered with the responsibility to deliver transactions to the ledger within a specific time bound. Furthermore, it controls the moments in which the honest party is activated, but it must ensure that the delay between two activations does not exceed a specific time bound. These limitations correspond to the standard, reasonable network assumptions and the security of LN depends on them.

Last but not least, we give the adversary the power to choose the moment of channel opening and closure, as well as the timings, directions and amounts of payments while the channel is open. These additional adversarial powers correspond to the choices that the honest party can make in a practical deployment. We choose this approach as it models the worst-case scenario, making our results stronger as well as conformant with the standard approach in cryptography. Allowing these choices to be made by the adversary has the added benefit of ensuring that the game is strictly 1-player, keeping the model simpler. The adversary wins if a channel closure request is put forward but, after the aforementioned time bound, the honest party has not received its rightful funds on-chain.

1.8 Architecture Overview

We now discuss our code architecture at a high level—Appendix A of the full version [9] contains a relevant diagram. We provide a simplified implementation of Bitcoin called Γ, which focuses on the capabilities related to LN

(Sect. 3 and `gamma.mlw`[2]). Furthermore, we implement the signature functionality [8]. It is used by the honest party, the adversary, and Γ to sign messages and verify signatures (Subsect. 1.3 and `signaturesFunctionality.mlw`). Our LN client can read the state of Γ and send transactions to it via a network queue controlled by the adversary. The honest client receives instructions to perform actions, such as to open a channel or carry out a payment. These instructions come from the adversary, but invalid instructions are ignored by the honest client (`honestPartyType.mlw` and `honestPartyInteractions.mlw`). Last but not least, we formally define funds security, as discussed in Sect. 2 (`honestPartyVsAdversary.mlw`).

In order to keep the proof tidy in the face of the complex interactions between the aforementioned components, we use a number of techniques (Sect. 4). We here highlight the two most salient ones. The LN client discussed above has to keep track of a complex state which includes many low-level details, such as which messages remain to be sent in order to conclude an in-flight payment. In order to keep these details separate from the proof, we identify a simple set of requirements on the client behavior (see Subsect. 4.2, Appendix C of the full version [9], and `honestPartyInterface.mlw`). We can thus separate our proof into two independent parts: We first prove that our LN implementation meets these requirements and we then prove that any implementation that satisfies these requirements enjoys funds security. We believe that our requirements must be satisfied by any secure LN implementation, therefore a proof of security of an existing production LN deployment boils down to just proving that it conforms to our requirements.

The second proof technique elucidates the meaning of coin ownership. Albeit a useful high-level concept, is not straightforward to define due to signed but non-processed transactions and multisig accounts. To that end, we define the `Evaluator` (Subsect. 4.4, Appendix B of the full version [9], and module `Evaluator` in `gamma.mlw`) which formally answers the question "How much money does a party own?" This abstraction greatly simplifies the proof effort. We believe this approach can be reused in similar verification projects.

1.9 Related Work

Formal Verification of Blockchain Infrastructure and Applications. Existing blockchain-related formal verification efforts revolve around two axes: Verifying consensus protocols and verifying smart contracts.

Formal verification of consensus protocols has been carried out in [10] and [11]. Similarly to both of these protocol analyses, the current work expresses the execution of multiple parties that communicate via the network, the delays of which are explicitly modeled. Moreover, similarly to [10] and [11], we verify end-to-end guarantees of the execution, not just static invariants.

Regarding the verification of smart contracts, a survey of tools for Ethereum smart contract analysis, including formal verification tools, can be found in [12].

---

[2] The full code can be found at https://anonymous.4open.science/r/LightingInWhy3-DD1C/—**README.md** contains relevant documentation.

Concrete examples are Manticore [13], EthVer [14], PRISM [15], and [16–18]. These tools focus on specific contract properties, whereas our work takes a whole-system approach, whereby the smart contract logic (i e., the LN transactions) only form one part of the entire system, the other parts being the explicit modeling of parties, the communication network they use, and the process of signing transactions.

Security Analyses of LN. A survey of results on LN security and attacks against it can be found in [19]. LN security has been formally modeled and proven in the UC setting in [20]. Most comparable to our work is [21], which builds upon [22] in an effort to formally verify the security of LN using TLA+.

Both [20] and [21] model the intricate details of funds security in the multi-hop payment setting, while our work focuses on a single channel. Due to the lack of multi-hop payments, the wormhole and griefing attacks [19] do not apply in our work. With respect to funds security, the main difference between our work and [20,21] is the framework used. Any small differences in the exact security guarantees result from framework differences, not from high-level security goals.

We now present a detailed comparison of our work with [21], starting with the similarities. Both works prove security for a specification of LN, as opposed to a specific implementation. Both approaches model signatures as ideal functionalities, removing their inherent randomness (the latter is problematic in the context of formal verification) in the process. Last but not least, in both cases non-determinism is used to model the adversary, including its exact leeway for arbitrary behavior.

On the other hand, the current work differs from [21] in the following respects: We model security using a game-based definition, proving specific security properties, whereas [21] uses a simplified version of UC-based modeling. We use the Why3 first-order proof system, which allows us to model infinite system states, whereas [21] uses the TLA+ model checker and only checks all possible scenarios up to a specific number of actions. Our modeling is limited to simple payments within a single channel, whereas [21] further models multi-hop payments over multiple channels. We provide a custom implementation of LN, upon which we base our specification of LN, which happens to be more abstract than the official specification (BOLT), whereas [21] verifies the BOLT specification itself. Last but not least, our formal verification effort is complete, whereas [21] constitutes an intermediate report of a proof effort that is still underway.

2 Security Model

The main security goal of this work is to guarantee that a Lightning party that honestly follows the protocol never loses money. In particular, an honest Lightning party that has sent and received a number of payments in the channel should be able to redeem on-chain its initial channel funds plus any funds received minus any funds sent within a bounded time after requesting channel closure. We call this *funds security*. Formally it is a property over 5 parameters:

- The honest party LN protocol `HonestParty`,
- The ledger protocol Γ,
- The party activation window `deltaWake` $\in \mathbb{N}$,
- The ledger delivery window `deltaNet` $\in \mathbb{N}$.
- The time needed for a channel to close `channelClosingTime` $\in \mathbb{N}$.

We define funds security in terms of a game, played between the adversary and the honest party. If the adversary cannot win no matter their actions, then funds security is guaranteed. This game is defined in the `honestPartyVsAdversary.mlw` file.

The game state consists of the following elements: the honest party state, the ledger state, the signature functionality state, and the collection of timestamped, pending ledger messages. It also tracks 4 variables: the last time the honest party was woken (`honestPartyLastWoken` $\in \mathbb{N}$), whether and when was the honest party first ordered to close its channel (`closeOrderTime` $\in \mathbb{N} \cup \{\bot\}$), the current time (`time` $\in \mathbb{N}$), and the expected funds of the honest party (`expectedAmount` $\in \mathbb{N}$).

Since channels are two-party constructions, the other party is presumed corrupted. We define an initial system state in which the ledger contains some coins for each of the two parties and the channel is not yet opened.

We next describe the types of moves that the adversary can make. All actions apart from `IncrementTime` are parametrized by additional arguments that the adversary chooses along with the move type, as explained below.

1. `SignMsg`: This message enables the adversary to sign any number of messages on behalf of the corrupted party. It also models signature malleability by allowing the adversary to create new signatures for messages already signed by the honest party (see Subsect. *Allowing public modification of signatures* in [23]).
2. `SendMsgToGamma`: The adversary generates an arbitrary message which is immediately processed by Γ. This models the ability of a *rushing* adversary to add transactions to the blockchain at any time, "skipping the queue". As we mentioned, Γ is a parameter of the game. Upon receiving a message, it reads the current time, verifies any signatures with the signature functionality, and returns its updated state.
3. `DeliverMsgToGamma`: This action gives the adversary control of the delivery of messages from `HonestParty` to Γ. The adversary chooses a message from the collection of pending messages. The message is removed from the collection and is immediately processed by Γ.
4. `IncrementTime`: This action increases the current system time by 1 unit. This action is only available if (i) there are no pending messages older than `deltaNet` -1 and (ii) `HonestParty` has been activated within the last `deltaWake` -1 rounds (i.e., `time` $-$ `honestPartyLastWoken` $<$ `deltaWake`).
5. `SendMsgToParty`: This action lets the adversary interact with `HonestParty` on behalf of the corrupted one. The adversary chooses a message to be

delivered to HonestParty, which the latter handles according to its implementation. The result of the HonestParty activation is accounted for as follows. The messages that HonestParty wants to send to Γ are added to the pending messages collection, honestPartyLastWoken is updated to time, and expectedAmount is updated if HonestParty has acknowledged receipt of a payment. During handling of the message, HonestParty may interact with the signature functionality. The exact format of messages that HonestParty expects depends on the concrete LN party protocol, which as mentioned before is a system parameter.

6. ControlEnvironment[3]: This action lets the adversary interact with HonestParty on behalf of the system. This action is handled by HonestParty in exactly the same way as adversarial instructions (i.e., SendMsgToParty) are. The only difference is that ControlEnvironment additionally may cause the system state to be directly updated. Here is an exhaustive list of all possible actions the system can prompt HonestParty to perform:
   (a) EnvOpenChannel: Orders HonestParty to initiate opening a channel with the counterparty.
   (b) TransferOnChain: Orders HonestParty to transfer its funds using an on-chain transaction, i.e., by spending coins from a public-key account. It fulfills two functions: (i) funding of a new channel and (ii) direct on-chain payment to the counterparty[4]. The system then decreases the party's expectedAmount accordingly.
   (c) TransferOnChannel: Similar to above, but using an already open channel. Once again, the party's expectedAmount is decreased.
   (d) CloseNow: Orders HonestParty to initiate the closing procedure of a previously opened channel. The variable closeOrderTime is set to time.
   (e) JustCheckGamma: Wakes up HonestParty to give it the chance to do any recurrent bookkeeping. This is needed to satisfy the periodic HonestParty wake-up requirement even when there is no concrete instruction for the party.

Those actions ensure that the interactions between the adversary and the honest party are modeled accurately. In particular, expectedAmount is tracked by the experiment (and not simply reported by the honest party), which guarantees that the value of expectedAmount matches its intuitive meaning: it decreases whenever the party is asked to pay the counterparty and increases every time the party acknowledges receiving a payment.

Last but not least, let us define the adversary's winning condition. It is also formally defined as adversaryWinningState in honestPartyVsAdversary.mlw.

---

[3] Actually, in the implementation both SendMsgToParty and ControlEnvironment are handled by SendMsgToParty, with appropriate arguments to distinguish between the two. We separate them here for clarity.

[4] Our work only needs the former function of TransferOnChain—still, the latter makes our model more complete for essentially no added code complexity.

Definition 1 (Funds Security). *The winning state for an adversary is one that satisfies the following:*

1. `closeOrderTime` $\neq \perp$,
2. `time` $\geq$ `closeOrderTime` + `channelClosingTime`,
3. *The honest party has less coins than* `expectedAmount` *on-chain (i.e., not counting those in the channel), as output by* Γ *when its function* `immediateAmountOnChain` *is called.*

We say that a system parametrized with the honest party LN protocol `HonestParty`, the ledger protocol Γ, `deltaWake`, `deltaNet`, and `channelClosingTime` **achieves** funds security *if no adversary can reach the winning state, no matter which sequence of actions it follows.*

Realistic LN implementations use practical constructions of digital signatures, therefore they can only achieve Funds Security against *probabilistic polynomial-time* (PPT) adversaries. As discussed earlier however, we model digital signatures as an ideal functionality, the security of which cannot be broken even by unbounded or non-computable adversaries. In the context of Why3 we model the adversary as unbounded for simplicity, but our ultimate security guarantee is with respect to practical digital signature constructions and therefore against bounded, PPT adversaries. Weakening the adversary from unbounded to PPT strictly shrinks the set of admissible adversaries, therefore the security guarantee obtained by the Why3 model is directly transferable to the bounded adversarial setting.

Let `channelTimelock` be the timelock after which a party can reclaim its funds from a commitment transaction. `channelTimelock` is a parameter of the `HonestParty` protocol. For any `deltaWake`, `deltaNet`, `channelClosingTime` $\in \mathbb{N}$: `channelClosingTime` $\geq$ 3· `deltaNet` + 2 · `deltaWake` + `channelTimelock` +1 and `channelTimelock` $\geq$ `deltaWake` + `deltaNet` + 1, we provide a concrete implementation of Γ that models a subset of the functionality of Bitcoin (Sect. 3), as well as an implementation of a subset of LN (Subsect. 1.5) such that funds security is guaranteed, as we formally verify (the main security result is lemma `honestPartyWins` in `honestPartyVsAdversary.mlw`).

3 Modeling Bitcoin

We use a high-level modeling of the ledger called Γ which captures the fragment of Bitcoin that is relevant to Lightning channels. In this section, we give a brief introduction to Bitcoin operation and then explain how we simplify it in order to express just what is necessary for the protocol.

In practical implementations, Bitcoin transactions are organized in a *directed acyclic graph* (DAG). Each transaction is a node with at least one *input* and one *output*. Each input is connected to exactly one output and each output to at most one input. Each output specifies the number of coins it contains. At any point in time, the DAG has some outputs that are not connected to any input: these are the *unspent transaction outputs* (UTXOs) and model all available coins. A new transaction can be added to the DAG if all its inputs are connected to UTXOs and the sum of the coins of its outputs are equal to the sum of the coins of the outputs that its inputs spend—this guarantees new coins are not created out of thin air. Furthermore, outputs contain *Script* that specify spending semantics. Script is a simple non-Turing-complete language with a limited expressiveness, including signature verification, hash checking and time checking. Each output locks its coins by specifying a Script statement. It can later be unlocked by providing an input with a corresponding witness. When a valid transaction is added to the DAG, the outputs it spends are not UTXOs anymore and its own outputs become UTXOs.

Our modeling keeps track of the set of transaction outputs, as well as whether they are unspent. It forgoes the DAG and the linearization of the transaction history. We limit our attention to a fixed set of scripts, enough to model all possible Lightning interactions:

- The public key account, known as "pay-to-public-key-hash" (P2PKH) in Bitcoin implementations[5],
- The 2-out-of-2 multisig—this is used to store the coins of an open Lightning channel during normal operation,
- The commitment transaction conditional output—this is used to unilaterally close an open channel.

We elaborate on the transitions associated with each script in the full version [9] and in our implementation (gamma.mlw).

Bitcoin has no official specification—this role is instead fulfilled by the reference implementation. A formal model for Bitcoin is presented in [24]. In the current work we intentionally avoid modeling parts of Bitcoin execution that are irrelevant to the Lightning participants. More specifically, we ignore all public keys other than those of the two channel parties and any script other than the aforementioned ones. We are confident that our simplified modeling is applicable to a full model of all Bitcoin transitions [24] when non-Lightning transactions are filtered out. We however leave proof of that our model is an abstract interpretation of [24] as future work.

For simplicity, we do not model on-chain fees in our work (this is in line with [24]). However, we believe that extending our work to include fees is conceptually straightforward. See Sect. 5 for more details.

4 Proof Strategy

LN consists of multiple moving parts that are interconnected in intricate ways. In order to manage the complexity of these interactions, we adhere to the following

---

[5] Similarly to [23], our modeling foregoes the use of public keys, opting for destination identifiers instead—this simplifies the model by avoiding the explicit formalization of the mechanics of cryptographic signatures.

principle. The system does not need to maintain the entire history of the past states, neither for the honest LN party nor for Γ. All useful knowledge on past states is instead compressed into constant-size invariants. The alternative would be to keep track of the entire execution history, which would be more aligned with human reasoning about distributed systems. Unfortunately, quantification over time complicates formally verified proofs, as it would require a number of interconnected inductive proofs. Our approach is more natural in the context of Hoare logic, as we adhere to a single induction step per protocol step.

4.1 Digital Signatures Ideal Functionality

From a cryptographic perspective, the security of any digital signatures construction is only *computational*, i.e., it can be broken by a sufficiently powerful adversary. As a standard, cryptographic literature only considers PPT adversaries. This is normally necessary because of the underlying computational assumptions, which are breakable by an unbounded adversary. In fact, replacing the aforementioned ideal functionality with a real signature scheme is only secure against such PPT adversaries. Unfortunately, quantifying over all PPT machines has historically proven exceedingly difficult [25] in the context of formal verification. We would thus like to categorically rule out the exponentially small probability of a successful forgery in a principled manner. We achieve this in two steps: Firstly, we allow the adversary in Why3 to be any function (even non-computable) using the any keyword of Why3. We then replace the signatures construction with an *idealized* digital signatures functionality (signaturesFunctionality.mlw) which never permits forgeries (not even with *negligible* probability), as defined in [23]. At a high level, this functionality plays the role of a "trusted signatures server" that is common for all parties. Parties request the signing and verification of messages. The functionality stores the message-party pair on signature request and responds whether the given message-party pair has been stored on verification request. Crucially, the functionality is incorruptible, making forgeries impossible even by a non-computable adversary.

A salient question is: why is the replacement of the construction with the functionality valid? The answer, coming from the *simulation-based cryptographic paradigm*, employs an *indistinguishability argument*, according to which *every* external PPT observer is unable to distinguish between interactions with the construction versus the functionality, except with negligible probability. Indeed, our ultimate security guarantee is provided with respect to a realistic signatures scheme (not an ideal functionality) and a PPT adversary (not an unbounded one). Using a non-computable adversary is merely a proof technique, necessary to tractably model the adversarial behavior in Why3. The indistinguishability argument enables us to transfer the ideal-world security property (formally verified by Why3) to the real world of practical digital signatures and PPT adversaries.

4.2 Encapsulation of Implementation-Aware Properties

Our work includes a novel implementation of a subset of the LN mechanism, an implementation of Bitcoin on which our LN implementation relies, as well as a formally verified proof of the *funds security* of our implementation. We chose to organize our proof so as to clearly separate the particularities of our custom LN implementation on the one hand and the general logic that every secure LN implementation must uphold on the other. Our proof is therefore separated into three parts: an implementation-specific part (honestPartyType.mlw and honestPartyImplementation.mlw) which is aware of the complexities and details of our LN implementation, an abstract specification which encapsulates a set of simpler invariants that any secure LN implementation must uphold (partyInterface.mlw), and an implementation-agnostic part of the proof that depends only on the specification (honestPartyVsAdversary.mlw).

Our abstract specification focuses on the high-level properties that clients have to satisfy in order to uphold security, such as the need to publish on-chain a known revocation transaction as soon as it becomes valid. This is very different from BOLT, which specifies the required behavior of clients, (e.g., reactions to specific messages), but does not stipulate logical properties. For more details on the interface, see Appendix C of the full version [9] or partyInterface.mlw.

4.3 goodSimpleParty

As our HonestParty LN protocol implementation progressed, it became increasingly complex and highly coupled with the rest of the system. Changes to low-level details of HonestParty LN protocol would ripple to the invariants and from there to the rest of the system. To mitigate this issue, we decided to introduce a simple, implementation-agnostic invariant that captures the essence of the properties that any secure LN implementation should satisfy (goodSimpleParty in partyInterface.mlw). This invariant is aware of only a subset of the information held by the HonestParty implementation, such as the received revocations and the commitment transaction that can be used to close the channel. This is the data that any reasonable LN implementation should be able to produce.

Unfortunately, one cannot prove that the goodSimpleParty invariant is preserved by the HonestParty transitions without additional dependencies. For this reason we also define a stronger, implementation-aware invariant (partyInvariant in honestPartyType.mlw) that implies goodSimpleParty. This invariant is visible only to HonestParty, not to the rest of the system. partyInvariant is more complex than goodSimpleParty: the former spans approximately 65 lines of code, whereas the latter just around 15 lines.

4.4 Funds Ownership

In this subsection we discuss what it means for an HonestParty to own coins in Γ. This is a subtle point, since, from the perspective of the chain, all channel funds are locked behind a 2-of-2 multisig, which usually does not imply exclusive ownership. However, an honest channel party should be able to consider some of these funds as its own. As a further example of funds ownership complications, consider an on-chain output controlled by a single public key *pk* and a signed, valid, published transaction that spends this output but is not (yet) part of the chain. These funds should not be considered as owned by the holder of the private key of *pk*. Our approach to resolving such ambiguities to ownership is to consider as owned those coins that a party can reliably and unilaterally move to its public key account—this way the tension in both of these scenarios vanishes.

To formalize this concept of ownership, consider a specific state of the Bitcoin ledger. Let an *Extractor* be a party which has some local state (e.g., private keys, signatures received by others) and can communicate with the ledger. We also consider an *Obstructor* with access to the ledger and the ability to take any action of the adversary, as described in Sect. 2. The Extractor has a single ID with respect to the signature functionality, whereas the Obstructor controls all other IDs. The Extractor's goal is to maximize the funds it can extract from the ledger into its private account(s), whereas the Obstructor tries to minimize them. Let *extractable value* be the value of such a game when both parties play optimally. We can now define the value owned by a given party at any instance of the execution of some Bitcoin-based protocol by identifying this party with the Extractor (thus allowing the party to diverge from the protocol) and the rest of the parties (along with the adversary) with the Obstructor. We then say that the funds owned by the party are equal to the extractable value. Observe that this definition of ownership does not depend on any specific protocol thus it can be used in settings other than LN.

Next, we discuss how the concept of ownership is leveraged in our proof of funds security. We say that the `HonestParty` has *solvency* at some point during the execution of the funds security game if the funds it owns are at least equal to `expectedAmount` (Sect. 2). Solvency has the intuitively appealing property that it refers to any given moment *during* the execution, as opposed to funds security which only concerns the *final state*. It is not hard to see that solvency implies funds security when the channel is closed. More precisely, funds security follows from solvency and the fact that the `HonestParty` can close the channel in bounded time. The proof of the latter fact is relatively straightforward (it is formalized as lemma `closingWorks` in `honestPartyVsAdversary.mlw`). The solvency part of the proof is more involved and it is discussed in Subsect. 4.5.

Finally, let us point out an important technical detail: Although the game-based definition of ownership is, in our opinion, both intuitive and theoretically appealing, it is also challenging to compute and reason about, as it involves evaluating an arbitrary min-max tree. Therefore, in our proof, we replace funds ownership with a more straightforward (i.e., free of min-max trees) but less intuitive `Evaluator` function (implemented as `partyExpectationsFull` in `gamma.mlw`), which provides a pessimistic under-approximation of the funds owned by the party. For further details, see Appendix B of the full version [9]. Similarly, we replace solvency with *evaluator solvency*, which states that the `Evaluator` never drops below `expectedAmount` during the execution of the protocol.

4.5 Evaluator Solvency Overview

As discussed in Subsect. 4.4, a central point of our effort is proving the preservation of evaluator solvency across state transitions. In this section we focus on the crux of the proof, which lies in the transitions of Γ and the `HonestParty`.

For the transitions of Γ, it is sufficient to prove that the `Evaluator` does not decrease (as `expectedAmount` does not change during such transitions). This is not hard to prove as the `Evaluator` mirrors the crucial aspects of funds ownership which, by definition, does not decrease during transitions of Γ. The proof is formalized in `gamma.mlw`.

The transitions of the `HonestParty` are harder to handle. To help with the proof, we define a relation `goodTransition`, which connects the states of the `simplePartyT` before and after the transition, as well as the messages sent by the party to Γ during the transition. This relation abstracts the properties that any LN implementation must guarantee to ensure evaluator solvency. In fact, it is agnostic of the exact implementation of `HonestParty`, which allows us to separate the proof from the implementation details.

5 Conclusion and Future Work

In this work we successfully modeled Lightning [3] channels using first-order logic in Why3 and proved funds security for honest channel parties. First-order logic allowed us to express naturally the security property and functionality of Lightning channels, as well as the low-level invariants encountered during formalization. During the proof effort, we realized that an in-depth understanding of funds ownership was necessary, which led us to define it robustly and formally. We believe that this approach can be reused in similar efforts in the future. Another relevant outcome is the `partyInterface` design, which was the result of a number of modularization attempts. It cleanly separates LN party implementation details with the interface it should provide, simplifying the proof.

There are a number of future directions for strengthening our modelling and architecture. To begin with, we believe that our work could be extended to two-party channels supporting HTLCs with a reasonable amount of effort. This will be a significant stepping stone towards formalizing the security of real-world LN implementations. Moreover, our modeling of Bitcoin can be improved to bring it to parity with already existing formalizations such as [24]. We expect that this task also needs a reasonable effort, but could face more unexpected roadblocks than adding HTLCs.

Another way of improving our Bitcoin model is to include transaction fees, which, for simplicity, we currently do not model. This would require the honest parties to set aside some on-chain funds to pay any fees that may arise. These funds would not be transferable by the `TransferOnChain` environment order. Thanks to the small maximum number of per-channel on-chain transactions (at most 3) and given a (weak) assumption of a maximum per-transaction fee, the amount to set aside is fixed. Thus, funds security could also be proved in the presence of transaction fees.

Last but not least, a more ambitious project would be to extend the security analysis to multi-hop payments over a network of LN channels. To that end, new ideas and insights would be required.

Acknowledgements. This work has been partly supported by the European Research Council (ERC) under the European Union's Horizon 2020 innovation program (grant PROCONTRA-885666). Furthermore, this work was partly supported by the German Research Foundation (DFG) via the DFG CRC 1119 CROSSING (project S7), by the German Federal Ministry of Education and Research and the Hessen State Ministry for Higher Education, Research and the Arts within their joint support of the National Research Center for Applied Cybersecurity ATHENE.

Disclosure of Interests. The authors have no competing interests to declare that are relevant to the content of this article.

References

1. Nakamoto, S.: Bitcoin: a peer-to-peer electronic cash system (2008)
2. Croman, K., et al.: On scaling decentralized blockchains. In: Financial Cryptography and Data Security, pp. 106–125. Springer (2016). https://doi.org/10.1007/978-3-662-53357-4_8
3. Poon, J., Dryja, T.: The bitcoin lightning network: scalable off-chain instant payments (2016). https://lightning.network/lightning-network-paper.pdf
4. Bobot, F., Filliâtre, J.C., Marché, C., Paskevich, A.: Why3: shepherd your herd of provers. In: Boogie 2011: First International Workshop on Intermediate Verification Languages, pp. 53–64. Wrocław, Poland (2011). https://hal.inria.fr/hal-00790310
5. Conchon, S., Coquereau, A., Iguernlala, M., Mebsout, A.: Alt-Ergo 2.2. In: SMT Workshop: International Workshop on Satisfiability Modulo Theories: Oxford, United Kingdom (2018). https://inria.hal.science/hal-01960203
6. Barrett, C.W., et al.: CVC4. In: Gopalakrishnan, G., Qadeer, S. (eds.) Computer Aided Verification - 23rd International Conference, CAV 2011, Snowbird, UT, USA, July 14–20, 2011. Proceedings, vol. 6806 of Lecture Notes in Computer Science, pp. 171–177. Springer (2011). https://doi.org/10.1007/978-3-642-22110-1_14
7. Barthe, G., Grégoire, B., Heraud, S., Béguelin, S.Z.: Computer-aided security proofs for the working cryptographer. In: Rogaway, P. (ed.) Advances in Cryptology – CRYPTO 2011, pp. 71–90. Springer, Berlin, Heidelberg (2011). https://doi.org/10.1007/978-3-642-22792-9_5
8. Canetti, R.: Universally composable signature, certification, and authentication. In: Proceedings. 17th IEEE Computer Security Foundations Workshop, 2004, pp. 219–233 (2004). https://doi.org/10.1109/CSFW.2004.1310743
9. Fabiański, G., Stefański, R., Litos, O.S.T.: A formally verified lightning network. arXiv:2503.07200 (2025)
10. Kukharenko, V., Ziborov, K., Sadykov, R., Rezin, R.: Verification of HotStuff BFT consensus protocol with TLA+/TLC in an industrial setting. In: Silhavy, R. (ed.) CSOC 2021. LNNS, vol. 228, pp. 77–95. Springer, Cham (2021). https://doi.org/10.1007/978-3-030-77448-6_9

11. Braithwaite, S., et al.: Tendermint blockchain synchronization: formal specification and model checking. In: Margaria, T., Steffen, B. (eds.) ISoLA 2020. LNCS, vol. 12476, pp. 471–488. Springer, Cham (2020). https://doi.org/10.1007/978-3-030-61362-4_27
12. di Angelo, M., Salzer, G.: A survey of tools for analyzing Ethereum smart contracts. In: 2019 IEEE International Conference on Decentralized Applications and Infrastructures (DAPPCON), pp. 69–78 (2019). https://doi.org/10.1109/DAPPCON.2019.00018
13. Mossberg M., et al.: Manticore: a user-friendly symbolic execution framework for binaries and smart contracts. In: 2019 34th IEEE/ACM International Conference on Automated Software Engineering (ASE), pp. 1186–1189 (2019). https://doi.org/10.1109/ASE.2019.00133
14. Mazurek, Ł.: EthVer: formal verification of randomized Ethereum smart contracts. In: Bernhard, M., et al. (eds.) Financial Cryptography and Data Security. FC 2021 International Workshops, pp. 364–380. Springer, Berlin, Heidelberg (2021). https://doi.org/10.1007/978-3-662-63958-0_30
15. Kwiatkowska, M., Norman, G., Parker, D.: PRISM 4.0: verification of probabilistic real-time systems. In: Gopalakrishnan, G., Qadeer, S. (eds.) CAV 2011. LNCS, vol. 6806, pp. 585–591. Springer, Heidelberg (2011). https://doi.org/10.1007/978-3-642-22110-1_47
16. Yang, Z., Dai, M., Guo, J.: Formal modeling and verification of smart contracts with spin. Electronics **11**(19) (2022). https://doi.org/10.3390/electronics11193091, https://www.mdpi.com/2079-9292/11/19/3091
17. Park, D., Zhang, Y., Rosu, G.: End-to-end formal verification of Ethereum 2.0 deposit smart contract. In: Lahiri, S.K., Wang, C. (eds.) CAV 2020. LNCS, vol. 12224, pp. 151–164. Springer, Cham (2020). https://doi.org/10.1007/978-3-030-53288-8_8
18. Hildenbrandt E., et al.: KEVM: a complete semantics of the Ethereum virtual machine. In: 2018 IEEE 31st Computer Security Foundations Symposium, pp. 204–217. IEEE (2018)
19. Tian, A., Ni, P., Liu, Y., Huang, L.: Blockchain-based payment channel network: challenges and recent advances. In: 2023 International Conference on Blockchain Technology and Information Security (ICBCTIS), pp. 187–194 (2023). https://doi.org/10.1109/ICBCTIS59921.2023.00036
20. Kiayias, A., Litos, O.S.T.: A composable security treatment of the lightning network. In: 2020 IEEE 33rd Computer Security Foundations Symposium (CSF), pp. 334–349 (2020). https://doi.org/10.1109/CSF49147.2020.00031
21. Grundmann, M., Hartenstein, H.: Towards a formal verification of the lightning network with TLA+ (2023)
22. Grundmann, M., Hartenstein, H.: Verifying payment channels with TLA+. In: 2022 IEEE International Conference on Blockchain and Cryptocurrency (ICBC), pp. 1–3 (2022). https://doi.org/10.1109/ICBC54727.2022.9805487
23. Canetti, R.: Universally composable signature, certification, and authentication. In: 17th IEEE Computer Security Foundations Workshop, (CSFW-17 2004), 28–30 June 2004, Pacific Grove, CA, USA, p. 219. IEEE Computer Society (2004). https://doi.org/10.1109/CSFW.2004.24, https://doi.ieeecomputersociety.org/10.1109/CSFW.2004.24

24. Atzei, N., Bartoletti, M., Lande, S., Zunino, R.: A Formal model of bitcoin transactions. In: Meiklejohn, S., Sako, K. (eds.) Financial Cryptography and Data Security - 22nd International Conference, FC 2018, Nieuwpoort, Curaçao, February 26 – March 2, 2018, Revised Selected Papers, vol. 10957 of Lecture Notes in Computer Science, pp. 541–560. Springer (2018). https://doi.org/10.1007/978-3-662-58387-6_29
25. Liao, K., Hammer, M.A., Miller, A.: ILC: a calculus for composable, computational cryptography. In: McKinley, K.S., Fisher, K. (eds.) Proceedings of the 40th ACM SIGPLAN Conference on Programming Language Design and Implementation, PLDI 2019, Phoenix, AZ, USA, June 22–26, 2019, pp. 640–654. ACM (2019). https://doi.org/10.1145/3314221.3314607

Strengthening Multi-hop Channels via Strategic Mesh Connections

Shuyang Tang[1] and Sherman S. M. Chow[2(✉)]

[1] School of Computer Science, Shanghai Jiao Tong University, Shanghai, China
[2] Department of Information Engineering, Chinese University of Hong Kong, Shatin, Hong Kong
smchow@ie.cuhk.edu.hk

Abstract. Scalable multi-hop cryptocurrency transactions are enabled by payment channel networks (PCNs) like the Lightning Network, which execute most transactions off-chain, greatly curbing on-chain activity. However, unrestricted channel formation often leads to centralization, creating a natural oligarchy where a few nodes gain disproportionate influence, weakening decentralization and raising risks of targeted attacks. Establishing a structured network in PCNs mitigates this issue by encouraging users to allocate channels strategically, resisting partitions.

Reframing PCN connectivity, we introduce the strategic mesh channel model that strengthens multi-hop connectivity by creating virtual channels that connect individual channels while retaining user autonomy. Melding theoretical optimization with practical deployment, our simulations based on our smart-contract implementation show that, with an appropriate participation rate, our design significantly enhances decentralization, connectivity, and attack tolerance over standard PCNs. Additionally, average users receive economic incentives to allocate channels strategically, driving broader adoption of this structured approach. Network resilience and fairness thus improve, challenging the assumption that decentralization presupposes unregulated, anarchic formation.

Keywords: Cryptocurrency · Off-chain Payments · Payment Channel

1 Introduction

Scalability challenges in blockchains, *e.g.*, constrained transaction throughput and long confirmation times, have spurred the creation of off-chain solutions. High-throughput off-chain transactions are made possible by *payment channels*

Sherman Chow (corresponding) is supported in part by the General Research Fund (CUHK 14210621) from the Research Grant Council, Hong Kong, and by Direct Grant (4055238) and the Strategic Impact Enhancement Fund (3135517) from the Chinese University of Hong Kong, Hong Kong.

and *payment channel networks* (PCN)[1], reducing on-chain transactions. Establishing a payment channel requires a deposit of money m as *custody*, which determines the maximum amount transferable within the channel at any time. Rather than executing every transaction on-chain, PCs facilitate direct off-chain asset transfers with instant confirmations but with fairness and reduced fees. Money held in custody serves as a deposit for final on-chain settlements and an escrow safeguard reinforcing fair dispute resolution in off-chain transactions. As multiple PCs interconnect, they form a PCN that enables multi-hop payments via intermediaries, routing transactions between users without direct links. Network-wide payments in a PCN incur costs proportional to the number of channels traversed, yet remain lower than on-chain fees because transactions require only local channel updates rather than global consensus.

Standard PCN schemes allow users to independently determine their network topology, commonly opting for neighboring nodes (*i.e.*, nodes sharing a channel) based on individual preferences. Ideally, a large-scale PCN would emerge, supporting practical (*i.e.*, well-connected) and decentralized multi-hop payments between any pair of users, ensuring strong and robust network connectivity. Given the current decentralized approach, the "price of anarchy" arises as users are incentivized to connect with well-connected peers to optimize their own connectivity. More often than not, networks evolve into suboptimal structures as a result. As users increasingly form connections with a limited set of well-connected nodes, these hubs amass undue sway, culminating in a natural oligarchy that concentrates control and renders the network vulnerable to adaptive attacks.

Having these observations, we introduce *strategic mediated connections*—a structured approach in which users establish part of their connections based on a predefined network design. As part of our model, the PCN is represented as an undirected graph, with edges corresponding to either *prescribed* channels or *open-choice* channels. To ensure a well-connected topology, the network is initialized at genesis with a (γm)-regular *basis graph*, in which each vertex connects to γm others. Compliance with this structure is enforced through a *participation rate* γ ($0 \leq \gamma \leq 1$), requiring each node to form the prescribed links according to this basis graph before freely creating the remaining $(1-\gamma)m$ open-choice channels. Handling new nodes, the system requires that they deposit custody of their channels in a smart contract that assigns them a vertex and automatically creates the assigned links. A node can form open-choice channels with others after satisfying this requirement.

Expecting all nodes to occupy one vertex in the predefined network structure is impractical, given varied client demands. Consequently, we allow users to occupy multiple nodes (vertices) and establish *super channels*—ideal channels with infinite *capacity* (the maximum admissible amount transferable through them) and zero fees—between them. Here, we set a parameter m for the number of channels; it is only a minimum requirement as participants may form multiple

---

[1] *e.g.*, Lightning (https://lightning.network/lightning-network-paper.pdf) and micropayment channels in bitcoinj (https://bitcointalk.org/?topic=244656.0.

sets of m channels.[2] Overall, this structure imposes constraints that enhance the network topology and decentralization, thus strengthening resistance to attacks.

1.1 Motivation from the Lightning Network Topology in Practice

Reviewing Findings on LN. The Lightning Network (LN) is currently the most widely used PCN. Tochner *et al.* [42] found that 60% (80%) of multi-hop channels pass through only 5 (15) nodes, highlighting a substantial concentration of traffic through a few central nodes. Similarly, Lisi *et al.* [23] revealed that 37.7% of nodes[3] have a degree of 1, whereas only 92 nodes exhibit a degree exceeding 100.

Most peripheral nodes have few connections, forming *bouquet* patterns (where many connect to a single central node). These "bouquet roots" constitute only 1% of the network yet connect to 2,285 peripheral nodes ("roses"), representing 29% of the network. Removing as few as 10 bouquet roots disconnects 10.4% of nodes and 6.4% of channels, underscoring the high centralization and suboptimal connectivity and clustering.

A further analysis of the latest LN topology is conducted using third-party data[4] (Table 1). We evaluate connectivity and local clustering via several metrics. First, we assess connectivity by counting the *cut channels* and *cut nodes* whose removal partitions the PCN into separate components. Fewer cut channels and nodes indicate improved resilience against network splits, which enhances resistance to censorship and network partitioning.

Next, we consider clustering metrics, which capture how interconnected a node's neighbors are. The *clustering coefficient* is defined as the average of the local clustering coefficients across all nodes, where a node's *local coefficient* is the fraction of connections among its neighbors. The clustering coefficient quantifies the likelihood that two nodes connected to the same node are also directly connected to each other, forming a triangle. A high value suggests transactions tend to concentrate within tightly-knit groups rather than being uniformly spread across the network, leading to liquidity centralization and routing inefficiencies. In contrast, a low coefficient suggests a more evenly connected network, reducing reliance on specific hubs and improving decentralization. Unlike cut nodes, which indicate the centralization of individual nodes, these metrics reflect clique-based centralization. *Transitivity* quantifies the proportion of actual triangles relative to potential triangles, where a value of 1 signifies that every path of length 2 connects to a neighbor of the starting node.

Finally, the *average distance* and *diameter* (*i.e.*, the worst-case distance) measure how efficiently transactions can be routed (see Sect. 2.2). Shorter routes generally reduce fees and increase success rates, thereby making the network

---

[2] Security concerns generally advise against a single participant spawning multiple nodes due to potential liveness and safety risks. However in our system, occupying each node requires substantial (redeemable) custody and non-redeemable fees, thereby encouraging users with higher transfer demands to occupy multiple nodes.
[3] This paper, *e.g.*, protocol specifications, may use vertex and node interchangeably.
[4] We use data from https://bitcoinvisuals.com/lightning on September 26, 2024.

more suitable for small-value transfers. Together, these metrics underscore the significant centralization within the LN, a trend that continues to intensify [45].

Table 1. A snapshot of LN on September 26, 2024

# Nodes	16,810	Average Distance	9.1
# Channels	54,432	Diameter	13
Channels per Node	6.9	Cut Channels (%)	49.7%
Clustering Coefficient (%)	12.3%	Cut Nodes (%)	12.8%
Transitivity (%)	2.7%		

Table 2. Properties of LPS Graphs for $(p,q) = (5,23)$ (left) and $(p,q) = (7,23)$ (right)

# Nodes	12,167	Av. Distance	4.31	# Nodes	12,167	Av. Distance	3.95
# Channels	36,501	Diameter	7	# Channels	48,668	Diameter	6
Channels/Node	6	Cut Channels	0%	Channels/Node	8	Cut Channels	0%
Clust. Coeff.	0.27%	Cut Nodes	0%	Clust. Coeff.	0.39%	Cut Nodes	0%
Transitivity	0.48%			Transitivity	0.53%		

Comparing LN with Ramanujan Graphs of Lubotzky–Phillips–Sarnak (LPS). To address issues reflected in these metrics, we consider LPS graphs [25], a family of Ramanujan expander graphs known for their high regularity and favorable spectral properties. Their relevance to PCNs is discussed in Sect. 2.3. Their construction relies on quotient spaces of the modular group and related groups such as projective special (PSL) groups and projective general linear (PGL) groups. See Sects. 1.2 and 4 for more details. Table 2 shows the same metrics for a comparable number of nodes. By our design, the average number of channels per node must be even (equal to $p+1$) and cannot be 7, as in Table 1. Thus, we present the cases for $p=5$ and $p=7$. Our analysis indicates a substantial improvement in topology metrics. We will later explore how to integrate these prescribed expander graphs with open-choice channels in a decentralized manner.

1.2 Technical Roadmap: High-Level Design and Research Methods

Smart Contract for Prescribed and Open-Choice Channels. Our smart contract Π_{sc} assigns a vertex $u \in \mathcal{S}$ from the prescribed graph $\mathcal{S}$ to user P_u provided the user deposits a custody amount mQ, where m is the number of channels per vertex and Q is the deposit per channel. It allows users to establish $(1-\gamma)m$ open-choice channels between this vertex and others. Counterintuitively, when the vertex is released to P_u, the γm prescribed channels are already established. The node-join subroutine operates similarly to channel setups in typical PCNs. Users can conduct off-chain transfers and update channel states, as described in Sect. 3.1. A key role of Π_{sc} is to secure channel withdrawals. As with bilateral PCs [20] (see Sect. 2.2), a dispute resolution mechanism is necessary (see Appendix B [39]). Multi-hop payments are handled using two routing methods, one for light nodes and one that optimizes canonical MF-based routing, detailed in Sect. 3.3.

Expander-Based Network Structure. Our prescribed structure $\mathcal{S}$ is configurable. We select the LPS expander graph for several reasons: (1) Expander graphs exhibit strong connectivity, yielding a robust topology that resists bisecting attacks and enhances decentralization. (2) They feature theoretically bounded and empirically small average distances and diameters, minimizing the number of hops required for multi-hop payments. (3) They often yield highly symmetric graphs, promoting fairness among vertices. (4) Their large expansion degrees (see Sect. 4) hinder clique formation and further boost decentralization. The LPS graph, defined by two odd primes p and q, results in a $(p+1)$-regular graph with $\frac{q^3-q}{2}$ (or $q^3 - q$) nodes if p is (not) a quadratic residue modulo q. More details are in Sect. 4.

Prototype, Evaluations, and Incentives. Our proposed Light Tower Protocol provides a concrete framework for implementing this structured approach to effectively establish strategic mediated connections. We implemented a prototype in Solidity (Sect. 5.1) and assessed its impact on decentralization (Sect. 5.2). Specifically, our experiments demonstrate that average-sized users are likely to generate higher revenues (Appendix G [39]), thereby incentivizing them to join our network.

Contributions. We summarize our contributions as follows.

- *Investigating Centralization in PCNs:* We empirically analyze the inherent centralization tendencies in the LN, illustrating how autonomous channel formation contributes to vulnerabilities and inefficiencies in existing PCNs.
- *Proposing a Structured, Modular Approach:* We introduce "strategic mediated connections," a pioneering methodology that integrates a prescribed network structure based on expander graphs into PCNs. This approach balances user freedom with network-wide benefits, enhancing decentralization and robustness without imposing excessive constraints. We instantiate this using LPS graphs, provide a detailed protocol for bilateral PCNs, explore alternative multi-hop routing and payment methods, and analyze its security.
- *Developing a Practical Implementation:* We design and implement a smart contract-based protocol for bilateral PCNs that shows the simplicity and viability of our approach. It includes secure channel establishment, multi-hop routing, and dispute resolution mechanisms that support deployment.

- *Showing Empirical Improvement via Simulation:* Extensive simulations validate our approach, showing marked improvements in network metrics like connectivity, resilience, and decentralization. Our results show that average users are economically incentivized to participate, which promotes adoption.
- *Bridging Theory and Practice in PCN Design:* Our work bridges the gap between theoretical constructs of optimal network topologies and their practical applications in real-world cryptocurrency networks, offering a scalable solution to centralization that can be readily implemented.

1.3 Related Works

Since their inception, various PCs have been proposed [11,17,20,36]. Multi-hop payments in PCNs prompted research on routing and bottlenecks [26,37]. Censorship [34] and distributed denial-of-service [24,32,42] attacks have threatened PCNs (notably in 2018[5]) and network centralization amplifies the impact and success of these attacks. Splitting attacks [21], which partition a PCN by removing minor nodes, have sparked heated debates.[6]

State channels [31] have been proposed to extend PC functionality, while virtual channels [12–14] enable multi-hop payments even when intermediary nodes are offline. Many other techniques, *e.g.*, rebalancing [19], atomic multi-channel updating [15], and trusted hardware [22], have also been discussed.

Many layer-two blockchain protocols were surveyed by Gudgeon *et al.* [18]. Sprites [31] coordinated multi-hop payments by smart contracts, reducing collateral overhead with partial withdrawals and deposits. Avarikioti *et al.* [4] first modeled PCN channel creation games to explore network structures and fee constraints for Nash equilibria. Later, Avarikioti *et al.* [6] defined a utility function for new LN users, provided an approximation algorithm for optimal solutions, and examined the parameter space for Nash equilibrium. These studies offer insight into user behavior and motivation under different network topologies.

Currently, no existing work has investigated how smart contract coordination can improve overall PCN topology. However, broader efforts to optimize cryptocurrency ecosystems while preserving decentralization and user autonomy have been explored, such as systematic market control of inflation via auction-based liquidity mechanisms [38]. Studies on PCN topology are linked to transaction structures, which adversaries can exploit to trace transactions in anonymous systems. Beyond unlinkability, maintaining the long-term sustainability of decentralized anonymity systems poses additional challenges [8].

2 Preliminaries

2.1 Notations and Assumptions

$A := B$ assigns B to A. m is the number of channels of a node, $[n]$ stands for $\{1, 2, \ldots, n\}$. N is the upper bound on the total number of nodes in the PCN, and Q is the custody of each payment channel. The power set of set S is $\mathcal{P}(S)$.

---

[5] www.trustnodes.com/2018/03/21/lightning-network-ddos-sends-20-nodes.
[6] www.reddit.com/r/CryptoCurrency/comments/f7csud.

We use cryptographic hash function $H(\cdot)$ and homomorphic one-way function (HOWF) $g(\cdot)$. $(a_0, a_1, \ldots)_P$ denotes the sequence of messages $\{a_i\}$ and P's signature on it. For off-chain messages, we may denote them by $\langle a_0, a_1, \ldots \rangle$. Each public key serves for signatures and encryption for simplicity (while using two keys is safer in practice), as well as the address of a user, often its sole identifier. A vertex in our PCN topology $\mathcal{S}$ represents either a user or an empty slot to be filled in the future. A user can occupy more than one vertex.

Off-chain communications occur via private channels without updating the blockchain. We suppose nodes can communicate privately and efficiently if they know the recipient's physical address. Alternatively, knowing the public key enables delivery via a less efficient public P2P network assumed asynchronous (with delayed, out-of-order, or lost messages). Channels between Π_{sc} and any party are assumed to be partially synchronized, with possible delays or out-of-order messages, but without losses. Since Π_{sc} is realized via smart contracts, interactions with Π_{sc} involve reading on-chain data and submitting transactions authenticated by blockchain consensus, so explicit authentication is omitted.

2.2 PC, PCN, and Multi-hop Payments

Payment Channels (PCs). Off-chain PCs improve the scalability of cryptocurrencies by enabling instant off-chain transfers without incurring on-chain costs for each transfer. In unilateral channels, the sender deposits custody funds into a contract address, typically equal to the channel's maximum transferable amount. Funds can then be transferred off-chain through messages acting as checks, allowing the receiver to claim the accumulated transfers from the sender's custody.

A basic unilateral channel construction is outlined in Appendix A [39] for illustration. However, this paper focuses on the more general bilateral channels.

Bilateral channels, unlike unilateral ones, support transfers in both directions, with balances represented as pairs of values that sum to a constant total. Both participants must deposit funds and jointly sign any channel state transitions. This complicates channel withdrawal, as both users must confirm them, while one user may intentionally fail to respond, affecting the channel's liveness. Therefore, when either user issues a withdrawal request, the other has to issue disputes within a specific time if necessary. If no dispute is raised, the withdrawal can be completed unilaterally. This creates demand for *watchtower services* [3,5,29], which address data availability issues of node withdrawal in bilateral channels.

Payment Channel Networks (PCNs). A PCN comprises all payment channels, often modeled as a graph where nodes represent participants and edges represent PCs. Nodes u and v are *adjacent* if a channel exists between them. The function $N: \mathcal{S} \to \mathcal{P}(\mathcal{S})$ maps each node u to its adjacent nodes (∂u). Two nodes are *connected* if a path of channels exists between them.

Routing and Multi-hop Locks. Routing in a multi-hop payment involves finding payment paths from payer A to payee B. Several methods for routing are discussed in Appendix E [39]. Once a route is determined, multi-hop locks freeze the selected channels before the transfer occurs. Various schemes implement multi-hop locks, such as *hashed time-lock contracts* (HTLC) [27], which lock passing channels that are unlocked upon either timeout or hash preimage revelation. *Anonymous multi-hop locks* (AMHL) [28] improve security through the use of HOWFs. A brief review of HTLC and AMHL is provided in Appendix A [39].

2.3 Expander Graphs

Expander graphs ensure robust connectivity even when multiple channels fail, as their uniform structure prevents reliance on a few highly connected hubs, mitigating network splits. Unlike scale-free networks, where liquidity and routing capacity cluster around dominant nodes, expander graphs distribute connectivity more evenly, improving decentralization and making the network resistant to censorship and targeted attacks. Their high expansion factor minimizes clustering and mitigates partitions, reducing bottlenecks that could otherwise constrain transaction flow. Additionally, their bounded diameter ensures that multi-hop payments require fewer intermediate nodes, cutting transaction fees and boosting payment success rates. These structural advantages are particularly relevant in PCNs, where liquidity distribution and routing efficiency are critical. By integrating expander-based channels with user-defined open-choice connections, our model balances decentralization, efficiency, and user autonomy, enhancing the resilience and economic sustainability of the network.

3 Our Proposed Protocol

We now present our Light Tower Protocol, designed to streamline understanding and implementation through a modular approach, with a basis graph detailed in Sect. 4. It consists of two parts: off-chain protocols, specifying private interactions between two nodes of a channel, and on-chain protocols, managing public user interactions and the smart contract Π_{sc}. Appendix C [39] lists the pseudocode.

3.1 Off-Chain Protocols

Off-chain protocols manage payment channels between nodes u and v. Vertex u (v) is occupied by the node with address (*i.e.*, public key) A (B). We refer to a user by their vertex u or address A interchangeably, depending on the context. The channel state is $\mathsf{rec} = (\mathsf{state}_0, \ldots, \mathsf{state}_\ell)$. The initial state (version $k = 0$) is $\langle u, v, 0, Q, 0, \_, \_, \_\rangle$, where $\_$ denotes empty. In general, a state has the form:

$$\langle u, v, k, R, \mathsf{frz}, I, \mathsf{sig}_A, \mathsf{sig}_B \rangle.$$

Here, R is the *balance* of node A, and $2Q - R$ is the balance of node B, where $2Q$ is the total capacity of the channel. frz is the *amount of frozen funds* (if any). I is a *hash image*, relevant only if $\mathsf{frz} \neq 0$. sig_A (sig_B) is a *signature* from A (B).

This tuple is symmetric and equivalent to $\langle v, u, k, 2Q - R, -\mathsf{frz}, I, \mathsf{sig}_B, \mathsf{sig}_A \rangle$ when Q is explicitly specified. We may refer to the same tuple using either form.

Initialization. The protocol exchanges the *physical* network addresses of u and v to establish off-chain communications. To initiate a handshake with B, A acquires the public key B from $\Pi_{\sf sc}$ and sends a handshake request in the form of $\langle {\sf handshake\text{-}req}, A, B, u, v, c = {\sf Enc}(B, {\sf addr}_A)\rangle$.

Upon receipt, B verifies via $\Pi_{\sf sc}$ that A is associated with u, then decrypts to recover ${\sf addr}_A = {\sf Dec}({\sf sk}_B, c)$. B then reciprocates by sending its encrypted network address to A, completing the setup of their off-chain communication.

Payment. A payment of amount a from A to B causes the state transition of

$$\langle u, v, k, R, 0, \_, {\sf sig}_A, {\sf sig}_B\rangle \mapsto \langle u, v, k+1, R-a, 0, \_, {\sf sig}'_A, {\sf sig}'_B\rangle,$$

where ${\sf sig}'_A$ (${\sf sig}'_B$) is a signature on new state $\langle u, v, k+1, R-a, {\sf frz}, I\rangle$ of A (B). The reverse process applies to payments from B to A. Notably, the action cannot be completed if the channel has frozen funds (${\sf frz} \neq 0$)[7].

Freezing. For multi-hop payments, either HTLC or AMHL applies, both requiring a hash preimage to unlock funds. These mechanisms apply to states where ${\sf frz} = 0$. To freeze an amount a (*e.g.*, from A), the state transition is

$$\langle u, v, k, R, 0, \_, {\sf sig}_A, {\sf sig}_B\rangle \mapsto \langle u, v, k+1, R-a, a, I, {\sf sig}'_A, {\sf sig}'_B\rangle,$$

where I is the hash/HOWF value of a uniformly random preimage, ${\sf frz} = a$ is frozen. In the symmetric case, the transition is $\langle u, v, k, R, 0, \_, {\sf sig}_A, {\sf sig}_B\rangle \mapsto \langle u, v, k+1, R+a, -a, I, {\sf sig}'_A, {\sf sig}'_B\rangle$.

Unfreezing. Without loss of generality, the frozen funds from A to B[8] should be released to B if B provides r such that $H(r) = I$. This corresponds to the state transition syntax

$$\langle u, v, k, R, {\sf frz}, I, {\sf sig}_A, {\sf sig}_B\rangle \mapsto \langle u, v, k+1, R, 0, r, \_, {\sf sig}'_B\rangle.$$

As will be shown in the dispute resolution phase, even if A is uncooperative, B can redeem the frozen funds using r. Furthermore, if a multi-hop payment fails and B refuses to revoke the state, B cannot claim the funds, and A is allowed to unilaterally withdraw.

Revoked Freezing. If multi-hop payment fails, A and B can collaboratively revoke the latest state by replacing the state $\langle u, v, k+1, R+a, a, I, {\sf sig}'_A, {\sf sig}'_B\rangle$ with $\langle u, v, k+1, R, 0, \_, {\sf sig}''_A, {\sf sig}''_B\rangle$. The two signatures on the new state of version number $k+1$ (rather than k) prohibit unnecessary disputes during withdrawal.

---

[7] States consist of eight fixed-length items for a simpler discussion. Hence, channels are modeled to hold at most one HTLC/AMHL at the same time. By extending the state, enriching dispute-resolving logic, and using threshold signatures (*e.g.*, [44]), we can leverage Turing-complete smart contracts to support more functionalities [30], *e.g.*, freezing multiple sums.

[8] For dispute resolution, the direction is traceable from the previous state.

A transition from state r_1 to state r_2 is *legal* if it complies with the transition syntax of any action above. We emphasize that a(n) *freezing (unfreezing) state* refers to a channel state triggered by a freezing (unfreezing) action, possibly in the past. It does not imply that the channel is currently frozen or unfrozen.

3.2 On-Chain Protocols

On-chain protocols manage public user interactions and the smart contract $\Pi_{\sf sc}$, which maintains the global state of the network and facilitates various on-chain operations. We detail the functionalities of $\Pi_{\sf sc}$, integrating necessary definitions of the structure on which it operates and other functions/mappings.

- **Vertices**: A countable set $\mathcal{S} = \{s_0, s_1, \ldots\}$ represents potential nodes in the network topology. An iterator function $\mathsf{nxt}\colon \mathcal{S} \to \mathcal{S}$ enumerates the set, where each node s_{i+1} is obtained by applying nxt to s_i without repetitions.
- **Occupation Mapping**: A function $\mathsf{occupied}\colon \mathcal{S} \to \{0,1\}$ indicates whether a vertex $u \in \mathcal{S}$ is occupied ($\mathsf{occupied}(u) = 1$) or not (0). Each occupied vertex u is associated with a user public key/address denoted by P_u.
- **Neighbor Function**: A mapping $\mathsf{N}\colon \mathcal{S} \to \mathcal{P}(\mathcal{S})$ assigns to each vertex u a set of neighboring vertices $\mathsf{N}(u)$. Adjacency is a symmetric relation, *i.e.*, for any $u, v \in \mathcal{S}$, if $v \in \mathsf{N}(u)$, then $u \in \mathsf{N}(v)$.
- **Hyperconnections**: A mapping $\mathsf{hyperConn}(u) = \{v \in \mathcal{S}\colon P_u = P_v\}$ returns all vertices occupied by the same user P_u, representing the concept of super-channels—ideal channels with infinite capacity and zero fees between a user's own vertices. These do not require actual storage or maintenance.

$\Pi_{\sf sc}$ consists of the following subroutines. Appendix D [39] provides a strawman instance of the prescribed structure for illustration.

Initiation. $\Pi_{\sf sc}$ is initiated with a tuple $(\mathcal{S}, s_0, \gamma, \mathsf{N}_0, \widetilde{\mathsf{nxt}}, m, Q)$.
- γ is a parameter defining the network's regularity.
- $\mathsf{N}_0\colon \mathcal{S} \to \mathcal{P}(\mathcal{S})$ then defines the topology as a (γm)-regular graph.
- $\mathsf{N}(u)$ is initialized with $\mathsf{N}_0(u)$ for each $u \in \mathcal{S}$.
- m is the maximum number of neighbors (channels) per vertex.
- Q is the base capacity assigned to each channel.
- $\mathcal{S}_q \subseteq \mathcal{S}$ is the set of withdrawn vertices, initially $\mathcal{S}_q := \emptyset$.
- The iterator is initialized with $\mathsf{it} := s_0$, the starting vertex. Its iterating function $\mathsf{nxt}(u)$ returns $v \leftarrow \widetilde{\mathsf{nxt}}(u)$ if $v \neq \bot$ (vacancies exist); else: it returns (and removes) a random element of $\mathcal{S}_q$ if $\mathcal{S}_q \neq \emptyset$, or $\bot$ otherwise.

Node join. A user P joins by submitting $(\mathtt{join}, P)_P$ and transferring a deposit mQ (to cover the maximum number of channels) to $\Pi_{\sf sc}$.
1. $\Pi_{\sf sc}$ sets the next unoccupied vertex it to P and updates as follows.
   - marks the vertex as occupied via $\mathsf{occupied}(\mathsf{it}) := 1$
   - associates the vertex with the user's address by $P_{\mathsf{it}} := P$
   - updates $\mathsf{hyperConn}(\cdot)$ accordingly: $\mathsf{hyperConn}(\mathsf{it}) := \{v \in \mathcal{S}\colon P_v = P\}$ and $\mathsf{hyperConn}(v) := \mathsf{hyperConn}(v) \cup \{\mathsf{it}\}$ for each $v \in \mathsf{hyperConn}(\mathsf{it})$.

2. Confirmation: Sends a confirmation (join-confirm, P, it, N(it)) to P, where N(it) is the set of neighbors for the assigned vertex; and moves to the next vertex: it := nxt(it).

Channel establishment. After joining, P_u can establish additional channels:
1. P submits (addEdge, $P_u, P_v, u, v, \sigma_v)_{P_u}$ to Π_{sc}, where u is a vertex occupied by P and v is the vertex with which P wants to establish a channel.
2. Π_{sc} checks: P_u and P_v occupy u and v, $|\mathsf{N}(u)|$ and $|\mathsf{N}(v)|$ do not exceed the maximum neighbors m, and (addEdge, $P_u, P_v, u, v, \sigma_v)_{P_u}$ is signed by P_u and P_v via σ_v.
3. If all pass, Π_{sc} updates $\mathsf{N}(u) \leftarrow \mathsf{N}(u) \cup \{v\}$ and $\mathsf{N}(v) \leftarrow \mathsf{N}(v) \cup \{u\}$.

Route query. To facilitate routing and connectivity, Π_{sc} allows users to query the network. Upon receiving (routeQ, u), Π_{sc} returns P_u, the address occupying vertex u if occupied(u) $= 1$; $\bot$ otherwise. This query looks up on-chain data, executes as a view function, and costs no gas.

Channel withdrawal. To withdraw a channel between u and v, P_u submits (withdrawal, $P_u, u, v, \mathsf{state}_p, \mathsf{state})$ to Π_{sc}, where state_p is the second-latest state and state is the latest channel state.
1. Π_{sc} parses the submitted states and verifies their integrity. Note that state_p can be empty when withdrawing from the initial state. Its inclusion ensures the signature of the counterparty is present, as the latest state might be a unilateral unfreezing lacking mutual agreement.
2. Π_{sc} forwards the withdrawal request to v and enters a dispute resolution period lasting Δ time units. During this period, Π_{sc} listens for additional messages and responds accordingly, as both parties may present further information or challenge the withdrawal (see Appendix B [39]).
3. After Δ time units (i.e., after the generation of a certain number of blocks), it removes v from $\mathsf{N}(u)$ and u from $\mathsf{N}(v)$, effectively nullifying the channel balances, and distributes the deposits back to u and v based on the agreed-upon final state state. Finally, if $\mathsf{N}(u) = \emptyset$, then $\mathcal{S}_q$ is updated to $\mathcal{S}_q \cup \{u\}$; similarly, if $\mathsf{N}(v) = \emptyset$, then $\mathcal{S}_q \leftarrow \mathcal{S}_q \cup \{v\}$.

3.3 Payments and Routings

Intra-channel transfers suffice for one-hop payments, but non-adjacent nodes require multi-hop payments for off-chain transfers. This involves routing and channel locks. Either HTLC or AMHL locks may be used, although the pseudocode in Appendix C [39] assumes AMHL. For routing, in addition to the canonical schemes, we overview two alternative approaches (detailed in Appendix E [39]).

For $\gamma > 0$, the first approach finds routes in the basis graph. Even lightweight nodes can compute routes locally with only a few parameters, without storing or monitoring all channels. This reduces storage and communication overhead.

The second approach mirrors existing flow-based routing. The sender treats the local copy of the global network as a flow graph and runs max-flow (MF) algorithms via augmenting paths. By slightly modifying the algorithm, the sender can identify routes with minimal fees if the network does not alter too rapidly.

This optimization taps into the *min-cost max-flow* (MCMF) concept, possibly implemented without the implementer's explicit awareness. Compared to the first approach, it uses both types of channels and trades higher routing overhead for improved quality of the probed paths.

4 Our Instantiation of the Prescribed Structure

An expander graph is a finite, undirected, and sparse graph with strong connectivity. Here, we assume an m-regular graph $G = (V, E)$, meaning that every vertex in V has m edges. The *adjacency matrix* of G is denoted by A_G. The *kernel metric* for expanders is the largest eigenvalue of A_G that is different from m, denoted λ_G. The *expansion degree*, defined as $h_G = \min_{X \subseteq V, 2|X| < |V|} \frac{|\partial X|}{|X|}$, is (tightly) bounded from below [40] and above [2] by λ_G. Thus, λ_G effectively quantifies the expansion. Also, the diameter D is bounded by $D \leq \log \frac{|V|}{\log(m/\lambda_G)}$ [9]. Smaller λ_G values yield better expansion, tighter upper bounds on the diameter, and improved connectivity.

We use an LPS-type Ramanujan graph for the prescribed channel structure. To construct a Ramanujan graph[9], we follow the method of Morgenstern [33], which extends the work of Lubotzky, Phillips, and Sarnak [25], *i.e.*, *LPS graphs*. We denote the resulting graph by LPS(p, q), where p and q are prime parameters.

For LPS graphs, the vertex count is $\frac{q^3-q}{2}$ if $(p|q) = 1$ and $q^3 - q$ if $(p|q) = -1$. LPS(p, q) is a $(p+1)$-regular Ramanujan graph if $q > 2\sqrt{p}$. Here, $(p|q)$ denotes the Legendre symbol. Appendix H [39] formally defines LPS graphs.[10]

5 Implementation and Experimental Analysis

5.1 Implementation

We implemented a smart contract to realize Π_{sc}, handling LPS-graph generation, vertex allocation, withdrawal, and dispute resolution in just 566 lines of *Solidity*.[11] This highlights the simplicity of our design. The main cost is in the graph setup. For $(p, q) = (3, 5)$, generating a 4-regular graph with 120 vertices on *Ethereum*[12] costs a total of 17,417,151 **gas**, broken down as follows:

---

[9] Ramanujan graphs are a kind of m-regular expander graphs with $\lambda_G \leq 2\sqrt{m-1}$. Asymptotically, a family of Ramanujan graphs is optimal since the lower bound for λ_G, given by $2\sqrt{m-1}(1-\frac{2}{D}) - \frac{2}{D}$ [1], approaches $2\sqrt{m-1}$ as the graph grows. This implies nearly optimized bisection bandwidth. Even better, due to their *discrepancy inequality* [10], Ramanujan graphs have a well-distributed number of edges between any collection of vertices, not just across bisections, further optimizing connectivity.
[10] Vertices in LPS graphs often correspond to elements of PGL$(2, \mathbb{F}_q)$ or PSL$(2, \mathbb{F}_q)$, congruence subgroups of GL$(2, \mathbb{F}_q)$/SL$(2, \mathbb{F}_q)$. Edges correspond to actions by elements in the group or certain generating sets within the group.
[11] https://github.com/htftsy/PcnTopology/blob/main/contract/PCN.sol.
[12] Raiden (https://raiden.network) is one of the PCNs built for Ethereum.

- 8,158,006 gas (46.8%) for contract construction,
- 1,049,921 gas (6.0%) for generating the symmetric group, and
- 8,209,224 gas (47.1%) for generating the LPS graph.

After graph generation, enrolling a vertex requires $703,515$ gas.[13] These are smart-contract computations of graphs and assignments. Notably, most costs arise from graph generation. These can be reduced by executing outside the contract and then forwarding the computation results with SNARK proofs, gossip protocols, or a data availability layer.

5.2 Experimental Analysis

We compute the following metrics for all relevant values of γ, ranging from 0 (open-choice PCN structure) to 1 (LPS graph) in increments of $1/(p+1)$.

Separation Metrics. We study the average and longest distances between two distinct nodes. The latter is also called diameter. These metrics capture the average and worst-case numbers of hops for multi-hop payments.

Minimal Cuts. Centralization leads to network bisection [21] after disabling only a few nodes. Thus, a long bisection width implies decentralization. We measured the number of cut nodes/edges defined in Sect. 1.1 using Tarjan's linear-time algorithm [41] to assess what it takes to bisect a network. Our construction, by design, yields no cut node/edge for all pairs (p, q) and almost all γ. To analyze connectivity trends as γ varies, we compute *the average minimal cuts*, defined as the expected fewest disabled channels disconnecting two nodes. Higher minimal cuts imply stronger connectivity and greater decentralization: Networks dominated by large bouquets of channels (Sect. 1.1) rooted in a few nodes exhibit lower minimal cuts, while larger cuts suggest smaller, more distributed bouquets.

Clustering. We also measure transitivity and the clustering coefficient (Sect. 1.1). For a fixed number of channels, lower values of these metrics reflect fewer nodes forming cliques, implying increased decentralization and global connectivity. These measures provide further evidence of improved decentralization.[14]

Evaluation Methods. We pick the following Ramanujan graphs. To simulate PCNs with $\sim 10^4$ or 10^5 nodes, we set $q = 23$ or 47 and vary p over $\{5, 7, 11, 17, 19\}$ or $\{5, 11, 13, 19, 23\}$. This results in networks with $12,167$ or $103,823$ nodes, forming m-regular graphs with $m \in \{6, 8, 12, 18, 20\}$ or $\{6, 12, 14, 20, 24\}$. Recall that the graph size is $q^3 - q$ if $(p|q) = -1$, and half that if $(p|q) = 1$. We omit the PSL cases like $(p, q) = (13, 23)$ to avoid sudden variations as p grows.

---

[13] At exchange rates of 2 10 PST, October 10, 2024, graph generation needs 0.152 ETH or 362.859 USD (3.02 USD per vertex). Afterward, enrolling a vertex takes 14.657 USD.
[14] Clustering metrics alone do not fully capture decentralization, *e.g.*, the highly centralized star-shaped network has zero transitivity and clustering coefficient.

Each $\gamma < 1$ instance involves open-choice channels, but real-world PCN data like LN is not fully applicable for modeling them. First, LN itself is small ($\sim 10^4$ nodes), limiting any analysis with scaling. Second, existing PCNs mostly involve developers and researchers whose behavior differs from larger user-oriented networks. Lastly, most LN nodes have similar forwarding tables, with 37.7% having a degree of 1, contrasting our case of $\gamma = 0$, where each node establishes $p+1$ channels. Thus, we simulate open-choice channels using random graphs.

We simulate PCNs by Barabási-Albert's algorithm [7], which follows power-law distributions, modeling new nodes linking to existing ones with probabilities proportional to their degrees, simulating the "rich-get-richer" effect.[15] We first generate a complete Ramanujan graph, retain a random γ-fraction of edges, and replace the rest using random sampling above.

Calculating average and longest distances takes $\mathcal{O}(N^2 \log N)$ time. To manage this for $N = 10^5$, we sample 30 nodes and calculate their shortest paths to all others. The average distance is the mean of these, while the longest is measured as the maximum observed. For the average min-cut, we sample 30 node pairs, convert the graph into a flow network between each pair, and compute the max-flow (min-cut) using the *max-flow min-cut theorem*. Transitivity is measured by sampling 10^5 random pairs of adjacent channels, and clustering coefficients are computed directly. Since our networks lack large bouquets, we can safely enumerate adjacent pairs without hitting $\Theta(N^2)$ complexity.

Finally, we sample 6 graphs for each (p, q), evaluate the metrics independently, and report the averages. Our open-source codes are available.[16]

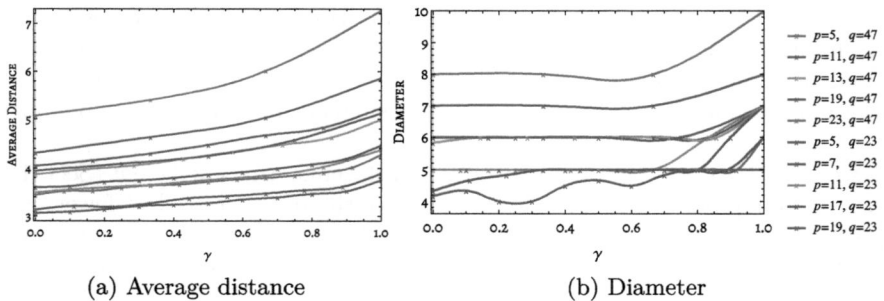

(a) Average distance (b) Diameter

Fig. 1. Evaluations of distance measures

---

[15] Some methods commonly used to model social networks are unsuitable. The Erdős-Rényi model [16], which uses uniform edge distribution (edges exist with a fixed probability), does not reflect typical PCN behavior. The Watts-Strogatz model [43] simulates the small-world phenomenon of social networks. However, real-world PCNs resemble *scale-free graphs* [7], where node degrees follow power-law distributions. A node's degree k occurs with a probability proportional to $k^{-\eta}$ for some parameter η.

[16] https://github.com/htftsy/PcnTopology.

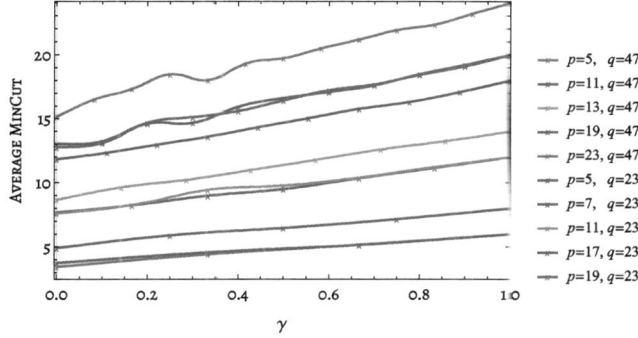

Fig. 2. Evaluation of minimal cuts

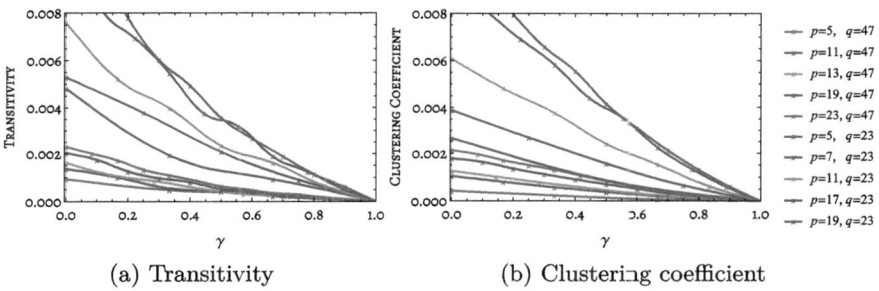

(a) Transitivity   (b) Clustering coefficient

Fig. 3. Evaluations of clustering measures

Evaluation Results. We assess separation metrics, minimal cuts, and clustering.

- *Separation Metrics.* Fig. 1 shows that average distance and diameter grow with γ, so average and worst-case hops increase as more prescribed channels are added. Open-choice channels, which follow power-law distributions, offer slightly better distance metrics but tend to cause centralization. Interestingly, the diameter exhibits sharp phase transitions: for $(p, q) = (13, 47)$ it remains at 6 until $\gamma = 1$, then jumps to 7. Such transitions are common in random graphs (and have broad implications for social networks).
- *Minimal Cuts.* Fig. 2 shows that the average minimal cut increases with γ, indicating improved connectivity and decentralization as more prescribed channels are added. The expander ($\gamma = 1$) yields the optimal minimal cut, where the most efficient partitioning involves cutting $p+1$ adjacency nodes. Interestingly, the curves for $q \in \{23, 47\}$ almost overlap for the same p, suggesting that network connectivity stays nearly constant as the graph extends. This underscores the high cost of censorship and network bisection.
- *Clustering.* Fig. 3 reveals a consistent decrease in transitivity and clustering coefficient as γ increases, illustrating enhanced decentralization.

Appendix G [39] analyzes user incentives through simulations, indicating that the system is friendly to average-sized users.

6 Conclusion

We have proposed a systematic methodology for improving connectivity and decentralization in PCNs. This methodology integrates strategically designed network structures. Our approach demonstrates clear advantages in network resilience and user incentivization, as validated through extensive simulations.

This framework offers a practical and scalable solution to the centralization issues in PCNs, making it well-suited for real-world deployment. The use of expander graphs to guide network structure balances user autonomy with enhanced network-wide benefits, which boosts the robustness and long-term sustainability of PCNs. Our study advances the development of decentralized, resilient PCNs, bridging the gap between theoretical network design and real-world deployment. Still, several challenges remain, opening avenues for future exploration in compatibility, security, scalability, and interoperability.

The principle of strategic mesh connection is likely to apply to commit chains and payment hubs. It shapes the network as symmetric and well-connected hypergraphs with long bisection widths, thereby improving the network topology. Future work could explore hybrid approaches and other applications, *e.g.*, integrating our techniques into leader-based layer-2 retail payment systems [35].

References

1. Alon, N.: Eigenvalues and expanders. Combinatorica **6**, 83–96 (1986)
2. Alon, N., Milman, V.D.: λ_1, isoperimetric inequalities for graphs, and superconcentrators. J. Comb. Theory Ser. B **38**, 73–88 (1985)
3. Avarikioti, G., Laufenberg, F., Sliwinski, J., Wang, Y., Wattenhofer, R.: Towards secure and efficient payment channels. arXiv:1811.12740 (2018)
4. Avarikioti, G., Scheuner, R., Wattenhofer, R.: Payment networks as creation games. In: CBT Workshop (Co-located with ESORICS), pp. 195–210 (2019)
5. Avarikioti, Z., Kokoris-Kogias, E., Wattenhofer, R., Zindros, D.: Brick: asynchronous incentive-compatible payment channels. In: FC-II, pp. 209–230 (2021)
6. Avarikioti, Z., Lizurej, T., Michalak, T., Yeo, M.: Lightning creation games. In: ICDCS, pp. 1–11 (2023)
7. Barabási, A.-L., Albert, R.: Emergence of scaling in random networks. Science **286**(5439), 509–512 (1999)
8. Chow, S.S.M., Egger, C., Lai, R.W.F., Ronge, V., Woo, I.K.Y.: On sustainable ring-based anonymous systems. In: CSF, pp. 568–583 (2023)
9. Chung, F.R.K.: Diameters and eigenvalues. J. Am. Math. Soc. **2**, 187–196 (1989)
10. Chung, F.R.K.: Spectral Graph Theory. American Mathematical Society (1997)
11. Decker, C., Wattenhofer, R.: A fast and scalable payment network with Bitcoin duplex micropayment channels. In: SSS, pp. 3–18 (2015)
12. Dziembowski, S., Eckey, L., Faust, S., Hesse, J., Hostáková, K.: Multi-party virtual state channels. In: EUROCRYPT Part I, pp. 625–656 (2019)
13. Dziembowski, S., Eckey, L., Faust, S., Malinowski, D.: Perun: virtual payment hubs over cryptocurrencies. In: SP, pp. 106–123 (2019)
14. Dziembowski, S., Faust, S., Hostáková, K.: General state channel networks. In: CCS, pp. 949–966 (2018)

15. Egger, C., Moreno-Sanchez, P., Maffei, M.: Atomic multi-channel updates with constant collateral in bitcoin-compatible payment-channel networks. In: CCS, pp. 801–815 (2019)
16. Erdős, P., Rényi, A : On random graphs I. Publicationes Mathematicae Debrecen **6**, 290–297 (1959)
17. Ersoy, O., Decouchant, J., Kumble, S.P., Roos, S.: SyncPCN/PSyncPCN: payment channel networks without blockchain synchrony. In: AFT, pp. 16–29 (2022)
18. Gudgeon, L., Moreno-Sanchez, P., Roos, S., McCorry, P., Gervais, A.: SoK: layer-two blockchain protocols. In: FC, pp. 201–226 (2020)
19. Khalil, R., Gervais, A.: Revive: rebalancing off-blockchain payment networks. In: CCS, pp. 439–453 (2017)
20. Kiayias, A., Litos, O.S.T.: A composable security treatment of the Lightning network. In: CSF, pp. 334–349 (2020)
21. Lin, J., Primicerio, K., Squartini, T., Decker, C., Tessone, C.J.: Lightning network: a second path towards centralisation of the bitcoin economy. New J. Phys. **22**(8), 083022 (2020)
22. Lind, J., Naor, O., Eyal, I., Kelbert, F., Sirer, E.G., Pietzuch, P.R.: Teechain: a secure payment network with asynchronous blockchain access. In: SOSP, pp. 63–79 (2019)
23. Lisi, A., Maesa, D.D.F., Mori, P., Ricci, L.: Lightnings over rose bouquets: an analysis of the topology of the bitcoin lightning network. In: COMPSAC, pp. 324–331 (2021)
24. Lu, Z., Han, R., Yu, J.: General congestion attack on HTLC-based payment channel networks. In: Tokenomics, pp. 2:1–2:15 (2021)
25. Lubotzky, A., Phillips, R., Sarnak, P.: Ramanujan graphs. Combinatorica **8**, 261–277 (1988)
26. Malavolta, G., Moreno-Sanchez, P., Kate, A., Maffei, M.: SilentWhispers: enforcing security and privacy in decentralized credit networks. In NDSS (2017)
27. Malavolta, G., Moreno-Sanchez, P., Kate, A., Maffei, M., Ravi, S.: Concurrency and privacy with payment-channel networks. In: CCS, pp. 455–471 (2017)
28. Malavolta, G., Moreno-Sanchez, P., Schneidewind, C., Kate, A., Maffei, M.: Anonymous multi-hop locks for blockchain scalability and interoperability. In: NDSS (2019)
29. McCorry, P., Bakshi, S., Bentov, I., Meiklejohn, S., Miller, A.: Pisa: arbitration outsourcing for state channels In: AFT, pp. 16–30 (2019)
30. Meng, W., et al.: Position paper on blockchain technology: smart contract and applications. In: NSS, pp. 474–483 (2018)
31. Miller, A., Bentov, I., Bakshi, S., Kumaresan, R., McCorry, P.: Sprites and state channels: payment networks that go faster than lightning. In: FC, pp. 508–526 (2019)
32. Mizrahi, A., Zohar, A.: Congestion attacks in payment channel networks. In: FC Part II, pp. 170–188 (2021)
33. Morgenstern, M.: Existence and explicit constructions of $q+1$ regular Ramanujan graphs for every prime power q. J. Comb. Theory Ser. B, **62**, 44–62 (1994)
34. Ndolo, C., Tschorsch, F.: Payment censorship in the lightning network despite encrypted communication. In: AFT, pp. 12:1–12:24 (2024)
35. Ng, L.K.L., Chow, S.S.D., Wong, D.P.H., Woo, A.P.Y.: LDSP: shopping with cryptocurrency privately and quickly under leadership. In: ICDCS, pp. 261–271 (2021)
36. Pass, R., Shelat, A. Micropayments for decentralized currencies. In: CCS, pp. 207–218 (2015)

37. Sivaraman, V., Venkatakrishnan, S.B., Alizadeh, M., Fanti, G., Viswanath, P.: Routing cryptocurrency with the spider network. In: HotNets, pp. 29–35 (2018)
38. Tang, S., Chow, S.S.M.: Towards decentralized adaptive control of cryptocurrency liquidity via auction. In: ICDCS, pp. 910–919 (2023)
39. Tang, S., Chow, S.S.M.: Strengthening multi-hop channels via strategic mesh connections. In: FC (2025). Pre-proceeding version with appendix
40. Tanner, R.M.: Explicit concentrators from generalized N-gons. SIAM J. Algebraic Discrete Methods **5**, 287–293 (1984)
41. Tarjan, R.E.: A note on finding the bridges of a graph. Inf. Process. Lett. **2**(6), 160–161 (1974)
42. Tochner, S., Zohar, A., Schmid, S.: Route hijacking and DoS in off-chain networks. In: AFT, pp. 228–240 (2020)
43. Watts, D.J., Strogatz, S.H.: Collective dynamics of 'small-world' networks. Nature **393**(6684), 440–442 (1998)
44. Wong, H.W.H., Ma, J.P.K., Chow, S.S.M.: Secure multiparty computation of threshold signatures made more efficient. In: NDSS (2024)
45. Zabka, P., Förster, K., Decker, C., Schmid, S.: Short paper: a centrality analysis of the lightning network. In: FC, pp. 374–385 (2022)

IvyAPC: Auditable Generalized Payment Channels

Ming Li[1], Yuxian Li[1,2]($\boxtimes$), Jian Weng[1], Yingjiu Li[3], Jiasi Weng[1], Junzuo Lai[1], and Robert H. Deng[2]

[1] Jinan University, Guangzhou, China
liyuxianjnu@gmail.com
[2] Singapore Management University, Singapore, Singapore
robertdeng@smu.edu.sg
[3] University of Oregon, Eugene, USA
yingjiul@uoregon.edu

Abstract. Payment channels (PCs) are instrumental in enhancing blockchain scalability. As PCs become more prevalent, the imperative for independent and robust auditing mechanisms grows. Despite the critical need, there has been no extensive research on auditing PCs to ensure provable security. Challenges include maintaining global consensus and chronological integrity of off-chain transactions. Moreover, collusive parties pose a threat by potentially launching attacks that could disrupt the auditor's ability to verify transaction integrity.

This paper introduces IvyApc, the novel protocol designed for the auditable PC framework. IvyApc addresses the aforementioned challenges through two innovative techniques: (i) Accountable Assertions with Flexible Public Keys: This mechanism imposes penalties on parties attempting collusion during the audit process; (ii) Chain-Linking of Off-Chain Transactions: It guarantees a verifiable sequence of transactions, safeguarding against tampering within PCs. We validate the IvyApc protocol within the Universal Composability framework, demonstrating its adherence to the security prerequisites of completeness and soundness for auditing purposes. A prototype of IvyApc has been developed and tested for compatibility with Bitcoin's PC infrastructure, showcasing its practical applicability.

Keywords: Payment channel · Auditability · Layer-two solution

1 Introduction

Auditing, essential for the external review of financial records, now extends to blockchain-based cryptocurrency transactions to meet finance's evolving needs [10,11,13,14,21,25–27]. Regulatory demands, such as New Jersey-AB 320 in Blockchain 2021 Legislation[1] prompt top accounting firms like Pricewaterhouse-

---

[1] https://www.ncsl.org/research/financial-services-and-commerce/blockchain-2021-legislation.aspx.

Coopers (PwC) [29] and Ernst & Young (EY) [16] to invest in tools like EY's Blockchain Analyzer for transaction analysis [9].

Despite extensive research on blockchain auditing, the focus remains narrow on on-chain transactions, overlooking off-chain transactions. This is particularly evident in Payment Channels (PCs) that allow multiple, unrecorded cryptocurrency exchanges, highlighting the necessity for expanded auditing practices [1, 4–6, 18, 19, 28, 30, 33]. The popularity of PCs like the Lightning [1] and Raiden Networks [3], their adoption in both academia and industry, underscores the need for their auditability.

Guidelines from the audit principle mentioned in Public Company Accounting Oversight Board [2] mandate auditors to ensure the completeness of annual financial reports and internal controls. This includes off-chain transactions, integral to blockchain finance, marking a departure from traditional audits due to significant challenges in auditing PCs, which is critical yet complex [2].

1.1 Challenges and Contributions

Lack of Order Information in Off-Chain Transactions. Most current PC protocols do not provide order information such as accurate timestamps for off-chain transactions, a feature not necessarily required by the protocols themselves but crucial for auditing purposes.

Lack of Global Consensus for Off-Chain Transactions. Off-chain transactions do not undergo the public consensus verification of blockchain, which is crucial for ensuring transaction validity on the blockchain [17]. This difference makes auditing off-chain transactions difficult, as off-chain transactions are verified locally by involved parties and auditors find it hard to collect all transactions.

Potential Collusions Among Transacting Parties. In PCs, the danger of collusion exists among transaction parties, who may submit incomplete off-chain transaction records to auditors, facilitating tax evasion and other malpractices. In extreme instances, they might only reveal the channel's opening and closing transactions, concealing all intermediate off-chain transactions. Further, collusive parties may alter the orders or contents of off-chain transactions or inject false off-chain transactions (e.g., fictitious charitable donations) into a PC.

To address these challenges, we propose IvyAPC, a universal and auditable PC framework incorporating generalized channels, a concept widely adopted in existing literature [4]. Our primary innovation lies in devising a strategy that compels transaction parties to accurately report off-chain transactions to auditors. This involves structuring off-chain transactions within a hash chain and creating a non-equivocation protocol that maintains hash chain validity, even amidst colluding attacks from transaction parties. Moreover, this non-equivocation protocol offers significant adaptability while using various payment systems, as discussed in Sect. 3. In the following, the contributions of this work are summarized:

- **Auditable generalized PC constructions**. We present IvyAPC, a protocol for auditable generalized PCs that enables auditors to detect misconduct in

off-chain transactions by colluding parties. We establish a formal audit framework, emphasizing two crucial security features: completeness and succinctness (see Sect §2.1). The core component of IvyAPC is the Accountable Assertions with a Flexible Public Key (AAFPK) mechanism, which is designed to create auditable off-chain transactions. Unlike traditional accountable assertions, AAFPK utilizes versatile public keys to support multiple assertions within the same context without compromising secret keys, thereby enhancing non-equivocation in decentralized systems.
- **Formal security analysis**. We model IvyAPC in the Universal Composability (UC) framework and prove its security properties in the UC framework. In particular, we solve the problem that was left in CCS'15 [32] regarding the composability of accountable assertions.
- **Implementation and Evaluation**. We implemented a prototype of IvyAPC [12]. Our experimental results indicate that, compared to generalized channels, IvyAPC requires an additional computation cost of less than 0.5 s and an additional communication cost of less than 9KB per payment.

2 Overview

In this section, we start by introducing an audit model for personal computers and formalize the IvyAPC protocol.

2.1 Audit Model for PCs

The main participants in IvyAPC are composed of two roles: (i) transacting parties $\mathcal{P} := \{A, B, ...\}$, i.e., payers or payees, and (ii) auditor $\mathcal{D}$, e.g., an accounting firm such as Deloitte or PWC. In particular, $\mathcal{D}$ performs an audit after a channel has been closed and requires accessing off-chain transactions from transacting parties according to regulation policies (e.g., for tax checks). Compared with traditional information systems auditing that concentrates on *who* participate in financial activities and *when* did they reach an agreement on *what* [11,22,24], the audit model in IvyAPC also considers the total *income* or *spend* which relies on the order of off-chain transactions. The contents of auditing in PCs can be illustrated as the following three objects: **(1) The parties** refers to the parties who participate in PCs to perform off-chain transactions. **(2) The timestamp** is a critical factor representing the parties performing the transaction activity over time. It refers to the moment that an off-chain transaction is generated between transacting parties[2]. **(3) The data** can illustrate the consensus results (e.g., income or expenditure) that transacting parties have achieved. It mainly refers to the outcomes reached by parties in PCs, e.g., token exchange.

IvyAPC extends the basic PC protocol by adding the Audit operation as follows. Specifically, an *audit trail* is generated by transacting parties and refers to the necessary auditing information for an off-chain transaction.

---
[2] Since an un-published transaction does not have the attribution of timestamp, we thus make use of block timestamp to mark the timestamp of un-broadcast commitment transactions.

Definition 1. (Auditable Payment Channel). *An auditable payment channel is defined as a tuple:* $\gamma := (\gamma.id, \gamma.us, \gamma.cash, \gamma.state, \gamma.ctList)$, *where* $\gamma.ctList := ((\mathcal{T}_{\text{off}_0}.tid, id_0), ..., (\mathcal{T}_{\text{off}_n}.tid, id_n))$ *refers to a list of off-chain transactions with the index that happened in a PC. IvyAPC is defined with respect to a blockchain* $\mathcal{L}$, *transacting parties* $\gamma.us := \{A, B\}$, *and an auditor* $\mathcal{D}$. *It proceeds with the five operations (*Create, Update, Close, Punish, Audit*):*

- Create$(A, B, x_A, x_B) \to 1/0$. *Two parties A and B collaboratively generate a funding transaction $\mathcal{T}_{\text{fund}}$ which has two deposits x_A and x_B, respectively. It initializes an empty list ctList to store revoked commitment transactions. If $\mathcal{T}_{\text{fund}}$ is published on blockchain $\mathcal{L}$, then an auditable payment channel $\gamma := (\gamma.id, \gamma.us, \gamma.cash, \gamma.state, \gamma.ctList)$ is created successfully by outputting 1; otherwise, output 0.*
- Update$(\gamma.id, \widetilde{state}) \to 1/0$. *Upon input an update state $\widetilde{state} := (\widetilde{\theta}_1, ..., \widetilde{\theta}_l)$, two parties collaboratively generate a new commitment transaction $\mathcal{T}_{\text{com}}$ with $\widetilde{state}$. If succeed, then add $(\mathcal{T}_{\text{off}}, id)$ to ctList and output 1, where id refers to the index of $\mathcal{T}_{\text{off}}$; otherwise, output 0.*
- Close$(\gamma.id) \to 1/0$. *Upon input the identifier $\gamma.id$ of an APC, this operation checks if it is authorized by both parties. If yes, output 1; else, output 0.*
- Punish$(\gamma.id)$. *This operation is executed at the end of each round. It checks if some output of $\mathcal{T}_{\text{fund}}$ has been spent. It punishes some party if it publishes a revoked commitment transaction or does not generate an audit trail following the IvyAPC protocol.*
- Audit$(\gamma.id, \mathcal{D}) \to 1/0$. *This operation is performed after γ has been closed. Upon receiving the audit information from both transacting parties, the auditor $\mathcal{D}$ verifies the validation of these information and reconstructs a final audit trail. $\mathcal{D}$ compares it with the published transaction on $\mathcal{L}$, and outputs 1 if it is equal; otherwise, it outputs 0.*

Particularly, a closed off-chain payment channel is *auditable* means that an auditor outputs "success (1)" if the payment channel satisfies the auditability requirements, and outputs "failure (0)" otherwise. This definition implies that an auditor can detect any changes made by rational users to the history of off-chain transactions committed in the channel, where the changes can be made either before or after the channel is closed. Note that we do not consider irrational users who may collude regardless of losing all their coins from a channel; such users may change transaction history before a channel is closed without being detected by an auditor.

Assume that A and B commit a sequence of off-chain transactions $(\mathcal{T}_{\text{com}_0}, \ldots, \mathcal{T}_{\text{com}_n})$ in a GC γ funded by $\mathcal{T}_{\text{fund}}$ and closed in $\mathcal{T}_{\text{com}_n}$. The corruption and collusion of the payer/payee P_1 or P_2 may present a modified history of off-chain transactions to an auditor $\mathcal{D}$. Following the current GC protocol [4], auditor $\mathcal{D}$ *cannot* detect any changes made to the original history of off-chain transactions (including changing of their orders, changing or hiding any subset of them, and inserting any new off-chain transactions among them) as long as the modified history is consistent with $\mathcal{T}_{\mathsf{fund}}$ and $\mathcal{T}_{\mathsf{com}_n}$; that is, each transaction in the modified history spends from the output of $\mathcal{T}_{\mathsf{fund}}$ and the last one of them updates the channel to the same state as $\mathcal{T}_{\mathsf{com}_n}$ does. Note that a change of the history of committed off-chain transactions in γ may be made either before or after ζ is closed. If it is made before γ is closed, colluding users may formulate $\mathcal{T}_{\mathsf{com}_n}$ for channel closure such that $\mathcal{T}_{\mathsf{com}_n}$ is consistent with the manipulated history.

Adversary Model. We consider a Probabilistic Polynomial Time (PPT) adversary who may corrupt any user, in which case it controls the internal state of the corrupted user and all the following messages that the user sends to others. For any off-chain payment channel, we assume that its users may collude but they remain *rational* in the sense that they get compensated by all coins in the channel if their transaction counterparties misbehave. Note that this assumption of rational users is not new, but has been commonly used and heavily relied on by the existing payment channel protocols [4]. In the presence of $\mathcal{A}$, we identify the *completeness* property for characterizing the security of any auditable payment channel protocol.

Definition 2. (Completeness). *An auditable payment channel protocol* IvyAPC := (Create, Update, Close, Punish, Audit) *is complete if the following security properties hold for auditing each closed payment channel:* **(1) Authenticity.** *Adherence to the* IvyAPC *protocol ensures the validity of each commitment transaction, a property verifiable by any honest blockchain node.* **(2) Zero-transaction Loss.** *The* IvyAPC *protocol mandates the inclusion of all commitment transactions generated before the final commitment in the audit scope.* **(3) Strict-transaction Order.** *The* IvyAPC *protocol guarantees that the sequence of commitment transactions submitted for auditing accurately reflects their chronological occurrence in reality.*

3 Accountable Assertions with Flexible Public Key

3.1 Extractable Chameleon Hash with Flexible Public Key

It is a randomized hash function that can easily compute collisions given a trapdoor and allows anyone to extract the trapdoor given two different messages and random number pairs [32]. Compared with conventional extractable chameleon hash, we extend it with the flexible public key (called ECHFPK), where a public key or secret key can be transformed into a new representative of the same equivalence class, i.e., the pair of old and new key are related through a hard relation R [7]. ECHFPK includes the following PPT algorithms: (GenCh, Ch, ChgChCPK ChgChCSK, Col, ExtractCsk):

- $(cpk, csk) \leftarrow$ GenCh(1^λ): The key generation algorithm inputs the security parameter λ and outputs a public key cpk and a secret key csk (i.e., a trapdoor).
- $h \leftarrow$ Ch($cpk, x; r$): The evaluation algorithm generates a hash value h with the public key cpk, a message x, and a random r.

- $cpk' \leftarrow \mathsf{ChgChCPK}(cpk, \omega)$: The public key transformation algorithm takes cpk of an equivalence class $[cpk]_R$ and a public parameter ω as inputs. It outputs a different representative public key cpk', where $cpk' \in [cpk]_R$.
- $csk' \leftarrow \mathsf{ChgChCSK}(csk, \omega)$: The secret key transformation algorithm takes a trapdoor csk and public parameter ω as inputs, and outputs a different representative secret key csk'. This algorithm is reversible that given csk', it allows anyone to recover the secret key csk with the public ω.
- $r_1 \leftarrow \mathsf{Col}(csk', x_0, r_0, x_1)$: The collision-finding algorithm inputs a trapdoor csk' and a triple x_0, r_0, x_1 and outputs a value r_1 such that $\mathsf{Ch}(cpk', x_0; r_0) = \mathsf{Ch}(cpk', x_1; r_1)$.
- $csk' \leftarrow \mathsf{ExtractCsk}(cpk', (x_0, r_0, x_1, r_1))$: The extraction algorithm takes a public key cpk' and a 4-tuple (x_0, r_0, x_1, r_1) as inputs, and outputs csk'.

Specifically, extractable chameleon hash function satisfies: *(i) collision-resistance (ii) uniformity, and (iii) extractability* [23,32]. The collision-resistance property states that the probability for a PPT adversary $\mathcal{A}$ to find a collision without a trapdoor is negligible. The uniformity property states that given two messages x_0 and x_1, for a uniformly random value r_0, the output of Col is also a uniformly distributed random value. The extractability property states that given two pairs (x_0, r_0) and (x_1, r_1), where $\mathsf{Ch}((\mathsf{cpk}', \mathsf{x}_0; \mathsf{r}_0))) = \mathsf{Ch}((\mathsf{cpk}', \mathsf{x}_1; \mathsf{r}_1)))$ and $x_0 \neq x_1$, the trapdoor csk' can be extracted. The public and secret key transformation algorithms are instantiated according to the instantiation of extractable chameleon hash [23,32].

3.2 Accountable Assertions with Flexible Public Key Definition

Accountable Assertions with Flexible Public Key (called AAFPK) allows parties to make multiple statements in the same context under different representative secret keys without exposing the secret key. Our core idea is based on ECHFPK supporting that a key pair (apk, ask) can be transformed into a different representative key pair (apk', ask'). Note that AAFPK satisfies extractability which exposes the secret key if an assertor makes two statements in the same context under the same secret key.

Definition 3. (AAFPK). *The AAFPK protocol is a tuple of PPT algorithms* $\widetilde{\Sigma}$:=*(Gen, Assert, Verify, ChgAPK, ChgASK, Extrtact) such that:*

- $(apk, ask, auxsk) \leftarrow \mathsf{Gen}(1^\lambda)$: *The key generation algorithm inputs a security parameter λ, and outputs a public key apk, a secret key ask, an auxiliary secret information $auxsk$. For each public key, there is exactly one secret key.*
- $ask' \leftarrow \mathsf{ChgASK}(ask, \omega)$: *The secret key transformation algorithm takes a representative secret key ask, and a public parameter ω as inputs, and outputs a different representative secret key ask'. The algorithm is reversible in that given ask', it allows anyone to recover the secret key ask with the public ω.*
- $apk' \leftarrow \mathsf{ChgAPK}(apk, \omega)$: *The public key transformation algorithm inputs a representative public key apk of equivalence class $[apk]_R$, and a public parameter ω, and outputs a different representative public key $apk' \in [apk]_R$.*

- $\tau / \perp \leftarrow$ Assert($ask', auxsk, ct, st$): The assertion algorithm takes a secret key ask', an auxiliary secret information $auxsk$, a context ct, a statement st as inputs. It outputs an assertion τ (or $\perp$ if the algorithm fails to execute).
- $1/0 \leftarrow$ Verify(apk', ct, st, τ): The verification algorithm takes a public key apk', a context ct, a statement st and an assertion τ as inputs, and outputs 1 if τ is a valid assertion.
- $ask'/ \perp \leftarrow$ Extract($apk', ct, st_0, st_1, \tau_0, \tau_1$): The extraction algorithm inputs a public key apk', a context ct, two statements st_0, st_1, two assertions τ_0, τ_1, and outputs either ask' or $\perp$ to indicate failure.

3.3 AAFPK Construction

Next, we present the construction of the AAFPK protocol. For simplification, here we mainly highlight the differences and refer the reader to [32] to see the construction of ECHFPK.

*.Key Generation. The key generation algorithm chooses L be a hash function: $\{0,1\}^* \rightarrow \{1, ..., m^{\ell-1}\}$, where m and ℓ are two positive integers that represent the branching and height of a tree. We assume that $L(\cdot)$ is modeled as a random oracle. It also chooses H_0, H_2 be hash functions which are modeled as random oracles, H_1 be a collision-resistant hash function, and PRF be a pseudo-random function. Then, this algorithm generates the secret key $ask := csk$, auxiliary secret information $auxsk := \kappa$, where $(cpk, csk) \leftarrow$ ECHFPK.GenCh(1^λ), $\kappa \in \{0,1\}^\lambda$ is a key for the PRF. It sets the public key as $apk := (cpk, z, L, H_0, H_1, H_2)$, where $z := H_0(y_1^1, ..., y_m^1)$, $y_i^1 := \text{Ch}(\text{PRF}_\kappa(id, i, 0); \text{PRF}_\kappa(id, i, 1))$, $i \in [m]$, id is an identifier for the position of the root node.

*.Secret Key Transformation. In this algorithm, the secret key, denoted as ask, is initially set to csk. It then transforms to become an updated secret key, ask', ensuring that ask and ask' belong to the same equivalence classes [20]. The transformation is performed using the function ChgASK(ask, ω), which effectively converts the secret key into another secret key within the same class, represented as $ask' :=$ ECHFPK.ChgChCSK(csk, ω). Here, ω stands for a specific public parameter chosen for this operation. It's important to note that this transformation allows the original secret key, ask, to be retrieved when given csk and ω. This feature ensures that the integrity of the secret key and link to its original form is maintained despite the update.

*.Public Key Transformation. This algorithm changes the public key $apk := (cpk, z, L, H_0, H_1, H_2)$ into an updated key $apk' := (cpk', z)$, where $cpk' :=$ ECHFPK.ChgChCPK(cpk, ω) and ω is a chosen public parameter. This transformation allows the original secret key, ask, to be retrieved when given csk and ω.

*.Assertion. The assertion algorithm takes ($ask', auxsk, ct, st$) as inputs. It computes the assertion path $\{Y_\ell, a_\ell, ..., Y_1, a_1\}$ from the leaf node Y_ℓ to the root node Y_1, where Y_ℓ stores the number $L(ct)$ and each node Y_j contains m entries $Y_j := \{y_1^j, ..., y_m^j\}$, $j \in [m]$ at positions $a_j \in \{1, ..., m\}$. To assert a statement st in the context ct which is stored in Y_ℓ, the assertion algorithm computes

$r'^{\ell}_{a_{\ell}} := \mathsf{Col}(csk', x^{\ell}_{a_{\ell}}, r^{\ell}_{a_{\ell}}, \mathsf{H}_1(st))$, where $(x^{\ell}_{a_{\ell}}, r^{\ell}_{a_{\ell}})$ refer to the values that were set when the tree was initially generated. The entry refers to the position $\mathsf{L}(ct)$ is calculated as: $y^{\ell}_{a_{\ell}} = \mathsf{H}_2(\mathsf{Ch}(cpk', \mathsf{H}_1(st); r'^{\ell}_{a_{\ell}}), r'^{\ell}_{a_{\ell}}) = \mathsf{H}_2(\mathsf{Ch}(cpk', x^{\ell}_{a_{\ell}}; r^{\ell}_{a_{\ell}}), r'^{\ell}_{a_{\ell}})$. Then the algorithm calculates other entries of Y_{ℓ} as: $y^{\ell}_i := \mathsf{Ch}(cpk', \mathsf{x}^{\ell}_i; \mathsf{r}'^{\ell}_i)$, where $i \in [m] \backslash a_{\ell}$. It stores the entries $\{y^{\ell}_1, ..., y^{\ell}_m\}$ to Y_{ℓ}, and lets $z_{\ell} := \mathsf{H}_0(y^{\ell}_1, ..., y^{\ell}_m)$ and $f_{\ell} := (y^{\ell}_1, ..., y^{\ell}_{a_{\ell}-1}, y^{\ell}_{a_{\ell}+1}, ..., y^{\ell}_m)$. Similarly, the algorithm calculates other nodes $(Y_{\ell-1}, a_{\ell-1}, ..., Y_1, a_1)$ as in the computation of (Y_{ℓ}, a_{ℓ}). The calculated assertion is $\tau := ((r'^{\ell}_{a_{\ell}}, f_{\ell}, a_{\ell}), ..., (r'^{1}_1, f_1, a_1))$, where $f_{\epsilon} := (y^{\epsilon}_1, ..., y^{\epsilon}_{a_{\epsilon}-1}, y^{\epsilon}_{a_{\epsilon}+1}, ..., y^{\epsilon}_m)$, where $\epsilon \in [\ell]$.

*.Verification. This algorithm takes (apk', ct, st, τ) as inputs, and parses apk' as (cpk', z) and τ as $((r'^{\ell}_{a_{\ell}}, f_{\ell}, a_{\ell}), ..., (r'^{1}_1, f_1, a_1))$. Then it reconstructs the path from the leaf node Y_l to the root node Y_1, where $Y_1 := (y^1_1, ..., y^1_m)$. If the constructed root $\mathsf{H}(y^1_1, ..., y^1_m)$ is equal to z, it outputs 1; otherwise, it outputs 0.

*.Extraction. This algorithm inputs $(apk', ct, st_0, st_1, \tau_0, \tau_1)$ and reconstructs the path from the leaf node to the root node for both (ct, st_0, τ_0) and (ct, st_1, τ_1). During the reconstruction, there will exist a node that forms a collusion in ECHFPK. That is, there exist values (x_0, r_0) and (x_1, r_1) that enables ECHFPK.Ch $(cpk', x_0; r_0)$ =ECHFPK.Ch$(cpk', x_1; r_1)$. According to the extraction algorithm of ECHFPK, the secret key csk' can be extracted as $csk' \leftarrow$ ECHFPK.ExtractCsk $(cpk', x_0, r_0, x_1, r_1)$. If no collusion is found, the extraction algorithm outputs $\bot$.

Remark. When the assertor chooses a different representative key pair, denoted as (apk', ask'), to generate the signature τ, the verifiers must use the ChgPK(apk, ω) algorithm. This algorithm allows them to compute and verify the corresponding public key apk' necessary for validating τ. However, if the assertor claims different statements within the same context using the same representative key pair, the verifiers are then able to deduce the secret key ask'. This is done by effectively 'removing' the public component ω from the known quantities, revealing the secret key ask.

Theorem 1. *If* $\mathsf{L}, \mathsf{H}_0, \mathsf{H}_2$ *are modeled random oracle and the extractable chameleon hash with flexible public key scheme ECHFPK is collision-resistant, the accountable assertions with flexible public key scheme described in §3.3 is unforgeable.*

Theorem 2. *Let* $\widetilde{\sum} =$ (Gen, ChgAPK, ChgASK, Assert, Verify, Extrtact) *be an accountable assertions with flexible public key protocol. Then* $\widetilde{\sum}$ *UC-realizes the ideal accountable assertions functionality* $\mathcal{F}_{\mathsf{AA}}$ *if and only if the AAFPK protocol is unforgeable.*

4 IvyAPC Protocol

4.1 Protocol Specification

This section details the specific framework of our tool, as referenced in Fig. 1. Our methodology requires that each extended GC γ presented for audit include at least one off-chain transaction and that it be closed by an off-chain transaction published on a blockchain. For simplicity, we conceptualize a complete transaction as comprising two distinct segments, symbolized by $\mathcal{T} := \{[\mathcal{T}], dat\}$. Here, $[\mathcal{T}] := \{in, out, v, tl\}$ represents the core payment component of $\mathcal{T}$, which lacks a signature. The dat refers to a data space, housing audit-relevant information (called audit trail)s.

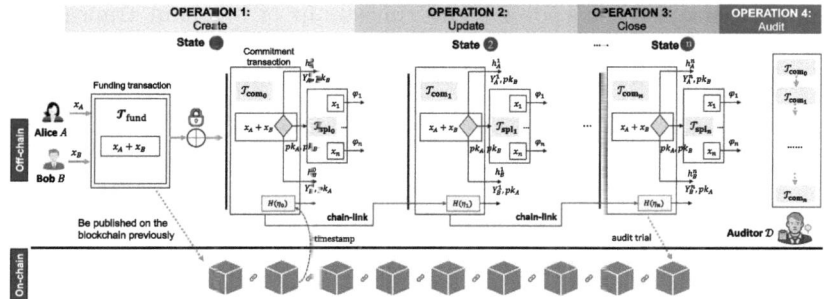

Fig. 1. An illustration of the IvyAPC protocol.

*.Create. Creating a payment channel involves three key steps for the transacting parties: generating the funding transaction $\mathcal{T}_{\mathsf{fund}}$, creating the initial commitment transaction $\mathcal{T}_{\mathsf{com}_0}$, and forming the initial split transaction $\mathcal{T}_{\mathsf{spl}_0}$. This procedure diverges from the GC protocol [4] in several crucial aspects: (i) *Assertion Exchange:* Transacting parties are required to exchange assertions using the AAFPK protocol during this operation. (ii) *Timestamping:* Each commitment transaction is marked with a timestamp using an on-chain transaction. (iii) *Digest Inclusion:* The digest of assertions and timestamps must be included in an unspent output.

The users A and B start by locally creating the funding transaction $[\mathcal{T}_{\mathsf{fund}}]$ and the commitment transaction $[\mathcal{T}_{\mathsf{com}_0}]$. To do this, each user generates their own set of keys A generates $(apk_A, ask_A, auxsk_A)$ and B generates $(apk_B, ask_B, auxsk_B)$, using the $\widetilde{\sum}$.Gen function with a security parameter λ. Here, apk stands for the public key, ask for the secret key, and $auxsk$, an auxiliary secret key, is derived by hashing ask, specifically $auxsk := \mathsf{H}_0(ask)$. The secret keys ask_A and ask_B are termed as *colluding secrets*. They are crucial for ensuring that any attempt by A and B to alter the history of off-chain transactions in γ can be penalized. Following the key generation, A and B exchange their public keys $(apk_A$ and $apk_B)$, ensuring that $apk_A \neq apk_B$. They then store the pair $\xi_0 = (apk_A, apk_B)$ locally as the *audit trail* for the funding transaction $[\mathcal{T}_{\mathsf{fund}}]$. Before signing and broadcasting $[\mathcal{T}_{\mathsf{fund}}]$ to the blockchain, they incorporate $h_0 = \mathsf{H}_1(\xi_0)$ into it. Here, h_0 is included as an unspendable transaction output, such as using the OP_RETURN in Bitcoin.

Then, each party generate their accountable assertions τ_A^0, τ_B^0 of $[\mathcal{T}_{\mathsf{com}_0}]$ under the context of $[\mathcal{T}_{\mathsf{fund}}]$ (written as ct). These assertions are generated using the

$\widetilde{\sum}$.Assert algorithm. Specifically, party A computes τ_A^0 as $\widetilde{\sum}$.Assert(ask$_A$, auxsk$_A$, $\mathsf{H}_1(0, [\mathcal{T}_{\mathsf{fund}}]), [\mathcal{T}_{\mathsf{com}_0}])$, and similarly, party B computes τ_B^0. To ensure that the assertions are indeed exchanged and linked to the transacting parties, IvyAPC requires each party to generate proof. This proof associates each party's private revocation key (r) with the other party's assertion (τ) using a hash function. For instance, after party A sends its assertion τ_A^0 to party B, party B verifies it with $\widetilde{\sum}$.Verify. Upon successful verification, B generates a proof $\varsigma_B^0 := \mathsf{H}_0(\tau_A^0 \| r_B^0)$. This mechanism also incorporates the timestamp of on-chain transactions to mark the commitment transactions' timing accurately. The audit trail from the first commitment transaction is captured in the format:

$$\eta_0 := (\tau_A^0, \tau_B^0, \varsigma_A^0, \varsigma_B^0, [\mathcal{T}_{\mathsf{fund}}], [\mathcal{T}_{\mathsf{com}_0}], n), \quad (1)$$
$$\text{where } \varsigma_A^0 := \mathsf{H}_0(\tau_B^0 \| r_A^0) \text{ and } \varsigma_B^0 := \mathsf{H}_0(\tau_A^0 \| r_B^0),$$

where r_A^0 and r_B^0 respectively refer to the private revocation key of party A and B, $n := 0$ refers to the first index of $\mathcal{T}_{\mathsf{com}_0}$.

Once transacting parties generate the complete commitment transaction $\mathcal{T}_{\mathsf{com}_0} := \{[\mathcal{T}_{\mathsf{com}_0}], \mathsf{H}(\eta_0)\}$ locally, they can exchange the (pre-)signature $\mathcal{T}_{\mathsf{spl}_0}$, $\mathcal{T}_{\mathsf{com}_0}$, and $\mathcal{T}_{\mathsf{fund}}$ as in [4]. Upon the publication of $\mathcal{T}_{\mathsf{fund}}$ on the blockchain, an auditable payment channel, denoted as γ, is successfully established.

*.Update. In this operation, transacting parties pay for each other by updating the state of the channel. That is, they collaboratively update the state of γ from $\gamma.cash := (x_A, x_B)$ to $\widetilde{\gamma.cash} := (\widetilde{x_A}, \widetilde{x_B})$. This process involves several key steps: (1) *Invalidation of the Old Commitment Transaction:* The parties agree to invalidate the previous commitment transaction. This step is crucial for ensuring that only the most recent state of the channel can be finalized on the blockchain. (2) *Generation of New Transactions:* A new commitment transaction and a corresponding split transaction are generated. These transactions reflect the updated balances $(\widetilde{x_A}, \widetilde{x_B})$ of the parties. Each off-chain transaction, $[\mathcal{T}_{\mathsf{com}_n}]$, is constructed to distribute the total coins $(x_A + x_B)$ in γ based on the latest agreed-upon balances. If transaction $[\mathcal{T}_{\mathsf{com}_n}]$ is published on a blockchain by party A (without loss of generality), it activates specific spending conditions according to the updated distribution of funds: *(1) Colluding Condition*: $(x_A + x_B)$ can be spent by a blockchain on-chain transaction that is verifiable w.r.t. X_A and X_B at any time after $[\mathcal{T}_{\mathsf{com}_n}]$ was published on blockchains. *(2) Publishing condition*: $(x_A + x_B)$ can be spent by B with a time lock Δ (n.e., after Δ time since $[\mathcal{T}_{\mathsf{com}_n}]$ was published on blockchains) if $[\mathcal{T}_{\mathsf{com}_n}]$ was revoked. *(3) Finalizing condition*: $(x_A + x_B)$ is spent by A and B for finalizing the channel state of γ with a time lock 2Δ if $[\mathcal{T}_{\mathsf{com}_n}]$ has not been revoked.

The *colluding condition* is used to punish a colluding user by their counterparty who can unilaterally spend all coins in γ if the history of committed off-chain transactions in γ is modified in their collusion attacks. Similar to the original GC protocol [4], the *publishing condition* is used to punish a user by their counterparty who can unilaterally spend all coins in γ if the user publishes a revoked off-chain transaction for channel closure. The only difference is that we add a time lock Δ to the publishing condition so that any collusion attack can be punished at a higher priority. The *finalizing condition* is also similar to that in the original GC protocol [4] except that its time lock is set to be twice as long to leave sufficient time for punishing any user publishing a revoked off-chain transaction before finalizing the channel state of γ. The parameter Δ serves as a system-wide constant, establishing a timeframe within which punitive actions can be executed on the blockchain to maintain channel integrity.

More concretely, a transacting party (e.g., A) first chooses a public parameter $\omega_A \in \mathbb{Z}_q^*$ and transforms the secret key $ask_A^n := \widetilde{\Sigma}.\mathsf{ChASK}(ask_A, n \cdot \omega_A) := ask_A \oplus n \cdot \omega_A$. It requires A to utilize a public parameter, e.g., $\omega_A := \mathsf{H}_0(\mathcal{T}_{\mathsf{fund}})$. When the n-th off-chain transaction $[\mathcal{T}_{\mathsf{com}_n}]$ ($n \geq 1$) is created in γ, users A and B exchange their accountable assertions τ_A^n, τ_B^n of $[\mathcal{T}_{\mathsf{com}_n}]$ under the context of $[\mathcal{T}_{\mathsf{fund}}]$, where $\tau_A^n \leftarrow \widetilde{\Sigma}.\mathsf{Assert}(ask_A, auxsk_A, ct, st_n)$ (i.e., $ct = \mathsf{H}_1(n, [\mathcal{T}_{\mathsf{fund}}])$ and $st_n := [\mathcal{T}_{\mathsf{com}_n}]$) and $\tau_B^n \leftarrow \widetilde{\Sigma}.\mathsf{Assert}(ask_B, auxsk_B, ct, st_n)$.

More concretely, a participant (e.g., A) selects a public parameter $\omega_A \in \mathbb{Z}_q^*$ and modifies their secret key to $ask_A^n := \widetilde{\Sigma}.\mathsf{ChASK}(ask_A, n \cdot \omega_A) := ask_A \oplus n \cdot \omega_A$, leveraging $\omega_A := \mathsf{H}_0(\mathcal{T}_{\mathsf{fund}})$. Upon generating the n-th off-chain transaction $[\mathcal{T}_{\mathsf{com}_n}]$ in γ, users A and B exchange their accountable assertions τ_A^n, τ_B^n of $[\mathcal{T}_{\mathsf{com}_n}]$ under the context of $[\mathcal{T}_{\mathsf{fund}}]$, where $\tau_A^n \leftarrow \widetilde{\Sigma}.\mathsf{Assert}(ask_A, auxsk_A, ct, st_n)$ (i.e., $ct = \mathsf{H}_1(n, [\mathcal{T}_{\mathsf{fund}}])$ and $st_n := [\mathcal{T}_{\mathsf{com}_n}]$) and $\tau_B^n \leftarrow \widetilde{\Sigma}.\mathsf{Assert}(ask_B, auxsk_B, ct, st_n)$.

Then, they embed the *hash chain* $h_n = Hash_1(h_{n-1} \| \xi_n)$ in $[\mathcal{T}_{\mathsf{com}_n}]$ before committing it[3] in γ. Specifically, upon receiving assertion τ_A^n from party A, party B first computes a new representative public key $apk_A^n = \widetilde{\Sigma}.\mathsf{ChAPK}(apk_A, n \odot \omega_A) := apk_A \odot n \cdot \omega_A$ and then verifies τ_A^n through using $\widetilde{\Sigma}.\mathsf{Verify}(apk_A^n, ct, st_n, \tau_A^n)$. If it outputs "1", party B generates a proof $\varsigma_B^n := \mathsf{H}_0(\tau_A^n \| r_B^n)$, where r_B^n refers to party B' private revocation key to be used in $[\mathcal{T}_{\mathsf{com}_n}]$. They exchange the proof and generate the audit trail η_n as in Equation (1). The timestamp value ts_n in η_n is set as the earliest timestamp in the latest block. After that, they construct and sign the complete commitment transaction $\mathcal{T}_{\mathsf{com}_n} := \{[\mathcal{T}_{\mathsf{com}_n}], (\mathsf{H}_0(\eta_n), \mathsf{H}_0(\eta_{n-1}))\}$ and split transaction $\mathcal{T}_{\mathsf{spl}_n}$.

*.Close. Transacting parties close the channel by publishing a commitment transaction to the blockchain. Under the revocation mechanisms, transacting parties can close the channel peacefully without disrupting the fairness between them. If a transacting party closes the channel by publishing a revoked commitment transaction on the blockchain or regenerating a commitment transaction without including the digest of all previous commitment transactions, IvyAPC allows the other party to redeem the deposit of that party.

*.Punish. This operation happens if (i) a transacting party publishes an old commitment transaction to the blockchain or (ii) makes two statements under the same representative secret key. For (i), suppose party A publishes an old

---

[3] In generalized channel [4], each off-chain transaction $[\mathcal{T}_{\mathsf{com}_n}]$ is constructed as a commitment transaction followed by a split transaction. The embedding should be performed on the commitment transaction as its unspendable transaction output.

commitment transaction, party B can utilize the pre-signature and complete signature of the transaction to calculate party A's secret witness y_A based on the extractability of adapter signature. With the witness y_A, party B can spend all the output of the channel. For (ii), party A's secret key ask_A would be extracted by B via $\widetilde{\Sigma}$.Extract. In both cases, B can spend the output of transaction $\mathcal{T}_{\text{com}_n}$ without interaction with A.

*.**Audit.** This operation is performed by auditor $\mathcal{D}$ who requires both transacting parties to provide information to be audited.

Given a channel γ, an auditor O may audit a sequence of off-chain transactions $\gamma.ctList := \{\mathcal{T}_{\text{com}_i}.tid, \mathcal{T}_{\text{spl}_i}.tid, n\}_{i \in [n]}$, audit trails $\{\eta_i\}_{i \in [n]}$, revocation secrets $\{r_\mathcal{P}^i\}_{i \in [n], \mathcal{P} \in \{A,B\}}$, assertions and their exchange proofs $\{\varsigma_\mathcal{P}^i, \tau_\mathcal{P}^i\}_{i \in [n], \mathcal{P} \in \{A,B\}}$, and public parameters $\{\omega_\mathcal{P}\}_{\mathcal{P} \in \{A,B\}}$. The auditor outputs "success" *iff* all of the following *audit conditions* are meet:

1. *Checking all transactions*: The funding transaction $\mathcal{T}_{\text{fund}}$ and the closing transaction $\mathcal{T}_{\text{com}_n}$ were published on-chain; the sequence of off-chain transactions is non-empty and all of them were committed in γ by their users; the signature of each commitment transaction is valid..
2. *Checking all audit trails*: Check if $\{\tau_\mathcal{P}^i\}_{i \in [n], \mathcal{P} \in \{A,B\}}$ and $\{\varsigma_\mathcal{P}^i, r_\mathcal{P}^i\}_{i \in [n], \mathcal{P} \in \{A,B\}}$ are correct, i.e., if $\mathsf{H}_0(r_\mathcal{P}^i) = h_\mathcal{P}^i$ and $\varsigma_\mathcal{P}^i = \mathsf{H}_0(\tau_\mathcal{P}^i || r_\mathcal{P}^i)$ hold.
3. *Checking hash chains*: Check $\mathsf{H}_0(r_\mathcal{P}^i) = h_\mathcal{P}^i$ and $\varsigma_\mathcal{P}^i = \mathsf{H}_0(\tau_\mathcal{P}^i || r_\mathcal{P}^i)$ for $1 \leq i \leq n$.
4. *Checking consistency between $\widetilde{\eta_n}$ and η_n*: Compute the latest audit information $\widetilde{\eta_n}$ according to the provided information $\{\gamma.ctList, \{\eta_i, \omega_\mathcal{P}, r_\mathcal{P}^i\}_{i \in [n], \mathcal{P} \in \{A,B\}}\}$, and verify whether the hash value of $\widetilde{\eta_n}$ is equal to hash value of η_n that is included in the closing transaction $\mathcal{T}_{\text{com}_n}$.
5. *Checking spending time of $\mathcal{T}_{\text{com}_n}$*: If $\mathcal{T}_{\text{com}_n}$ was spent on the blockchain, it was spent after 2Δ time since $\mathcal{T}_{\text{com}_n}$ was published on the blockchain.

If the information submitted for audit is the original history of off-chain transactions committed in γ and associated audit trails, it is clear that the auditor outputs "success" following our methodology. Next, we clarify that our methodology enables the auditor to output "failure" if a modified history of off-chain transactions and associated audit trails (if any) are submitted for audit.

5 Security Analysis

Let sequence $(\bar{\mathcal{T}}_{\text{com}_1}, \ldots, \bar{\mathcal{T}}_{\text{com}_m})$ for $m \geq 1$ denote the original history of the off-chain transactions committed in channel γ funded by $\mathcal{T}_{\text{fund}}$ and closed by $\mathcal{T}_{\text{com}_{\text{last}}}$. For each $\bar{\mathcal{T}}_{\text{com}_i}$ in the original history, we assume that users A and B already generated an audit trail and embedded a hash chain $\bar{h}_i$ (out of scope is that the users do not follow the extended GC in the first place). Let sequence $(\mathcal{T}_{\text{com}_1}, \ldots, \mathcal{T}_{\text{com}_l})$ denote a changed history of committed off-chain transactions in γ. In the following analysis we make a non-trivial assumption: (i) the changed history is non-empty (i.e., $n \geq 1$), (ii) $\mathcal{T}_{\mathsf{com}_i}$ is committed by both A and B, (iii) the i-th audit trail is generated for $\mathcal{T}_{\mathsf{com}_i}$ following our methodology, and (iv) a hash chain h_i is embedded in each $\mathcal{T}_{\mathsf{com}_i}$ following our methodology; otherwise, an auditor can trivially output "failure" by checking the first three *audit conditions* mentioned above. Any changes made to the original history in γ can be categorized into the exclusive cases:

– *Case I (i.e., arbitrary-ordering attack):* $\{i : \bar{\mathcal{T}}_{\mathsf{com}_i} \neq \mathcal{T}_{\mathsf{com}_i}, 1 \leq i \leq m\} \neq \emptyset$.
– *Case II (i.e., discarding attack):* $1 \leq n < m$ and $\bar{\mathcal{T}}_{\mathsf{com}_i} = \mathcal{T}_{\mathsf{com}_i}$ for $i \leq n < m$.
– *Case III (i.e., injection attack):* $1 \leq m < n$ and $\bar{\mathcal{T}}_{\mathsf{com}_i} = \mathcal{T}_{\mathsf{com}_i}$ for all $i \leq m < n$.

Case I means that at least one off-chain transaction in the original history was changed, which refers to the *arbitrary-ordering attack*. Let $m_0 = \min\{i : \bar{\mathcal{T}}_{\mathsf{com}_i} \neq \mathcal{T}_{\mathsf{com}_i}, 1 \leq i \leq m\}$. Since both A and B need to commit the changed off-chain transaction, $\mathcal{T}_{\mathsf{com}_{m_0}}$, it requires collusion between A and B. If A and B in collusion made the change *after* γ was closed, then the audit trail η_{m_0} for the changed transaction $\mathcal{T}_{\mathsf{com}_{m_0}}$ is different from the audit trail $\bar{\eta}_{m_0}$ for the original transaction $\bar{\mathcal{T}}_{\mathsf{com}_i}$; thus, the auditor can output "failure" by checking the consistency between $\mathcal{T}_{\mathsf{com}_{\mathsf{last}}}$ and $\mathcal{T}_{\mathsf{com}_n}$ (i.e., the 4-th audit condition): The auditor can detect that the hash chain $\bar{h}_m$ embedded in $\mathcal{T}_{\mathsf{com}_{\mathsf{last}}}$ (which is computed partly from $\bar{\eta}_{m_0}$) is different from the hash chain h_n embedded in $\mathcal{T}_{\mathsf{com}_n}$ (which is computed partly from η_{m_0}).

On the other hand, if A and B in collusion made the change from $\bar{\mathcal{T}}_{\mathsf{com}_{m_0}}$ to $\mathcal{T}_{\mathsf{com}_{m_0}}$ *before* γ was closed, they embed h_n into $\mathcal{T}_{\mathsf{com}_{\mathsf{last}}}$ such that the auditor cannot detect any inconsistency between $\mathcal{T}_{\mathsf{com}_{\mathsf{last}}}$ and $\mathcal{T}_{\mathsf{com}_n}$. In this case, the auditor can still output "failure" by checking the spending time of $\mathcal{T}_{\mathsf{com}_{\mathsf{last}}}$ (i.e., the 5-th audit condition). The auditor can detect that $\mathcal{T}_{\mathsf{com}_{\mathsf{last}}}$ was spent within Δ time since $\mathcal{T}_{\mathsf{com}_{\mathsf{last}}}$ was published on the blockchain. This is because A and B need to compute their accountable assertions $\tau_A^{m_0}, \tau_B^{m_0}$ and exchange them for constructing a valid audit trail η_{m_0}. The user, say A w.l.o.g., who receives $\tau_B^{m_0}$ before B receives $\tau_A^{m_0}$ (or B receives no $\tau_A^{m_0}$), can extract B's colluding secret $ask'_B := \widetilde{\Sigma}.\mathsf{Extract}(apk'_B, ct, st_{m_0}, \bar{st}_{m_0}, \tau_B^{m_0}, \bar{\tau}_B^{m_0})$. Recall that in the original history, A had already received B's accountable assertion $\bar{\tau}_{B,m_0}$ in constructing $\bar{\eta}_{m_0}$. Now A can publish $\bar{\mathcal{T}}_{\mathsf{com}_{m_0}}$ on the blockchain as $\mathcal{T}_{\mathsf{com}_{\mathsf{last}}}$ and punish B by spending all coins in γ within Δ time under the colluding condition of $\bar{\mathcal{T}}_{\mathsf{com}_{m_0}}$. A rational A will do so because if A does not punish B but sends its accountable assertion $\tau_A^{m_0}$ to B, then B can punish A by publishing $\bar{\mathcal{T}}_{\mathsf{com}_{m_0}}$ and spending all coins in γ under the colluding condition of $\bar{\mathcal{T}}_{\mathsf{com}_{m_0}}$.

Case II means that no off-chain transaction in the original history was changed but a last segment of it was missing in the changed history, which refers to the *discarding attack*. In this case, each off-chain transaction in the changed history was ever revoked by A and B. If the change was made *after* γ was closed, then the auditor can output "failure" by checking the consistency between $\mathcal{T}_{\mathsf{com}_{\mathsf{last}}}$ and $\mathcal{T}_{\mathsf{com}_n}$ (i.e., the fourth audit condition): The auditor can detect that the hash chain $\bar{h}_m$ embedded in $\mathcal{T}_{\mathsf{com}_{\mathsf{last}}}$ is different from the hash chain h_n embedded in $\mathcal{T}_{\mathsf{com}_n}$. On the other hand, if the change was made *before* γ was closed, a user, A w.l.o.g., could publish $\mathcal{T}_{\mathsf{com}_n}$ for channel closure (i.e., $\mathcal{T}_{\mathsf{com}_{\mathsf{last}}} = \mathcal{T}_{\mathsf{com}_n}$) such that the auditor cannot detect any inconsistency between $\mathcal{T}_{\mathsf{com}_{\mathsf{last}}}$ and $\mathcal{T}_{\mathsf{com}_n}$. In this case, the auditor can still output "failure" by checking the spending time of $\mathcal{T}_{\mathsf{com}_{\mathsf{last}}}$ (i.e., the fifth audit condition). The auditor can detect that $\mathcal{T}_{\mathsf{com}_{\mathsf{last}}}$ was spent in $[\Delta, 2\Delta)$ time since $\mathcal{T}_{\mathsf{com}_{\mathsf{last}}}$ was published on the blockchain. This is because a rational B punishes user A for publishing a revoked off-chain transaction $\mathcal{T}_{\mathsf{com}_n}$ on the blockchain under the publishing condition of $\mathcal{T}_{\mathsf{com}_n}$.

Case III means that no off-chain transaction in the original history was changed but additional off-chain transactions were appended in the changed history. If the change was made *after* γ was closed, then the auditor can output "failure" by checking the consistency between $\mathcal{T}_{\mathsf{com}_{\mathsf{last}}}$ and $\mathcal{T}_{\mathsf{com}_n}$. The auditor can detect that the hash chain $\bar{h}_m$ embedded in $\mathcal{T}_{\mathsf{com}_{\mathsf{last}}}$ is different from the hash chain h_n embedded in $\mathcal{T}_{\mathsf{com}_n}$. Further, if the change was made *before* γ was closed, both A and B committed the additional off-chain transactions $\mathcal{T}_{\mathsf{com}_{m+1}}, \ldots, \mathcal{T}_{\mathsf{com}_n}$, computed their audit trails, and embedded their hash chains following our assumption. If γ was not closed on $\mathcal{T}_{\mathsf{com}_n}$ but on a revoked transaction, the auditor can output "failure" by detecting that $\mathcal{T}_{\mathsf{com}_{\mathsf{last}}}$ was spent in $[\Delta, 2\Delta)$ time since $\mathcal{T}_{\mathsf{com}_{\mathsf{last}}}$ was published on the blockchain. If γ was closed on $\mathcal{T}_{\mathsf{com}_n}$ (i.e., $\mathcal{T}_{\mathsf{com}_{\mathsf{last}}} = \mathcal{T}_{\mathsf{com}_n}$), then the changed history ($\mathcal{T}_{\mathsf{com}_1}, \ldots, \mathcal{T}_{\mathsf{com}_n}$) can be treated as a new original history in γ since A and B continued committing additional off-chain transactions beyond the old original history before the channel was closed. Our above analysis on any changes made to the old original history can be applied recursively to any changes made to the new original history.

6 Instantiation and Implementation

6.1 Implementation

Our work is implemented using C++ and Javascript. It depends on the full source code of *libsecp256k1* [15] to perform elliptic curve computations, and accountable assertions [31] to realize the AAFPK protocol. Bitcoin environment was built locally on a personal computer ("Intel(R) Core(TM) i5-5200U CPU @ 2.20GHz", 4GB RAM). We make use of *bitcoinjs-lib* [8] as a programming lib to interact with Bitcoin. The implementation is publicly available [12]. To evaluate the performance of IvyAPC, we modeled two parties as two clients in the computer and conducted the experiments by letting them generate 100 commitment transactions in a channel (i.e., $n = 99$). At the time of writing, the average price of Bitcoin is 10 satoshis per byte citebitcoinfees or 0.0039 USD per byte.

6.2 Evaluation Results

Compared with GCs [4], IvyAPC does not reduce the number of on-chain or off-chain transactions. Thus, we mainly present its extra computation and storage costs in generating audit trails in commitment transactions.

*.Computation Cost. Table 1a shown the computation cost of the AAFPK protocol. The results show that the public and secret key transform algorithms are efficient and take no more than 1 μs. The performance of the assertion and verification algorithm is as efficient as [32] which takes about 4.3 ms and 5.1 ms, respectively. Besides, the computation cost of an audit trail includes the assertion generation, verification, and exchange proof generation as in Eq. (1), which takes 121.3 ms on average (considering local communication cost between two parties). In addition, we allow one party to extract the secret key of the other party in case of dishonest behavior. The Extract algorithm recovers a transformed secret key first and removes the public parameter to obtain the secret, which takes 5.4 ms on average.

*.Storage Cost. Regarding the storage cost, we mainly evaluate the size and transaction fees concerning the funding and commitment transactions. The results are shown in Table 1b. Specifically, each commitment transaction contains a hash value for storing audit information, resulting in an extra cost of 32 bytes compared with GCs [4]. The size of a funding transaction and a commitment transaction are about 744 bytes and 1303 bytes, respectively, resulting in the cost of 2.90 USD and 5.08 USD on the Bitcoin blockchain. To generate an audit trail in a commitment transaction, a transacting party is required to send an assertion and its exchanging proof to the other party, which takes 4192 bytes. Besides, to provide the whole history of commitment transactions to the auditor, one party needs to store $100*(2\ \tau|+|\mathcal{T}_{com}|+2*|\varsigma|+|\mathcal{T}_{on}.ts|)$, where the size of an assertion τ, ς, and $|\mathcal{T}_{on}\ ts|$ are 4160 bytes, 32 byte, 8 bytes, respectively. To audit 100 commitment transactions, one party is required to store about 0.92MB.

Table 1. Computation and Storage Costs of the AAFPK Protocol

Operation	Average Time
ChgAPK/ChgASK	1.0 μs
Assert	4.3 ms
Verify	5.1 ms
Extract	5.4 ms

Operation	Size (bytes)	Cost (USD)
Funding Transaction	744	2.90
Commitment Transaction	1303	5.08
Audit Trail in a Commitment Transaction	4192	-

7 Conclusion

Payment Channels (PCs) have emerged as a pivotal solution for enhancing blockchain scalability. In this study, we tackled the auditing challenges associated with off-chain transactions and introduced IvyApc—a comprehensive, auditable protocol tailored for PCs. Our contributions are twofold: (i) Audit Model: We established a formal audit model that delineates the security criteria necessary for PC audits. (ii) Accountable Assertions Scheme: We devised the Accountable Assertions Scheme with Flexible Public Key (AAFPK) and integrated it into the IvyApc framework. Through rigorous proofs, we have affirmed that IvyApc fulfills the stringent security standards set by our audit model within the UC framework. Moreover, practical implementation tests confirm that IvyApc is not only theoretically sound but also viable for real-world applications.

Acknowledgement. This was supported by the National Natural Science Foundation of China (Nos. 2020YFB1005600, 62102165, 62472198, U2001205,62332007, U22B2028, 62302192, U23A20303), the Science and Technology Major Project of Tibetan Autonomous Region of China (No. XZ202201ZD0006G), the Natural Science Foundation of Guangdong Province (No. 2024A1515010086), and the Science and Technology Program of Guangzhou (Nos. 2024A03J0464, 2024A04J3691), Guangdong Basic and Applied Basic Research Foundation (No. 2023B1515040020) National Joint Engineering Research Center of Network Security Detection and Protection Technology, Guangdong Key Laboratory of Data Security and Privacy Preserving, Guangdong Hong Kong Joint Laboratory for Data Security and Privacy Protection, and the Ripple University Blockchain Research Initiative.

References

1. Lightning network (2022)
2. Public company accounting oversight board (2022)
3. Raiden network (2022)
4. Aumayr, L., et al.: Generalized bitcoin-compatible channels. Cryptology ePrint Archive **2020**, 476 (2020)
5. Aumayr, L., et al.: Bitcoin-compatible virtual channels. In: S&P, pp. 901–918. IEEE (2021)
6. Aumayr, L., Thyagarajan, S.A., Malavolta, G., Monero-Sánchez, P., Maffei, M.: Sleepy channels: bitcoin-compatible bi-directional payment channels without watchtowers. Cryptology ePrint Archive (2021)
7. Backes, M., Hanzlik, L., Kluczniak, K., Schneider, J.: Signatures with flexible public key: introducing equivalence classes for public keys. In: Asiacrypt, pp. 405–434. Springer (2018)
8. BitcoinJS: bitcoinjs-lib. https://github.com/bitcoinjs/bitcoinjs-lib (2024), Accessed 27 Apr 2024
9. Bonyuet, D.: Overview and impact of blockchain on auditing. Int. J. Digit. Account. Res. **20**, 31–43 (2020)
10. Chatzigiannis, P., Baldimtsi, F.: Miniledger: compact-sized anonymous and auditable distributed payments. In: ESORICS, pp. 407–429. Springer (2021)
11. Chatzigiannis, P., Baldimtsi, F., Chalkias, K.: Sok: auditability and accountability in distributed payment systems. In: ACNS, pp. 311–337. Springer (2021)
12. Consortium, A.C.: Auditable channel consortium implementation. https://github.com/AuditableChannel-Consortium (2024), Accessed 27 Apr 2024
13. Dagher, G.G., Bünz, B., Bonneau, J., Clark, J., Boneh, D.: Provisions: Privacy-preserving proofs of solvency for bitcoin exchanges. In: CCS, pp. 720–731 (2015)
14. Daian, P., et al.: Flash boys 2.0: Frontrunning in decentralized exchanges, miner extractable value, and consensus instability. In: S&P, pp. 910–927. IEEE (2020)
15. Developers, B.C.: libsecp256k1. https://github.com/bitcoin/secp256k1 (2024), Accessed 27 Apr 2024

16. EY Global: Building a better working world. https://www.ey.com/en_gl (2024), Accessed 27 Apr 2024
17. Garay, J., Kiayias, A., Leonardos, N.: The bitcoin backbone protocol: Analysis and applications. In: Eurocrypt, pp. 281–310. Springer (2015)
18. Ge, Z., Gu, J., Wang, C., Long, Y., Xu, X., Gu, D.: Accio: Variable-amount, optimized-unlinkable and nizk-free off-chain payments via hubs. In: CCS, pp. 1541–1555 (2023)
19. Glaeser, N., Maffei, M., Malavolta, G., Moreno-Sanchez, P., Tairi, E., Thyagarajan, S.A.K.: Foundations of coin mixing services. In: CCS, pp. 1259–1273 (2022)
20. Hanser, C., Slamanig, D.: Structure-preserving signatures on equivalence classes and their application to anonymous credentials. In: Asiacrypt, pp. 491–511. Springer (2014)
21. Jiang, Y., Li, Y., Zhu, Y.: Auditable zerocoin scheme with user awareness. In: ICCSP, pp. 28–32 (2019)
22. Kogan, B., Jajodia, S.: An audit model for object-oriented databases. In: Proceedings Seventh Annual Computer Security Applications Conference, pp. 90–91. IEEE Computer Society (1991)
23. Krawczyk, H., Rabin, T.: Chameleon hashing and signatures (1998)
24. Latham, D.C.: Department of defense trusted computer system evaluation criteria. Department of Defense (1986)
25. Li, Y., et al.: Auditpch: Auditable payment channel hub with privacy protection. TIFS (2024)
26. Naganuma, K., Yoshino, M., Sato, H., Suzuki, T.: Auditable zerocoin. In: EuroS&PW, pp. 59–63. IEEE (2017)
27. Narula, N., Vasquez, W., Virza, M.: zkledger:privacy-preserving auditing for distributed ledgers. In: NSDI, pp. 65–80 (2018)
28. Poon, J., Dryja, T.: The bitcoin lightning network: scalable off-chain instant payments (2016)
29. PricewaterhouseCoopers global: building trust for today and tomorrow. https://www.pwc.com/gx/en.html (2024), Accessed 21 Feb 2024
30. Qin, X., et al.: Blindhub: bitcoin-compatible privacy-preserving payment channel hubs supporting variable amounts. In: S&P, pp. 2462–2430. IEEE (2023)
31. or Random, R.: Acccuntable assertions. https://github.com/real-or-random/accas (2024), Accessed 27 Apr 2024
32. Ruffing, T., Kate, A., Schröder, D.: Liar, liar, coins on fire! penalizing equivocation by loss of bitcoins. In: CCS, pp. 219–230 (2015)
33. Thyagarajan, S.A.K., Malavolta, G.: Lockable signatures for blockchains: scriptless scripts for all signatures. In: S&P, pp. 937–954. IEEE (2021)

A Framework for Combined Transaction Posting and Pricing for Layer 2 Blockchains

Shouqiao Wang[1(✉)], Davide Crapis[2], and Ciamac C. Moallemi[1]

[1] Columbia University, New York, USA
shwang27@gsb.columbia.edu
[2] Ethereum Foundation, Zug, Switzerland

Abstract. This paper presents a comprehensive framework for transaction posting and pricing in Layer 2 (L2) blockchain systems, focusing on challenges stemming from fluctuating Layer 1 (L1) gas fees and the congestion issues within L2 networks. Existing methods have focused on the problem of optimal posting strategies to L1 in isolation, without simultaneously considering the L2 fee mechanism. In contrast, our work offers a unified approach that addresses the complex interplay between transaction queue dynamics, L1 cost variability, and user responses to L2 fees. We contribute by (1) formulating a dynamic model that integrates both posting and pricing strategies, capturing the interplay between L1 gas price fluctuations and L2 queue management, (2) deriving an optimal threshold-based posting policy that guides L2 sequencers in managing transactions based on queue length and current L1 conditions, and (3) establishing theoretical foundations for a dynamic L2 fee mechanism that balances cost recovery with congestion control. We validate our framework through simulations.

1 Introduction

The scalability roadmap for Ethereum is rapidly coming to fruition, marked by the deployment of numerous Layer 2 (L2) blockchains that have significantly enhanced the network's capacity and efficiency. Major L2 solutions like Optimism, Arbitrum, and others have attracted assets worth billions of dollars and are processing millions of transactions daily. These platforms offload transaction processing from the main Ethereum blockchain (L1), enabling higher throughput and lower fees for users while maintaining the security guarantees of the underlying network.

A pivotal development facilitating this growth is Ethereum Improvement Proposal 4844 (EIP-4844), which has unlocked ample data availability for L2 rollups. By introducing a new transaction type that carries ephemeral data (blobs), EIP-4844 allows L2 blockchains to post large amounts of data to L1 at significantly reduced costs. This enhancement has resulted in very low fees for L2 users, further incentivizing adoption and driving transaction volumes.

However, the burgeoning L2 ecosystem faces two critical challenges:

1. **Fluctuating L1 Fees and Posting Costs:** The cost of posting transactions from L2 to L1 is subject to significant variability due to fluctuating L1 gas prices. These fluctuations impact the operational costs of rollups, making it challenging to predict and manage expenses effectively. This issue is poised to become even more pronounced as data availability demand begins to match supply, potentially increasing the cost and variability of data blobs used in rollup operations.
2. **Limited Capacity and Congestion Pricing:** Despite their enhanced capacity, L2 rollups have finite resources and may experience congestion during periods of high demand. To manage this, they might need to implement congestion fees, adjusting transaction costs to regulate network usage and maintain performance standards.

Addressing these challenges is essential for the sustainable growth of L2 solutions. Current studies have predominantly focused on the problem of optimal posting strategies to L1 in isolation, without concurrently considering the L2 fee mechanism. Practical systems have employed heuristic approaches to set L2 fees. Notably, Arbitrum Nitro has introduced a decoupled fee structure that separates fees into components aimed at recovering L1 posting costs and managing L2 congestion, drawing inspiration from Ethereum s EIP-1559 mechanism. However, these methods lack rigorous theoretical underpinnings, leaving a gap in understanding the optimal interplay between posting strategies and pricing mechanisms.

In this paper, we develop a comprehensive transaction management framework for L2 blockchain systems that captures the complex interplay between transaction queue dynamics, posting strategies, and gas price fluctuations. For the first time, we jointly consider the problems of posting and pricing, providing a unified approach to optimize both aspects simultaneously. Our model operates in discrete time, aligned with L1 block intervals, and incorporates realistic behaviors of both transaction arrivals influenced by L2 fees and L1 gas price movements.

We explicitly set up the objectives of balancing operational costs and controlling congestion within the L2 network. By formulating an objective function that incorporates both posting costs and queuing delays, we aim to derive strategies that optimize the cumulative operational cost over time while maintaining network performance. Furthermore, we establish the first theoretical results for L2 pricing mechanisms under this framework, subject to technical assumptions that we validate through robust simulations.

Our primary contributions are as follows:

1. **Joint Modeling of Posting and Pricing Strategies:** We introduce a dynamic [1.] model that simultaneously considers the optimal posting of transactions from L2 to L1 and the L2 fee mechanism. This joint approach captures the dependencies between transaction queue dynamics, L1 gas price fluctuations, and user behavior in response to L2 fees.
2. **Optimal Posting Strategy with Threshold Policy:** We derive an optimal posting strategy for the L2 sequencer using dynamic programming techniques.

We prove that a threshold policy is optimal, where the sequencer decides to post all pending transactions or none based on a critical queue length that depends on the current L1 gas price. This finding simplifies the decision-making process and provides practical guidelines for L2 operators.
3. **Theoretical Foundations for L2 Pricing Mechanisms:** We establish the first theoretical results for L2 pricing, explicitly formulating the objectives of cost recovery and congestion control. By modeling the transaction arrival rate as a function of the L2 fee, we develop a dynamic fee adjustment strategy that ensures budget balance and manages network congestion. We prove the existence and uniqueness of optimal fees and show that with our fee adjustment mechanism, fees converge to the optimal fees, under some technical conditions. We also demonstrate the robustness of our approach in more general and practical settings through simulations.

The remainder of the paper is structured as follows. In Sect. 2, we detail our transaction management model, including the dynamics of the transaction queue, L1 gas price modeling, cost structure, compensation mechanism, and the formulation of the objective function. Section 3 is dedicated to deriving the optimal posting strategy. We employ dynamic programming techniques to establish the Bellman equation for our system and prove that a threshold policy is optimal for the sequencer's decision-making process. In Sect. 4, we focus on the design of the L2 fee mechanism. We analyze how the L2 fee influences transaction arrival rates and develop a dynamic fee adjustment strategy that achieves budget balance and congestion control. We establish the first theoretical results for L2 pricing under this framework and present an adaptive algorithm for fee updates. Section 5 provides an analysis of the proposed mechanisms, including the assumptions made, convergence results, and discussions on practical implications. We validate our theoretical findings through simulations, demonstrating the robustness of our approach under various realistic network conditions.

1.1 Literature Review

Existing literature on decentralized L1 blockchains such as Bitcoin and Ethereum has extensively examined fee market designs, often using game-theoretic models to investigate how auction-based or monopolistic pricing schemes affect miner incentives, user behavior, and network throughput [2,9,18,19]. Roughgarden [15] provides an economic analysis of Ethereum's EIP-1559, highlighting dynamic base-fee adjustments for congestion control. Further refinements in L1 fee mechanisms appear in works by Leonardos et al. [10], who analyzed fee market dynamics and demonstrated that optimal fee mechanisms can be achieved despite inherent market chaos, and Crapis et al. [6], who investigated optimal dynamic fees for blockchain resources, introducing models that adjust to network conditions to optimize fee structures. Additionally, Crapis [4] has provided an analysis of the fee market under EIP-4844, discussing its implications for L1 fee dynamics. While these studies primarily focus on decentralized settings where miners or validators collectively enforce protocol rules, our work centers on a more centralized

L2 context, where a single operator unilaterally defines both posting and pricing policies, thereby departing from the standard L1-centric paradigm. Although congestion and blockspace constraints remain central concerns, L2 rollups face the additional challenge of covering volatile posting costs on L1, which substantially shapes the L2 fee design. By jointly modeling L2 queue dynamic and L1 gas prices dynamics, our framework emphasizes maximizing throughput while achieving budget balance on the L2, thus bridging a key gap in the existing literature.

Studies on optimal posting strategies for L2 rollups have emerged to tackle the challenges posed by unpredictable L1 gas prices and the imperative for timely data finalization. Mamageishvili and Felten [12] propose a Q-learning approach to determine the optimal moment for a rollup to publish transactions on L1, modeling a trade-off between waiting for favorable gas prices and incurring delay costs under a quadratic delay cost model. Although their work offers valuable insights into the batch posting decision, it does not address the design of L2 fee mechanisms or account for the dynamics of user demand driven by network congestion. In contrast, our work considers user demand dynamics via an L2 fee model while adopting a linear delay cost framework. By rigorously proving a threshold policy property, we implement a policy iteration algorithm that is significantly more efficient than the Q-learning method. Similarly, Bar-On and Mansour [1] build on related ideas by offering threshold-based policies for specific classes of cost functions, thereby providing analytical insights into optimal posting schedules. However, their analysis is confined solely to the posting decision and does not examine how user fees might be dynamically set to influence transaction arrivals. In contrast, our framework jointly addresses both posting and pricing decisions, capturing the intricate interplay between volatile L1 gas costs and user-driven congestion. Moreover, we design and rigorously prove key properties of our dynamic L2 fee mechanism under relaxed assumptions. Furthermore, Crapis et al. [5] investigate the economics of EIP-4844, focusing on blob posting strategies and equilibrium cost-sharing among rollups. While their analysis highlights important trade-offs for rollups operating under blob constraints, our work focuses specifically on batch posting. Additionally, we incorporate a dynamic L2 fee mechanism to actively manage network congestion. By unifying the optimal posting strategy and L2 fee mechanism, our approach enables L2 systems to simultaneously maximize throughput and maintain budget balance, thereby offering a comprehensive and robust solution that extends beyond the scope of the aforementioned works.

2 Model

In what follows, we describe the main components of our transaction management framework for a Layer 2 blockchain system. This framework not only captures the dynamics of the transaction queue and gas prices but also outlines a decision model for optimizing transaction posting costs and waiting costs over time. We consider a realistic transaction processing scenario where both the demand for transaction posting and fluctuating gas prices are modeled in discrete time, indexed by t.

Queue Dynamics. The L2 queue length at time t, denoted by Q_t, evolves according to the following equation:

$$Q_{t+1} = Q_t - S_t + A_t,$$

where S_t is the number of transactions posted in the t_{th} L1 block, and A_t represents the number of incoming transactions between the t_{th} and $(t+1)_{\text{th}}$ L1 block time. While A_t is modeled as an independent and identically distributed process conditioned on a specific Layer 2 gas price g, the distribution of A_t can vary as g changes, which captures the dynamic interplay between the transactions processed and new ones arriving.

L1 Gas Price Dynamics. The L1 gas price P_t, which is exogenous to the L2 structures, follows a mean-reverting process, i.e., it tends to move back toward a long-term average over time, with dynamics given by

$$P_{t+1} = \theta\mu + (1-\theta)P_t + \sigma\omega_t,$$

where θ controls the rate of mean reversion towards the long-term average μ, σ is the volatility parameter, and ω_t follows an i.i.d. standard normal distribution. This is also known as an autoregressive AR(1) process.

The mean-reverting behavior of P_t is particularly realistic in the context of Ethereum's EIP-1559 update, which introduces a mechanism for adjusting transaction fees that inherently aims to stabilize block sizes around a target size. Specifically, the gas fee for the next block increases if the current demand exceeds the target, and decreases if it falls below. If current demand exceeds the target then prices will increase, but as the demand subsequently responds to the increased prices, it will decrease, and in turn drive down future prices. This inherently leads to a mean-reverting dynamic. See [15] for an economic analysis of EIP-1559. Using a mean-reverting process to model P_t captures the realistic features of EIP-1559 while simplifying the model for better analysis. This approach is also supported in the literature; for example, [13] employ a fractional Ornstein-Uhlenbeck process to model gas fees, which is also a type of mean-reverting process.

Cost Structure. The cost incurred at the t_{th} L1 block is given by:

$$c(Q_t, S_t, P_t) = a(Q_t - S_t) + (b_0 + b_1 S_t)P_t \mathbf{1}_{\{S_t > 0\}},$$

where a is the proportional penalty on the number of waiting transactions after posting, b_0 is the fixed cost when transactions are posted, and b_1 scales linearly with the number of posted transactions, reflecting the sensitivity of the cost to the number of transactions. Observe that charging a linear penalty on the number of waiting transactions in each time step is equivalent to charging a linear penalty in the total number of time steps each transaction waits [11]. To see this more clearly, note that at each time step, every waiting transaction incurs a cost of a. If a transaction waits over multiple time steps, it thus accumulates the sum of these step-by-step penalties. Interchanging the summation over time and over transactions (an argument analogous to summation by parts) demonstrates that this is precisely the same as penalizing the total waiting time for each transaction. Hence, the first term in the cost structure is fundamentally a penalty on queuing delay.

Compensation Mechanism. To mitigate user dissatisfaction due to transaction delays and to align the incentives of the sequencer, the L2 platform could implement a compensation mechanism. For every L1 block of delay experienced by a transaction, the platform refunds the user an amount proportional to the delay, calculated as a times the number of delayed L1 blocks.

This compensation ensures that from the user's perspective, the utility remains consistent irrespective of the transaction posting time. Simultaneously, this approach aligns the incentives of the L2 sequencer with the cost function $c(Q_t, S_t, P_t)$ they are optimizing. By providing such refunds, the L2 sequencer demonstrates a commitment to minimizing transaction delays, rather than exploiting these for potential profit. This transparent compensation also reinforces trust in the platform's operational integrity.

Objective Function. The overall objective is to minimize the expected cumulative discounted cost, given by:

$$J(Q_t, P_t) = \min_{\{S_s\}} \mathbb{E}\left[\sum_{s \geq t} \gamma^{s-t} \left(a(Q_s - S_s) + (b_0 + b_1 S_s)P_s \mathbf{1}_{\{S_s > 0\}}\right) \bigg| Q_t, P_t\right],$$

where γ is the discount factor that captures the present value of future costs. The aim is to strike a balance between reducing the delay cost and managing posting costs effectively over time.

3 Optimal Posting Strategy

We continue our analysis of the optimal posting strategy under the assumption that the arrivals A_t are i.i.d., given a fixed Layer 2 fee. This section builds upon the established objective function and focuses on optimizing the transaction posting mechanism under dynamic gas price conditions. The decision variable, S_t, determines the number of transactions to post per L1 block. It is optimized by evaluating immediate costs and forecasting future system states to enhance transaction processing efficiency on Layer 2.

Theorem 1. *Threshold Policy.* *For any state (Q_t, P_t), the optimal posting strategy S_t^* satisfies:*

$$S_t^* = \begin{cases} Q_t & \text{if } Q_t > Q^*(P_t), \\ 0 & \text{if } Q_t \leq Q^*(P_t), \end{cases}$$

where $Q^*(P_t)$ is a critical threshold dependent on the gas price P_t.

Proof. Due to space constraints, we defer the proof to the full version [17]. □

The threshold policy mandates a binary decision: either clear the queue by posting all transactions or withhold all transactions when conditions do not favor posting, based on the queue length relative to a dynamic threshold $Q^*(P_t)$. This straightforward, binary approach greatly simplifies operational decisions by removing intermediate options, which streamlines the posting mechanism and enhances system efficiency by ensuring that decisions are consistently aligned with current economic conditions.

By leveraging the threshold structure of the optimal policy, we significantly simplify the decision-making process in our Markov Decision Problem[1] [14]. This structure transforms the action space from $\{0, 1, \cdots, Q\}$ to just two discrete options 0 or Q. Utilizing this binary action space, we implemented an efficient policy iteration algorithm. At each iteration, we evaluate the expected total cost for both possible actions by calculating the immediate cost and the expected future cost based on the current value function estimate. By directly comparing these two options, we can promptly update the policy without exhaustively searching over all possible actions. In contrast, [12] employs a Q-learning algorithm for the optimal posting strategy without utilizing a threshold policy, resulting in a computation time of approximately 72 h for a single run, whereas our method completes in just about 6 s.

4 Layer 2 Pricing

In our model, we assume a uniform L2 fee per transaction, simplifying the varying costs typically seen due to different gas usages per transaction in reality. The fee mechanism in our analysis, similar to many L2 platforms, fundamentally addresses two critical objectives: maintaining budget balance and managing congestion. Therefore, our strategy seeks to optimize network throughput within the framework established by these baseline conditions, ensuring that enhancements in throughput do not compromise our commitment to budget balance and effective congestion management.

The objectives of the fee mechanism in our study, and similarly in many L2 platforms, are twofold: to maintain budget balance and to manage congestion effectively. A similar idea is also mentioned in [3]. The goal is to satisfy the minimum level of these two objectives; under this condition, we maximize the chain throughput. Our mechanism is well-suited for implementation on most optimistic rollup platforms, such as Arbitrum, Base, and Optimism.

Arrival Rate. We denote the arrival rate of transactions by $\lambda(g)$, which represents the expected number of incoming transactions between L1 block times, $\mathbb{E}[A(t;g)]$, where $A(t;g)$ represents the random variable of the number of incoming transactions between L1 block times, whose distribution varies as a function

---
[1] A Markov Decision Problem models sequential decision-making, where a system transitions between states based on chosen actions, with the goal of minimizing expected costs or maximizing rewards.

of the fee g. In our model, we assume that $A(t; g)$ follows a Poisson distribution [8], which is commonly used to describe event counts that have independent increments and occur with a constant rate. We further assume a linear relationship between the arrival rate and the fee:

$$\lambda(g) = \lambda_0 - kg,$$

where λ_0 is the maximum potential arrival rate when the fee is zero, and k is a constant that captures the sensitivity of the arrival rate to changes in the fee. If the fee exceeds the threshold $g > \lambda_0/k$, the arrival rate becomes zero, i.e., no arrivals occur. The linear demand curve assumption is supported by empirical analysis of [16]. While this assumption simplifies the analysis of the root existence condition, our fee mechanism is robust and applicable to a broad range of arrival rate models.

Budget Balance. Budget balance is achieved when the total fees collected from transactions match the total operational costs of processing those transactions within the L2 framework. To establish this equilibrium, we define the fee f to satisfy the following condition under the stationary distribution:

$$\mathbb{E}\left[A(t; f)f - c(S_t^*, Q_t, P_t; f)\right] = 0, \tag{1}$$

where $c(S_t^*, Q_t, P_t; f)$ is the cost associated with the optimal posting strategies given the L2 fee f. The root of this equation, $f = f^*$, defines the fee level at which the network achieves budget balance, ensuring financial sustainability by perfectly aligning revenues with costs.

Property 1. $\mathbb{E}\left[c(S_t^*, Q_t, P_t; f)\right]$ is strictly monotonically decreasing with respect to f.

Proof. Due to space constraints, we defer the proof to the full version [17]. □

Corollary 1. *The expected profit and loss per L1 block, given by*

$$\mathbb{E}\left[A(s; f)f - c(S_s^*, Q_s, P_s; f)\right],$$

is strictly monotonically increasing for $f \in [0, \lambda_0/(2k)]$.

Proof. The corollary is straightforward, since

$$\mathbb{E}\left[A(s; f)f - c(S_s^*, Q_s, P_s; f)\right] = \lambda(f)f - \mathbb{E}[-c(S_s^*, Q_s, P_s; f)]$$
$$= (\lambda_0 - kf)f - \mathbb{E}[c(S_s^*, Q_s, P_s; f)],$$

where the product $(\lambda_0 - kf)f$ is strictly monotonically increasing for $f \in [0, \lambda_0/(2k)]$, and the expected cost $\mathbb{E}[c(S_s^*, Q_s, P_s; f)]$ is strictly monotonically decreasing due to Property 1. □

Property 2. The arrival rate $\lambda(f) = 0$ if and only if $\mathbb{E}\left[c(S_t^*, Q_t, P_t; f)\right] = 0$.

Property 3. The cost function $\mathbb{E}\left[c(S_t^*, Q_t, P_t; f)\right]$ can be bounded by a decreasing linear function. Specifically,

$$\mathbb{E}\left[c(S_t^*, Q_t, P_t; f)\right] \leq (b_0 + b_1\lambda_0 - b_1 kf)\mu.$$

Proof. Due to space constraints, we defer the proof to the full version [17]. □

Theorem 2. *Existence of Unique Budget Balance Fee.* *If*

$$\frac{\lambda_0^2}{4k} \geq (b_0 + b_1\lambda_0)\mu,$$

then there exists a unique fee $f^* \in [0, \lambda_0/(2k)]$ that achieves budget balance, being the root of the equation defined in Eq. (1).

Proof. Due to space constraints, we defer the proof to the full version [17]. □

The condition outlined in the theorem ensures that there is a fee level, f^*, which precisely balances the revenues from transaction fees with the costs of transaction processing, thereby achieving budget balance. Setting the fee below f^* results in revenues that fail to cover the operational costs, leading to financial losses for the platform. Conversely, setting the fee above f^* may generate surplus revenue, potentially turning a profit.

Target Arrival Rate. In managing the L2 network, it is critical to recognize the system's maximum capacity for executing transactions. The target arrival rate, denoted as $\bar{\lambda}$, is set based on this maximum capacity to ensure the network operates efficiently without being overwhelmed by an excessive volume of transactions.

Congestion Control. To align the actual arrival rate of transactions with the target $\bar{\lambda}$, a congestion control fee p is utilized. The fee that precisely balances the incoming transaction rate with the network's capacity is p^*, defined by the root of the equation:

$$\mathbb{E}[\bar{\lambda} - A(t; p)] = 0. \tag{2}$$

The fee p^* ensures that the number of transaction arrivals matches the target arrival rate $\bar{\lambda}$.

Theorem 3. *Existence of Unique Congestion Control Fee.* *If*

$$\frac{\lambda_0}{2} \leq \bar{\lambda} \leq \lambda_0,$$

then there exists a unique fee $p^* \in [0, \lambda_0/(2k)]$ that achieves congestion control, being the root of the equation defined in Eq. (2).

Proof. This proof is straightforward, because we only need to solve

$$0 = \mathbb{E}[\bar{\lambda} - A(t; p^*)] = \bar{\lambda} - \lambda(p^*) = \bar{\lambda} - \lambda_0 + kp^*.$$

The equation has a unique root $p^* = (\lambda_0 - \bar{\lambda})/k$. The value $p^* \in [0, \lambda_0/(2k)]$ if and only if $\lambda_0/2 \leq \bar{\lambda} \leq \lambda_0$. □

The condition outlined in the theorem ensures that there is a fee level, p^*, which precisely aligns the actual transaction arrival rate with the target rate $\bar{\lambda}$, effectively managing congestion. Setting the fee below p^* may lead to network overload, while setting it above p^* can result in underutilization of network capacity.

Optimal Fee Strategy. Our fee mechanism is strategically designed to simultaneously achieve budget balance and manage congestion, fundamental conditions for the stable operation of an L2 platform. To this end, the fee must be set at least as high as f^* to cover operational costs and ensure financial sustainability, and at least as high as p^* to regulate the flow of transactions and prevent system overload.

Given our goal to maximize network throughput, which ideally involves keeping fees as low as possible, the optimal fee charged is $\max(f^*, p^*)$. This strategy ensures that fees are not set higher than necessary to meet the foundational requirements, allowing the platform to process the maximum number of transactions without compromising financial viability or operational stability. By charging $\max(f^*, p^*)$, we maintain a balance that supports the highest possible throughput within the constraints of budget balance and congestion management.

4.1 L2 Fee Mechanism

In this part, we introduce a dynamic fee mechanism designed to achieve both budget balance and congestion control while maximizing throughput. When considering only budget balance, we have a fee mechanism based on updating the fee f. Similarly, when considering only congestion control, we have a fee mechanism based on updating the fee p. Since we may not know in advance whether the budget balance fee f^* is greater than the congestion control fee p^*, we propose an adaptive approach that updates both fees based on observed network conditions to determine the optimal fee.

Fee Update Mechanism for Budget Balance. For the budget-balancing fee f, we define its update rule as:

$$f_{t+1} = \Pi_{[0, \lambda_0/(2k)]} \left(f_t - a \cdot X(t; f_t) \right),$$

where $\Pi_{[x_a, x_b]}(x)$ projects x onto the interval $[x_a, x_b]$ to ensure the fee remains within feasible bounds, and $a > 0$ is a step size parameter that controls the magnitude of each fee update, i.e., larger values lead to more aggressive adjustments, while smaller values yield more conservative changes. Here, $X(t; f_t)$ represents the cumulative profit or loss over the t-th posting period when using fee f_t, defined as:

$$X(t; f_t) = \sum_s \left(A(s; f_t) f_t - c(S_s^*, Q_s, P_s; f_t) \right).$$

In this expression, $A(s; f_t)$ is the observed number of arrivals during the s-th L1 block time after applying fee f_t and $c(S_s^*, Q_s, P_s; f_t)$ is the cost associated with the optimal posting strategy at the s-th L1 block given fee f_t. The summation over s aggregates over multiple L1 block intervals within the t-th posting period. Specifically, suppose that after the $(t-1)$-th posting, the queue is empty, thanks to Theorem 1, the Threshold Policy. During the t-th posting period, transactions arrive over several L1 block intervals. We may decide not to post immediately, accumulating transactions and observing the profit and loss in each interval (the revenue from fees minus the cost). We sum these values until we decide to post, obtaining $X(t; f_t)$.

The update rule aims to achieve financial sustainability by aligning fees with operational costs. If $X(t; f_t) < 0$, it suggests the current fee is not covering costs, prompting an increase in f_{t+1}. Conversely, if $X(t; f_t) > 0$, there is room to reduce the fee in f_{t+1} without undermining financial health, potentially boosting transaction volume.

Fee Update Mechanism for Congestion Control. For the congestion control fee p, we define its update rule as:

$$p_{t+1} = \Pi_{[0, \lambda_0/(2k)]} \left(p_t - b \cdot Y(t; p_t) \right),$$

where $b > 0$ is a step size parameter. Here, $Y(t; p_t)$ represents the cumulative difference between the target arrival rate and the actual arrivals over the t-th posting period when using fee p_t, defined as:

$$Y(t; p_t) = \sum_s \left(\bar{\lambda} - A(s; p_t) \right).$$

In this expression, $A(s; p_t)$ is the observed number of arrivals during the s-th L1 block time after applying fee p_t, and $\bar{\lambda}$ is the target arrival rate that the network aims to maintain to avoid congestion. The summation over s captures the total effect over multiple L1 block intervals within the t-th posting period.

The congestion control fee is adjusted to align the actual transaction flow with the target arrival rate. A negative $Y(t; p_t)$ indicates congestion, suggesting a need to increase p_{t+1} to reduce the incoming transaction rates. Conversely, a positive $Y(t; p_t)$ suggests the capacity to handle more transactions, allowing a fee reduction.

Adaptive Fee Selection Mechanism. Since we do not know whether $f^* \leq p^*$ or $f^* > p^*$, we adopt an adaptive mechanism that updates both fees based on observed network performance to determine the optimal fee.

Let g_t represent the fee applied during the t-th posting period, and let δ_t be an indicator variable, representing whether g_t is updated based on the fee update mechanism for budget balance or congestion control. If g_t is updated based on the budget balance fee update mechanism, the indicator variable $\delta_t = 1$; otherwise, the indicator variable $\delta_t = 0$.

Define $\zeta(t) = \max\{s \leq t : \delta_s = 1\}$ and $\eta(t) = \max\{s \leq t : \delta_s = 0\}$, which represent the last time we have updated the budget balance fee and congestion control fee up to time t respectively. The decision variable δ_{t+1} and the fee g_{t+1} for the next posting period are updated according to the following rules:

- **If $\delta_t = 1$:**
  - If $Y(t; g_t) < 0$, indicating network congestion, we set $\delta_{t+1} = 0$ to switch to the congestion control fee sequence. The corresponding fee update rule
  $$g_{t+1} = \Pi_{[0, \lambda_0/(2k)]} \left(g_{\eta(t)} - b \cdot Y(\eta(t); g_{\eta(t)}) \right).$$
  - If $Y(t; g_t) \geq 0$, we keep $\delta_{t+1} = 1$, continuing with the budget balance fee sequence. The corresponding fee update rule
  $$g_{t+1} = \Pi_{[0, \lambda_0/(2k)]} \left(g_{\zeta(t)} - a \cdot X(\zeta(t); g_{\zeta(t)}) \right).$$
- **If $\delta_t = 0$:**
  - If $X(t; g_t) < 0$, indicating that revenues fail to cover operational costs, we set $\delta_{t+1} = 1$. This decision switches back to the budget balance fee update mechanism for the next period
  $$g_{t+1} = \Pi_{[0, \lambda_0/(2k)]} \left(g_{\zeta(t)} - a \cdot X(\zeta(t); g_{\zeta(t)}) \right).$$
  - If $X(t; g_t) \geq 0$, indicating financial stability, we keep $\delta_{t+1} = 0$, continuing with the congestion control fee sequence. The corresponding fee update for the next period
  $$g_{t+1} = \Pi_{[0, \lambda_0/(2k)]} \left(g_{\eta(t)} - b \cdot Y(\eta(t); g_{\eta(t)}) \right).$$

This method shares similarity with the multi-armed bandit problem, where we iteratively select the fee update mechanism between different objectives based on observed performance. It enables the system to adaptively switch between fee mechanisms as necessary, optimizing for either budget balance or congestion control in response to real-time conditions. This mechanism is particularly robust, adept at handling non-stationary network conditions and ensuring that fees stay close to the ideal level despite fluctuations. Through this adaptive approach, the system maintains crucial controls over budget and congestion, thereby enhancing throughput and ensuring consistent operational efficiency.

4.2 Analysis

We analyze the theoretical results for the L2 fee mechanism, considering some relaxations such as decreasing step size and i.i.d. Layer 1 gas fee prices. This analysis aims to establish a robust understanding of the dynamics underpinning the fee update mechanism within a theoretical framework.

Proposition 1. *For any feasible fee g, where $0 \leq g \leq \lambda_0/(2k)$, the expected value of $X(t; g)$ under the stationary distribution can be expressed as:*

$$\mathbb{E}[X(t; g)] = \mathbb{E}[\tau(g)] \cdot \mathbb{E}[A(s; g)g - c(S_s^*, Q_s, P_s; g)],$$

where $\tau(g)$ is the number of L1 blocks between two consecutive postings, which empty the queue according to Theorem 1. Therefore, if g^* is the fee level such that $\mathbb{E}[A(f^*)f^* - c(S_s^*, Q_s, P_s; f^*)] = 0$, then $\mathbb{E}[X(t; f^*)] = 0$. Similarly, for the congestion control metric:

$$\mathbb{E}[Y(t;g)] = \mathbb{E}[\tau(g)] \cdot \mathbb{E}[\bar{\lambda} - A(s;g)].$$

Consequently, if p^* is the fee level where $\mathbb{E}[\bar{\lambda}-A(s;p^*)] = 0$, then $\mathbb{E}[Y(t;p^*)] = 0$.

Proof. Due to space constraints, we defer the proof to the full version [17]. □

To underpin a well-founded theoretical result, we incorporate the following considerations:

1. **Decreasing Step Size.** The step size parameters a_t and b_t decrease over time, defined as $a_t = a/(t+1)$ and $b_t = b/(t+1)$.
2. **Independent and Identically Distributed L1 Gas Fee.** We assume that the L1 gas fee sequence $\{p_s\}$ follows an independent and identically distributed distribution.
3. **Multiple Observations.** For each fee update, we consider κ postings and use the observations of all these postings to select the fee update mechanism.

Given these considerations, our fee update rules can be described as follows:

- If $\delta_t = 1$ and $\sum_{s=\kappa t+1}^{s=\kappa(t+1)} Y(s; g_t) \geq 0$, or if $\delta_t = 0$ and $\sum_{s=\kappa t+1}^{s=\kappa(t+1)} X(s; g_t) < 0$, we set $\delta_{t+1} = 1$, and the fee update rule

$$g_{t+1} = \Pi_{[0, \lambda_0/(2k)]} \left(g_{\zeta(t)} - a_{i(t)} \cdot \frac{\sum_{s=\kappa\zeta(t)+1}^{s=\kappa(\zeta(t)+1)} X(s; g_{\zeta(t)})}{\kappa} \right),$$

where $i(t) = \sum_{s=1}^{t} \mathbf{1}\{\delta_s = 1\}$, represents the total number of budget balance fee updates up to t.

- If $\delta_t = 1$ and $\sum_{s=\kappa t+1}^{s=\kappa(t+1)} Y(s; g_t) < 0$, or if $\delta_t = 0$ and $\sum_{s=\kappa t+1}^{s=\kappa(t+1)} X(s; g_t) \geq 0$, we set $\delta_{t+1} = 0$, and the fee update rule

$$g_{t+1} = \Pi_{[0, \lambda_0/(2k)]} \left(g_{\eta(t)} - b_{j(t)} \cdot \frac{\sum_{s=\kappa\eta(t)+1}^{s=\kappa(\eta(t)+1)} Y(s; g_{\eta(t)})}{\kappa} \right),$$

where $j(t) = t - i(t)$, represents the total number of congestion control fee updates up to t.

Theorem 4. *Assuming the conditions and relaxations defined above hold, consider the dynamic fee update mechanisms with δ_t indicating whether the fee update is for budget balance or congestion control. Define:*

- $i(t) = \sum_{s=1}^{t} \mathbf{1}\{\delta_s = 1\}$, *the total number of budget balance fee updates up to t,*
- $j(t) = t - i(t)$, *the total number of congestion control fee updates up to t,*
- $f_{i(t)} = g_{\zeta(t)}$, *linking the budget balance fee to the last update up to t,*

– $p_{j(t)} = g_{\eta(t)}$, linking the congestion control fee to the last update up to t.

Suppose the condition $\lambda_0^2/(4k) \geq (b_0 + b_1\lambda_0)\mu$ for the existence of unique budget balance fee in Theorem 2, and the condition $\lambda_0/2 \leq \bar{\lambda} \leq \lambda_0$ for the existence of unique congestion control fee in Theorem 3 hold. Then, the following properties hold almost surely as $t \to \infty$:

1. Both $i(t) \to \infty$ and $j(t) \to \infty$.
2. The sequences $f_t \to f^*$ and $p_t \to p^*$.
3. The long-run average proportions of updates,

$$\frac{i(t)}{t} \to \pi_f \quad \text{and} \quad \frac{j(t)}{t} \to \pi_p,$$

where (π_f, π_p) is the stationary distributions under the transition matrix P. Here, P governs the transition of δ_t when the fee is fixed at the optimal levels, i.e., $g_t \equiv f^*$ for $\delta_t^* = 1$ and $g_t \equiv p^*$ for $\delta_t^* = 0$.
4. If $f^* \neq p^*$, as the number of observations $\kappa \to \infty$, the stationary distribution

$$(\pi_f, \pi_p) \to (\mathbf{1}\{f^* > p^*\}, \mathbf{1}\{f^* < p^*\}).$$

As $\kappa \to \infty$, the convergence rate

$$|\pi_f - \mathbf{1}\{f^* > p^*\}| = |\pi_p - \mathbf{1}\{f^* < p^*\}| = O(1/\sqrt{\kappa}).$$

Proof. Due to space constraints, we defer the proof to the full version [17]. □

According to Theorem 4, the sensitivity of our adaptive fee selection mechanism to network fluctuations can be moderated by adjusting the parameter κ, which determines the number of postings observed before a fee update. By increasing κ, the mechanism aggregates more data across multiple L1 block intervals before reconsidering fee changes. This extended observation window tends to smooth out short-term volatility and reduces the frequency of switching between fee update rules, thereby decreasing the likelihood of erratic fee adjustments driven by transient network effects.

In practical terms, the fee mechanism described in Sect. 4.1 sets $\kappa = 1$ because real-world systems are inherently non-stationary. Updating the fee for each posting, similar to how EIP-1559 updates fees for each block, allows the mechanism to quickly adapt to changing network conditions and improve robustness. Updating fees after observing a larger set of postings (i.e., increasing κ) presents a trade-off. On one hand, it improves stability by reducing sensitivity to short-term fluctuations, leading to more consistent fee decisions. On the other hand, it may diminish the mechanism's responsiveness to rapid changes in network conditions. This reduced agility may compromise robustness, as fees might not adapt swiftly to evolving demand patterns during extended observation periods.

5 Simulation

In this section, we empirically evaluate our L2 fee mechanism through a series of simulations designed to test its performance under varying conditions. Initially corroborating the theoretical model, we progressively introduce more realistic scenarios shifting from i.i.d., which assumes the L1 gas fees are independent and identically distributed across time, providing a simplified theoretical setting, to non-i.i.d., which models the fees via a mean-reverting process to capture temporal dependence and better reflect real-world dynamics, price distributions and from decreasing to constant step sizes. These simulations aim to assess whether the fees f_n and p_n stay close to their theoretical optimal values f^* and p^* under less idealized conditions, providing insight into the mechanism's robustness and practical applicability.

5.1 Simulation Setup

We conduct simulations to evaluate the performance of our L2 fee mechanism across four distinct scenarios, which vary by the nature of L1 gas fee conditions, either i.i.d. or non-i.i.d., and the approach of step sizes, either decreasing or constant. For each scenario, we assess how well the fee mechanism approaches the theoretical optimal fees f^* and p^*, as well as analyze the long-term frequency of selecting either the budget balance or congestion control fee update mechanisms. These simulations are crucial for understanding how well the mechanism can maintain its efficiency and effectiveness in different market conditions.

Price Generation. For i.i.d. scenarios, prices are generated from a predefined normal distribution. For non-i.i.d. scenarios, prices are generated using the mean-reverting AR(1) process, as defined in Sect. 2.

Step Size Configuration: For decreasing step sizes, we use $a_t = a/t$ and $b_t = b/t$, where a and b are predefined. For constant step sizes, a_t and b_t are fixed throughout the simulation.

Parameters Setup. Our parameters are calibrated as follows:

- **L1 gas fee parameter.** We use the L1 base fee data during the second half of February 2024 to get the mean and variance. Then for the i.i.d. case, we set its mean $\mu = 3.86 \times 10^{-8}$ and standard deviation $v = 1.93 \times 10^{-8}$. For the non-i.i.d. case, we set $\mu = 3.86 \times 10^{-8}$, $\theta = 0.1$ and $\sigma = 8.41 \times 10^{-9}$.
- **Arrival rate parameter.** The typical L2 transaction fee is around 0.09 USD, equivalent to 3.6×10^{-5} ETH at an ETH price of 2500 USD. Some historical data shows an average of 120 transactions per L1 block time before EIP-4844. We model the transaction decline by setting a fee cap at 0.27 USD, or 1.08×10^{-4} ETH, above which no transactions occur. This setup defines a linear arrival rate model with parameters $\lambda_0 = 180$ and $k = 1.67 \times 10^6$, based on these two fee thresholds.
- **Single observation.** We set $\kappa = 1$, which means that for each fee update, we only consider the current posting to determine the fee update mechanism.

5.2 Simulation Results

Decreasing Step Size and i.i.d. L1 Fee Case. The simulation validates the theoretical results for decreasing step sizes with i.i.d. L1 fee, as shown in the full version [17]. Each graph demonstrates the corresponding parameter converges in the long run. These outcomes support the use of the decreasing step size approach in achieving target efficiency in a stationary environment.

Decreasing Step Size and non-i.i.d. L1 Fee Case. In the absence of a formal theorem for almost surely convergence of the sequence f_t, p_t, $i(t)/t$ and $j(t)/t$ under non-i.i.d. conditions, our simulations serve as a critical empirical test. The results, as shown in the full version [17], indicate that despite the complexity introduced by the non-i.i.d. nature of L1 fees, all of these parameters still demonstrate a tendency towards convergence over an extended period. This performance suggests that our fee mechanism is robust even in more complicated and realistic L1 gas fee conditions.

Constant Step Size And Non-i.i.d. L1 Fee Case. This scenario arguably presents the most practical and realistic conditions for the implementation of our L2 fee mechanism. While we lack a formal convergence theorem for this case, the simulation results, as shown in the full version [17], are promising, showing that the fees f_n and p_n tend to stabilize close to f^* and p^* over time. The histograms indicate that this stabilization occurs within a reasonable neighborhood given the simulation environment. This observation aligns with the theorems presented in Chap. 8 of [7], which discusses the convergence behavior for constant step-size cases, indicating asymptotic convergence within a neighborhood of the root. Moreover, the simulation indicates that the relative frequencies $i(t)/t$ and $j(t)/t$ of selecting different update mechanisms appear to converge. Although almost surely convergence may not hold in highly stable environments, the robustness and adaptability of our fee mechanism are essential for effectively managing the dynamic and often unstable conditions encountered in real-world applications.

6 Conclusion

This paper presents a framework to optimize transaction posting and dynamic fee mechanisms in L2 blockchain systems. By integrating models for transaction arrivals, queue dynamics, and cost structures, we showed that an optimal threshold policy can dictate when to post transactions to L1, balancing operational costs and system performance.

On the pricing side we developed an L2 fee mechanism that achieves both budget balance and congestion control. Our analysis established the existence and uniqueness of fee levels that satisfy these objectives and examined the convergence properties of the adaptive update mechanism. Simulations confirm that the method efficiently adjusts fees to maintain stability and manage congestion.

Overall, our work bridges transaction posting strategies and fee design, offering a principled method that enhances operational efficiency, financial viability, and congestion management. This integrated perspective paves the way for more resilient and scalable L2 platforms and opens avenues for future research. For example, extending the framework to include blob transactions and other complex settings could further refine our approach to handle diverse transaction types and evolving network demands.

References

1. Bar-On, Y., Mansour, Y.: Optimal publishing strategies on a base layer. arXiv preprint arXiv:2312.06448 (2023)
2. Basu, S., Easley, D., O'Hara, M., Sirer, E.G.: Towards a functional fee market for cryptocurrencies. arXiv preprint arXiv:1901.06830 (2019)
3. Lee, B., et al.: Arbitrum nitro: a second-generation optimistic rollup (2022)
4. Davide Crapis. Eip-4844 fee market analysis. https://ethresear.ch/t/eip-4844-fee-market-analysis/15078 (2023)
5. Crapis, D., Felten, E.W., Mamageishvili, A.: Eip-4844 economics and rollup strategies. arXiv preprint arXiv:2310.01155 (2023)
6. Crapis, D., Moallemi, C.C., Wang, S.: Optimal dynamic fees for blockchain resources. CoRR, abs/2309.12735 (2023)
7. Harold, J., Kushner, G., George, Y.: Stochastic approximation and recursive algorithm and applications. Appl. Math. **35**(10) (1997)
8. Katti, S.K., Vijaya Rao, A.: Handbook of the poisson distribution (1968)
9. Lavi, R., Sattath, O., Zohar, A.: Redesigning bitcoin's fee market. ACM Trans. Econ. Comput. **10**(1), 1–31 (2022)
10. Leonardos, S., Reijsbergen, D., Monnot, B., Piliouras, G.: Optimality despite chaos in fee markets. CoRR, abs/2212.07175 (2022)
11. Little, J.D.C., Graves, S.C.: Little's law. Building intuition: insights from basic operations management models and principles, pp. 81–100 (2008)
12. Mamageishvili, A., Felten, E.W.: Efficient rollup batch posting strategy on Base Layer. CoRR, abs/2212.10337 (2022). arXiv:2212.10337, https://doi.org/10.48550/arXiv.2212.10337
13. Meister, B.K., Price, H.C.: Gas fees on the ethereum blockchain: from foundations to derivative valuations. Front. Blockchain, **7**, 1462666 (2024)
14. Puterman, M.L.: Markov decision processes: discrete stochastic dynamic programming. John Wiley & Sons (2014)
15. Roughgarden, T.: Transaction fee mechanism design for the ethereum blockchain: an economic analysis of EIP-1559. arXiv preprint arXiv:2012.00854 (2020)
16. Stephenson, M., Zach, A.: Getting the pricing right in crypto (2024). https://panteracapital.com/research-getting-the-pricing-right-in-crypto/
17. Crapis, D., Moallemi, C.C., Wang, S.: A framework for combined transaction posting and pricing for layer 2 blockchains. arXiv preprint arXiv:2505.19556 (2025)
18. Yaish, A., Zohar, A.: Correct cryptocurrency asic pricing: are miners overpaying? In 5th Conference on Advances in Financial Technologies (AFT 2023). Schloss Dagstuhl-Leibniz-Zentrum für Informatik (2023)
19. Yao, A.C.C.: An incentive analysis of some bitcoin fee designs. arXiv preprint arXiv:1811.02351 (2018)

X-Transfer: Enabling and Optimizing Cross-PCN Transactions

Lukas Aumayr[1,5], Zeta Avarikioti[2,5], Iosif Salem[3,6], Stefan Schmid[3], and Michelle Yeo[4(✉)]

[1] University of Edinburgh, Edinburgh, UK
[2] TU Wien, Vienna, Austria
[3] TU Berlin, Vienna, Austria
[4] National University of Singapore, Singapore, Singapore
michellexyeo@gmail.com
[5] Common Prefix, Abu Dhabi, UAE
[6] ZeroPoint Technologies, Gothenburg, Sweden

Abstract. Blockchain interoperability solutions allow users to hold and transfer assets among different chains, and in so doing reap the benefits of each chain. To fully reap the benefits of multi-chain financial operations, it is paramount to support interoperability and cross-chain transactions also on Layer-2 networks, in particular payment channel networks (PCNs). Nevertheless, existing works on Layer-2 interoperability solutions still involve on-chain events, which limits their scalability and throughput. In this work, we present X-TRANSFER, the first secure, scalable, and fully off-chain protocol that allows payments across different PCNs. We formalize and prove the security of X-TRANSFER against rational adversaries with a game theoretic analysis. In order to boost efficiency and scalability, X-TRANSFER also performs transaction aggregation to increase channel liquidity and transaction throughput while simultaneously minimizing payment routing fees.

Keywords: Payment channel networks · Layer-2 · interoperability · optimization · transaction aggregation · cryptocurrencies

1 Introduction

Payment channel networks (PCNs) [9,17,18,32,35,39] are a promising solution to mitigate the limited transaction throughput of blockchains [16]. Two parties that wish to transact with each other can open a payment channel between themselves by depositing funds into a "common account" on the blockchain only to be used in this channel. Whenever the parties transact with each other, they update the distribution of funds in the channel by decreasing the funds of the sender and increasing the funds of the receiver by the payment amount. To close a payment channel, parties can publish the last agreed distribution of funds on-chain either cooperatively or unilaterally. As such, with just a constant number of blockchain transactions, any two parties can make an unlimited number of costless transactions between themselves. A network of users and payment channels between pairs of users constitute a payment channel network (PCN), which also allows for multi-hop routing of payments between users that are not directly connected through intermediary nodes [35]. Examples of PCNs are Bitcoin's Lightning Network [35] and Ethereum's Raiden [2].

An important open problem in PCNs is to design secure and scalable cross-PCN payment solutions in order to fully unlock their interoperability potential, complementing existing cross-chain solutions on the blockchain itself [1,27,36]. Existing solutions for cross-blockchain payments rely on *bridges* [1,13,27,29, 36,37,43], which condition the occurrence of some transaction on a destination blockchain given the occurrence of a specific event on a source blockchain. These solutions, however, still involve on-chain events and thus do not fully leverage the scalability that fully off-chain solutions can provide. The main challenge in adapting these solutions to the *purely off-chain* setting is the absence of global events off-chain, as off-chain state updates only occur among pairs of users in payment channels. This makes conditioning the occurrences of off-chain state updates an extremely difficult exercise in coordination and incentive-alignment, and remains an open challenge.

Our Contributions. In this paper, we present X-TRANSFER, the first secure and scalable cross-PCN transaction protocol that relies purely on off-chain events. X-TRANSFER comprises of an aggregation followed by an execution phase. For the aggregation phase, we assume a specific "star" topology among all PCNs whereby users are connected to a single "hub node" that forms the center of the star. The reason for this realistic assumption (more details in Sect. 3.1) is twofold: first, it is necessary in order to ensure that solving the transaction aggregation problem is feasible (we show it is polynomial in the number of transactions and exponential in the number of PCNs), and second, we use the specific assumptions about hub nodes (that there is at least one PCN that contains wallets of all hub nodes and channels between them) in order to execute transactions securely in the second execution phase of X-TRANSFER. During the aggregation phase, multiple transactions across PCNs are aggregated such that the resulting aggregated transactions occur simultaneously rather than sequentially. In this way, transactions could "cancel" each other out which reduces transaction fees and increases liquidity. Furthermore, our optimization problem in the transaction aggregation phase involves both maximizing the total volume of transactions selected for aggregation while minimizing the volume of cross-PCN transactions which involves heftier cross-PCN transaction fees. In doing so, we ensure the largest amount of throughput possible across all PCNs while ensuring that fees are kept minimal.

In the second execution phase, the aggregated transactions are executed. To ensure balance security (i.e., that the balance of involved users across PCNs does not change apart from what they should send or receive) of involved users, we first simultaneously execute the transactions only among the hubs. This effectively executes all cross-PCN transactions. We then show that assuming all involved parties are rational, using incentive alignment arguments and strategically-chosen execution time parameters, we can ensure that the execution of all cross-PCN aggregated transactions is the off-chain variant of the "global event" necessary to induce updates of all subsequent aggregated transactions in all PCNs. We employ Thora [4], an existing single-PCN atomic channel update protocol, to ensure all hub-to-hub channels and well as channels within each PCN can be atomically updated.

We summarize our contributions as follows:

- We present the building blocks of X-TRANSFER, the first purely off-chain cross-PCN transaction protocol which also performs aggregation/optimization, in Sect. 3. We also include formal definitions of the desiderata of X-TRANSFER (which includes security, privacy, feasibility and optimality definitions) as well as model assumptions.
- We detail both the aggregation and execution phases of X-TRANSFER in Sect. 4, including the design principles behind the protocol.
- We analytically show that X-TRANSFER achieves the aforementioned desiderata of security, privacy, feasibility and near-optimality in Sect. 5.
- We perform an empirical evaluation of X-TRANSFER's performance in Appendix I in our extended technical report [5] under the metrics of transaction throughput and computational overhead. We show that X-TRANSFER achieves at least twice as much throughput compared to the baseline of no aggregation with little additional overhead.

1.1 Related Work

PCNs. Payment channels [6,7,9,11,17,21,22,31,32] emerged as a promising technology to improve blockchain transaction throughput. Originally introduced by Spilman [39], the first bidirectional channels followed with the Lightning Network [35] and Duplex Micropayment Channels [18]. See [20] for a recent survey.

Transaction Aggregation. Transaction aggregation in PCNs is the problem of finding an optimal subset of transactions that maximizes the total satisfiable transaction volume with a minimal number and volume of actual transactions carried out. Typically, this is done by finding transactions that "cancel" each other out. In the context of PCNs, the problem was first proposed and studied in [40] but only for the single PCN setting. To make the computational problem tractable, [40] proposed a "star topology" where clients connect directly to several hubs arranged in a clique. Our work extends the problem considered in [40] to the multiple PCN setting where transactions across several PCNs can cancel each other out. Although we also adopt a similar star topology as in [40] in each PCN, a novel and key focus of our work is finding the optimal set and volume of cross-PCN monetary flows, as well as ensuring that the resulting aggregated transactions can be executed across PCNs atomically. We also note that both the centralized [25,38] and decentralized [14,15] variants of the netting problem (interbank liabilities are aggregated and settled) are also similar to the problem studied in our work. In particular, the work of [14] uses smart contracts on the blockchain. In our work, though, we focus on off-chain aggregation of cross-PCN transactions, which avoids the usage of costly blockchain transactions.

Atomic Cross-Chain Payments. In the single PCN setting, there are several tools [4,8,30,35] that govern the atomic updates of channel states. Our work, however, addresses atomic channel updates across multiple PCNs. Jia et al. [28] propose using a trusted third party (TTP) to open and close a payment channel between two users in different blockchains. Guo et al. [26] present a protocol for cross-PCN channels using expensive cryptography. Zhang and Qian [44] propose a hub-based cross-PCN structure, but their protocol relies heavily on deposits to prevent rational users from deviating, such as by failing to execute a transfer and stealing funds. These deposits serve as an incentive for hubs to follow the protocol. In contrast, X-TRANSFER does not rely on a TTP and is lightweight, requiring neither expensive cryptography nor substantial deposits – only small deposits for paying fees to the hubs for their services. Alba [37] is a decentralized bridge [1,13,27,29,36,37,43] that can condition executions on the destination blockchain on off-chain events. However, Alba's executions still occur on (and thus involve) the destination blockchain, whereas our protocol enforces fully off-chain conditional executions.

2 Background and Notation

Payment channel networks (PCNs). Several payment channels opened on the same blockchain form a payment channel network (PCN). A node on a PCN represents a channel party, and an edge represents a channel among the two nodes/parties it connects. Refer to Appendix A in our extended technical report [5] for more details about routing in PCNs and payment fees.

Thora [4]. Thora is a single-PCN channel state update protocol that ensures that any number of (possibly disjoint) channels in a PCN can be updated atomically. The key idea behind Thora's atomic updates is the preparation and signing of a specific "enable-payment" transaction that allows receiving parties to enforce payments from their corresponding sending parties in their payment channels. Indeed, after setting up Thora, every recipient has this transaction along with its necessary signatures. If the corresponding sender refuses to update, the recipient can post the enable-payment transaction. As long as one such enable-payment transaction appears on the blockchain (which should only happen during a dispute), every other involved user can enforce their promised payments. In the optimistic case, nothing goes on-chain.

Thora achieves two properties: (i) *atomicity* ensures that either all channels update or revert, and malicious users cannot deviate from this outcome except by forfeiting their money to the honest parties, and (ii) *strong value privacy*, which ensures that the update value of any channel out of the set of to-be-updated channels is only known to the two channel users in the optimistic case. We describe further details of Thora in Appendix C of our extended technical report [5].

Transaction Aggregation and Wiser [40]. For transaction aggregation, we will build upon Wiser, a single-PCN private aggregation and execution protocol. Wiser consists of 2 phases: transaction aggregation and execution. In the aggregation phase, transactions are chosen to maximize the total demand in the network. To ensure privacy, parties secret share their transactions and channel balances, and then the optimization problem is solved using multiparty computation (MPC) among a selected number of delegates. Thora is used to execute all transactions atomically during the transaction execution phase.

Notation and Transaction Model. For $n \in \mathbb{N}$, we use $[n]$ to denote the set $\{1, \ldots, n\}$. Let $\epsilon > 0$ be the smallest amount of cryptocurrency funds that can be sent in the blockchain. We use H to denote a globally available cryptographic hash function, e.g., SHA256. We assume all underlying blockchains implement an Unspent Transaction Output (UTXO) model [3,33]. In this model, transactions are mappings between inputs and outputs. We can write a transaction as $t_i = [o_j^1, o_j^2, o_k^1, \ldots] \mapsto [o_i^1, o_i^2, \ldots]$ where i, j, k are transaction identifiers. We further denote a UTXO output $o = (x|C)$ as having a monetary value of x coins, which are only spendable if the Boolean expression C evaluates to TRUE. In our work we are mainly interested in 3 types of literals in C: (1) timelocks, where we simply use a constant to denote that it evaluates to TRUE after the specified amount of time has elapsed. (2) hashlock, where we use $H(s)$ to denote that it evaluates to TRUE when one provides the preimage s of $H(s)$. (3) signature locks, where we use σ_{u_i} to denote that it evaluates to TRUE if the signature of user u_i is provided. When multisignatures between a specific set of k parties $u_1, \ldots, u_k$ are required, we specify them as $\sigma_{u_1,\ldots,u_k}$. We use $\#$ to denote UTXO inputs that are irrelevant to a given transaction design, e.g., $t_i = \# \mapsto [o_i^1, o_i^2, \ldots]$.

3 Model

3.1 System Model and Assumptions

We assume we have k PCNs, each supporting a different blockchain, whose users wish to interact with each other. We restrict each PCN to a single hub node and several client nodes, and we denote the hub node in the ith PCN as h_i for $i \in [k]$. The nodes in each PCN are arranged in a star topology with the hub as the star center. We adopt this topological assumption to make the computation of the cross-chain transaction aggregation problem tractable. We stress, however, that this assumption corresponds to the high degree of centralization observed in the Lightning Network in reality [34,42], is also adopted in previous work [40], and is shown to be stable [10,12]. We further assume each hub node has wallets in all other PCNs, and there exists a PCN that contains all channels between hubs. We make the reasonable assumption that the capacities of the inter-hub channels are a lot larger than the capacity of channels between clients and hubs, as cross-PCN transfers could potentially be a lot larger than transfers within a PCN. Although we do not specify the requisite capacity of these inter-hub channels, we assume for the rest of the paper that the capacity of these channels is large enough to handle all cross-PCN transfers. Finally, we assume that hub nodes only participate in routing transactions in the protocol, and do not send or receive transactions. Let $G_i = (V_i, E_i)$ represent the ith PCN.

The input to the problem is a set of transactions $\mathcal{T} := \{(x_i, s_i, r_i)\}_{i=1}^n$ where x_i represents the size of the ith transaction in the list, and s_i, r_i represent the sender and recipient of the ith transaction. Note that s_i and r_i can be in different PCNs. A payment x_i can be sent from $s_i \in G_1$ to $r_i \in G_2$ in the following way: s_i sends x_i to h_1 along the channel (s_i, h_1). Assuming G_2 is the PCN that contains the channel between h_1 and h_2, h_1 sends x_i to h_2 along the channel (h_1, h_2). Finally, h_2 sends x_i to r_i along the channel (h_2, r_i). As these between-hub channels effectively shift payments from one PCN to another, we call these between-hub channels *cross-PCN channels*.

We assume payments going through cross-PCN channels are significantly more expensive compared to payments routed within a PCN. The main reason behind this assumption is that the hubs have to lock funds in several PCNs in order to provide this service to users, which incurs a high opportunity cost. Additionally, if users were to go with a traditional swap, the user would have to find a trusted service provider, which would incur high fees, or use atomic swaps on the blockchain, which also incur a larger cost in terms of gas fees to run the smart contracts [19,27]. Formally, suppose we have a transaction (x_i, s_i, r_i) with s_i, r_i in different PCNs. Denote the payment path the transaction takes from s_i to r_i as $\pi = (e_1, e_2, \ldots, e_m)$ where $e_j \in \pi$ can either be channels within a single PCN or cross-PCN channels. Let us further suppose the total number of cross-PCN channels in π is $m' < m$. Then, the fee incurred for this transaction would be $\sum_{j=1}^{m-m'} f(x_i) + m'\alpha$ for some affine function f and large positive constant α.

Assumptions. We further make some usual assumptions concerning cryptographic primitives, the underlying blockchains, the communication model, and the adversary. In particular, we assume the existence of secure communication channels between users. We also assume all underlying blockchains are censorship-resistant, and also satisfy persistence and liveness as defined in [24]. In addition, we assume a synchronous network model, i.e., there is a known network delay that bounds the time needed for any user to receive any incoming message. We assume that all PCNs operate using the same underlying tokens. Further, we assume all parties (hubs and clients) are rational, i.e., they may deviate from the honest protocol execution if they may increase their profit. Finally, we assume that hubs and clients are not colluding. We discuss collusion and potential mitigation in Sect. 6 of our extended technical report [5].

3.2 Desired Properties

In the following, we define the desiderata of our protocol.

Firstly, X-Transfer should maintain the safety of channel funds for users that follow the protocol, encompassed by the following property.

Definition 1 (Balance security). *No honest party loses more than a negligible amount of funds[1] as a result of participating in* X-TRANSFER.

Moreover, our protocol should ensure that users incur minimal fees.

Definition 2 (Fee Minimization). *The solution of* X-TRANSFER *should execute the list of transactions* T *such that the total fees are minimized.*

The computational complexity of the problem depends on the aggregation, which is a hard optimization problem. Accordingly, we postulate computational efficiency in the sense that a solution must be fixed-parameter tractable, i.e., polynomial in the number of transactions:

Definition 3 (Computational Feasibility). *The aggregation problem is fixed-parameter linear, i.e., polynomial in the number of input transactions n and exponential in the number of PCNs k.*

This is reasonable since transactions likely involve only a few PCNs.

Privacy is a key aspect of PCN protocols, as payment channels inherently protect users' balances and transactions. We adapt the privacy definition from [40] to multiple PCNs, providing an informal description below and leaving the formal definition to Appendix D of our extended technical report [5]. Uninvolved users learn only that they do not participate. Involved parties know the flow output on their incident channels and their direct counterparties. Receiving parties also learn all other recipients within the same PCN. Hub nodes additionally learn the set of involved users across all participating PCNs.

4 The X-TRANSFER Protocol

This section outlines the design principles and details of X-TRANSFER. We first provide an overview, followed by a detailed description of its phases, covering both the optimization solution and transaction execution. An example implementation with three PCNs is presented in Appendix F in our extended technical report [5].

4.1 Protocol Overview

X-TRANSFER proceeds in two phases: an aggregation phase and an execution phase. In the aggregation phase, our protocol privately computes an aggregation of the input transactions such that the resulting aggregation optimizes transaction throughput while minimizing fees. Then, each user u receives a monetary

---

[1] In the aggregation phase of X-TRANSFER, we require that hub clusters that are disconnected from other hub clusters are connected by a payment channel that sends negligible amount of funds $\epsilon > 0$ between them. Total connectivity of hubs is required to ensure atomicity of execution in the execution phase of X-TRANSFER, and this will be the only portion of X-TRANSFER where additional funds of ϵ are transferred.

flow $\mathbf{f}(e)$ representing either inflow or outflow of funds to or from u for all channels incident to u. The user u needs to check whether the computed flow is correct (that is, u will not lose money if the flow is executed). The actual execution of the transactions happens after all users have verified the correctness of the flow computation. To ensure that the computed flow is executed atomically both within and across PCNs, our protocol employs Thora to execute transactions within each PCN as well as cross-PCN transactions, with carefully chosen Thora time parameters to connect all these executions together. Figure 1 depicts a high-level overview of both phases of our protocol.

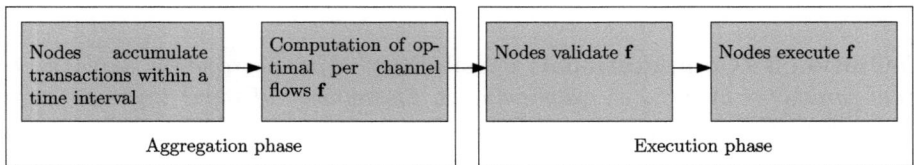

Fig. 1. X-TRANSFER phases for cross-PCN transaction aggregation

4.2 Aggregation Phase

Secret Sharing Inputs. The aggregation phase begins after sufficiently many transactions have been accumulated. To preserve the privacy of the input transactions and channel balances, our protocol requires each party to secret-share their transactions and their balance information along their incident channels. These shares are given to a group of delegates that will validate the correctness of the inputs, i.e., check that no party submits a transaction that exceeds their balance in their channel with their hub, and compute the solution of the transaction aggregation optimization problem using multiparty computation (MPC) [41]. We stress that our protocol is agnostic to the type of secret sharing scheme, MPC protocol, as well as how the delegates are chosen, so long as the group of delegates satisfies the trust assumptions of the underlying MPC protocol.

Optimization Problem. The optimization problem is to maximize the volume of successful transactions (throughput) while minimizing the flow amounts (or fees since they are linear in the flows). Recall that in every PCN, clients connect directly to a hub, and the hub-to-hub balances are assumed to be high enough to accommodate for all input transactions. Thus, we can independently find the subset $\mathcal{T}^* \subseteq \mathcal{T}$ that maximizes transaction volume and is feasible and then find the flows routing the transactions in $\mathcal{T}^*$. We will solve the first problem by reducing it to the optimization problem solved in Wiser [40] (in FPL[2] time

---

[2] FPL (Fixed Parameter Linear) is a complexity class where a decision problem has time complexity $O(f(k) \cdot |x|)$, with x and k as inputs. The complexity is *linear in* $|x|$ but can be *arbitrary* (often exponential) in k. FPL is a subset of FPT (Fixed Parameter Tractable), which includes problems that are computationally hard but remain tractable when exponential complexity is confined to a specific parameter k.

complexity) and the second one with a polynomial-time greedy algorithm, which we prove to use $k-1$ links (where k is the number of hubs), as required by X-TRANSFER's execution phase. Thus, the total time complexity is in FPL.

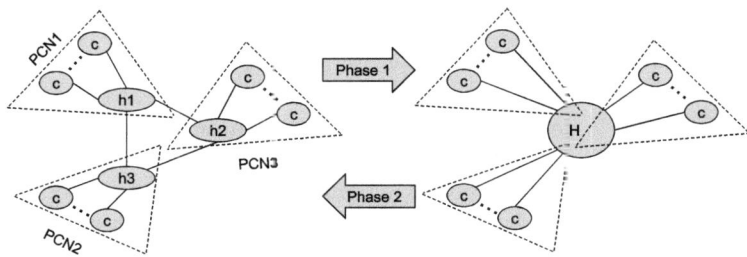

Fig. 2. Sample graph structures for the optimization problem. Clients connect directly to the hub of each PCN and every hub is connected to all other hubs. We contract the hub clique to one node $\mathcal{H}$ for phase 1 (finding the subset $\mathcal{T}^* \subseteq \mathcal{T}$ that maximizes throughput) and find the flows realizing $\mathcal{T}^*$ in the original graph in phase 2.

In more detail, to find the subset $\mathcal{T}^* \subseteq \mathcal{T}$ that maximizes the transaction volume and respects channel capacities, we replace the hub-to-hub network with a single node $\mathcal{H}$ (see Fig. 2 for details). The resulting topology is a star graph in which all clients in all PCNs connect to $\mathcal{H}$. This abstraction takes advantage of the much larger capacity of hub-to-hub channels compared to client-to-hub channels, thus relegating the problem of optimally realising $\mathcal{T}$ to client-to-hub channels. We model our optimization problem as an integer linear program (ILP) as follows:

max $\sum_{i=1}^{n} |t_i| x_i$, subject to

$$\sum_{i:\, t_i=(u,*,*)} |t_i| x_i - \sum_{j:\, t_j=(*,u,*)} |t_j| x_j \leq c(u, \mathcal{H}), \text{ for every client } u \quad (1)$$

such that $x_i \in \{0, 1\}$ is a decision variable for choosing whether a transaction $t_i = (s, r, x)$ is included in the output solution or not, $|t_i| = x$ is the transaction amount, $c(u, v)$ is the capacity of channel (u, v), and $*$ denotes any existing value.

The ILP states that we aim at finding an assignment of values to the x_i variables, such that the volume is maximized, while for every client-to-hub channel the sum of outgoing flow minus the incoming flow is bounded by the channel capacity. This is the exact same transaction aggregation problem of Wiser in one PCN, which is shown to be NP-hard [40, Theorem 1]. It can be solved in $O(n(k\Delta)^{k^2})$ time through the work of [23, Theorem 8], where $\Delta = \max_{i \in [n]} |t_i|$, i.e., the maximum transaction amount (or a bound on that), n is the number of transactions, and k is the number of hubs. That is, the complexity is linear in the number of transactions and exponential in the maximum transaction amount and the number of hubs. Therefore, it belongs to the FP_ complexity class.

Given the optimal transaction subset $\mathcal{T}^*$ from the ILP, we now have to compute the cheapest flows realizing it in the actual network. Since the client-to-hub flows are already computed in the first phase, we need to compute the flows on exactly $k-1$ links connecting the hubs and realizing the computed flows. We formally describe a polynomial-time greedy algorithm to solve this problem in Appendix E.1 in our extended technical report [5]. Informally, the algorithm works by aggregating the total inflow and outflow of each hub node from the solution specified by $\mathcal{T}^*$ and using this to define supply (resp. demand) hubs as hubs that need to send (resp. receive) funds to (resp. from) other hubs. The supply and demand hubs are sorted in descending order, and for each demand amount specified by a demand hub, we add hub-to-hub links with as many supply hubs as needed to fulfill the demand. The supply hubs are re-sorted and the procedure is repeated. The following lemma (proof in Appendix G.1 in our extended technical report [5]) shows that our greedy algorithm outputs at most $k-1$ hub-to-hub links.

Lemma 1 *Let $|E_{greedy}|$ the number hub-to-hub of links created by our greedy algorithm and $|\mathcal{H}_s|$, $|\mathcal{H}_d|$ be the number of supply and demand hubs, respectively. Then, $\max\{|\mathcal{H}_s|,|\mathcal{H}_d|\} \leq |E_{greedy}| \leq k-1$.*

Finally, note that if the algorithm outputs less than $k-1$ hub-to-hub links, we simply add links of size $\epsilon > 0$ to connect any disconnected hub components.
Restricting the Topology Among Hubs to a Path. At this point, we note that the above greedy algorithm connects all hubs in a DAG topology, which we denote as G. In X-TRANSFER, we restrict the topology of the hub-to-hub channels to a path. The main reason for this restriction is that we use some secret from receiving hubs (i.e., hubs that only receive funds from other hubs) to link all payments together during the execution phase to ensure atomicity. However, the setting with more than one receiving hub opens a vulnerability whereby the first receiving hub that reveals their secret can get their funds stolen. We describe these vulnerabilities in detail in Appendix E.2 in our extended technical report [5]. To convert the DAG topology G among the hubs into a path topology P, we employ another polynomial-time algorithm (see Algorithm 3 in Appendix E.2 in [5]) to create a path topology P from G while maintaining the invariant of *balance conservation* of the vertices, i.e., the difference between the sum of all incoming and outgoing edges is the same for all vertices in G and in P. We leave the details of the procedure to Appendix E.2 in our extended technical report [5].
Computing Execution Time Parameters for Execution Phase. In addition to the path graph representing the flow of funds between hubs, the aggregation phase of X-TRANSFER also outputs some time parameters which determines the sequence of both cross-PCN and within-PCN fund transfers in the execution phase of X-TRANSFER. The reason why these time parameters are computed during the aggregation and not the execution phase is mainly to preserve privacy. We present an informal description of the procedure as well as give an intuition of correctness and leave the formal description and details to Appendix E.3 in our extended technical report [5].

Informally, let us denote the client-to-hub flows in a PCN as outputted by the ILP as the *net flow* of the PCN. We observe that we can classify PCNs into three categories: PCNs that have positive, negative, or zero net flow. Positive (resp. negative) net flow PCNs have hubs that have positive (resp. negative) *inflow* of funds from their clients, and neutral net flow PCNs have zero out or inflow. Now assuming that the hub-to-hub flows have already been executed, we note that hubs with positive or neutral net flow will have incentive to execute the within-PCN transfers to receive funds from the process[3]. These PCNs are deemed "safe" and will have smaller execution time parameters. We now state two crucial observations that underlie the correctness of our procedure: (1) there always exists a recipient in an "unsafe" PCN (let us call it G_i) with a corresponding sender in a safe PCN. G_i can then be added to the safe set and given a larger execution time parameter, which allows enough time for senders in safe PCNs to propagate necessary information to their recipients. As we use Thora to update channels within PCNs (more details in Sect. 4.3), the recipient in G_i can use this information to enforce all payments in the case where h_i refuses to execute the channel updates in G_i. (2) This process always terminates with all PCNs labeled safe. We show this with the proof of Lemma 3 in Appendix E.3 in our extended technical report [5].

4.3 Execution Phase

The execution phase starts once each user u verifies the aggregation output, following a flow validation process similar to [40].

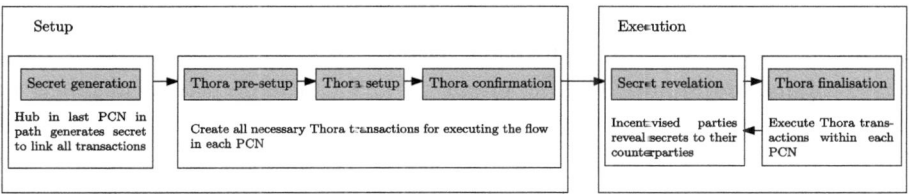

Fig. 3. X-Transfer Execution phase stages

Recall that the output of the aggregation phase is a path topology which defines a depth-ordering $h_1, \ldots, h_k$ among the hubs (and corresponding PCNs), as well as time parameters for each PCN which determines their execution order. The main design challenge of the execution protocol is to ensure the atomicity of transactions: as long as one transaction is executed in our protocol, all other (involved PCNs as well as cross-PCN) transactions should also be executed. We stress that this challenge stems from the fact that there does not exist any off-the-shelf protocol that guarantees atomicity for cross-PCN transactions. Indeed,

---

[3] The argument in the case for why neutral net flow PCNs are incentivized to execute the within-PCN transfers even though their balance does not change is mainly due to the fact that they gain some funds as compensation when X-TRANSFER gets executed successfully. More details in Sect. 6 of our extended technical report [5].

while Thora ensures the atomicity of transactions within a single PCN, there are no atomicity guarantees for transactions going out of the PCN.

Strawman Protocol. A simple strawman protocol to address the lack of atomicity between PCNs would be to use 1 Thora for each PCN to execute the transactions inside the PCN (i.e., transactions between clients and hubs). Then, since we assume that (1) hubs have wallets in each PCN, (2) there is at least one PCN (say G_j) in which all hubs have channels with each other, and (3) the hubs are connected in a path topology, we can set up hashed timelock contracts (HTLCs, see Appendix A in [5] for details) between the hubs in G_j to handle the cross-PCN transfers. Nevertheless, this strawman protocol leaves a glaring issue unresolved: hubs can steal funds from other hubs in an attack similar to the wormhole attack as described by [30]. In fact, unlike the classic wormhole attack where the victim simply loses out on the payment fees, the attack is more devastating in our setting as it actually impairs the balance security of our protocol. We illustrate this with a simple example with four PCNs G_1, G_2, G_3 and G_4 with corresponding hubs h_1, h_2, h_3, h_4. We assume an aggregated flow of x_1 coins going from h_1 to h_2, x_2 coins going from h_2 to h_3, and x_3 coins going from h_3 to h_4. If we use HTLCs locked with a secret generated by h_4 to transfer funds between the hubs, h_4 could collude with h_2 and skip revealing the secret to h_3 by directly revealing the secret to h_2, resulting in a loss of x_2 funds for h_3 and hence balance security of our protocol. Although this would mean that h_4 will lose out on getting x_3 coins, h_2 would profit from not sending x_2 coins to h_3. Thus, if x_2 is sufficiently larger than x_3, the total profit of h_4 and h_2 would be larger under the attack. Hence, it is imperative that X-TRANSFER imposes *an atomic method for updating channels between hubs.*

Atomic Channel Updates Between Hubs. To ensure that channel updates between hubs are atomic, that is, either no hub can update their channels or all hubs have the means to do so, X-TRANSFER uses another Thora protocol to update the channels among the hubs. In doing so, the channel updates are guaranteed to be atomic from the Thora protocol. Nevertheless, at this point there are still a few problems left unanswered, chief of which is *a method that links all of these payments together.*

Secret Generation. A simple way to link all the transactions (both transactions within all PCNs and cross-PCN transactions) would be to use a common secret as an additional hashlock on the transactions, making all transactions unspendable unless the secret is revealed. The choice of which parties should generate the secret is important, as not all parties have an incentive to reveal the secret at a later stage so as to force the transactions to go through. For instance, consider a simple example with three PCNs G_1, G_2 and G_3 with an aggregated flow of x_1 coins going hub $h_1 \in G_1$ to hub $h_2 \in G_2$, and x_2 coins going from h_2 to h_3 (see Fig. 6 in Appendix F of our extended technical report [5] for a depiction of this setting). Because h_1 has a net cash outflow, using h_1 to generate the secret would lead to h_1 only revealing the secret to the users in G_1 but not h_2, thus gaining a profit of x. To counter this, *we only allow secret generation to be done by the hub in the last PCN as defined by the path topology* returned from the aggregation phase of X-TRANSFER(i.e., h_k). While common secrets linking transactions play a crucial role in ensuring balance security during the execution of the protocol, there can still be violations of balance security if the setup or execution order is bad. Thus, a related challenge is *defining a setup and execution order such that balance security is preserved.*

Setup and Execution Order. We first highlight a problematic scenario with a bad setup order and then show how X-TRANSFER avoids this. Consider again the simple case of 3 PCNs illustrated in Fig. 6 in Appendix F of our extended technical report [5]. If the Thora updating the channel between the hubs is set up before the individual PCN Thoras, as h_3 knows the secret, h_3 can enforce the channel updates and steal x_2 coins from h_2 even before the other Thoras are set up. Thus, X-TRANSFER ensures that all within PCN Thoras are set up first before the Thora updating all inter-hub channels is set up. In this way, there is no incentive for the secret-generating hub to reveal the secret at any point during setup. This is because the secret generating hub, as the hub in the last PCN in the within-hub transaction path and thus is receiving funds from other PCNs, is in a positive balance *after executing the transactions in their PCN and without executing the inter-hub transactions.*

During the Thora setup, each PCN uses the Thora time parameter as output from the aggregation phase, with the additional Thora between the hubs assigned a time parameter T_0 such that T_0 is smaller than all other time parameters as returned from the aggregation phase. This ensures that the Thora responsible for updating cross-PCN transfers executes first. Once these cross-PCN transfers have been executed, the net flow positions of all other hubs together with the assigned time parameters ensure that there is at least one user (hub or client) in each PCN that is incentivized to enforce the Thora execution in each PCN (stated and proved in Lemma 3 in Appendix E.3 and Lemma 6 in Appendix H.1 in our extended technical report [5]).

X-Transfer Execution Phase Details. The actual execution phase of X-TRANSFER can be broken down into 2 stages: setup and execution. Figure 3 depicts all intermediate steps in both stages of the execution phase, and a formal description of the execution stage of X-TRANSFER is detailed in Algorithm 1. The setup stage begins with h_k sampling a secret s as well as computing a hash of the secret $H(s)$. $H(s)$ is then broadcasted to all the hubs and will be used as an additional hashlock on all transactions.

Once all hubs have verified that they have received $H(s)$, all individual PCN Thoras are set up to handle the updates of the transactions inside each PCN (Lines 3 and 4 in Algorithm 1). The time parameter that is used as input to the Thora setup phase for each PCN G_i is the time parameter T_i corresponding to G_i returned from the aggregation phase. Here we stress that this process can be done in parallel. Once all individual PCN Thoras are set up and the correctness of the setup stage is verified, an additional Thora is set up in G_j to handle the updates of all cross-PCN transactions. The time parameter used for this Thora is $T_0 < T_i \forall i$. Note that the Thora pre-setup, setup, and confirmation stages in our protocol follow almost exactly as described in [4], with the exception that

Protocol 1: Execution Phase of X-TRANSFER

Data: PCNs $G_1, \ldots, G_k$, times $T_0, T_1, \ldots, T_k$, blockchain delay parameter Δ
Result: Broadcasted secret $\mathfrak{s}$, Updated incident channels
/* Secret Generation   */
1 h_k generates a random secret $\mathfrak{s}$
2 h_k broadcasts $H(\mathfrak{s})$ to all other hubs
/* Thora setup   */
3 Each PCN G_i runs Algorithm 5 in Appendix E.4 of our extended technical report [5] with inputs $G_i, \Delta, H(\mathfrak{s})$
4 Each PCN G_i runs Algorithm 6 in Appendix E.4 of our extended technical report [5] with inputs $G_i, T_i, \Delta, H(\mathfrak{s})$
5 Thora confirmation on G_i follows as per Thora protocol (see Algorithm 7 in our extended technical report [5])
6 After confirming that each Thora is set up correctly, hubs $h_1, \ldots h_k$ set up another Thora in PCN G_j with the involved channels being their inter-hub channels and time parameter T_0
/* Thora Execution   */
7 h_k reveals $\mathfrak{s}$ to hubs, enabling the update of the inter-hub channels as per the Thora protocol
8 Doing so reveals $\mathfrak{s}$ to each hub, which enables the updates of each involved channel in each PCN as per the Thora protocol.

some transactions are locked with all the extra hashlocks generated during secret generation. We detail these changes in Algorithms 5,6, and 7 in Appendix E.4 in our extended technical report [5].

After the setup, the protocol moves on to the actual execution, which begins with h_k revealing the secret $\mathfrak{s}$ to the other hubs. The hubs verify that $\mathfrak{s}$ is the preimage of $H(\mathfrak{s})$. Thereafter, the hubs can use $\mathfrak{s}$ to enforce the inter-hub channel updates, which execute the cross-PCN transactions. Following that, the Thoras handling the updates of the channels within each PCN can be executed. Note that all channel updates follow exactly as per the Thora protocol.

5 Analysis

In this section, we show that X-TRANSFER satisfies all desired properties outlined in Sect. 3.2. We will provide informal arguments and description of techniques used to show how these properties are satisfied and leave all formal statements and proofs to Appendix H in our extended technical report [5].

Informally, balance security is preserved in the aggregation phase due to the definition of the optimization problem, the correctness of the underlying solver, as well balance conservation in the conversion from a DAG to path hub topology. We show balance security is preserved in the execution phase of X-TRANSFER by first defining an underlying extensive form game induced by the execution phase of X-TRANSFER. Thereafter, we show that following the protocol as stipulated by X-TRANSFER is a strict subgame perfect equilibrium in the underlying game, which rules out unilateral deviations from rational players at any step of the execution phase of X-TRANSFER. A key ingredient in the proof of execution phase balance security is the computed Thora time parameters as well as the correctness of the algorithm in the proof of Lemma 3 in Appendix E.3 in our extended technical report [5], which shows that as long as the Thora protocol among the hubs is executed, all PCNs will eventually execute their Thora and update their channels. Computational feasibility of X-TRANSFER stems from a similar analysis to [40], with the additional terms in the complexity coming from sorting the list of hubs for the greedy algorithm to connect the flows within hub components. We note that the DAG hub topology satisfies optimality but our path hub topology solution is not optimal and we provide a worst-case example in Appendix H.2 in our extended technical report [5]. Nevertheless in Appendix E.2 in our extended technical report [5] we conjecture that the DAG solution is impossible without the use of on-chain events, and in Appendix H.2 in our extended technical report [5] we detail heuristics to minimize the cost of our path topology solution. Finally, X-TRANSFER achieves privacy so long as the delegates satisfy the assumptions of the underlying MPC protocol.

6 Conclusion

In this work, we presented the first fully off-chain cross-PCN transaction aggregation protocol. We analytically show that X-TRANSFER is secure, private, computationally feasible, and near-optimal. We envision our work as a first step in achieving secure, fully off-chain interoperability. That said, our work also relies on some assumptions (for instance the path topology) and would it would be an interesting direction for future work to alleviate these assumptions.

Acknowledgments. This work was partially supported by MOE-T2EP20122-0014 (Data-Driven Distributed Algorithms), the Austrian Science Fund (FWF) through the SFB SpyCode project F8512-N, the project CoRaF (grant agreement ESP68-N), the WWTF through project 10.47379/ICT22045, the German Research Foundation (DFG), grant SPP 2378 (ReNO), 2023-2027, and Input Output (http://iohk.io) through their funding of the Edinburgh Blockchain Technology Lab.

References

1. Arbitrum, https://arbitrum.io/, Accessed Sept 2024
2. Raiden network, https://raiden.network/, Accessed 4 Oct 2024
3. Androulaki, E., Cachin, C., De Caro, A., Kokoris-Kogias, E.: Channels: horizontal scaling and confidentiality on permissioned blockchains. In: Lopez, J., Zhou, J., Soriano, M. (eds.) ESORICS 2018. LNCS, vol. 11098, pp. 111–131. Springer, Cham (2018). https://doi.org/10.1007/978-3-319-99073-6_6
4. Aumayr, L., Abbaszadeh, K., Maffei, M.: Thora: atomic and privacy-preserving multi-channel updates. In: CCS, pp. 165–178. ACM (2022)
5. Aumayr, L., Avarikioti, Z., Salem, I., Schmid, S., Yeo, M.: X-transfer: enabling and optimizing cross-PCN transactions. IACR Cryptol. ePrint Arch. (2025)

6. Aumayr, L., et al.: Bitcoin-compatible virtual channels. IACR Cryptology ePrint Archive, Report 2020/554 (2020)
7. Aumayr, L., et al.: Generalized bitcoin-compatible channels. IACR Cryptology ePrint Archive, Report 2020/476 (2020)
8. Aumayr, L., Moreno-Sanchez, P., Kate, A., Maffei, M.: Blitz: secure multi-hop payments without two-phase commits. In: USENIX Security Symposium, pp. 4043–4060. USENIX Association (2021)
9. Avarikioti, G., Kokoris-Kogias, E., Wattenhofer, R.: Brick: asynchronous state channels. CoRR abs/1905.11360 (2019)
10. Avarikioti, Z., Heimbach, L., Wang, Y., Wattenhofer, R.: Ride the lightning: The game theory of payment channels. In: Financial Cryptography. Lecture Notes in Computer Science, vol. 12059, pp. 264–283. Springer (2020)
11. Avarikioti, Z., Litos, O.S.T., Wattenhofer, R.: Cerberus channels: incentivizing watchtowers for bitcoin. In: International Conference on Financial Cryptography and Data Security, pp. 346–366. Springer (2020)
12. Avarikioti, Z., Lizurej, T., Michalak, T., Yeo, M.: Lightning creation games. In: ICDCS, pp. 1–11. IEEE (2023)
13. Bünz, B., Kiffer, L., Luu, L., Zamani, M.: Flyclient: super-light clients for cryptocurrencies. In: SP, pp. 928–946. IEEE (2020)
14. Cao, S., Yuan, Y., De Caro, A., Nandakumar, K., Elkhiyaoui, K., Hu, Y.: Decentralized privacy-preserving netting protocol on blockchain for payment systems. In: Bonneau, J., Heninger, N. (eds.) FC 2020. LNCS, vol. 12059, pp. 137–155. Springer, Cham (2020). https://doi.org/10.1007/978-3-030-51280-4_9
15. Chapman, J., Garratt, R., Hendry, S., McCormack, A., McMahon, W.: Project jasper: are distributed wholesale payment systems feasible yet? (2017)
16. Croman, K., et al.: On scaling decentralized blockchains. In: Clark, J., Meiklejohn, S., Ryan, P.Y.A., Wallach, D., Brenner, M., Rohloff, K. (eds.) FC 2016. LNCS, vol. 9604, pp. 106–125. Springer, Heidelberg (2016). https://doi.org/10.1007/978-3-662-53357-4_8
17. Decker, C., Russell, R.: eltoo : A simple layer 2 protocol for bitcoin (2018). https://api.semanticscholar.org/CorpusID:49253813
18. Decker, C., Wattenhofer, R.: A fast and scalable payment network with bitcoin duplex micropayment channels. In: Pelc, A., Schwarzmann, A.A. (eds.) Stabilization, Safety, and Security of Distributed Systems, pp. 3–18. Springer International Publishing, Cham (2015)
19. DeCred: decred-compatible cross-chain atomic swapping. https://github.com/decred/atomicswap
20. Dotan, M., Pignolet, Y.A., Schmid, S., Tochner, S., Zohar., A.: Survey on blockchain networking: context, state-of-the-art, challenges. In: Proc. ACM Computing Surveys (CSUR) (2021)
21. Dziembowski, S., Eckey, L., Faust, S., Malinowski, D.: Perun: virtual payment hubs over cryptocurrencies. In: IEEE Symposium on Security and Privacy, pp. 327–344 (2017)
22. Egger, C., Moreno-Sanchez, P., Maffei, M.: Atomic multi-channel updates with constant collateral in bitcoin-compatible payment-channel networks. In: Proceedings of the 26th ACM SIGSAC Conference on Computer and Communications Security, pp. 801–815. ACM (2019)
23. Eisenbrand, F., Weismantel, R.: Proximity results and faster algorithms for integer programming using the steinitz lemma. ACM Trans. Algorithms (TALG) **16**(1), 1–14 (2019)

24. Garay, J., Kiayias, A., Leonardos, N.: The bitcoin backbone protocol: analysis and applications. In: Oswald, E., Fischlin, M. (eds.) EUROCRYPT 2015. LNCS, vol. 9057, pp. 281–310. Springer, Heidelberg (2015). https://doi.org/10.1007/978-3-662-46803-6_10
25. Güntzer, M.M., Jungnickel, D., Leclerc, M.: Efficient algorithms for the clearing of interbank payments. Eur. J. Oper. Res. **106**(1), 212–219 (1998). https://doi.org/10.1016/S0377-2217(97)00265-8
26. Guo, Y., Xu, M., Yu, D., Yu, Y., Ranjan, R., Cheng, X.: Cross-channel: scalable off-chain channels supporting fair and atomic cross-chain operations. IEEE Trans. Comput. **72**(11), 3231–3244 (2023)
27. Herlihy, M.: Atomic cross-chain swaps. In: Proceedings of the 2018 ACM Symposium on Principles of Distributed Computing, pp. 245–254 (2018)
28. Jia, X., Yu, Z., Shao, J., Lu, R., Wei, G., Liu, Z.: Cross-chain virtual payment channels. IEEE Trans. Inf. Forensics Secur. **18**, 3401–3413 (2023). https://doi.org/10.1109/TIFS.2023.3281064
29. Madathil, V., Thyagarajan, S A.K., Vasilopoulos, D., Fournier, L., Malavolta, G., Moreno-Sanchez, P.: Cryptographic oracle-based conditional payments. In: NDSS. The Internet Society (2023)
30. Malavolta, G., Moreno-Sanchez, P., Schneidewind, C., Kate, A., Maffei, M.: Anonymous multi-hop locks for blockchain scalability and interoperability. In: NDSS. The Internet Society (2019)
31. McCorry, P., Bakshi, S., Bentov, I., Meiklejohn, S., Miller, A.: Pisa: arbitration outsourcing for state channels. In: AFT (2019). https://doi.org/10.1145/3318041.3355461
32. Miller, A., Bentov, I., Bakshi, S., Kumaresan, R., McCorry, P.: Sprites and state channels: payment networks that go faster than lightning. In: Goldberg, I., Moore, T. (eds.) FC 2019. LNCS, vol. 11598, pp. 508–526. Springer, Cham (2019). https://doi.org/10.1007/978-3-030-32101-7_30
33. Nakamoto, S.: Bitcoin: a peer-to-peer electronic cash system. https://bitcoin.org/bitcoin.pdf (2008)
34. Pietrzak, K., Salem, I., Schmid, S., Yeo, M.: Lightpir: privacy-preserving route discovery for payment channel networks. In: Networking. pp. 1–9. IEEE (2021)
35. Poon, J., Dryja, T.: The bitcoin lightning network: scalable off-chain instant payments. https://lightning.network/lightning-network-paper.pdf (2015)
36. Scaffino, G., Aumayr, L., Avarikioti, Z., Maffei, M.: Glimpse: on-demand pow light client with constant-size storage for DEFI. In: USENIX Security Symposium, pp. 733–750. USENIX Association (2023)
37. Scaffino, G., Aumayr, L., Bastankhah, M., Avarikioti, Z., Maffei, M.: Alba: the dawn of scalable bridges for blockchains. IACR Cryptol. ePrint Arch, 197 (2024)
38. Shafransky, Y.M., Doudkin, A.A.: An optimization algorithm for the clearing of interbank payments. Eur. J. Oper. Res. **171**(3), 743–749 (2006). https://doi.org/10.1016/j.ejor.2004.09.003
39. Spilman, J.: Anti dos for tx replacement. https://lists.linuxfoundation.org/pipermail/bitcoin-dev/2013-April/002433.html (2013)
40. Tiwari, S., Yeo, M., Avarikioti, Z., Salem, I., Pietrzak K., Schmid, S.: Wiser: increasing throughput in payment channel networks with transaction aggregation. In: AFT, pp. 217–231. ACM (2022)
41. Yao, A.C.C.: Protocols for secure computations. In: 23rd Annual Symposium on Foundations of Computer Science (sfcs 1982), pp. 160–164 (1982). https://api.semanticscholar.org/CorpusID 62613325

42. Zabka, P., Förster, K., Decker, C., Schmid, S.: Short paper: a centrality analysis of the lightning network. In: Financial Cryptography. Lecture Notes in Computer Science, vol. 13411, pp. 374–385. Springer (2022)
43. Zamyatin, A., Harz, D., Lind, J., Panayiotou, P., Gervais, A., Knottenbelt, W.J.: XCLAIM: trustless, interoperable, cryptocurrency-backed assets. In: IEEE Symposium on Security and Privacy, pp. 193–210. IEEE (2019)
44. Zhang, X., Qian, C.: A cross-chain payment channel network. In: ICNP, pp. 1–11. IEEE (2023)

DeFi

am-AMM: An Auction-Managed Automated Market Maker

Austin Adams[1], Ciamac C. Moallemi[2,3](✉), Sara Reynolds[4], and Dan Robinson[3]

[1] Whetstone Research, New York, USA
austin@whetstone.cc
[2] Columbia University, New York, USA
ciamac@gsb.columbia.edu
[3] Paradigm, New York, USA
dan@paradigm.xyz
[4] Uniswap Labs, New York, USA
sara@uniswap.org

Abstract. Automated market makers (AMMs) have emerged as the dominant market mechanism for trading on decentralized exchanges implemented on blockchains. This paper presents a single mechanism that targets two important unsolved problems for AMMs: reducing losses to informed orderflow, and maximizing revenue from uninformed orderflow. The "auction-managed AMM" works by running a censorship-resistant onchain auction for the right to temporarily act as "pool manager" for a constant-product AMM. The pool manager sets the swap fee rate on the pool, and also receives the accrued fees from swaps. The pool manager can exclusively capture some arbitrage by trading against the pool in response to small price movements, and also can set swap fees incorporating price sensitivity of retail orderflow and adapting to changing market conditions, with the benefits from both ultimately accruing to liquidity providers. Liquidity providers can enter and exit the pool freely in response to changing rent, though they must pay a small fee on withdrawal. We prove that under certain assumptions, this AMM should have higher liquidity in equilibrium than any standard, fixed-fee AMM.

1 Introduction

Liquidity providers (LPs) for automated market makers (AMMs) want to minimize their losses to arbitrageurs while maximizing fee revenue from retail flow. Each of these is a major unsolved problem in AMM design. Minimizing losses to arbitrageurs (which can be characterized as "loss-vs-rebalancing," or LVR)

The second author is supported by the Briger Family Digital Finance Lab at Columbia Business School, and is an advisor to Paradigm and to fintech companies. The authors wish to thank Agostino Capponi, Mallesh Pai, and Anthony Zhang for helpful comments.

requires either setting high fees or relying on some other mechanism to capture the profits from information or latency arbitrage and mitigate losses to agents (arbitrageurs), who possess superior information on the market value of the asset and snipe stale prices posted by the AMM. Meanwhile, the optimal fee for a given asset pair depends on how retail volume for that pair responds to fees—a difficult problem that is not easy to model. Moreover, the optimal fee may be dynamic and vary with other market variables such as volatility or overall market volume. In standard fixed-fee AMMs (ff-AMMs), these problems compound and interfere with each other: liquidity providers must choose a pool with fees high enough to reduce arbitrage opportunities while still low enough to capture value from retail flow. Additionally, liquidity providers must make this choice statically and for themselves, and if they disagree, liquidity ends up fragmented across multiple pools.

In this paper, we propose the auction-managed AMM (am-AMM), a new AMM design that targets both LVR reduction and fee optimization with one mechanism. The mechanism incentivizes sophisticated market participants to capture some of the value leaked by the AMM, and also lets those market participants set fees at a level that optimizes revenue from retail traders. The pool maintains synchronous composability with other onchain contracts, does not require price oracles, and is resistant to censorship. It also ensures *accessibility*, meaning that liquidity on the pool can always be traded against with some capped fee. Under certain assumptions, we prove that the am-AMM will attract more liquidity than *any* fixed-fee constant product AMM pool (with any fee up to the cap), in equilibrium.

The am-AMM is a constant-product AMM. The AMM utilizes an onchain censorship-resistant "Harberger lease" auction to find the highest bidder. The current highest bidder in the ongoing auction, known as the *manager*, pays rent to liquidity providers. In exchange, the manager can dynamically set the swap fee rate (up to some maximum cap), and receives all swap fees collected by the pool. This allows the manager to capture small arbitrage opportunities each block by trading on the pool, since they can trade with effectively zero fee. It also incentivizes them to set the swap fee in order to maximize revenue from uninformed flow. Liquidity providers can enter and exit the pool freely (though they pay a small withdrawal fee).

The am-AMM has some drawbacks. It may provide even fewer protections against sandwich attacks than a fixed-fee AMM, since the pool manager's ability to trade without fees allows them to profit by pushing any publicly visible transaction to its limit price. It also could contribute to centralization of block builder infrastructure. We think these limitations and drawbacks warrant future study, as does the problem of making this feature work with concentrated liquidity [4].

Related Literature. While automated market makers are newer compared to many financial market primitives, the literature on the subject is growing rapidly. The concept of AMMs can be traced back to [16] and [26]. Early literature on the current implementations of AMMs includes [6,7,10,20], and [17].

Implementation details of automated market makers are described in [3] and [4]. Furthermore, [2] describes a forthcoming platform for customizable AMMs.

Our paper builds directly on the loss-vs-rebalancing framework established in [23] and [22] as a model for evaluating designs for AMMs. Contemporaneous with the this paper, [21] analyze liquidity provision in AMMs with a similar model of LP profitability and noise trader demand as the present paper.

The idea described in this paper is an instance of an *ex ante* auction for the right to capture the arbitrage profit from the block, an idea first proposed by Alex Herrmann from Gnosis as the "MEV capturing AMM" (McAMM) in [19]. This paper extends that concept to allow the manager to also select the fee charged to retail traders and collect those fees, thus using a similar mechanism to address an independent problem. Also, unlike the McAMM, the auction proposed here guarantees the property of *accessibility*—people can trade against the pool even if the current manager has not submitted a transaction in this block.

Our paper also proposes a way to optimize fees that takes into account the difficult-to-model demand function for retail orderflow. Some AMMs, such as Uniswap v3 [4] address this problem by letting liquidity providers choose between different static "fee tiers." This puts the responsibility for optimizing fees on individual liquidity providers, can lead to some fragmentation of liquidity. Other automated market makers have implemented dynamic fees on individual pools, including Trader Joe v2.1 [24], Curve v2 [13], and Mooniswap [9], as well as [25]. [11] propose a design involving dynamic fees and dynamic price impact functions. While innovative, these dynamic fee implementations are not necessarily optimized for maximizing liquidity. The am-AMM is a first attempt at a provably incentive-compatible dynamic fee, where the fee is set by the market in a way that should always attract more liquidity than any fixed-fee AMM.

2 Auction Design

The auction is designed to set up a censorship-resistant version of the two-stage game modelled in Sect. 3.2, where (1) potential managers bid for the right to set and earn the trading fee in a future block; and (2) liquidity providers respond by adding or removing liquidity. The auction uses a delay parameter K. The rules of the auction are designed so that both the rent and the pool manager for block N are locked in as of block $N - K$.

Harberger Lease. The right to be the manager of a pool is set in a special onchain auction we call a "Harberger lease" (named after the "Harberger taxes" popularized by [27]). This is a continuously held English auction where bids are expressed in terms of rent per block. The *top bid* at any given time determines the manager for the pool, who pays the rent to liquidity providers in the pool for as long as that bid is active.

The rent is denominated and paid in pool tokens, and is paid out of the pool manager's deposit to all pool LP token holders proportional to their stake (thus effectively increasing the value of those pool tokens). This ensures that pool tokens remain fungible and that rent is compounded automatically.

Bidding Rules. Each bid specifies a per-block rent R. When the bid is placed, it must include a *deposit* D, which must be a multiple of R and must be at least $R \cdot K$. Newly placed bids do not become active immediately, but are delayed by K blocks. When either a new high bid becomes active, or the current pool manager's deposit is depleted, the new high bidder *usurps* the current pool manager. The contract enforces a minimum bid increment.

The top bid cannot be cancelled, but can reduce its deposit as long as it leave a minimum deposit of $D_{\text{top}} \geq R_{\text{top}} K$. The contract keeps track of the *next* bid (which is either the next-highest bid after the current top bid, or a bid that is higher than the top bid but is not yet active). If the top bid does not have enough rent to pay for K blocks—that is, if $\frac{D_{\text{top}}}{R_{\text{top}}} < K$, then the next bid cannot be canceled, but must leave at least enough deposit such that $\frac{D_{\text{top}}}{R_{\text{top}}} + \frac{D_{\text{next}}}{R_{\text{next}}} \geq K$.

Pool Manager Rights. The current pool manager can adjust the swap fee for the next block at any time, subject to a fixed *fee cap* $f_{\max}$. The pool manager also receives all swap fees collected by the pool. Since the pool manager receives swap fees, they are effectively able to swap on the pool with zero fee. This means that they can capture arbitrages from small price movements that no other arbitrageur would be able to profitably capture. However, if the price moves by more than the current fee in a single block—in other words, if it moves outside the "no-trade region" [22]—then some of the profit could leak to other arbitrageurs, as discussed in Sect. 3.2.

Censorship Resistance. The delay parameter K should be chosen such that there is a negligible probability that anyone can censor the base layer for K blocks in a row. This prevents someone from stealing MEV from a high-volatility block by usurping the current manager and then censoring arbitrage transactions for K blocks. It also ensures that liquidity providers can respond to changes in rent by adding or removing liquidity before the new rent takes effect.

Withdrawal Fees. Liquidity providers are free to enter or exit at any time. This allows them to respond to anticipated changes in rent during the K-block delay. However, when liquidity providers exit, they must pay a small withdrawal fee to the current manager. This prevents liquidity providers from withdrawing liquidity after volatility is realized but before the current manager has the opportunity to execute an arbitrage transaction. As shown in Appendix B, even a very small withdrawal fee—less than 0.13 basis points, if the fee cap is 1%—can ensure that strategic liquidity provider withdrawals cannot reduce the manager's profit from a given arbitrage opportunity below the amount assumed in Sect. 3. This fee could alternatively be replaced with a withdrawal delay for a similar effect.

3 Theory

Our starting point is a model inspired by [23] and [22], which consider an AMM trading a risky asset (denoted by x) versus the numéraire (denoted by y), and that the risky asset has a fundamental price at all times (for example, on an infinitely deep centralized exchange). As in [22], we assume that traders can only trade on the pool at discrete block generation times.

Our setting is consistent with and can be structurally microfounded in the full setting of [22], which assumes that blocks arrival times follow a Poisson process and that the asset's price follows geometric Brownian motion parameterized by volatility $\sigma > 0$, but our theorems do not depend on those assumptions. Instead we describe the model primitives in reduced form, with weaker assumptions, and provide examples that show that those models would satisfy the assumptions.

We will restrict to the case of a constant product market maker,[1] with invariant $\sqrt{xy} = L$, where we denote the reserve quantities by (x, y) and the pool liquidity level by L. If the price of the risky asset is given by P, the value of the pool reserves is given by $V(L) \triangleq 2\sqrt{P}L$, as a function of the available liquidity L. We assume the pool charges a proportional trading fee $f \in [0, f_{\max}]$.

We consider a setting where there are two types of traders: (1) noise traders, who trade for idiosyncratic reasons and generate fee income for the pool; and (2) arbitrageurs, who seek to exploit price differences between the pool and the fundamental price, and create adverse selection costs for the pool. Here, the P&L of LPs is a jump process, stochastically jumping at instances of block generation. We will consider the expected aggregate instantaneous rate of P&L of LPs per unit time, where we are averaging over stochasticity in future price changes, or, equivalently, assuming that exposure to market risk of the risky asset has been hedged.

Noise Traders. We assume there exists a population of noise traders that trade for idiosyncratic reasons (e.g., convenience of executing on chain) and not for informational reasons. Hence, economically, in our model noise traders serve exclusively to generate fee income for the pool. Given pool fee $f \geq 0$ and liquidity $L \geq 0$, denote by $H(f, L)$ the expected total volume of noise trades arriving per unit time, denominated in the numéraire, so that $fH(f, L)$ is the total rate per unit time of fee revenue generated by the noise traders. We will assume that:

Assumption 1 (Noise trader demand) *For $L > 0$, define*

$$H_0(f, L) \triangleq H(f, L)/V(L),$$

to be the expected noise trader volume per unit time per unit of pool value, we assume that $H_0(\cdot, \cdot)$ is a continuous function satisfying:

---

[1] The key property of the constant product market maker we use is that the arbitrage profits and arbitrage excess scale linearly with pool value, where the constant of proportionality does not depend on the price. This property holds more generally for geometric mean market makers, and our results would trivially extend there. Beyond that, when considering more general invariant curves, there may be additional second order effects due to the price changing over time horizon of the LP investment. If price movements over the scale of the LP investment horizon are not large, these effects may not be significant, and we would expect the high level insights of our model to continue to apply to general invariant curves.

1. For all $L > 0$, $H_0(f, L)$ is a decreasing function of f.
2. For all $f \in [0, f_{\max}]$, $H_0(f, L)$ is strictly decreasing function of L. Moreover, $H_0(f, L) \downarrow 0$ as $L \to \infty$, and $H_0(f, L) \uparrow \infty$ as $L \to 0$.

Part 1 asserts that noise trader demand is decreasing in the price (fee) charged. Part 2 implies that the noise trader is sub-linear in pool value or liquidity, i.e., noise trader demand is satiated.

Example 1. Consider $H(f, L) \triangleq c_0 L^\alpha \exp(-c_1 f)$, where $c_0, c_1 > 0$ and $\alpha \in (0, 1)$ are parameters that could be estimated from transaction data, and may be time varying or may depend on other market parameters such as volatility or broader market volume. This liquidity dependence is consistent with the model proposed by [18].

Arbitrageur Profits. We assume there is a competitive and deep market of arbitrageurs monitoring prices in the AMM and exploiting price differences between the AMM and the fundamental price. Denote by $\mathsf{ARB\_PROFIT}(f, L)$ the expected profit to arbitrageurs per unit time, given fee $f \in [0, f_{\max}]$ and liquidity $L \geq 0$. We make the following assumption:

Assumption 2 (Arbitrageur profits) *For $L > 0$, we assume that*

$$\mathsf{ARB\_PROFIT}(f, L) = \mathsf{AP}_0(f) V(L),$$

where $\mathsf{AP}_0(\cdot)$ is a continuous, decreasing function.

Assumption 2 guarantees that arbitrage profits scale *linearly* with the pool value or liquidity, in contrast to noise trader volume. This is because we assume, by nature of engaging in riskless activity, arbs have access to infinite capital for arbitrage activity, and arbitrage demand will not be satiated so long as arbitrage opportunities are available. Assumption 2 also implies that, holding liquidity fixed, arbitrageur profits are decreasing in the fee f, this is because the fee is a friction that limits arbitrage.

This assumption does not depend on a particular model for either the asset price's behavior or for block generation times, but we show that it can be structurally microfounded in one such model, as illustrated here:[2]

Example 2. Consider a setting where the risky asset's price follows geometric Brownian motion parameterized by volatility $\sigma > 0$ and blocks are generated at the arrivals of a Poisson process of rate Δt^{-1}, with Δt being the average interblock time. [22] establish that, when $\Delta t < 8\sigma^2$,

$$\mathsf{ARB\_PROFIT}(f, L) = \frac{\sigma^2}{8} \frac{1}{1 + \frac{f}{\sigma\sqrt{\Delta t/2}}} \frac{e^{+f/2} + e^{-f/2}}{2(1 - \sigma^2 \Delta t/8)} V(L). \qquad (1)$$

This satisfies Assumption 2.

---
[2] See Sect. 4 for further discussion.

3.1 Fixed-Fee AMM Model

As a benchmark, we consider the standard AMM design with a fixed fee $f \in [0, f_{\max}]$, which we refer to as a *fixed-fee AMM* (ff-AMM). Following the discussion above, we define the instantaneous rate of aggregate expected P&L of LPs in this pool in excess of the risk free rate according to

$$\Pi_{\text{ff}}^{\text{LP}}(f, L) \triangleq fH(f, L) - \text{ARB\_PROFIT}(f, L) - rV(L)$$
$$= (fH_0(f, L) - \text{AP}_0(f) - r) V(L), \quad (2)$$

where the first term in the sum is the revenue from noise traders, the second term is the loss to arbs, and the final term is a capital charge, where $r > 0$ is the risk-free rate. Under free entry and exit of LPs, we define the equilibrium in the fixed-fee AMM according to a zero profit condition:

Lemma 1 (ff-AMM equilibrium). *Given fee $f \in [0, f_{\max}]$, define a liquidity level $L^* > 0$ to be a competitive equilibrium if LPs earn zero profit in excess of the risk free rate, i.e., $\Pi_{\text{ff}}^{\text{LP}}(f, L^*) = 0$. Then, for any $f \in [0, f_{\max}]$, a unique equilibrium level of liquidity $L^* = L_{\text{ff}}(f)$ exists.*

3.2 Auction-Managed AMM Model

In this section, we consider the auction-managed AMM design.

Arbitrageur Excess. In the am-AMM, the pool manager collects all of the fee revenue, and therefore, effectively, can also trade against the pool without paying any fees. Therefore, the pool will suffer adverse selection costs of ARB_PROFIT$(0, L)$, independent of the fee level f. However, the manager does not collect all of these fees as income. Instead, note that whenever the mispricing in the pool exceeds the fee f, some of that mispricing can be profitably captured by agents other than the manager. We denote by ARB_EXCESS(f, L) the instantaneous rate of expected arbitrage profit per unit time forgone by the manager. We assume that:

Assumption 3 (Arbitrageur excess) *For $L > 0$, we assume that*

$$\text{ARB\_EXCESS}(f, L) = \text{AE}_0(f)V(L),$$

with $\text{AE}_0(f)$ a continuous, decreasing function that satisfies $\text{AE}_0(f) \leq \text{AP}_0(f)$, for all $f \in [0, f_{\max}]$, and where the inequality is strict if $f > 0$.

Assumption 3 is largely analogous to Assumption 2, and can be similarly microfounded by a stochastic model, as shown in Example 4, but does not depend on that model. The strict inequality assumption simply asserts that *some* of the arbitrage profit is captured by the manager.

Example 3. One extreme setting is the McAMM design of [19]. There, no trades can occur in an AMM in a given block unless the pool manager has a transaction earlier in the block to "unlock" the pool. Hence the pool manager is guaranteed to be the first transaction in everyblock and can capture all arbitrage profits. In this case, ARB_EXCESS$(f, L) = 0$.

Example 4. In Sect. 4, we develop structural microfoundations of a model for arbitrageur excess in the setting of [22], where the risky asset's price follows geometric Brownian motion parameterized by volatility $\sigma > 0$ and blocks are generated at the arrivals of a Poisson process of rate Δt^{-1}, with Δt being the average interblock time. In that setting, we assume that (1) the pool manager fully monetizes any arbitrage where the mispricing is less than the fee f, and (2) when the mispricing exceeds the fee f, other arbitrageurs correct the mispricing back to the fee level f before the pool manager can trade, and hence the pool manager is only able to monetize the portion of the arbitrage up to f. Then, we establish that, when $\Delta t < 8\sigma^2$,

$$\mathsf{ARB\_EXCESS}(f, L) = \frac{\sigma^2}{8} \exp\left(-\frac{f}{\sigma\sqrt{\Delta t/2}}\right) \frac{e^{+f/2} + e^{-f/2}}{2(1 - \sigma^2 \Delta t/8)} V(L). \quad (3)$$

This satisfies the conditions of Assumption 3.

Comparing Example 2 and Example 4, we see that $\mathsf{ARB\_EXCESS}(f, L) \ll \mathsf{ARB\_PROFIT}(f, L)$ in the sense that

$$\frac{\mathsf{ARB\_EXCESS}(f, L)}{\mathsf{ARB\_PROFIT}(f, L)} = \frac{\mathsf{AE}_0(f, L)}{\mathsf{AP}_0(f, L)} = \left(1 + \frac{f}{\sigma\sqrt{\Delta t/2}}\right) \exp\left(-\frac{f}{\sigma\sqrt{\Delta t/2}}\right),$$

which is exponentially vanishing in $f/\sigma\sqrt{\Delta t}$.

Equilibrium. We imagine a game that proceeds in two steps: (1) agents bid rent R, the agent with the highest rent wins the auction and is declared the pool manager, with the right to determine the trading fee f and earn all fees; and (2) LPs determine aggregate liquidity L given R. Based on the discussion above, the P&L of the manager per unit time is given by

$$\Pi_{\mathsf{am}}^{\mathsf{MGR}}(R, L) \triangleq \max_{f \in [0, f_{\max}]} \{fH(f, L) + \mathsf{ARB\_PROFIT}(0, L)$$
$$- \mathsf{ARB\_EXCESS}(f, L) - R\}$$
$$= \max_{f \in [0, f_{\max}]} \{fH_0(f, L) + \mathsf{AP}_0(0) - \mathsf{AE}_0(f)\} V(L) - R.$$

The maximization is because the manager is free to set the fee, and we assume they will do so to maximize P&L. The first term captures the fact that the manager retains all fee revenue. The second and third terms capture the fact that the manager earns arbitrage profits as if it pays no fees, except for the arbitrage excess. The final term captures the fact that the manager pays rent. On the other hand, the LPs in aggregate earn P&L per unit time given by

$$\Pi_{\mathsf{am}}^{\mathsf{LP}}(R, L) \triangleq R - \mathsf{ARB\_PROFIT}(0, L) - rV(L) = R - (\mathsf{AP}_0(0) + r)V(L).$$

Here, the first term is the rent payment made by the manager, the second term is the adverse selection cost (which is as if no fees are charged), and the third term is the cost of capital. Given these definitions, we have that:

Theorem 1 (am-AMM equilibrium). (R^*, L^*) *is a competitive equilibrium of the am-AMM if the zero profit conditions*[3]

$$\Pi_{am}^{MGR}(R^*, L^*) = 0, \qquad \Pi_{am}^{LP}(R^*, L^*) = 0,$$

are satisfied. An equilibrium (R^*, L^*) *must exist, with equilibrium fees*

$$f^* \in \underset{f \in [0, f_{max}]}{\operatorname{argmax}} \ f H_0(f, L) - AE_0(f), \qquad (4)$$

and satisfies $L^* > L_{ff}(f)$, *for all* $f \geq 0$. *Therefore, in equilibrium, the am-AMM will have higher liquidity than any ff-AMM.*

Theorem 1 establishes that the equilibrium liquidity for the am-AMM is larger than that of any ff-AMM. Beyond that, it gives insight into the equilibrium fee f^* set in the am-AMM: from (4), the pool operator will seek to set the fee to maximize noise trader revenue adjusted for arbitrageur excess. As a comparison consider the fee level f_{opt} that exclusively maximizes noise trader revenue, i.e.,

$$f_{opt} \in \underset{f \in [0, f_{max}]}{\operatorname{argmax}} \ f H_0(f, L^*). \qquad (5)$$

If we assume that the revenue function $f \mapsto f H_0(f, L^*)$ is concave, and the arbitrageur excess function $AE_0(f)$ is convex, then a comparison of first order conditions for (4)–(5) reveals that $f_{opt} \leq f^*$, i.e., the am-AMM will set fees higher than is purely revenue optimal. However, by virtue of the optimality of f^* in (4), we have that

$$f_{opt} H_0(f_{opt}, L^*) - f^* H_0(f^*, L^*) \leq AE_0(f_{opt}) - AE_0(f^*) \leq AE_0(f_{opt}). \qquad (6)$$

In the arbitrageur excess model of Example 4, $AE_0(f_{opt})$ may be very small (since it is exponentially vanishing in blocktime, for example), and in such cases (6) would imply that f^* is also nearly optimal from a noise trader revenue perspective.

4 A Structural Model for Arbitrageur Excess

In this section, we will derive the structural model for arbitrageur excess of Example 4, following the arbitrageur profits model of [22] and of Example 2.

Fee Structure. In order to simplify formulas, [22] uses a fee structure wherein a proportional fee of $e^{+\gamma} - 1 = \gamma + o(\gamma)$ is charged for purchases of the risky asset from the pool, while a proportional fee of $1 - e^{-\gamma} = \gamma + o(\gamma)$ is charged for sales of the risky asset to the pool—these are symmetric fees in log-price space. This is different than the setting in this paper, where we assume a fee proportional f

---

[3] Here, we assume that entry and exit are frictionless for LPs, ignoring the withdrawal fees. This is justified if the liquidity provision decision horizon is sufficiently long so that, amortized over its length, the withdrawal fees are de minimus.

which is the same for buys or sells—that is, symmetric in (linear) price space. In order to facilitate comparison with [22], we will make the approximation $f = \gamma$. As illustrated in Example 1 of [22], for practical parameter values, this does not make a significant difference.

Asset Price Dynamics. Denote by P_t the fundamental price of the asset, which follows a geometric Brownian motion with drift $\mu > 0$ and volatility $\sigma > 0$, and denote by $\tilde{P}_t$ the implied spot price of the asset in the pool. Define $z_t \triangleq \log P_t/\tilde{P}_t$ to be the log-mispricing at time t. When t is not a block generation time, Itô's lemma implies that z_t is governed by the stochastic differential equation

$$dz_t = \left(\mu - \tfrac{1}{2}\sigma^2\right) dt + \sigma \, dB_t, \tag{7}$$

where B_t is a Brownian motion. We will make the symmetry assumption that $\mu = \tfrac{1}{2}\sigma^2$, so that z_t is a driftless, (scaled) Brownian motion.

Block Time Dynamics. We assume that blocks are generated according to a Poisson process with mean interarrival time Δt. Denote the block generation times by $0 < \tau_1 < \tau_2 < \ldots$. At instances $t = \tau_i$ when blocks are generated, we imagine that

1. If the $|z_{t-}| \geq f$ (i.e., the mispricing immediately before block generation exceeds the fee), we imagine an arbitrageur is able to trade until the mispricing is equal to the fee, and thus earns profits that are not captured by the pool operator. These profits then become part of arbitrageur excess. Following the derivation of [22], the instaneous profit from arbitrageur excess when price is $P = P_t$ and the mispricing is $z = z_{t-}$ due to buying (respectively, selling) is given by

$$A_+(P, z) \triangleq \left[P\left\{x^*\left(Pe^{-z}\right) - x^*\left(Pe^{-f}\right)\right\} + e^{+f}\left\{y^*\left(Pe^{-z}\right) - y^*\left(Pe^{-f}\right)\right\}\right]\mathbb{I}_{\{z > +f\}} \geq 0,$$

$$A_-(P, z) \triangleq \left[P\left\{x^*\left(Pe^{-z}\right) - x^*\left(Pe^{+f}\right)\right\} + e^{-f}\left\{y^*\left(Pe^{-z}\right) - y^*\left(Pe^{+f}\right)\right\}\right]\mathbb{I}_{\{z < -f\}} \geq 0.$$

Here, the holdings of the pool when implied price is P are given by $x^*(P) \triangleq L/\sqrt{P}$, $y^*(P) = L\sqrt{P}$.

2. After the arbitrageur trades, the pool operator corrects any remaining mispricing, so that $z_t = 0$.

Intensity of Arbitrageur Excess. The intensity or instaneous rate of arbitrageur excess per dollar of pool value per unit time is given by

$$\mathsf{AE}_0(f) = \frac{\mathsf{ARB\_EXCESS}(f, L)}{V(L)} = \frac{1}{\Delta t}\mathsf{E}\left[\frac{A_+(P, z) + A_-(P, z)}{V(L)}\right],$$

where the expectation is over $z = z_\tau$ at the next block generation time τ, i.e., $z \sim N(0, \sigma^2\tau)$ with $\tau \sim \mathrm{Exp}(\Delta t^{-1})$.

Observe that

$$\frac{A_+(P,z)}{V(L)} = \frac{1}{2L\sqrt{P}} \left[P\left\{x^*\left(Pe^{-z}\right) - x^*\left(Pe^{-f}\right)\right\} + e^{+f}\left\{y^*\left(Pe^{-z}\right) - y^*\left(Pe^{-f}\right)\right\}\right] \mathbb{I}_{\{z>+f\}}$$

$$= \tfrac{1}{2}\left[\left\{e^{+z/2} - e^{+f/2}\right\} + e^{-f}\left\{e^{-z/2} - e^{-f/2}\right\}\right]\mathbb{I}_{\{z>+f\}}$$

$$= \tfrac{1}{2}e^{+f/2}\left[e^{+(z-f)/2} - 2 - e^{-(z-f)/2}\right]\mathbb{I}_{\{z>+f\}},$$

$$\frac{A_-(P,z)}{V(L)} = \frac{1}{2L\sqrt{P}} \left[P\left\{x^*\left(Pe^{-z}\right) - x^*\left(Pe^{+f}\right)\right\} + e^{-f}\left\{y^*\left(Pe^{-z}\right) - y^*\left(Pe^{+f}\right)\right\}\right] \mathbb{I}_{\{z<-f\}}$$

$$= \tfrac{1}{2}\left[\left\{e^{+z/2} - e^{-f/2}\right\} + e^{-f}\left\{e^{-z/2} - e^{+f/2}\right\}\right]\mathbb{I}_{\{z<-f\}}$$

$$= \tfrac{1}{2}e^{-f/2}\left[e^{+(z+f)/2} - 2 + e^{-(z+f)/2}\right]\mathbb{I}_{\{z<-f\}},$$

Taking expectations of the first term, conditioned on the block generation time τ, we have $z \sim N(0, \sigma^2 \tau)$, so that

$$\mathbb{E}\left[\frac{A_+(P,z)}{V(L)}\,\bigg|\,\tau\right] = -e^{\frac{f}{2}} + \frac{1}{2}\left(e^f + 1\right)e^{\frac{\sigma^2\tau}{8}} - \frac{1}{2}e^f e^{\frac{\sigma^2\tau}{8}} \operatorname{erf}\left(\frac{\sigma^2\tau + 2f}{2\sqrt{2}\sigma\sqrt{\tau}}\right)$$
$$+ \frac{1}{2}e^{\frac{\sigma^2\tau}{8}} \operatorname{erf}\left(\frac{\sigma^2\tau - 2f}{2\sqrt{2}\sigma\sqrt{\tau}}\right) + e^{\frac{f}{2}} \operatorname{erf}\left(\frac{f}{\sigma\sqrt{\tau}\sqrt{2}}\right).$$

Taking expectations over $\tau \sim \operatorname{Exp}(\Delta t^{-1})$, assuming that $\Delta t < 8\sigma^2$,

$$\frac{1}{\Delta t}\mathbb{E}\left[\frac{A_+(P,z)}{V(L)}\right] = \frac{\sigma^2}{8}\exp\left(-\frac{f}{\sigma\sqrt{\Delta t/2}}\right)\frac{e^{+f/2}}{2\left(1 - \sigma^2\Delta t/8\right)}.$$

Similarly, for the other term,

$$\frac{1}{\Delta t}\mathbb{E}\left[*\frac{A_-(P,z)}{V(L)}\right] = \frac{\sigma^2}{8}\exp\left(-\frac{f}{\sigma\sqrt{\Delta t/2}}\right)\frac{e^{-f/2}}{2\left(1 - \sigma^2\Delta t/8\right)}.$$

Combining these results yields the arbitrageur excess expression in (3).

Discussion. The expressions (1) for arbitrageur profits and (3) for arb excess have an interesting common structure. In both cases, the expressions can be decomposed into the product of (1) the probability that an arbitrageur can trade at the next block time; and (2) the expected profit conditioned on trade. In the arbitrageur profits expression, the probability of trade is given by

$$\frac{1}{1 + \frac{f}{\sigma\sqrt{\Delta t/2}}},$$

while in the arbitrageur excess expression, it is given by

$$\exp\left(-\frac{f}{\sigma\sqrt{\Delta t/2}}\right).$$

In both cases, however, the expected profit conditioned on trade is the same. Thus, the fact that arbitrageur excess is less than arbitrageur profits is driven by the fact that the probability of trade is (exponentially) less. This, in turn, is because the pool operator drives the mispricing to zero at the end of every block, making large mispricings at the beginning of the next block unlikely.

5 Discussion

Advantages. One desirable characteristic of the auction-managed AMM is that it shifts the strategic burden of determining the optimal fee from passive LPs to the pool manager, who, in turn will set the fee according to (4), which seeks to set fees to optimize revenue from noise traders, adjusted by arb excess paid to arbitraguers. This makes sense, since the pool manager is assumed to be a more sophisticated entity that can perform off-chain modeling and analysis to estimate noise trader sensitivity and losses to arbs.

Our model captures the most visible and salient features that drive noise trader demand (the fee and the liquidity). However, as argued by [22] and [28], noise traders may also be concerned with the accuracy of prices in the pool. Relative to an outside reference price (e.g., the price on infinitely deep centralized exchange), noise traders pay an effective spread which is the sum of the trading fee of the pool (deterministic, positive) and the relative mispricing of the pool (stochastic, could be positive or negative). In general noise traders will prefer pools with less relative mispricing. An additional benefit of the am-AMM over the ff-AMM is that the quoted prices are more accurate. This is because the pool operator of an am-AMM faces no fees in performing arbitrage trades against the pool, and is able to correct smaller price discrepancies.

There is also an important transfer of risk between the LPs and the pool manager: in the am-AMM, the LPs earn rent payments instead of noise trader fees. Since these rent payments are determined *ex ante*, in equilibrium, they incorporate the expected value of future noise trader fee revenue, in contrast to the actual noise trader fee revenue, which arrives in a lumpy and stochastic fashion and goes to the pool manager. Although it is beyond the scope of the analysis we have presented (which assumes risk neutrality), this risk transfer is likely welfare improving since the pool manager is likely a larger and better capitalized entity than a typical passive LP, and is thus less risk averse.

Drawbacks. The auction-managed AMM is not without drawbacks. First, the pool manager's ability to effectively trade on the pool with zero spread exacerbates the "sandwich attack" problem with onchain AMMs, as discussed generally by [1,12,29]. A party that can trade with zero fees can profit by pushing any publicly visible swap transaction to its limit price. This is a meaningful drawback—which could hurt swappers or ultimately discourage retail flow, thus potentially invalidating the assumption in Sect. 3 that retail flow is only a function of liquidity and fee—but known mitigations for general sandwich attacks could be applied, such as verifiable sequencing rules [14], private relays [1], or offchain filler auctions [5].

Second, the *ex ante* auction for the arbitrage opportunity could have effects on the market for block building. The pool manager's exclusive right to capture some arbitrage profit from a pool could give them an advantage in the block builder auction, similar to the advantages enjoyed by builders with private orderflow discussed by [15]. Additionally, while the am-AMM allows any party to bid on the pool manager position, parties with greater sophistication or access to private orderflow may be more likely to win the auction. On the other hand, by capturing some arbitrage profit and reducing the power of block proposers, the am-AMM could mitigate some of the harmful pressures that MEV puts on the blockchain consensus mechanism. We think these possible consequences warrant further study.

Lastly, one disadvantage of the am-AMM over the McAMM discussed by [19] is that the current manager does not capture the "arbitrage excess" that results from single-block price movements beyond the no-trade region, as discussed in Sect. 3. This creates an incentive for the manager to set a higher fee than the one that optimizes total fee revenue. This could be fixed by requiring the manager to unlock the pool at every block, at the cost of sacrificing the accessibility property.

Future Work. In this paper, we focus on constant product market makers. Extending this design to other AMMs—and particularly to concentrated liquidity AMMs, in which different liquidity providers may have different returns during the same period and may go in or out of range as a result of price changes—is left for future work.

Implementing this mechanism is also left for future work. Since we first made this paper available, there has been at least one open-source third-party implementation [8].

A Proofs

Proof (Proof of Lemma 1). Given fixed $f \in [0, f_{\max}]$, define $G(L) \triangleq fH_0(f, L) - \mathsf{AP}_0(f) - r$. By Assumption 1(2) and Assumption 2, this is a continuous function, and

$$\lim_{L \to 0} G(L) = \infty, \quad \lim_{L \to \infty} G(L) = -\mathsf{AP}_0(f) - r < 0.$$

By the intermediate value theorem, there exists $L^* > 0$ with $G(L^*) = 0$, comparing with (2), this must be an equilibrium. This equilibrium is unique since $G(\cdot)$ is strictly monotonic.

Proof (Proof of Theorem 1). First, we will prove that the equilibrium (R^*, L^*) exists. Solving for R^* in the condition $\Pi_{\text{am}}^{\text{MGR}}(R^*, L^*) = 0$ and substituting into $\Pi_{\text{am}}^{\text{LP}}(R^*, L^*) = 0$, we have that L^* must satisfy $G(L^*) = 0$ where

$$G(L) \triangleq \max_{f \in [0, f_{\max}]} fH_0(f, L) - \mathsf{AE}_0(f) - r.$$

From Assumption 1 and Assumption 2, this function is continuous, and

$$\lim_{L \to \infty} G(L) = \max_{f \in [0, f_{\max}]} -\mathsf{AE}_0(f) - r = -\mathsf{AE}_0(0) - r < 0.$$
$$\lim_{L \to 0} G(L) \geq \lim_{L \to 0} fH_0(f, L) - \mathsf{AE}_0(f) - r = \infty > 0,$$

for any $f \in (0, f_{\max}]$. By the intermediate value theorem, an equilibrium (R^*, L^*) must exist.

In order to compare with the ff-AMM, define

$$L_{\max} \triangleq \max_{f \in [0, f_{\max}]} L_{\text{ff}}(f),$$

to be the maximum level of liquidity that can be achieved in the ff-AMM, and denote by f^* the maximizing fee. Define

$$R_{\max} \triangleq (\mathsf{AP}_0(0) + r)V(L_{\max}).$$

From the zero profit condition $\Pi_{\text{am}}^{\mathsf{LP}}(R_{\max}, L_{\max}) = 0$, it is clear that a rent payment of $R_{\max}$ will incentivize liquidity $L_{\max}$. Under such a rent payment, the pool manager earns profits

$$\begin{aligned}\Pi_{\text{am}}^{\mathsf{MGR}}(R_{\max}, L_{\max}) &= \left(\mathsf{AP}_0(0) + \max_{f \in [0, f_{\max}]} fH_0(f, L_{\max}) - \mathsf{AE}_0(f)\right)V(L_{\max}) - R_{\max} \\ &\geq (\mathsf{AP}_0(0) + f^*H_0(f^*, L_{\max}) - \mathsf{AE}_0(f^*))V(L_{\max}) - R_{\max} \\ &= (\mathsf{AP}_0(0) + \mathsf{AP}_0(f^*) + r - \mathsf{AE}_0(f^*))V(L_{\max}) - R_{\max} \\ &= (\mathsf{AP}_0(0) + \mathsf{AP}_0(f^*) + r - \mathsf{AE}_0(f^*))V(L_{\max}) - (\mathsf{AP}_0(0) + r)V(L_{\max}) \\ &= (\mathsf{AP}_0(f^*) - \mathsf{AE}_0(f^*))V(L_{\max}) \\ &> 0.\end{aligned}$$

Here, the first inequality follows from the suboptimality of f^* for the am-AMM, and we also use the fact that $\Pi_{\text{ff}}^{\mathsf{LP}}(f^*, L_{\max}) = 0$ since it is an equilibrium for the ff-AMM. The last equality follows from Assumption 3.

Since the pool manager earns positive profits when the rent is $R_{\max}$, and equilibrium rent R^* musty satisfy $R^* > R_{\max}$, therefore and equilibrium fee-auction AMM utility $L^* > L_{\max}$.

B Withdrawal Fees

Here, we show that a withdrawal fee of $1 - \frac{2 \cdot \sqrt{f_{cap}}}{f_{cap}+1}$ is sufficient to protect managers from strategic liquidity withdrawals. With a fee cap of 1%, this comes out to approximately 0.00001238%, or about 0.1238 basis points—a $12.38 fee on a $1 million position.

Our goal is to set a withdrawal fee to prevent opportunistic withdrawals of liquidity (in response to arbitrage opportunities) from reducing manager profits. Under our assumptions, the manager's profit from a given arbitrage opportunity is capped once the price moves by f_{cap}, the maximum allowable swap fee. Any larger price move results in MEV for the block proposer (since any arbitrageur can capture the excess portion with a swap), rather than profit for the manager. Therefore, we only need to set a withdrawal fee that is greater than the value from arbing that liquidity in response to an increase of a factor of f_{cap}. (A decrease by a factor of f_{cap} will result in a smaller arbitrage opportunity.)

For this proof, we use the same conventions as Sect. 3, where reserves are expressed in terms of two assets x and y, asset y is defined as the numéraire for all prices and valuations, and "liquidity" for a position is defined as $\sqrt{xy}$ where x and y are the position's reserves of assets x and y, respectively.

Suppose without loss of generality that a liquidity provider is providing 1 unit of liquidity, and the current midpoint price on the AMM is p_{amm}. Since $p_{amm} = \frac{y_{now}}{x_{now}}$ and $x_{now} \cdot y_{now} = 1$, the liquidity provider's current reserves of assets X and Y are $x_{now} = \frac{1}{\sqrt{p_{amm}}}$ and $y_{now} = \sqrt{p_{amm}}$.

We suppose price has increased by f_{cap}, making the true price $p_{true} = f_{cap} \cdot p_{amm}$.

The current valuation of the liquidity is:

$$v_{now} = p_{true} \cdot x_{now} + y_{now} = f_{cap} \cdot p_{amm} \cdot \frac{1}{\sqrt{p_{amm}}} + \sqrt{p_{amm}} = (1 + f_{cap}) \cdot \sqrt{p_{amm}} \tag{8}$$

The valuation of the liquidity after the manager arbitrages the pool to p_{true} ($f_{cap} \cdot p_{amm}$) would be:

$$v_{after} = f_{cap} \cdot p_{amm} \cdot \frac{1}{\sqrt{f_{cap} \cdot p_{amm}}} + \sqrt{f_{cap} \cdot p_{amm}} = 2 \cdot \sqrt{f_{cap} \cdot p_{amm}} \tag{9}$$

To prevent strategic withdrawal from being profitable for liquidity providers at the expense of managers, we can impose a withdrawal fee of $\frac{v_{now} - v_{after}}{v_{now}}$, which simplifies to:

$$f_{withdrawal} = \frac{v_{now} - v_{after}}{v_{now}} = 1 - \frac{2 \cdot \sqrt{f_{cap}}}{1 + f_{cap}} \tag{10}$$

References

1. Adams, A., Chan, B.Y., Markovich, S., Wan, X.: The costs of swapping on the uniswap protocol. arXiv preprint arXiv:2309.13648 (2023)
2. Adams, H., et al.: Uniswap v4 core [draft] (2023). https://github.com/Uniswap/v4-core/blob/main/docs/whitepaper-v4.pdf
3. Adams, H., Zinsmeister, N., Robinson, D.: Uniswap v2 core (2020). https://uniswap.org/whitepaper.pdf
4. Adams, H., Zinsmeister, N., Salem, M., Keefer, R., Robinson, D.: Uniswap v3 core (2021). https://uniswap.org/whitepaper-v3.pdf
5. Adams, H., et al.: Uniswapx (2023). https://uniswap.org/whitepaper-uniswapx.pdf
6. Angeris, G., Chitra, T.: Improved price oracles: constant function market makers. In: Proceedings of the 2nd ACM Conference on Advances in Financial Technologies, pp. 80–91 (2020)
7. Angeris, G., Kao, H.-T., Chiang, R., Noyes, C., Chitra, T : An analysis of uniswap markets. arXiv preprint arXiv:1911.03380 (2019)
8. BidDog. Biddog: Open source implementation of am-amm auctions (2024). https://github.com/Bunniapp/biddog. Accessed 22 May 2024

9. Bukov, A., Melnik, M.: Mooniswap by 1inch.exchange (2020). https://mooniswap.exchange/docs/MooniswapWhitePaper-v1.0.pdf
10. Capponi, A., Jia, R.: The adoption of blockchain-based decentralized exchanges. arXiv preprint arXiv:2103.08842 (2021)
11. Cartea, Á., Drissi, F., Sánchez-Betancourt, L., Siska, D., Szpruch, L.: Automated market makers designs beyond constant functions. Available at SSRN 4459177 (2023)
12. Daian, P., et al.: Flash boys 2.0: frontrunning in decentralized exchanges, miner extractable value, and consensus instability. In: 2020 IEEE Symposium on Security and Privacy (SP), pp. 910–927. IEEE (2020)
13. Michael Egorov and Curve Finance (Swiss Stake GmbH). Automatic market-making with dynamic peg (2021). https://classic.curve.fi/files/crypto-pools-paper.pdf
14. Ferreira, M.V.X., Parkes, D.C.: Credible decentralized exchange design via verifiable sequencing rules. arXiv preprint arXiv:2209.15569 (2022)
15. Gupta, T., Pai, M.M., Resnick, M.: The centralizing effects of private order flow on proposer-builder separation. arXiv preprint arXiv:2305.19150 (2023)
16. Hanson, R.: Logarithmic markets coring rules for modular combinatorial information aggregation. J. Prediction Mark. **1**(1), 3–15 (2007)
17. Hasbrouck, J., Rivera, T.J., Saleh, F.: The need for fees at a dex: how increases in fees can increase dex trading volume. Available at SSRN (2022)
18. Hasbrouck, J., Rivera, T.J., Saleh, F.: An economic model of a decentralized exchange with concentrated liquidity. Working Paper (2023)
19. Herrmann, A.: Mev capturing amm (mcamm) (2022). https://ethresear.ch/t/mev-capturing-amm-mcamm/13336
20. Lehar, A., Parlour, C.A.: Decentralized exchanges. Available at SSRN 3905316 (2021)
21. Ma, J., Crapis, D.: The cost of permissionless liquidity provision in automated market makers. arXiv preprint arXiv:2402.18256 (2024)
22. Milionis, J., Moallemi, C.C., Roughgarden, T.: Automated market making and arbitrage profits in the presence of fees. arXiv preprint arXiv:2305.14604 (2023)
23. Milionis, J., Moallemi, C.C., Roughgarden, T., Zhang, A.L.: Automated market making and loss-versus-rebalancing (2022). https://doi.org/10.48550/ARXIV.2208.06046
24. MountainFarmer, Louis, Hanzo, Wawa, Murloc, and Fish. Joe v2.1 liquidity book (2022). https://github.com/traderjoe-xyz/LB-Whitepaper/blob/main/Joe%20v2%20Liquidity%20Book%20Whitepaper.pdf
25. Nezlobin, A.: Twitter thread (2023). https://twitter.com/0x94305/status/1674857993740111872
26. Othman, A., Pennock, D.M., Reeves, D.M., Sandholm, T.: A practical liquidity-sensitive automated market maker. ACM Trans. Econ. Comput. (TEAC) **1**(3), 1–25 (2013)
27. Posner, E.A., Glen Weyl, E.: Radical Markets: Uprooting Capitalism and Democracy for a Just Society. Princeton University Press, Princeton (2018)
28. Rao, R., Shah, N.: Triangle fees (2023). arXiv:2306.17316
29. Zhou, L., Qin, K., Torres, C.F., Le, D.V., Gervais, A.: High-frequency trading on decentralized on-chain exchanges. In: 2021 IEEE Symposium on Security and Privacy (SP), pp. 428–445. IEEE (2021)

The Case of FBA as a DEX Processing Model

Tiantian Gong[1](✉), Zeyu Liu[1], and Aniket Kate[2,3]

[1] Yale University, New Haven, USA
{tiantian.gong,zeyu.liu}@yale.edu
[2] Purdue University, West Lafayette, USA
aniket@purdue.edu
[3] Supra Research, Miami, USA

Abstract. We investigate the welfare loss of the *continuous* and *discrete* order matching models in blockchain-based decentralized exchanges (DEX) that use order books to record outstanding orders. *Continuous processing* matches each incoming transaction against the current order book. The *discrete processing* model, i.e., *frequent batch auction* (FBA), executes transactions discretely in batches with a uniform price double auction: Orders are first matched according to *price*, then the exact transaction order if competing orders specify the same price.

We find that FBA imposes less **welfare loss** and provides better **liquidity** than continuous processing in typical scenarios, e.g., when few parties are *privately informed* about asset valuations. Even otherwise, it achieves better social welfare and liquidity provision in the following settings: when price takers and public information reflecting asset value changes arrive sufficiently frequently compared to private information, when the priority fees (for faster transaction inclusion into blockchains) are small, or when the market is more balanced on both buy and sell sides. Our empirical analysis of the BTC-USD and ETH-USD transactions on a DEX named dYdX indicates that FBA can reduce transaction costs by $21\% - 37\%$.

1 Introduction

Blockchain-based decentralized exchanges (DEX) enable users to trade assets without relying on intermediary authorities through blockchain transactions. They are valued at several billion USD and are expected to grow multifold in the coming years. DEXes typically take one of the two following forms. (1) In a limit order book-based design (e.g., Penumbra [24,30], Uniswap limit orders [25], CoW Swap [12]), each transaction is a limit order (which specifies the direction[1], the price, and quantity of trade), and orders are matched individually. A set of outstanding limit orders is called a limit order book. (2) An automated market maker design (e.g., Uniswap [1]) features automatic algorithmic trading where

---

This work is mostly done while the author was a Ph.D. candidate at Purdue University.
[1] Sell or buy.

the settling price ensures a certain predefined function behaves in a predetermined way.

In this paper, we analyze order book-based DEX designs with a focus on comparing two applicable *transaction processing models*, i.e., *continuous* processing (CLOB, continuous limit order book) where transactions are handled one by one in order or *discrete* frequent batch auction (FBA) where transactions are aggregated at a certain frequency and settled in a double auction (i.e., bids are from both sellers and buyers). Similar to traditional centralized exchanges (CEXs), many order book-based DEX designs follow the CLOB model. Two main metrics to compare the performance of the two designs are (1) *welfare loss*, which measures the extra transaction costs paid by a common user and is determined by the adverse selection risk (explained below) and the adopted processing model (either CLOB or FBA); and (2) *liquidity provision*, which measures the extent to which an on-demand user's transaction is settled (against the order book)[2]. We evaluate the suitability of FBA in the blockchain setting by uncovering scenarios where FBA provides better welfare and liquidity.

Why Consider FBA. While FBA is less considered, it can potentially fit the DEX setting better. In addition to discussions in the context of centralized exchanges [8,16], there are several other intuitive reasons. First, inherently, blockchains already treat time as discrete when ordering and assembling transactions into blocks, the same as in FBA. Second, when transactions are executed continuously (via CLOB), one can observe and act on the "future" if the pending transaction pool is not fully hidden, thus rendering one of CLOB's main advantages moot. Similarly, latencies in block generation and message transmission along with priority fees allow even more space for latency arbitrage rents in DEXes, making CLOB even less favorable. Lastly, a common critique of FBA, the non-execution risks caused by non-transparent pre-trade order book, is alleviated in public blockchains where at least part of the transactions are overt.[3]

Analysis Framework. In the DEX we consider three types of players: (1) *common investors* who submit inelastic trading orders, (2) *informed traders* who submit trades after observing publicly or privately available information about asset valuation jumps, and (3) (many) *arbitrageurs* who can apply market-making (i.e., placing orders to facilitate trades) and front-running strategies. Arbitrageurs are addressed as *liquidity providers* (LPs) when applying the market-making strategy, and as *front-runners* when front-running investors, traders, or other LPs. Our focus is then on how LPs set up their quotes, which decide the amount by which the asking price exceeds the bid price, i.e., the bid-ask spread.

Putting ourselves in LPs' shoes, common investors are price takers and thus the *source of profits*. Informed traders and front-runners cause *losses* to LPs by reacting to information faster, which is also called *adverse selection risk* [8,17].

---

[2] The bid-ask spread is usually viewed as a proxy for measuring liquidity.
[3] In centralized exchanges employing FBA [11], quotes are hidden until being matched. For CEX, displaying orders directly could violate certain regulations [7], e.g., Rule 610 in Regulation National Market System.

Hence, the arrival rates of common investors and the changes in public or private information about asset valuation affect how LPs determine the bid-ask spread. An LP does not set it to be too high, considering that other arbitrageurs can improve on it (i.e., setting a lower spread) to trade with common investors and earn a profit. The LP does not make it too small either, to absorb the potential loss from adverse selection. Here, the *markup* set aside to tolerate this adverse selection risk is the *welfare loss* of our interest. It is considered a "loss" of the welfare of common investors and traders because this portion of the spreads does not need to be paid when there is no adverse selection. Aside from the welfare loss, we are also interested in *liquidity provision*, which is measured with the bid-ask spread itself. Overall, the spread consists of the markup (i.e., the welfare loss) and the price impact of new incoming orders (because it may reflect public or private information about the underlying asset's price changes).

1.1 Contributions

In summary, we make two contributions. First, we analyze the theoretical benefits of employing FBA (frequent batch auction) as the transaction processing model for DEX compared to CLOB (continuous limit order book). Specifically, we uncover typical market conditions where FBA provides better welfare and liquidity. Second, we conduct empirical analysis to straightforwardly compare the transaction costs under the two processing approaches.

Welfare and Liquidity Provision. For welfare loss, if there is *no* private information in DEXes, then FBA always imposes a *zero* welfare loss while CLOB has a positive welfare loss. If a specific DEX design allows privately informed parties, e.g., a board member or a developer capable of dictating protocol updates, adverse selection is present under FBA. In this case, FBA inflicts positive welfare loss. In this setting with private information, we find that first, FBA imposes less welfare loss than CLOB if common investors and public information concerning asset value changes arrive sufficiently often compared to private information. This is because, under FBA, LPs have more time to respond to public information, and less private information reduces adverse selection. Second, the smaller the transaction priority fees [15] are, the higher the markups under CLOB are, as compared to under FBA.[4] This is because the profits from front-running increase as costs decline, resulting in the LPs charging higher markups to counter adverse selection. Finally, a more balanced market decreases the welfare loss for FBA, making it typically less than the welfare loss under CLOB. In essence, when sufficiently many transactions are accumulated and matched among themselves, the welfare loss in FBA decreases.

In terms of liquidity provision, FBA has smaller bid-ask spreads (thus better liquidity provision) under similar conditions.

Empirical Analysis. Overall, if the public blockchain that performs the DEX function has much less private information than public information, FBA pro-

---
[4] Average fee per transaction is $1.18 for Ethereum between September 11-October 10 in 2024, during which the average daily price changes of ETH is $49.37.

vides lower welfare loss and better liquidity. More specifically, assuming that the system has little private information, using real-world transactions acquired from the dYdX exchange [21] from January 2023 to October 2024, we find that empirically there is a 21%-37% increase in transaction costs when the transactions are executed with CLOB compared with using FBA.

2 Model and Definitions

In this section, we specify the system and trading system models and then introduce game theoretic concepts.

2.1 System Model

A set of n processes called validators run a secure blockchain system that mitigates *transaction order manipulation attacks* with order-fair atomic broadcast (of-ABC) [10] (Definition 1). Up to f validators are Byzantine and behave arbitrarily. They communicate via reliable authenticated point-to-point channels. More specifically, they are connected with Byzantine fault-tolerant first-in-first-out (FIFO) *consistent broadcast links* [10] that securely deliver messages. The network is *partially synchronous* where the network imposes some known bounded message delay after a global stabilization time (GST).

Definition 1. (Differentially of-ABC [10]). *A secure κ-differentially of-ABC protocol satisfies:*

1. **Agreement**: *If a message m is delivered by some correct process, then m is eventually delivered by every correct process.*
2. **Integrity**: *No message is delivered more than once.*
3. **Weak validity**: *If all processes are correct and broadcast a finite number of messages, every correct process eventually delivers these broadcast messages.*
4. **Total order**: *Let m and m_0 be two messages, P_i and P_j be correct processes that deliver m, m_0. If P_i delivers m before m_0, P_j also delivers m before m_0.*
5. **κ-differential order fairness**: *If $b(m; m_0) > b(m_0; m) + 2f + \kappa$ (where $b(x; y)$ counts the number of processes that consistent-broadcast x before y), then no correct process delivers m_0 before m.*

Note that we can adopt alternative order manipulation techniques. We only need to re-calibrate the front-running success probability.

Front-running Success Probability. Suppose after observing the transaction m_i of a user i, arbitrageur j decides to front-run m_i with transaction m_j. To compute j's success probability in of-ABC, we assume the distribution of latencies on different communication links is known. The links connecting the validators have latency distribution F_v; the links between common users (i.e., investors and traders) and validators have latency distribution F_{it}; the links between arbitrageurs and validators have latency distribution F_a.

Let D be the random variable for the latency differences to independently deliver two messages on a communication link between validators. Let D follow distribution $\tilde{F}_{lt}$. For example, if F_v is instantiated with normal distribution $N(1,1)$, then $\tilde{F}_{lt}$ follows distribution $N(0,2)$. Let $\tilde{F}_{lt}^C$ be the CDF of $\tilde{F}_{lt}$. Assuming the worst case where j sees m_i immediately after it arrives at some validator, j then immediately sends m_j to a validator, and j always wins when neither transaction is broadcast first by more than $(2f + \kappa)$ validators. We denote j's winning probability as $p^\star$ and compute it as follows: $p^\star = 1 - \mathbb{P}[b(m_i; m_j) > b(m_j; m_i) + 2f + \kappa] = 1 - \sum_{s=2f+\kappa-1}^{n-1} \binom{n-1}{s} [\tilde{F}_{lt}^C(0)]^s [1 - \tilde{F}_{lt}^C(0)]^{n-1-s}$

If Byzantine validators do not relay messages, we replace $(n-1)$ with $(n-f-1)$. In the above example where $F_v \sim N(1,1)$ and $\tilde{F}_{lt} \sim N(0,2)$, we have $p^\star = 0.75$ for $n = 10, f = 3, \kappa = 1$ and $p^\star = 0.95$ for $n = 31, f = 10, \kappa = 1$.

2.2 Trading System

We adapt the dynamic trading models in Eibelshäuser and Smetak [14] and Budish et al. [8] in traditional centralized exchanges to the blockchain-based DEX. The frequency of the batch auction is every one or multiple blocks. We denote the length of this period as I.

We consider an asset X with changing fundamental value V_t at time t ($t \in [0, T]$, for some $T > 0$). We assume an observable signal that equals the fundamental value of the asset and evolves according to a compound Poisson jump process, drawn from a symmetric distribution F_{jp} with arrival rate λ_{jp}, bounded support, and zero mean. The fundamental value jump can be observed as both *public* and *private* information. We capture the absolute value of the jump with the random variable J.

We model three types of risk-neutral[5] trading players:

- **Investors** who arrive stochastically with probability λ_i and have inelastic demand, with buying and selling being equally likely.
- **Informed traders** who can observe both the public information arriving stochastically with probability λ_{pb} and the private information arriving stochastically with probability λ_{pr}. Both types of information affect V_t positively or negatively with equal probability.
- r **arbitrageurs** who can apply market-making or front-running strategy. They can also observe and respond to the public information mentioned above (arriving with probability λ_{pb}). At time t, they intend to sell at a price higher than V_t or buy at a price lower than V_t.

The arbitrageurs here can be trading firms and arbitrage bots, among others. As mentioned in Sect. 1, a front-running arbitrageur can front-run LPs, investors, and traders. Unlike in the modeling in centralized exchanges, the front-runner now can act after others have already submitted transactions.

---
[5] i.e., obtaining the same amount in expectation generates the same utility.

Trading System States. We capture the history information at time t with $\mathcal{H}_t$, which is observable by all. The state of the trading system at time t is a tuple $S_t = (P_t, J_t, (\boldsymbol{b_t}, \boldsymbol{a_t}), \mathbf{g})$, where $P_t = \mathbb{E}[V_t|\mathcal{H}_t]$ is the expected value of the fundamental value of the asset given the observed history, J_t is sampled from distribution J (i.e., $J_t \sim J$), $(\boldsymbol{b_t}, \boldsymbol{a_t})$ are quotes of the bid and ask prices, and $\mathbf{g}$ records the probabilities that arbitrageurs respond to investors' and traders' orders with front-running at each level of the order book.

Fees. The exchange collects fees from both sides of each settled trade. There are a base fee and a priority fee F which can promote the order of a transaction during tie-breaking. In the analysis, we disregard the base fee since it is the same for all transactions and is burnt in some systems [15].

2.3 Definitions Solution Concepts

In the trading game, r arbitrageurs are the strategic players and aim to maximize their utilities by playing the best strategy. A *strategy* is a probabilistic distribution over possible actions, with all mass condensed at one action for a pure strategy. A *solution concept* then describes a profile or snapshot of all players' strategies with certain desired properties, e.g., Nash equilibrium discourages unilateral deviation. We naturally adopt stationary Markov Perfect Equilibrium (MPE) [27] for CLOB since the parameters of player and information arrival rates in the stochastic game are time-independent.

Definition 2. (Stationary MPE *[27]*)**.** *A Nash equilibrium (NE) is a strategy profile s where no player increases utility by unilaterally deviating from s. A subgame perfect equilibrium (SPE) is a strategy profile s that forms an NE for any subgame of the original game. An MPE is an SPE in which all players play Markov strategies, i.e., strategies that depend only on the current state of the game. A stationary MPE is an MPE where strategies are time-independent.*

We utilize a weaker notion, Order Book Equilibrium (OBE) for FBA since stationary MPE does not always exist for FBA [9]. Intuitively, this is because under FBA, when an arbitrageur provides liquidity at the bid-ask spread that equals costs from market-making, other arbitrageurs do not have the incentive to undercut (by improving the current quotes). Since others do not undercut, the arbitrageur has the incentive to widen the spread to increase profits, which is a unilateral action to increase the player's utility. But this would result in others undercutting the widened quotes. We first define OBE and discuss why adopting the weaker notion still gives a fair comparison.

Definition 3. (OBE [9]**).** *Given state S_t, an OBE at time t is a set of orders submitted by all arbitrageurs such that the following hold: There exist (1) no safe profitable price improvements and (2) no other safe profitable deviations.*

Here, a profitable price improvement is safe if it remains strictly profitable after other arbitrageurs take profitable responses, e.g. liquidity withdrawals, after the improvement. A profitable deviation is safe if it remains strictly profitable after other arbitrageurs react with safe profitable price improvements or liquidity withdrawals. Price improvements are liquidity provisions improving current quotes, and liquidity withdrawals are cancellations of limit orders. See [9] for formal justifications for OBE. OBE is weaker than MPE in the sense that it allows the existence of unilateral deviations that increase utility as long as they can be made unprofitable by others' reactions. This is reasonable as FBA leaves time for others to respond to one's actions, and thus any reasonable player would not. Therefore, the players in CLOB and FBA would follow the corresponding equilibrium (MPE and OBE, the strongest equilibrium respectively), and the induced welfare losses are comparable.

3 DEX Under CLOB and FBA

We now model DEXes under the CLOB and FBA. We then detail the events and provide the equilibrium analysis focusing on welfare loss and liquidity provision.

3.1 Order of Events

We abstract the DEX as run by validators maintaining a secure blockchain. Arbitrageurs, investors and traders submit transactions by sending messages to one or more validators, who then broadcast received messages to each other. In the following stochastic trading game $\mathcal{G}$, we capture the arrival of the three types of players and how the validators order and execute the transactions.

Trading game $\mathcal{G}$: Repeat the following for asset X with initial value V_0.

(a) Arbitrageurs place orders on the exchange.
(b) One of the following events is then triggered:
   (1) An investor arrives with probability λ_i and submits an order to the exchange. This may change order book quotes $(\boldsymbol{b_t}, \boldsymbol{a_t})$ at time t but not to the fundamental value.
   (2) A private information event occurs with probability λ_{pr}, resulting in a jump in fundamental value, and an informed trader submits an order to the exchange. This may change the order book quotes.
   (3) A public information event occurs with probability λ_{pb}, resulting in a jump in fundamental value, and arbitrageurs can submit withdrawals of existing orders, place new orders, or front-run stale quotes.
   (4) Null event. The fundamental value and order books do not change.
(c) Each validator accumulates transactions and steps (a) and (b) are repeated until the validators can order transactions and output a block according to the underlying blockchain protocol.
(d) *CLOB*. After outputting a block, the validators running the exchange execute the transactions sequentially in the proposed order.
   FBA. Depending on the auction frequency, after outputting one or multiple blocks, the validators execute the transactions by clearing the market with a uniform price double auction: (1) the validators first gather the orders in the current batch and all previous outstanding orders; (2) they aggregate the bids and asks; (3) if there are intersections, the market clears where supply meets demand, at a uniform price. When there are conflicting ties, priority fees lift the execution order of transactions, and further ties are broken uniformly at random. Unmatched orders that are not canceled enter into the next trading game as outstanding orders.

3.2 MPE Under CLOB

As described before, we aim to solve for the markup of LPs. It is contingent on the profits from satisfying investors' orders and the costs of defending against adverse selection. We denote the expected fundamental value of asset X conditioned on history and a new sell or buy order respectively as $\mathbb{E}[V_t|\mathcal{H}_t, buy]$ and $\mathbb{E}[V_t|\mathcal{H}_t, sell]$. For clarity, without loss of generality, we let each level of the book be one unit order. Let Q be the maximum number of units investors need and p_j be the probability of an investor transacting j units ($j = 1, \ldots, Q$). We state the results for the quotes on the limit order book (LOB) under CLOB as follows.

Theorem 1. *There exists a stationary MPE in trading game $\mathcal{G}$ under CLOB processing. Bid and ask prices at the k-th level of the LOB in equilibrium satisfy*

$$b_t^k = \mathbb{E}[V_t|\mathcal{H}_t, sell] = P_t - \frac{s_k}{2}, a_t^k = \mathbb{E}[V_t|\mathcal{H}_t, buy] = P_t + \frac{s_k}{2}$$

where s_k satisfies

$$\lambda_i \sum_{j=k}^{Q} p_j \frac{s_k}{2} - \lambda_{pr}(1 + p^\star \frac{\mathbf{g}_k}{\mathbf{g}_k(r-2)+1})\bar{J}_k - \lambda_{pb}\bar{J}_k + (\lambda_i + \lambda_{pr})\mathbf{g}_k\mathsf{F} = 0$$

Here, $\bar{J}_k = \mathbb{P}[J > \frac{s_k}{2}]\mathbb{E}[J - \frac{s_k}{2}|J > \frac{s_k}{2}]$, and $\mathbf{g}_k$ is the probability that an arbitrageur front-runs traders and investors at the k-th level. In equilibrium, $\mathbf{g}_k$ is then updated to take the value that maximizes profits from front-running traders and investors, i.e., $\lambda_{pr}p^\star \frac{\mathbf{g}_k}{\mathbf{g}_k(r-2)+1}\bar{J}_k - (\lambda_i + \lambda_{pr})\mathbf{g}_k\mathsf{F}$. The expected price impact of an incoming k-unit order is $\Delta_k = \tilde{J}_k \frac{\lambda_{pr}}{\lambda_{pr}+\lambda_i}$ with $\tilde{J}_k = \mathbb{P}[J > \frac{s_k}{2}]\mathbb{E}[J|J > \frac{s_k}{2}]$; the expected markup from liquidity providers is $(\lambda_{pr} + \lambda_i)(\frac{s_k}{2} - \Delta_k)$.

We defer the proof to the full version [18]. The key to the proof is that in equilibrium, market-making and front-running strategies yield the same profits because arbitrageurs can choose strategies freely.

Interpret Theorem 1. The spread s at each level of the order book consists of (1) profits for market-making and (2) the part to absorb the price impact Δ from orders driven by private information. The price impact exists because arbitrageurs cannot distinguish common trades that do not carry information (which affects asset fundamental values) from privately informed trades. The expected welfare loss of investors and traders is contained in the profits, i.e., $(\lambda_{pr}+\lambda_i)(\frac{s}{2}-\Delta)$, which we address as markups. They are affected by the arrival rates of investors (λ_i), private information (λ_{pr}), and public information (λ_{pb}), the front-running probability $(\mathbf{g})$ and its success probability $(p^\star)$, priority fees F, jump size, the number of arbitrageurs (r), and transaction sizes. Below, we discuss how the markup within the spread is affected intuitively. In Sect. 4.3, we show how these formulas are reflected using real-life data, and in our full version [18], we additionally provide an example demonstrating this theorem.

What Affects the Markups Under CLOB From the theorem, overall, the markup from LPs in equilibrium increases with the jump size, public information releases, the front-running probability, and its success probability. It decreases with private information arrivals, fees, and the number of arbitrageurs. Fix a specific front-running probability $\mathbf{g}$, the markup first increases as the investor arrival rate rises and then decreases as it continues to grow. This is because λ_i raises market-making profits from common investors. In the meantime, it also lowers the profits from front-running traders due to increased costs (i.e., front-running arbitrageurs attack unprofitable common trades more often). Since arbitrageurs can choose freely between market-making and front-running, more arbitrageurs adopt the market-making strategy when market-making is more profitable. The competition reduces the markup until equilibrium is reached, where the profits from both strategies are equal.

3.3 OBE Under FBA

Under FBA, we only need to process excessive demand or supply since only those transactions need to be fulfilled by LPs. We assume the withdrawals and updates of existing quotes can be completed in time during the batch auction interval. Let Z_I denote the excess demand (demand minus supply) during a batch interval I. $Z_I \leq Q + 1$ ($Q \geq 0$ is an integer) is bounded. We borrow $\bar{J}_k$ and $\tilde{J}_k$ from Theorem 1 and formally state the result for FBA in Theorem 2.

Theorem 2. *There exists an OBE in pure strategies in trading game $\mathcal{G}$ under FBA processing. If $|Z_I| \leq Q + 1$, bid and ask quotes in equilibrium satisfy*

$$\begin{cases} b^k_{(I)} = P_I - \Delta_k - M_k & Z_I < 0 \\ a^k_{(I)} = P_I + \Delta_k + M_k & Z_I > 0 \end{cases}, \quad k = 1, \ldots, Q+1$$

where $\Delta_k = \tilde{J}_k \frac{\lambda_{pr}}{\lambda_{pr}+\lambda_i}$ is the expected price impact from informed traders, $M_k = \sum_{u=k}^{Q} \Delta_u \prod_{v=k}^{u} \alpha_v$ for $k = 1, \ldots, Q$, and $M_{Q+1} = 0$ are the markups from LPs, $\alpha_k = \frac{q_{k+1}}{q_k + q_{k+1}}$ and $q_k = \mathbb{P}[Z_I = k| \; |Z_I| \leq Q+1]$. The expected markup per unit time is $\frac{2}{I} \sum_{k=1}^{Q} k q_k M_k$.

The proof utilizes induction on k. Intuitively, first, the ask quote for the $(Q+1)$-th level LOB has 0 markup as otherwise, another arbitrageur can improve on it to settle the $(Q+1)$-th transaction. This means that the last quote reflects only the price impact. In the induction process, given the $(k+1)$-th quote ($k \leq Q$), we can determine the k-th markup by considering safe price improvements or other deviations in different cases of Z_I, which can take values from k (with probability q_k), $k+1$ (with probability q_{k+1}), to $Q+1$ (with probability q_{Q+1}), and different cases of an LP, who may already own a lower-level quote, an upper-level quote, or no existing quote. We defer the full proof to the full version [18].

Interpret Theorem 2. Same as before, the spread consists of the markup and the cushion for absorbing the price impact from adverse selection. The expected markup or welfare loss is influenced by the arrival rates of investors (λ_i), privately informed traders (λ_{pr}), the jump size, and the excessive demand. Again, we discuss these relationships below and show real-world data-based analysis in Sect. 4.3. In our full version [18], we provide an example with small parameters demonstrating Theorem 2.

What Affects the Markups Under FBA. Overall, the welfare loss in equilibrium increases with the jump size, private information releases, and excessive demand, and decreases with investor arrivals. First, when the jump size or private information arrival rates are larger or the investor arrival rates are smaller, the adverse selection is more severe, and the expected price impact rises. This in turn results in higher markups. Second, when there is more excessive demand (or supply), then the markups on the ask (or bid) quotes grow to incorporate more levels of price impacts on the LOB.

4 Welfare Loss and Liquidity Provision

We compare the welfare loss and liquidity provision under CLOB and FBA in equilibrium in Sect. 4.1 and Sect. 4.2, and give an empirical analysis with real-world data in Sect. 4.3. In our full version [18], we additionally discuss an example with small parameters.

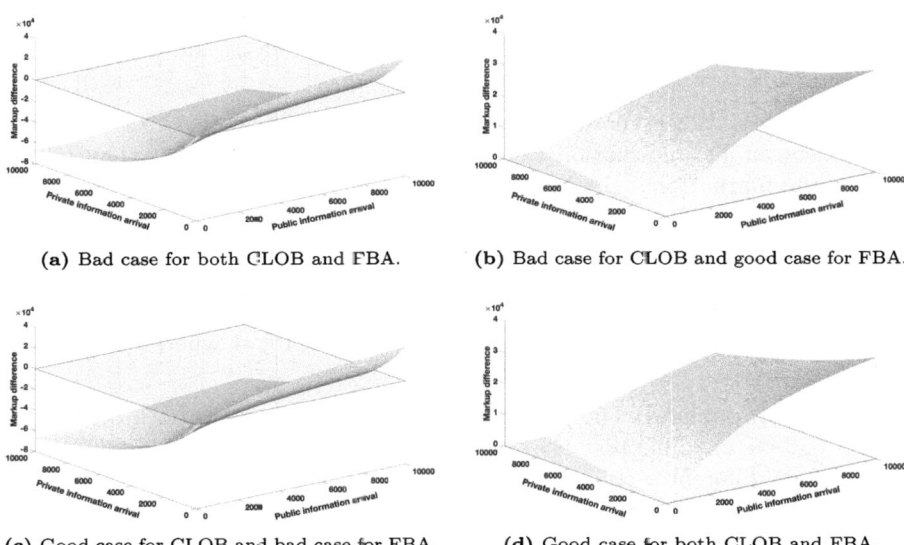

Fig. 1. The markup difference between CLOB and FBA with respect to public and private information arrivals. Positive regions are where FBA has fewer markups, i.e., less welfare loss. The investor arrival rate λ_i is set to 5000. Increasing (decreasing) λ_i pushes the surface up (down).

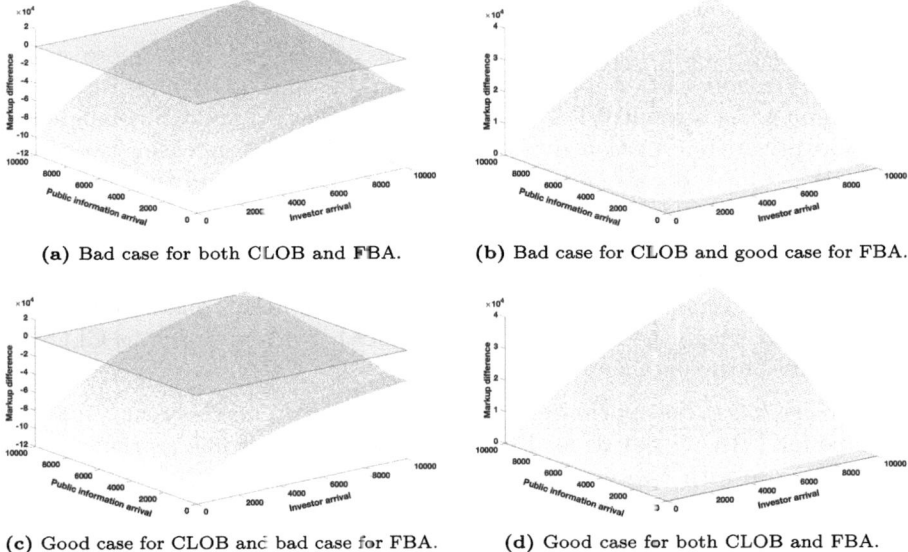

Fig. 2. The markup difference between CLOB and FBA with respect to public information and investor arrivals. The private information arrival rate λ_{pr} is set to be 5000. Increasing (decreasing) λ_{pb} pushes the surface down (up).

4.1 Welfare Loss

This section compares FBA and CLOB under special cases and general conditions and ends with the main takeaways.

Special Cases. When there are no privately informed traders ($\lambda_{pr} = 0$) but there exists public information ($\lambda_{pb} > 0$), FBA is strictly better than CLOB because the markup in FBA becomes zero while the markup in CLOB is still positive. As depicted in Figs. 1 and 3, FBA always suffers less welfare loss when $\lambda_{pr} = 0$. When there is no public information ($\lambda_{pb} = 0$) but there exists private information ($\lambda_{pr} > 0$), FBA has positive markups that increase with λ_{pr}. For CLOB, the markups tend to zero for small λ_{pr} but remain positive and also increase with λ_{pr} otherwise. This is also portrayed in Fig. 1 where the markups for both processing models approach zero.

General Comparison. The parameters affecting markups in both models are $\lambda_i, \lambda_{pr}, \lambda_{pb}$. We examine how they affect the markup differences in CLOB and FBA in four different settings (a)-(d). In setting (a), we pick the bad case for the remaining effective parameters for both CLOB and FBA. This means a high front-running success probability, small priority fees for CLOB, and high excessive demand for FBA. Parameters in settings (b)-(d) are set similarly to reflect the combinations of good- and bad-case scenarios for the two models. Additionally, in FBA, the excess demand Z_I follows a truncated Skellam distribution as the arrival rates of investors and traders follow the compound Poisson jump process. Therefore, when computing the markup differences, we consider the upper bound for the markup in FBA. This means that FBA can perform *strictly better* than the predictions.

Public Versus Private Information. Overall, as shown in Fig. 1, more public information renders FBA appealing since markups in CLOB increase due to front-running. As a result, FBA performs better when λ_{pb} is high compared to λ_{pr}. More private information gives CLOB an advantage by increasing the spread in CLOB. As for the state of the market, if it is one-sided and there is a large excessive demand, CLOB outperforms FBA and FBA realizes lower welfare loss only when λ_{pr} is small. When the market is balanced and submitted orders are mostly settled among themselves, FBA has lower welfare loss when λ_{pb} surpasses λ_{pr} by a smaller amount. This can also be observed in Figs. 2 and 3: in the good cases for FBA where the market is more balanced, FBA outperforms CLOB in the majority of the parameter regions.

Investor arrivals versus public information. We know from Theorem 2 that the markups for FBA do not depend on public information while markups under CLOB increase with λ_{pb}. As a result, FBA performs better in terms of welfare as λ_{pb} increases, which is also evident in Fig. 2. Investor arrivals have a mixed effect. FBA experiences a smaller price impact as λ_i grows larger, diminishing its markup. CLOB also faces a smaller price impact. And larger λ_i decreases the profits from front-running and more arbitrageurs compete as LPs, reducing the markups. Overall, FBA realizes better social welfare if sufficiently many market participants are price takers or are publicly informed.

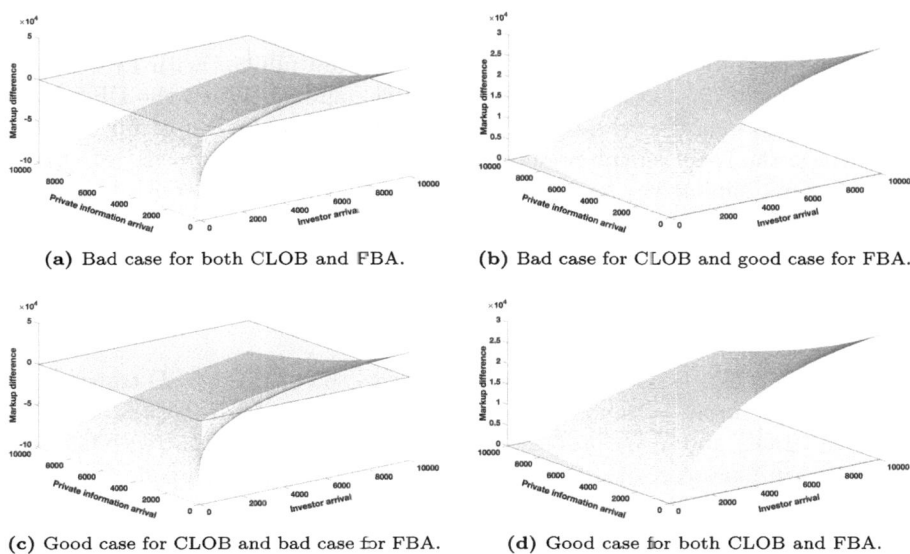

Fig. 3. The markup difference between CLOB and FBA with respect to private information and investor arrivals. The public information arrival rate λ_{pb} is set to be 5000. Increasing (decreasing) λ_{pb} pushes the surface up (down).

Investor arrivals versus private information. As described in Sect. 3.3, FBA's welfare loss decreases with the investor arrival rate and increases with private information. CLOB's induced welfare loss decreases with λ_{pr} and also eventually decreases with λ_i. As shown in Fig. 3, in the bad case for FBA, its markups are amplified by the excessive demand and only larger λ_i absorbs this effect. In the good case for FBA, its markups are already small even when λ_i is minute.

Main Takeaways. In a nutshell, we believe FBA is more suitable for the setting of blockchain systems, since we believe blockchain markets tend to have (a lot) more public information than private information. For example, for Bitcoin and Ethereum, all the core codes and projects are open-sourced, and the transactions are overt on-chain. Furthermore, the main goal of blockchain systems is to be decentralized and to have less hidden information. Under this belief, FBA tend to have less welfare loss, as also shown in Sect. 4.3.

4.2 Liquidity Comparisons from Bid-Ask Spread

We now turn to compare the two execution models from a liquidity provision perspective, with the bid-ask spread being the proxy quantity that we examine. The spread consists of the price impact from orders driven by information about assets' valuation changes, and markups from LPs.

We additionally include the figures depicting how $\lambda_i, \lambda_{pb}, \lambda_{pr}$ affect the spreads in FBA and CLOB in our full version [18], and state the main takeaway below. Similar to the analysis with welfare loss, λ_{pr} approaching 0 always benefits liquidity provision in FBA. For a larger λ_{pr}, FBA has better liquidity provision only when λ_i, λ_{pb} are sufficiently high with respect to λ_{pr}. When the market is thin or one-sided and more orders are fulfilled with LPs' orders, this requirement on λ_i and λ_{pb} is even more demanding. When the DEX has a more balanced market and a larger proportion of the orders can be filled among themselves, the requirement is looser.

Therefore, similar to the previous section, we conclude that FBA provides better liquidity in the blockchain settings, under the assumption that the blockchain market has much more public information than private information.

4.3 Empirical Analysis

We sample 707,267 BTC-USD transactions and 786,727 ETH-USD transactions on dYdX [21] from January 2023 to October 2024 via Tardis [33]. We then simulate CLOB and FBA processing on the order book at the receiving time (measured in nanoseconds) of each transaction. The simulation code and result summary are available here [3]. We compute the realized spread [20] as the welfare loss. We trim outliers in the computed realized spread value with three median absolute deviations for a more robust comparison.

For BTC-USD, the realized spread of CLOB has a mean of 0.0864 and a median of 0.0643; the realized spread of FBA has mean values (0.0688, 0.0652, 0.0632) and median values (0.0520, 0.0490, 0.0476) for auction frequency of 5, 10, and 15 s. CLOB inflicts 24%-37% more transaction costs. As shown in Fig. 4a, the realized spread for FBA, especially with 5-second auction frequency is more concentrated at the smaller end. The actual clearing price is on average 1.06, 1.74, and 2.20 better than the posted prices of settled trades under FBA with auction frequency of 5, 10, and 15 s. A longer auction period allows for the arrival of more transactions, bringing about more and at least not worse trading opportunities.

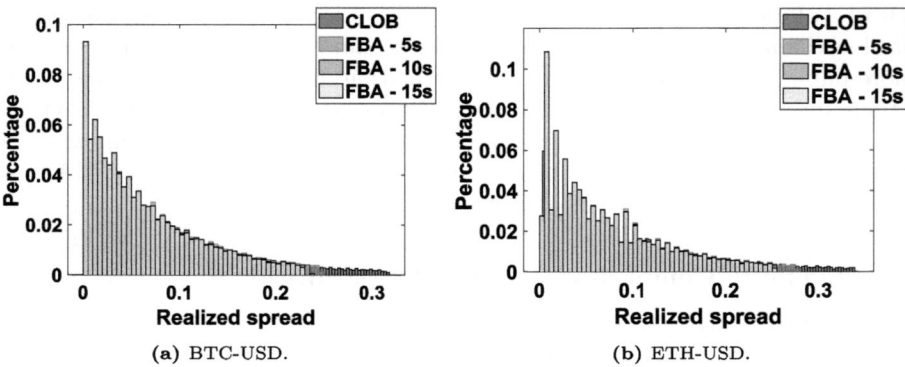

(a) BTC-USD.   (b) ETH-USD.

Fig. 4. Distribution of realized spread (with outliers trimmed) from simulations on sampled transactions. The bars for depicting the four execution methods are placed on top of each other. The bars for FBA with 15-second auction frequency concentrate on the lower end, while the rest stretch to higher realized spread, with CLOB having the rightmost bars.

For ETH-USD, the realized spread of CLOB has a mean value 0.0950 and a median value 0.0710. FBA has mean realized spreads of $(0.0770, 0.0720, 0.0709)$ and median realized spreads of $(0.0586, 0.0550, 0.0544)$ for auction frequency of 5, 10, 15 s. CLOB has 21%-34% more transaction costs. The clearing price is on average 0.05, 0.11, and 0.12 better than the posted prices of the settled trades under FBA with an auction frequency of 5, 10, and 15 s

In summary, for the two trading targets during the sampled time window, FBA reduces welfare loss and saves transaction costs for users. Note that for the lack of more suitable datasets, we acquired the tick-level order book snapshots and transactions from an exchange utilizing CLOB. If FBA had been adopted, more transactions could have been settled since placed orders can be matched against each other, while the order books could have had different spreads.

5 Related Work

Batch auction-based DEX. Penumbra [30] adopts FBA as the processing model. CoW Swap [12] combines batch auctions with trade intents where users specify the assets and the amounts to trade. Users' intents are then settled via direct matching among intents for the same tokens and opposite sides.

Manipulation-Aware DEX Design. We mention mechanisms that update transaction *execution* rules to mitigate order manipulation attacks in DEX because they are closely related to this work. For general order manipulation mitigation techniques that update *ordering* algorithms, we refer the readers to comprehensive surveys like [19]. Fair-TraDEX [28] combines FBA with commit-then-reveal style transaction masking where users commit to transactions and later reveal the contents upon finalization. Each user needs to make deposits in an escrow service so that they are incentivized to post correct commitments. Similarly, Injective [23] and Penumbra [30] utilize FBA for executing transactions on proof-of-stake blockchains, with Penumbra being a private chain. It additionally hides transactions' trading amounts. Masking transaction limits may not eliminate all manipulation opportunities. In P2DEX [6], servers run secure multi-party computation (MPC) to match orders. This introduces computation overhead and latencies and adds constraints inherent to the adopted MPC. SPEEDEX [31] approximates the clearing price in a block in general equilibrium where demand meets supply given a set of static orders. The equilibrium does not capture participants' strategies, acquired information, or sequential moves. Xavier et al. [34] alternatively consider a greedy sequencing rule in two-token constant product AMM. Since this sequencing rule ensures good properties only inside a block, sequencers can push submitted transactions to future blocks.

Comparison of CLOB and FBA in Centralized Exchanges. It has been shown that compared with CLOB, FBA leads to lower transaction costs [2], decreases adverse selection and spreads [29,32], achieves an optimal trade-off between liquidity and price discovery [5], and increases market quality [13,22,26]. However, the severity of the inefficiency of liquidity provision under FBA can exceed the inefficiency from latency arbitrage under CLOB [14]. This liquidity provision inefficiency of FBA originates from bid shading[6] in UPDA: every equilibrium in multi-unit uniform price auctions is inefficient due to bid shading [4].

6 Concluding Remarks and Future Directions

We explore the adoption of FBA as a DEX processing model as compared to CLOB. Specifically, we compare the welfare loss and liquidity provision under FBA and CLOB at their respective market equilibrium.

Our analysis reveals that FBA leads to a lower welfare loss and better liquidity provision under specific conditions, including scenarios where there is no or less private information compared with common investors and public information, where the priority fees for transaction inclusion are small relative to the asset's valuation jump size, or when the market is more balanced. Performance improvement in these settings is mainly because, under FBA, liquidity providers have time to react to information, and common users can settle trades among themselves in more balanced markets.

In future research, several avenues of investigation could be pursued as extensions of this work: (1) compare other aspects of the FBA and CLOB processing models in the DEX context, e.g., price discovery, (2) introduce competition among DEXes instead of modeling a single exchange, and (3) devise and solve for stronger solution concepts for the stochastic trading game.

Acknowledgement. This work was supported in part by the National Science Foundation (NSF) under grant CNS1846316 and a Purdue Research Foundation (PRF) research grant.

References

1. Adams, H., Zinsmeister, N., Salem, M., Keefer, R., Robinson, D.: Uniswap v3 core. Tech. rep., Uniswap, Tech. Rep. (2021)
2. Aldrich, E.M., López Vargas, K.: Experiments in high-frequency trading: comparing two market institutions. Exp. Econ. **23**(2), 322–352 (2020)
3. Anonymized: Simulation source code. https://drive.google.com/drive/folders/1XtnstLf5oOY8KTp_YMOwpNbHgs01JpGC?usp=share_link
4. Ausubel, L.M., Cramton, P.: Demand reduction and inefficiency in multi-unit auctions (2002)
5. Baldauf, M., Mollner, J.: High-frequency trading and market performance. J. Financ. **75**(3), 1495–1526 (2020)
6. Baum, C., David, B., Frederiksen, T.K.: P2dex: privacy-preserving decentralized cryptocurrency exchange. In: ACNS, pp. 163–194 (2021)
7. Budish, E., Cramton, P., Shim, J.: Implementation details for frequent batch auctions: slowing down markets to the blink of an eye. Am. Econ. Rev. **104**(5), 418–424 (2014)

---

[6] (Non-unit-demand) bidders' tendency to bid less than true valuations for later units.

8. Budish, E., Cramton, P., Shim, J.: The high-frequency trading arms race: frequent batch auctions as a market design response. Q. J. Econ. **130**(4), 1547–1621 (2015)
9. Budish, E., Lee, R.S., Shim. J.J.: A theory of stock exchange competition and innovation: will the market fix the market? Tech. rep, National Bureau of Economic Research (2019)
10. Cachin, C., Mićić, J., Steinhauer, N., Zanolini, L.: Quick order fairness. In: FC pp. 316–333 (2022)
11. Corporation, T.S.E. Taiwan stock exchange. https://www.twse.com.tw/en/
12. CoW: cow protocol. https://docs.cow.fi/cow-protocol
13. Economides, N., Schwartz, R.A.: Electronic call market trading. In: The Electronic Call Auction: Market Mechanism and Trading, pp. 87–99. Springer (2001)
14. Eibelshäuser, S., Smetak, F.: Frequent batch auctions and informed trading (2022)
15. ethereum.org: Priority fees in ethereum. https://ethereum.org/en/developers/docs/gas/#priority-fee
16. Farmer, D., Skouras, S.: Review of the benefits of a continuous market vs. randomised stop auctions and of alternative priority rules (policy options 7 and 12). Manuscript, Foresight. Government Office for Science (2012)
17. Glosten, L.R., Milgrom, P.R.: Bid, ask and transaction prices in a specialist market with heterogeneously informed traders. J. Financ. Econ. **14**(1), 71–100 (1985)
18. Gong, T., Liu, Z., Kate, A.: The case of FBA as a DEX processing model (2025). https://arxiv.org/abs/2302.01177, full version of this work that appeared at FC'25
19. Heimbach, L., Wattenhofer, R.: Sok: preventing transaction reordering manipulations in decentralized finance. In: Proceedings of the 4th ACM Conference on Advances in Financial Technologies, pp. 47–60 (2022)
20. Indriawan, I., Pascual, R., Shkilko, A.: On the effects of continuous trading. Available at SSRN 3707154 (2020)
21. Juliano, A.: dydx. https://github.com/dydxprotocol (2023)
22. Kandel, E., Rindi, B., Bosetti, L.: The effect of a closing call auction on market quality and trading strategies. J. Finan. Intermediation **21**(1), 23–49 (2012)
23. Labs, I.: Injective. https://injective.com/about
24. Labs, M.: sui. https://github.com/MystenLabs/sui (2023)
25. Labs, U.: Uniswap limit order book. https://blog.uniswap.org/limit-orders (2024)
26. Madhavan, A.: Trading mechanisms in securities markets. the Journal of Finance **47**(2), 607–641 (1992)
27. Maskin, E., Tirole, J.: Markov perfect equilibrium: I. observable actions. J. Econ. Theory **100**(2), 191–219 (2001)
28. McMenamin, C., Daza, V., Fitzi, M., O'Donoghue, P.: Fairtradex: a decentralised exchange preventing value extraction. In: ACM CCS DeFi Workshop'22, pp. 39–46 (2022)
29. Menkveld, A.J., Zoican, M.A.: Need for speed? exchange latency and liquidity. Rev. Finan. Studies **30**(4), 1188–1228 (2017)
30. Penumbra: Penumbra zswap. https://protocol.penumbra.zone
31. Ramseyer, G., Goel, A., Mazières, D.: Speedex: a scalable, parallelizable, and economically efficient digital exchange. arXiv preprint arXiv:2111.02719 (2021)
32. Riccò, R., Wang, K.: Frequent batch auctions vs. continuous trading: evidence from taiwan. Continuous Trading: Evidence from Taiwan (November 19, 2020) (2020)
33. Tardis.dev: Tardis.dev node. https://github.com/tardis-dev/tardis-node (2023)
34. Xavier Ferreira, M.V., Parkes, D.C.: Credible decentralized exchange design via verifiable sequencing rules. In: Proceedings of the 55th Annual ACM Symposium on Theory of Computing, pp. 723–736 (2023)

Securely Computing One-Sided Matching Markets

James Hsin-Yu Chiang[1](✉), Ivan Damgård[1], Claudio Orlandi[1], Mahak Pancholi[2], and Mark Simkin[3]

[1] Aarhus University, Aarhus, Denmark
[2] IMDEA Software Institute, Madrid, Spain
[3] Flashbots, George Town, Cayman Islands

Abstract. Top trading cycles (TTC) is a famous algorithm for trading indivisible goods between a set of agents such that all agents are as happy as possible about the outcome. In this paper, we present a protocol for executing TTC in a privacy-preserving way. To the best of our knowledge, it is the first of its kind. As a technical contribution of independent interest, we suggest a new algorithm for determining all nodes in a functional graph that are on a cycle. The algorithm is particularly well suited for secure implementation in that it requires no branching and no random memory access. Finally, we report on a prototype implementation of the protocol based on somewhat homomorphic encryption.

1 Introduction

Barter economies, where agents directly exchange goods amongst each other, are one of the oldest forms of commerce. While historically barter was restricted to physical goods or services, nowadays barter is gaining popularity as a form of commerce in the context of cryptocurrencies and decentralized finance. In this digital realm, the goods that are being traded are so-called tokens, which may represent assets, intellectual property rights, equities, bonds, or services.

In our work, we consider one of the most archetypical forms of barter, known as one-sided matching markets, introduced by Shapley and Scarf [41]. Here, we have n agents, each holding one (indivisible) good as well as an ordered preference list over the n goods. The agents are willing to engage in a joint trading protocol and each agent would like to get their most preferred good. The protocol should ensure that all agents are as "happy" as they could be, once trading has finished, i.e., no subset of agents can still perform trades amongst each other that would leave all agents in the subset better off. Shapley and Scarf [41] showed that, for arbitrary preference lists, a sequence of trades that makes everybody happy always exists and presented an algorithm, known as the *top trading cycles* (TTC) algorithm[1], that efficiently computes the necessary trades.

The one-sided matching problem is not only a very intuitive game-theoretic problem, but its instances can be found in several real-world scenarios, with the

---
[1] Attributed to David Gale.

TTC algorithm being used for effective solutions in many cases; for example, assigning an optimal allocation of schools for pupils [1–3,30], public housing allocation [42], and mutual housing exchange, etc.

The TTC algorithm has several attractive game-theoretic properties. Roth and Postlewaite [38] showed that, if the preferences of each agent are strict[2], the algorithm finds the unique allocation of goods to agents. Later, Roth [37] showed that all agents are incentivized to be truthful, i.e. that no agent can obtain a better good by being dishonest about their claimed preference list.

The appealing game-theoretic features of the TTC algorithm make it a useful tool for extending the potential of barter trading in the context of trading digital tokens in decentralized finance. Let's say that a particular token represents a particular service, and a user in possession of a token x would like to exchange it for y, and if not y, then for z Traditionally, the bulk of digital tokens that are exchanged are limited to exchange between a pair of users, and only for preference over one token at a time. With TTC, users can post their preferences in the beginning as a ranked preference list of all offers from all other participating users[3], and receive the optimal exchange solution.

Unfortunately, a naive implementation of TTC would require all involved agents to publicly reveal their preference lists, which in turn would also reveal who is obtaining which good. When transaction privacy is required, this is not a viable solution. However, there has been no prior work studying secure-TTC.

A first (naive) approach outlined in Sect. 1.3 is to implement a privacy-preserving version of TTC would be to simply convert the TTC algorithm to a circuit in a straightforward way and evaluate it using a generic Multiparty Computation (MPC) engine. This would result in a rather inefficient solution, typically requiring $O(n^2 \log(n))$ sequential oblivious RAM accesses for n agents. The large number of memory accesses required is a severe bottleneck, as random memory accesses are notoriously difficult to implement in secure computation. We discuss this in more detail in Sect. 1.3. A main contribution of this work, discussed in more detail in the following, is to come up with a new equivalent formulation of the TTC algorithm that is much better suited for secure computation because it is algebraic in nature and requires no memory accesses.

1.1 Our Contribution

In this work, we present a protocol that allows n agents to efficiently compute all the desirable trades in a given one-sided matching market, without revealing any unnecessary private information. Our protocol hides each agent's preference list and agents only learn about the trades they are personally involved in. Surprisingly, our work is the first to address this question, as far as we are aware of. Our protocol does not require any random memory accesses or any expensive branching operations; for this reason, it integrates well with secure computation frameworks for arithmetic circuits.

---

[2] In the sense that no agent likes two goods equally.
[3] A user can reject offers from other parties, by ordering its own offer above theirs.

As a technical building block that may be of independent interest, we construct a simple and (asymptotically) highly efficient protocol for determining the nodes that are part of a cycle on a hidden functional[4] graph (Sect. 3).

Our new secure TTC protocol can be realized from any MPC framework that offers basic arithmetic in a prime field of cardinality larger than the number of parties. We prove our protocol to be UC-secure in the semi-honest, dishonest majority setting (Sect. 4.1) and we show that each protocol subtask induces a multiplicative depth that is *logarithmic* in the number of participants.[5]

We experimentally evaluate our TTC protocol by building a prototype implementation[6] based on somewhat homomorphic encryption (SHE), also known as leveled-HE. Although our current implementation can still be optimized in several ways, it already shows that the approach has the potential in practice, e.g., the entire protocol can be done for 25 users in a few minutes. Such practical runtimes are achieved by heavily exploiting purpose-built and general SIMD (Same-Instruction Multiple-Data) techniques for SHE schemes that natively support SIMD operations. Our implementation is based on the OpenFHE [4] framework and the BGV cryptosystem [10]. We provide benchmarks for various parameter settings (Sect. 5).

Our construction can be implemented based on any secure computation framework offering basic arithmetic in finite fields. So an obvious question is whether it would be more efficient to use a secret-sharing MPC protocol, like SPDZ [19], rather than SHE. However, secret-sharing-based MPC incurs a large number of communication rounds, which becomes the main bottleneck as soon as the number of parties or the round trip time of the network is large enough. While our objective in this work is not to compare secret-sharing and FHE in general and for all parameter ranges, we provide a discussion on the two implementation methods in the appendix of the full paper version [18], targeted at our setting. We conclude that secret-sharing based MPC will be slower as soon as the network roundtrip time is large enough (40ms in our example setting).

Upgrading to malicious security can be done using standard techniques in a relatively straightforward way. Although the resulting protocol would be less efficient, we expect that the overhead would not necessarily be prohibitive. We discuss this extension in more detail in the appendix of the full paper version [18].

1.2 Related Work

In the following, we discuss research domains closely related to our work.

Matching Algorithms. Beyond one-sided matching markets, many other types of matching problems have been studied in the literature. These include: The stable marriage problem of Gale and Shapley [23], with its privacy-preserving variants

---

[4] A directed graph is said to be functional if all vertices have out-degree at most one.
[5] In comparison to a naive implementation that would require a multiplicative depth linear in the number of parties.
[6] Source code has been open-sourced here.

presented in [20,22,24,32,35,45]. The housing allocation problem of Hylland and Zeckhauser [29]. The kidney exchange problem of Roth, Sönmez, and Ünver [39], with the privacy-preserving versions being recently proposed in [8,12–14]. From a technical perspective, the ideas for computing stable marriages or performing kidney exchange privately do not appear to be useful for solving the problem considered in this work; the former is incomparable, while the latter is a more restricted setting. On the other hand, we observe that the protocols in our work can easily be adapted to solve the housing allocation problem as well. In the appendix of the full paper version [18] we provide a more detailed discussion about related matching algorithms.

Secure Graph Computations. Looking ahead, our protocol is based on the original TTC algorithm which repeatedly interprets agents as graph vertices, preferences as edges, and attempts to identify agents that are part of a graph cycle. While there are many works [6,7,9,34,44] on secure computation of graph algorithms, such as determining the shortest path between two nodes in a graph, for performing depth/breadth-first search, and computing the maximum flow of a graph, these tools, however, do not seem amenable to securely and efficiently determining *which* agents are part of a cycle. The difficulty of our task is best illustrated by considering Floyd's famous cycle finding algorithm for functional graphs. While this algorithm has a simple condition for checking whether a cycle exists, it is not obvious how to modify it, such that it allows for efficiently *listing* all vertices that are part of the cycles.

1.3 Technical Overview

To understand the ideas behind our approach, let us first review the TTC algorithm itself and see why naively using secure computation techniques is unlikely to yield an efficient protocol.

The Top Trading Cycles Algorithm. Recall that we have n agents, each holding a private preference list, sorting all n goods from most to least desirable. In the TTC algorithm, in each round, every agent points at the agent with the good they desire the most. Viewing the agents as vertices and who they point to as edges, we get a functional graph with n vertices and n edges. Such graphs always have at least one cycle. Any agent that is part of a cycle will trade their good, i.e. they will receive the good they desire and they will give their good to whoever is pointing at them. All agents that were involved in trades leave the procedure and all remaining agents repeat this process by now pointing to their most preferred good among those that are still available. Eventually, the algorithm terminates with all agents having performed trades, possibly with themselves.

Demands to a privacy-preserving solution. We will aim to construct a protocol that allows each party to only learn the trade she is involved in. In particular, the protocol must not leak the round in which her trade was decided, nor ask her to post a new preference every round depending on the current availability.

Instead, all parties must supply a complete preference list up front, and then the protocol must securely update the preferences between cycle finding steps "inside" the secure computation.

A Naive Approach. Let us focus on just one round of the TTC algorithm, where agents would like to determine whether they are part of a cycle or not. In the following, implicitly assume that all computations are done either on secret shared or encrypted values, depending on the precise secure computation framework that is used.

First, every agent securely inputs the index of the agent with their most preferred good, among those that are still present (ignoring for now how precisely this would even be done). Interpret all those pointers as an array A of length n, encoding a graph with out-degree equal to 1. Now the agents will jointly perform n steps to securely traverse the graph starting from the vertex representing their index as follows: Initially, each agent i has an associated value $v_i = 1$ and is located at vertex i. At each step, each agent i securely looks up the successor of the vertex they are currently at in A and moves to that vertex. Let j be this vertex, then agent i updates $v_i := v_i \cdot (i-j)$. If an agent i is part of a cycle, then it will have returned to their initial node within n steps at least once, and thus $v_i = 0$ after n steps.

While this solution does indeed allow each agent to determine whether they are part of a cycle, it also requires each agent to perform n memory lookups in array A *securely*. When implemented via a naive circuit, this would require one linear scan of A per access per agent. A more intelligent approach is to use secure computation protocols for RAM programs [25], which can perform efficient memory accesses (as low as $O(\log(n))$) access per RAM access). Many protocols for secure RAM computation have already been proposed [11,15,21,27,33,36,40,43,45], but those are either restricted to a constant number of parties, require an honest majority among the parties, or are significantly less efficient than circuit-based secure computation protocols. Consequently, it would be desirable to have a protocol that does not require any random memory accesses and can be expressed nicely as a circuit.

In any case, for both naive RAM and circuit approaches, one round of TTC would require $O(n)$ sequential memory accesses, amounting to a multiplicative depth of $O(n)$ per round. As opposed to this, our solution only requires $O(\log(n))$ multiplicative depth per round of TTC.

Our Solution. The main idea underlying our approach is to view the graph through its adjacency matrix and to exploit certain structural properties of these matrices that are specific to functional graphs. The adjacency matrix M of a graph with n vertices is an $n \times n$ matrix, where entry $(i,j) \in \{1,\ldots,n\} \times \{1,\ldots,n\}$ is one, if there is an edge from node i to node j and zero otherwise. It is well known that for any $k \in mathbbN$, the entry (i,j) in M^k equals the number of walks from node i to node j of length k. Intuitively, this would already allow for checking whether vertex i is on a cycle by computing all powers $M^1,\ldots,M^n$ of the adjacency matrix M and checking whether in any of them, there is a non-zero entry at (i,i), i.e. whether there is a walk of some length $\ell \in \{1,\ldots,n\}$ from vertex i to itself. This would work but requires n separate matrix-matrix multiplications. In this work, we build upon this basic idea but reduce the number of matrix-matrix multiplications to $\log(n)$.

What we prove in this work, is that computing $\boldsymbol{u} = \boldsymbol{1} \cdot M^n$, where $\boldsymbol{1}$ is the row vector of length n with all entries being one, allows for determining the vertices that are on cycles. Concretely, we prove that for each $i \in \{1,\ldots,n\}$, the i'th value in $\boldsymbol{u}$ is non-zero if and only if vertex i is on a cycle, provided the underlying graph is a functional graph. Note that computing M^n can be done with $\log(n)$ matrix-matrix multiplications via repeated squaring. Furthermore, note that this approach does not require any random memory accesses at all and is purely algebraic in nature.

While efficiently determining which vertices are on a cycle in a given functional graph is one of the more difficult steps, there are several other technical difficulties that need to be overcome, e.g., the secure updating of preferences, alluded to above. We will highlight those and our corresponding solutions in detail in the technical sections of this work.

2 Preliminaries

Notation. We denote scalars as x, vectors as $\boldsymbol{v}$, matrices as A, and A^T as the transpose of A. We write $\boldsymbol{1}$ to denote the vector of length n, where all entries are 1. We write $\boldsymbol{v} \cdot \boldsymbol{w}$ to denote Hadamard product, i.e. element-wise multiplication of vectors. We write $v_1 \to v_2$ to denote a directed edge from vertex v_1 to v_2. For a value a, we write $[a]$ to denote the encryption of value a.

Secure Multiparty Computation. We prove security in the UC framework [16,17] with semi-honest and static corruptions, and $\mathcal{F}'$-hybrid setting. The security requirement is captured by showing indistinguishability between the real-world and ideal-world experiments, where in the ideal-world all of the computation is done via an ideal functionality $\mathcal{F}$. For a brief summary and formal definition, see the Appendix in the full paper version [18].

Ideal Functionality: Top Trading Cycles. We describe the algorithm of Shapley and Scarf [41], as already discussed in Sect. 1.3, in the UC functionality F_{TTC} in Fig. 1.

Leveled Homomorphic Encryption. To instantiate our TTC protocol we will use a leveled homomorphic encryption scheme (leveled-HE). The standard definition is reproduced in the Appendix of the full paper version [18]. Specifically, our protocol is implemented with the BGV cryptosystem [10], which offers ciphertext slots over which "same instruction multiple data" (SIMD) parallelism can be exploited without additional overhead (Sect. 4.2).

Ideal Functionality: Arithmetic Black Box. This functionality, called F_{ABB} (reproduced in the appendix of [18]) provides an interface for doing a series of basic arithmetic operations on secret values in a secure manner, and to open the

---

F_{TTC}

F_{TTC} is an n party functionality and runs with clients $\{C_1,\ldots,C_n\}$.

Input: For $i \in \{1,\ldots,n\}$, receive preference list $\boldsymbol{x}^{(i)}$ from client C_i.
Top Trading Cycle: Initialize the set of available clients $\mathcal{C} := \{C_1,\ldots,C_n\}$.
While $\mathcal{C} \neq \emptyset$, do:
1. For each $C_i \in \mathcal{C}$, let $\mathsf{top}_i := C_j$ be its first preference such that $C_j \in \mathcal{C}$.
2. Build a graph $\mathcal{G} := (V, E)$, where $V := \mathcal{C}$, and $(v_i \rightarrow v_j) \in E$ if $\mathsf{top}_i := C_j$.
3. Find all cycles in $\mathcal{G}$.
4. For each $v_i \in V$, if v_i lies on a cycle such that $v_i \rightarrow v_j$, store (On Cycle, i, j), and remove C_i from $\mathcal{C}$.

Output: Output (On Cycle, i, j) to client C_i where tuple (On Cycle, i, j) is stored internally.

Fig. 1. Functionality for Secure Top Trading Cycles

final output towards a particular participant. Trivially, by design, no information about the intermediate values is leaked to participants.

At a high level, F_{ABB} receives commands from two types of computing devices: from clients it receives an input vector of fixed length ℓ (via INPUT command), and then it allows servers $S_1,\ldots,S_m$ to securely perform element-wise additions (via ADD) and multiplications (via MULT) by making a single call to the functionality, i.e., ℓ parallel additions or multiplications can be computed at the cost of a single call. Additionally, the servers can securely *cycle* vector elements (via ROT) by any number of slots and direction; this operation is called *rotation*. At last, the participants can open the final output towards a particular client (via OPEN).

In the client-server setting, we can UC-realize F_{ABB} using a leveled-HE encryption scheme in the $F_{\mathsf{KeyGenDec}}$ hybrid (reproduced in appendix of [18]). $F_{\mathsf{KeyGenDec}}$ allows servers and clients to obtain a public-key for the leveled-HE scheme where the associated secret-key is stored inside the functionality. Given the public-key, clients can encrypt secret inputs and send them to a server S_1, who then evaluates homomorphic operations over ciphertexts locally with Eval algorithm of the leveled-HE scheme.

We give the details of this realization in the appendix of the full version [18]. The security of this realization can be formally stated in the following theorem. The proof is similar to that in [19], but for completeness we present the main proof ideas in the appendix of [18].

Theorem 1. *Let* LHE := (KeyGen, Enc, Dec, Eval) *be a leveled-HE scheme that is correct, IND-CPA secure, and is circuit private. Then* F_{ABB} *can be UC-realized by a protocol with* LFHE *in the* $F_{\mathsf{KeyGenDec}}$-*hybrid against any static, passive adversary corrupting up to* $m - 1$ *servers and* $n - 1$ *clients.*

3 Basic Algorithms

As part of our overall solution, we will require solutions for two smaller problems. First, for each node in the graph, we need to decide if the node is on a cycle or not. Second, after a round of cycle finding is over, we need to compute the new preferences of all clients for the next round. Both of our solutions for these sub-tasks are designed to be easy to implement within secure computation.

Cycle finding. For determining the parties that are on a cycle, we will exploit properties of the adjacency matrix of the corresponding functional graph. Let matrix M be the adjacency matrix, where entry $M_{i,j}$ is 1 if the graph has a vertex from node i to node j and 0 otherwise. It is well known that $M_{i,j}^k$ is the number of paths of length k from node i to node j. As explained earlier, a simplistic way to exploit this would be to compute $M^2, M^3, ..$ and for each node i test, if any value $M_{i,i}^k$ is non-zero. If we, however, exploit the fact that we have a *functional graph*, i.e., all out-degrees are 1, then we obtain a significantly more efficient solution: node i is on a cycle if the i'th index in the vector $\mathbf{1}M^n$ is non-zero.

Specifically, we show the following technical lemma (proof in appendix of [18]):

Lemma 1. *Let M be the adjacency matrix of a functional graph with n nodes, let $\mathbf{1}$ be a row vector where all entries are 1 and let $\mathbf{u} = \mathbf{1}M^n$. Then $\mathbf{u}_i$ is non-zero if and only if node i is on a cycle. Moreover, $\mathbf{u}_i$ is a non-negative integer and $\mathbf{u}_i \leq n$.*

Using this lemma, we can securely decide whether nodes are on cycles by computing $\mathbf{1}M^n$ and checking which entries are 0. We can do this efficiently with leveled-HE, since matrix multiplications can be done using one layer of parallel multiplications (and some additions), thus matrix exponentiation to power n can be done using $\log n$ multiplicative depth via standard repeated squaring.

Preference Computation. Here, we assume that the preference list of client C_i is given as an $n \times n$ permutation matrix N_i, such that multiplying a vector by N_i will reorder the input entries in order of preference. We assume that the list of available goods is given as a vector $\mathbf{h}$, where $\mathbf{h}_j = 1$ if good number j is currently available, and 0 otherwise. As we shall see, such a list is readily available, once a cycle finding stage is done.

Our goal here is to compute the adjacency matrix of the graph for the next cycle finding stage. That is, for each C_i, we want to compute vector $\mathbf{w}^{(i)}$ where $\mathbf{w}_j^{(i)} = 1$ if house j is the one party i prefers among the available houses, and 0 otherwise. Viewing these individual vectors as a single matrix, we obtain our desired adjacency matrix. We can compute these vectors as follows:

1. Let vector $\mathbf{a}^{(i)} = N_i \mathbf{h}$.
2. Compute the vector $\mathbf{b}^{(i)}$ as follows:
   $j = 1$ to n, set $\mathbf{b}_j^{(i)} = \mathbf{a}_j^{(i)} \prod_{k<j}(1 - \mathbf{a}_k^{(i)})$.

3. Let $\boldsymbol{w}^{(i)} = N_i^{-1} \boldsymbol{b}^{(i)}$.

For correctness, note that in vector $\boldsymbol{a}^{(i)}$, the first 1 corresponds to the good C_i prefers the most among the available ones. The formula for computing $\boldsymbol{b}^{(i)}$ preserves the first 1 in $\boldsymbol{a}^i$ but will zero out everything else. Thus, as desired, $\boldsymbol{w}^{(i)}$ will contain a 1 in the position of the good C_i prefers, and 0 s elsewhere.

The reason for using this specific way of computing the adjacency matrix is that it can be done in depth $\log n$ and that we can exploit known algorithms for parallel prefix computation, such that the second step above only requires $O(n)$ multiplication, while still being logarithmic depth.

4 TTC Protocols: Generic and SIMD Optimized

In this section, we present two protocols for computing the TTC algorithm securely. In Sect. 4.1, we present our main and generic protocol (Π_{TTC}) using basic secure arithmetic operations provided by F_{ABB}. We chose to first explain a simple version of our protocol, without any optimizations, to expose the central ideas of our TCC protocol. Π_{TTC} is generic since, to implement this, F_{ABB} can be realized by different techniques such as an MPC, or computation over ciphertexts.

Later, in Sect. 4.2, we improve upon this by exploiting SIMD operations offered by leveled-HE schemes. Our optimised TTC protocol ($\Pi_{\mathsf{TTC-SIMD}}$) utilizes the SIMD interface of F_{ABB} to significantly reduce the number of multiplications by up to a factor of n^2, where n is the number of clients. This allows us to demonstrate practical runtimes with our implementation in Sect. 5.

4.1 Generic TTC Protocol

In this section, we present our main protocol (Π_{TTC} in Fig. 2) for computing the top trading cycles algorithm securely. We state correctness in Lemma 2, security in Theorem 2, and state the multiplicative depth of Π_{TTC} in Theorem 3 (proofs are stated in appendix of [18]).

Client-Server Model. We consider computations in the standard client-server model with n clients and m servers. The clients own the input and initialize F_{ABB} with it. The servers then do the computation over these inputs by repeatedly calling F_{ABB}, without any further involvement of the clients. Only towards the end, when the output is computed, the clients are again involved to learn the output. In the appendix of [18], we show how to realize F_{ABB} using a leveled-HE scheme.

Overview of Protocol Π_{TTC}. The protocol description appears in Fig. 2. It includes three sub-protocols: Exponentiate, NotEqualZero and PreserveLeadOne, explained below.

Input: The clients first input their preference over goods in form of permutation matrices (N_i), which order offered goods by their preference, and their transpose to F_{ABB}. The clients also initialize vectors h and o, which record the availability of goods, and the allocated goods, respectively. Once the client inputs are stored in F_{ABB}, subsequent parts of the protocol are performed by the servers calling arithmetic operations on the values stored in F_{ABB}.

Subsequently, one round of TTC algorithm consists of three steps: (i) compute current preference matrix (M) according to the available clients and their available preference, (ii) compute cycles and identify parties on the cycles, and (iii) update goods' availability and clients' assignments. These steps are repeated n times, since the TTC algorithm requires n rounds of cycle finding.

Preference Computation: The client's permutation matrix (N_i) is used to reorder h by preference (Sect. 3). Then, PreserveLeadOne is used to isolate the most preferred, available good. Finally, applying the transpose gives us the i'th row of the adjacency matrix M. Recall from Sect. 3, given input sequence $x_1, ..., x_n$, to preserve the first 1, we compute $y_j = x_j \prod_{k<j}(1 - x_k)$ for $j = 1$ to n. Here, note that $\prod_{k<j}(1 - x_k)$ for $j = n$ represents the sequence of all prefix multiplications on $(1 - x_1), ..., (1 - x_{n-1})$; prefix multiplication is known to be computable in $\lceil \log(n) \rceil$ multiplicative depth [28], and we illustrate an example of prefix multiplication in the appendix of [18].

Compute Cycles: Let M be the adjacency matrix obtained in the previous step. The servers evaluate Exponentiate to compute M^n. We apply square-and-multiply to compute matrix exponentiation; to obtain M^n, first compute $M^2, M^4, ... M^{2^k}$, where $k = \lfloor \log(n) \rfloor$. Given $(i_k, \cdots, i_0)$, the binary representation of n, we then multiply terms $M^{i_0} \cdot M^{2 \cdot i_1} \ldots \cdot M^{2^k \cdot i_k}$ in binary tree fashion with $\lceil \log(\lfloor \log_2(n) \rfloor) \rceil$ depth. The resultant matrix is multiplied by a n-dimensional vector of ones, obtaining vector u with non-zero values in the i'th position, if the i'th client is on a cycle (as shown in Lemma 1).

Next, we map each non-zero element of u to 1 with NotEqualZero so that the i'th index of u is 1 if the client C_i is on a cycle, and otherwise 0. Naively, this could be done by exploiting Fermat's little theorem $x^p \equiv x \mod p$, which implies that the exponentiation of $u_i \in u$ to the power of $p - 1$ equals 1 if u_i is non-zero, and 0 otherwise. However, for a large plaintext modulus p, computing u_i^{p-1} remains concretely inefficient. Instead, we exploit the fact that values in u never exceed n (Lemma 1), and can simply compute NotEqualZero$(u_i) := 1 - n! \cdot \prod_{j=1}^{j=n}(j - u_i)$; multiplying n terms only requires $O(\log(n))$ multiplicative depth and is independent of the plaintext modulus p.

Update Availability of Goods and Client's Assignment: Lastly, after each cycle finding round, we update clients' output vector o and availability of goods h. We recover the index of each client's preferred good from the current adjacency matrix (M) and assign it to the output, if the output is unassigned $o_i = 0$. Finally, the availability of goods is computed from the output vector.

Lemma 2. *(Correctness) Π_{TTC} (Fig. 2) implements the top trading cycle algorithm (specified in F_{TTC}).*

Theorem 2. Π_{TTC} *(Fig. 2) UC-realizes* F_{TTC} *(Fig. 1) in the* F_{ABB}*-hybrid model against a passive adversary corrupting up to* $m-1$ *servers and* $n-1$ *clients.*

Multiplicative depth of Π_{TTC}. We have highlighted the multiplicative depth of subroutines Exponentiate, Not Equal Zero and PreserveLeadOne. The following theorem and proof states that given n client inputs, Π_{TTC} incurs a maximum multiplicative depth of $O(\log(n))$, for a single round of TTC, and $O(n\log(n))$ overall. We refer to the appendix of [18] for the proof for all theorems.

Theorem 3. *Protocol* Π_{TTC} *evaluated on* n *client preference lists privately input to hybrid functionality* F_{ABB} *incurs a maximum multiplicative depth of* $O(n\log(n))$ *on values output from* F_{ABB}.

4.2 TTC Protocol with SIMD Optimizations

Whilst Π_{TCC} can be evaluated in $O(\log(n))$ multiplicative depth per cycle finding round, the concrete complexity remains high (Fig. 3). For example, NotEqualZero and PreserveLeadOne all require secure multiplication of n values in F_{ABB}. These operations are each repeated n times for each client, incurring $O(n^2)$ multiplications per cycle finding round. In each round, building the adjacency matrix and matrix exponentiation incur $O(n^3)$ and $O(n^3\log(n))$ total multiplications, resp.

Our $\Pi_{\mathsf{TTC-SIMD}}$ protocol detailed in the appendix of [18] exploits the full SIMD interface of F_{ABB} to reduce the total complexity of Π_{TTC} whilst retaining multiplicative depth of $O(\log(n))$, thereby enabling *practical runtimes* of secure TTC in our implementation (Sect. 5). In $\Pi_{\mathsf{TTC-SIMD}}$, steps (1),(2), and (3) have improved asymptotic complexity over Π_{TTC} by up to a factor of n^2 (see comparison in Fig. 3). Here, it is important to also consider rotations as "expensive" operations as these incur runtimes in the same order of magnitude as multiplications when F_{ABB} is instantiated with leveled-HE (See comparison of multiplication and rotation runtimes in appendix of [18]).

In the rest of the section we focus on an overview of $\Pi_{\mathsf{TTC\text{-}SIMD}}$, introducing additional sub-protocols needed to exploit SIMD operations effectively. Since, each sub-protocol retains the multiplicative depth of $O(\log(n))$ of $\Pi_{\mathsf{TTC\text{-}SIMD}}$, we only discuss the total number of operations needed. In Fig. 5, we provide the concrete number of addition, multiplication, and rotation operations needed for each of the three main steps in $\Pi_{\mathsf{TTC-SIMD}}$. We refer to the appendix of [18] for a more detailed description of $\Pi_{\mathsf{TTC\text{-}SIMD}}$.

PrefixAdd$_{\mathsf{L/R}}$ and PrefixMult$_{\mathsf{L/R}}$ protocols compute the sum/product of all prefixes of a vector with only $\log(n)$ additions/multiplications and rotations. Here, we only explain PrefixAdd for left (and right) directions; computation for PrefixMult is analogous. PrefixAdd$_{\mathsf{L}}$ (PrefixAdd$_{\mathsf{R}}$) outputs a vector where index i stores the sum of all input elements up to (starting from) index i.

We adapt parallel prefix arithmetic from [28] to the setting of SIMD operations in F_{ABB}. First, an n-length vector is padded with 0 s (for PrefixMult we

$\Pi_\mathsf{TopTradingCycle}$

Parties $\mathcal{C} = \{C_1, \ldots, C_n\}$ interact with F_ABB to initialize their inputs. Then, computing servers $\mathcal{S} = \{S_1, \ldots, S_m\}$ interact with hybrid functionality F_ABB exclusively to securely evaluate the top trading cycle algorithm. Values in F_ABB are denoted by $[\cdot]$ for which a unique object identifier (id) is known to all servers. Servers execute stateless subroutines PreserveLeadOne, Exponentiate, and NotEqualZero on values stored in F_ABB.

Input: On receiving a preference list $\boldsymbol{x}^{(i)} \in \mathbb{Z}_p^n$ as input, each client C_i locally computes the permutation matrix $N_i \in \mathbb{Z}_p^{n \times n}$ such that $\boldsymbol{x}^{(i)} = N_i \times (1, \ldots, n)^T$, and privately inputs N_i and N_i^{-1} to F_ABB. Servers jointly initialize availability $[\boldsymbol{h}] \leftarrow 0^n$ and output vectors $[\boldsymbol{o}] \leftarrow 1^n$ in F_ABB.

Cycle Finding: For round $r \in (1, \ldots, n)$, servers jointly perform the following.

1. Update adjacency matrix:
   (a) For $i \in (1, \ldots, n)$:
      i. Let $\left[\boldsymbol{a}^{(i)}\right] \leftarrow ([N_i] | [\boldsymbol{h}])$
      ii. Let $\left[\boldsymbol{b}^{(i)}\right] \leftarrow \mathsf{PreserveLeadOne}(\left[\boldsymbol{a}^{(i)}\right])$
      iii. Let $\left[\boldsymbol{w}^{(i)}\right] \leftarrow [N_i^{-1}] \times \left[\boldsymbol{b}^{(i)}\right]$
   (b) Store matrix $[M] \in \mathbb{Z}^{n \times n}$ with i'th row $\left[\boldsymbol{w}^{(i)}\right]^T$

2. Compute cycles:
   (a) $[\boldsymbol{u}] \leftarrow 1^n \times \mathsf{Exponentiate}([M], n)$
   (b) $[\boldsymbol{u}_i] \leftarrow \mathsf{NotEqualZero}([\boldsymbol{u}_i])$ for $i \in n$.

3. Update assignments & availability:
   (a) For $i \in (1, \ldots, n)$:
      i. $[\boldsymbol{t}_i] \leftarrow \sum_{j \in [n]} j \cdot [M_{i,j}]$
      ii. $[\boldsymbol{o}_i] \leftarrow [\boldsymbol{t}_i] \cdot [\boldsymbol{u}_i] + [\boldsymbol{o}_i] \cdot (1 - [\boldsymbol{u}_i])$
   (b) If round $r \neq n$, $i \in (1, \ldots, n)$:
      i. $[\boldsymbol{h}_i] \leftarrow (1 - \mathsf{NotEqualZero}([\boldsymbol{o}_i]))$

Open assignments: Clients call F_ABB to privately open $[\boldsymbol{o}_i]$ to C_i for $i \in (1, \ldots, n)$.

Fig. 2. Top trading cycle in the F_ABB-hybrid model.

	Mults/Rots in each cycle finding round			Mult. Depth
	(1) Adj Matrix	(2) Cycle Comp	(3) Avail Update	
Π_TCC	$O(n^3)$	$O(n^3 \log(n))$	$O(n^2)$	$O(\log(n))$
$\Pi_\mathsf{TCC\text{-}SIMD}$	$O(n^2)$	$O(n \log(n))$	$O(n \log(n))$	

Fig. 3. Asymptotic complexities of Π_TCC and $\Pi_\mathsf{TCC\text{-}SIMD}$.

pad with 1 s) to length $n' \geq 2^{k+1} - 1$, where $k = \lceil \log_2(n) \rceil$. For example, to compute PrefixAdd$_L$ for vector $[1, 2, \ldots, 8]$, we pad 0 s to obtain $[1, 2, \ldots, 8, 0^7]$, and then proceed in levels. For level $i \in [0, \lceil \log_2(n) \rceil - 1]$, we rotate the intermediate vector to the *right* by 2^i slots (see illustration of prefix arithmetic in appendix of [18]). The unrotated vector from the preceding level is then added element-wise in SIMD-fashion with a single addition call to F_{ABB}. After $\lceil \log_2(n) \rceil$ levels, we obtain the resultant vector where each element holds the sum of all elements of the input vector with lower slot indices. This requires only $O(\log_2(n))$ total additions, and rotations. These prefix algorithms are essential to implement InnerProd and PreserveLeadOne in SIMD with concrete efficiency.

InnerProd is a task needed to update assignments and availability. The InnerProd over n-sized vectors $[v]$, $[w]$ can be computed with a single multiplication and evaluating the additive prefix over the result:

$$\mathsf{PrefixAdd}_R([v] \cdot [w]) = \left[\sum_{i \in [m]} v_i w_i, \sum_{j \in [m-1]} v_j w_j, \ldots \right]$$

The inner product scalar is then located in the first slot position, and if necessary can be *extracted* by multiplying with a fresh encryption of $[1, 0, \ldots]$. This incurs a total multiplicative complexity of 1 (or 2 if extraction is required).

PreserveLeadOne is adapted for SIMD operations by padding the input vector x with 1 s, and then executing SIMD operations on the following:

$$[x, 1, \ldots, 1] \cdot \mathsf{rot}(\mathsf{PrefixMult}_L([1] - [x, 1, \ldots, 1]), 1, \mathsf{right}) \quad (1)$$

Here, the padding with 1's maintains the correctness of the prefix multiplication following the rotation of vector elements. This incurs $\lceil \log_2(n) \rceil + 2$ multiplications, and $\lceil \log_2(n) \rceil + 1$ rotations.

NotEqualZero is a pure SIMD algorithm, that computes element-wise only; it does not call rotations in F_{ABB}. Each vector index represents a separate parallel execution. NotEqualZero for all elements in input vector $[v]$, is evaluated as;

$$\mathsf{NotEqualZero}_n([v]) = [1] - [n!^{-1}] \prod_{i \in [n]} ([i] - [v]) \quad (2)$$

Here, let $[i]$ and $[n!^{-1}]$ denote $[i, \ldots, i]$ and $[n!^{-1}, \ldots, n!^{-1}]$ with the same dimension as the input vector. By moving the factor -1 out of the product term and considering cases of even or odd n, we rewrite as follows to avoid negation by multiplication;

$$\mathsf{NotEqualZero}_n([x]) = \begin{cases} [1] + [-n!^{-1}] \prod_{i \in [n]} ([x] + [-i]) & n \text{ even} \\ [1] + [n!^{-1}] \prod_{i \in [n]} ([x] + [-i]) & n \text{ odd} \end{cases} \quad (3)$$

NotEqualZero in SIMD-fashion and input range $[0, n]$ incurs $n+1$ multiplications and additions $\lceil \log_2(n+1) \rceil$.

SIMD Matrix Operations: For matrix-matrix products, we implement the technique by Jiang et al. [31], which requires only $O(n)$ multiplications for multiplying two $n \times n$-matrices. For matrix-vector products, we implement Halevi and Shoup [26] which also exhibits $O(n)$ multiplicative complexity. These techniques encrypt entire matrices (or their diagonals) in a single ciphertext and are reproduced in the appendix of [18] for the readers convenience.

5 Implementation

We benchmark the local running times of the server performing the computation to realize our proposed protocol $\Pi_{\text{TCC-SIMD}}$; in the semi-honest setting, a single dedicated computation server is tasked with computing operations over leveled-HE ciphertexts. Since these only permit computation of bounded depth, the computation server must periodically interact with a set of key servers holding key shares to refresh the ciphertexts and reset the ciphertext noise. The interactive ciphertext refresh runtime component is highly dependent on the network conditions, but can remain small compared to the local computing time for ideal network conditions. We provide estimates for ciphertext refreshing amongst 3 key servers for a wide range of network conditions in the appendix of [18], which also facilitates a comparison with secret-sharing based MPC. In this section, we focus on the local leveled-HE computation runtime. The computational runtime component of $\Pi_{\text{TCC-SIMD}}$ for 5 clients is 14 s, which increases to 2 min for 15 clients and 8 min for 25 clients.

Benchmarking Computational Overheads. We illustrate the running times for varying numbers of clients. In addition to SIMD parallelization, we implement our protocol with hardware parallelization across threads for each single server; in the semi-honest setting, a single dedicated computation server.

Figure 4 shows the total local runtime for varying number of clients. We emphasize that the TTC protocol runs an additional round for every additional client, whilst each individual round increases in complexity, which explains the increase in runtimes with increasing number of clients. In Fig. 5, the running times are depicted for each phase of a single TTC round (and different numbers of clients); whilst updating the adjacency matrix appears to be quasi-linear in the number of clients with sufficient parallelisation, the matrix exponentiation in the cycle computation phase is not, suggesting observable bottlenecks in memory bandwidth.

We implement our $\Pi_{\text{TTC-SIMD}}$ protocol with the OpenFHE [4] library with AVX2 support, using their implementation of the BGV cryptosystem [10]. The main parameters of ring-LWE variant of BGV are the plaintext modulus p, ciphertext modulus q and ciphertext ring dimension N. Large ciphertext moduli are required to accommodate the noise growth of ciphertexts during homomorphic operations.

OpenFHE exposes automated parameter generation to derive parameters for a given plaintext modulus which (1) achieve a desired multiplicative depth and (2) a level of standardized security (e.g. equivalent to 128 bits) [5]. We set $p = 65537$, a plaintext modulus recommended by library authors for general applications over integers. This modulus allows for homomorphic computations

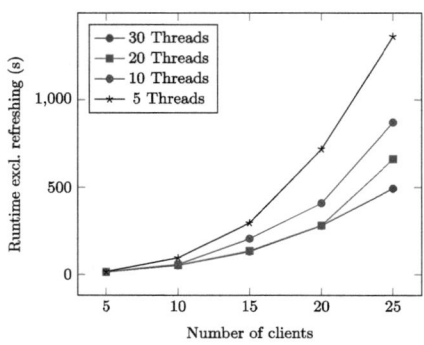
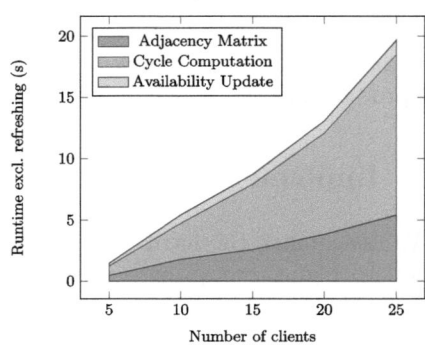

Fig. 4. TTC runtimes for different thread counts (excl. refreshing).

Fig. 5. TTC single round runtime (excl. refreshing) with 38 threads.

with a multiplicative depth of ~ 11. Using this parameterization, we obtain up to 32768 plaintext slots in each ciphertext.

We assume that all computations are performed by three servers of which at most two are corrupt. We ran our experiments on a PC with an 48-core Intel CPU and 96 GB of RAM, and varying number of threads (Fig. 4). Our implementation of $\Pi_{\text{TCC-SIMD}}$ already provides ciphertext level parallelisation; remaining protocol steps which can be parallelised at the hardware level are run with varying number of threads. We note that runtimes for n clients do not measurably improve beyond n threads, as single-thread performance and memory bandwidth become performance bottlenecks.

Comparison with secret-sharing based MPC. We show in the appendix of [18] that leveled-HE is superior to secret-sharing based approaches for realistic, public network conditions, where the roundtrip latency exceeds ≈ 40 ms.

References

1. Abdulkadiroglu, A.: Generalized matching for school choice. Unpublished paper, Duke University. [1311, 1312] (2011)
2. Abdulkadiroğlu, A., Pathak, P.A., Roth, A.E.: Strategy-proofness versus efficiency in matching with indifferences: redesigning the nyc high school match. Am. Econ. Rev. **99**(5), 1954–1978 (2009)
3. Abdulkadiroğlu, A., Pathak, P.A., Roth, A.E., Sönmez, T.: The Boston public school match. Am. Econ. Rev. **95**(2), 368–371 (2005)
4. Al Badawi, A., et al.: OpenFHE: open-source fully homomorphic encryption library. In: Proceedings of the 10th Workshop on Encrypted Computing & Applied Homomorphic Cryptography, pp. 53–63. WAHC'22, Association for Computing Machinery, New York, NY, USA (2022). https://doi.org/10.1145/3560827.3563379
5. Albrecht, M., et al.: Homomorphic encryption standard. In: Lauter, K., Dai, W., Laine, K. (eds.) Protecting Privacy through Homomorphic Encryption, pp. 31–62. Springer, Cham (2021). https://doi.org/10.1007/978-3-030-77287-1_2

6. Aly, A., Cuvelier, E., Mawet, S., Pereira, O., Van Vyve, M.: Securely solving simple combinatorial graph problems. In: Sadeghi, A.-R. (ed.) FC 2013. LNCS, vol. 7859, pp. 239–257. Springer, Heidelberg (2013). https://doi.org/10.1007/978-3-642-39884-1_21
7. Araki, T., et al.: Secure graph analysis at scale. In: Vigna, G., Shi, E. (eds.) ACM CCS 2021: 28th Conference on Computer and Communications Security, pp. 610–629. ACM Press, Virtual Event, Republic of Korea Nov 15–19 (2021). https://doi.org/10.1145/3460120.3484560
8. Birka, T., Hamacher, K., Kussel, T., Möllering, H., Schneider, T.: SPIKE: secure and private investigation of the kidney exchange problem. BMC Med. Inf. Decis. Making **22**(1), 253 (2022)
9. Blanton, M., Steele, A., Aliasgari, M.: Data-oblivious graph algorithms for secure computation and outsourcing. In: Chen, K., Xie, Q., Qiu W., Li, N., Tzeng, W.G. (eds.) ASIACCS 13: 8th ACM Symposium on Information, Computer and Communications Security, pp. 207–218. ACM Press, Hangzhou, China May 8–10, (2013)
10. Brakerski, Z., Gentry, C., Vaikuntanathan, V.: (Leveled) fully homomorphic encryption without bootstrapping. In: Goldwasser, S. (ed.) ITCS 2012: 3rd Innovations in Theoretical Computer Science, pp. 309–325. Association for Computing Machinery, Cambridge, MA, USA Jan 8–10 (2012). https://doi.org/10.1145/2090236.2090262
11. Braun, L., Pancholi, M., Rachuri, R., Simkin, M.: Ramen: souper fast three-party computation for RAM programs. In: Meng, W., Jensen, C.D., Cremers, C., Kirda, E. (eds.) Proceedings of the 2023 ACM SIGSAC Conference on Computer and Communications Security, CCS 2023, Copenhagen, Denmark, November 26-30, 2023. ACM (2023)
12. Breuer, M., et al.: Solving the kidney exchange problem using privacy-preserving integer programming. In: 19th Annual International Conference on Privacy, Security & Trust, PST 2022, Fredericton, NB, Canada, August 22-24, 2022, pp. 1–10. IEEE (2022)
13. Breuer, M., Meyer, U., Wetzel, S.: Privacy-preserving maximum matching on general graphs and its application to enable privacy-preserving kidney exchange. In: Joshi, A., Fernández, M., Verma, R.M. (eds.) CODASPY '22: Twelveth ACM Conference on Data and Application Security and Privacy, Baltimore, MD, USA, April 24 - 27, 2022, pp. 53–64. ACM (2022)
14. Breuer, M., Meyer, U., Wetzel, S.: Efficient privacy-preserving approximation of the kidney exchange problem. CoRR **abs/2302.13880** (2023). https://doi.org/10.48550/arXiv.2302.13880
15. Bunn, P., Katz, J., Kushilevitz, E., Ostrovsky, R.: Efficient 3-party distributed ORAM. In: Galdi, C., Kolesnikov, V. (eds.) SCN 2020. LNCS, vol. 12238, pp. 215–232. Springer, Cham (2020). https://doi.org/10.1007/978-3-030-57990-6_11
16. Canetti, R.: universally composable security: a new paradigm for cryptographic protocols. In: 42nd Annual Symposium on Foundations of Computer Science. pp. 136–145. IEEE Computer Society Press, Las Vegas, NV, USA Oct 14–17 (2001). https://doi.org/10.1109/SFCS.2001.959888
17. Canetti, R., Lindell, Y., Ostrovsky, R., Sahai, A.: Universally composable two-party and multi-party secure computation. In: 34th Annual ACM Symposium on Theory of Computing, pp. 494–503. ACM Press, Montréal, Québec, Canada May 19–21 (2002). https://doi.org/10.1145/509907.509980
18. Chiang, J.H., Damgård, I., Orlandi, C., Pancholi, M., Simkin, M.: Securely computing one-sided matching markets. IACR Cryptol. ePrint Arch. (2024). https://eprint.iacr.org/2024/1657

19. Damgård, I., Pastro, V., Smart, N., Zakarias, S.: Multiparty computation from somewhat homomorphic encryption. In: Safavi-Naini, R., Canetti, R. (eds.) CRYPTO 2012. LNCS, vol. 7417, pp. 643–662. Springer, Heidelberg (2012). https://doi.org/10.1007/978-3-642-32009-5_38
20. Doerner, J., Evans, D., shelat, a.: Secure stable matching at scale. In: Weippl, E.R., Katzenbeisser, S., Kruegel, C., Myers, A.C., Halevi, S. (eds.) ACM CCS 2016: 23rd Conference on Computer and Communications Security. pp. 1602–1613. ACM Press, Vienna, Austria Oct 24–28, (2016). https://doi.org/10.1145/2976749.2978373
21. Doerner, J., shelat, a.: Scaling ORAM for secure computation. In: Thuraisingham, B.M., Evans, D., Malkin, T., Xu, D. (eds.) ACM CCS 2017: 24th Conference on Computer and Communications Security, pp. 523–535. ACM Press, Dallas, TX, USA Oct 31 – Nov 2 (2017). https://doi.org/10.1145/3133956.3133967
22. Franklin, M., Gondree, M., Mohassel, P.: Improved efficiency for private stable matching. In: Abe, M. (ed.) CT-RSA 2007. LNCS, vol. 4377, pp. 163–177. Springer, Heidelberg (2006). https://doi.org/10.1007/11967668_11
23. Gale, D., Shapley, L.S.: College admissions and the stability of marriage. Am. Math. Mon. **69**(1), 9–15 (1962)
24. Golle, P.: A private stable matching algorithm. In: Di Crescenzo, G., Rubin, A. (eds.) FC 2006. LNCS, vol. 4107, pp. 65–80. Springer, Heidelberg (2006). https://doi.org/10.1007/11889663_5
25. Gordon, S.D., et al.: Secure two-party computation in sublinear (amortized) time. In: Yu, T., Danezis, G., Gligor, V.D. (eds.) ACM CCS 2012: 19th Conference on Computer and Communications Security, pp. 513–524. ACM Press, Raleigh, NC, USA Oct 16–18 (2012). https://doi.org/10.1145/2382196.2382251
26. Halevi, S., Shoup, V.: Algorithms in HElib. Cryptology ePrint Archive, Report 2014/106 (2014). https://eprint.iacr.org/2014/106
27. Hamlin, A., Varia, M.: Two-server distributed ORAM with sublinear computation and constant rounds. In: Garay, J.A. (ed.) PKC 2021. LNCS, vol. 12711, pp. 499–527. Springer, Cham (2021). https://doi.org/10.1007/978-3-030-75248-4_18
28. Hillis, W.D., Steele Jr, G.L.: Data parallel algorithms. Commun. ACM **29**(12), 1170–1183 (1986). https://dl.acm.org/doi/pdf/10.1145/7902.7903
29. Hylland, A., Zeckhauser, R.: The efficient allocation of individuals to positions. J. Polit. Econ. **87**(2), 293–314 (1979)
30. Jacobs, R.: Chicago booth (2019). https://www.chicagobooth.edu/review/when-students-are-matched-schools-who-wins
31. Jiang, X., Kim, M., Lauter, K., Song, Y.: Secure outsourced matrix computation and application to neural networks. In: Proceedings of the 2018 ACM SIGSAC conference on computer and communications security, pp. 1209–1222 (2018). https://doi.org/10.1145/3243734.3243837
32. Keller, M., Scholl, P.: Efficient, oblivious data structures for MPC. In: Sarkar, P., Iwata, T. (eds.) ASIACRYPT 2014. LNCS, vol. 8874, pp. 506–525. Springer, Heidelberg (2014). https://doi.org/10.1007/978-3-662-45608-8_27
33. Keller, M., Yanai, A.: Efficient maliciously secure multiparty computation for RAM. In: Nielsen, J.B., Rijmen, V. (eds.) EUROCRYPT 2018. LNCS, vol. 10822, pp. 91–124. Springer, Cham (2018). https://doi.org/10.1007/978-3-319-78372-7_4
34. Meng, X., Kamara, S., Nissim, K., Kollios, G.: GRECS: graph encryption for approximate shortest distance queries. In: Ray, I., Li, N., Kruegel, C. (eds.) ACM CCS 2015: 22nd Conference on Computer and Communications Security. pp. 504–517. ACM Press, Denver, CO, USA Oct 12–16 (2015). https://doi.org/10.1145/2810103.2813672

35. Mondal, A., Panda, P., Agarwal, S., Aly, A., Gupta, D.: Fast and secure oblivious stable matching over arithmetic circuits. Cryptology ePrint Archive, Paper 2023/1789 (2023). https://eprint.iacr.org/2023/1789
36. Noble, D., Falk, B.H., Ostrovsky, R.: Metadoram: breaking the log-overhead information theoretic barrier. IACR Cryptol. ePrint Arch. (2024)
37. Roth, A.E.: Incentive compatibility in a market with indivisible goods. Econ. Lett. **9**(2), 127–132 (1982)
38. Roth, A.E., Postlewaite, A.: Weak versus strong domination in a market with indivisible goods. J. Math. Econ. **4**(2), 131–137 (1977)
39. Roth, A.E., Sönmez, T., Ünver, M.U.: Kidney exchange. Q. J. Econ. **119**(2), 457–488 (2004)
40. Sasy, S., Vadapalli, A., Goldberg, I.: PRAC: round-efficient 3-party MPC for dynamic data structures. IACR Cryptol. ePrint Arch. (2023)
41. Shapley, L., Scarf, H.: On cores and indivisibility. J. Math. Econ. **1**(1), 23–37 (1974)
42. Thakral, N.: The public-housing allocation problem. Technical report, Harvard University, Tech. rep. (2016)
43. Vadapalli, A., Henry, R., Goldberg, I.: Duoram: a bandwidth-efficient distributed ORAM for 2- and 3-party computation. In: Calandrino, J.A., Troncoso, C. (eds.) 32nd USENIX Security Symposium, USENIX Security 2023, Anaheim, CA, USA, August 9-11 (2023). USENIX Association (2023)
44. Wang, Q., Ren, K., Du, M., Li, Q., Mohaisen, A.: SecGDB: graph encryption for exact shortest distance queries with efficient updates. In: Kiayias, A. (ed.) FC 2017. LNCS, vol. 10322, pp. 79–97. Springer, Cham (2017). https://doi.org/10.1007/978-3-319-70972-7_5
45. Zahur, S., et al.: Revisiting square-root ORAM: efficient random access in multiparty computation. In: 2016 IEEE Symposium on Security and Privacy. pp. 218–234. IEEE Computer Society Press, San Jose, CA, USA May 22–26 (2016). https://doi.org/10.1109/SP.2016.21

Robust Double Auctions for Resource Allocation

Arthur Lazzaretti[1]([✉]), Charalampos Papamanthou[1,2],
and Ismael Hishon-Rezaizadeh[2]

[1] Yale University, New Haven, USA
[2] Lagrange Labs, San Francisco, USA

Abstract. In a zero-knowledge proof market, we have two sides. On one side, bidders with proofs of different sizes and some private value to have this proof computed. On the other side, we have distributors (also called sellers) which have computational power available to process the proofs by the bidders, and these distributors have a certain private cost to process these proofs (dependent on the size). More broadly, this setting applies to any online resource allocation where we have bidders who desire a certain amount of a resource and distributors that can provide this resource. In this work, we study how to devise double auctions for this setting which are truthful for users, weak group strategy proof, weak budget balanced, computationally efficient, and achieve a good approximation of the maximum welfare possible by the set of bids. We denote such auctions as *robust*.

1 Introduction

Consider the setting of a zero-knowledge proof market, where bidders are interested in having a zero-knowledge proof computed for a circuit they have (for a certain price) and distributors (also referred to as sellers) are willing to perform the proof computation for these bidders (for a certain price). In the middle, we have an auctioneer who is in charge of matching bidders and distributors as well as deciding the final prices—how much each matching bidder has to pay and how much each matching distributor is receiving. Clearly, there are incentives in this setting: the bidders want to have their proof computed for the least amount of money as possible, and the distributors want to maximize their revenue given their cycles of compute. How should the auctioneer decide which bidders to match with which distributors and at what prices?

In particular, our auction setup is the following: The market has n bidders interested in circuits of different complexities and sizes. Each bidder i has circuit of size k_i (measured in required cycles computation) and private value v_i for having the zero-knowledge proof for this circuit computed. The market also has t distributors, each distributor j with a different computation capacity (units of computation) u_j they can provide per round, and a cost per compute cycle c_j.

A. Lazzaretti —Work done during author's time at Lagrange Labs.

Our auction setup has a series of caveats. The bidders are only interested in a certain number of cycles of compute, corresponding to the number of cycles needed to prove their circuit, and no less. In the literature, this has been coined as a "single-minded bidder" [4] (we will also call them knapsack bidders). Distributors do not have this same "all-or-nothing" constraint. They are happy to sell however many cycles of compute they have available, for the same price per cycle. Furthermore, since proofs can be (and most times need to be) distributed we do not impose any constraints on a bidder being assigned to one or multiple distributors. Due to the above, and in order to simplify the model, we in many places consider a distributor with u_j units of capacity to instead be u_j different distributors selling one cycle of compute at cost c_j. More generally, as modeled, this setting encompasses a double auction of any resource where the bidder is interested in only a certain quantity of this resource and no less. Other examples can include storage, general computation, ML training ad space or time and others. (For a physical example, consider a chair auction, where bidders have different sized tables and either want chairs for their whole table, or no chairs at all.)

Related Works on Double Auctions. Two-sided markets are used throughout the web for a myriad of different settings and goods, stocks and futures, currencies, ad sales [2], among others [7,13,20] and therefore double auctions have been very well studied. In particular, knapsack auctions have been studied in the single-sided auction setting [2,4] (multiple bidders, single distributor) but not in the double-auction setting. On the other hand, double auctions have been studied in the case where bidders are interested in a single item, or are interested in many items, but have a *diminishing* value per additional item of interest—as opposed to a value dictated by a knapsack constraint. Another line of work looks at bundles, when sellers are restricted to selling one item per commodity. (We give a more detailed overview of related work in Appendix A.)[1]

The problem we pose is to define a knapsack double auction mechanism which has the following properties:

- Truthfulness: The best strategy for auction participants is to report their private values to the auctioneer.
- (Weak) Group-Strategy Proofness: For any group of colluding participants, for at least one of the participants in the group, the best strategy is still to bid truthfully over participating in the collusion.
- Welfare-Maximization: Across all possible assignments that satisfy the knapsack constraint, you pick the ones with the largest sum of private values.
- Weak Budget-Balanced: The auctioneer does not lose money from facilitating the auction.
- Computational Efficiency: The mechanism runs in polynomial time in the size of the inputs.

---

[1] Recent work by Wang et al. [23] studies a similar setting but with important differences. We discuss this in a dedicated subsection.

These properties are standard notions considered for auction mechanisms. We define a double auction to be robust if it satisfies all these properties, with the caveat of the welfare-maximization being an approximate notion (we leave the exact approximation to be defined in Appendix 5). This is because by the Myerson-Satterthwaite theorem [19], no auction mechanism can satisfy all of these properties at once (even without the weak group-strategy proofness requirement). Next, we consider existing mechanisms to check whether they may satisfy our needs.

Vickrey-Clarke-Groves (VCG) Knapsack Double Auction [5,9,11,22]. Applying the double-auction version of the classical Vickrey-Clarke-Groves (VCG) auction naively fails: It is not computationally efficient, not budget balanced [16] (although it is collusion-proof [6]). There has been some VCG-style approaches to this idea which either do not achieve budget balance or do not give a welfare analysis in the general setting. We expand on this in related work.

Pay-as-bid Double Auction. Another option would be an orderbook-style approach, where bidders and distributors report their cost and transact whenever there is a match in ranges. In this case, notice that the one to bid first can have an incentive to strategize based on expected demand and other bids it sees within the orderbook. In addition, the auction has discriminatory pricing (the same item can be sold for different prices). This makes the auction not truthful (this is because for certain bidder and distributor distributions, an individual bidder could increase their utility by bidding something other than their true private value).

1.1 Our Contribution

This leads us to question whether we can devise a framework for knapsack double auction mechanisms that are *robust* as defined above. Unfortunately, we show that achieving a perfectly welfare-maximizing solution and a computationally efficient solution is impossible, since it is equivalent to the knapsack problem which is known to be NP. Therefore, we tweak our definition of robustness to allow for an approximate welfare-maximization.

Our contribution in this work is to show that there is a class of knapsack double auctions that satisfy the properties above (with the approximate welfare-maximization). We achieve this through a modular approach, inspired by the composition framework of Dütting et al. [10].

Dütting et al. [10] established a framework where the input is two ranking algorithms, for user bids and distributors bids respectively, a composition rule and a payment rule, and the output is a double auction mechanism. They show that for the scenario where multiple bidders and distributors interested in buying/selling a single item, if the ranking algorithms, composition rule and payment rule exhibited certain properties, then we could conclude that the resulting double auction mechanism was truthful, weak GSP, welfare-maximizing (to a certain extent) and WBB.

In our work, we follow the same approach, extending their framework to the knapsack setting, where bidders are interested in only a certain number of items (or no items) and distributors don't have this constraint. Extending the framework requires entirely new definitions, proofs and techniques. This general framework allows for more flexibility in devising what we call knapsack double auctions by encompassing most current knapsack solutions. Specifically, we don't show that a single specific mechanism satisfies the properties above, but instead show that the properties hold for a whole class of functions that satisfy our constraints. (The work of extending the composition framework to some cross-auction constraints was posed as an interesting open question by the work in [10]; this work answers that open question in establishing the feasibility of establishing a composition framework which can support cross-auction constraints.)

2 Preliminaries

In this section we work through definitions and some background that will be necessary when approaching our problem.

2.1 Double Auctions

We will study an asymmetric double auction setting. It is a two sided market with n bidders and t distributors. There is one item type for sale. Each distributor has u units to sell at a price c each[2], and each bidder is interested in either getting k units, or no units. We call this bidder a 'single minded bidder' or a 'knapsack bidder'. For the special case where $k = 1$ for every bidder, this degrades to the multi-bidder multi-distributor single item auction, which is covered [10]. In this setting (where $k = 1$ for every bidder) there have been other works that are robust [17].

A set of bidders and distributors is *feasible* if there are at least as many distributors as the sum of the items desired by the set of bidders, $\sum_{i \in [N]} k_i$.

Each bidder i has a value v_i and size k_i, and each distributor j has a unit capacity u_j and a *cost per unit* c_j, all of these are bounded from above and below by some maximum and minimum value. We will denote by $\boldsymbol{b} = (\boldsymbol{v}, \boldsymbol{k})$ the value and size profile of each bidder. We will denote by $b_i = (v_i, k_i)$ the bid representing the value and size of the i-th bidder. We denote by $\boldsymbol{d}$ the cost profile of all distributors. We will denote by $d_j = (u_j, c_j)$ the unit capacity and cost per unit of distributor j.

We define a double auction mechanism as a tuple of two deterministic functions:

- The allocation rule $x(\cdot, \cdot)$: It takes in the inputs of bidders and distributors and outputs the set of *winning*[3] bidders and distributors. For every $i \in [n]$, we

---

[2] To simplify the exposition, where appropriate we will split a distributor into u single-unit distributors.

[3] Where we define winning bidders and distributors to be those who actually transact as a result of the auction.

let $x_i(\boldsymbol{b},\boldsymbol{d}) \in \{0,1\}$ to denote whether bidder i was a winning bidder. Symmetrically, we define $x^j(\boldsymbol{b},\boldsymbol{d})$ to denote a vector of size $m = \sum_{\ell \in [t]} u_\ell$ where each index denotes whether each unit of a certain distributor was allocated, in order.
- The payment rule $p(\cdot,\cdot)$: The payment rule takes in the same inputs as $x(\cdot,\cdot)$ and outputs the price each winning bidder is required to pay, and payment each distributor is entitled to receive. We will denote $p_i(\boldsymbol{b},\boldsymbol{d})$ to be the price to be paid by bidder i and $p^j(\boldsymbol{b},\boldsymbol{d})$ the payment to be received by distributor j for each unit (again p^j is of size m, we break each distributor up for the assignment). For any non-winning bidder/distributor units, this value is 0.

We can then define the welfare of bidder i from acquiring k_i units to be $x_i(\boldsymbol{b},\boldsymbol{d}) \cdot v_i - p_i(\boldsymbol{b},\boldsymbol{d})$ (the price paid when a user is not selected is 0). Analogously we define the welfare of distributor j for selling a unit to be $p^j(\boldsymbol{b},\boldsymbol{d}) - x^j(\boldsymbol{b},\boldsymbol{d}) \cdot c_j$. Finally, we can define the welfare of the auctioneer holding the auction. This is just the difference between the prices paid by the bidders and the payments made to the distributors, $\sum_{i \in [n]} p_i(\boldsymbol{b},\boldsymbol{d}) - \sum_{j \in [m]} p^j(\boldsymbol{b},\boldsymbol{d})$.

Now, we can define the *welfare of the auction mechanism* as the sum of the welfare of all participating parties. After summing and cancelling some terms, we get that:

$$W(\boldsymbol{b},\boldsymbol{d}) = \sum_{i \in [n]} x_i(\boldsymbol{b},\boldsymbol{d}) \cdot v_i - \sum_{j \in [m]} x^j(\boldsymbol{b},\boldsymbol{d}) \cdot c_j .$$

Because we also account for the auctioneer's welfare, the welfare is actually independent of the payment rule. Intuitively this means that our welfare definition does not necessarily capture payment 'fairness' as in who should the excess welfare belong to. However, this will be (partially) covered by our truthfulness which holds for both sides.

2.2 Properties for Double Auction Mechanisms

We now define the properties we want double auction mechanisms to satisfy more formally.

Truthfulness: A double auction mechanism is *truthful* if for every bidder or distributor, reporting the private value (resp. the true cost) for the good(s) is a best strategy. Furthermore, any participating bidder or distributor cannot get negative utility.

Formally, this means that, for any bidder $i \in [n]$ with truthful input $b_i = (v_i, k_i)$, and for any b'_i:

$$x_i(\boldsymbol{b},\boldsymbol{d}) \cdot v_i - p_i(\boldsymbol{b},\boldsymbol{d}) \geq x_i((b'_i, \boldsymbol{b}_{-i}), \boldsymbol{d}) \cdot v_i - p_i((b'_i, \boldsymbol{b}_{-i}), \boldsymbol{d}) .$$

Furthermore, for any bidder $i \in [n]$ that bids truthfully, $x_i(\boldsymbol{b},\boldsymbol{d}) \cdot v_i - p_i(\boldsymbol{b},\boldsymbol{d}) \geq 0$. It is defined symmetrically for distributors.

Weak Group Strategy Proofness (WGSP): A double auction mechanism is WGSP if for any input bid and cost vectors $\boldsymbol{b}, \boldsymbol{v}$ to the mechanism, for every set

$A \subseteq (B \bigcup S)$, subset of the participating bidders and distributors, and every alternative reporting bid and/or cost inputs the participants in A can pick together, there is always at least one party in A who is no better off by participating in A than it is reporting truthfully. This means that a colluding set of parties cannot skew the auction so that all colluding parties get better utility from the auction.[4]

(Weak) Budget Balancing ((W)BB): A double auction mechanism is budget balanced if the auctioneer neither gains nor loses utility from conducting the auction. It is *weak* budget balanced if the auctioneer does not lose utility (in this case the auctioneer can gain utility).

Welfare Maximizing: A double auction mechanism is welfare maximizing if the welfare $W(\cdot,\cdot)$ output by the mechanism for any input sets b, d is exactly $\mathsf{OPT}(b,d)$, where we define OPT as follows:

$$\mathsf{OPT}(b = (v,k), d = (u,c)) = \max_{B,S: B \subseteq [n], S \subseteq [m] \text{ s.t. } \sum_{i \in B} k_i \leq |S|} \left\{ \sum_{i \in B} v_i - \sum_{j \in S} c_j \right\}.$$

We will use this function $\mathsf{OPT}(b,d)$ throughout to denote the maximum possible welfare achievable by a set of bidders and distributors. We say that a mechanism is ϵ−welfare maximizing if for any b, d, $W(b,d) \geq \epsilon \cdot \mathsf{OPT}(b,d)$.

Notice that given a blackbox algorithm to solve $\mathsf{OPT}(b,d)$ for any b, d, we can construct a solver to the knapsack problem by assigning all costs equals 0 and picking the number of distributors equal the weight of the knapsack and assigning bidders with size equal value equal weight. This implies that computing $\mathsf{OPT}(b,d)$ is at least as hard as knapsack and therefore not solvable in polynomial time.

Computationally Efficient: A double auction mechanism is computationally efficient if for any input b, d, both of its functions $x(\cdot,\cdot)$ and $p(\cdot,\cdot)$ can be computed in time polynomial in the size of the input.

2.3 Relevant Prior Work on Double Auctions and Compositions

We first outline a known characterization of double auctions with respect to truthfulness. For that, we will need two definitions.

Definition 21 (Monotone Allocation Rule [10]). *An allocation rule is $x(\cdot,\cdot)$ is monotone if for every input set b, d, every winning bidder (resp. distributor) who raises his value (resp. lowers his cost) while other bids and costs remain static is still a winner.*

---

[4] Group Strategy Proofness (without the weak) says no group can collude to make some party better off while the others don't lose anything. This cannot be satisfied by any double auction mechanism [10] so we don't consider it.

This monotone allocation rule just states that bidders should never be removed from the winning set for bidding more (resp. distributors should not be removed from the winning set for bidding a lower cost.) Next we define a threshold payment rule.

Definition 22 *(Threshold Payments [10]). The threshold payment for bidder i (resp. for distributor j), given inputs b_{-i}, d (resp. b, d_{-j}) and a monotone allocation rule $x(\cdot, \cdot)$, are respectively:*

$$\inf_{v_i : x_i(b,d)=1} v_i , \quad \sup_{c_j : x^j(b,d)=1} c_j .$$

What this is saying is that the threshold payment is the minimum value this winning bidder would need to bid to still be accepted. The intuition is symmetrical for distributors.

Theorem 21 *(Truthful Double Auction Mechanisms [10]). A double auction mechanism is truthful if and only if the allocation rule is monotone and the payment rule applies threshold payments.*

The theorem above assumes that participants with a value of 0 always receive or pay 0.

Ranking Algorithms for Compositions [10]. The only definition we use (almost) as-is from [10] is the definition for ranking algorithms for single unit distributors. In their work, they use this definition to compose single unit distributors and single unit bidders. Although we use the same general framework, our definitions need changes in order to suit the new multi-unit singleminded bidders and multi-unit sellers, so we redefine them in the next section, along with new definitions of monotonicity and consistency, which are also properties defined previously but which require changes to make sense in the multi-unit setting.

3 A New Composition Framework

In this section, we establish our new composition framework which encompasses single minded bidders interested in multiple items. We will call these *asymmetric* compositions, which compose a bidder with a knapsack constraint on its value, with distributors that are interested in selling a single item.

3.1 Ranking Algorithms

We will use one-sided *ranking algorithms* for user and operator bids to be used for our composition.

Definition 31 (Knapsack Ranking). *A knapsack ranking algorithm $r(\boldsymbol{b})$ is a deterministic algorithm that takes in a vector of n single minded bids of the form $b_i = (v_i, k_i)$, where v_i is the value this bidder assigns to getting k_i items, and outputs an ordered list of tuples. We will denote $r_i(\boldsymbol{b})$ to be the $i-$th element of the ordered output of r.*

In this definition, the ordering itself could be dependent of v_i, k_i, or both. We will see in the next sections the properties we will need from this ordering algorithm in order to achieve our desired properties.

Definition 32 (Cost Ranking). *A cost ranking algorithm $\hat{r}$ takes in a vector of distributor bids $\boldsymbol{d}$ with each bid j of the form $\boldsymbol{d}_j = (u_j, c_j)$, where u_j is the unit capacity and c_j is the cost per unit of distributor j. The output $\hat{r}(\boldsymbol{d})$ is a ordered list of tuples. We will denote $\hat{r}_j(\boldsymbol{d})$ to be the j-th available unit in $\hat{r}(\boldsymbol{d})$.*

Similar to above, we leave how exactly the order is picked open, however, specifically for the case of distributors, in our setting the only ordering that makes sense is to sort the distributors in increasing order by cost.

Notation. Notice that we have used a slightly different notation for indexing each ranking. Whereas we index the knapsack ranking by tuple, we index the cost ranking per unit. For example, if $\hat{r}(\boldsymbol{d}) = (5,3),(2,7)$ then $\hat{r}_4(\boldsymbol{d}) = 3$ (there are 5 units of cost 3 and 2 units of cost 7).

Definition 33 (Asymmetric Composition Rule). *An asymmetric composition rule for ranking algorithms for multi-unit single-minded bidders (resp. distributors) and simple distributors (resp. bidders) receives as input a knapsack user bid $b = (v, k)$ and a cost per item c and outputs either 1 (accept) or 0 (reject).*

We now define the composition rule which will be the one we use the most throughout the paper.

Definition 34 (t-Threshold Asymmetric Composition Rule). *The $t-$threshold composition rule takes in a bid $b = (v, k)$, the value attributed to this bid and the number of items this bid requires, and a cost c, and outputs 1 (accept) if and only if $v - k \cdot c \geq t$, where t is a non-negative threshold in $\mathbb{R}$.*

The $0-$threshold composition rule accepts any bidder whose value is greater than the cost to add this bidder to the winning set. For any non-zero threshold t, it means we require a fixed positive welfare in order to accept the bidder.

Basically it means that every unit must individually add positive welfare by accepting this bidder, in order for the bidder to be accepted. Since we send the minimum price out of the k best-priced units available, this ensures that.

3.2 Asymmetric Composition

Here we formally define the core primitive we need, the asymmetric composition. This asymmetric composition will take in a knapsack ranking and a single-unit ranking, along with an asymmetric composition rule, and outputs an allocation rule $x(\cdot,\cdot)$. An asymmetric composition along with a payment rule $p(\cdot,\cdot)$ defines a double auction mechanism. Then, we can prove statements of the form: 'If the ranking algorithms and composition rule satisfy properties A and B, with payment rule C then the double auction mechanism output by their asymmetric composition satisfies property D'. We define an asymmetric composition below.

Definition 35 (Asymmetric Composition). *An asymmetric composition, determined by a knapsack ranking algorithm r, a cost ranking algorithm $\hat{r}$, and a composition rule, greedily determines an allocation as follows. Let n be the number of bidders, t be the number of distributors and m be the total number of units available across all distributors.*

- *For each $j \in [m]$:*
  1. *Let $I_j = \{\}$.*
  2. *For $i \in [n]$: Apply the composition rule on $(r_i(\boldsymbol{b}), \hat{r}_j(\boldsymbol{d}))$. If it outputs 1 and $k_i + \sum_{\ell \in I_j} k_\ell \leq j$, $I_j = I_j \bigcup \{i\}$.*
- *For each $j \in [m]$, let $w_j = \sum_{i \in I_j} v_i - \sum_{i \in [j]} \hat{r}_i(\boldsymbol{d})$.*
- *Let j^* be the j with the largest corresponding w_j for $j \in [m]$. Output I_{j^*} and the set of distributors with costs $\{\hat{r}_j(\boldsymbol{d})\}_{j \in [j^*]}$.*

This defines our asymmetric composition given two ranking algorithms. Note that we can also define a slightly different asymmetric composition denoted a *trade-reduced* asymmetric composition. In a trade-reduced asymmetric composition, we remove the least efficient distributor *that was selected by the algorithm*. This distributor will set the price.

Definition 36 (Trade-Reduced Asymmetric Composition). *A Trade-Reduced Asymmetric Composition runs exactly as Definition 35 except after the algorithm we run one additional step:*

- *Remove all units from the least-efficient (worst-ranked) distributor from the accepted set. Also remove any bidders that no longer fit after this distributor is removed.*

When creating a composition using a threshold asymmetric composition rule (Definition 34), we will see that it will be necessary to trade-reduce our composition in order to achieve incentive compatibility.

4 Incentive Compatibility

In this section, we will determine incentive compatibility of knapsack double auctions defined via our composition framework. Specifically, we will show what properties our ranking algorithms and composition rule must follow so that the resulting double auction is truthful for both sides (no party has an incentive to misreport their true value) and also weak group strategy proof (for every group formed, at least one member of the group has no incentive to join it).

4.1 Properties

We start by defining some properties that will be necessary to show both truthfulness and WGSP. We denote a player to be any bidder or distributor participating in the auction.

Definition 41 (Monotone Knapsack Ranking). *We denote a knapsack ranking algorithm to be monotone if a player's ranking both:*

- *(Weakly) Improves with quality: For every bidder i, and bid set $\boldsymbol{b}$, if bidder i changes its bid $b_i = (v_i, k_i)$ to a bid $b_{i'} = (v_{i'}, k_i)$ with $v_{i'} > v_i$, it follows that $r_i(b_{i'}, \boldsymbol{b}_{-i}) \leq r_i(\boldsymbol{b})$ (defined symmetrically for distributors).*
- *(Weakly) Deteriorates with size: For every bidder i and bid set $\boldsymbol{b}$, if bidder i changes its bid $b_i = (v_i, k_i)$ to $b_{i'} = (v_i, k_{i'})$ with $k_{i'} > k_i$, it holds that $r_i(b_{i'}, \boldsymbol{b}_{-i}) \geq r_i(\boldsymbol{b})$ (defined symmetrically for distributors).*

This differs from previous work since we require two properties, both improvement with quality and deterioration with size. This is a natural extension of the monotone ranking algorithm defined in [10], which did not consider single-minded bidders.

Definition 42 (Consistent Knapsack Ranking). *A knapsack ranking algorithm r is consistent if for any two bidders $i \neq i'$ and any bid set $\boldsymbol{b}$, $r_i(\boldsymbol{b}) < r_{i'}(\boldsymbol{b})$ implies that at least one of the following conditions must hold:*

1. $v_i \geq v_{i'}$
2. $k_i \leq k_{i'}$

Here, we must ensure at least one of the two conditions holds for our ranking algorithm to be consistent. Either the value is greater or the size is smaller for one bid to be ranked over another. Notice that bids with different value and different size can be incomparable. In the case where $k = 1$ for all bidders, the definition is equivalent to the consistency definition in [10]. We also apply their definition of monotonicity and consistency for our cost rankings, which depend only on the cost (but inversely) and not on the number of units (since the distributors are not single minded). We do not redefine them here, but monotonicity would require only the first point of Definition 41, and consistency requires only the first point of Definition 42.

Definition 43 (Monotone Asymmetric Composition). *Consider two different inputs to a asymmetric composition rule, with both bidders having same size n: inputs (b_i, c), $(b_{i'}, c')$, and assume that $v_{i'} \geq v_i$ and for each $i \in [n]$, $k_i \geq k'_i$. The composition rule is monotone if for any such two inputs, if the composition rule accepts (b_i, c) then it accepts $(b_{i'}, c')$.*

These two properties will be important to show our incentive compatibility.

4.2 Truthfulness

Here, we show that we can use our definitions from before to show that a composition that follows certain rules will always be truthful.

Theorem 41 *(Truthful Composition).* *A trade-reduced asymmetric composition that is monotone and composed of a consistent and monotone knapsack ranking algorithm and a consistent and monotone cost ranking algorithm, using a monotone composition rule and applying threshold payments is a truthful double auction mechanism.*

The proof of this theorem was deferred to the full version of the work [15].

We cannot protect against sybil attacks unless we include additional assumptions on the distribution. Potentially every distributor would have an incentive to place a bid for one unit of computation for a price immediately less than its own, in order to increase its revenue in the case that it can set its own price. For this work, we do not consider sybil attacks.

4.3 Weak Group Strategy Proofness

Next, we look at how our composition fares against groups of bidders strategically coordinating their bids. Specifically, as we have seen, achieving Group Strategy Proofness is not possible for double auctions [10], therefore, we look to show that our asymmetric composition satisfies weak group strategy proofness.

Theorem 42 *(Weak Group Strategy Proofness).* *An asymmetric composition of monotone, consistent ranking algorithms with a monotone composition rule and applying threshold payments is a Weak Group Strategy Proof double auction mechanism.*

The proof of this theorem was deferred to the full version of the work [15].

5 Welfare and Budget Balancing of Compositions

Other than incentive compatibility, there are two more properties of the auction we care about. Welfare and budget balancing. Recall we define these in Sect. 2. We go into each of these in detail below.

5.1 Welfare

First, we look at the social welfare of the double auction mechanism resulting from our asymmetric composition. Precisely, given the guarantees of welfare achieved by single sided auctions defined by each ranking algorithm, we would like to make a statement about the social welfare of the composition of both into our double auction. For example, in [10] they show that for single unit auctions, a composition of two second price auctions (which provide optimal social welfare) into a double auction provides optimal social welfare. Recall that for knapsack auctions there is no efficient algorithm that solves for the optimal solution in polynomial time, so we will be most likely working with approximations in order to keep the algorithm efficient. In this subsection, we lower bound the welfare of the double auction mechanism resulting from our asymmetric composition below. To do this, we first must define a set of parameters which will be necessary in doing so.

Quantifying how exhaustive the composition rule is: We will quantify how exhaustive the composition rule by a parameter which tells us how large the set of bidders and distributors is when compared to the size of the set of bidders and distributors in the optimal allocation would be. Specifically, we use $s(\boldsymbol{b}, \boldsymbol{d})$ to output a number between 0 and $\sum_{i \in [n]} k_i$ to be the number of items allocated by our composition. We will denote $s'(\boldsymbol{b}, \boldsymbol{d})$ to denote how many items would have been allocated with the same ranking algorithms and an unconstrained composition rule, and finally we will denote $s^*(\boldsymbol{b}, \boldsymbol{d})$ to be the number of items the optimal solution would have allocated. Concretely, in our case this will quantify how much damage the trade reduction does to our welfare.

Quantifying how close to optimal our ranking algorithms are: We will use parameters $\alpha, \beta \geq 1$ to quantify how close to optimal the solution to the one sided algorithms are for any number q of allowed allocation items. Let us define $v_{\mathsf{OPT}}(q)$ to be the value of the feasible solution with at most q bidders that maximizes total value (analogously, we define $c_{\mathsf{OPT}}(q)$ for distributors, but minimizing cost). Then, we say that a ranking algorithm ALG is an α approximation of the optimal if for any $q > 0$, for any bid vector $\boldsymbol{b}$,

$$v_{\mathsf{ALG}}(q) \geq \frac{1}{\alpha} \cdot v_{\mathsf{OPT}}(q).$$

Similarly for distributors we say that a ranking algorithm is a β approximation of optimal if for any q, for any distributor costs report $\boldsymbol{d}$,

$$c_{\mathsf{ALG}}(q) \leq \beta \cdot c_{\mathsf{OPT}}(q).$$

Note that our ranking algorithm is *perfect* if $\beta = 1$.

Quantifying how difficult the problem instance is: The parameter $\gamma(\boldsymbol{b}, \boldsymbol{d}) = v_{\mathsf{OPT}}(s^*(\boldsymbol{b}, \boldsymbol{d})/c_{\mathsf{OPT}}(s^*(\boldsymbol{b}, \boldsymbol{d}))$ quantifies how hard the problem is by taking the ratio of the optimal cost profile for distributors and optimal value profile for distributors. It has been used also in prior works as the same measurement in related problems [10,21]. A large ratio means that there is a lot more value than cost and therefore there are likely to be a surplus of high value bids and therefore approximating the problem instance is not as hard. It also means that the optimal welfare is large. When there is a ratio close to one the optimal solution is close to 0 and tight, and therefore harder to approximate.

Proving Welfare of an Asymmetric Composition Now we use these to show our theorem on welfare, which uses the parameters above to quantify the optimality of our asymmetric composition.

To do this, first we define a *linear* knapsack ranking algorithm and a *perfect* standard ranking algorithm.

Definition 52 (Linear Knapsack Ranking). *A linear knapsack ranking algorithm is a ranking algorithm which sorts user bids of the form $b_i = (v_i, k_i)$ by using as a sorting key the expression $C(v_i/k_i)$ for any $C \geq 1$.*

This means that the bids with the largest value over size ratio (with some multiplicative weight constant greater than one) are ranked first.

Lemma 51. *A linear knapsack ranking is monotone and consistent.*

Proof. It is easy to verify that our linear knapsack ranking satisfies both our properties.

Definition 52 (Perfect Cost Ranking). *A perfect cost ranking in the unconstrained standard setting is a distributor ranking where for we use only cost to rank the distributors. We sort distributors by smallest cost and output $\hat{r}(d)$ such that the i−th element and we rank distributors by smallest cost. We call it perfect since it achieves optimal welfare from the point of view of distributor selection.*

Now we give our theorem. For the theorem below we consider only auction mechanisms which execute at least one trade, meaning $s(b, d) \geq 1$.

Theorem 52 (Approximate Welfare). *Consider input (b, d) for which $\mathsf{OPT}(b, d) \geq 0$. The asymmetric composition of a linear knapsack ranking algorithm that is an α approximation of the optimal assignment, and a perfect cost ranking, using a monotone composition rule achieves welfare at least:*

$$\frac{s(b,d)}{s'(b,d)} \cdot \frac{\frac{\gamma(b,d)}{\alpha} - 1}{\gamma(b,d) - 1} \cdot \mathsf{OPT}(b,d).$$

The proof of this theorem was deferred to the full version of the work [15].

The steps in the proof follow along the same lines as the proof in [10], except the arguments are different since we use a different composition rule and different ranking algorithms.

5.2 Budget Balancing

The second property we examine is the budget balancing of the double auction mechanism resulting from our asymmetric composition. Specifically, while we cannot guarantee strong budget balancing (the auctioneer will not gain or lose money from the trade), what we can show is that the double auction mechanism resulting from an asymmetric composition is weak budget balanced (the auctioneer will not lose money from running the auction. We show this below:

Theorem 52 (Weak Budget Balanced Asymmetric Composition). *A trade-reduced monotone asymmetric composition of a linear knapsack ranking and a consistent, monotone standard ranking algorithms using a monotone composition rule and applying threshold payments is weak budget balanced.*

The proof of this theorem was deferred to the full version of the work [15].

With this, we have shown that our composition can be weak budget balanced when using the correct ranking algorithms. Next, we look at how to use this.

6 Concrete Instantiations and Applications

Now, we move to look at what these ranking algorithms actually look like. It is clear to see that for the single-unit ranking we can always just sort by cost. This ranking is monotone and consistent.[5] Similarly, for our knapsack algorithm, notice that any sorting of users using as sorting value some expression of the form $f(v_i)/g(k_i)$ for any functions f, g would satisfy the consistent and monotone ranking definitions. However, we are only able to show approximate welfare optimality and weak budget balancing for linear knapsack ranking algorithms.

Specifically, if we instantiate our knapsack ranking to use plainly v_i/k_i in order to sort each bid. Ranking items in this fashion for the knapsack problem has been shown to give a $1/2$ approximation to the best knapsack solution for any size, meaning this ranking achieves an $\alpha = 2$ approximation in the parameters defined in Sect. 5. The sort-by-cost ranking for distributors achieves a $\beta = 1$ optimal solution which then means that a composition of these two algorithms provides a robust auction mechanism with welfare that is close to $1/2$ of the optimal welfare for problem instances with large enough γ. We formalize this below (recall the definition of CPT from Sect. 2):

Lemma 62. *For any user bid vector $\boldsymbol{b}$ and distributor cost bid vector $\boldsymbol{d}$, an asymmetric composition by sorting user bids by v_i/k_i as our knapsack ranking algorithm and a cost ranking algorithm sorting distributors by their cost c_j, using the 0−threshold composition rule and threshold payments is a robust double auction mechanism which achieves welfare at least:*

$$\frac{\frac{\gamma(\boldsymbol{b},\boldsymbol{d})}{2} - 1}{\gamma(\boldsymbol{b},\boldsymbol{d}) - 1} \cdot \mathsf{OPT}(\boldsymbol{b},\boldsymbol{d}).$$

Proof. It follows directly from previous results shown here plus the fact that our knapsack ranking algorithm can approximate knapsack up to a factor of $1/2$.

Notice that for large $\gamma(\boldsymbol{b},\boldsymbol{d})$ this approaches a $1/2$ approximation of the optimal welfare.

One can also define a more general theorem. Any linear knapsack ranking algorithm which provides an α approximation to knapsack, paired with the optimal distributor sorting algorithm, can be converted into a robust double auction mechanism with a $1/\alpha$ approximation to the optimal welfare for problem instances with large enough γ.

---

[5] We leave it more general in case other constraints cause some distributors to be more appealing than others.

6.1 Applications of Interest

Our knapsack double auctions can be useful for a suit of diverse online auctions. In the blockchain space, where there is typically not one provider, but a heterogenous network of providers for computation, storage, among other things, knapsack auctions become very relevant.

As is, our auctions can cover any setting where the bidders have some knapsack constraint on the amount of resource they want, and distributors don't. As modeled, it is also necessary that bidders don't care whether their service is provided by one or many distributors, as long as it is satisfied. Although most modern services are parallelizable, it could be also very interesting to expand our work to the case where we do not actually want a user's bid to be split among different distributors. Another interesting thing to consider would be whether we can have a truthful mechanism that optimizes only for bidder welfare. Or maybe dropping distributor truthfulness in favor of some notion of fairness for distributors (on how often they get to sell).

One technicality that is necessary to be dealt with is sybil attacks. We assume that the usage of the network is by known clients with a reputation. The auctioneer which is in charge of the auction can work to detect and dissuade sybil attacks through authentication, staking, and slashing.

7 Protocol Modifications and Tradeoffs

In the full version of the work [15, Appendix B], we also an discuss additional modifications to the protocol which might be of interest in practice. Specifically, we discuss a property orthogonal to some which we discuss in that paper, which is the issue of *fairness*. Fairness, informally, refers to any distributor willing to provide a unit for a price less than the agreed-upon price having equal chance of being assigned it (proportional to the distributor's size). This comes up because for distributors, one important factor for willingly participating in auctions is predictability of the expected return. This is talked about by FileCoin storage providers as paramount for their business [1]. Thus, we believe fairness is a good way to capture this. Unfortunately, fairness is at odds with other desired properties of auctions.

8 Conclusion

In this work, we pushed our understanding of double auctions by providing a composition system for knapsack double auctions. Our main motivation for the exploration was a zero-knowledge proof market, although we identified many other settings where such a double auction could be useful. Many questions still remain open in this setting. The two we find more compelling are:

- Can we achieve a closer approximation to the optimal welfare? Ideally we could achieve a $(1 - \epsilon)$ approximation of the welfare for any epsilon. Our

framework outlines what is necessary for such result: a monotone and consistent ranking algorithm that can achieve such approximation, along with a way to relate this algorithm to the welfare (if it is not linear).
- Can we provide robust double auctions when both bidders and distributors have a knapsack constraint? And how does this affect the welfare? This setting can be relevant when bidders want their units to come from a single provider (an example could be non-parallelizable computation).

A Related Work

Auctions have been thoroughly studied in many different settings. In the interest of clarity and completeness, we outline below some settings we found to be similar to the prover network setting we study here, although with some important differences which we also discuss. In the full version of the work [15], we also include a more complete treatment of related work.

A.1 Combinatorial/Knapsack Auctions

The study of combinatorial auctions was initially studied by McMillan [18] in the setting where there are several different item types and users might be interested in only a set of them (these are also called package auctions). This setting was also studied in other works [3,4,14]. Along with the fact that this setting is not exactly equivalent to ours where users are interested in varying quantities of 'the same' item, these works also only talk about one-sided auctions. Two works were identified that work in the setting of multiple sellers. The work by Gujar and Narahari [12] and the work by Chu [8]. In [12] the mechanism is not budget balanced and in [8] to the best of our understanding the welfare analysis does not extend to the case where sellers sell multiple items of the same kind, which is the case in our setting.

References

1. FileCoin Docs — RCI (2023)
2. Aggarwal, G., Hartline, J. D.: Knapsack auctions. In: Proceedings of the seventeenth annual ACM-SIAM symposium on Discrete algorithm - SODA '06, pp. 1083–1092, Miami, Florida. ACM Press (2006)
3. Ausubel, L. M., Milgrom, P.R.: Package bidding vickrey vs. ascending auctions. Revue économique, 53(3):391–402, Publisher: Sciences Po University Press (2002)
4. Blumrosen, L., Nisan, N.: Combinatorial Auctions. In: Tardos, E., Nisan, N., Roughgarden, T., Vazirani, V. V (eds) Algorithmic Game Theory, pp. 267–300. Cambridge University Press, Cambridge (2007)
5. Chawla, S.: Lecture notes in algorithmic game theory (2011)
6. Che, Y.-K., Kim, J.: Optimal collusion-proof auctions. J. Econ. Theory 144(2), 565–603 (2009)

7. Chen, X., Zhu, G., Ding, H., Zhang, L., Zhang, H., Fang, Y.: End-to-end service auction: a general double auction mechanism for edge computing services. IEEE/ACM Trans. Netw. **30**(6), 2616–2629 (2022)
8. Chu, L.: Truthful bundle/multiunit double auctions. Management Science, 55(7):1184–1198. Publisher: INFORMS (2009)
9. Clarke, E. H.: Multipart pricing of public goods. Public Choice, 11:17–33, Publisher: Springer (1971)
10. Dütting, P., Roughgarden, T., Talgam-Cohen, I.: Modularity and greed in double auctions. In: Proceedings of the fifteenth ACM conference on Economics and computation, EC '14, pp. 241–258, New York, NY, USA. Association for Computing Machinery (2014)
11. Groves, T.: Incentives in Teams. Econometrica, 41(4):617–631, 1973. Publisher: [Wiley, Econometric Society]
12. Gujar, S., Narahari, Y.: Optimal multi-unit combinatorial auctions with single minded bidders. In: 2009 IEEE Conference on Commerce and Enterprise Computing, pp. 74–81. ISSN: 2378-1971 (2009)
13. Jin, A., Song, W., Wang, P., Niyato, D., Ju, P.: Auction mechanisms toward efficient resource sharing for cloudlets in mobile cloud computing. IEEE Transactions on Services Computing, 9(6):895–909. Conference Name: IEEE Transactions on Services Computing (2016)
14. Kasberger, B., Teytelboym, A.: The Combinatorial multi-round ascending auction (2024). arXiv:2203.11783
15. Lazzaretti, A., Papamanthou, C., Hishon-Rezaizadeh, I.: Robust Double Auctions for Resource Allocation. Publication info, Preprint (2024)
16. Leyton-Brown, K.: Lecture notes - multiunit auctions (2008)
17. McMillan, J.: Selling spectrum rights. J. Econ. Perspectives, 8(3):145–162. Publisher: American Economic Association (1994)
18. McMillan, J.: Selling spectrum rights. J. Econ. Perspectives, 8(3):145–162, 1994. Publisher: American Economic Association
19. Myerson, R. B., Satterthwaite, M. A.: Efficient mechanisms for bilateral trading. J. Econ. Theory, 29(2):265–281 (1983)
20. Ng, J. S., et al.: A double auction mechanism for resource allocation in coded vehicular edge computing. IEEE Transactions on Vehicular Technology, 71(2):1832–1845. Conference Name: IEEE Transactions on Vehicular Technology (2022)
21. Roughgarden, T., Sundararajan, M.: Quantifying inefficiency in cost-sharing mechanisms. J. ACM, 56(4):23:1–23:33 (2009)
22. Vickrey, W.: Counterspeculation, auctions, and competitive sealed tenders. The Journal of Finance, 16(1):8–37, 1961. Publisher: [American Finance Association, Wiley]
23. Wang, W., Zhou, L., Yaish, A., Zhang, F., Fisch, B., Livshits, B.: Mechanism Design for ZK-Rollup Prover Markets (2024). arXiv:2404.06495

Zero-Knowledge and Its Applications

Verifying Jolt zkVM Lookup Semantics

Carl Kwan[1]($^\boxtimes$), Quang Dao[2], and Justin Thaler[3,4]

[1] The University of Texas at Austin, Austin, USA
carlkwan@cs.utexas.edu
[2] Carnegie Mellon University, Pittsburgh, USA
qvd@andrew.cmu.edu
[3] Georgetown University, Washington, D.C., USA
[4] a16z Crypto Research, Menlo Park, USA

Abstract. Lookups are a popular way to express repeated constraints in state-of-the art SNARKs. This is especially the case for *zero-knowledge virtual machines* (zkVMs), which produce succinct proofs of correct execution for programs expressed as bytecode according to a specific instruction set architecture (ISA). The Jolt zkVM (Arun, Setty & Thaler, Eurocrypt 2024) for RISC-V employs Lasso (Setty, Thaler & Wahby, Eurocrypt 2024), an efficient lookup argument for massive structured tables, to prove correct execution of instructions. Internally, Lasso performs multiple lookups into smaller "subtables", then combines the results.

We present an approach to formally verify Lasso-style lookup arguments against the semantics of instruction set architectures. We demonstrate our approach by formalizing and verifying all Jolt 32-bit instructions corresponding to the RISC-V base instruction set (RV32I) using the ACL2 theorem proving system. Our formal ACL2 model has undergone extensive validation against the Rust implementation of Jolt. Due to ACL2's bitblasting, rewriting, and developer-friendly features, our formalization is highly automated.

Through formalization, we also discovered optimizations to the Jolt codebase, leading to improved efficiency without impacting correctness or soundness. In particular, we removed one unnecessary lookup each for four instructions, and reduced the sizes of three subtables by 87.5%.

1 Introduction

Cryptographic proof systems [17] are essential to the scalability and privacy of modern blockchains. Succinct Non-interactive Arguments of Knowledge (SNARKs) [14,24] allow participants to prove arbitrary NP computations, generating short on-chain proofs that can be efficiently verified. In other words, SNARKs allow untrusted provers to establish that they know a "witness" satisfying some property, such as a correct batch of blockchain transactions that advance the blockchain from one state to another.

This work was partially performed while the first and second authors were interns at a16z crypto research.

A special case of SNARKs are zero-knowledge virtual machines (zkVMs),[1] which enable succinct proofs of program execution for computer programs compiled to bytecode for some instruction set architecture (ISA). zkVMs enable developers to write programs in high-level programming languages, and for untrusted provers to then prove that they ran the program correctly. In contrast, older toolchains for SNARK deployment often involve hand-crafting circuits or constraint systems, a highly error-prone process requiring domain-specific expertise. Because of these benefits, there has been an explosion of zkVMs for various instruction sets such as RISC-V [20,30,34], EVM [28,31,41], MIPS [39], Cairo [16] and others.

zkVMs often rely on *lookup arguments* to efficiently represent high-degree constraints that are needed to implement virtually all instruction sets. These arguments allow for proving the correctness of a sequence of lookup operations into some pre-determined tables. The performance of lookup arguments typically scales with the size of the table;[2] however, a recent work by Setty et al. called Lasso [33] overcomes this limitation (for a large useful class of tables). The key idea of Lasso is that for specific tables that satisfy a form of *decomposability*: a lookup on the large table (say of size 2^{64}) can be performed via a sequence of lookups on much smaller subtables (say of size 2^{16}). This powerful observation forms the basis of the Jolt RISC-V zkVM [2], which represents every RISC-V instruction as one or more decomposable lookups, realizing the "lookup singularity" vision outlined by Whitehat [37]. Jolt's implementation [20] is currently among the fastest zkVMs [29] and, thanks to its lookup-centric approach, is both simpler and more auditable than competitors [36].

While Jolt may be simpler than other zkVMs, it is still a complicated piece of software. The current implementation [20] contains at least 25,000 lines of code (and growing), with at least 2000 lines dedicated to specifying lookups. Given the large surface area, it is crucial to *formally verify* that Jolt lookups are actually performing the right operations. This is not merely a theoretical concern: vulnerabilities in SNARK designs and implementations are quite common, with soundness bugs present in both protocol specifications [13,27] and implementations [12,25]. Another class of bugs are those affecting the constraint system (so-called "front-end") used to represent computations [9]. These front-end vulnerabilities are also prevalent in SNARK implementations; for Jolt, a bug in the Lasso lookup front-end could allow a malicious prover to produce an accepting proof for a different program than the one the verifier thinks it is verifying.[3]

In light of these concerns, our goal is to **formally verify the semantic correctness of lookups in the Jolt zkVM**, ensuring that the lookups for each instruction actually produce the expected result for that instruction.

---

[1] Many zkVMs are only succinct and not zero-knowledge, but in keeping with the common vernacular we will refer to them as zkVMs.
[2] This dependency is present in either the prover cost or the preprocessing cost.
[3] This would be problematic, for instance, if the program does signature verification, and the prover produces a valid proof without knowing the secret key.

1.1 Our Results

We answer this goal with the following contributions:

1. We present a *general methodology* for formally verifying lookup semantics in Jolt (or any proof system that relies on Lasso-style decomposable lookups).
2. We instantiate this methodology with a formalization of all RISC-V base instructions (RV32I) in Jolt using the ACL2 theorem prover [1]. Our formalization is *highly automated* thanks to various features of ACL2.

Our formalization and artifacts are publicly available.[4] Our approach achieves correctness guarantees for Jolt lookups while maintaining the flexibility needed to work with an evolving system like Jolt. We now elaborate on our results.

Jolt Subtables and Instructions. In Jolt, subtables are parametrized by a size parameter $m \in \mathbb{N}$. For each m, a subtable consists of a function

$$T_m : \{0,1\}^m \times \{0,1\}^m \to \mathbb{F},$$

which on input (x, y) returns the (x, y)-th entry of the subtable, and a polynomial

$$P_m \in \mathbb{F}[X_0, \ldots, X_{m-1}, Y_0, \ldots, Y_{m-1}]$$

purported to be the *multilinear extension* (MLE) of T_m (see Sect. 2.1 for background on MLEs). Here $\mathbb{F}$ is the underlying finite field used in Jolt (of size at least 2^{128}). The statement we want to formally verify is that P_m is indeed the MLE of T_m, i.e. that

$$P_m(x,y) = T_m(x,y) \quad \text{for all} \quad x, y \in \{0,1\}^m. \tag{1}$$

In particular, Eq. (1) only needs to hold for parameters m that are used in Jolt; currently, Jolt only uses $m = 8$, giving us subtables of size $2^{16} = 65536$. This number is small enough that we can directly test for correctness between the materialized version and the MLE version. Nevertheless, formalizing the model of MLEs and proving correctness against the subtable functions is an interesting mathematical result in their own right.[5] We present a formal model of MLEs for some subtables and prove Eq. (1) for larger bit-widths such as $m \in \{16, 32, \ldots\}$ (see Sect. 4.1 for an example). In future work, we plan to extend this to arbitrary $m \in \mathbb{N}$.

We next describe Jolt instructions. Each instruction in Jolt is parameterized by a word size $W \in \{32, 64\}$,[6] comes with an expected semantics, and a purported alternative way to achieve the same semantics using lookups into subtables. The alternative way proceeds as follows:

---
[4] https://github.com/kwancarl/acl2-jolt.
[5] Formal modeling of MLEs will also help any future "back-end" verification effort, which establishes security of the argument system using the fact that these are indeed multilinear polynomials.
[6] Currently, Jolt only supports 32-bit instructions, with 64-bit planned for the future.

1. First, the operands of the instruction are split into $C = W/m$ chunks:

$$\mathsf{Chunk}(x, y) = (z_0, \ldots, z_{C-1}) \in \left(\{0,1\}^{2m}\right)^C.$$

2. Second, the chunks are then used to lookup into a list of subtables

$$L = ((\mathsf{ST}_0, \mathsf{idx}_0), \ldots, (\mathsf{ST}_{n-1}, \mathsf{idx}_{n-1})),$$

where for each j, ST_j is a subtable (of a given size m_j) and $\mathsf{idx}_j \in \{0, \ldots, C-1\}$ is the index of the chunk that will be used to query the subtable. In other words, lookup results are computed as

$$\mathsf{Lookup}(L, z_0, \ldots, z_{C-1}) = \left(T_j[z_{\mathsf{idx}_j}]\right)_{j=0}^{n-1}.$$

3. Finally, we produce the final result from the subtable lookups using a function $\mathsf{Combine}(\text{lookup results}) \in \mathbb{F}$, whose range should be in $\{0, \ldots, 2^W - 1\}$.

For a concrete example, the 32-bit AND instruction splits the operands $(x, y) \in \left(\{0,1\}^{32}\right)^2$ into 4 chunks of 16 bits $(x_i, y_i) \in \left(\{0,1\}^8\right)^2$, looks up each chunk in the AND subtable, then concatenates the lookup results, which should be equal to the bit-wise AND of the two operands. See the IACR Cryptology ePrint Archive version of this paper [21] for a list of all instructions. The relation we formally verify is that the lookup process (performing steps 1, 2, and 3) gives the expected result of the instruction. In other words, the following equation holds for all $W \in \{32, 64\}$ and $x, y \in \{0,1\}^W$:

$$\mathsf{ExpectedResult}(x, y) = (\mathsf{Combine} \circ \mathsf{Lookup} \circ \mathsf{Chunk})(x, y). \tag{2}$$

Theorem 1.1. *Equation (2) holds for every* Jolt *instruction in the base RV32I instruction sets.*

Figure 1 visualizes our results. We further elaborate on our approach in Sect. 3, and fully work out an example verified instruction in Sect. 4.

Automation and Extensibility. Our formalization is highly automated, thanks to ACL2's built-in automated rewriting and verified model checking libraries. Our theorems are discharged with minimal user intervention, requiring only simple connecting lemmas. At a minimum, our contribution requires expertise with various formal methods tools (e.g. theorem provers, model checkers, specification languages), the insight to apply the appropriate method for a particular application, and the ability to model real-world and mathematical systems. Our more significant contribution is in developing an extensible theory which can automatically discharge the correctness of *families* of Jolt instructions. Doing this requires finding a pattern of theorems that enables a tool (e.g. ACL2) to automatically rewrite formal statements involving Lasso-style lookups and Jolt instructions into true statements. We illustrate this in Sect. 3.

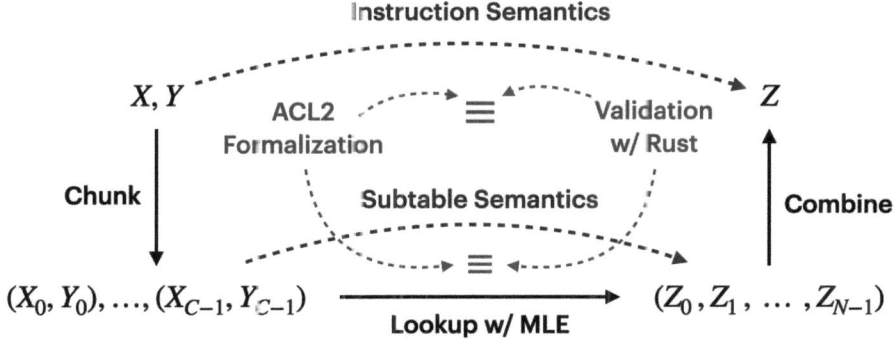

Fig. 1. Overview of our formalization. The main contents of our work are the **green** equivalences, which we prove for all subtables and instructions in the base RV32I & RV64I instruction sets. Our result assumes that Lasso correctly proves the expected decomposable lookups with respect to the black arrows.

In most cases, once we proved correctness of 32-bit instructions, extending to 64-bit versions requires only restatements of definitions and theorems. Initial experiments indicate that our approach scales to formally verifying parts of the RISC-V M-extension, which was recently added to Jolt; we leave a full write-up of this effort to future work.

Validation with Rust. Since we develop our formal model in ACL2, it is crucial to validate that these models correspond to the Rust implementation [20]. Subtables are small enough (of size at most 2^{16}) that we exhaustively check for correctness between ACL2 and Rust. Since instructions cannot be exhaustively checked, we perform validation on randomly-chosen inputs, and scope our formal model so that the only points of potential differences are in commonly-used subroutine helper functions (such as Chunk and Combine functions).

Efficiency Benefits of Our Formalization. We remove one unused lookup for each of the comparison instructions (SLT, SLTU, BGE, and BGEU), which constitute 4 out of 19 instructions in total. We discover this optimization through our ACL2 formalization, as ACL2 tooling could automatically recognize that a lookup went unused, producing an error message. Furthermore, we recognize that the sizes of shift-related subtables can be significantly smaller than the current implementation. This is because only the last 5 bits of the shift amount operand are relevant to 32-bit shift instructions; thus, we can use $2^8 \times 2^5 = 2^{13}$-sized subtables instead of the 2^{16}-sized subtables that is currently used.

We contacted the Jolt developers to integrate these optimizations. The first (removing unused lookups) was already integrated, and the second (smaller shift subtables) is currently under review. For more details, see Sect. 5.

Non-Goals. Since our focus is on verifying lookup semantics, it is necessary for us to black-box other parts of the Jolt codebase. In particular, we assume that the underlying "back-end" argument systems (such as Lasso) are secure, and correctly prove all specified relations (such as all lookups). We also do not model other parts of the front-end such as R1CS and offline memory-checking [32]. As Jolt is a large codebase, we believe our approach is a pragmatic compromise that allows for incremental verification. In future work, we plan to incorporate other front-end components into our formal model.

1.2 Related Works

A growing body of work has applied techniques from *formal methods* to rule out bugs in SNARK front-ends, with various tradeoffs between the automation of the tool and the guarantee it provides. Many focus on verifying ZK circuits, specifically in R1CS format [10,11,23,26]. Some even use ACL2 [10]. Some work involves detecting under-constrained circuit bugs [26], aiming for high automation but not necessarily full formal correctness. On the other hand, there are formalization results that prove full formal correctness of either a VM front-end such as Cairo [3,4], zkWasm [8], or of R1CS or Plonkish circuits via special DSLs [11,23]. Our work differs from these in the following aspects. First, we target verifying (a particular form of) lookups that are used inside general-purpose zkVMs, whereas other works focus on verifying arithmetic constraints such as R1CS, Plonk-ish, or AIR. Second, we aim for full functional correctness, unlike other works that aim only to detect, e.g. under-constrained circuits. Finally, despite full formal guarantees, we do not compromise on automation, by leveraging desirable features of ACL2.

Cairo. The work most relevant to ours is the formal verification effort for the Cairo ecosystem [16], which consists of a high-level programming language, an ISA, and a compiler from the high-level language to the ISA. The first work [3] verified the correctness of an AIR encoding for the Cairo ISA, while the second work [4] augmented the Cairo compiler with tools that allow for proving correctness of compiled programs, without needing to verify the overall compiler.

There are a few key differences between Cairo and our work with Jolt. Cairo is a particularly simple VM that is specifically designed to be SNARK friendly, and pertains to an ad hoc language and architecture. Users who wish to produce proofs of programs will need to either use the Cairo language, or compile down to the Cairo ISA from another high-level language. This contrasts with the existing mature compiler, tooling, and infrastructure for RISC-V, which is Jolt's target architecture. Finally, Cairo's verification efforts are highly manual. As Cairo changes, it is unknown how the formal proofs may change. Our efforts in this work aim to enable automatic, extensible, and scalable verification as Jolt matures.

zkWasm. Another recent work [8] by the CertiK team focuses on the zkWasm project [40], verifying the correctness of arithmetic constraints for the zkWasm VM. It is difficult to compare their efforts to ours, since CertiK has not yet put forth a peer-reviewed publication, instead releasing a code preview with all proofs omitted, and several high-level blog posts. Nevertheless, the same comments regarding Cairo's lack of automated verification can also be made about CertiK's formalization. While Wasm is a more complex ISA than Cairo, the particular form of constraint system used to model Wasm instructions are quite different from Jolt's, and hence the verification effort is orthogonal to ours. In particular, zkWasm relies on Plonkish/Halo2-style constraints [18], while Jolt uses decomposable lookups along with R1CS and memory-checking.

Backend Verification. Finally, some recent works focused on verifying SNARK backends, such as verifying soundness for Linear-PCP-based SNARKs [5] and for the sum-check protocol [6]. These are complementary to our efforts, which focus solely on the front-end.

2 Preliminaries

2.1 Jolt and Lasso Basics

Multilinear Extensions. Given a function $f : \{0,1\}^n \to \mathbb{F}$, its *multilinear extension (MLE)* $\widetilde{f} : \mathbb{F}^n \to \mathbb{F}$ is the unique multilinear polynomial that agrees with f on all inputs in $\{0,1\}^n$.

Decomposable Lookup Relations and Lasso. We describe the type of lookup tables that can be proved efficiently by Lasso. In the original paper [33], it is referred to as having a *Surge-only structure* (SOS); in this work, we simply refer to this property as being *decomposable*.

Definition 2.1 (Decomposable Lookup Table). *Let* $T : \{0,1\}^n \to \mathbb{F}$ *be a lookup table for some* $n \geq 1$ *and finite field* $\mathbb{F}$. *Given a divisor* $c \geq 1$ *of* n, *some* $m \geq 1$, *a mapping* $i : [m] \to [c]$, *and a low-degree polynomial* $g : \mathbb{F}^m \to \mathbb{F}$, *we say that* T *is* (c, m, i, g)-*decomposable if there exist a sequence of subtables* $T_1, \ldots, T_m : \{0,1\}^{n/c} \to \mathbb{F}$ *such that:*

1. *The multilinear extensions* $\widetilde{T}_1, \ldots, \widetilde{T}_m$ *of* $T_1, \ldots, T_m$ *can be evaluated in* $O(\log(n/c))$ *time;*
2. *For all* $x \in \{0,1\}^n$, *writing* $x = (x_1, \ldots, x_c) \in (\{0,1\}^{n/c})^c$, *we have:*

$$T(x) = g\left(T_1(x_{i(1)}), \ldots, T_m(x_{i(m)})\right). \qquad (3)$$

Given a (c, m, i, g)-decomposable lookup table T and a commitment scheme cm for field elements, we define the (committed) decomposable lookup relation as:

$$\mathcal{R}_{T,c,m,i,g,\mathsf{cm}} := \{(c, (y, x)) \mid c = \mathsf{cm}(y) \land y = T(x)\}.$$

Lasso is an argument system for proving correctness of decomposable lookup relations. In this paper, we will assume that Lasso is complete and sound, meaning that it correctly proves Eq. (3) for any (c, m, i, g)-decomposable lookup table T. Our focus will be to show that the lookup relations in Jolt that are proved by Lasso in fact represent the intended semantics of RISC-V instructions.

2.2 ACL2 Basics

ACL2 is a highly automated theorem proving system, which also supports programming in Common Lisp. It has seen success in verifying hardware, software, and cyber-physical systems at companies such as Intel, AMD, ARM, Collins Aerospace, and more [19]. Some Jolt-relevant ACL2 successes include highly-efficient formal executable models of x86, Y86, JVM, and RISC-V ISAs [15,22]. While ACL2 handily supports reasoning about software and general-purpose mathematics, it has seen outsized impact verifying low-level systems, motivating much tool development in this direction. This makes ACL2 well-suited to verifying the front-end of Jolt or other zkVMs.

Table 1. Common ACL2 functions, macros, and other commands used in this paper.

Command	Description
defun	Define a function symbol
define	Define a function symbol, enforce guard checking, and more
b*	Binder for local variables; often used to simplify control flow
defthm	Name and prove a theorem
cons	Construct a pair or list
car	Return the head of a list
cdr	Return the second element of a cons pair
logcar	Return the least significant bit of a number
logcdr	Return all but the least significant bit of a number
part-select	Return a bitvector part of an integer
natp	Recognizer for natural numbers
bitp	Recognizer for bits
unsigned-byte-p	Recognizer for unsigned numbers fitting a specified bit width
def-gl-thm	Name and prove a theorem using GL symbolic simulation

Table 1 lists some common ACL2 functions and macros used in this paper. For brevity, we omit the extensive details of the ACL2 rewriting system and heuristics. For this paper, it is sufficient to know that ACL2 will automatically attempt to rewrite formal statements into known equivalent statements. For example, the following is a theorem which is automatically proven in ACL2:

$$\text{(defthm foo (equal (- a a) 0))}$$

The function defthm above introduces a theorem named foo stating that $a-a = 0$. When ACL2 proves foo, it also automatically introduces a rewrite rule which will automatically attempt to replace terms of the form (- a a) with 0 in future proofs. A typical ACL2 theorem will involve: (1) hypotheses (if any); and (2) the theorem conclusion. More details on the ACL2 rewriting system can be found in the ACL2 documentation [38].

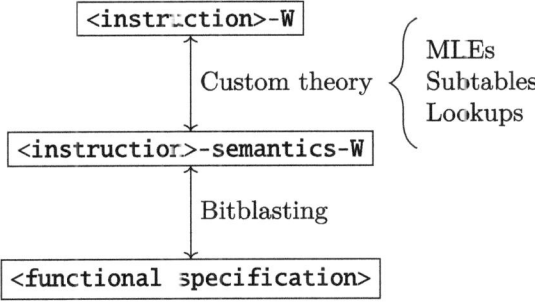

Fig. 2. Approach to verifying Jolt instructions, where $W \in \{32, 64\}$

Another instrument in the ACL2 toolkit is the use of *bitblasting*. Bitblasting is the process of reducing theorems on finite domains into decision problems on bitvectors, making them amenable to SAT-like decision procedures. ACL2 supports bitblasting via several frameworks. We use GL, which supports bitblasting via BDDs or external SAT solvers [35]. The internal GL BDD-based model checker and proof procedures are fully written in and verified with ACL2. In addition to a hypothesis and conclusion, a typical GL theorem event will involve bindings which assign bits to represent variables in the theorem statement.

GL's symbolic simulation of large sets of boolean functions with BDD-based procedures has successfully verified many large-scale industrial designs. However, model checking with SAT or BDDs has its limits, either due to what is expressible in the language or due to scalability issues. For sophisticated verification efforts involving various high-level protocols, low-level machinery, and their interactions – such as Jolt – a unified approach combining bitblasting with light user-guided theorem proving is more effective. Often, the expedient approach to verification with ACL2 is to setup a theory with the appropriate theorems which enable ACL2 heuristics to automatically discharge the final desired theorems. We will describe such an approach in the context of Jolt lookups.

3 General Approach to Lookup Formalization

Formalizing each Jolt instruction in ACL2 broadly involves proving two parts:

(A) the multilinear extensions (MLEs) involved in the lookups are equivalent to their respective intended behavior; and
(B) the composition of chunking the inputs, lookups to materialized subtables, and combining the results is equivalent to the intended instruction semantics.

A particular Jolt instruction may involve multiple lookups, but otherwise part (A) is a straightforward exercise in equational reasoning. In fact, part (A) is amenable to bitblasting if we restrict our attention to Jolt-specific bitwidths.

Part (B) involves combining new definitions, intermediate semantic layers, bitblasting, and theory management to automatically trigger rewrite rules that discharge the desired final theorem with very little user-interaction. It is the part that we focus on in this section. A summary of our approach is visualized in Fig. 2, and a full example of an instruction is given in Program 4.

The first step in part (B) is to define and verify the necessary subtables for each Jolt instruction. We make a distinction between subtables which are indexed by one or two parameters, and define analogous functions for each. Since many subtables are intended to be the same size, we have a single function which generates the indices based on upper limits for x and y (for subtables indexed by two parameters). Lookup functions are built on top of existing ACL2 association list and related libraries. Some subtables are further parameterized (e.g. by word sizes or chunk index) but all lookup functions take a subtable and either one or two parameters. A common pattern of theorems and rewrite rules enable us to readily verify that lookups to these subtables return the expected result. These theorems often state the return "type" and correctness of supporting functions.

For every Jolt instruction, we define an equivalent instruction which replaces the lookup stage with their intended semantics; otherwise, they contain identical chunking and combining stages. We name this intermediary semantics representation `<instruction>-semantics-32` and simply bitblast their correctness. Then we define the Jolt instructions themselves, which we simply name `<instruction>-32`. Because they only differ with respect to lookups, proving the Jolt instructions equivalent to their intermediate versions reduces to the theorems we prove about the subtables and lookups.

We restrict our use of bitblasting to theorems about lower-level functions or intermediate steps. Correctness theorems for each subtable and the associated MLEs are simply stored as ACL2 rewrite rules. Clause processing with lookup arguments is not mature in GL or ACL2; a naïve attempt to bitblast or otherwise prove the correctness of `sltu-32` or any direct implementation of a Jolt instruction will open too many function definitions. Part of this is exacerbated by the concrete values of $W = 32$ and $m = 8$ in the 32-bit version of Jolt instructions. Certain executions in proof attempts with such instructions are no longer symbolic and tables of size 2^{16} can literally be materialized. On their own, such tables can be exhaustively checked for correctness, but layering on top various chunking and combining functions can easily cause the state space to be intractable or misdirect the theorem prover. Instead, for top-level theorems, we control the rules space, preventing the rewriter from expanding the function definition in most proofs, enabling it to focus only on the correctness lemmas, and providing it with a simple chain of equivalences to obtain the final desired theorem.

4 Formalization Example: Set Less Than (Unsigned)

In this section, we describe the process of formalizing and verifying an example Jolt instruction, set less than (unsigned), abbreviated by SLTU. We begin with

Program 1: ACL2 Formalization of $\widetilde{\mathsf{Eq}}_m$

```
1  ;; Equality of two bits, computes x * y + (1 - x) * (1 - y)
2  (define b-eq-w ((x bitp) (y bitp))
3    (b-xor (b-and x y) (b-and (b-xor 1 x) (b-xor 1 y))) ...)
4
5  ;; Equality of two bitvectors, computes: Prod (xi * yi + (1 - xi) * (1 - yi))
6  (define eq-w ((x :type unsigned-byte) (y :type unsigned-byte))
7    (b* (((unless (and (natp x) (natp y)))      0)       ;; Edge cases
8         ((if (xor (bitp x) (bitp y)))          0)
9         ((if (and (bitp x) (bitp y)))   (b-eq-w x y))   ;; Base case
10        (x-0     (logcar x))                            ;; LSB of x
11        (y-0     (logcar y))                            ;; LSB of y
12        (x-rest  (logcdr x))                            ;; Rest of x
13        (y-rest  (logcdr y)))                           ;; Rest of y
14       (b-and (b-eq-w x-0 y-0) (eq-w x-rest y-rest))))  ;; Recursive case
15  ///
16  ;; eq-w correctness theorem for arbitrary unsigned ints
17  (defthmd eq-w-equal-equiv
18    (implies (and (natp x) (natp y)) (equal (eq-w x y) (if (equal x y) 1 0)))))
```

the modelling and verification of the MLEs, corresponding to part (A) of the approach described in Sect. 3. Then we verify the top-level Jolt instruction itself, corresponding to part (B).

4.1 Formalizing MLEs for Subtables

Given $x, y \in \{0, 1\}^W$, the SLTU instruction returns 1 if $x < y$ and 0 otherwise, treating x and y as unsigned integers. To get a multilinear extension formula for SLTU, we use two other MLEs, $\widetilde{\mathsf{Eq}}_m$ for "equality" and $\widetilde{\mathsf{Ltu}}_m$ for "less than (unsigned)", a helper polynomial. The construction of the former is straightforward:

$$\widetilde{\mathsf{Eq}}_m(X, Y) = \prod_{i=0}^{m-1} \left((1 - X_i)(1 - Y_i) + X_i \cdot Y_i \right) \qquad (4)$$

checks whether bitvector chunks X and Y of length m are equal. The i-th factor in the product of Eq. (4) above checks whether the i-th bits in X and Y are the same, returning 1 if so and 0 otherwise. Thus if X and Y mismatch in any position, the entire product is 0. Otherwise, the product is 1.

We embed $\widetilde{\mathsf{Eq}}_m$ into ACL2 and prove it is indeed equivalent to the mathematical semantics of an "equal" function. The entire sequence of events is displayed in Program 1. We define two functions: b-eq-w, which computes whether two bits are equal; and eq-w, which calls b-eq-w recursively along the lengths of two bitvectors. The b* macro in eq-w is a binder that also supports convenient features [7], similar to the Common Lisp let*. The desired theorem is eq-w-equal-equiv, which states that eq-w (or Eq. (4)) is equivalent to equality when x and y are unsigned integers.

The MLE for "less than (unsigned)" is defined by

$$\widetilde{\mathsf{Ltu}}_m(X, Y) = \sum_{i=0}^{m-1} (1 - X_i) \cdot Y_i \cdot \widetilde{\mathsf{Eq}}_i(X_{<i}, Y_{<i}) \qquad (5)$$

Program 2: ACL2 Formalization of $\widetilde{\mathsf{Ltu}}_m$

```
1  ;; Compute the MLE for LTU
2  (define ltu-w ((x :type unsigned-byte) (y :type unsigned-byte)) ...
3    (b* (((unless (and (natp x) (natp y)))                             0)  ;; Edge case
4         ((if (and (zerop (integer-length x)) (zerop (integer-length y)))) 0)  ;; Base case
5         (x-0    (logcar x))                                               ;; LSB of x
6         (y-0    (logcar y))                                               ;; LSB of y
7         (x-rest (logcdr x))                                               ;; Rest of x
8         (y-rest (logcdr y))                                               ;; Rest of y
9         (ltu-0  (b-and (b-and (b-xor 1 x-0) y-0) (eq-w x-rest y-rest)))) ;; Summand
10        (b-xor ltu-0 (ltu-w x-rest y-rest))))                             ;; Recursive case
```

Intuitively, $\widetilde{\mathsf{Ltu}}_m(X,Y)$ recognizes when $X < Y$ because a summand will be nonzero only if the $(i-1)$-th most significant bits are equal, Y_i is high, and X_i is low, i.e. when i is the most significant bit position which determines $X < Y$. We easily verify Eq. (5) is correct for large bitwidths by defining an ACL2 function ltu-w which computes $\widetilde{\mathsf{Ltu}}_m$ and using GL to bitblast its correctness theorem ltu-w-equiv-<-32.

4.2 Verifying an Instruction Involving Subtable Lookups

Now that the MLEs for the SLTU subtables are verified, we proceed with materializing the subtables. We model subtables in ACL2 as association lists, i.e. lists of pairs where the first element in the pair acts as a key and the second element acts as a value. For subtables associated with MLEs, the keys are the operands and the values are the expected results. To make this concrete, consider materialize-eq-subtable in Program 3. Evaluating the function on a list of X and Y operands, such as ((1 . 1) (1 . 0) (0 . 1) (0 . 0)), returns the following subtable:

(((1 . 1) . 1) ((1 . 0) . 0) ((0 . 1) . 0) ((0 . 0) . 1)).

As expected, the values in the subtable are 1 only when X and Y are equal and 0 otherwise. By proving a small number of intermediate lemmas, we automatically obtain a correctness theorem for $\widetilde{\mathsf{Eq}}_m$'s subtable in the form of lookup-eq-subtable-correctness in Program 3. This theorem states that if the operands of interest are indexed in the subtable, then the lookup value is 1 if the operands are equal and 0 otherwise. Very similar functions and theorems are formalized for $\widetilde{\mathsf{Ltu}}_m$; the only substantial difference is that = is replaced with <. The command (create-tuple-indices x-hi y-hi) simply creates the list

((x-hi . y-hi) ... (1 . 1) (1 . 0) (0 . 1) (0 . 0)),

and (tuple-lookup i j subtable) returns the subtable value at (i . j).

We are now ready to tackle SLTU itself. Each Jolt instruction has three stages: chunk, lookup, and combine. For SLTU, integers $x, y \in \{0,1\}^{W=32}$ are chunked into subvectors of size $m = 8$ so that

$$x = x_0\|x_1\|x_2\|x_3, \qquad y = y_0\|y_1\|y_2\|y_3 \qquad (6)$$

Program 3: ACL2 Formalization of Eq$_m$ Subtable

```
;; Given a list of (x y) operands, materialize a list of key-value pairs
;;    key: (x y)       value: (if (= x y) 1 0)
(defun materialize-eq-subtable (idx-lst)
  (b* (((unless (alistp idx-lst))    nil)    ;; Edge case
       ((if (atom idx-lst))           nil)    ;; Base case
       ((cons hd tl)              idx-lst)    ;; Bind head & tail in the index list
       ((unless (consp hd))          nil)    ;; Edge case
       ((cons x y)                    hd))    ;; Bind x & y operands in the head
      ;; Construct a key-value pair and append it to the rest of the eq subtable
      (cons (cons hd (if (= x y) 1 0)) (materialize-eq-subtable tl))))
...
;; Lookup values within the bounds of the subtable are equivalent to "="
(defthm lookup-eq-subtable-correctness
  (implies (and (natp i) (natp j)  (natp x-hi) (natp y-hi) (<= i x-hi) (<= j y-hi))
           (b* ((indices  (create-tuple-indices x-hi y-hi))
                (subtable (materialize-eq-subtable indices)))
               (equal (tuple-lookup i j subtable) (if (= i j) 1 0)))) ... )
```

in preparation for the subtable lookups. Lookups are performed using interwoven chunks as indexes, setting

$$Z_0 := \text{Ltu}_m [x_0 \| y_0], \quad Z_1 := \text{Ltu}_m [x_1 \| y_1], \quad Z_2 := \text{Ltu}_m [x_2 \| y_2], \quad Z_3 := \text{Ltu}_m [x_3 \| y_3],$$
$$W_0 := \text{Eq}_m [x_0 \| y_0], \quad W_1 := \text{Eq}_m [x_1 \| y_1], \quad W_2 := \text{Eq}_m [x_2 \| y_2]. \quad (7)$$

Then combining the results gives

$$\text{SLTU}(x,y) = \sum_{i=0}^{3} Z_i \prod_{j=0}^{i-1} W_j = Z_0 + Z_1 \cdot W_0 + Z_2 \cdot W_0 \cdot W_1 + Z_3 \cdot W_0 \cdot W_1 \cdot W_2. \quad (8)$$

Verifying that Eq. (8) is indeed equivalent to (if (< x y) 1 0) is the ultimate objective, which is Program 4.

We first formalize a version of SLTU without subtables, instead directly calling the intended function of the lookups in this intermediary semantics version of the instruction, which we call sltu-semantics-32. The bindings which involve part-select correspond to Eq. (6). The next sequence of bindings is semantically equivalent to the lookup stage in Eq. (7). The final expression returned is equivalent to Eq. (8). Verification is again a straightforward application of GL. Finally, we define the Jolt version of SLTU, sltu-32. The function sltu-32 is identical to sltu-semantics-32 except that we actually materialize the subtables and perform lookups. We prove it equivalent to the version without lookups, sltu-semantics-32, giving us a chain of equivalences which enable us to conclude that Jolt SLTU is correct.

5 Optimizations and Impact to Jolt's Codebase

An ACL2 analysis of Jolt forces the development of a formal specification for the Jolt components we verify. Formal specification in itself is already an important contribution to any project. Jolt was originally announced in the form of

Program 4: ACL2 Formalization of Jolt SLTU Instruction.

```
1   ;; SLTU without subtables, just lookup semantics
2   (define sltu-semantics-32 ((x (unsigned-byte-p 32 x)) (y (unsigned-byte-p 32 y)))
3     (b* (((unless (unsigned-byte-p 32 x)) 0)                ;; Edge cases
4          ((unless (unsigned-byte-p 32 y)) 0)
5          (x8-3 (part-select x :low  0 :width 8))            ;; Chunk
6          (x8-2 (part-select x :low  8 :width 8))
7          (x8-1 (part-select x :low 16 :width 8))
8          (x8-0 (part-select x :low 24 :width 8))
9          (y8-3 (part-select y :low  0 :width 8))
10         (y8-2 (part-select y :low  8 :width 8))
11         (y8-1 (part-select y :low 16 :width 8))
12         (y8-0 (part-select y :low 24 :width 8))
13         (z0   (if (< x8-0 y8-0) 1 0))                      ;; Lookup semantics
14         (z1   (if (< x8-1 y8-1) 1 0))
15         (z2   (if (< x8-2 y8-2) 1 0))
16         (z3   (if (< x8-3 y8-3) 1 0))
17         (w0   (if (= x8-0 y8-0) 1 0))
18         (w1   (if (= x8-1 y8-1) 1 0))
19         (w2   (if (= x8-2 y8-2) 1 0))
20         (?w3  (if (= x8-3 y8-3) 1 0)))                     ;; ignore w3
21      (+ z0 (* z1 w0) (* z2 w0 w1) (* z3 w0 w1 w2))))       ;; Combine
22
23  ;; Correctness of SLTU intermediate semantics layer
24  (gl::def-gl-thm sltu-semantics-32-correctness
25    :hyp (and (unsigned-byte-p 32 x) (unsigned-byte-p 32 y))
26    :concl (equal (sltu-semantics-32 x y) (if (< x y) 1 0))
27    :g-bindings (gl::auto-bindings (:mix (:nat x 32) (:nat y 32))))
28
29  ;; Define SLTU with subtable lookups
30  (define sltu-32 ((x (unsigned-byte-p 32 x)) (y (unsigned-byte-p 32 y))) ...
31    (b* (((unless (unsigned-byte-p 32 x)) 0)                ;; Edge cases
32         ((unless (unsigned-byte-p 32 y)) 0)
33         (x8-3 (part-select x :low  0 :width 8))            ;; Chunk
34         (x8-2 (part-select x :low  8 :width 8))
35         (x8-1 (part-select x :low 16 :width 8))
36         (x8-0 (part-select x :low 24 :width 8))
37         (y8-3 (part-select y :low  0 :width 8))
38         (y8-2 (part-select y :low  8 :width 8))
39         (y8-1 (part-select y :low 16 :width 8))
40         (y8-0 (part-select y :low 24 :width 8))
41         (indices     (create-tuple-indices (expt 2 8) (expt 2 8)))  ;; Materialize subtables
42         (ltu-subtable (materialize-ltu-subtable indices))
43         (eq-subtable  (materialize-eq-subtable  indices))
44         (z0   (tuple-lookup x8-0 y8-0 ltu-subtable))       ;; Perform Lookups
45         (z1   (tuple-lookup x8-1 y8-1 ltu-subtable))
46         (z2   (tuple-lookup x8-2 y8-2 ltu-subtable))
47         (z3   (tuple-lookup x8-3 y8-3 ltu-subtable))
48         (w0   (tuple-lookup x8-0 y8-0  eq-subtable))
49         (w1   (tuple-lookup x8-1 y8-1  eq-subtable))
50         (w2   (tuple-lookup x8-2 y8-2  eq-subtable))
51         (?w3  (tuple-lookup x8-3 y8-3  eq-subtable)))      ;; ignore w3
52      (+ z0 (* z1 w0) (* z2 w0 w1) (* z3 w0 w1 w2)))        ;; Combine
53    ///
54  ;; Equivalence between sltu-32 & its intermediate semantics version
55    (defthm sltu-32-sltu-semantics-32-equiv
56      (equal (sltu-32 x y) (sltu-semantics-32 x y))
57      :hints (("Goal" :in-theory (enable sltu-semantics-32)))))
58
59  ;; Correctness of Jolt SLTU
60  (defthm sltu-32-correctness
61    (implies (and (unsigned-byte-p 32 x) (unsigned-byte-p 32 y))
62             (equal (sltu-32 x y) (if (< x y) 1 0))))
```

an academic paper, eliding some implementation details. Conversely, the Rust implementation of Jolt contains many undocumented engineering efforts. For example, some MLEs have no mathematical specification beyond their function. Issues such as these are now identified and documented.

We discovered several optimizations to Jolt during the course of our formalization, which were caught automatically by ACL2 and our framework. Consider again the formalization of SLTU in Program 4. Note that the lookup w3 is prefixed by a ?. The b* macro enforces that all bindings should be used in the body unless otherwise indicated, such as with ?. Indeed, w3 is not used to evaluate SLTU but this lookup is still listed in the Jolt paper and previous versions of the Jolt codebase. The same applies for the SLT, BGEU, and BGE instructions.[7] The efficiency gain from this optimization depends on how often these 4 instructions are used, since the prover only "pays" for instructions that get executed. Nevertheless, instruction overhead is linear in the number of lookups necessary; for an instruction like SLTU which originally required 8 lookups, we achieve a 12.5% speedup in prover time by saving 1 lookup.

We also discovered that all shift subtables in the Jolt codebase can be reduced in size. The maximum meaningful shift for 32-bit integers is $32 = 2^5$. Thus a shift subtable need only be size $2^8 \times 2^5 = 2^{13}$, with 2^8 indices for the chunk to be shifted and 2^5 indices for the shift parameter. However, the Jolt Rust implementation materializes a $2^8 \times 2^8 = 2^{16}$ subtable for shifts. Our formalization exhibits a proof that we can reduce Jolt's three shift subtables by 87.5%. This directly translates to reduced cost for shift operations.

6 Conclusion and Future Work

We present a formal model of Lasso-style lookup arguments, and verify all 32-bit base Jolt instruction lookups using ACL2 in a highly automated and validated manner. We also demonstrate the utility of ACL2-based formalization via identifying possible optimizations, resulting in performance improvements for Jolt.

Our work takes the first step towards full formal correctness of Jolt's frontend, demonstrating that an incremental approach to front-end verification (starting with instruction lookups) is both feasible and useful. We have begun verifying the M-extension to Jolt, and plan to extend our formalization to include the other two components of Jolt's front-end (R1CS and memory-checking) in future work.

Acknowledgements. The authors would like to thank Daejun Park, Michael Zhu, Sam Ragsdale, and Srinath Setty for their helpful comments and feedback.

Disclosures. Justin Thaler is a Research Partner at a16z crypto and an investor in various blockchain-based platforms, as well as in the crypto ecosystem more broadly (for general a16z disclosures, see https://www.a16z.com/disclosures/.

---

[7] BLT and BLTU are also RISC-V instructions which benefit from this optimization, but in the Rust code base they are implemented via other comparison instructions.

References

1. ACL2. https://cs.utexas.edu/~moore/acl2/
2. Arun, A., Setty, S.T.V., Thaler, J.: Jolt: SNARKs for virtual machines via lookups. In: Joye, M., Leander, G. (eds.) EUROCRYPT 2024, Part VI. LNCS, vol. 14656, pp. 3–33. Springer, Cham (2024). https://doi.org/10.1007/978-3-031-58751-1_1
3. Avigad, J., Goldberg, L., Levit, D., Seginer, Y., Titelman, A.: A verified algebraic representation of cairo program execution. In: Proceedings of the 11th ACM SIGPLAN International Conference on Certified Programs and Proofs, pp. 153–165 (2022)
4. Avigad, J., Goldberg, L., Levit, D., Seginer, Y., Titelman, A.: A proof-producing compiler for blockchain applications. In: 14th International Conference on Interactive Theorem Proving (ITP 2023). Schloss Dagstuhl-Leibniz-Zentrum für Informatik (2023)
5. Bailey, B., Miller, A.: Formalizing soundness proofs of linear PCP SNARKs. In: Balzarotti, D., Xu, W. (eds.) USENIX Security 2024. USENIX Association (2024)
6. Bosshard, A.G., Bootle, J., Sprenger, C.: Formal verification of the sumcheck protocol. In: 2024 IEEE 37th Computer Security Foundations Symposium (CSF), pp. 205–219. IEEE Computer Society (2024)
7. ACL2 XDOC: B* (2024). https://www.https://www.cs.utexas.edu/~moore/acl2/manuals/latest/?topic=ACL2____B_A2. Accessed 10 Oct 2024
8. CertiK: Verification of zkwasm in coq (2024). https://github.com/CertiKProject/zkwasm-fv
9. Chaliasos, S., Ernstberger, J., Theodore, D., Wong, D., Jahanara, M., Livshits, B.: SoK: what don't we know? Understanding security vulnerabilities in SNARKs. In: Balzarotti, D., Xu, W. (eds.) USENIX Security 2024. USENIX Association (2024)
10. Chin, C., Wu, H., Chu, R., Coglio, A., McCarthy, E., Smith, E.: Leo: a programming language for formally verified, zero-knowledge applications. Cryptology ePrint Archive, Report 2021/651 (2021). https://eprint.iacr.org/2021/651
11. Coglio, A., McCarthy, E., Smith, E., Chin, C., Gaddamadugu, P., Dellepere, M.: Compositional formal verification of zero-knowledge circuits. Cryptology ePrint Archive, Report 2023/1278 (2023). https://eprint.iacr.org/2023/1278
12. Dao, Q., Miller, J., Wright, O., Grubbs, P.: Weak fiat-shamir attacks on modern proof systems. In: 2023 IEEE Symposium on Security and Privacy, pp. 199–216. IEEE Computer Society Press (2023)https://doi.org/10.1109/SP46215.2023.10179408
13. Gabizon, A.: On the security of the BCTV pinocchio zk-SNARK variant. Cryptology ePrint Archive, Report 2019/119 (2019). https://eprint.iacr.org/2019/119
14. Gennaro, R., Gentry, C., Parno, B., Raykova, M.: Quadratic span programs and succinct NIZKs without PCPs. In: Johansson, T., Nguyen, P.Q. (eds.) EUROCRYPT 2013. LNCS, vol. 7881, pp. 626–645. Springer, Heidelberg (2013). https://doi.org/10.1007/978-3-642-38348-9_37
15. Goel, S., Hunt, W.A., Kaufmann, M., Ghosh, S.: Simulation and formal verification of x86 machine-code programs that make system calls. In: 2014 Formal Methods in Computer-Aided Design (FMCAD), pp. 91–98 (2014). https://doi.org/10.1109/FMCAD.2014.6987600
16. Goldberg, L., Papini, S., Riabzev, M.: Cairo – a Turing-complete STARK-friendly CPU architecture. Cryptology ePrint Archive, Report 2021/1063 (2021). https://eprint.iacr.org/2021/1063

17. Goldwasser, S., Micali, S., Rackoff, C.: The knowledge complexity of interactive proof-systems (extended abstract). In: 17th ACM STOC, pp. 291–304. ACM Press (1985). https://doi.org/10.1145/22145.22178
18. Plonkish arithmetization - the halo2 book. https://zcash.github.io/halo2/concepts/arithmetization.html
19. Hunt, W.A., Kaufmann, M., Moore, J.S., Slobodova, A.: Industrial hardware and software verification with ACL2. Philos. Trans. Roy. Soc. London Ser. A **375**(2104) (2017). https://doi.org/10.1098/rsta.2015.0399
20. Jolt (2024). https://github.com/a16z/jolt
21. Kwan, C., Dao, Q., Thaler, J.: Verifying jolt zkVM lookup semantics. Cryptology ePrint Archive, Paper 2024/1841 (2024). https://eprint.iacr.org/2024/1841
22. Liu, H.: Formal Specification and Verification of a JVM and its Bytecode Verifier. The University of Texas at Austin (2006)
23. Liu, J., et al.: Certifying zero-knowledge circuits with refinement types. In: 2024 IEEE Symposium on Security and Privacy (SP), pp. 1741–1759. IEEE (2024)
24. Micali, S.: CS proofs (extended abstracts). In: 35th FOCS, pp. 436–453. IEEE Computer Society Press (1994). https://doi.org/10.1109/SFCS.1994.365746
25. Nguyen, W.D., Boneh, D., Setty, S.: Revisiting the nova proof system on a cycle of curves. In: 5th Conference on Advances in Financial Technologies (2023)
26. Pailoor, S., et al.: Automated detection of under-constrained circuits in zero-knowledge proofs. Proc. ACM Program. Lang. **7**(PLDI), 1510–1532 (2023)
27. Parno, B.: A note on the unsoundness of vnTinyRAM's SNARK. Cryptology ePrint Archive, Report 2015/437 (2015). https://eprint.iacr.org/2015/437
28. Polygon zkevm (2024). https://polygon.technology/polygon-zkevm
29. Ragsdale, S., Zhu, M., Thaler, J.: Understanding Lasso and Jolt, from theory to code (2024). https://a16zcrypto.com/posts/article/building-on-lasso-and-jolt/
30. Risc zero (2024). https://risczero.com/
31. Scroll - native zkevm layer 2 for ethereum (2024). https://scroll.io/
32. Setty, S.: Spartan: efficient and general-purpose zkSNARKs without trusted setup. In: Micciancio, D., Ristenpart, T. (eds.) CRYPTO 2020. LNCS, vol. 12172, pp. 704–737. Springer, Cham (2020). https://doi.org/10.1007/978-3-030-56877-1_25
33. Setty, S.T.V., Thaler, J., Wahby, R.S.: Unlocking the lookup singularity with Lasso. In: Joye, M., Leander, G. (eds.) EUROCRYPT 2024, Part VI. LNCS, vol. 14656, pp. 180–209. Springer, Cham (2024). https://doi.org/10.1007/978-3-031-58751-1_7
34. Succinct (2024). https://succinct.xyz/
35. Swords, S., Davis, J.: Bit-blasting ACL2 theorems. Electron. Proc. Theor. Comput. Sci. **70**, 84–102 (2011). https://doi.org/10.4204/eptcs.70.7
36. Thaler, J.: Approaching the 'lookup singularity': introducing Lasso and Jolt (2024). https://a16zcrypto.com/posts/article/introducing-lasso-and-jolt/
37. Whitehat, B.: Lookup singularity (2024). https://zkresear.ch/t/lookup-singularity/65/7
38. ACL2 XDOC: User manual for the ACL2 theorem prover (2024). https://www.cs.utexas.edu/~moore/acl2/manuals/current/manual/. Accessed 10 Oct 2024
39. Zkm (2024). https://www.zkm.io/
40. Delphinus lab (2024). https://delphinuslab.com/
41. Zksync (2024). https://zksync.io/

Prooφ: A ZKP Market Mechanism

Wenhao Wang[1](✉), Lulu Zhou[1], Aviv Yaish[1], Fan Zhang[1], Ben Fisch[1], and Benjamin Livshits[2]

[1] Yale University, New Haven, CT, USA
{wenhao.wang,lulu.zhou,aviv.yaish,f.zhang,benjamin.fisch}@yale.edu
[2] Imperial College London, London, UK
livshits@ic.ac.uk

Abstract. Zero-knowledge proofs (ZKPs) are computationally demanding to generate. Their importance for applications like ZK-Rollups has prompted some to outsource ZKP generation to a market of specialized provers. However, existing market designs either do not fit the ZKP setting or lack formal description and analysis.

In this work, we propose a formal ZKP market model that captures the interactions between users submitting ZKP tasks and provers competing to generate proofs. Building on this model, we introduce *Prooφ*, an auction-based ZKP market mechanism. We prove that *Prooφ* is incentive compatible for users and provers, and budget balanced. We augment *Prooφ* with system-level designs to address the practical challenges of our setting, such as Sybil attacks, misreporting of prover capacity, and collusion. We analyze our system-level designs and show how they can mitigate the various security concerns.

1 Introduction

Zero-knowledge proofs (ZKPs) enable efficient verification of computation and are used by blockchain scalability solutions (e.g., ZK-Rollups [26,28,30]), user authentication [3], data oracles [32], and many more. Despite recent efficiency improvements, generating ZKPs remains computationally expensive [7], often requiring specialized infrastructure (e.g., GPU or ASIC). This has naturally led to the emergence of *ZKP markets* [1,13,24] that allow users to outsource proof generation to specialized provers. Ideally, an effective market will not only improve user experience but also lower user costs by fostering competition among provers. However, since such markets operate in an open and decentralized environment, challenges arise because users and provers might be malicious.

Market designs by both industry and academia [1,13,25,28] are limited. For example, the elegant work of Gong et al. [14] considers a market comprising one user and multiple provers. However, proving multiple user transactions in batches is a key performance optimization in ZK-Rollups. Moreover, ZKP applications, such as ZK-Rollups, are already serving a substantial user base [18], highlighting the need for mechanisms that address multi-user scenarios. On the other hand, the mechanism advanced by the commercial prover market Gevulot [13] supports multiple users but relies on a fixed fee for all tasks, implying users willing to pay more may have to wait longer than those willing to pay less. A survey of the literature (see Sect. 2) shows that other proposed mechanisms either do not apply to our setting or lack formal specifications and analysis.

This Work. We formally model ZKP markets and dissect several designs. In particular, we propose *Prooφ*, a ZKP market mechanism that comprises a *core auction mechanism* and *system-level designs*. At a high level, the core mechanism of *Prooφ* runs an auction between users and provers and allocates a set of low-cost provers with another set of high-value user tasks. We formally analyze the properties of the core mechanism and show that it is budget-balanced and guarantees incentive compatibility of market participants. We then introduce system-level designs to enhance the core mechanism and mitigate security threats that the core auction mechanism alone cannot address, and provide an analysis of how these designs defend against untruthful capacity bids, Sybil attacks, and collusion. The main challenges lie in modeling the ZKP market to capture the setup of practical systems, achieving desired security properties through game-theoretic designs (e.g., with auctions) and system-level designs (e.g., using cryptography), and developing rigorous formal analysis.

1.1 ZKP Market Model

We consider a model comprising users, who have ZKP generation tasks, and provers, who finish user tasks for rewards. The market operates in rounds of auctions, and each auction handles a specific *type* of tasks, i.e., tasks of the same circuit and ZKP scheme. In each auction, users submit tasks and specify a fee f for each task. The fee reflects how much the user values this task, also called the *value* of a task. Meanwhile, each prover specifies a capacity s, i.e., the number of tasks they can handle within a predefined time frame (tailored to application needs), and their unit cost p i.e., the cost to finish one given task. Given user tasks and provers' capacities and unit costs, a market mechanism decides *allocation* and *payments*: it selects a subset of tasks that are to be proven, and for each one, the prover that would generate the associated proof, the user's payment, and the amount that can be collected as revenue by the prover. Note that user payments and the prover's revenue may differ from user-chosen fees.

Our model explicitly captures the fact that practical provers produce proofs in batch, by allocating user tasks in batches. Assigning tasks of the same type to one prover is more efficient than assigning them to different provers, as it avoids context-switching costs (e.g., loading proving keys and circuits to the memory) and can leverage efficient batch proofs available in some ZKP schemes [4,9,17]. Although we use ZK-Rollup terminologies, our market model applies to other systems that include a market of verifiable services, such as zkLogin [3], where users need to generate ZKPs to authenticate their identity.

1.2 Our Core Market Mechanism: $Proo\varphi$

Inspired by second-price auction mechanisms such as VCG [29] and classic double auction mechanisms [19], we present our core ZKP market mechanism named $Proo\varphi$. In this mechanism, we guarantee incentive compatibility by paying each allocated prover the "second price", i.e., the price reported by the unallocated prover with the lowest cost, and ensuring each allocated prover's capacity is used in full. Concretely, the mechanism first hypothetically allocates the highest-paying user tasks to the lowest-cost provers and stops when reaching a task with a fee that no longer covers the cost of the prover. The mechanism then selects this hypothetical set of provers excluding the one with the highest unit cost, and selects the highest value tasks up to the capacity of the selected provers. The core mechanism of $Proo\varphi$ is specified below.

Core Mechanism of $Proo\varphi$

- The mechanism collects user bids $\{f_i\}_{i=1}^n$, and prover bids $\{(s_j, p_j)\}_{j=1}^N$ with $f_1 \geq \cdots \geq f_n$ and $p_1 \leq \cdots \leq p_N$. Let $\bar{S}_j := \sum_{i=1}^{j} s_i$ denote the sum of the first j provers' capacities.
- The mechanism determines the largest ℓ such that $p_{j+1} \leq f_{(\bar{S}_j+1)}$, i.e., $\ell = \arg\max_j \{p_{j+1} \leq f_{(\bar{S}_j+1)}\}$. The first ℓ provers are allocated in full, with the first $\bar{S}_\ell$ user tasks.
- Each selected user is charged $f_{\bar{S}_\ell+1}$. Each selected prover with index $j \in [1, \ell]$ is $s_j \cdot p_{\ell+1}$.

To provide intuition, we run the mechanism through a simple example.

Example 1. Suppose a market with 8 tasks with values $(10, 10, 10, 10, 9, 9, 1, 1)$, and 3 provers with capacities s_i and costs p_i such that $(s_1, p_1) = (4, 0), (s_2, p_2) = (2, 1), (s_3, p_3) = (2, 10)$. When all parties are bidding honestly, we have $\ell = 1$. The first $\bar{S}_\ell = \sum_{j=1}^{\ell} s_j = 4$ task are allocated, and are charged $f_{\bar{S}_\ell+1} = 9$. Prover 1 is paid $p_{\ell+1} = 1$ per task, and has utility $(1 - 0) \times 4 = 4$.

One interpretation is that we first greedily match high-paying tasks with low-cost provers until none are left. E.g., p_1 is matched f_1 through f_4, and so on. Then, we compare a prover k's cost p_k with the highest fee of her matched tasks (which is precisely $f_{\bar{S}_{k-1}+1}$). E.g., compare p_1 with f_1, p_2 with f_5, and p_3 with f_7. Let's call a prover *feasible* if $p_k \leq f_{\bar{S}_{k-1}+1}$. Finally, the mechanism allocates *all but the last* feasible provers to their full capacity and calls the number of allocated provers ℓ. In this example, p_1 and p_2 are feasible, so $\ell = 1$. The last feasible prover's cost and its highest-paying task's fee set the prices for provers and users, respectively. I.e., provers are paid $p_{\ell+1}$ and users are charged $f_{\bar{S}_\ell+1}$.

We prove $Proo\varphi$ achieves several desirable properties. It is *budget-balanced* (Proposition 1), i.e., the payments to provers are always covered by the fees collected from users. Moreover, it is *incentive compatible* for users and provers to bid honestly (Propositions 2 and 3).

1.3 Implementing $Proo\varphi$ in an Open ZKP Market

The core mechanism alone leaves certain security threats open, thus we enhance it with system-level solutions, including slashing, fixing prover capacity bids over multiple rounds, and encrypting bids to hide information required for profitable deviations such as misreporting of prover capacity, Sybil attacks, and collusion. When considering risk-averse actors (in line with previous work making the same assumption [5,6,8,23]), our solutions thwart possible risk-free threats.

Incorrect or Missing Proofs. To ensure the correctness and timeliness of the completion of the ZKP tasks, we require provers to deposit collateral when joining the protocol, and seize the collateral of provers who generate incorrect ZKPs or do not generate them in a timely manner (as detailed in Sect. 5.1).

Misreporting Capacity. The core $Proo\varphi$ mechanism is incentive compatible for provers, meaning that they truthfully report their *proving costs*. However, provers may profitably deviate in other ways, such as by misreporting their *capacity*. In Proposition 4, we prove that such deviations are worthwhile only when the bids of other users and provers satisfy a narrow condition, implying that dishonest provers would have to monitor user bids and adjust their reported capacities correspondingly. Following this observation and given that a prover's capacity is not likely to change drastically in a short amount of time, the threat can be mitigated by restricting the changes of the capacity bid over time; for example, a prover can only change the capacity every n rounds by m folds (where n, m are parameters, possibly adjusted via, e.g., community votes in a DAO).

Table 1. Summary of prover market designs.

Protocol	User Payment	Prover Selection	Payment to Provers
$Proo\varphi$	second price	lowest price	second price × allocated capacity
=nil;	limit order book	limit order book	limit order book
Taiko	posted price	random selection	prover-specified payment
Scroll	first price	random selection	partially subsidized
Gevulot	posted price	random selection	posted price × allocated capacity

Sybil Attacks. A malicious prover could pose as multiple actors (provers or users) and mount *Sybil attacks*: a prover may create several Sybil provers or submit "fake" user tasks [10]. In Proposition 6, we prove that the threat of such attacks is limited. Particularly, a prover splitting into multiple provers never harms the social welfare if such an attack is profitable. In the other case, where a prover generates fake user bids to gain more profit, we show that such attacks are only profitable when the bids of the other users and provers satisfy certain conditions. We show in Proposition 5 that if the prover has no information on the bids submitted by other parties, there always exists a possible configuration of these bids that would result in the prover having a loss. Therefore, this type of Sybil attack can be mitigated by concealing user and prover bids from the provers, i.e., making the auctions sealed-bid.

Collusion. Collusion can occur among different actors, e.g., users and provers or among a group of provers. In Propositions 7 and 8, we show that for the collusion to be definitely profitable, the colluders need to have full information of the other parties' bids. Therefore, these types of collusion can be intuitively mitigated using a similar approach as we use for Sybil attacks, i.e., hiding the bids of other parties from provers. Still, our protocol cannot properly circumvent all collusion (e.g., all provers can collude with each other and form a monopoly), but it is common for mechanism designs to disregard collusion [14,15].

2 Related Work

Commercial Mechanisms for ZKP Markets. Several commercial platforms suggested ZKP market mechanisms without formal analysis. Gevulot [13] uses posted prices to determine the set of provers (i.e., the same predetermined fee per task is paid to selected provers); Taiko [25] lets provers set their prices; Scroll [28] selects and partially subsidizes the lowest-cost provers and pays them with their bid; =nil; [1] facilitates price discovery by maintaining a limit order book for each circuit with buy orders from users and sell orders from provers. An order is executed when the buying and selling prices meet. In Table 1, we list the protocols across three dimensions: how provers are selected ("Prover Selection"), how user payments are determined ("User Payment"), and how the profit of provers is decided ("Payment to Provers").

Other Computation Outsourcing Mechanisms. Thyagarajan et al. [27] propose OpenSquare, a Verifiable Delay Function (VDF) market that incentivizes maximum server participation, which is resistant to censorship and single-point failures. In a broader sense, ZKP markets are computation outsourcing markets. In V3rified [14], the fee mechanism for computational tasks is categorized into revelation ones (i.e., an auction where provers bid their costs) and non-revelation ones (the client posts its task with a given fee) and characterize their power and limitations. The protocols in V3rified cannot be directly applied to our model, as they are tailored for multiple provers proving one user task.

Double Auctions. Our setting is of a two-sided market: on the demand side, users submit transactions that require proving, while on the supply side, provers provide proving capacity. Double auctions are commonly used to coordinate trade in such markets, i.e., to choose which agents get to trade and at what prices. While there is some overlap between the "traditional" setting explored by auction theory literature and the ZKP market setting, we note that the latter introduces new challenges: provers may collude, either amongst themselves or with users, and provers have a capacity parameter to bid. McAfee [19] presents a mechanism that is incentive compatible, individually rational, and budget-balanced for unit-demand buyers and unit-supply sellers (i.e., each buyer wishes to purchase a single item, and each seller offers a single item for sale). Huang, SchellerWolf, and Sycara [15] show a mechanism that is also incentive compatible, individually rational, and budget-balanced for multi-unit buyers and sellers (i.e., buyers may want multiple items, and suppliers may sell multiple items). However, their work assumes public capacity information and no collusion, and they are not a direct generalization of our mechanism to multi-item buyers. Although outside the scope of our work, we refer readers interested in a broad review of the literature to the survey of Parsons, Rodriguez-Aguilar, and Klein [21], which covers a variety of auction formats, including double auctions.

3 Model

3.1 ZKP Market

In a ZKP market, user-specified ZKP generation tasks are outsourced to specialized parties (i.e., provers) for a price. The market is specified by a core mechanism and a system-level protocol. We now elaborate on these components.

Roles. We use n to denote the number of users in the market, and each user has a ZKP generation task. Each user task has a value f that the user is willing to pay to complete the task. There are N provers in the market willing to complete ZKP generation tasks for rewards. Each prover has a ZKP generation capacity s, i.e., the number of tasks it can complete within a fixed time window, and a unit cost p, i.e., its cost to complete one ZKP task. Note that in our model, we assume that each prover's total cost is the sum of the costs of all its tasks. Besides users and provers, a coordinator (or auctioneer) is responsible for collecting bids from users and provers and executing the market system and mechanism. For instance, when applied to ZK-Rollups, the centralized sequencer can be the auctioneer.

Core Market Mechanism. In each round, the market mechanism selects a set of user tasks that can be proven and an allocation of the tasks to the provers. Additionally, the core mechanism determines the amount of fee that needs to be collected from each user and determines the payment to each prover.

Market System. The market system specifies the additional steps and requirements for users and provers during the execution of the market mechanism. An example is that the provers deposit some collateral before they are eligible to submit bids in the market. The goal of the market system is to work in synergy with the market mechanism to secure the market against security threats.

Utilities. Here we introduce the utility of the market participants. We assume that all parties are myopic, i.e., they are only concerned with their utility within one round of market. We further assume that the auctioneer is trusted and therefore does not have a utility to maximize. For a user whose valuation of its task is f and pays f', if the task is selected, its utility is $f - f'$; otherwise, if the task is not selected, its utility is $-f'$. For a prover whose unit cost is p, and is paid w and allocated s' tasks, then its utility is $w - s' \cdot p$.

3.2 Threat Model

Both users and provers can act strategically and deviate from the protocol arbitrarily. The attacks on the market may occur in the following forms.

Incorrect or Missing ZKPs. Provers may fail to generate correct ZKPs in the allotted time, whether intentionally or otherwise.

Misreporting Bids. Both users and provers may not bid truthfully. If any actor can benefit from misreporting its bid, we consider this as an attack.

Sybil Attacks. Besides misreporting bids, a user or a prover may pose as multiple actors and submit fake bids. Sybil attacks can occur when a prover submits bids as fake users or a prover submits bids as fake provers.

Collusion. Users and provers may collude to bid strategically to increase their joint utility. Not all forms of collisions harm players outside the coalition, but those that do are considered a security threat.

Remark 1. Previous work on TFMs typically adopted a non-Bayesian perspective, including when analyzing different possible threats, i.e., misreporting values, Sybil attacks, and collusion [2,5,11,12,22]. In practice, blockchain actors such as Bitcoin miners who invest resources to receive rewards may prefer to minimize the financial risk entailed in their operation, with prior work seeing this as an explanation for the popularity of mining pools. Therefore, we follow previous work that modeled actors as risk-averse [6,8,23,31], who will deviate from the honest behavior only if it would certainly improve their payoffs [5]. We note that alternative models could lead to interesting future work (see Sect. 6).

3.3 Desiderata

Following prior work [19,22], we devise a desiderata for ZKP market mechanisms.

Budget Balance. In a ZKP market, the fees collected from users in each round should cover the payment to provers, a property called *budget balance*.

Definition 1 (Budget Balance (BB)). *A mechanism is* budget-balanced *if the fees collected from the users are no less than the sum of payment to provers.*

Incentive Compatibility. Our mechanism should incentivize actors to truthfully report their values, i.e., it should satisfy Definition 2. In Definitions 3 and 4 we provide the corresponding definitions for users and provers, respectively.

Definition 2 (Dominant Strategy Incentive Compatibility (DSIC)). *A mechanism is dominant strategy incentive compatible if it is always best for each participant to bid its true valuation.*

Definition 3 (User DSIC (UDSIC)). *A mechanism UDSIC if the mechanism is DSIC for users.*

Definition 4 (Prover DSIC (PDSIC)). *A mechanism is PDSIC if it is DSIC for provers to bid their costs honestly.*

Here we note that with PDSIC, it is still possible that a prover may misreport its capacity and get extra utility.

Sybil Proofness. Provers submitting bids under fake identities should not negatively impact social welfare if creating Sybils is profitable. Recall that provers can bid under fake prover or user identities. We define them respectively as *prover Sybil proofness* (Definition 5) and *user Sybil proofness* (Definition 6).

Definition 5 (Prover Sybil Proofness). *A mechanism is prover-Sybil-proof if other parties' utilities are not reduced when any prover profits from creating prover Sybils.*

Definition 6 (User Sybil Proofness). *A mechanism is user-Sybil-proof if others' utilities are not reduced when any prover profits from creating user Sybils.*

Collusion Resistance. A ZKP market mechanism is collusion resistant if a coalition of provers and users (Definition 7) or a coalition of provers (Definition 8) results in higher joint utility and harms the utility of other parties.

Definition 7 (User Collusion Resistance). *A ZKP market mechanism is user collusion resistant if a coalition of provers and users cannot simultaneously result in higher joint utility and harm the utility of other parties.*

Definition 8 (Prover Collusion Resistance). *A ZKP market mechanism is prover collusion resistant if a coalition of provers cannot simultaneously result in higher joint utility and harm the utility of other parties.*

4 Core Mechanism of *Prooφ*

In this section, we analyze the game-theoretic properties of the core mechanism (as specified in Sect. 3.3): we prove that it satisfies Budget Balance (Proposition 1), UDSIC (Proposition 2), and PDSIC (Proposition 3). In the interest of space, we defer some of the proofs to the full version of the paper.

Budget Balance. A ZKP market mechanism is budget-balanced if the fees collected from all users are no less than the total payments to the provers.

Proposition 1. *The Prooφ mechanism is BB.*

Proof. According to the *Prooφ* mechanism, each allocated task is charged $f_{\bar{s}_\ell+1}$, and each allocated prover is paid the unit price $p_{\ell+1}$. Since the mechanism guarantees that $f_{\bar{s}_\ell+1} \geq p_{\ell-1}$, it must be budget-balanced. □

User Incentive Compatibility. A ZKP market mechanism is UDSIC if the mechanism is DSIC for users (Definition 3). In Proposition 2, we prove that the core mechanism of *Prcoφ* is UDSIC.

Proposition 2. *The Prooφ mechanism is UDSIC.*

Proof. We show that for any user, bidding differently than its valuation is not profitable. Suppose user i changes its bid from f_i to f. We re-label the modified user bids as $f'_1 \geq \cdots \geq f'_n$. Similarly, we use primed variables throughout the proof to denote variables after user i changes its bid, and those without primes denote variables before that. I.e., ℓ' is the number of allocated provers and $\bar{S}'_{\ell'}$ the allocated number of tasks after i's change. Note that prover bids do not change by assumption, so $p'_j = p_j$ and $\bar{S}'_j = \bar{S}_j$ for all $j = 1, \cdots, N$.

We say a task has *rank* i if its fee is the i-th highest among all tasks. We denote the rank of user i's task before and after the deviation with $R(i)$ and $R'(i)$, respectively. We now discuss the utility of user i in two cases: when the task is allocated before the change (i.e., $R(i) \in [1, \bar{S}_\ell]$), and when it is not.

Case 1: User i is allocated before changing the bid. By the assumption that user i's task is allocated before deviation, the fee f_i is at least $f_{\bar{S}_\ell+1}$, i.e., $f_i \geq f_{\bar{S}_\ell+1}$. By the definition of our mechanism, $p_{\ell+1} \leq f_{\bar{S}_\ell+1}$ (as shown in Fig. 1) We now consider two sub-cases, based on whether $f < f_{\bar{S}_\ell+1}$ or not, i.e., whether the modified fee is less than the "second" price before deviating.

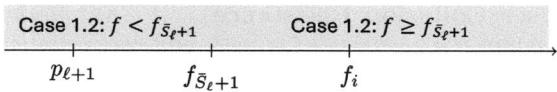

Fig. 1. Two of the sub-cases examined in the proof of Proposition 2.

If $f \geq f_{\bar{S}_\ell+1}$, we show that the task of user i is still allocated, and the second price does not change. Otherwise, if $f < f_{\bar{S}_\ell+1}$, we show that the task of user i is not allocated. In both, the utility of user i does not increase.

Case 1.1: $f \geq f_{\bar{S}_\ell+1}$. We now show that in this case, user i is still allocated and the payment $f'_{\bar{S}'_{\ell'}+1}$ remains the same as $f_{\bar{S}_\ell+1}$.

Firstly, we show that $R'(i) \leq \bar{S}_\ell$. By assumption ($f \geq f_{\bar{S}_\ell+1}$ and $f_i \geq f_{\bar{S}_\ell+1}$), tasks with a rank greater than $\bar{S}_\ell$ before the deviation will have the same rank after the deviation. Figure 2 shows an intuitive example.

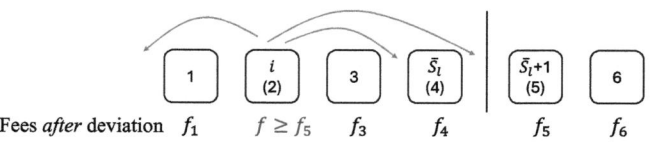

Fig. 2. Example used in case 1.1 to show $R'(i) \leq \bar{S}_\ell$. Labels show the ranks of tasks before i's deviation. After the deviation, i's new rank $R'(i) \leq 4$, because $f \geq f_{\bar{S}_\ell+1}$.

In this example, $i = 2$ and $\bar{S}_\ell = 4$. After user i changes its bid such that $f \geq f_{\bar{S}_\ell+1}$, tasks with rank 5 and 6 will still have the same rank, so $R'(i)$ can only be in $[1,4]$. In general, it follows that $R'(i) \leq \bar{S}_\ell$.

Secondly, we prove that $\ell' = \ell$, by showing that $\ell' \geq \ell$ and $\ell' \leq \ell$. To see that $\ell' \geq \ell$, recall that $\ell \stackrel{\text{def}}{=} \arg\max_j\{p_{j+1} \leq f_{\bar{S}_j+1}\}$, and $\ell' \stackrel{\text{def}}{=} \arg\max_j\{p'_{j+1} \leq f'_{\bar{S}'_j+1}\}$. As argued previously, $f'_{\bar{S}_\ell+1} = f_{\bar{S}_\ell+1}$ and $R'(i) \leq \bar{S}_\ell$ (c.f. Figure 2). In addition, note that $p'_{\ell+1} = p_{\ell+1}$ and $\bar{S}'_\ell = \bar{S}_\ell$ since prover bids are not changed, indicating $f'_{\bar{S}_\ell+1} = f'_{\bar{S}'_\ell+1}$. It follows then $p'_{\ell+1} = p_{\ell+1} \leq f_{\bar{S}_\ell+1} = f'_{\bar{S}_\ell+1} = f'_{\bar{S}'_\ell+1}$. Since ℓ' is the maximum of all such ℓ's, we have $\ell' \geq \ell$.

To see $\ell' \leq \ell$, consider any $\ell^* > \ell$. We have $p_{\ell^*+1} > f_{\bar{S}_{\ell^*}+1}$ by the definition of ℓ. Note that $f'_{\bar{S}_{\ell^*}+1} = f_{\bar{S}_{\ell^*}+1}$, since $\bar{S}_{\ell^*}+1 > \bar{S}_\ell$ by the definition of $\bar{S}$, and that tasks with a rank greater than $\bar{S}_\ell$ will have the same rank after the deviation (as argued previously). Further recall that $p'_{\ell^*+1} = p_{\ell^*+1}$ and $\bar{S}_{\ell^*} = \bar{S}'_{\ell^*}$ since prover bids are not changed. It follows that $p'_{\ell^*+1} = p_{\ell^*+1} > f_{\bar{S}_{\ell^*}+1} = f'_{\bar{S}_{\ell^*}+1} = f'_{\bar{S}'_{\ell^*}+1}$. Since $p'_{\ell^*+1} > f'_{\bar{S}'_{\ell^*}+1}$ for any $\ell^* > \ell$, ℓ must be at least maximum, i.e., $\ell' \leq \ell$.

In summary, $\ell' = \ell$. We now can derive $\bar{S}'_{\ell'}$, the number of allocated tasks after the deviation: $\bar{S}'_{\ell'} = \bar{S}'_\ell = \bar{S}_\ell$. Since $R'(i) \leq \bar{S}_\ell = \bar{S}'_{\ell'}$ as argued previously, task i remains allocated after the deviation. The payment after deviating is $f'_{\bar{S}'_{\ell'}+1} = f'_{\bar{S}_\ell+1} = f_{\bar{S}_\ell+1}$, as before. Thus, the utility of user i remains the same.

The proof for case 1.2 (when $f < f_{\bar{S}_\ell+1}$, user i's task will not be allocated after the user changes its bid) is similar to that for case 1.1; the proof for case 2 is more involved as it incorporates more sub-cases. □

Prover Incentive Compatibility. Considering the prover side, recall that a ZKP market is PDSIC if the mechanism is DSIC for the provers to bid their costs honestly. We show that the *Prooφ* mechanism is PDSIC.

Proposition 3. *The Prooφ mechanism is PDSIC.*

Proof. We show that it is not profitable for any prover to bid other than its valuation. Recall that the users' bids satisfy $f_1 \geq \cdots \geq f_n$, and the provers' bids satisfy $p_1 \leq \cdots \leq p_N$. We assume that the prover j changes its bid from p_j to p, and suppose after the bid change, the new user bids are $f'_1 \geq \cdots \geq f'_n$, and the new prover bids are $p'_1 \leq \cdots \leq p'_N$. (All notations with primes denote the variables after prover j changes its bid, but note that the user bids are not changed, i.e., $f'_i = f_i$ for all $i = 1, \cdots, n$.) Let ℓ' be the number of allocated provers is and $\bar{S}'_{\ell'}$ be the number of allocated tasks.

A prover is said to have *rank* j if its cost is the j-th lowest among all provers. We denote the rank of prover j before and after changing its bid with $R(j)$ and $R'(j)$. We now discuss the utility change of prover j in two cases: when the prover is allocated before the change (i.e., $R(j) \leq \ell$), and when it is not.

Case 1: Prover j is allocated before changing the bid. By the assumption that prover j is allocated, the cost p_j is at most $p_{\ell+1}$, i.e., $p_j \leq p_{\ell+1}$. By the mechanism we have $p_{\ell+1} \leq f_{\bar{S}_\ell+1}$. The proof proceeds in two cases depending on whether $p > p_{\ell+1}$, i.e., the cost p is greater than the "second-price" of the provers. If $p \leq p_{\ell+1}$, we show that prover j is still allocated, and the second price does not change. Otherwise, we prover that prover j is not allocated. In either case, prover j's utility does not increase.

Case 1.1: $p \leq p_{\ell+1}$. We now show that in this case, prover j will still be allocated and the payment $s_j \cdot p'_{\ell'+1}$ remains the same as $s_j \cdot p_{\ell+1}$.

First, we show that $R'(j) \leq \ell$. By assumption, we have $p \leq p_{\ell+1}$ and $p_j \leq p_{\ell+1}$, thus provers with rank greater than ℓ before prover j changes its bid will have the same rank after it changes its bid. It follows that $R'(j) \leq \ell$.

Second, we show that $\ell' = \ell$, as $\ell' \geq \ell$ and $\ell' \leq \ell$. Recall that by definition, $\ell = \arg\max_k \{p_{k+1} \leq f_{\bar{S}_k+1}\}$, and $\ell' = \arg\max_k \{p'_{k+1} \leq f'_{\bar{S}'_k+1}\}$. To see that $\ell' \geq \ell$, note that $\bar{S}'_\ell = \bar{S}_\ell$ and $p'_{\ell+1} = p_{\ell+1}$, because the provers with rank greater than ℓ before prover j changes its bid will have the same rank after prover j changes its bid (as argued previously). Further recall that $f'_{\bar{S}_\ell} = f_{\bar{S}_\ell}$ since user bids are not changed. It follows that $p'_{\ell+1} = p_{\ell+1} \leq f_{\bar{S}_\ell+1} = f'_{\bar{S}_\ell+1} = f'_{\bar{S}'_\ell+1}$. So, $\ell' \geq \ell$ by the definition of ℓ'.

To see $\ell' \leq \ell$, consider any $\ell^* > \ell$, and $p_{\ell^*+1} > f_{\bar{S}_{\ell^*}+1}$ by the definition of ℓ. Because the provers with rank greater than ℓ before prover j changes its bid will have the same rank after prover j changes its bid (as argued previously), $p'_{\ell^*+1} = p_{\ell^*+1}$ and $\bar{S}'_{\ell^*} = \bar{S}_{\ell^*}$. Note that $f'_{\bar{S}_{\ell^*}+1} = f_{\bar{S}_{\ell^*}+1}$ since user bids are not changed. It follows that $p'_{\ell^*+1} = p_{\ell^*+1} > f_{\bar{S}_{\ell^*}+1} = f'_{\bar{S}_{\ell^*}+1} = f'_{\bar{S}'_{\ell^*}+1}$. Since $p'_{\ell^*+1} > f'_{\bar{S}'_{\ell^*}+1}$ for any $\ell^* > \ell$, $\ell' \leq \ell$ by the definition of ℓ'. In summary, $\ell' = \ell$.

We now have the allocation after prover j changes its bid: $p'_{\ell'+1} = p'_{\ell+1} = p_{\ell+1}$. Therefore, prover j will still be allocated. Moreover, since the payment to of prover j is $p'_{\ell'+1} \cdot s_j = p_{\ell+1} \cdot s_j$, the utility of prover j will remain the same.

The proof of case 1.2 (when $p > p_{\ell+1}$, prover j will not be allocated after it changes its bid) and the proof of case 2 are more involved. □

5 Implementing *Proo*φ in an ZKP Market

In the previous section, we have shown that *Proo*φ has desirable game-theoretic properties. However, the core mechanism alone leaves certain security threats open. In this section, we present system-level designs to mitigate them. As before, missing proofs are given in the full version of the paper.

5.1 Missing or Incorrect ZKPs

It is possible that an allocated prover does not generate the required ZKPs. To address this concern, we require each prover to deposit collateral when joining the protocol. The collateral is used to refund users whose tasks were not generated on time. Specifically, suppose the market designer sets a public "refund" limit for user tasks that are not completed, up to a value of $\bar{p}$. This effectively serves as an upper bound on user valuations: if the refund $\bar{p}$ seems too low to some users, they can choose not to send their task to the ZKP market. Then, a prover with capacity s needs to maintain a deposit of at least $\bar{p} \cdot s$ when it bids (s, p). Note that $p < \bar{p}$. If the prover does not finish the allocated task in time, its deposit will be confiscated (causing it to lose $s \cdot \bar{p}$ utility) and used to refund $\bar{p}$ to each affected user, which is no less than the fees they paid. We note that this way of setting the collateral matches industry-adopted practices such as [24].

5.2 Misreporting Capacity

Proposition 3 proved that provers are incentivized to bid their costs honestly. However, a prover may misreport its *capacity*, as demonstrated in Example 2.

Example 2. We continue with Example 1, where when all parties bid honestly, $\ell = 1$ and prover 1 gets $(1 - 0) \times 4 = 4$ utility. However, when prover 1 bids capacity 1 instead of 4, $\ell = 2$ and prover 1 gets $(10 - 0) \times 1 = 10$ utility. The allocation is shown pictorially as follows.

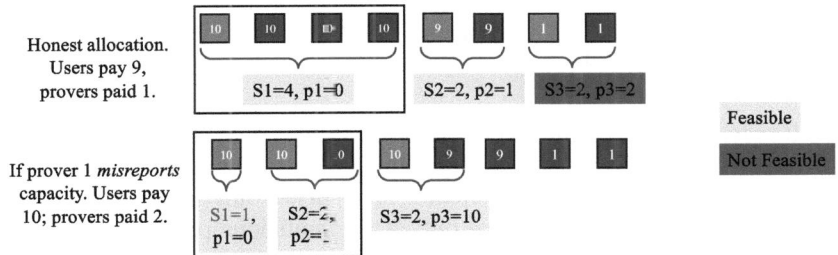

This example suggests that reporting a lower capacity in some cases can render more provers feasible, increasing the prover's payment. Worst yet, fewer users are allocated in the market, and those allocated must pay more. However, in Proposition 4, we observe that the above attack is profitable only under specific market conditions. The mitigation we propose is based on this observation.

Proposition 4. *When a prover $j < N$ submits a smaller capacity bid than its true capacity, there will always be some prover and user bids that result in the prover receiving lower utility compared to if it had bid honestly, assuming all other provers are bidding honestly.*

Mitigation: Fixing Capacity. As the profitability of the above attack depends on user bids, one mitigation is to have provers submit their capacity bids before users. The uncertainty of user bids creates a risk for provers. Another approach is to fix prover capacity for several rounds, to prevent provers from strategically adjusting capacities based on market conditions. In practice, a prover's capacity is unlikely to change drastically in a short amount of time.

5.3 User Sybil Proofness

We show in Example 3 the core mechanism alone is not user Sybil proof, i.e., provers can profit by creating fake user bids.

Example 3. Suppose there are 8 user tasks with values $(10, 10, 10, 2, 2, 2, 2, 2)$, and 3 provers with capacities s_i and costs p_i $(s_1, p_1) = (4, 0), (s_2, p_2) = (2, 2), (s_3, p_3) = (2, 9)$. When all parties bid honestly, we have $\ell = 1$ and prover 1 can make $(2 - 0) \times 4 = 8$. However, prover 1 can create 4 Sybil tasks with a bid of 9. Then we have $\ell = 2$, and prover 1 will make $\underbrace{(9 - 0) \times 4}_{\text{prover reward}} - \underbrace{9 \times 3}_{\text{task cost}} = 9$.

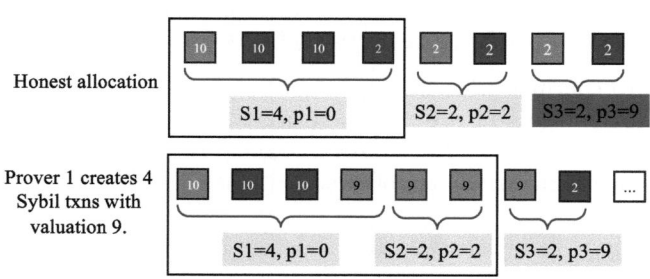

Intuitively, creating high-paying tasks can sometimes render more provers feasible, increasing all provers' utility. This can also reduce user utility. We observe that creating user Sybils benefits the attacker only under specific conditions and that the attack is possible only if the malicious prover knows all user bids.

Proposition 5. *When a prover $j < N$ submits Sybil user bids, there will always be some prover and user bids that result in prover j receiving lower utility compared to if it had acted honestly, assuming all other provers are honest.*

Mitigation: hiding bids Based on this observation, the above attacks can be mitigated by *encrypting all user and prover bids* to hide the necessary information required by profitable Sybil attacks, i.e., making the auctions sealed-bid.

Remark 2. If provers are risk-averse and thus would try to avoid worst-case outcomes (as assumed by prior work, see Remark 1), Proposition 5 suffices to thwart the threat of a deviating prover sending Sybil user bids. One may consider a Bayesian setting, where different solutions may be needed to ensure that such deviations lower an attacker's *expected* utility (see Sect. 6).

5.4 Prover Sybil Proofness

Recall that a mechanism is prover Sybil proof if no prover finds it profitable to submit bids as multiple provers. We show that the $Proo\varphi$ mechanism is not prover Sybil proof, as demonstrated in Example 4. Intuitively, prover ℓ may split into multiple provers and get allocated some proof generation capacity.

Example 4. Suppose there are 8 user tasks, where 3 of them have value 10, and 5 of them have value 3. Also, suppose there are 3 provers in the ZKP market. The capacities s_i and costs p_i of the provers are $(s_1, p_1) = (4, 0), (s_2, p_2) = (2, 2), (s_3, p_3) = (2, 9)$. When all parties are bidding honestly, we have $\ell = 1$, and prover 2 will get zero utility. Instead, prover 2 can split into two provers, one with bid $(1, 2)$ and the other with bid $(1, 3)$. Then ℓ will increase to 2, and the split prover with bid $(1, 2)$ will be allocated and get 1 utility.

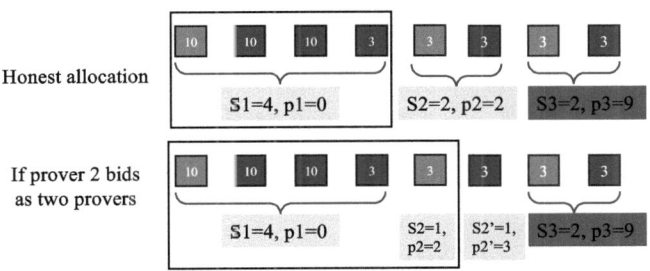

We analyze prover Sybil attacks and show in Proposition 6 that profitable attacks contribute to social welfare and thus do not harm users.

Proposition 6. *Suppose a prover j with capacity s_j splits into p Sybil provers, where the k-th split has cost bid $p_{j,k}$ and capacity bid $s_{j,k}$, with $\sum_k s_{j,k} = s_j$. Then if the Sybil attack is profitable, the social welfare will increase.*

5.5 Collusion

A mechanism is vulnerable to collusion if a coalition of provers and/or users finds it profitable to coordinate and bid strategically. In this paper, we focus on two types of collusion in a ZKP market; one is a prover colluding with a user, and the other is a set of provers colluding with each other. We note that potential collusion among market agents is typically not discussed in related work [14,15]. Here, we consider the possibility of collusion and show that it is not much of a threat with proper implementation of the mechanism. Specifically, we assume a coalition of colluding participants can freely communicate; i.e., colluders have private communication channels with each other, while honest actors not in the coalition are independent and do not communicate with any other party.

In case a prover colludes with a user, we show in Proposition 7 that this benefits the attacking coalition only under specific conditions.

Proposition 7. *When a prover and a user collude by deviating from their honest bids, there will always be other prover and user bids that cause the coalition to receive lower joint utility, assuming all other parties are honest.*

In the proof, we show in a case-by-case manner that all profitable deviations require the coalition to know the bids of the other parties.

Following this result, the previous mitigation (hiding bids) also mitigates such collusion by creating uncertainty about profitability. I.e., a prover-user coalition cannot be sure that they will profit by bidding strategically.

When a set of provers form a coalition and bid strategically, if the provers in the coalition have the same cost then this is equivalent to a single prover splitting into prover Sybils. As in Proposition 6, such coalitions do not harm the ZKP market. On the other hand, we show in Proposition 8 that two provers colluding can only benefit the provers in the coalition when the other parties have specific bids, which again is mitigated by encrypting user and prover bids.

Proposition 8. *When two provers with different costs collude by changing their bids, there will always be other prover and user bids that result in the coalition receiving lower joint utility compared to if they had bid honestly, assuming all other parties are bidding honestly.*

6 Conclusions and Future Work

We have presented $Proo\varphi$, a mechanism designed to address the demands of ZKP markets, where proofs are generated in batches. $Proo\varphi$ consists of a core auction mechanism that matches low-cost provers with high-value user tasks. We formally analyze the mechanism and show that it ensures incentive compatibility for both users and provers and that it is budget-balanced. We also introduce system-level designs such as slashing, fixing prover capacity bids over multiple auction rounds, and encrypting bids, to address security challenges that are not handled by the core mechanism alone. We analyze how our measures mitigate security concerns including untruthful capacity bids, Sybil attacks, and collusion.

Future Work. Following the literature [2,5,11,22], we consider a non-Bayesian setting. One possible direction for future work is to extend the model to a Bayesian one where actors may deviate to increase *expected* payoffs. For example, provers can send Sybil user bids to "simulate" a reserve price for users, thus potentially increasing revenue. Analyzing this manipulation could be interesting from the perspective of the adversaries, who should surmount several practical difficulties. First, attackers should have robust estimates for the distribution of user valuations and the distribution of the number of users. Second, in a permissionless setting, price gouging may not be profitable in the long run: it can allow new actors to offer lower prices while still making a profit [16]. Moreover, long-term dynamics may result in lower-paying transactions accumulating until allocating the pent-up demand becomes profitable for provers [20].

Acknowledgments. The authors wish to thank Matter Labs for research discussions and support with several aspects of this work. Wenhao Wang was supported in part by the ZK Fellowship from Matter Labs.

References

1. =nil; Proof Market. https://docs.nil.foundation/proof-market/market/economics
2. Bahrani, M., et al.: Transaction fee mechanism design in a post- MEV world. In: 6th Conference on Advances in Financial Technologies (AFT '24) 29:1–29:24 (2024). https://doi.org/10.4230/LIPIcs.AFT.2024.29
3. Baldimtsi, F., et al.: zklogin: privacy-preserving blockchain authentication with existing credentials. In: Proceedings of the 2024 on ACM SIGSAC Conference on Computer and Communications Security, pp. 3182–3196 (2024). https://doi.org/10.1145/3658644.3690356
4. Chen, B., et al.: HyperPlonk: Plonk with linear-time prover and highdegree custom gates. In: Annual International Conference on the Theory and Applications of Cryptographic Techniques. Springer (2023). https://doi.org/10.1007/978-3-031-30617-4_17
5. Chung, H., Shi, E.: Foundations of transaction fee mechanism design. In: Proceedings of the 2023 Annual ACM-SIAM Symposium on Discrete Algorithms (2023). https://doi.org/10.1137/1.9781611977554.ch150
6. Cong, L.W., et al.: Decentralized mining in centralized pools. Rev. Financial Stud. **34**(3), 1191–1235 (2020). ISSN: 0893-9454. https://doi.org/10.1093/rfs/hhaa040
7. Ernstberger, J., et al.: zk-Bench: a toolset for comparative evaluation and performance benchmarking of SNARKs. In: Galdi, C., Phan, D.H., Eds., Security and Cryptography for Networks, pp. 46–72. Springer Nature Switzerland, Cham (2024). ISBN: 978-3-031-71070-4. https://doi.org/10.1007/978-3-031-71070-4_3
8. Fisch, B., et al.: Socially optimal mining pools. In: Devanur, N.R., Lu, P., Ed., Web and Internet Economics, pp. 205–218. Springer, Cham (2017). https://doi.org/10.1007/978-3-319-71924-5_1
9. Gabizon, A., et al.: Plonk: Permutations over Lagrange-bases for oecumenical non-interactive arguments of knowledge. Cryptol. ePrint Arch. (2019). https://ia.cr/2019/953
10. Gafni, Y., Tennenholtz, M.: Optimal mechanism design for agents with DSL strategies: the case of sybil attacks in combinatorial auctions. In: Electronic Proceedings in Theoretical Computer Science, vol. 379, pp. 245–259 (2023). ISSN: 2075-2180. https://doi.org/10.4204/eptcs.379.20
11. Gafni, Y., Yaish, A.: Barriers to collusion-resistant transaction fee mechanisms. In: Proceedings of the 25th ACM Conference on Economics and Computation. EC '24 (2024). https://doi.org/10.1145/3670865.3673469
12. Gafni, Y., Yaish, A.: Discrete & Bayesian transaction fee mechanisms. In: Leonardos, S., et al. eds. Mathematical Research for Blockchain Economy. MARBLE '24. Springer, Cham (2024). https://doi.org/10.1007/978-3-031-68974-1_8
13. Gevulot Docs: Economics. https://docs.gevulot.com/gevulot-docs/network/fees
14. Gong, T., et al.: V3rified: Revelation vs Non-Revelation Mechanisms for Decentralized Verifiable Computation (2024). arXiv: 2408.07711
15. Huang, P., et al.: Design of a multi–unit double auction E–Market. In: Comput. Intell. **18**(4), 596–617 (2002). https://doi.org/10.1111/1467-8640.t01-1-00206
16. Huberman, G., et al.: Monopoly without a monopolist: an economic analysis of the bitcoin payment system. Rev. Econ. Stud. (2021). https://doi.org/10.1093/restud/rdab014
17. Kate, A., et al.: Constant-size commitments to polynomials and their applications. In: Advances in Cryptology - ASIACRYPT. Springer (2010)
18. Layer 2 Activity. https://l2beat.com/scaling/activity

19. Preston McAfee, R.: A dominant strategy double auction. J. Econ. Theory (1992). https://doi.org/10.1016/0022-0531(92)90091-u
20. Nisan, N.: Serial Monopoly on Blockchains. **2311**, 12731 (2023). https://doi.org/10.48550/arXi
21. Parsons, S., et al.: Auctions and bidding: a guide for computer scientists". In: ACM Comput. Surv. (2011). https://doi.org/10.1145/1883612.1883617
22. Roughgarden, T.: Transaction fee mechanism design. J. ACM **71**(4) (2024). ISSN: 0004-5411. https://doi.org/10.1145/3674143
23. Roughgarden, T., Shikhelman, C.: Ignore the extra zeroes: variance- optimal mining pools. In: Financial Cryptography and Data Security, pp. 233–249. Springer (2021). https://doi.org/10.1007/978-3-662-64331-0_12
24. Roy, U., et al.: Succinct Network: Prove the World's Software (2024). https://www.provewith.us/
25. Taiko Tokenomics. https://github.com/taikoxyz/taiko-mono/blob/42bbc5/packages/protocol/docs/tokenomics_staking.md
26. The Starknet Book. https://book.starknet.io/title-page.html
27. Thyagarajan, S.A.K., et al.: OpenSquare: decentralized repeated modular squaring service. In: Proceedings of the 2021 ACM SIGSAC Conference on Computer and Communications Security (2021). https://doi.org/10.1145/3460120.3484809
28. Transaction Fees on Scroll. https://docs.scroll.io/en/developers/transaction-fees-on-scroll/
29. Vickrey, W.: Counter speculation, auctions, and competitive sealed tenders. J. Finan. **16**(1) (1961). https://doi.org/10.2307/2977633
30. Workflow of a zkSync Era transaction: from generation to finalization. https://blog.quarkslab.com/zksync-transaction-workflow.html
31. Yaish, A., Zohar, A.: Correct Cryptocurrency ASIC Pricing: are miners overpaying? In: 5th Conference on Advances in Financial Technologies, vol. 282, pp. 2:1–2:25 (2023). https://doi.org/10.4230/LIPIcs.AFT.2023.2
32. Zhang, F., et al.: DECO: liberating web data using decentralized oracles for TLS. In: Proceedings of the 2020 ACM SIGSAC Conference on Computer and Communications Security, pp. 1919–1938 (2020). https://doi.org/10.1145/3372297.3417239

SoK: Trusted Setups for Powers-of-Tau Strings

Faxing Wang[1,2(✉)], Shaanan Cohney[1], and Joseph Bonneau[2,3]

[1] University of Melbourne, Parkville, Australia
lingerwan123@gmail.com, shaanan@cohney.info
[2] New York University, New York, USA
[3] a16z Crypto Research, Menlo Park, USA

Abstract. Many cryptographic protocols rely upon an initial *trusted setup* to generate public parameters. While the concept is decades old, trusted setups have gained prominence with the advent of blockchain applications utilizing zero-knowledge succinct non-interactive arguments of knowledge (zk-SNARKs), many of which rely on a "powers-of-tau" setup. Because such setups feature a dangerous trapdoor which undermines security if leaked, multiparty protocols are used to prevent the trapdoor from being known by any one party. Practical setups utilize an elaborate public ceremony to build confidence that the setup was not subverted. In this paper, we aim to systematize existing knowledge on trusted setups, drawing the distinction between setup *protocols* and *ceremonies*, and shed light on the different features of various approaches. We establish a taxonomy of protocols and evaluate real-world ceremonies based on their design principles, strengths, and weaknesses.

1 Introduction

Consider the following well-known cryptographic setup procedure: sampling two independent generators in a finite group $g, h \in \mathbb{G}$. Doing so is necessary for a variety of schemes, such as Pedersen commitments [1] and (notoriously) the Dual_EC pseudorandom bit generator [2]. For any two such generators in a cyclic group, there exists a value τ such that $g^\tau = h$ (the discrete logarithm of h to the base g). The value τ is variously called a *trapdoor*, *backdoor* or *toxic waste* [3] in that disclosure of τ undermines the security properties of the system.

The risk of disclosure motivates a variety of approaches to sample g and h such that *no party learns* τ. Given some public constant c and a hash function H which outputs elements in the group $\mathbb{G}$ [4], it suffices to choose $g = H(c||0), h = H(c||1)$. This fits into the class of *public-coin* protocols: all parties can see the value c, which could be sampled from a randomness beacon or the output of a multi-party randomness protocol [5].

Unfortunately, some schemes inherently require secrets or *private coins*. The best-known example is *powers-of-tau* setups, in which the output is a sequence of elements $(g^\tau, g^{\tau^2}, g^{\tau^3}, \cdots, g^{\tau^k})$ in a finite group. Amongst the "Cambrian explosion" of zero-knowledge proof systems [6] used in modern blockchain applications, the most efficient protocols rely on a powers-of-tau-like string. These protocols have real stakes, some with billions of dollars on the line if the trusted setup is compromised. They power proofs for many applications, including scaling blockchains via zk-rollups [7], connecting disparate blockchains via zkBridges [8], and facilitating anonymous payments [9].

Setting up the powers-of-tau string is easy with a simple *trusted setup*: a trusted party can generate the string and promise not to use the trapdoor τ maliciously. It is cliched to note that placing trust in a single entity is risky, as that entity is a single-point-of-failure inherently exposed to targeted attacks. It is also impossible to generally cryptographically prove trapdoor deletion since digital data can be arbitrarily copied and pasted.[1] Another potential solution is to outsource setup to a secure hardware enclave [16–19]. However, this model is reliant on significant assumptions as to the security of the enclave, which has been found not to hold in real implementations, [20–22]. Instead, practical instantiations bootstrap trust from a multi-party trusted setup protocol. In a typical powers-of-tau setup protocol, each participant ends up with a share τ_i such that $\tau = \prod \tau_i$. An appealing feature is that all parties must collude to reconstruct τ, and if any party deletes their τ_i then τ can never be recovered (ensuring forward secrecy even if an honest party is later corrupted).

While in principle such a protocol could be run once and re-used for many applications, in practice, it is difficult to find a universally trusted party, leading to a number of disparate trusted setups for different applications. Additionally, some proof systems require additional application-specific parameters, requiring distinct setups. Hence, the blockchain space has already seen dozens of powers-of-tau setup protocols. While notions of a trusted setup have long been known in the literature, in practice, the bulk of practical instantiations have been powers-of-tau setups ocurring within the past several years, making them the most important case study for trusted setups.

In this work, we systematize the emerging body of knowledge on trusted setups, specifically for powers-of-tau strings.

Protocols vs. Ceremonies. While there are widespread discrepancies in terminology within both the research literature and zk-SNARKs community, we draw a distinction between trusted setup *protocols* and trusted setup *ceremonies*:

- Trusted setup *protocols* which are specified purely mathematically, enabling an arbitrary group of n participants to construct public parameters. They often utilize abstractions such as a public bulletin board or broadcast channels, and come with a rigorous cryptographic security proof.
- Trusted setup *ceremonies* are real-world instantiations of these protocols. They operate with a specific user base or organization and aim to provide operational security, verifiability and social trust among the intended user base. Ceremonies require, for example, implementing the adopted protocol

---

[1] Surprisingly, under specific settings and using quantum computation, it is theoretically possible to produce a proof-of-deletion [10–15], but we will not consider these approaches in detail here.

in software, choosing participants, instantiating required tools like bulletin boards, and ensuring public access to data output during the protocol run.

The research literature often conflates these two notions, but we draw a distinction as it allows us to define desiderata for each independently. Both are essential to achieve security. In the current research literature, protocols are highly formalized and often come with formal proofs, while ceremonies are often loosely described and practitioners have had to design many details on the fly. The purpose of this work is not to solve the significant challenge of formalizing all aspects of ceremonies. However, though practitioners have now conducted cryptographic ceremonies over a significant time period, there has until now been insufficient scrutiny of practices at a systematic level. This work aims to partially fill that gap, by reviewing past practices, and presenting the first step towards understanding ceremonies (and their tradeoffs) in context.

Types of Setups. Adapting from GMR [23], we refer to a setup which requires generating and erasing secrets as a private-coin setup, whereas a secret-free setup is called a public-coin setup. Public-coin setups are often called *transparent setups* [24,25] in the context of zk-SNARKs. They do not constitute a trusted setup as the trapdoor, though it may be guaranteed to exist mathematically, does not become available to any computationally-bounded party.

By contrast, many zk-SNARK systems (e.g. the popular Groth16 [26]) require a circuit-specific private-coin setup and a new setup for any new circuit to be proved. In contrast, a *universal setup* [27,28] is one-size-fits-all that can be used in proving any circuit. Once complete, multiple statements can be proved by reusing the materials from the ceremony assuming bounded-size statements. *Updatable setups* [29] enable the parameters to be updated at any time, with cumulative security: if any update is done securely, the trapdoor is hidden permanently. Note that both *universal* and *updatable* setups are independent of any specific circuit.

Why Trusted Setups? From a security standpoint, transparent setups are obviously superior to trusted setups (even universal or updatable ones). Given this, why do we care about the trusted setup model at all? For better or for worse, SNARKs built with private-coin *circuit-specific* setups provide the most efficient proof size, prover time, and verification time. Even if the trusted setup is very complex and slow, it is a one-time cost (which may only be borne by large, powerful nodes participating) and the system may enjoy substantial performance benefits in the long run. For these reasons, as we will see, in practice many real-world blockchain systems have chosen to undertake the risks and costs of trusted setups. Hence, we consider it crucial to design the most secure and efficient trusted setups possible.

Scope. Reviewing and evaluating all the existing *trusted setups* and *ceremonies* is far beyond this SoK. In particular, we focus on powers-of-tau strings and derivatives, though there are many other important types of setups such as groups-of-unknown-order [30]. We also exclude trusted ceremonies like DNSSEC since the corresponding underlying protocols are not trusted setups (they are signing ceremonies which must be repeated periodically).

Paper Organization. We begin with an overview of trusted setup protocols and categorizes which applications require which type of protocol in Sect. 2. In Sect. 3 we discuss practical trusted setup ceremonies, introducing a set of desirable properties for ceremonies and surveying over ceremonies which have been conducted. We conclude (Sect. 4) with insights from all the ceremonies we cover above and open research questions.

We present key notation and notions we will use henceforth. PPT denotes probabilistic polynomial time. We set λ as our security parameter. We use $\mathsf{negl}(\lambda)$ to denote a negligible function that vanishes faster than the inverse of any polynomial of λ. We denote uniform sampling x from a set A as $x \leftarrow_\$ A$. For a cyclic group $\mathbb{G}$ with a generator of order q, we denote its generators as g and h.

2 Trusted Setup Protocols

We begin by formalizing the notion of a trusted setup *protocol* as a purely mathematical representation of a trusted setup (Sect. 2.1). We then systematize the core ideas of setup protocols for powers-of-tau-like strings (Sect. 2.2).

2.1 Trusted Setup Protocol Formalization

We present a generic definition of trusted setup protocols with formally defined security properties. Our definition aims to capture the core notion of a *process*, which enforces internal computations and communicates with other *processes* through corresponding external *input* and *output* channels. They proceed in rounds, with only one party active in each round.

General Framework: A *process* captures a family of probability distributions among multiple runs indexed by security parameters. A *process* could have multiple runs. A run of a *process* not only includes the *process* description but also the security parameter and all random coins. Note that *processes* could be composed to form a new *process*. We denote *process* A composed with *process* B as $A \| B$. Typically, we model *process* as probabilistic polynomial-time systems of probabilistic polynomial-time interactive Turing machines (PPT ITM).

Channels are categorized into two types of visibility: *private, public*. A *public* channel can be seen as broadcasting, whereas *private* channel is modeled as point-to-point (P2P) communication. With external input channels I and output channels O, we denote the set of all *processes* by $\Pi(I, O)$. We denote $I_A = I_B$ if the same data is transmitted in channels I_A, I_B, and I_A and I_B connect the same endpoints.

We proceed with our formal definition of *trusted setup protocols*:

Definition 1. *A trusted setup protocol is a tuple,*
$$TS = (S, C, OUT, \{\Pi_p\}_{p \in S}, \{\Pi'_p\}_{p \in S}, t, s), \text{ where:}$$

- $S = (p_1, \cdots, p_n; op)$ *is a finite set of* participants $p_{i \leq n}$ *and a special participant* operator op. C *contains all the channels of TS;*
- $I, O \in C$ *are channels connecting participants in S such that $O(p \in S)$ and $O(p_1 \in S)$ are disjoint for all $p \neq p_1$ and $I(p)$ and $I(p_1)$ are disjoint for all $p \neq p_1$ as well. We call $I(p)$ and $O(p)$ the set of external* input *and* output *channels of participant p respectively;*
- *Explicitly, we define OUT to be output of a trusted setup. Note that post-ceremony materials (PCM) are included in OUT;*
- $\Pi_{p \in S} \subseteq \Pi(I(p), O(p))$, *is the set of* all the possible runs *of a participant p;*
- $\Pi'_{p \in S} \subseteq \Pi_{p \in S}$, *is the set of* all the honest runs *of a participant p. Note that the behaviors of participants are reflected in their corresponding runs. Thus, our definition captures both* honest *and* dishonest *participants. An instance of TS is a process in the form of $\pi = (\pi_{p_1} || \cdots , || \pi_{p_n})$ where $\pi_{p_i} \in \Pi_{a_i}$. We call a participant p_i honest if $\pi_{p_i} \in \Pi'_{p_i \in S}$. As trusted setups tolerate corrupted participants, we call a process π honest if the number of corrupted participants is within the corruption threshold t;*
- *s is the trapdoor of a trusted setup, which is supposed to be known to no one during the lifetime of the trusted setup.*

Desired Properties of Trusted Setup Protocols. We propose the following security properties for a trusted setup protocol:

1. **Correctness**: a correct trusted setup should comply with the trusted setup procedure and produce the deterministic output to any two participants on accepted inputs from honest participants. Consider two instances $\pi, \bar{\pi}$ of a trusted setup with the same input $I = \bar{I}, (I, \bar{I}) \in C, \bar{C}$. For any PPT distinguisher D, a correct trusted setup satisfies

$$\Pr\left[\begin{matrix} OUT \leftarrow \pi(S, C, t) \\ \overline{OUT} \leftarrow \pi(S, \bar{C}, t) \end{matrix} \mid 1 \leftarrow D(OUT, \overline{OUT})\right] \leq \mathsf{negl}(\lambda) \quad (1)$$

Informally we define correctness with the following observation: if the output is deterministic, then anyone with the trapdoor t can rerun the trusted setup and get the identical output.

2. γ-ϵ **trapdoor-confidentiality**: Trusted setup contain a secret (the trapdoor). Let s be the trapdoor of the setup procedure π. A trusted setup provides γ-ϵ trapdoor confidentiality if, for any PPT adversary $\mathcal{A}$ wh$[p_A]_{A \leq t}$ up to the threshold t.

$$\Pr\left[s' \leftarrow \mathcal{A}(S, C, [\pi^i(I,O)]_{i \in \gamma}, OUT) \mid s' = s\right] \leq \mathsf{negl}(\lambda) \quad (2)$$

where π^i indicates that $\mathcal{A}$ is allowed to repeat the instance π with the same S, I, O up to γ times. We model a powerful $\mathcal{A}$ who is able to rewind the instance π of TS. To win the game, the $\mathcal{A}$ must derive the trapdoor with non-negligible probability.

3. **Consistency**: a consistent trusted setup is an *instance* π *of TS* that outputs OUT_i to a participant process π_{p_i} and OUT_j to party j,

$$\Pr\left[\pi_{p_i}, \pi_{p_j} \in \Pi'_{p \in S} | OUT_i = OUT_j\right] = 1 \qquad (3)$$

Trusted setup results are intended to be publicly accessible to anyone. More importantly, every honest party's view of the output should be consistent—even for those who did not commit contributions.

4. (m, ϵ)**-Robustness.** we define a trusted setup to be $(m\text{-}\epsilon)$ robust if and only if the following holds: Let m be the number of participants, $\pi_{p_j\, j \in m} \subseteq \pi$ be the instances of trusted setup TS under the control of $\mathcal{A}$. Then, for channels C with inputs I and outputs O the distribution of the trusted setup output OUT must satisfy:

$$\Pr\begin{bmatrix} [\pi_{p_j}]_{j \in m}, \pi_{p_j} \notin \Pi'_{p \in S} \\ m \leq t < n \\ OUT \leftarrow \pi(S, C, t) \\ \overline{OUT} \leftarrow \pi(\bar{S}, \bar{C}, t) \end{bmatrix} | OUT \approx \overline{OUT} \leq 1 - \mathsf{negl}(\lambda)[\epsilon] \qquad (4)$$

where $\bar{S}$ is a set full of honest participants and $\overline{OUT}$ and $\bar{C}$ is the corresponding output and channels of the same instance π. The intuition is that an adversary $\mathcal{A}$ who controls m participants must not be able to bias the output of the trusted setup in a non-neglible fashion.

2.2 Powers-of-Tau Setup Protocols

Table 1. Non-transparent proof systems and their SRS. l linear relations for the left and right inputs. Assume a circuit is of size $N = 2^n$, M is the upper bound of the number of multiplication gates and m is the number of multiplication gates in the circuit. n_k is the number of nonzero entries in R1CS(-lite) matrices encoding the circuit. a is the number of wires in the circuit.

SNARKs	SRS size	Universal	Proof Size	Year	Constraint system
Marlin [28]	$(3n_k + 3)\, \mathbb{G}_1, 2\, \mathbb{G}_2$	✓	$13\, |\mathbb{G}_1| + 8\, |F|$	2019	R1CS, sparse matrices
Plonk [31]	$3N\, \mathbb{G}_1, 1\, \mathbb{G}_2$	✓	$7\, |\mathbb{G}_1| + 7\, |F|$	2019	Plonkish [31]
Sonic [27]	$4M\, \mathbb{G}_1, 4M\, \mathbb{G}_2$	✓	$20\, |\mathbb{G}_1| + 16\, |F|$	2019	Hadamard Product Constraint [32]
Lunar [33]	$M\, \mathbb{G}_1, M\, \mathbb{G}_2$	✓	$11\, |\mathbb{G}_1| + 2\, |F|$	2020	R1CSLite, sparse matrices
Basilisk [34]	$M\, \mathbb{G}_1, 1\, \mathbb{G}_2$	✓	$10\, |\mathbb{G}_1| + 3\, |F|$	2021	Plonk constraints
Vampire [35]	$(12M + n_K)\, \mathbb{G}_1, (4M + n_k)\, \mathbb{G}_2$	✓	$4\, |\mathbb{G}_1| + 2\, |F|$	2022	R1CSLite, sparse matrices
Gemini [36]	$(N + 2)\, \mathbb{G}_1, 2\, \mathbb{G}_2$	✓	$3n\, \mathbb{G}_2$	2022	R1CS
Tesutdo [37]	$\sqrt{N}\mathbb{G}_1, \sqrt{N}\mathbb{G}_2,$	✓	$\frac{\sqrt{N}}{2}\mathbb{G}_t, \frac{\sqrt{N}}{2}\mathbb{G}_1, \frac{\sqrt{N}}{2}\mathbb{G}_2$	2023	R1CS [38]
Pari [39]	$4a\, \mathbb{G}_1$	✗	$2\, \mathbb{G}_1 + 2\, |F|$	2024	Square R1CS [40]
Polymath [41]	$(2a + 24m)\, \mathbb{G}_1,$	✗	$3\, \mathbb{G}_1 + 1\, |F|$	2024	SAP [26]
Groth16 [26]	$(a + 2m)\, \mathbb{G}_1, m\, \mathbb{G}_2$	✗	$2\, \mathbb{G}_1, 1\, \mathbb{G}_2$	2016	R1CS,QAP [38]
BCTV14 [42]	$(6a + m + l)\, \mathbb{G}_1, m\, \mathbb{G}_2$	✗	$7\, \mathbb{G}_1, 1\, \mathbb{G}_2$	2014	R1CS,QAP
Pinocchio [43]	$(7a + m - 2l)\, \mathbb{G}$	✗	$8\, \mathbb{G}$	2013	R1CS,QAP

Table 2. Polynomial Commitment Schemes (PCS). We separate *univariate* PCS and *multilinear* PCS with the dashline. DL is discrete logarithm, RO is random oracle, GUO is groups-of-unknown-order. We let d be the degree of the univariate polynomial, $\mathbb{G}_1, \mathbb{G}_2,$ and $\mathbb{G}_T$ be generators of bilinear groups, λ be the security parameter, and $\mathbb{F}$ be a finite field. For the v-variate multilinear polynomial, $n = 2^v$.

PCS		SRS size	Setup	Open proof size	Prove	Verify
KZG [44]	Pairing	$O(d)$ $\mathbb{G}_1$	Univ	1 $\mathbb{G}_1$	$O(d)$	$O(1)$
Bulletproof [45]	DL	$O(d)$ $\mathbb{G}$	Trans	$2\log d$ $\mathbb{G}$	$O(d)$	$O(d)$
FRI [46]	RO	$O(1)$ $\mathbb{G}$	Trans	$\lambda \log^2(d)$ $\mathbb{G}_1$	$O(\lambda d)$	$O(\lambda \log^2(d))$
DARK [24,32]	GUO	$O(1)$ $\mathbb{G}$	Trans	$\lambda \log^2(d)$ $\mathbb{G}_1$	$O(\lambda d)$	$O(\lambda \log^2(d))$
Dory [25]	Pairing	$O(d)$ $\mathbb{G}$	Trans	$6\log(d)$ $\mathbb{G}_1$	$O(d^{1/2})$	$O(\log d)$
Dew [47]	GUO	$O(1)$ $\mathbb{G}$	Trans	66 $\mathbb{G}_2$	$O(d^3/\log d)$	$O(\log d)$
Behemoth [48]	Pairing	$O(d)$ $\mathbb{G}$	Trans	47 $\mathbb{G}_2$ + 19 $\mathbb{F}$	$O(d^3/\log d)$	$O(1)$
KZG [44]	Pairing	$O(n)$ $\mathbb{G}_1$	Univ	v $\mathbb{G}_1$	$O(n)$	$O(v)$
Dory [25]	Pairing	$O(n)$ $\mathbb{G}_1$	Trans	$6v\mathbb{G}_T$	$O(n)$	$O(v)$
Bulletproof [49]	GUO	$O(n)$ $\mathbb{G}_1$	Univ	$2v$ $\mathbb{G}$	$O(n)$	$O(n)$
Gemini [36]	Pairing	$O(n)$ $\mathbb{G}_1$	Univ	$(v+4)\mathbb{G}_1 + (v+1)\mathbb{F}$	$O(n)$	$O(n)$
Brakedown [46]	Coding	$O(n)$ $\mathbb{G}$	Trans	$\sqrt{\lambda n}\mathbb{F}$	$O(n)$	$\sqrt{\lambda n}$
Orion [50]	Coding	$O(n)$ $\mathbb{G}_1$	Trans	$\lambda v^2 \mathbb{G}_1$	$O(n)$	$O(\lambda v^2)$
Zeromorph [51]	Pairing	$O(n)$ $\mathbb{G}_1$	Univ	$v + 3\mathbb{G}_1$	$O(n)$	$O(\lambda v^2)$
Orion+ [52]	Pairing	$O(n)$ $\mathbb{G}_1$	Univ	$4v\mathbb{G}_1$	$O(n)$	$O(v)$
BaseFold [53]	Coding	$O(n)$ $\mathbb{G}_1$	Trans	$4v\mathbb{G}_1$	$O(n)$	$O(v)$
Ideal PCS	TBA	$O(1)$ $\mathbb{G}$	Trans	$O(1)\mathbb{G}$	$O(d)$	$O(1)$

We summarize popular powers-of-tau-based proof systems in Table 1 and polynomial commitment schemes (PCS) in Table 2 (where we highlight the ideal polynomial commitment scheme in red). These two applications are inherently related, many SNARK proof systems are built on KZG commitments [44] which benefit from fast verification and constant-size proofs. In return for these advantages, of course, is the required trusted setup. Transparent proof systems remain significantly more expensive in proof and/or verification time. Developing a PCS with transparent setup, constant-sized proof, and constant verification is still an open question.

KZG commitments depend inherently on an SRS powers-of-tau tuple. Knowledge of the trapdoor τ completely undermines the binding property, which in turn breaks the soundness of every SNARK proof system built on it. This has motivated considerable work on generating the powers-of-tau SRS in a distributed manner, ideally in the dishonest majority model where the trapdoor τ is secure so long as one participant has behaved honestly (and deleted the toxic waste corresponding to their particular contribution to the protocol).

We introduce a toy protocol to illustrate this approach.

Toy Powers-of-Tau Setup Protocol. Intuitively, our goal is for parties to contribute secrets to the SRS such that no single party knows the combined and final τ of the SRS. The simplest protocol relies on sequential contributions by participants. That is, upon receiving the powers-of-tau string $S = (g^\tau, g^{\tau^2}, g^{\tau^3}, \cdots, g^{\tau^k})$ from the last participant, participant j samples a random τ_j and obfuscates S by raising each element to the corresponding powers of τ_j:

$$S' = (g^{\tau\tau_j}, g^{(\tau\tau_j)^2}, g^{(\tau\tau_j)^3}, \cdots, g^{(\tau\tau_j)^k})$$

At first glance, this scheme works so long as one participant is honest. However, a malicious participant might *adaptively* generate their secret τ to bias the final SRS. For this reason, some protocols [54–57] aim to eliminate the adaptive bias by adding a mandatory commitment layer beforehand. In this case, each party is required to commit to their secret before contributing it and running the remainder of the protocol. Thus each τ_j is guaranteed to be independent even under an adaptive adversary. Obviously, asking parties to commit their τ_j at minimum incurs another round of interaction. In addition, this imposes a significant additional constraint as the participants must be known and remain online throughout the trusted setup, which could take multiple days to finalize in practice.

Additional Re-randomization. A key of Bowe, Gabizon and Miers [66] is that the last powers-of-tau SRS can be mixed with another random τ' from a public, independent, source. As a result even an adaptively chosen τ_j can not bias the outcome and parties are no longer required to remain online during the setup. Bowe, Gabizon and Miers [66] instantiated the random source with the *random beacon* [58] primitive, designed to periodically produce fresh randomness. This allows the design of a protocol without the commitment phase. Further it permits constructions wherein participants can join the round-robin contribution process in an ad-hoc manner. Participants are thus able to join the SRS trusted setup in their reserved time slot and add their contributions, after which they are free to leave. Restrictions on the identity and the time of participants are also removed. This approach leads us to the MMORPG framework [66].

MMORPG Trusted Setups. MMORPG (Massively Multiparty Open Reusable Parameter Generation) is a protocol for generating the SRS used by Groth16 [26] (a pairing-based zk-SNARK). The MMORPG approach has seen broad adoption in systems such as Semaphore [59], TornadoCash [60], and Aztec [61]. Groth16 is not a universal proof system—instead, proofs apply only for the specific program for which they were generated. This leads to a two-phase design, with an initial universal phase and a circuit-specific phase. The universal phase is conducted according to the powers-of-tau private-coin trusted setup we mentioned above. The second phase is a circuit-specific phase that tailors the construction to the specific program for which proofs are to be generated.

Generally, an MMORPG private-coin trusted setup involves three types of entities: the coordinator, the participants, and a randomness beacon (which may be a multiparty protocol itself [5,62,63]). We describe it in more detail as follows:

1. The coordinator initializes the protocol by executing a procure $\mathsf{Init}(k, g)$ with the prescribed size of the powers-of-tau tuple k, and a group generator g. After initialization, the coordinator chooses the first party who expressed interest in joining the protocol and sends them the initial powers-of-tau tuple PoT_0^1.
2. After receiving the powers-of-tau tuple from the coordinator (or prior participant), the participant (p_i) first checks the correctness of prior contributions to the string. After checking for correctness, p_i picks a random τ_i to update the power-of-tau tuple in the way we mentioned in the toy proposal and then generates the corresponding correctness proof of their contribution. Specifically, every participant must provide a zero-knowledge proof of the following three properties to ensure the correctness of the tuple: First, the participant must prove knowledge of their corresponding τ_i. Second, the participant must show that the structure of the string has been preserved: each exponent should be the square of the prior exponent. Third, the participant showed the update was non-degenerative (where a malicious p_i erases all prior contributions by using a contribution $\tau_i = 0$). p_i then transmits the tuple and its correctness proof.
3. The coordinator receives the update from p_n, checks the correctness of p_n's contribution, and samples a random contribution τ^1 from the *randomness beacon*. Note that as long as the beacon is secure (unpredictable, live, and unbiased), the protocol remains secure—even if all the participants are malicious. The coordinator finalizes the powers-of-tau phase by updating with τ^1 and generating the corresponding correctness proof.
4. After generating the powers-of-tau tuple, the coordinator first converts the statement to an equivalent arithmetic circuit and then linearly combines elements in the PoT according to the circuit C to initialize the SRS_0^1 for the second phase protocol.
5. The coordinator begins the second phase by transmitting the SRS from phase one SRS_0^1 over to the first registered phase two participant. Similar to phase 1, participants contribute their secrets to the SRS. Each participant checks the correctness of the last contribution, samples a random secret, and updates the SRS with the secret.
6. In the final step, the coordinator checks the SRS_m^2 transmitted from the prior participant, retrieves another output τ^2, from the random beacon, and updates the SRS with τ^2 to finalize the output of the whole protocol.

Remark 1. Note that for clarity, we assume that each participant passes their contribution consecutively to the next participant, and everyone verifies the correctness of the tuple from the last round. In practice, communication is centralized through the coordinator, who also verifies the correctness proofs. In addition, transcripts of the whole protocol are stored and made available to the public for further inspection, and a mandatory correctness check is not compulsory for participants.

Remark 2. Note that both phases are necessary to finalize an *SRS*, though essentially, participants in both phases work in the same manner. That is because the corresponding circuit-dependent SRS is a linear combination of the final $\tau = \prod_{i=1}^{n} \tau_i$. The additional contribution from the *random beacon* provides an important property: even where participants collude, no set will know the final powers-of-tau tuple $(g^\tau, g^{\tau^2}, g^{\tau^3}, \cdots, g^{\tau^k})$. Therefore, to transform powers-of-tau to the Groth16 SRS the coordinator must ensure the powers-of-tau process has been finalized with the random beacon.

Remark 3. A simplified and optimized version of the MMORPG framework is Snarky Ceremonies [64]. Snarky ceremonies are a more general framework that captures both circuit-specific [26,43,65] and updatable SRS [27,28,31]. By relaxing the security definition, it removes the need for random beacons as slightly biased SRS is not sufficient to break SNARKs. We summarize existing proposals for trusted setup protocol in Table 3.

Table 3. Trusted Setup Protocols. We denote the number of participants in a protocol as n. Protocol with an additional round of applying a random beacon is denoted as ∗. We use rounds for the communication complexity, individual-rounds for communications of individuals in running the protocol, corruption to denote the threshold of corruption, round-robin to indicate if protocols are running in round-robin communication model, decentralized to distinct whether a central coordinator is necessary, incentive to indicate if participants are incentively driven to be hoenst, UC to indicate if protocols are proven to be UC-Secure, target for their design goals.

Protocols	Rounds	Individual-Rounds	Corruption	Round-robin	Decentralized	Incentive	UC-secure	Target
BCDTV15 [54]	$O(n)$	$O(n)$	$n-1$	✗	✗	✗	✗	General
BGG17 [55]	$O(1)$	4	$n-1$	✗	✗	✗	✗	Pinocchio
BGM17 [66]	$O(n)\ast$	1	n	✓	✗	✗	✗	Groth16
KMSV21 [64]	$O(n)$	1	$n-1$	✓	✗	✗	✗	Groth16
KKK21 [67]	$O(n)\ast$	1	$n-1$	✓	✓	✓	✓	General
CDKS22 [68]	$O(\sqrt{n})$	$O(\sqrt{n})$	$n-1$	✗	✓	✗	✓	PoT
NRBB22 [69]	$O(n)\ast$	1	$n-1$	✓	✓	✗	✗	PoT

3 Ceremonies

Trusted setup protocols can not be executed on paper. Instead, public trust in these setup protocols is based on "celebrating" a ceremony to convince the public that the protocol was run correctly and securely. Ceremonies are often conducted with requirements on real-world conduct—(for example lack of conflicts-of-interest or collusion between participants, geographic diversity, rules mandating recording of proceedings). Such elements are designed to bootstrap social trust in the systems, beyond provabile mathematical notions.

We attempted to identify all real-world ceremonies conducted to date to construct a powers-of-tau string, proving a tabulation of more than 40 instances Table 4. We note that all of the ceremonies we were able to find are variations of the MMORPG framework [54,66]. We collected details from various projects with their corresponding trusted setup ceremonies based on an exhaustive online search for the *trusted setup ceremony* keyword on Google (yielding 18 pages in total). The details of many ceremonies, like Hermez, are already missing and scattered despite being conducted only a few years prior to our study. In these cases, we attempted to find their corresponding ceremony pages and blog posts using the Internet Archive [70]. Since 2022, ceremony information can be found on one page thanks to the DefinitelySetup project [71].

3.1 Desired Properties of Ceremonies

Based on our study of real-world trusted setup ceremonies, as well as the public communication around trusted setup ceremonies we have observed in practice, we distill a set of desirable properties. We propose a set of properties by the acronym **"ADOPT"**, that an ideal ceremony should follow:

- **A**vailability says that the protocol runs for a sufficient period of time that all participants have time to broadcast contributions. Due to the round-robin nature of protocols, it is important to leave enough time for many contributors. cannot be suppressed by a denial-of-service attack.
- **D**ecentralization means the absence of reliance on a central coordinator. This coordinator might be a target for attacks, or could censor specific contributors.
- **O**pen indicates that the ceremony welcomes any interested participant to join and contribute.
- **P**ersistent means that a ceremony maintains its published information for future verification or extension even after the ceremony is finished. Note that this may require ensuring long-term access to a non-trivial amount of data (i.e. multiple gigabytes).
- **T**ransparency requires that the ceremony documents all procedures for public scrutiny, including the exact protocol specification to enable independent implementation, as well as all procedures, identities of operators and contributors, data formats for intermediate transcripts, etc.

Note that none of the ceremonies we observed actually satisfied all five properties, in particular the Decentralization property. Ensuring all the above properties without a centralized coordinator requires some form of multi-party computation (MPC). In general, conducting a secure MPC without an honest majority or a trusted coordinator is impossible. Fortunately, the general MPC impossibility results on identifiable abort [72,73] and output delivery guarantee [74,75] under a dishonest majority model, do not apply to ceremonies. Ceremonies can operate in a fashion where an execution is attempted, and if it fails, rounds can proceed by excluding parties that contributed to the failure—without losing their security. As all the ceremonies that operate in a round-robin manner can easily identify individual malicious behaviors, aborts are easily identifiable. Given this, a malicious party's only option is to abort the ceremony to prevent others from learning the output with their contribution. However, since all ceremonies implement a timeout mechanism and the output is independent of individual contributions, contributors who deliberately attempt to abort the process can be excluded from future executions of the ceremony.

As noted above, we also observed widespread problems with the Persistence and Transparency goals. Many projects did not provide clear, complete documentation sufficient for an independent third-party implementation for contribution or for verification, requiring participants to download and run the reference source code to participate. Many projects also have not persisted the intermediate values or in some cases even the final results of the ceremony, making it impossible retroactively to assess or extend their powers-of-tau string. A case study of the Sprout ceremony can be found in our full version.

3.2 Recovering from a Compromised SRS

We now present, as a case study, an illustrating real-world example of how a trusted setup can fail, outlining properties that could be preserved even under a *subverted SRS*. We also note that *recovering* from a compromised setup is itself a second type of ceremony, designed to build public trust.

The most prominent example was in the ZCash Sprout ceremony [54]. In this case, the problem was not with the ceremony but the protocol itself. Specifically, Gabizon [110] found a small but critical vulnerability in the private-coin SRS protocol as described in the research paper by Ben-Sasson et al. [65], which was the protocol used in the ZCash Sproud ceremony. Ben-Sasson et al. [65] described an extra, unneeded parameter, which was generated in the ZCash Sprout ceremony, but could be exploited by an adversary to generate proof of any statement based on a single valid proof. This implies that an adversary can generate arbitrary proofs for any statement given a single proof—allowing an adversary to mint ZCash coins at will. Note that the vulnerability (which we present below for illustrative purposes) is not a result of the ceremony itself but is a flaw in the underlying protocol.

Abstractly, for n polynomials $P_j(x_j) = \sum_{i=0}^{n} a_{i,j} x_j^i, j \in n$, the SRS of P_j described in [65] is $g^{P_j(\tau)}, g^{\alpha P_j(\tau)}, \alpha \leftarrow_r \mathbb{F}$. For a prover, with public input $w_{in} = w_0, \cdots, w_m$ and witness $w_{m+1}, \cdots, w_n$, the proof $\pi[0]$ is $\prod_{i=m+1}^{n} (g^{P_i(\tau)})^{w_i}$ and $\pi[1] = \prod_{i=m+1}^{n} (g^{\alpha P_i(\tau)})^{w_i}$. A valid proof will pass the check $\pi[0]^\alpha = \pi[1]$. Obviously, SRS like $g^{P_j(\tau), j \in m}$ are redundant and are never used. So a malicious prover with a valid π could generate valid proofs to other public inputs $w'_{in} = w'_0, \cdots, w'_m$, $\pi'[0] = \pi[0] \prod_{i=1}^{m} (g^{P_i(\tau)})^{w_i - w'_i}, \pi'[1] = \pi[1] \prod_{i=1}^{m} (g^{\alpha P_i(\tau)})^{w_i - w'_i}$. Essentially, $\pi'[0] = g^{\sum_{i=0}^{n} P_i(\tau) w_i - \sum_{i=m+1}^{n} P_i(\tau) w'_i}$, $\pi'[1] = g^{\sum_{i=0}^{n} \alpha P_i(\tau) w_i - \sum_{i=m+1}^{n} \alpha P_i(\tau) w'_i}$. Therefore, $\pi'[0]^\alpha$ will always be $\pi'[1]$.

Table 4. SNARK Ceremonies up-to-date in alphabetic order. PPOT denotes the index of the powers-of-tau contributions from the PPOT ceremony. "Update" denotes if it is an updatable ceremony. The "Data" and "Time" columns measure the costs to each participant in the ceremony. For a ceremony running over on multiple circuits, we denote time and size as the amounts of efforts for one to contribute to all circuits. "Available" indicates whether all the transcripts of a ceremony are still publicly accessible. We denote a ceremony with both phases in MMORPG as "MMORPG", whereas a ceremony only runs the first phase as "MMORPG-1" and the one only runs the second phase as "MMORPG-2".

Project	PPOT	Update	System	Data	Time	# Contrib	Curve	Type	Available
Aleo universal [76]	N/A	✓	Marlin [28]	44 GB	9.56 h	146	BLS12_377	Powers-of-tau	✗
Aleo inner [76]	N/A	✗	Groth16 [26]	771 MB	40 min	1059	BLS12_377	MMORPG	✗
Aleo outer [76]	N/A	✗	Groth16 [26]	2.56 GB	42 min	1036	BW6_761	MMORPG	✗
Anon Aadhaar V2 [77]	54	✗	Groth16 [26]	583 MB	6.81 min	105	BN254	MMORPG-2	✓
Axiom [78]	78	✓	KZG [44]	-	-	-	BN254	MMOPRG-1	✓
Aztec [61]	N/A	✗	Sigma [79]	5.71 GB	3.3 h	176	BN254	MMORPG-1	✓
Celo Plumo [80]	N/A	✗	Groth16 [26]	Unknown	10 h	111	BLS12_377	MMORPG	✗
clr.fund [81]	54	✗	Groth16 [26]	252 MB	10 min	2562	BN254	MMORPG-2	✗*
DeGate [82]	71	✗	Groth16 [26]	370 GB	14 h	5	BN254	MMORPG-2	✗
Email Wallet [83]	54	✗	Groth16 [26]	2.83 GB	50 min	29	BN254	MMORPG-2	✗*
FileCoin Mainnet [84]	19	✗	Groth16 [26]	52G	6 h	17	BLS12-381	MMORPG-2	✓
	19	✗		77 GB	3 h	19		MMOPRG-1	✓
FileCoin SnapDeals [85]	19	✗	Groth16 [26]	25 GB	30 min	12	BLS12-381	MMORPG-2	✓
Fractal Cash [86]	30	✗	Groth16 [26]	17.4 MB	2 min	7	BN256	MMORPG-2	✓
Hermez [87]	54*	✗	Groth16 [26]	92 GB	9 horus	6	BN254	MMORPG-2	✓
KZG ceremony [88]	N/A	✗	KZG [44]	7.21 MB	3 min	141416	BLS12-381	MMORPG-2	✓
Loopring [89]	11	✗	Groth16 [26]	75 GB	5.0 h	16	BN254	MMORPG-2	✗*
MACI [90]	54	✗	Groth16 [26]	1.23 GB	10 min	45	BN254	MMORPG-2	✗*
MACI v1.2 [91]	54	✗	Groth16 [26]	2093 MB	33 min	41	BN254	MMORPG-2	✓
MACI V2 [92]	54	✗	Groth16 [26]	2010 MB	20.5 min	246	BN254	MMORPG-2	✓
Manta [93]	72	✗	Groth16 [26]	30 MB	10 min	4382	BN254	MMOPRG	✓
Namada [94]	ZCash POT	✗	Groth16 [26]	80.8 MB	2 min	2510	BLS12-377	MMORPG-2	✓
Panther [95]	54	✗	Groth16 [26]	38.5 MB	60 s	11	BN254	MMORPG-2	✓
PPOT [96]	N/A	✓	N/A	97 GB	24 h	80	BN254	Powers-of-tau	✗*
RLN [97]	54	✗	Groth16 [26]	68.2 MB	17 min	62	BN254	MMORPG-2	✗*
RISCZERO [98]	54	✗	Groth16 [26]	3452 MB	25 min	238	BN254	MMORPG-2	✓
Semaphore [59]	25	✗	Groth16 [26]	208 MB	10 min	360	BN256	MMORPG-2	✗*
Semaphore V4 [99]	54	✗	Groth16 [26]	102 MB	25 min	389	BN254	MMORPG-2	✓
Tornado cash [100]	30	✗	Groth16 [26]	10.64 MB	3 s	1114	BN256	MMORPG-2	✓
Unirep v2 [101]	54	✗	Groth16 [26]	41.8 MB	2 min	5347	BN254	MMORPG-2	✗*
ZCash Sprout [102]	N/A	✗	BCTV14 [65]	7 GB	2 days*	6	BN254	BGG	✓
Zcash Sapling [103]	N/A	✗	Groth16 [26]	1.1 GB	2.5 h	87	BLS12-381	MMORPG-1	✓
	N/A	✗		741 MB	40 min	91		MMORPG-2	✓
ZKOPRU [104]	54	✗	Groth16 [26]	400 MB	40 min	369	BN254	MMORPG-2	✓
ZKP2P [105]	23	✗	Groth16 [26]	8.2 GB	82 min	25	BN254	MMORPG-2	✗*
ZKP2P v2.4 [106]	54	✗	Groth16 [26]	17.1 GB	71 min	8	BN254	MMORPG-2	✓
ZKP2P Domain [107]	54	✗	Groth16 [26]	1662 MB	34.5 min	17	BN254	MMORPG-2	✓
ZKSync [108]	N/A	✓	PLONK [31]	5.71 GB	3.3 h	176	BN256	MMORPG-1	✓
ZK Ticket [109]	54	✗	Groth16 [26]	3.62 MB	2.5 min	17	BN254	MMORPG-2	✗*

The above flaw was implemented by the practical Zcash ceremony directly from the paper [65], and the results were widely published before the bug was noticed. This brings up two natural questions. First, what occurs when an adversary is able to set the SRS and how much security can one retain under a maliciously generated SRS? Second, how can a practical project recover from a compromised SRS?

Noting that circuit-specific SRS in SNARKs [26] depends on the circuit's corresponding statement, a modified SRS undermines the protocol by leading to a different statement. Further, if the secure trapdoor τ is not random, the verifier can learn one bit of the witness by checking the proof. Last, a sophisticated adversary could set all strings to 0 except the string on the chosen spot. This leaks one bit of the witness to the verifier, which inevitably breaks the zero-knowledge property. More details can be found in [111].

Bellare, Fuchsbauer and Scafuro [112] studied subversion-resistant zk-SNARKs and systematically answered the extent to which security can be retained in the event of a subverted SRS: one generated by a malicious party who knows the trapdoor. Following the principle of trust-but-verify, subversion-resistant zk-SNARKs additionally allow a prover to verify if a generated SRS is well-formed. Thus, it bypasses trust and the need for a trusted third party. Bellare, Fuchsbauer and Scafuro [112] provides a counterintuitive result: even where an SRS/URS is subverted, it is possible to nonetheless retain *soundness of the overall protocol* even while preserving the zero-knowledge property. However, the paper also provides a negative result: one can not retain both *subversion-soundness* (a property requiring that it is hard for an adversary to generate a malicious CRS) and classical zero-knowledge properties at the same time. This is a result of the existence of a simulator that can output valid proofs of false statements under a valid proof.

In the event of the Sprout ceremony, the bug was discovered by Zcash engineers in March 2018 [113]. After confirmation, the published ceremony transcripts containing the additional were quietly removed. As there was no way to fix the vulnerability if anybody had downloaded and cached the transcripts, the bug was kept under embargo until after the already-planned second setup ceremony, Sapling, was conducted in November 2018. At this point, after the network had hard-forked away from using the parameters from the vulnerable Sprout ceremony, the bug was publicly disclosed in February 2019. There is (fortunately) no evidence that the bug was ever exploited.

4 Concluding Discussion

We conclude with outlining key lessons from our systematization. First are research goals emerging from our systematization of protocols, followed by lessons from our systematization of ceremonies:

4.1 Research Directions for Trusted Setup Protocols

Reducing the Size of SRS from Linear to Sublinear. For a comparison of the size of the SRS for different schemes, we refer the reader to [47,48]. Recent work [37] shows that SNARKs can be built with a linear-time prover, constant-sized proofs, and square root-sized SRS. It is also possible [114] to achieve a sublinear prover with a linear-sized SRS, and a constant-sized proof. It is still an open question to construct a SNARK-proof system with a sublinear prover, sublinear SRS, and constant-sized proof. This would dramatically alleviate participants'/coordinators' loads to participate in expensive SRS setup ceremonies.

Accelerating SNARK Ceremonies via Reusing SRS: note that the powers-of-tau ceremony can be upgraded to a perpetual version. We defer the discussion of the perpetual powers-of-tau (PPOT) ceremony to our full vervison. Powers-of-tau strings relieve new zk-SNARK players from generating system parameters from scratch. To properly launch a publicly trustworthy zk-SNARK system, they only have to fork any PPOT contribution out to continue their specific phase 2 ceremony. Moreover, noticeably, the phase 2 ceremony is significantly lightweight compared to the powers-of-tau ceremony. As reported in [66], phase 2 runs 4x faster than phase 1 while incurring 3x less transmission overhead.

Asynchronous Ceremonies: Existing ceremonies are designed in a synchronized model, which requires contributors to register to reserve a timeslot for online contribution or a contributor has to queue in a line until its turn to formally join a ceremony. To activate a fully *come-contribute-go* ceremony paradigm, one requires an asynchronous ceremony. Initial work is done by Das et al. [115], outlining an asynchronous powers-of-tau ceremony that significantly improves the sequential MMORPG protocol. However, it is still far away from an optimal asynchronous PPOT setup since it introduces $O(\lambda n^3)$ communication overhead overall. This protocol [115] only targets the power-of-tau setup, though we can trivially extend it to phase 2 since both phases essentially work in the same manner. It's still not a fully asynchronous protocol as participants in phase 2 have to wait for the central coordinator to finalize the polynomial SRS $g^{P(\tau)}$. It remains an open challenge to design a fully asynchronous protocol that is capable of handling the whole ceremony without a centralized coordinator.

Fully Decentralized and Asynchronous Ceremonies: A further enhancement is to get rid of the centralized coordinator completely. Nikolaenko et al. [69] designed and evaluated an on-chain powers-of-tau ceremony to eliminate the assumption of the centralized coordinator. For the phase 2 circuit-dependent ceremony, Kerber et al. [67] observed that updatable SRS [27–29] generation can be integrated as part of a consensus protocol so that no additional security assumptions or off-chain computation are needed for the security of the SRS. Both [69] and [67] open the door to providing incentives for honest participants. However, it is still a synchronous ceremony requiring sequential updates. Still, it opens the possibility of a fully *decentralized* and *asynchronous* phase one ceremony for zk-SNARKs integrated with [115]. Furthermore, we envision a fully asynchronous and decentralized ceremony that is capable of handling both phases of zk-SNARKs' protocols.

Curve Transformation: So far, the PPOT ceremonies in practice have been performed on the fixed BN254 curve [116]. However, deployed applications may be built on other curves. For example, ZCash uses BLS12-381 [117]. Practitioners face trade-offs when considering implementing their applications in a specific curve. However, outputs from the PPOT ceremony are incompatible with applications that rely on a different curve. An interesting research question is to design an efficient transformation scheme to enable using the output of power-of-tau ceremonies on the BN254 curve for other pairing-friendly popular curves [118].

The transparency requirement requires not only a commitment to open-sourcing code, but also requires explainable system parameters. This is an often overlooked point in SNARK ceremonies when deciding to run it on the BN254 curve. There are concerns that the base point [119] (generator) may be too small (the generator's x coordinate is chosen to be one) to be secure. Though the generator is fast for pairing, it is not a truly random point.

4.2 Lessons for Trustworthy Setup Ceremonies

We summarize the following six lessons for running a sound and trustworthy ceremony, many of which were not explicitly followed in multiple ceremonies we studied. Note that those are universal principles distilled from the MMOPRG ceremony that can be beneficial to all ceremonies.

Multiple Open-Sourced Implementations and Third-Party Auditing: to reduce the risk of coordinated failure due to software bugs, contributors should be encouraged to implement their own version of the ceremony and several official implementations should be sanctioned, with third-party audits. The MPC protocol [120] of the Sprout Ceremony is open-sourced and is audited by a third party – NCC [121]. The ceremony code of generating *SRS* for ZCash depends on a specific circuit, and ZCash functions are open-sourced and audited. A model example is the recent Ethereum KZG ceremony [122], community members not only implement the ceremony in command-line with different programming languages to hedge potential security issues in libraries [123], but also provide web-based interfaces implemented based on arkworks [124] and gnark [125], which are more user-friendlier. This effort results in 10 different implementations.

Diverse Participation: To boost the confidence that all participants in the ceremony are not colluding, the ceremony should include people from different backgrounds and interests. This may require active recruitment by the organizers. To counter a critique of anonymous participation, the Sprout Ceremony chose participants from academia, the ZCash founder team, an independent Bitcoin core developer, Peter Todd, who is skeptical and critical of the ceremony, and the whistleblower Edward Snowden. People of unrelated interests and even criticism prevent the ceremony from the interior collusion and counterfeits of the ZCash team.

Air-Gapped and One-Time Machines: To minimize the risk of vulnerabilities, air-gapped machines should be the only places processing participants' contributions to the ceremony Some ceremonies have gone beyond that, for example requiring that every machine was from a random store and it was exclusive to the ceremony. In this manner most cyber-attacks can be prevented since the machines will never be connected to any network during their lifetime. To jointly finish an MPC in the Sprout ceremony, an additional networked laptop was used to burn the communication transcripts onto a disc so that air-gapped machines can talk to each other. Every laptop was physically destroyed after the Sprout Ceremony. In that case, the ceremony is solely vulnerable to participants' willful collusion.

Geographically Isolation: participants should be selected from diverse geogrpahic locations and isolated worldwide to lower the chance that all of them could be targeted physically.

Diversed Source of Randomness: participants should be encouraged to secure their contributions as much as they can by sampling randomness from diverse physical sources. Creative ideas include [126]: sampling randomness from space aboard the Crypto 2 satellite, from the random fluctuations of a lava lamp, from scatted biscuits over the floor after feeding a pet, or from the noisy city Sydney, and so forth.

Publicly Verifiable Operation Log: all communications from the ceremony should be stored permanently and made public for later attestation. The logs cannot convince the public that the participants did not collude, but can enable them to verify that the transcript is consistent with the protocol. Additionally, old transcripts can be used to extend a ceremony in the future by adding additional contributions. For example, restored transcripts from the Sprout Ceremony guaranteed that the updated CRS of ZCash after the Sapling Ceremony (a newer and larger ceremony) is genuine from the original six participants (not substituted by any others who might keep his τ).

Acknowledgements. Faxing Wang is supported by Melbourne research scholarship. Joseph Bonneau was additionally supported by DARPA Agreement HR00112020022 and NSF Grant CNS-2239975. The views and conclusions contained in this material are those of the authors and do not necessarily reflect the official policies or endorsements of the United States Government, DARPA, a16z Crypto, or any other supporting organization.

References

1. Pedersen, T.P.: Non-interactive and information-theoretic secure verifiable secret sharing. In: CRYPTO (1991)
2. Barker, E., Kelsey, J.: Recommendation for Random Number Generation Using Deterministic Random Bit Generators. NIST Special Publication (2006)
3. Wilcox, Z.: The Design of the Ceremony (2016). http://electriccoin.co/blog/the-design-of-the-ceremony/

4. Faz-Hernandez, A., Scott, S., Sullivan, N., Wahby, R.S., Wood, C.A.: Hashing to Elliptic Curves. RFC 9380 (2023)
5. Choi, K., Manoj, A., Bonneau, J.: SoK: distributed randomness beacons. In: IEEE Security & Privacy (2023)
6. Ben-Sasson, E.: The Cambrian Explosion of Crypto Proofs (2020)
7. Nazirkhanova, K., Neu, J., Tse, D.: Information dispersal with provable retrievability for rollups. In: ACM AFT (2022)
8. Xie, T., et al.: zkbridge: trustless cross-chain bridges made practical. In: ACM CCS (2022)
9. Miers, I., Garman, C., Green, M., Rubin, A.D.: Zerocoin: anonymous distributed e-cash from bitcoin. In: IEEE Security & Privacy (2013)
10. Bartusek, J., Khurana, D.: Cryptography with certified deletion. In: CRYPTO (2023)
11. Broadbent, A., Islam, R.: Quantum encryption with certified deletion. In: TCC (2020)
12. Garg, S., Goldwasser, S., Vasudevan, P.N.: Formalizing data deletion in the context of the right to be forgotten. In: Eurocrypt (2020)
13. Hiroka, T., Morimae, T., Nishimaki, R., Yamakawa, T.: Quantum encryption with certified deletion, revisited: public key, attribute-based, and classical communication. In: Asiacrypt (2021)
14. Poremba, A.: Quantum proofs of deletion for learning with errors (2023)
15. Bartusek, J., Khurana, D., Poremba, A.: Publicly-verifiable deletion via target-collapsing functions (2023)
16. Costan, V., Devadas, S.: Intel SGX explained. Cryptology ePrint Archive, Paper 2016/086 (2016)
17. Costan, V., Lebedev, I., Devadas, S.: Sanctum: minimal hardware extensions for strong software isolation. In: USENIX Security (2016)
18. Lee, D., Kohlbrenner, D., Shinde, S., Asanović, K., Song, D.: Keystone: an open framework for architecting trusted execution environments. In: EuroSys (2020)
19. Pinto, S., Santos, N.: Demystifying arm trustzone: a comprehensive survey. ACM Comput. Surv. (2019)
20. Van Bulck, J., et al.: Foreshadow: extracting the keys to the intel SGX kingdom with transient Out-of-Order execution. In: USENIX Security (2018)
21. van Schaik, S., et al.: SoK: SGX.Fail: how stuff gets eXposed. In: IEEE Security & Privacy (2024)
22. Zhang, Z., Tao, M., O'Connell, S., Chuengsatiansup, C., Genkin, D., Yarom, Y.: BunnyHop: exploiting the instruction prefetcher. In: USENIX Security (2023)
23. Goldwasser, S., Micali, S., Rackoff, C.: The knowledge complexity of interactive proof-systems. SIAM J. Comput. (1989)
24. Bünz, B., Fisch, B., Szepieniec, A.: Transparent SNARKs from DARK compilers. In: EUROCRYPT (2020)
25. Lee, J.: Dory: efficient, transparent arguments for generalised inner products and polynomial commitments. In: TCC (2021)
26. Groth, J.: On the size of pairing-based non-interactive arguments. In: Eurocrypt (2016)
27. Maller, M., Bowe, S., Kohlweiss, M., Meiklejohn, S.: Sonic: zero-knowledge snarks from linear-size universal and updatable structured reference strings. In: ACM CCS (2019)
28. Chiesa, A., Yuncong, H., Maller, M., Mishra, P., Vesely, N., Ward, N.: Marlin: preprocessing zkSNARKs with universal and updatable SRS. In: Eurocrypt (2020)

29. Groth, J., Kohlweiss, M., Maller, M., Meiklejohn, S., Miers, I.: Updatable and universal common reference strings with applications to zk-SNARKs. In: CRYPTO (2018)
30. Chen, M., et al.: Diogenes: lightweight scalable RSA modulus generation with a dishonest majority. In: IEEE Security & Privacy (2021)
31. Gabizon, A., Williamson, Z.J., Ciobotaru, O.: PLONK: permutations over lagrange-bases for oecumenical noninteractive arguments of knowledge. Cryptology ePrint Archive, Paper 2019/953 (2019)
32. Bootle, J., Cerulli, A., Chaidos, P., Groth, J., Petit, C.: Efficient zero-knowledge arguments for arithmetic circuits in the discrete log setting. In: Eurocrypt (2016)
33. Campanelli, M., Faonio, A., Fiore, D., Querol, A., Rodríguez, H.: Lunar: a toolbox for more efficient universal and updatable zkSNARKs and commit-and-prove extensions. In: Asiacrypt (2021)
34. Ràfols, C., Zapico, A.: An algebraic framework for universal and updatable SNARKs. In: CRYPTO (2021)
35. Lipmaa, H., Siim, J., Zając, M.: Counting vampires: from univariate sumcheck to updatable zk-snark. In: Asiacrypt (2022)
36. Bootle, J., Chiesa, A., Yuncong, H., Orru, M.: Gemini: elastic SNARKs for diverse environments. In: Eurocrypt (2022)
37. Campanelli, M., Gailly, N., Gennaro, R., Jovanovic, P., Mihali, M., Thaler, J.: Testudo: linear time prover SNARKs with constant size proofs and square root size universal setup. In: Latincrypt (2023)
38. Gennaro, R., Gentry, C., Parno, B., Raykova, M.: Quadratic span programs and succinct NIZKs without PCPs. In: Eurocrypt (2013)
39. Dellepere, M., Mishra, P., Shirzad, A.: Garuda and pari: smaller and faster snarks via equifficient polynomial commitments. ePrint Archive (2024)
40. Groth, J., Maller, M.: Snarky signatures: minimal signatures of knowledge from simulation-extractable snarks. In: CRYPTO (2017)
41. Lipmaa, H.: Polymath: groth16 is not the limit. In: CRYPTO (2024)
42. Ben-Sasson, E., Chiesa, A., Tromer, E., Virza, M.: Scalable zero knowledge via cycles of elliptic curves. In: CRYPTO (2014)
43. Parno, B., Howell, J., Gentry, C., Raykova, M.: Pinocchio: nearly practical verifiable computation. In: IEEE Security & Privacy (2013)
44. Kate, A., Zaverucha, G.M., Goldberg, I.: Constant-size commitments to polynomials and their applications. In: Asiacrypt (2010)
45. Bünz, B., Bootle, J., Boneh, D., Poelstra, A., Wuille, P., Maxwell, G.: Bulletproofs: short proofs for confidential transactions and more. In: IEEE Security & Privacy (2018)
46. Ben-Sasson, E., Bertov, I., Horesh, Y., Riabzev, M.: Fast Reed-Solomon interactive oracle proofs of proximity. In: ICALP (2018)
47. Arun, A., Ganesh, C., Lokam, S., Mopuri, T., Sridhar, S.: Dew: a transparent constant-sized polynomial commitment scheme. In: PKC (2023)
48. Seres, I.A., Burcsi, P.: Behemoth: transparent polynomial commitment scheme with constant opening proof size and verifier time. ePrint (2023)
49. Papamanthou, C., Shi, E., Tamassia, R.: Signatures of correct computation. In: TCC (2013)
50. Xie, T., Zhang, Y., Song, D.: Orion: zero knowledge proof with linear prover time. In: CRYPTO (2022)
51. Kohrita, T., Towa, P.: Zeromorph: zero-knowledge multilinear-evaluation proofs from homomorphic univariate commitments. J. Cryptol. (2024)

52. Chen, B., Bünz, B., Boneh, D., Zhang, Z.: Hyperplonk: plonk with linear-time prover and high-degree custom gates. In: EurocryptO (2023)
53. Zeilberger, H., Chen, B., Fisch, B.: Basefold: efficient field-agnostic polynomial commitment schemes from foldable codes. In: CRYPTO (2024)
54. Ben-Sasson, E., Chiesa, A., Green, M., Tromer, E., Virza, M.: Secure sampling of public parameters for succinct zero knowledge proofs. In: IEEE Security & Privacy (2015)
55. Bowe, S., Gabizon, A., Green, M.D.: A multi-party protocol for constructing the public parameters of the Pinocchio zk-SNARK. In: FC (2019)
56. Abdolmaleki, B., Baghery, K., Lipmaa, H., Siim, J., Zajac, M.: UC-secure CRS generation for SNARKs. In: Africacrypt (2019)
57. Aggelakis, A.,et al.: A non-interactive shuffle argument with low trust assumptions. In: CT-RSA (2020)
58. Rabin, M.O.: Transaction protection by beacons. J. Comput. Syst. Sci. (1983)
59. Semaphore trusted setup. https://github.com/privacy-scaling-explorations/semaphore-phase2-setup
60. Tornado.cash trusted setup ceremony app. https://github.com/tornadocash/trusted-setup-server
61. Aztec trusted ceremony. https://medium.com/aztec-protocol/aztec-crs-the-biggest-mpc-setup-in-history-has-successfully-finished-74c6909cd0c4
62. Raikwar, M., Gligoroski, D.: SoK: decentralized randomness beacon protocols. In: Australasian Conference on Information Security and Privacy (2022)
63. Kavousi, A., Wang, Z., Jovanovic, P.: SoK: public randomness. In: Euro S&P (2024)
64. Kohlweiss, M., Maller, M., Siim, J., Volkhov, M.: Snarky ceremonies. In: Asiacrypt (2021)
65. Ben-Sasson, E., Chiesa, A., Tromer, E., Virza, M.: Succinct non-interactive zero knowledge for a von neumann architecture. In: USENIX Security (2014)
66. Bowe, S., Gabizon, A., Miers, I.: Scalable multi-party computation for zk-SNARK parameters in the random beacon model. Cryptology ePrint Archive, Paper 2017/1050 (2017)
67. Kerber, T., Kiayias, A., Kohlweiss, M.: Mining for privacy: how to bootstrap a snarky blockchain. In: Financial Crypto (2021)
68. Cohen, R., Doerner, J., Kondi, Y., Shelat, A.: Guaranteed output in $o(\sqrt{n})$ rounds for round-robin sampling protocols. In: Eurocrypt (2022)
69. Nikolaenko, V., Ragsdale, S., Bonneau, J., Boneh, D.: Powers-of-tau to the people: decentralizing setup ceremonies. In: ACNS (2024)
70. Internet Archive. The internet archive (2024). https://archive.org/
71. Definitely Setup. Definitely setup project (2024). https://github.com/privacy-scaling-explorations/DefinitelySetup
72. Ishai, Y., Ostrovsky, R., Seyalioglu, H.: Identifying cheaters without an honest majority. In: TCC (2012)
73. Ishai, Y., Ostrovsky, R., Zikas, V.: Secure multi-party computation with identifiable abort. In: CRYPTO (2014)
74. Cleve, R.: Limits on the security of coin flips when half the processors are faulty. In: STOC (1986)
75. Ishai, Y., Patra, A., Patranabis, S., Ravi, D., Srinivasan, A.: Fully-secure MPC with minimal trust. In: TCC (2022)
76. Aleo trusted setup. https://setup.aleo.org/
77. Anon adahaar trusted ceremony. https://ceremony.pse.dev/projects/AnonAadhaarV2TrustedSetupCeremony

78. Axiom trusted ceremony. https://docs.axiom.xyz/docs/transparency-and-security/kzg-trusted-setup
79. Damgård, I.: On σ-protocols. Technical report (2002)
80. Celo plumo trusted ceremony. https://blog.celo.org/the-plumo-ceremony-ac7649e9c8d8
81. CLR-fund trusted ceremony. https://blog.clr.fund/trusted-setup-completed
82. Degate trusted setup. https://medium.com/degate/degate-completes-zk-trusted-setup-ceremony-4752301e379f
83. Email wallet trusted ceremony. https://ceremony.pse.dev/projects/Email%20Wallet%20Trusted%20Setup%20Ceremony
84. Filecoin mainnet trusted setup. https://filecoin.io/blog/posts/trusted-setup-complete/
85. Filecoin snapdeal trusted setup. https://filecoin.io/blog/posts/trusted-setup-complete-for-network-v15-upgrade/
86. Fractal cash trusted setup ceremony. https://medium.com/@fractalcash/fractal-cash-announces-trusted-setup-ceremony-652445cfe176
87. Hermez trusted setup ceremony. https://github.com/hermeznetwork/phase2ceremony_4
88. Ethereum KZG ceremony. https://github.com/ethereum/kzg-ceremony
89. Loopring trusted setup ceremony. https://loopring.org/#/ceremony
90. Maci v1 trusted setup ceremony. https://ceremony.pse.dev/projects/Maci%20v1%20Trusted%20Setup%20Ceremony
91. Maci v1 trusted setup ceremony. https://ceremony.pse.dev/projects/MACI%20V1.2.0%20Trusted%20Setup%20Ceremony
92. Maci v2 trusted setup ceremony. https://ceremony.pse.dev/projects/MACI%20v2%20Trusted%20Setup%20Ceremony
93. Manta trusted setup. https://cointelegraph.com/news/manta-network-conducts-record-breaking-trusted-setup-ceremony-4-000-contribute
94. Namanda trusted setup. https://namada.net/trusted-setup
95. Panther trusted setup ceremony. https://github.com/pantherprotocol/preZKPceremony
96. Ppot trusted setup. https://perpetualpowersoftau.com/
97. Rln trusted setup ceremony. https://ceremony.pse.dev/projects/RLN%20Trusted%20Setup%20Ceremony
98. Risczero trusted setup ceremony. https://ceremony.pse.dev/projects/RISC%20Zero%20STARK-to-SNARK%20Prover
99. Semaphore v4 trusted setup ceremony. https://ceremony.pse.dev/projects/Semaphore%20V4%20Ceremony
100. Tornadocash trusted setup ceremony. https://tornado-cash.medium.com/the-biggest-trusted-setup-ceremony-in-the-world-3c6ab9c8fffa
101. Unirep trusted setup ceremony. https://ceremony.unirep.io/
102. Zcash sprout setup ceremony. https://electriccoin.co/blog/the-design-of-the-ceremony/
103. Zcash sapling MPC. https://electriccoin.co/blog/completion-of-the-sapling-mpc/
104. Zkopru trusted setup ceremony. https://medium.com/privacy-scaling-explorations/zkopru-trusted-setup-ceremony-f2824bfebb0f
105. Zkp2p trusted setup. https://ceremony.pse.dev/projects/ZKP2P%20Trusted%20Setup%20Ceremony
106. Zkp2p v2 trusted setup. https://ceremony.pse.dev/projects/ZKP2P%20Trusted%20Setup%20Ceremony%20V2

107. Zkp2p domain trusted setup. https://ceremony.pse.dev/projects/ZKP2P%20Domain%20Marketplace
108. Zksync trusted setup. https://docs.lite.zksync.io/userdocs/security/#universal-crs-setup
109. Zkticket trusted setup. https://ceremony.pse.dev/projects/ZK%20Ticket%20Trusted%20Setup%20Ceremony
110. Gabizon, A.: On the security of the BCTV Pinocchio zk-SNARK variant. Cryptology ePrint Archive, Paper 2019/119 (2019)
111. Campanelli, M., Gennaro, R., Goldfeder, S., Nizzardo, L.: Zero-knowledge contingent payments revisited: attacks and payments for services. In: ACM CCS (2017)
112. Bellare, M., Fuchsbauer, G., Scafuro, A.: NIZKs with an untrusted CRS: security in the face of parameter subversion. In: Asiacrypt (2016)
113. Swihart, J.: Zcash counterfeiting vulnerability successfully remediated. ECC Blog (2019)
114. Choudhuri, A.R., Garg, S., Goel, A., Sekar, S., Sinha, R.: Sublonk: sublinear prover plonk. Cryptology ePrint Archive, Paper 2023/902 (2023)
115. Das, S., Xiang, Z., Ren, L.: Powers of tau in asynchrony. In: NDSS (2024)
116. Barreto, P. S.L.M., Naehrig, M.: Pairing-friendly elliptic curves of prime order. In: SAC (2006)
117. Barreto, P.S., Lynn, B., Scott, M.: Constructing elliptic curves with prescribed embedding degrees. In: SCN (2003)
118. Bellés-Muñoz, M., Whitehat, B., Baylina, J., Daza, V., Muñoz-Tapia, J.L.: Twisted edwards elliptic curves for zero-knowledge circuits. Mathematics (2021)
119. Buterin, V., Reitwiessner, C.: EIP-197: Precompiled contracts for optimal ate pairing check on the elliptic curve alt_bn128 (2017)
120. Multi-party computation protocol for the key-generation step of Pinocchio zkSNARKs. https://github.com/zcash/mpc
121. NCC Group Research Blog. Zcash cryptography and code review
122. KZG ceremony (2023). https://github.com/ethereum/kzg-ceremony
123. Kim, S., Woo, S., Lee, H., Oh, H.: Vuddy: a scalable approach for vulnerable code clone discovery. In: IEEE Security & Privacy (2017)
124. arkworks contributors. arkworks zkSNARK ecosystem (2022). https://arkworks.rs
125. Botrel, G., Piellard, T., El Housni, Y., Kubjas, I., Tabaie, A.: Consensys/gnark: v0.9.0 (2023). https://doi.org/10.5281/zenodo.5819104
126. KZG Ceremony Special Contributions (2023). https://github.com/ethereum/kzg-ceremony/blob/main/special_contributions.md

Short Paper: Curve Forests
Transparent Zero-Knowledge Set Membership with Batching and Strong Security

Matteo Campanelli[1], Mathias Hall-Andersen[2],
and Simon Holmgaard Kamp[3(✉)]

[1] Offchain Labs, New York, USA
matteo@offchainlabs.com
[2] ZKSecurity, Aarhus, Denmark
mathias@hall-andersen.dk
[3] CISPA Helmholtz Center for Information Security, Saarbrücken, Germany
simonhkamp@gmail.com

Abstract. Zero-knowledge for set membership is a building block at the core of several privacy-aware applications, such as anonymous payments, credentials and whitelists. We propose a new efficient construction for the *batching* variant of the problem, where a user intends to show knowledge of several elements (a batch) in a set without any leakage on the elements. Our construction is transparent—it does not requires a trusted setup—and based on Curve Trees by Campanelli, Hall-Andersen and Kamp (USENIX 2023). Our first technical contribution consists in techniques to amortize Curve Trees costs in the batching setting for which we crucially exploit its algebraic properties. Even for small batches we obtain ≈2× speedups for proving, ≈3× speedups for verification and ≈60% reduction in proof size. Our second contribution is a modifications of a key technical requirement in Curve Trees (related to so called "permissible points") which arguably simplifies its design and obtains a stronger security property. In particular, our construction is secure even for the case where the commitment to the set is provided by the adversary (in contrast to the honest one required by the original Curve Trees).

1 Introduction

Zero-knowledge proofs are a cryptographic technique that enables someone to prove they possess knowledge of a secret without disclosing the secret itself. Various applications rely on these proofs being both short and computationally efficient. A growing application of zero-knowledge proofs is to *set membership*: given a compact digest of a set S (also called *accumulator*), the goal is to later show knowledge of an element in S without revealing the element itself. This is particularly useful in areas like privacy-preserving distributed ledgers, anonymous broadcasting, financial identity management, and asset governance (see [2]).

This work was done while the author was at Aarhus University and is partially funded by the Concordium Foundation.

Batching: Applications and Challenges. In this work we consider the *batching* variant of the set membership problem: where we want to show that several elements are in a set (all at the same time). The batching setting is immediately applicable to scenarios we already mentioned: privacy-preserving ledgers (proving multiple transactions at the same time) and to decentralized identities (or DID, where a user may want to prove it possesses *several* identity-related attributes to convince someone else they are eligible for a loan, voting, etc.). Besides these concrete application settings, zero-knowledge for batch set membership can itself be used as a tool to obtain more complicated cryptographic proofs. For example, they can be used to build lookup arguments as argued in [18] (which in turn can be used to build zkVMs [1,5]).

The applications we mentioned so far assume an *honestly generated* accumulator. This is the case for example in blockchains where updates are (in principle) observed by all participants and agreed to through a consensus. If a proof system for set-membership is secure even for the (harder) setting where the accumulator may be provided by a malicious actor, then we can unlock even more applications[1]. These includes, for example, zero-knowledge for machine learning: as argued in [4], it is possible to represent key features of a decision tree as a set and then use zero-knowledge for set membership (referred to as a lookup in that paper) to prove correct classification. We refer to the discussion in [7, Section 7] for other example applications of settings where a user provides a hidden, but potentially malicious digest to a set of features.

Our Goal. In this paper we aim at providing an efficient solution to the batching set membership problem and to extend its spectrum of applications as much as possible, by achieving security for the malicious-accumulator setting. We now discuss what features an *acceptable* solution should have.

A trivial solution to the batching problem is one that performs a set membership proof for each of the elements in the batch. This is not an interesting solution since its proving and verification time, as well as the bandwidth required, are growing *linearly* with the batch size (which may be unacceptable in several applications). We desire a solution where we can amortize the total costs in these metrics when proving/verifying a batch.

Another aspect we will focus on in this work is the requirement for a *transparent* setup. What this means is that the system should work securely and efficiently without a one-time step run by a trusted entity (the setup)[2].

Our Starting Point: Curve Trees—Background and Limitations. The starting point for our work is the recent construction of Curve Trees by Campanelli, Hall-Andersen and Kamp [10]. This construction is interesting for three

---

[1] One intuition for why this is harder problem is that the adversary may provide a cleverly malformed accumulator on which it can cheat later. Hereby we refer to this scenario as the *malicious-accumulator* setting.
[2] Trusted setups can be emulated by multi-party computations but this keeps being complex, costly and risky. Trusted setups often defy the point of "removing as much trust as possible" often pursued in distributed ledgers.

reasons: *i) efficiency*, it currently represents the current state of art for transparent zero-knowledge set membership in terms of number of constraints[3]; *ii)impact*, it may soon constitute the backbone for proofs in the privacy-preserving cryptocurrency Monero[4]; *iii)techniques*, since every node in a Curve Tree is a point on an elliptic curve, this gives us a broad set of algebraic tricks we can exploit.

Unfortunately, as of today, Curve Trees does not provide any form of batching besides the *trivial* one outlined above (we note that it allows to amortize verification of several proofs through techniques from [3] but it does not improve bandwidth or proving time). Also, the construction relies on the accumulator being provided honestly. As mentioned, this does match the requirements of settings like distributed ledgers, but at the same time prevents others applications.

Our contributions In this work:

- We provide a non-trivial batching version of Curve Trees that trades a larger accumulator for a more efficient prover and smaller proof. We dub this construction a *Curve Forest* because of the key idea at its core: an accumulator is now encoding not a single tree, but several ones (each constructed in a particular way). At proving time we exploit the redundant representation of multiple trees and "merge" several opening proofs as much as possible through (standard) techniques from the DLOG setting. Even for small batches, our construction obtains $\approx 2\times$ speedups for proving, $\approx 3\times$ speedups for verification and $\approx 60\%$ reduction in proof size compared to the original [10].
- We show how to remove an idiosyncratic requirement during the building process for Curve Trees and how this can lead to stronger security. The specific requirement is that of having nodes being of a specific form, i.e. being *permissible points*. Enforcing the requirements require additional steps while computing the digest. While these steps are shown to be *efficient on average* in [10], they are not guaranteed to always be. We show how to build a Curve Tree structure without permissible points. As a result we obtain a modest efficiency improvement, but also stronger security, in particular making the scheme applicable in the scenario where the accumulator may be untrusted.

We stress that these modifications to Curve Trees cannot be securely combined in their current form and elaborate on this in the full version.

Related Work. Given that this work and Curve Trees overlap significantly in scope and approach, most of the work related to this paper is the same as the one in [10], to which we refer the reader. The discussion points in the full version [9]

---

[3] More than as a proof system, Curve Trees can be thought of as a way to reduce set membership to an efficient relation on a cycle of elliptic curves with DLOG. Other transparent solutions (e.g., ZCash Orchard) can achieve better concrete performance than Curve Trees when applying a more sophisticated proof system, e.g., Halo2 rather than Bulletproofs [3]. Using Halo2 to prove the Curve Trees relation would provide analogous speedups and potentially lead to the most efficient approach.

[4] For the last year the Monero community has been actively developing a prototype to which it may switch and that includes Curve Trees as a core tool. See https://www.getmonero.org/2024/04/27/fcmps.html.

will generally also apply to this work. Among additional works related to the more specific setting in this paper, we cite works on zero-knowledge lookups, such as the already mentioned Caulk [18], cq+ [4], the segment-lookup argument in Sublonk [13] and the recent zkLasso [5][5]. With the exception of the last one, these are not transparent. Works such as [14] provide notions of hiding almost complementary to ours: the set and its actual size remain hidden, while the elements of which we are proving membership is revealed. In this work and in Curve Trees, the set of <u>commitments</u> to the elements are not required to stay private; the commitment(s) of which we are proving membership–and especially the respective opening(s)—are always hidden. We also cite two state-of-the-art constructions on zero-knowledge for batch set-membership [6] and [16], which are not transparent ([6] is not transparent in its most efficient instantiation based on RSA and LegoGro16 [8]).

Outline. After providing some background, we describe the problem of permissible points and our solution in Sect. 3. We then combine these ideas with others specific to batching in Sect. 4. Section 5 provides an experimental evaluation.

2 Preliminaries

Basic Building Blocks. We assume familiarity with elliptic curves. We denote by $\mathbb{E}[\mathbb{F}_q] \subseteq \mathbb{F}_q \times \mathbb{F}_q$ the set of points in (x, y) on the elliptic curve $\mathbb{E}$ [15]. The curve points form an Abelian group $(\mathbb{E}[\mathbb{F}_q], +)$; we use "additive notation". We always assume that the order of $\mathbb{E}[\mathbb{F}_q]$ denoted by $p := |\mathbb{E}[\mathbb{F}_q]|$ is prime. We call the prime field $\mathbb{F}_p \cong \mathbb{Z}/(p\mathbb{Z})$ the *scalar field* of $\mathbb{E}[\mathbb{F}_q]$ and denote by $[s] \cdot G$ the "scalar multiplication" operation. We denote by $\langle s, G \rangle = \sum_i [s_i] \cdot G_i$ the "inner product" between a vector of scalars $s \in \mathbb{F}_p^n$ and a list of group elements $G \in \mathbb{E}[\mathbb{F}_q]^n$. We will be using 2-cycles (or simply cycles) of elliptic curves. These consist of two elliptic curves $\{\mathbb{E}_{(evn)}, \mathbb{E}_{(odd)}\}$ and two prime fields $\{\mathbb{F}_p, \mathbb{F}_q\}$ such that: $p = |\mathbb{E}_{(evn)}[\mathbb{F}_q]|$ and $q = |\mathbb{E}_{(odd)}[\mathbb{F}_p]|$. In other words: the base/scalar fields of the two curves are complementary. A point on a curve is a pair; we denote by $x(G)$ and $y(G)$ the coordinates of a point G. We sometimes abuse this notation by extending it to a vector of points in the natural way (e.g., $x(\boldsymbol{G})$).

Recall Pedersen commitments: commit to a vector $\boldsymbol{v} \in \mathbb{F}_p^\ell$ with randomness r we compute $C = \mathsf{Com}(\boldsymbol{v}; r) = \langle \boldsymbol{v}, \boldsymbol{G} \rangle + [r] \cdot H \in \mathbb{E}[\mathbb{F}_q]$ where $\boldsymbol{G}, +$ are random group elements. We assume familiarity with the DLOG assumptions, on which binding of Pedersen relies (see, e.g., Assumption 1 in [10]). We will exploit the rerandomization properties of Pedersen: $C \xrightarrow{\text{rernd}} C'$ through $C' \leftarrow C + [\tilde{r}] \cdot H$.

---

[5] This is work is possibly one of the others with the strongest potential for efficiency in this setting. The treatment in the original paper [5] is of zkLasso as a theoretical tool for non-malleability of zkVMs. We leave a full comparison as future work, but mention that several of the caveats for Hyrax [17] already discussed in [§1.1.5] [9] will probably apply to zkLasso (especially its "generalized" version, which is the one required for our setting).

Batch Zero-Knowledge for Set Membership on the Back of a Napkin.
We briefly review syntax and properties for zero-knowledge set membership. We directly provide a syntax for the batching setting (the standard setting is a special case). Our presentation slightly deviates from the abstractions used in [10], but it is equivalent.

We already outlined the goal of such a system in the introduction (to which we hereby refer to as a BatchZKSet scheme). It consists of the following algorithms:

Setup(1^λ) → pp produces public parameters (NB: these are transparent).
Accum(pp, $S = \{C_1, \ldots, C_N\}, m$) → A deterministically accumulates a set of (Pedersen) commitments of size N (usable to prove batches of size m).
PrvBatch (pp, $S, B = (C_1, \ldots, C_m)$) → $\left(\hat{C} = \left(\hat{C}_1, \ldots, \hat{C}_m\right), \pi\right)$ returns a proof showing $B \subseteq S$ together with "masked handles" $\hat{C}$[6].
VfyBatch(pp, $A, \hat{C}, \pi$) — 0/1 checks that handles in $\hat{C}$ refer to elements in set S.

The presentation above is for batches *on the same set*, but it can be directly extended to batches with multiple sets $S_1, \ldots, S_m$. The properties we require[7] are a form of *binding*—no adversary can claim something is in the set if it was not in the original S—and *hiding*—I cannot learn anything from a membership proof and its handle, except that the handle "opens" to *some* element in S.

Background on Curve Trees. The design of a curve tree is simple and relies on the hardness of discrete logarithm and the random oracle model (ROM) for its security. A curve tree can be described as a shallow Merkle tree where the leaves are points over an elliptic curve (and so are the internal nodes). Like Merkle trees, Curve Trees uses a hash, but the hash at each level is a specific Pedersen hash. There are three caveats to this: *i)* what one really uses is not a straightforward Pedersen hash of the children (each child being a curve point is a pair (x, y) but that is not exactly what we are hashing); *ii)* in a sense the hash function changes a little at each level (we have two curves, $\mathbb{E}_{(evn)}, \mathbb{E}_{(odd)}$ and we use them respectively for even and odd layers) and we alternate the curve at each layer (we require the two curves to be on a cycle); *iii)* differently from a standard Merkle tree we need zero-knowledge. To prove membership in zero-knowledge we use commit-and-prove [8] capabilities of a proof system like Bulletproofs [3] (or some other DLOG-based proof system), i.e., a proof system where the verifier takes as input a commitment—a Pedersen commitment, in our case—and can efficiently verify a relation on the *opening* of that commitment.

Curve Trees from 5000 ft: The protocol is building a tree where the N leaves are the accumulated set and is parameterized by *arity* ℓ and *depth* D (s.t. $N = \ell^\mathsf{D}$).

- The parameters are two vectors of $\ell + 1$ generators $\boldsymbol{G}_{(evn)} \in \mathbb{E}^\ell_{(evn)}$, $H_{(evn)} \in \mathbb{E}_{(evn)}$ and $\boldsymbol{G}_{(odd)} \in \mathbb{E}^\ell_{(odd)}$, $H_{(odd)} \in \mathbb{E}_{(odd)}$. The groups $\mathbb{E}_{(evn)}$ and $\mathbb{E}_{(odd)}$ are related to elliptic curves on a 2-cycle.

---

[6] These "handles" are rerandomized version of $C_1, \ldots, C_m$ that can be used for verification without revealing which original accumulated commitments we are referring.
[7] We will not formalize these properties here; see [10] for the non batching case.

- To accumulate a set $S = \{C_1, \ldots, C_N\}$ we build a tree proceeding as follows until we reach the root: the leaves are the elements of S; at each level we group the elements into vectors $C'_1, \ldots, C'_\ell$ of size ℓ and make an inner (parent) node as the Pedersen commitment $C_{\text{par}} = \langle \text{x}(C'), G \rangle$, where G are generators for the curve corresponding to the level. Notice we are alternating curve each time, e.g., if elements C' are in $\mathbb{E}_{(\text{evn})}$, then $C_{\text{par}} \in \mathbb{E}_{(\text{odd})}$[8].
- Zero-knowledge membership: in order to show membership of some leaf $C \in \mathbb{E}_{(\text{evn})}$, we basically provide a *hiding* path on algebraic Merkle Tree we obtained. First we give a hiding handle for the leaf $C^* \leftarrow C + [r] \cdot H_{(\text{evn})}$ to the verifier; we then send analogous hiding handles C^*_{par} for all the parents along the path to the root; for each level i we then two prove two facts for handles C^*_i and C^*_{i-1} (alleged child and parent respectively): *a)* C^*_{i-1} can be opened as $\langle \mathbf{x}, G \rangle + [r] \cdot H$; *b)* for some $\hat{x}$ in $\mathbf{x}$ and some $\hat{y}$ it holds that $(\hat{x}, \hat{y}) \xrightarrow{\text{rernd}} C^*_i$. In other words, *a)* shows that C^*_{i-1} is the (rerandomized) parent of children with x coordinates $\mathbf{x}$ and *b)* shows that one of them (the one with x being $\hat{x}$) is rerandomized in C^*_i.

The steps *a)* and *b)* above are grouped by curve (i.e., all the even layers will be proved together and same for the odd ones). Each group of constraints will be proved with a Bulletproofs execution on the related field. This way, most "openings" of curve points in *a)* and *b)* will be represented as inner products with *native* field arithmetic. This is a main reason behind the scheme's efficiency.

3 Removing Permissible Points and Stronger Security

In our presentation of Curve Trees accumulation we intentionally skipped an important detail for sake of clarity. The reader may notice that an internal node in the tree uses only the x coordinate of a point. Without introducing extra nuances, the resulting approach would be insecure. Since there can be two points on a curve with the same first coordinate ((x, y) and (x, −y)) either of them could be used in the proof for step *b)* above (but only one of them has been accumulated!). In order to ensure an efficient check, the authors of [10] propose that, at accumulation time, points need to be made "permissible" by being "shifted" several times until a simple test defined by a universal hash function passes for y but not −y (see [10, Section 6.1]). This same test will be carried out on y at step *b)* at proving time, with soundness being ensured by −y not passing the test. It is possible to show that on average a constant number of shifts will give a permissible point.

Issues with Permissibility. We have already discussed one issue earlier: permissibility provides a solution only for the case where the accumulator is computed honestly. We now discuss additional limitations of requiring permissible points. First, it does complicate the implementation of the Curve Trees approach. Since it is using a *universal* hash function, this should be in principle

---

[8] This leaves out requirements on permissibility, which we discuss in the next section.

sampled independently of the leaf/node we are inserting into the tree. As honest inputs to the function are random, the function can be fixed while keeping the permissibility step efficient *in expectation*. But we cannot a priori dismiss it having an *extremely long running time* for *some* inputs. It is not even clear that such points would be hard to find. If possible, this may potentially lead to DoS attacks when this construction is applied in distributed ledgers (an attacker could find many of these points and release them all as transactions at the same time).

Our Solution. Instead of "making points permissible" and taking their x coordinate, we propose that a child is shifted by a common known group element Δ before we commit to the x coordinate in the parent. We elaborate below.

SETUP. For each curve, in addition to the usual generators we also sample two additional ones, $\Delta_{(evn)} \in \mathbb{E}_{(evn)}$ and $\Delta_{(odd)} \in \mathbb{E}_{(odd)}$.

ACCUMULATING/COMPUTING PARENT. Given children commitments $C_{(evn)} \in \mathbb{E}_{(evn)}$ compute the parent as follows

$$C_{par} = \langle \mathbf{x}, G_{(odd)} \rangle \in \mathbb{E}_{(odd)}, \quad \text{where } \mathbf{x} = \text{x}\left(C_{(evn)} + \Delta_{(evn)}\right) \in \mathbb{F}^\ell_{|\mathbb{E}_{(odd)}|}$$

That is, for each child C, we first add the Δ generator and take the x-coordinate of the result. We then compute a commitment to the resulting list of x-coordinates. If working in the other curve at any given layer, we adapt the above accordingly.

PROVING MEMBERSHIP. We adopt the syntax from the preliminaries. We perform steps *a)* and *b)* as above but with the minor differences:

- while the public input for the parent remains the same (the handle C^*_{i-1}), for the child the public input will be $C^\dagger_i := C^*_i + \Delta$. That is, step *b)* is now showing $(\hat{x}, \hat{y}) \xrightarrow{\text{rernd}} C^\dagger_i$ (NB: this adds no extra constraints).
- we add constraints to check $(\hat{x}, \hat{y})$ is on the curve.

Finally, we explicitly require the prover to show knowledge of the DLOGs of the leaf node handle C^*_D (already ordinarily done in common applications).

Security. Consider an adversary $\mathcal{A}$ successfully claiming two distinct $v \neq v'$ are in the same leaf[9]. This is not something we can *immediately* reduce to DLOG; it can be reduced, however, to $\mathcal{A}$ knowing (r, r') s.t. $C_{leaf} = [v]G + [r]H, C'_{leaf} = [v']G + [r']H$ with $\text{x}(C + \Delta) = \text{x}(C' + \Delta)$. But this implies also $\text{y}(C + \Delta) = -\text{y}(C' + \Delta) \implies C + \Delta = -(C' + \Delta) \implies C + C' = [-2]\Delta$, and the latter *can* be reduced to finding a non-trivial DLOG relation. It is crucial for this proof that $\mathcal{A}$ knows DLOGs for the leaves which motivates the last extra proof we introduced above. While we do not frame this security statement in a full formal framework, it is straightforward to do so extending the one in [12] and

---

[9] This approach can easily be adapted, *mutatis mutandis*, to the more general case where the adversary is not trying to cheat on the same leaf node.

incorporating it into the original security proof for Curve Trees. We stress that our argument above essentially argues that the resulting accumulator (the root of the tree) has binding properties even if generated by a malicious party.
A formalization of the security notion we achieve is in the full version [11].

4 Batching Proofs of Set Membership

The first place to look for an optimization for Curve Trees batching is the rerandomization check (in step $b)$) as this is the only non-native operation and the source of roughly 90% of the constraints in the circuit. Our solution tries to eliminate as many rerandomization checks as possible when proving a batch. As a warm up to our approach: recall that proving a batch involves proving m paths in the tree. Could we show a "batched rerandomization" by summing all internal nodes on each level of the path and showing rerandomization of the resulting "multi-node"? As Pedersen commitments are homomorphic, the resulting "multi-path" hides the original nodes and the prover can open the nodes individually. However, the nodes are all commitments created from the same set of generators. So, considering a set of paths that all start by choosing the first branch of the root. If we let the first branch of the root be committed to a value x, then in the sum of the root nodes the first generator is multiplied by $m \cdot x$. This can be opened honestly to x for all m paths, but it can also be "opened" to m values that sum to $m \cdot x$.

We salvage the strawman idea above by applying it with a twist: we use m independent curve trees constructed from independent sets of generators (the blinding generators will instead, crucially, stay the same). That is for $\mathbb{E}_{(evn)}$ we need m independent length ℓ generators $\boldsymbol{G}^1_{(evn)}, \ldots, \boldsymbol{G}^m_{(evn)}$ but only a single common blinding generator $H^{(evn)}$, and likewise for $\mathbb{E}_{(odd)}$. Now the sum of nodes on the same level across the m different paths can be viewed as a single Pedersen commitment with $\ell \cdot m$ generators, and it is not possible to mix and match entries. We describe the relation for opening an odd parent multi-node to a rerandomized sum of its even children, for even parents the same relation is used with odd and even reversed.

$$\left\{ \begin{pmatrix} i^1, \ldots, i^m, r, \delta, \\ \mathbf{x}^1, \ldots, \mathbf{x}^m, \\ \mathbf{y}^1, \ldots, \mathbf{y}^m \end{pmatrix} : \begin{array}{c} C = \sum_{j=1}^{m} \langle [\mathbf{x}^j], \boldsymbol{G}^j_{(odd)} \rangle + [r] \cdot H_{(odd)} \\ \bigwedge_{j=1}^{m} (\mathbf{x}^j_{ij}, \mathbf{y}^j) \in \mathbb{E}_{(evn)} \\ \wedge \hat{C} + [m]\Delta_{(evn)} = \sum_{j=1}^{m} (\mathbf{x}^j_{ij}, \mathbf{y}^j) + [\delta] \cdot H_{(evn)} \end{array} \right\}$$

At the leaf level all the trees contain the same set of commitments and in particular those commitments use the same generators. So the above optimization would be unsound. Instead, we treat the rerandomized sum of the parents of the selected leaves as a parent in the regular select and rerandomize relation, except the ith child must in the circuit be selected from the ith set of generators.[10] We give the relation for opening rerandomized leaves.

$$\left\{ \begin{pmatrix} i^1,\ldots,i^m,r, \\ \delta_1,\ldots,\delta_m \\ \mathbf{x}^1,\ldots,\mathbf{x}^m, \\ \mathbf{y}^1,\ldots,\mathbf{y}^m \end{pmatrix} : \begin{array}{l} C = \sum_{j=1}^{m} \langle [\mathbf{x}^j], \boldsymbol{G}^j_{(\text{odd})} \rangle + [r] \cdot H_{(\text{odd})} \\ \bigwedge_{j=1}^{m} (\mathbf{x}^j_{ij}, \mathbf{y}^j) \in \mathbb{E}_{(\text{evn})} \\ \bigwedge_{j=1}^{m} \hat{C}_j + \Delta_{(\text{evn})} = (\mathbf{x}^j_{ij}, \mathbf{y}^j) + [\delta_j] \cdot H_{(\text{evn})} \end{array} \right\}$$

An inclusion in [10] requires selecting and rerandomizing D commitments on the path towards a leaf and sending these points in addition to the proof. Expressed as R1CS constraints: selecting requires ℓ while rerandomization requires $O(\lambda)$. For m inclusions this gives $O(m \cdot \text{D} \cdot (\ell + \lambda))$ constraints. The proof consists of m paths of D rerandomized commitments and $O(\log(m \cdot \text{D} \cdot (\ell + \lambda)))$ points when the constraints are enforced with Bulletproofs. With the batching trick presented above: $(\text{D}-1) \cdot (m-1)$ *rerandomizations* in the circuit are replaced with *curve additions* which are enforced by $O(1)$ constraints. Asymptotically the number of constraints in the resulting circuit is $O(m \cdot (\text{D} \cdot \ell + \lambda))$ and only the m selected leaves and a single path of D constraints need to be sent. In Sect. 5 we evaluate the concrete effects of this.

5 Implementation and Evaluation

We provide an implementation of Curve Trees with the improvements described in this paper, namely removing the permissibility requirement as described in Sect. 3 and allowing efficient batching of multiple proofs of inclusion as described in Sect. 4. We then benchmarks proofs of m inclusions using m separate select-and-rerandomize relations in a single circuit and using a single Curve Tree against using proving/verifying a batch with m independent Curve Trees proofs. In both cases we use curve trees without permissible points. The experiment was run on a Macbook with an M2 Pro chip and 16 GB RAM and the results are given in Table 1. The implementation is available at https://github.com/simonkamp/curve-trees.

---

[10] Alternatively one could ensure that the commitments being "selected and rerandomized" also have independent generators for each membership in a batch.

Table 1. Comparison for costs of proving inclusion in the accumulator for various batch sizes using either Curve Trees or our batching construction (Curve Forests) with $D = 4$ and $\ell = 256$, i.e. with 2^{32} commitments. All timings are in milliseconds. The last column specifies the amortized cost of verifying 100 proofs using standard techniques.

	Batch	Constraints	$|\pi|$ (bytes)	Prove	Vfy	AmortizedVfy
Curve Trees [10]	2	9,320	3,446	3,978	44	2.74
	4	18,640	4,270	7,932	87	5.77
	8	37,280	5,786	15,417	169	12.54
Curve Forests	2	6,620	2,927	2,014	24	1.59
	4	10,540	3,059	4,071	34	2.41
(this work)	8	18,380	3,323	8,151	60	4.35

References

1. Arun, A., Setty, S.T.V., Thaler, J.: Jolt: SNARKs for virtual machines via lookups. LNCS, pp. 3–33 (2024)
2. Benarroch, D., Campanelli, M., Fiore, D., Gurkan, K., Kolonelos, D.: Zero-knowledge proofs for set membership: efficient, succinct, modular. LNCS, pp. 393–414 (2021)
3. Bünz, B., Bootle, J., Boneh, D., Poelstra, A., Wuille, P., Maxwell, G.: Bulletproofs: short proofs for confidential transactions and more. In: 2018 IEEE Symposium on Security and Privacy, pp. 315–334. IEEE Computer Society Press (2018)
4. Campanelli, M., Faonio, A., Fiore, D., Li, T., Lipmaa, H.: Lookup arguments: improvements, extensions and applications to zero-knowledge decision trees. In: PKC 2024, Part II. LNCS, pp. 337–369 (2024)
5. Campanelli, M., Faonio, A., Russo, L.: SNARKs for virtual machines are non-malleable. Cryptology ePrint Archive, Paper 2024/1551 (2024)
6. Campanelli, M., Fiore, D., Han, S., Kim, J., Kolonelos, D., Oh, H.: Succinct zero-knowledge batch proofs for set accumulators. In: Yin, H., Stavrou, A., Cremers, C., Shi, E. (eds.) ACM CCS 2022, pp. 455–469. ACM Press (2022)
7. Campanelli, M., Fiore, D., Khoshakhlagh, H.: Witness encryption for succinct functional commitments and applications. In: PKC 2024, Part II. LNCS, pp. 132–167 (2024)
8. Campanelli, M., Fiore, D., Querol, A.: LegoSNARK: modular design and composition of succinct zero-knowledge proofs. In: Cavallaro, L., Kinder, J., Wang, X., Katz, J. (eds.) ACM CCS 2019, pp. 2075–2092. ACM Press (2019)
9. Campanelli, M., Hall-Andersen, M., Kamp, S.H.: Curve trees: practical and transparent zero-knowledge accumulators. Cryptology ePrint Archive, Paper 2022/756 (2022)
10. Campanelli, M., Hall-Andersen, M., Kamp, S.H.: Curve trees: practical and transparent zero-knowledge accumulators, pp. 4391–4408. USENIX Association (2023)
11. Campanelli, M., Hall-Andersen, M., Kamp, S.H.: Curve forests: transparent zero-knowledge set membership with batching and strong security. Cryptology ePrint Archive, Paper 2024/1647 (2024)
12. Campobasso, M., Allodi, L.: Know your cybercriminal: evaluating attacker preferences by measuring profile sales on an active, leading criminal market for user impersonation at scale, pp. 553–570. USENIX Association (2023)

13. Choudhuri, A.R., Garg, S., Goel, A., Sekar, S., Sinha, R.: SublonK: sublinear prover PlonK. Cryptology ePrint Archive, Report 2023/902 (2023)
14. Ghosh, E., Ohrimenko, O., Papadopoulos, D., Tamassia, R., Triandopoulos, N.: Zero-knowledge accumulators and set algebra. In: Cheon, J.H., Takagi, T. (eds.) ASIACRYPT 2016. LNCS, vol. 10032, pp. 67–100. Springer, Heidelberg (2016). https://doi.org/10.1007/978-3-662-53890-6_3
15. Miller, V.S.: Use of elliptic curves in cryptography. In: Williams, H.C. (ed.) CRYPTO 1985. LNCS, vol. 218, pp. 417–426 (1986)
16. Srinivasan, S., Karantaidou, I., Baldimtsi, F., Papamanthou, C.: Batching, aggregation, and zero-knowledge proofs in bilinear accumulators. In: Yin, H., Stavrou, A., Cremers, C., Shi, E. (eds.) ACM CCS 2022, pp. 2719–2733. ACM Press (2022)
17. Wahby, R.S., Tzialla, I., Shelat, A., Thaler, J., Walfish, M.: Doubly-efficient zkSNARKs without trusted setup. In: 2018 IEEE Symposium on Security and Privacy, pp. 926–943. IEEE Computer Society Press (2018)
18. Zapico, A., Buterin, V., Khovratovich, D., Maller, M., Nitulescu, A., Simkin, M.: Caulk: lookup arguments in sublinear time. In: Yin, H., Stavrou, A., Cremers, C., Shi, E. (eds.) ACM CCS 2022, pp. 3121–3134. ACM Press (2022)

Modeling Bitcoin and Incentives

A Composability Treatment of Bitcoin's Transaction Ledger with Variable Difficulty

Juan Garay[1], Yun Lu[2], Julien Prat[3], Brady Testa[1(✉)], and Vassilis Zikas[4]

[1] Texas A&M University, College Station, USA
{garay,btesta}@tamu.edu
[2] University of Victoria, Victoria, Canada
yunlu@uvic.ca
[3] CREST, École Polytechnique, IP Paris, Palaiseau, France
Julien.Prat@ensae.fr
[4] Georgia Tech, Atlanta, USA
vzikas@gatech.edu

Abstract. As the first proof-of-work (PoW) permissionless blockchain, Bitcoin aims at maintaining a decentralized yet consistent transaction ledger as protocol participants ("miners") join and leave as they please. This is achieved by means of a subtle PoW difficulty adjustment mechanism that adapts to the perceived block generation rate, and important steps have been taken in previous work to provide a rigorous analysis of the conditions (such as bounds on dynamic participation) that are sufficient for Bitcoin's security properties to be ascertained.

Such existing analysis, however, is *property-based*, and as such only guarantees security when the protocol is run **in isolation**. In this paper we present the first (to our knowledge) simulation-based analysis of the Bitcoin ledger in the dynamic setting where it operates, and show that the protocol abstraction known as the *Bitcoin backbone* protocol emulates, under certain participation restrictions, Bitcoin's intended specification. Our formulation and analysis extend the existing Universally Composable treatment for the fixed-difficulty setting, and develop techniques that might be of broader applicability, in particular to other composable formulations of blockchain protocols that rely on difficulty adjustment.

1 Introduction

Nakamoto's introduction of the Bitcoin protocol [27] put forth the novel notion of blockchains to solve the continuous (distributed) consensus problem (cf. [12]), also known in the distributed computing literature as *state machine replication* [31]. Nakamoto's protocol was designed to emulate the concept of a secure financial ledger: Users would be able to spend or receive BTCs provided they own

---

The full version of this paper appears in [18].

© International Financial Cryptography Association 2026
C. Garman and P. Moreno-Sanchez (Eds.): FC 2025, LNCS 15751, pp. 233–248, 2026.
https://doi.org/10.1007/978-3-032-07024-1_14

the BTCs they are trying to use, while being prevented from "double-spending" them. Broadly speaking, the security of Bitcoin is guaranteed by the cryptographic primitive known as *Proof of Work* (PoW) [10], in which participants known as "miners" solve moderately difficult cryptographic puzzles to earn the right to insert the next block. As of 2024, the Bitcoin protocol is still up and "humming," boasting a market cap of over USD 1.3T.

This nascent protocol quickly garnered the attention of wide range of researchers who investigated its properties and vulnerabilities. One of the first rigorous and property-based treatments of blockchains was presented by Garay *et al.* [13]. They examined the basic case of static difficulty (i.e., fixed but unknown number of participants) and defined two properties: *common prefix* and *chain quality*. A third property, *chain growth*, was also discussed in [13], and made explicit in [22]. They provide an abstract description of the Bitcoin protocol as a distributed protocol, termed the *Bitcoin backbone*, and then proceed to demonstrate that, under specific parameter assumptions, the protocol upholds the aforementioned properties in the cryptographic sense—i.e., they hold except with negligible probability in the security parameter. The initial formalization in [13] assumed a synchronous network. Subsequently, Pass *et al.* [28] examined the blockchain protocol also in the static participation setting, but in the more realistic bounded-delay network setting (sometimes also referred to as the "partially synchronous" setting [9]), where there is an (unknown) upper bound on the communication delay, proving similar properties.

The Need for a Composable Ledger. The above first works paved the way for a deeper understanding of the Bitcoin protocol and proved tight conditions for their security properties. However, while such property-based analysis is an excellent first approximation for proving the security of cryptographic protocols, and has traditionally been the first step in any cryptographic study of novel protocol concepts, it is known that, especially in the presence of malicious protocol participants, who might arbitrarily misbehave, such a property-based treatment tends to miss important aspects of the functionality offered by the primitive being analyzed, which might affect its security under more adversarial scenarios [6,8]. In addition, such property-based analysis typically gives guarantees about the protocol running *in isolation*, which might no longer hold when the protocol is run alongside other protocols (or even another execution of the same protocol) and/or used by other protocols as a subroutine. This is particularly problematic for ledger protocols, such as Bitcoin, which, on one hand, has spawned several variants of itself running in parallel and has seeded a plethora of alternative blockchain-based ledger protocols, and on the other hand, it is meant to be utilized by higher-level constructions for many applications such as secure transactions, fair contract signing, NFTs, and more.

The literature has recognized the above shortcomings of the property-based treatment, and has proposed the *simulation paradigm* as the means to offer such stronger composable security guarantees. In more detail, in simulation-based security (cf. [5,20,24,25,30]), the first step is to completely describe the desired behavior that the distributed protocol/primitive *should* have even in the presence of an attacker, instead of listing some properties that *should not* be violated. The idea is to capture the desired behavior of the primitive by defining how a (centralized) *fully trusted* party—the so-called *ideal functionality*—could best offer the services of the distributed protocol to its users. The simulation-based paradigm, then, requires that any attack (captured by a cryptographic adversary) to the protocol can be simulated as an attack to (an invocation) of the ideal functionality. Formally, this means that for any adversary attacking the actual protocol, there exists an ideal adversary (the *simulator*) attacking the (ideal evaluation of) the functionality which yields an indistinguishable input/output behavior between the real and the ideal execution.

Importantly, by requiring that no (computationally bounded) distinguisher be able to discern between the real and ideal executions—not even one that spawns/observes executions of other protocols in parallel, or creates higher-level protocols that utilize the primitive being analyzed—the paradigm ensures that the protocol is secure for its specification/functionality in any context. This yields so-called *composition theorems* that solve the property-based definitions' nuisances pointed to above. Namely, the protocol's security guarantees remain the same even when the protocol being composed with other protocols (or itself), or when it is used as a subroutine in a higher-level protocol.

The first simulation-based analysis of the Bitcoin (backbone) protocol was done by Badertscher *et al.* [2], who used the state-of-the-art and by far most commonly used simulation-based security framework, namely, Canetti's Universal Composability (UC) framework [7]. In a nutshell, they captured, for the first time, the behavior of the Bitcoin backbone protocol by means of a UC functionality, called the *Bitcoin Ledger* functionality; provided a UC abstraction of the backbone protocol; and proved that it UC-emulates the above functionality. Along the way, they also provided the way to capture assumptions such as an honest majority of hashing power—which has been known to be necessary even for the property-based security analyses [13,28]—by defining appropriate resources as UC *hybrid* functionalities[1], and providing a UC-friendly way for capturing such assumptions by means of so-called *functionality wrappers* (cf. [19])[2]. For example, the above assumption of an honest majority of hashing power was captured by abstracting the hash function as a random-oracle hybrid (functionality) and wrapping it to enforce that the adversarially controlled parties/miners (collectively) are allowed less queries than the honest miners (cf. [17]).

Beyond Fixed-Difficulty Analysis. As discussed, all the above analyses assume an abstraction of Bitcoin in which the difficulty value for a PoW to be successful is fixed and the number of parties in the protocol is always within some fixed bound. While this analysis is very useful as a first step, it does not capture reality—indeed, because of its "permissionlessness," Bitcoin is a dynamic protocol, where

---

[1] Those are functionalities available to the protocol in the real world that abstract resources that the protocol might use.
[2] Recall that the primary purpose of this technique is to fine-tune those ideal functionalities that, while conveying the essence of the cryptographic task at hand, might lack the level of detail required by the particular setting or realization.

participants join and leave the network unpredictably and at will. To account for this, Bitcoin changes the difficulty of the PoW according to the density of the recently produced blocks and the corresponding timestamps: If blocks are being produced too quickly, then the difficulty increases, while if blocks are being produced too slowly, then the difficulty decreases. It is known that there are attacks against such a difficulty adjustment mechanism, as presented in [4,11,26], making the formal examination of Bitcoin's blockchain protocol in the dynamic difficulty setting imperative.

In fact, shortly after the first property-based analyses of the Bitcoin backbone protocol, Garay et al. [14] were able to extend their treatment to this variable difficulty realm. In more detail, this was achieved in [14] by parameterizing the environment—which in [14] is in charge of spawning and removing parties—in such a way that it is (γ, s)-respecting. In a nutshell, within any s rounds of the protocol execution, the ratio between the largest and smallest number of participants must be bounded by γ. It is worth noting that this use of the term *environment* in [14] is not intended to capture simulation-based indistinguishability, and is therefore different from its utilization in UC—in fact, restricting the environment in such a way would preclude universal composition!

Thus, the above state of affairs left, once again, an important open question/gap in the literature:

Can we devise a UC treatment of (the) Bitcoin (backbone protocol) which incorporates, as in [14], the dynamic participation of miners?

Our work answers the above question in the affirmative, by providing such an analysis. Interestingly, such an analysis needs to adapt the original UC Ledger functionality from [3] to make a list of features explicit, such as the trade-offs between liveness/chain-growth and chain quality. In passing, we note that while such a UC treatment of *proof-of-stake* blockchain protocols with dynamic availability exists [1], to our knowledge, no such analysis was previously done for PoW-based blockchains, which, given both the timing of the protocols and their market relevance, is somewhat surprising.

The balance of the paper is organized as follows. In Sect. 2 we present some basic blockchain terminology, network assumptions and the resources available to the protocol, and an abridged Universal Composability background. In Sect. 3 we present our UC abstraction of Bitcoin's PoW-based lottery system in the dynamic participation setting, while in Sect. 4 we present our formulation of the ideal ledger functionality supporting dynamic participation. Finally, in Sect. 5 we present our ledger protocol abstraction, ModularLedger, which realizes the ideal ledger functionality above while using the PoW lottery functionality. Due to space limitations, complementary material, detailed specifications of functionalities and protocols, as well as proofs, are presented in the full version of this paper [18].

2 Preliminaries

2.1 Blockchain Essentials

We present the fundamentals of PoW-based blockchains below. We refer the reader to [13,29] for a more detailed discussion of the topic in the fixed difficulty setting, and to [14] in the variable difficulty setting.

Blockchain Basics. A *blockchain* $\mathcal{C} = \mathbf{B}_1, \ldots, \mathbf{B}_n$ is a (finite) sequence of blocks where each *block* $\mathbf{B}_i = \langle \mathsf{p}_i, \mathsf{st}_i, \mathsf{n}_i, T_i, t_i \rangle$ is a quintuple consisting of the (hash) *pointer* to the previous block p_i, the *state block* st_i containing transactions, the target for the hash value T_i, the timestamp t_i, and the *nonce* n_i. The *head* of a chain $\mathcal{C}$ is denoted $\mathsf{head}(\mathcal{C}) = \mathbf{B}_n$, and *length* $\mathsf{length}(\mathcal{C}) = n$. The sequence of the first $\mathsf{length}(\mathcal{C}) - k$ blocks of $\mathcal{C}$, i.e. ($\mathcal{C}^{\lceil k} = \mathbf{B}_1, \ldots, \mathbf{B}_{length(\mathcal{C})-k}$) is denoted $\mathcal{C}^{\lceil k}$. Note that $\mathcal{C}^{\lceil k}$ itself is also a valid chain. If we have two chains $\mathcal{C}_1, \mathcal{C}_2$, and write $\mathcal{C}_1 \preceq \mathcal{C}_2$, we mean that $\mathcal{C}_1$ is a prefix of $\mathcal{C}_2$.

In a blockchain $\mathcal{C}$, the state $\vec{\mathsf{st}} = \mathsf{st}_1 \parallel \cdots \parallel \mathsf{st}_n$ contains the data of the ledger, i.e., transactions in Bitcoin. To allow for an abstract representation of this information, we map each state block $\vec{\mathsf{st}} = \mathsf{blockify}_\mathcal{B}(\vec{N})$ following the notation introduced in [23] and adopted in [2]. Here, $\vec{N}$ is a vector of transactions. A special type of initial block called the *genesis block* also exists. It is defined as $\mathbf{G} = \langle \bot, \mathsf{gen}, \bot, T_0, 0 \rangle$. gen is the genesis state, while T_0 refers to the initial target difficulty for the PoW.

To account for dynamic participation of parties and thus fluctuations in hashing power, Bitcoin performs a *target recalculation* procedure in which participants take the time stamps of the previous m blocks, and compare the average time to generate a block against the ideal time b_tgt (in Bitcoin, $m = 2016$ and $\mathsf{b}_\mathsf{tgt} = 10\,\mathrm{min}$). Further, a *dampening filter* τ prevents the change in difficulty over a single epoch from exceeding a multiple of $[\frac{1}{\tau}, \tau]$. This is necessary to avoid certain attacks on the target recalculation function, such as the 'difficulty raising attack' [4], in which an adversary forges his timestamps to successfully manipulate the difficulty. In Bitcoin, τ is set to 4.

When discussing the validity of a chain, we make a distinction between *syntactic correctness* and *semantic correctness*. In a nutshell, syntactic correctness refers to the structure of the metadata (e.g., pointers, timestamps, difficulty, etc.), while semantic correctness ensures that the data itself is meaningful and properly formed, such as having valid transactions.

In more detail, *syntactic correctness* is defined with regards to a blockchain $\mathcal{C}$, an initial difficulty parameter (the 'target') $T_0 \in [2^\kappa]$ where κ is a security parameter, a hash function $H : \{0,1\}^* \to \{0,1\}^\kappa$ such that for all $i > 1$ blocks $\mathbf{B}_i \in \mathcal{C}$, we have that $H[\mathbf{B}_{i-1}] = \mathsf{p}_i$. That is, the hash of a block should be the same as the pointer in the next block. Note that in the dynamic participation setting, the difficulty is not a constant, and is dependent on the previous timestamps. We require that if $i < j$ then two timestamps t_i, t_j must satisfy $t_i < t_j$. Additionally, for chain $\mathcal{C}^{\lceil i}$ and the corresponding state $\vec{\mathsf{st}} = \vec{\mathsf{st}}_1 \parallel, \ldots, \parallel, \vec{\mathsf{st}}_i$, it holds that $H[\mathbf{B}_i] < \mathsf{gettarget}(\vec{\mathsf{st}})$ is true for all $i > 1$. The function gettarget, described in Sect. 3.2, calculates the target based on previous timestamps and is used within the overall algorithm for checking syntactic correctness.

Blockchains can also have multiple blocks that extend a single block, branching out into multiple directions. For example, a fork at block $\mathbf{B}_{i-1}$ would have $H[\mathbf{B}_{i-1}] = \mathsf{p}_i = \mathsf{p}_{i'}$ where $i \neq i'$. Near universally, this is an undesirable event. This is naturally represented as a tree $\mathcal{T}$. Because participants in the protocol will potentially have differing views from each other, a tree structure is a natural representation of a party's overall view.

Semantic correctness is defined with respect to the state $\vec{\mathsf{st}}$ encoded in the chain. We follow the approach of [2] and model semantic correctness via a predicate $\mathsf{ValidTx}_\mathfrak{B}$, and an associated predicate isvalidstate. Such predicates are dependent on the particular blockchain application being analyzed. In addition, semantic validity requires that the state begins with a genesis state, and that the beginning of each block contains a "coinbase" transaction which entitles the block miner to claim the block reward and fees.

A chain $\mathcal{C}$ is valid if it satisfies syntactic correctness and semantic correctness: for $\vec{\mathsf{st}}$ associated with $\mathcal{C}$, we have $\mathsf{validStruct}_\mathfrak{B}^{m,T_0,\tau,\mathsf{b}_{\mathsf{tgt}}}(\mathcal{C}) \wedge \mathsf{isvalidstate}(\vec{\mathsf{st}})$ is true. In the variable difficulty setting, the "longest chain" is the chain which cumulatively has the largest difficulty, implemented by algorithm maxvalid.

There have been property-based treatments of blockchains in the variable difficulty setting, notably [14] and the follow-up work in [15]. These elaborate on the need to restrict the rate at which parties join and leave the protocol in order to prove the protocol cryptographically secure (i.e., that the protocol satisfies certain properties, except with negligible probability). Intuitively, the ideal properties rely on the difficulty remaining (somewhat) stable over the execution of the protocol. This requires the participation in the protocol to not fluctuate too much over a defined period. To this end, they propose the following notion of a (γ, s)-respecting sequence. Let n_r be the number of active parties in round r:

Definition 1 ([14]). *For $\gamma \in \mathbb{R}^+$, a sequence is called $(n_r)_{r \in \mathbb{N}}$ (γ, s)-respecting if for any set S of at most s consecutive rounds, $\max_{r \in S} n_r \leq \gamma \cdot \min_{r \in S} n_r$.*

That is, within any s number of consecutive rounds, the ratio between the minimum and maximum number of parties is bounded by γ. In [14], the sequence of parties executing the protocol $\mathbf{n} = \{n_r\}_{r \in \mathbb{N}}$ is thus required to be a (γ, s)-*respecting sequence*. This restriction is necessary to prove two properties: *common prefix* and *chain quality*, discussed further in [18].

2.2 Protocol Resources and Network Assumptions

In this section we describe the resources, specified as ideal UC functionalities (described in more detail [18]), available to the protocol in the dynamic participation setting. We also describe assumptions about the network model.

- **The clock:** $\bar{\mathcal{G}}_{\text{CLOCK}}$ [2,21] is a global functionality ensuring that the protocol proceeds in synchronized rounds.[3] Specific to the variable difficulty setting, the clock also provides the timestamps used in the target recalculation function. $\bar{\mathcal{G}}_{\text{CLOCK}}$ works by enforcing protocol participants to register with a REGISTER command. Note that this enforces a regularity condition necessary for global functionalities, and having individual parties register with the functionality before interacting with it. We refer to the session id for the clock as cid. In a nutshell, the clock CLOCK-READ keeps track of a counter τ_{cid}, associated with each different session, a party set $\mathcal{P}$, and variable d_P associated with each party P. After receiving inputs from every party in the session, the clock increments its value. Registered parties in a valid session can query the clock by sending a message (CLOCK-READ, cid), to whom $\bar{\mathcal{G}}_{\text{CLOCK}}$ returns (CLOCK-READ, cid, τ_{cid}).
- **The random oracle:** $\mathcal{F}_{\text{RO}}$ models an idealized hash function. $\mathcal{F}_{\text{RO}}$ keeps an internal table H of input-output pairs. Upon receiving input $x \in \{0,1\}^*$ from a party, the functionality queries $H[x]$. If the value is present, then it returns $H[x]$. If it is not, then a value y is sampled uniformly at random from $\{0,1\}^\kappa$, and is saved in the table as $H[x] = y$. This value is returned to the party that requested it. In Bitcoin, $\mathcal{F}_{\text{RO}}$ is used in particular for the computation and verification of PoWs. Restricting the number of queries to the oracle is accomplished by means of a wrapper $\mathcal{W}^q(\mathcal{F}_{\text{RO}}^\kappa)$, which ignores queries beyond the allotted amount.
- **The message diffusion functionality:** $\mathcal{F}_{\text{DIFF}}$. This functionality allows parties to broadcast messages across the Bitcoin network, to share new transactions and extensions to the blockchain. $\mathcal{F}_{\text{DIFF}}$ maintains a party set, and a list of messages for which it keeps track of the current time remaining before the message can be received (see below).

We use $\mathcal{F}_{\text{DIFF}}$ presented above as our mechanism for communication among parties. Because the UC framework natively operates in the asynchronous model, where messages are not guaranteed to be delivered in order, it is necessary to model eventual, bounded delivery—the so-called 'bounded-delay network' model (cf. [9]; see also [21]), where there exists an unknown delay Δ in the delivery of messages, measured in number of rounds. $\mathcal{F}_{\text{DIFF}}$ is based on the model described in [2,16,28]. In particular, this means that Δ is unknown to the participants in the protocol, an immediate consequence of which is that a protocol operating in this circumstance cannot use Δ directly (say, as a time-out). Our formulation incorporates this fact, even under arbitrary protocol composition. Initially, the delay is set to 0. The adversary then sets the delay parameter Δ by passing (SET-DELAY, sid, n) to $\mathcal{F}_{\text{DIFF}}$, which it stores.

Any message sent by a party $P_s \in \mathcal{P}$ to $\mathcal{F}_{\text{DIFF}}$ with command (MULTICAST, sid, m), is stored internally in a buffer with a timer associated with each copy of the message to be sent to all parties. The adversary is forwarded the content

---
[3] The underlying assumption here, following [2,15], is that Bitcoin's timestamping mechanism works and can be abstracted as such ideal functionality. See [15] for its detailed analysis.

of the message, along with all of the message IDs. It then can swap message IDs and enforce arbitrary delays (up to Δ).

3 Modeling Bitcoin's Dynamic Participation in the UC Framework

We introduce the abstraction of the PoW-based lottery system in the dynamic participation and variable difficulty setting. We follow the convention in [2] to incorporate these aspects into a 'State Exchange' functionality ($\mathcal{F}_{\mathsf{StX}}(\mathcal{P}, \Delta, p_H, p_A)$; see below for details). This modular approach allows for simplified analysis. Here, this means that we first analyze the lottery procedure before applying it to the Bitcoin backbone protocol. When parameters are clear from context or unneeded, we also refer to this as $\mathcal{F}_{\mathsf{StX}}$. At a high level, $\mathcal{F}_{\mathsf{StX}}$ handles extending the chain state, and propagating the resulting chains to the other participants while obeying the delay constraint. Upon receiving (SUBMIT-NEW, sid, $\vec{\mathsf{st}}$, st) from a party, $\mathcal{F}_{\mathsf{StX}}$ runs a Bernoulli experiment with the given probability, extending the state on success. $\mathcal{F}_{\mathsf{StX}}$ also stores an internal buffer $\vec{M}$ of states that parties may not have yet received; those parties can send (FETCH-NEW, sid) to retrieve them if the message delay has been satisfied.

The formulation in [2], however, only applies to the fixed number of participants and difficulty setting. Here we extend the formulation to the dynamic participation/variable difficulty setting by applying the "functionality wrapping" technique (cf. [19]; see also [17]). We will then show that this (wrapped) functionality is UC-realized by a protocol we call StateExchange, in the $(\mathcal{W}^q(\mathcal{F}^\kappa_{\mathrm{RO}}), \mathcal{F}_{\mathrm{DIFF}})$-hybrid model. Later on, in Sect. 4, we will use this functionality to realize, under certain constraints, a ledger functionality that captures Bitcoin in the permissionless setting where it is intended to operate. A glossary of parameters that will be used in our specifications and analyses can be found in the full version [18].

3.1 The Lottery Mechanism

As mentioned above, the 'State Exchange' functionality $\mathcal{F}_{\mathsf{StX}}(\mathcal{P}, \Delta, p_H, p_A)$ from [2] for the static setting handles the process of extending the state of the blockchain as well as propagating the result of the extension to the other participants. In particular, it takes as parameters $\mathcal{P}$, the party set for that invocation, Δ, the maximal delay for a message, and p_H (p_A), the probability of an honest party (resp., corrupted party) successfully querying the functionality to extend the state. (The full specification of the static functionality can be found in [18].)

Next, we introduce our wrapped functionality, which will manage the current set of active parties, compute the target value for the PoW accordingly, and capture the restrictions on the environment (recall Definition 1) that will ensure the realization of the underlying functionality. Let stx-params = $\{T_0, m, \mathsf{b}_{\mathsf{tgt}}, \tau, \gamma, s\}$. The full specification of our wrapper functionality, $\mathcal{W}^{\mathsf{stx\text{-}params}}(\mathcal{F}_{\mathsf{StX}}(\mathcal{P}, \Delta, p_H, p_A))$, appears below. We proceed to describe its various aspects.

A Composability Treatment of Bitcoin's Transaction Ledger 241

Functionality $\mathcal{W}^{\text{stx-params}}(\mathcal{F}_{\text{StX}}(\mathcal{P}, \Delta, p_H, p_A))$

The functionality maintains a party set $\mathcal{P} \leftarrow \emptyset$, and a set $C = \{C_1, \ldots, C_n\}$, where $C_i = |\mathcal{P}|$ at round i. The functionality maintains a set of trees for each party $\mathcal{T}_P$ of 3-tuple $(\vec{\text{st}}, \vec{T}, \vec{\tau_s})$, where each $\vec{\text{st}}$ is unique. The functionality also maintains a value $\Delta \in \mathbb{N}$, initialized to 0. It also registers with the global clock functionality $\bar{\mathcal{G}}_{\text{CLOCK}}$

Setting the delay :
Upon receiving (SET-DELAY, sid, d) from the adversary $\mathcal{A}$, if $d \in \mathbb{N}$ and SET-DELAY has never been received by this functionality, then set $\Delta = d$. Return (SET-DELAY, sid, ok)

Registration :
Upon receiving any REGISTER or DE-REGISTER command, sends (CLOCK-READ, cid) to $\bar{\mathcal{G}}_{\text{CLOCK}}$ to receive the answer (CLOCK-READ, cid, τ_L)
- Upon receiving (REGISTER, sid) from some party P (or from $\mathcal{A}$ on behalf of a corrupted P) Let i refer to the current round
  1. If $|\mathcal{P}| + 1 > \gamma \cdot C_j$ for any $j \in [\tau_L - s, \tau_L]$, then return (REGISTER, $sid, \bot$). Otherwise, proceed.
  2. Set $\mathcal{P} = \mathcal{P} \cup \{P\}$, set $C[\tau_L] = |\mathcal{P}|$ and initialize the tree $\mathcal{T}_P \leftarrow \textbf{gen}$ where each rooted path corresponds to a valid state the party has received. Return (REGISTER, sid, P) to the caller.
- Upon receiving (DE-REGISTER, sid) from some party $P \in \mathcal{P}$ (or from $\mathcal{A}$ on behalf of a corrupted $P \in \mathcal{P}$)
  1. If $|\mathcal{P}| - 1 < \gamma \cdot C_j$ for any $j \in [\tau_L - s, \tau_L]$, then do nothing. Otherwise, proceed.
  2. Set $\mathcal{P} := \mathcal{P} \setminus \{P\}$, set $C[\tau_L] = |\mathcal{P}|$, and return (DE-REGISTER, sid, P) to the caller.

Submit/receive new states :
- Upon receiving (SUBMIT-NEW, $sid, \vec{\text{st}}, \text{st}$) from some participant $P_s \in \mathcal{P}$, if isvalidstate$_B(\vec{\text{st}} \parallel \text{st}) = 1$ and $(\vec{\text{st}}, \cdot, \cdot) \in \mathcal{T}_P$, then do the following:
  1. Set $T \leftarrow \textbf{gettarget}_{m, T_0, \tau, \text{btgt}}(\vec{\text{st}})$
  2. Set $p_H \leftarrow 1 - (1 - \frac{T}{2^\kappa})^q$, $p_A \leftarrow \frac{T}{2^\kappa}$ and forward (SUBMIT-NEW, $sid, \vec{\text{st}}, \text{st}$) to $\mathcal{F}_{\text{StX}}(\mathcal{P}, \Delta, p_H, p_A)$
  3. Upon response (SUCCESS, sid, B), if $B = 1$, then add $(\vec{\text{st}} \parallel \text{st}, T, \tau_L)$ to $\mathcal{T}_P$ and send (CONTINUE, sid) to $\mathcal{F}_{\text{StX}}(\mathcal{P}, \Delta, p_H, p_A)$.
  4. Send (SUCCESS, sid, B, T, τ_L) to P_s
- Upon receiving any other input, forward the request to $\mathcal{F}_{\text{StX}}(\mathcal{P}, \Delta, p_H, p_A)$, and return its response.

Because it is necessary to capture certain restrictions to guarantee the basic blockchain properties—common prefix, chain quality and chain growth—we do so by having the wrapper reject any communication that would violate these restrictions. This applies in particular to the case of the (γ, s)-respecting sequence, which occurs during registration and de-registration; if the environment activates participants so that they attempt to register/deregister too quickly, $\mathcal{W}^{\text{stx-params}}(\mathcal{F}_{\text{StX}}(\mathcal{P}, \Delta, p_H, p_A))$ ignores the message. The set C provides the necessary context from previous rounds so that the wrapper knows how many participants were present, and is able to determine if a violation occurs.

The wrapper handles the party management, passing off the current party set as a parameter to $\mathcal{F}_{\mathbf{StX}}$ to handle the message handling and state extension. Upon receiving a request to attempt to extend the state, $\mathcal{W}^{\mathsf{stx\text{-}params}}(\mathcal{F}_{\mathbf{StX}})$ first calculates the target difficulty from the provided $\vec{\mathtt{st}}$. From this, $\mathcal{W}^{\mathsf{stx\text{-}params}}(\mathcal{F}_{\mathbf{StX}})$ calculates the appropriate probabilities p_H, p_A, then passes off the result to $\mathcal{F}_{\mathbf{StX}}(\mathcal{P}, \Delta, p_H, p_A)$.

The wrapper also handles timestamps and PoW target values by storing the corresponding entry for each $\mathtt{st}$ in the tree. This is necessary to properly handle any calculations of the PoW difficulty in future calls to the ideal functionality, as well as be able to calculate the probabilities p_A, p_H.

Thus, from the perspective of $\mathcal{F}_{\mathbf{StX}}(\mathcal{P}, \Delta, p_H, p_A)$, the functionality operates as if it were in the static-difficulty case per invocation. Upon receiving message (SUBMIT-NEW, $sid, \vec{\mathtt{st}}, \mathtt{st}$) from the wrapper $\mathcal{W}^{\mathsf{stx\text{-}params}}(\cdot)$, functionality $\mathcal{F}_{\mathbf{StX}}(\mathcal{P}, \Delta, p_H, p_A)$ samples a Bernoulli distribution with the probabilities passed in as a parameter. If $B = 1$, the party 'wins' the lottery, and the result is forwarded back to the wrapper, which, upon responding to continue, $\mathcal{F}_{\mathbf{StX}}(\mathcal{P}, \Delta, p_H, p_A)$ creates new messages with separate message ids into its internal buffer $\vec{M}$.

Regarding message delays, the adversary $\mathcal{A}$ can enforce a delay up to Δ on the state propagation messages by sending (DELAY, sid, T, mid) to the wrapper, which forwards it to $\mathcal{F}_{\mathbf{StX}}(\mathcal{P}, \Delta, p_H, p_A)$ as a parameter. Additionally, the adversary is able to swap messages in the buffer, given two $\mathsf{mid}, \mathsf{mid}'$, provided they exist. Note that modeling the delay Δ as a value that the adversary sets instead of a parameter to the functionality is necessary since we are operating under the assumption that Δ itself is finite but **unknown**. Having Δ be fixed as a parameter would leak information about the delay and as such violate this assumption. Passing off Δ from the wrapper to $\mathcal{F}_{\mathbf{StX}}$ does not expose the value to the participants, as all interaction with the functionality occurs through the wrapper, which instead keeps it hidden.

Finally, note that the honest and adversarial probabilities are not equal, similarly to the analysis in [13] and [2]. This is because the adversary is not obligated to follow the protocol. The honest parties do follow the protocol, and this means that their probability of success is the probability of receiving at least one success within the q PoW-solving (mining) attempts. When the probability of solving a PoW is p, this results in the expression $1 - (1-p)^q$.

3.2 Implementing the Lottery Mechanism

To implement the State Exchange functionality, it is necessary for the protocol to implement the PoW system, as well as to handle the message diffusion. As usual, the party is expected to register and deregister with the relevant functionalities, $\mathcal{F}^{bc}_{\mathrm{DIFF}}$ and $\mathcal{W}^q(\mathcal{F}^{\kappa}_{\mathrm{RO}})$. Toward the first aim, upon receiving (SUBMIT-NEW, $sid, \vec{\mathtt{st}}, \mathtt{st}$), the party first checks the validity of the state, and if it finds a corresponding state in its tree, then it attempts to run the hash calculation q times (recall that it is assumed that the parties have a bound q on the number of RO calls per round [13,14]).

If the party 'wins' the PoW lottery through the RO calls, the extended state is appended to the tree $\mathcal{T}$. The process then propagates the message via $\mathcal{F}_{\text{DIFF}}^{bc}$. To implement the fetching aspects of the State Exchange functionality, the party sends (FETCH, sid) to $\mathcal{F}_{\text{DIFF}}^{bc}$, parses the output for valid chains, adds them to $\mathcal{T}$, and then extracts the states from the chains. The protocol is depicted in [18].

Note that in contrast to [2], protocol StateExchange takes additional parameters as well, which are used by the extendchain algorithm. Upon executing the protocol for the first time, the party P is expected to first register with $\mathcal{F}_{\text{DIFF}}^{bc}$ and $\mathcal{W}^q(\mathcal{F}_{\text{RO}}^{\kappa})$. StateExchange uses two subroutines: isvalidstate and extendchain, both introduced in [2]. The former is responsible for taking a state vector as input and ensuring that all blocks in the state are composed of valid transactions, including the first transaction which is required to be a coinbase transaction. isvalidstate is presented in [18]; extendchain is depicted [18] as well. extendchain takes in the epoch length m, the expected block generation time $\mathsf{b_{tgt}}$, the initial difficulty T_0, the number of RO queries per round q, the dampening factor τ, and the chain and state $\mathcal{C}, \mathsf{st}$ respectively. StateExchange uses the algorithm gettarget, which first computes the new target value based on the previous timestamps, and for q attempts, the party calculates the hash of the block, which is accepted if its value is below the previously derived target. The party will also periodically fetch messages from the network to receive new chains $\mathcal{C}_1, \ldots, \mathcal{C}_k$ that other parties have been working on, storing the valid chains in its own internal tree. We present the target recalculation algorithm gettarget below.

We now state the main result of this section. (Proof in full version [18].)

Theorem 1. *Protocol* StateExchange$^{q,T_0,\tau,m}(P)$ *UC-realizes functionality* $\mathcal{W}^{\text{stx-params}}(\mathcal{F}_{\mathsf{StX}})$ *in the* $(\mathcal{W}^q(\mathcal{F}_{\text{RO}}^{\kappa}), \mathcal{F}_{\text{DIFF}}^{bc})$-*hybrid model.*

Algorithm gettarget$^{m,T_0,\tau,\mathsf{b_{tgt}}}(\vec{\mathsf{st}})$

1. Calculate $i = \lfloor \frac{|\mathsf{st}|}{m} \rfloor$
2. If $i = 0$, then return $T = T_0$
3. Parse $\vec{\mathsf{st}} = (st_1, T_1, t_1) \| \ldots (st_n, T_n, t_n)$
4. Set $\mathsf{T_{diff}} = t_{i \cdot m - 1} - t_{(i-1) \cdot m}$
5. Set $T = \frac{\mathsf{T_{diff}}}{m \cdot \mathsf{b_{tgt}}} \cdot T_{(i-1) \cdot m}$.
6. If $T > \tau T_{(i-1) \cdot m}$, then set $T = \tau T_{(i-1) \cdot m}$. If $T < \tau T_{(i-1) \cdot m}$, then set $T = \frac{\tau}{T_{(i-1) \cdot m}}$.
7. Return T

---

4 The Ledger Functionality with Dynamic Participation

In this section we present our formulation of the ledger functionality supporting dynamic participation. We follow a similar approach to the previous section's, by appropriately "wrapping" the ledger functionality for the static setting in [2], which participants interact with instead. In a nutshell, [2]'s static functionality $\bar{\mathcal{G}}_{\text{LEDGER}}$ abstracts the process of maintaining and extending a distributed ledger. (The full specification of $\bar{\mathcal{G}}_{\text{LEDGER}}$ is presented in [18].)

Let ledger-params = {windowSize, γ, Validate, ExtendPolicy, Blockify, predict-time}, where windowSize, $s \in \mathbb{N}$ and $\gamma \in \mathbb{R}$. We refer to our dynamic-participation functionality as $\mathcal{W}^{\text{ledger-params}}(\bar{\mathcal{G}}_{\text{LEDGER}})$. The list of parameters capture the restrictions that are sufficient for the protocol in Sect. 5 below to UC-realize the ledger. The full specification of $\mathcal{W}^{\text{ledger-params}}(\bar{\mathcal{G}}_{\text{LEDGER}})$ is given below, followed by an explanation of its various aspects.

Functionality $\mathcal{W}^{\text{ledger-params}}(\bar{\mathcal{G}}_{\text{LEDGER}})$

Parameters: windowSize, $s \in \mathbb{N}, \gamma \in \mathbb{R}$; Algorithms Validate, ExtendPolicy, Blockify, predict-time.

Clock-time: The functionality maintains a variable τ_L that is kept in-sync with clock-time: Upon any activation (and thus also initialization), the ledger first sends (CLOCK-READ, cid) to $\bar{\mathcal{G}}_{\text{CLOCK}}$ to receive the answer (CLOCK-READ, cid, τ_L), then proceeds with the remaining actions.

Variables and initialization: The functionality initializes state, s_{ep}, NxtBC, $\vec{\mathcal{I}}_H^T \leftarrow \epsilon$, buffer $\leftarrow \emptyset$, $\Delta = 0$ as well as party sets $\mathcal{P}, \mathcal{H}, \mathcal{P}_{DS} \leftarrow \emptyset$. It also keeps track of the cardinality per round of the party sets, indexed by i, i.e $(\mathcal{P}_i, \mathcal{H}_i, \mathcal{P}_{DS,i})$ The functionality also keeps track of a set $C = \{C_1, \dots, C_n\}$, where $C_i = |\mathcal{P}|$ at round i.

Setting Delay:
Upon receiving (SET-DELAY, sid, d) from the adversary $\mathcal{A}$, if $d \in \mathbb{N}$ and SET-DELAY has never been received by this functionality, then set $\Delta = d$.

γ, s **Restriction Enforcement:**
- Upon receiving (REGISTER, sid) from some party P (or from $\mathcal{A}$ on behalf of a corrupted P), if $|\mathcal{P}| + 1 > \gamma \cdot C_j$ for any $j \in [\tau_L - s, \tau_L]$, then do nothing. Otherwise, forward the request to $\bar{\mathcal{G}}_{\text{LEDGER}}$.
- Upon receiving (DE-REGISTER, sid) from some party $P \in \mathcal{P}$ (or from $\mathcal{A}$ on behalf of a corrupted $P \in \mathcal{P}$), if $|\mathcal{P}| - 1 < \gamma \cdot C_j$ for any $j \in [\tau_L - s, \tau_L]$, then do nothing. Otherwise, forward the request to $\bar{\mathcal{G}}_{\text{LEDGER}}$.

Party Set Management:
Upon any other input I received from a party $P_i \in \mathcal{P}$ or from the adversary $\mathcal{A}$ the following steps are taken:
1. If $P_i \in \mathcal{H}$ or if I is a corruption message from $\mathcal{A}$ targeting $P_i \in \mathcal{H}$, then update $\vec{\mathcal{I}}_H^T \leftarrow \vec{\mathcal{I}}_H^T \parallel (I, P_i, \tau_L)$. If a party P_i gets corrupted, additionally update $\mathcal{H} \leftarrow \mathcal{H} \setminus \{P_i\}, \mathcal{P}_{DS} \leftarrow \mathcal{P}_{DS} \setminus \{P_i\}$
2. Let $\hat{P} := \{P \in \mathcal{P}_{DS} | \tau_P^{reg} < \tau_L - 4\Delta\}$. Set $\mathcal{P}_{DS} := \mathcal{P}_{DS} \setminus \{\hat{P}\}$.
3. If the message was not received from $\bar{\mathcal{G}}_{\text{LEDGER}}$, forward the message, along with the appropriate parameters and variables that this functionality stores.

Restrictions

1. Upon any message (RESOURCE-CHECK, sid, p, x) from $\bar{\mathcal{G}}'_{\text{LEDGER}}$, where $x \in \{0,1\}^*$, $p \in \{\text{LEDGER-STARTUP}, \text{LEDGER-GROWTH}\}$
   - If $p = \text{LEDGER-STARTUP}$, parse x as $\vec{\tau}_{\text{state}}, \vec{\text{hf}}, \vec{T}$, do the following:
     (a) Find the minimum interval in the timestamps during startup. Let $j \in [0, \tau_L - \texttt{maxTime}_{\text{window}}], i \in [j + \texttt{maxTime}_{\text{window}}, \tau_L]$.
     Then $lr \leftarrow \min_{j,i}(\frac{\texttt{windowSize}+|n\in[|\vec{\tau}_{\text{state}}|]:j\leq\vec{\tau}_{\text{state}}[n]\leq i|}{i-j+1})$
     (b) $ar \leftarrow \sum_{i=s \wedge \vec{\text{hf}}[i]=1}^{t}(T_i)$
     (c) If $lr < \frac{\texttt{windowSize}}{\texttt{maxTime}_{\text{window}}} \vee ar > \delta - 3\epsilon$, then set $\texttt{inv} = 1$
   - If $p = \text{LEDGER-GROWTH}$, parse x as $\vec{\tau}_{\text{state}}, \vec{\text{hf}}, \vec{T}$, do the following:
     (a) For all (s,t) such that $s \in [1, |\vec{\tau}_{\text{state}}| - \ell + 1]$ and $t \in [s+\ell-1, |\vec{\tau}_{\text{state}}|]$ set $\texttt{inv} \leftarrow 1$ if $\sum_{i=s}^{t}(T_i) < \texttt{chaingrowth}(s,t)$ for any s,t
     (b) $ar \leftarrow \max_{s=1,\ldots,|\vec{\tau}_{\text{state}}|-(\ell+2\Delta)+1; t=s+(\ell+2\Delta)-1\ldots,|\vec{\tau}_{\text{state}}|}($
     $\sum_{i=s \wedge \vec{\text{hf}}[i]=1}^{t}(T_i))$
     (c) If $ar < \delta - 3\epsilon$, then set $\texttt{inv} = 1$
2. Return (RESOURCE-CHECK, $\texttt{inv}$) to $\bar{\mathcal{G}}_{\text{LEDGER}}$

Our ledger formulation also enforces the γ, s restrictions in order to prevent too many parties from entering or leaving in a short time. The wrapper also handles party management for the honest parties $\mathcal{H}$, the party set $\mathcal{P}$, and the honest but de-synchronized parties $\mathcal{P}_{DS}$. The latter is necessary to model, as a de-synchronized party is effectively unable to extend the blockchain with its computing resources. Worse, under the model, the parties may end up inadvertently extending the adversary's chain.

Assuming the above restrictions are satisfied, our wrapper forwards all of the queries it receives to the ledger. In ExtendPolicy and DefaultExtension($\vec{\mathcal{I}}_H^T$, state, buffer, NxtBC, s_{ep}), the ledger functionality forwards the necessary information back to the wrapper in order to compute whether the proposed ledger extension has a high-enough number of honestly generated blocks, and that the ledger is not introducing blocks too slowly. DefaultExtension($\vec{\mathcal{I}}_H^T$, state, buffer, NxtBC, s_{ep}) is triggered upon an adversarial attempt to include an extension that is not admissible (e.g., by including too many adversarial blocks in one period). This default extension is disadvantageous for the adversary, and so the adversary will attempt to prevent its invocation.

The adversary can also set the state slackness via the command SET-SLACK, supplemented with a list of (P_i, state$_i$) pairs. The adversary is allowed to violate this constraint for the case of de-synchronized parties, as they do not yet have a complete view of what is going on in the network.

5 Bitcoin as a Variable-Difficulty Ledger Protocol

In this section we present our ledger protocol, ModularLedger, which realizes the functionality $\mathcal{W}^{\text{ledger-params}}(\bar{\mathcal{G}}_{\text{LEDGER}})$ above. Due to space limitations, the protocol's full specification is presented in [18]; here we give a high-level overview. The protocol assumes access to the $\mathcal{W}^{\text{stx-params}}(\mathcal{F}_{\text{StX}})$ functionality from Sect. 3.2. A party first sends (REGISTER, sid) to $\mathcal{W}^{\text{stx-params}}(\mathcal{F}_{\mathbf{StX}})$ and awaits its response. If the party receives an affirmative response (REGISTER, sid, P), the party proceeds to register with $\mathcal{F}_{\text{DIFF}}^{\text{tx}}$ and $\bar{\mathcal{G}}_{\text{CLOCK}}$. Otherwise, the party is considered to be unregistered. This process is similar for de-registration.

The reason this sequential approach is necessary is to enforce the (γ, s)-respecting sequence on the party protocol. In order to keep the $\mathcal{F}_{\text{DIFF}}^{\text{tx}}, \bar{\mathcal{G}}_{\text{CLOCK}}$ functionalities canonical, we enforce the (γ, s) requirement on the $\mathcal{W}^{\text{stx-params}}$ $(\mathcal{F}_{\mathbf{StX}})$ side. If we had allowed the registration for $\mathcal{F}_{\text{DIFF}}^{\text{tx}}, \bar{\mathcal{G}}_{\text{CLOCK}}$ to occur simultaneously with the registration for $\mathcal{W}^{\text{stx-params}}(\mathcal{F}_{\mathbf{StX}})$, then a mismatch could occur in party sets for the functionalities when $\mathcal{W}^{\text{stx-params}}(\mathcal{F}_{\mathbf{StX}})$ rejects registration, rendering the party registered with some of the functionalities, but not the others.

To extend the ledger, parties first execute LedgerMaintenance. Here, the party first runs the FetchInformation sub-protocol, where the party fetches the most recent messages from $\mathcal{W}^{\text{stx-params}}(\mathcal{F}_{\mathbf{StX}})$ and then updates its own local chain. Then, the party gathers the transactions in its buffer, formats them with a coinbase transaction, and encodes them in a state. The ExtendState sub-protocol is then invoked, where the party attempts to query the (wrapped) lottery functionality to determine if it is allowed to extend the state. Of course, this operation corresponds to solving successful PoWs. As in [2], the protocol is run in an (MAINTAIN-LEDGER, $sid, minerID$)- interruptible manner. The idea is that when a party passes a message to another machine, it loses control of the execution, despite the fact that the remaining steps are necessary for the correctness of the protocol. This interruptiblity requirement can be satisfied by storing an anchor; for a protocol of m steps, if we relinquish activation on step $i < m$, then we store $i+1$ in the associated anchor; otherwise, we store $i = 2$. We are now ready to state our main theorem.

Theorem 2. *Assume that the parameter constraints specified in [18] are satisfied. Then protocol* ModularLedger$^{T_0, m, b_{\text{tgt}}, q, \tau, windowSize}$ *UC-realizes* $\mathcal{W}^{\text{ledger-params}}$ $(\bar{\mathcal{G}}_{\text{LEDGER}})$ *in the* $(\bar{\mathcal{G}}_{\text{CLOCK}}, \mathcal{W}^{\text{stx-params}}(\mathcal{F}_{\mathbf{StX}}), \mathcal{F}_{\text{DIFF}})$*-hybrid model.*

References

1. Badertscher, C., Gazi, P., Kiayias, A., Russell, A., Zikas, V.: Ouroboros genesis: composable proof-of-stake blockchains with dynamic availability. In: Lie, D., Mannan, M., Backes, M., Wang, X. (eds.) ACM CCS 2018, pp. 913–930. ACM Press (2018)
2. Badertscher, C., Maurer, U., Tschudi, D., Zikas, V.: Bitcoin as a transaction ledger: a composable treatment. In: Katz, J., Shacham, H. (eds.) CRYPTO 2017. LNCS, vol. 10401, pp. 324–356. Springer, Cham (2017). https://doi.org/10.1007/978-3-319-63688-7_11
3. Badertscher, C., Maurer, U., Tschudi, D., Zikas, V.: Bitcoin as a transaction ledger: a composable treatment. In: Katz, J., Shacham, H. (eds.) CRYPTO 2017, Part I. LNCS, vol. 10401, pp. 324–356. Springer, Heidelberg (2017)

4. Bahack, L.: Theoretical bitcoin attacks with less than half of the computational power (draft). Cryptology ePrint Archive, Paper 2013/868 (2013). https://eprint.iacr.org/2013/868
5. Camenisch, J., Krenn, S., Küsters, R., Rausch, D.: iUC: flexible universal composability made simple. In: Galbraith, S.D., Moriai, S. (eds.) ASIACRYPT 2019, Part III. LNCS, vol. 11923, pp. 191–221. Springer, Heidelberg (2019)
6. Canetti, R.: Security and composition of multiparty cryptographic protocols. J. Cryptol. **13**(1), 143–202 (2000)
7. Canetti, R.: Universally composable security. J. ACM **67**(5), 28:1–28:94 (2020)
8. Cohen, R., Garay, J., Zikas, V.: Completeness theorems for adaptively secure broadcast. In: Handschuh, H., Lysyanskaya, A. (eds.) Advances in Cryptology - CRYPTO 2023, pp. 3–38. Springer, Cham (2023)
9. Dwork, C., Lynch, N.A., Stockmeyer, L.J.: Consensus in the presence of partial synchrony. J. ACM **35**(2), 288–323 (1988)
10. Dwork, C., Naor, M.: Pricing via processing or combatting junk mail. In: Brickell, E.F. (ed.) Advances in Cryptology - CRYPTO 1992, 12th Annual International Cryptology Conference, Santa Barbara, California, USA, 16–20 August 1992, Proceedings. Lecture Notes in Computer Science, vol. 740, pp. 139–147. Springer (1992)
11. Eyal, I., Sirer, E.G.: Majority is not enough: Bitcoin mining is vulnerable (2013)
12. Garay, J.A., Kiayias, A.: SoK: a consensus taxonomy in the blockchain era. In: Jarecki, S. (ed.) CT-RSA 2020. LNCS, vol. 12006, pp. 284–318. Springer, Heidelberg (2020)
13. Garay, J., Kiayias, A., Leonardos, N.: The bitcoin backbone protocol: analysis and applications. In: Oswald, E., Fischlin, M. (eds.) EUROCRYPT 2015. LNCS, vol. 9057, pp. 281–310. Springer, Heidelberg (2015). https://doi.org/10.1007/978-3-662-46803-6_10
14. Garay, J.A., Kiayias, A., Leonardos, N.: The bitcoin backbone protocol with chains of variable difficulty. In: Katz, J., Shacham, H. (eds.) CRYPTO 2017, Part I. LNCS, vol. 10401, pp. 291–323. Springer, Heidelberg (2017)
15. Garay, J.A., Kiayias, A., Leonardos, N.: Full analysis of nakamoto consensus in bounded-delay networks. IACR Cryptol. ePrint Arch. 277 (2020)
16. Garay, J.A., Kiayias, A., Leonardos, N.: The bitcoin backbone protocol: analysis and applications. J. ACM **71**(4), 25:1–25:49 (2024)
17. Garay, J., Kiayias, A., Ostrovsky, R.M., Panagiotakos, G., Zikas, V.: Resource-restricted cryptography: revisiting MPC bounds in the proof-of-work era. In: Canteaut, A., Ishai, Y. (eds.) EUROCRYPT 2020. LNCS, vol. 12106, pp. 129–158. Springer, Cham (2020). https://doi.org/10.1007/978-3-030-45724-2_5
18. Garay, J.A., Lu, Y., Prat, J., Testa, B., Zikas, V.: A composability treatment of bitcoin's transaction ledger with variable difficulty. IACR Cryptol. ePrint Arch. 1823 (2024)
19. Garay, J.A., MacKenzie, P.D., Yang, K.: Strengthening zero-knowledge protocols using signatures. J. Cryptol. **19**(2), 169–209 (2006)
20. Goldwasser, S., Micali, S., Rackoff, C.: The knowledge complexity of interactive proof-systems. In: Proceedings of Seventeenth Annual ACM Symposium on Theory of Computing, STOC 1985, pp. 291–304 (1985)
21. Katz, J., Maurer, U., Tackmann, B, Zikas, V.: Universally composable synchronous computation. In: Theory of Cryptography Conference, pp. 477–498. Springer (2013)

22. Kiayias, A., Panagiotakos, G.: Speed-security tradeoffs in blockchain protocols. Cryptology ePrint Archive, Paper 2015/1019 (2015). https://eprint.iacr.org/2015/1019
23. Kiayias, A., Zhou, H.-S., Zikas, V.: Fair and robust multi-party computation using a global transaction ledger. In: Fischlin, M., Coron, J.-S. (eds.) EUROCRYPT 2016. LNCS, vol. 9666, pp. 705–734. Springer, Heidelberg (2016). https://doi.org/10.1007/978-3-662-49896-5_25
24. Lindell, Y.: How to Simulate It – A Tutorial on the Simulation Proof Technique, pp. 277–346. Springer, Cham (2017)
25. Maurer, U., Renner, R.: Abstract cryptography. In: Chazelle, B. (ed.) ICS 2011, pp. 1–21. Tsinghua University Press (2011)
26. Meshkov, D., Chepurnoy, A., Jansen, M.: Revisiting difficulty control for blockchain systems. Cryptology ePrint Archive, Paper 2017/731 (2017). https://eprint.iacr.org/2017/731
27. Nakamoto, S.: Bitcoin: a peer-to-peer electronic cash system (2008). http://bitcoin.org/bitcoin.pdf
28. Pass, R., Seeman, L., Shelat, A.: Analysis of the blockchain protocol in asynchronous networks. In: Coron, J.-S., Nielsen, J.B. (eds.) EUROCRYPT 2017. LNCS, vol. 10211, pp. 643–673. Springer, Cham (2017). https://doi.org/10.1007/978-3-319-56614-6_22
29. Pass, R., Shelat, A.: Micropayments for decentralized currencies. In: Ray, I., Li, N., Kruegel, C. (eds.) ACM CCS 2015, pp. 207–218. ACM Press (2015)
30. Pfitzmann, B., Waidner, M.: Composition and integrity preservation of secure reactive systems. In: Gritzalis, D., Jajodia, S., Samarati, P. (eds.) ACM CCS 2000, pp. 245–254. ACM Press (2000)
31. Schneider, F.B.: Implementing fault-tolerant services using the state machine approach: a tutorial. ACM Comput. Surv. **22**(4), 299–319 (1990)

Rapidash: Atomic Swaps Secure Under User-Miner Collusion

Hao Chung[1], Elisaweta Masserova[1(✉)], Elaine Shi[1],
and Sri AravindaKrishnan Thyagarajan[2]

[1] Carnegie Mellon Unviersity, Pittsburgh, USA
[2] University of Sydney, Sydney, Australia

Abstract. Cross-chain trading is fundamental to blockchains and Decentralized Finance (DeFi). A way to achieve such trading in a truly decentralized manner, i.e., without trusted third parties, is by using *atomic swaps*. However, recent works revealed that Hashed Time-Lock Contract, a key building block of the existing atomic swaps, is entirely insecure in the presence of user-miner collusion. Specifically, a user can bribe the miners of the blockchain to help it cheat.

In this work, we give the first and rigorous formal treatment of fair trading on blockchains, where users and miners may enter arbitrary binding contracts on the side. We propose RAPIDASH, a new atomic swap protocol, and prove its incentive-compatibility in the presence of user-miner collusion. Specifically, we show that RAPIDASH satisfies a coalition-resistant Nash equilibrium absent external incentives. We give instantiations of RAPIDASH that are compatible with Bitcoin and Ethereum, and incur only minimal overheads in terms of costs for the users.

1 Introduction

A major challenge in blockchain technology is ensuring interoperability across multiple blockchains. Cross-chain trading, which allows users to exchange different cryptocurrencies, is a crucial step in obtaining such interoperability. While there are multiple ways to achieve such cross-chain trading, an ideal solution would allow users to trade their coins without relying on a centralized platform and without using intermediate currencies. Atomic swaps [8] achieve exactly that – they allow users to exchange assets across two blockchains without a trusted third party. The atomicity guarantee ensures that, in the end, either both users successfully exchange their assets or they retain their original assets. Atomic swaps are fundamental to many applications, driving significant efforts in the blockchain community to develop secure and efficient solutions [8–11].

Such protocols typically rely on Hashed Time-Lock Contracts (HTLCs). These allow Alice to sell her secret to Bob, i.e., perform a *knowledge-coin exchange*. HTLC typically assumes that both Alice and Bob are aware of the hash derived from Alice's secret To assure Bob that the hash truly corresponds to the correct secret, Alice can give a zero-knowledge proof, such as [12].[1] Then,

---
[1] A similar strategy is used in, e.g., zero knowledge contingent payments [2].

Bob deposits v coins into a smart contract. If Alice reveals the preimage of the hash, i.e., the secret, before a specified timeout T, Alice obtains v coins. Otherwise, after timeout T, Bob can request his deposit back. In practice, to ensure that only Bob learns the secret, Alice can encrypt the secret using Bob's public key and use the *encryption* of the secret as the preimage, instead of the secret itself. Current atomic swap implementations [1,16] work by composing two HTLCs in a way that lets Alice reveal her secret to get Bob's coin from the first HTLC. Bob later uses the revealed secret to get Alice's coin from the second HTLC.

Unfortunately, MAD-HTLC [18] recently showed that a single HTLC instance is already incentive-incompatible and vulnerable to very cheap bribery attacks, where a malicious Bob can bribe the miners to ignore Alice's transaction until the timeout T and get both the secret and his money back. This attack renders the atomic swap solution above insecure as well. MAD-HTLC identified bribe opportunities on the Bitcoin and Ethereum main networks where a few dollars bribe yielded tens of thousands of dollars in reward. MAD-HTLC proposed a solution that addresses the bribing attack. Unfortunately, this solution itself opens up new attacks (cf. the meta-game analysis in our full version [3]). Indeed, as the authors acknowledge, *MAD-HTLC does not provide any provable guarantees in the presence of general user-miner collusion*. Given MAD-HTLC's deficiency, there seems to be little hope of achieving secure atomic swaps. However, in this work, we overcome the challenges and build an atomic swap that is secure under arbitrary user-miner collusion. In particular, **our scheme is secure even if colluding users and miners enter into legally binding side-contracts (even in the physical world)**, a much more generic attack vector than the bribery attacks proposed in MAD-HTLC. Note that general forms of miner-user collusion are not merely a hypothetical problem – such collusion is prevalent in the real world, especially in the context of miner extractable value, which has become one of the most important problems in the blockchain community. Middleman platforms such as Flashbots facilitate such collusion, resulting in a billion-dollar eco-system.

1.1 Our Contributions

We formalize the problem of blockchain-based fair exchange given user-miner collusion (Sect. 2). To the best of our knowledge, we are the first to give a formal treatment in this area. Towards this, we adopt the notion of *cooperative strategy proofness* (CSP fairness) [5,14,21]. It guarantees that, absent external incentives, any coalition of players is incentivized to play honestly as long as the coalition does not control 100% of the mining power. In other words, honest behavior is a *coalition-resistant Nash equilibrium*.

To build a CSP-fair atomic swap, we first build a new *knowledge-coin exchange* protocol, RAPIDASHKC. It achieves the same functionality as an HTLC, but can be formally proven to satisfy CSP fairness (see the proof intuition in Sect. 3). While RAPIDASHKC is a key building block in our atomic swap, we show that surprisingly, the naive composition of two RAPIDASHKC instances does *not* result in a secure atomic swap scheme (Sect. 4). Instead, to obtain a secure atomic swap, we carefully combine central ideas from our RAPIDASHKC in a non-black-box way with additional techniques.

We show that our solution is practical and compatible not only with the Turing complete languages such as Ethereum's Solidity [6], but also with the limited scripting language of Bitcoin. For the latter, we rely only on the most commonly used Bitcoin scripts and exploit Bitcoin's transaction model. Assuming generic smart contracts, our schemes are very simple to implement. In Solidity, our atomic swap requires only 252 lines of code, and we deploy the corresponding smart contracts on the Goerli testnet. We further implement and evaluate our knowledge-coin exchange RAPIDASHKC, and compare it to HTLC, MAD-HTLC, and He-HTLC [19], which aim to achieve similar functionality.

In summary, we make the following contributions:

- We formalize the knowledge-coin exchange and atomic swap problems, and propose definitions that account for user-miner collusion.
- We give an atomic swap construction that satisfies CSP-fairness. Along the way, we design a CSP secure knowledge-coin exchange protocol.
- We implement and evaluate our schemes. We give instantiations both for Bitcoin and Ethereum.

Concurrent Work. The concurrent He-HTLC [19] has results that are closely related to ours. Both works were initially completed in May 2022, and have undergone several revisions since. While He-HTLC considers only knowledge-coin exchange, main technical challenges arise in the atomic swap. In particular, as we show, directly composing two knowledge-coin instances does not yield a secure atomic swap. Rapidash provides a tailored solution for this problem.

2 Formalizing Blockchain-Based Fair Exchange

2.1 Our Model

Blockchain. We assume that a blockchain is an append-only ledger consisting of a number of ordered blocks, each of which contains *transactions* possibly involving *money*. We call a subset of the players in the system who are allowed to create blockchain blocks *miners*. We assume that the network delay is 0; i.e., posted transactions are seen by everyone immediately. Thus, when miners choose the transactions to include in a block for time step t, they can see transactions posted at time t. See "On network delay" in Sect. 3 for a discussion on network delay. While in a practical instantiation, each party may also need to pay a small *transaction fee* for their transaction to be confirmed, for simplicity, we ignore these fees in our theoretical model since we need not rely on them to achieve our security guarantees. Adding an ϵ-small transaction fee in a practical instantiation will only introduce $O(\epsilon)$-slack to our game theoretic guarantees.

We assume that a blockchain provides a way to set up *smart contracts*, which are modeled as ideal functionalities that are 1) aware of money; and 2) whose states are publicly observable. A smart contract can have one or more *activation points*. Each transaction is associated with a unique identifier, and consists of the following information: 1) an activation point of a smart contract, 2) a non-negative amount of money, and 3) an arbitrary message. When the transaction is executed, the corresponding activation point of the smart contract is invoked and the computation specified by this contract takes place, accompanied by the possible transfer of money. Money can be transferred from and to the following entities: smart contracts and players' pseudonyms. Without loss of generality, we may assume that players cannot directly send and receive money among themselves; however, they can send money to or receive money from smart contracts. The balance of a smart contract is the difference between the amount of money it has received and sent, and must always be non-negative.

For simplicity, we assume an idealized mining process; i.e., in each time step t, an ideal functionality picks a winning miner with probability proportional to each miner's mining power (or amount of stake for Proof-of-Stake blockchains). Whenever a miner is selected to mine a block, it can include an arbitrary subset of the outstanding transactions into the block, and order them arbitrarily. The miner can also create new transactions and include them in the mined block.

Convention for Writing Smart Contracts. We use the following style of pseudo-code to express smart contracts. ping denotes an empty message.

A toy contract

- **Parameters:** time T. Alice deposits $\$d_a$, Bob deposits $\$d_b$.

A_{fast}: On receiving ping from Alice: send $\$d_b$ to Alice.
A_{wait}: After T, on receiving ping from Alice: send $\$d_a + \$d_b$ to Alice.
B_{other}: On receiving ping from Bob: send $\$d_a$ to Bob.

The leading letter defines the *type* of the activation point. All activation points of the same type are *mutually exclusive*, i.e., if A_{wait} has been invoked, neither A_{fast} nor A_{wait} can be invoked anymore. If an activation point constrained some time interval (e.g., after block height T), then any attempted invocation outside this interval is deemed invalid and not counted. An activation point cannot be invoked if the balance is lower than the amount it is supposed to send out. For example, if A_{wait} has been invoked, B_{other} cannot be invoked anymore.

Above, Alice and Bob each deposit some coins into the contract. Once *all* deposits are in place, the contract is *active* and its activation points can be used. In practice, the contract should allow each player to withdraw its deposit if the other player has not made its deposit yet. However, once the contract is active, the distribution of money is only possible through the activation points.

System Participants. In addition to the miners, we consider *users*, who can post transactions, but do not necessarily participate in block creation. All users and miners are *interactive Turing machines* who can send and receive money.

(Adversarial) Strategy Space. The behavior of a deviating player can be any probabilistic polynomial time (PPT) algorithm (which takes into account the existence of money). For example, at any time deviating players can post new transactions or smart contracts, deposit money into smart contracts, attempt to find hash function preimages, abort from the protocol, or send arbitrary, even ill-formed messages to other players or smart contracts. Colluding miners about to mine a block can further, e.g., choose to censor certain transactions.

We explicitly exclude consensus- or network-level attacks—there is an orthogonal and complementary line of work that focuses on this topic [7,13,15].

Coalition. We consider users Alice and Bob, who wish to trade between themselves using blockchains. Either can form a coalition with some of the miners. We assume that coalition members share all information they know, e.g., when the secret seller colludes with a miner, the miner is assumed to know the secret. Signing keys are also shared inside the coalition.[2] The coalition's strategy space is the union of its members' strategy spaces. As in standard cryptographic literature, we do not consider coalitions including *both* Alice and Bob.

2.2 Game Theoretic Definitions of Blockchain-Based Fair Exchange

We now formalize the properties essential for blockchain-based trading. Our notions use an application-dependent *utility* function, which we later specify explicitly for each primitive. In the following, λ is the security parameter.

CSP Fairness. We first review the notion of *cooperative strategy proofness (CSP fairness)*, formulated in [4,5,14,17,21]. Intuitively, CSP fairness is achieved if a profit-driven coalition that wants to maximize its own utility has no incentive to deviate from the honest protocol, as long as all other players play by the rules. In this sense, the honest protocol achieves a *coalition-resistant Nash Equilibrium*.

Definition 2.1 (CSP fairness). *A protocol satisfies γ-CSP-fairness, iff the following holds. Let $\mathcal{C}$ be any coalition that controls at most a $\gamma \in [0,1)$ fraction of the mining power, and possibly includes either Alice or Bob. Then, for any probabilistic polynomial-time (PPT) strategy $S_\mathcal{C}$ of $\mathcal{C}$, there exists a negligible function $\mathsf{negl}(\cdot)$ such that except with $\mathsf{negl}(\lambda)$ probability, we have*

$$\mathsf{util}^\mathcal{C}(S_\mathcal{C}, HS_{-\mathcal{C}}) \leq \mathsf{util}^\mathcal{C}(HS_\mathcal{C}, HS_{-\mathcal{C}}), \tag{1}$$

where $HS_\mathcal{C}$ denotes the honest strategy of $\mathcal{C}$, $HS_{-\mathcal{C}}$ denotes the honest strategy of anyone other than $\mathcal{C}$, and $\mathsf{util}^\mathcal{C}(X_\mathcal{C}, Y_{-\mathcal{C}})$ is the expected utility of the coalition

---

[2] This model is standard in both in game theory (when modeling cooperative strategies), and in cryptography literature. Allowing coalition members to share information and coordinate increases the coalition's power, thus making our notions stronger.

$\mathcal{C}$ when $\mathcal{C}$ is executing strategy X and the remaining players (denoted by $-\mathcal{C}$) execute strategy Y.[3]

For simplicity, we ignore the transaction fee in our model. When accounting the transaction fee $\$f$, our results can be generalized if Eq. (1) is modified as $\mathsf{util}^\mathcal{C}(S_\mathcal{C}, HS_{-\mathcal{C}}) \leq \mathsf{util}^\mathcal{C}(HS_\mathcal{C}, HS_{-\mathcal{C}}) + O(f)$.

Dropout Resilience. In blockchain-based trading, it is crucial to provide *dropout resilience*; i.e., to protect an honest player if the counterparty drops out. In practice, such a drop out can happen due to mistakes, misconfiguration, or unforeseen circumstances; e.g., Alice may lose her hardware wallet. We define it as follows:

Definition 2.2 (Dropout resilience). A protocol is dropout resilient, iff as long as at least $1/\mathsf{poly}(\lambda)$ fraction of the mining power is honest, then with $1 - \mathsf{negl}(\lambda)$ probability, an honest Alice (or Bob) is guaranteed to have non-negative utility even when Bob (or Alice) is honest but drops out during the protocol's execution.

2.3 Defining Knowledge-Coin Exchange

Imagine that Alice has a secret pre_s and Bob offers to pay Alice $\$v$ amount of coins in exchange for pre_s. We assume that the secret pre_s is worth $\$v_a$ and $\$v_b$ to Alice and Bob, respectively. That is, Alice loses utility $\$v_a$ if pre_s is released to someone else, and Bob gains $\$v_b$ if he learns pre_s. We assume that $\$v_b > \$v > \$v_a$, i.e., Alice has the incentive to sell the secret pre_s for $\$v$ coins.

For $X \in \{\text{CSP fairness, dropout resilience}\}$, we say that a knowledge-coin exchange satisfies X, if it satisfies X with respect to the utility function below.

Utility. Let $\beta \in \{0,1\}$ be such that $\beta = 1$ if and only if Bob outputs pre_s at the end of the protocol. Let $\$d_a \geq 0$ and $\$d_b \geq 0$ be the amount of money Alice and Bob deposit into the smart contract, respectively. Let $\$r_a \geq 0$ and $\$r_b \geq 0$ be the payments that Alice and Bob obtain from all smart contracts during the protocol. Then, Alice's and Bob's utilities, $\$u_a$ and $\$u_b$, are defined as

$$\$u_a = -\$d_a + \$r_a - \beta \cdot \$v_a, \qquad \$u_b = -\$d_b + \$r_b + \beta \cdot \$v_b.$$

We further define the utility for the miners. Fix a miner. Let $\$d_m$ be the money that the miner deposits into the smart contracts belonging to this protocol, and let $\$r_m$ be the payment received by the miner in the current protocol instance. A miner's utility, denoted $\$u_m$, is defined as $\$u_m = -\$d_m + \$r_m$.

Finally, the joint utility of the coalition is simply the sum of every coalition member's utility. Let $\mathcal{C}$ be any subset of players, and $-\mathcal{C}$ to denote all parties of the protocol that are not in $\mathcal{C}$. Let $S_\mathcal{C}$ and $S'_{-\mathcal{C}}$ be the strategies of $\mathcal{C}$ and $-\mathcal{C}$. We use $\mathsf{util}^\mathcal{C}(S_\mathcal{C}, S'_{-\mathcal{C}})$ to denote the expected joint utility of $\mathcal{C}$ when $\mathcal{C}$ adopts the strategy $S_\mathcal{C}$ and the remaining parties adopt the strategy $S'_{-\mathcal{C}}$.

---

[3] The formal definition of the utility function util is given in Sects. 2.3 and 2.4 in the context of knowledge-coin exchange and atomic swap, respectively.

2.4 Defining Atomic Swap

Suppose Bob has x_b coins on BobChain (denoted $Ḃx_b$), and Alice has x_a coins on AliceChain (denoted $Åx_a$). Bob wants to exchange his $Ḃx_b$ for Alice's $Åx_a$.

We may assume that Alice and Bob are not in the same coalition. Therefore, we have three types of coalitions: 1) Alice-miner coalition (or Alice alone); 2) Bob-miner coalition (or Bob alone); and 3) miner-only coalition.

Given a player or coalition, we assume that it has some specific valuation of each unit of coins on AliceChain and BobChain. We use the notation $\$AV(\cdot)$ to denote the valuation function of Alice (or an Alice-miner coalition); specifically, $\$AV(Ḃx_b + Åx_a) = \$v_a^B \cdot x_b + \$v_a^A \cdot x_a$ where $\$v_a^B \geq 0$ and $\$v_a^A \geq 0$ denote how much Alice or the Alice-miner coalition values each coin on BcbChain and AliceChain, respectively. Similarly, we use $\$BV(\cdot)$ to denote the valuation function of Bob (or a Bob-miner coalition), and we use $\$MV(\cdot)$ to denote the valuation function of a miner-only coalition. In the following, we make the following assumption which justifies why Alice wants to exchange her $Åx_a$ with Bob's $Ḃx_b$, and vice versa.

Assumption: $\$AV(Ḃx_b - Åx_a) > 0$, $\$BV(Åx_a - Ḃx_b) > 0$.

The assumption is necessary to prove CSP fairness as it ensures that no PPT strategy outperforms the honest strategy. However, our protocol additionally guarantees that when the honest case yields negative utility, the best utility a strategic party can achieve is zero—equivalent to not participating in the protocol.

Finally, we define atomic swap's utility function.

Utility. Let $\mathcal{C}$ be any subset of players, and let $S_\mathcal{C}$ and $S'_{-\mathcal{C}}$ be the strategies of $\mathcal{C}$ and $-\mathcal{C}$. Let $Åd_a^A, Ḃd_a^B \geq 0$ be the cryptocurrencies that Alice or an Alice-miner coalition deposit into the smart contracts; let $År_a^A, Ḃr_a^B \geq 0$ be the payment Alice or an Alice-miner coalition receive from all smart contracts during the protocol. Now, we can define the utility $\text{util}^\mathcal{C}(S_\mathcal{C}, S'_{-\mathcal{C}})$ when $\mathcal{C}$ consists of Alice or the Alice-miner coalition as follows:

$$\text{util}^\mathcal{C}(S_\mathcal{C}, S'_{-\mathcal{C}}) = \$AV(År_a^A - Åd_a^A + Ḃr_a^B - Ḃd_a^B).$$

We define $Åd_b^A, Ḃd_b^B, År_b^A, Ḃr_b^B$ analogously for Bob (or the Bob-miner coalition), and $År_m^A, Ḃr_m^B, Åd_m^A, Ḃd_m^B$ for the miner-only coalition. We define the utility $\text{util}^\mathcal{C}(S_\mathcal{C}, S'_{-\mathcal{C}})$ when $\mathcal{C}$ consists of Bob or a Bob-miner coalition as

$$\text{util}^\mathcal{C}(S_\mathcal{C}, S'_{-\mathcal{C}}) = \$BV(År_b^A - Åd_b^A + Ḃr_b^B - Ḃd_b^B),$$

and the utility $\text{util}^\mathcal{C}(S_\mathcal{C}, S'_{-\mathcal{C}})$ when $\mathcal{C}$ is a miner-only coalition as

$$\text{util}^\mathcal{C}(S_\mathcal{C}, S'_{-\mathcal{C}}) = \$MV(År_m^A - Åd_m^A + Ḃr_m^B - Ḃd_m^B).$$

3 Knowledge-Coin Exchange

As a first step toward our atomic swap, we design a knowledge-coin exchange allowing Alice to sell Bob the secret preimage pre_s of a publicly known hash h_s.

3.1 Our Construction

To achieve this, Bob creates a smart contract, and deposits payment \$$v$ along with a collateral \$$c_b$ into it. The contract will facilitate the exchange of pre_s for Bob's money. It is parametrized by the hash h_s and an extra hash h_b generated by Bob. To obtain h_b, Bob generates $pre_b \leftarrow \{0,1\}^\lambda$ uniformly at random and computes $h_b = H(pre_b)$. Bob holds on to the preimage, but keeps it secret. We distinguish between: **(1)** an efficient **default** path, **(2)** a **refund** path to allow Bob obtain its money back if Alice drops out, and **(3)** a **burn** path, which is a novel technique we introduce to punish misbehavior. We now discuss each case.

Default Path. In the default case Alice simply waits until Bob deposited his money and sends pre_s to the activation point P_{default} of the smart contract in Fig. 1. P_{default} then sends Bob's payment to Alice and returns the collateral to Bob. If both players are honest and there are no network delays, the protocol completes at this point. In the remaining two paths, we ensure that in case of either misbhavior or unstable network, the honest party is still protected.

Refund Path. This path ensures that if Alice did not send pre_s to P_{default} on time, Bob can recover his money. To achieve this, a standard HTLC simply has an activation point which returns Bob's money upon obtaining a request from him after a deadline T. However, as MAD-HTLC showed, this is insecure [18]. Briefly, Bob can bribe the miners to ignore Alice's transaction to P_{default} (which contains pre_s), and instead include Bob's refund transaction. This way, Bob obtains both the secret and his coins (minus a small bribe) back. To prevent such attacks, we need to disincentivize Bob from attempting to get a refund once Alice's secret pre_s is publicly known. Towards this, we let Bob generate a hash h_b at the beginning of the protocol, and split the refund process into two steps: First, Bob must announce his intent to obtain a refund by sending a preimage of h_b to an activation point P_{refund} which can only be triggered after time T_1. Then, after T_2 time has passed since the activation of P_{refund}, Bob can obtain his refund by sending a message to the activation point C_{refund}. As we show below, using the helper hash h_b in combination with the timelock on Bob obtaining his refund is key to ensuring that Bob is disincentivized from misbehaving.

Burn Path. The goal of the burn path is to disincentivize parties from misbehaving. Note that currently, Alice has no incentive to misbehave: She only has the choice of either revealing her secret and obtaining Bob's payment, or not revealing the secret and thus forgoing the money. Bob, however, could attempt to bribe the miners to not include Alice's transaction for T_1+T_2 time, and including his own refund transactions instead. Thus, we must ensure that miners have a "better choice". For this, we introduce the *bomb* – an activation point C_burn, which, given preimages of both Alice's h_s and Bob's h_b, sends a small amount of Bob's coins to the party who submitted these preimages, and burns the rest. Note that if Bob attempts to misbehave after Alice's secret is publicly known, as we split the refund path into two parts, both Alice's and Bob's preimages are known after Bob invoked P_refund. Thus, miners have at least T_2 time to submit both pre_s and pre_b to C_burn and obtain the reward. Thus, Bob would need to corrupt every miner who mines a block during this window to ensure that miner chooses to *not* activate C_burn. In the following, we will describe how to set the parameters T_2, c_b, and the amount of the reward obtained in C_burn to ensure that it is irrational for Bob to attempt the attack. Similarly, by setting the parameters in this way we can provably ensure that a malicious Alice is disincentivised from attempting to activate C_burn instead of the default P_default.

RapidashKC Contract. We give our formal knowledge-coin exchange smart contract below. Activation points of the same type are mutually exclusive.

/* Params: $(h_s, h_b, T_1, T_2, \$v, \$c_b, \$\epsilon)$, Bob deposits $\$v + \$c_b$. */
P_default: On receiving z from Alice s.t. $H(z) = h_s$, send $\$v$ to Alice and $\$c_b$ to Bob.
P_refund: Time T_1 or greater: on receiving z from Bob s.t. $H(z) = h_b$, do nothing.
C_refund: At least T_2 after P_refund is activated: on receiving ping from anyone, send $\$v + \$c_b$ to Bob.
C_burn: On receiving (z_1, z_2) from any P s.t. $H(z_1) = h_s$ and $H(z_2) = h_b$, send $\$\epsilon$ to player P. All remaining coins are burnt.

Fig. 1. RapidashKC contract.

RapidashKC Protocol. Informally, we have Bob deposit $\$v + \$c_b$ into Rapidashkc (let $t = 0$ denote the corresponding time), and have Alice post pre_s as soon as Bob has done so. If Alice has not posted a valid preimage by deadline T_1, Bob submits the refund request to P_refund (and revealing his secret pre_b). T_2 time after submitting his request, Bob can obtain his refund by sending ping to C_refund. Further, if anyone knows both pre_s and pre_b, they can send those to C_burn to obtain a small reward ϵ, and *burn all remaining coins*.

We now give the formal RapidashKC protocol, i.e., the formal description of the sequence of actions that an honest Alice, Bob, and miner must follow. Note that when we give the description for Alice, we do *not* assume that Bob and the miners follow the protocol. The same holds for Bob.

> **RAPIDASHKC protocol**
>
> **Alice**: Alice sends pre_s to P_{default} at $t = 0$.
>
> **Bob**: If Alice failed to send pre_s to P_{default} before T_1, Bob sends pre_b to P_{refund} at time $t = T_1$. Then, T_2 time after P_{refund} is activated, he sends ping to C_{refund}.
> If either P_{default} or C_{burn} is successfully activated, Bob outputs the corresponding pre_s value included in the corresponding transaction. Otherwise, Bob outputs $\perp$.
>
> **Miner**: Every miner M watches all transactions posted to P_{default}, P_{refund}, and C_{burn}. If M observes the correct values of both pre_s and pre_b in these transactions, it sends (pre_s, pre_b) to C_{burn}. Further, M always includes all outstanding transactions in every block it mines. If multiple transactions are posted to C_{burn}, M places its own ahead of others (thus invalidating the others).

Theorem 3.1 (CSP fairness and dropout resilience). *Suppose that the hash function $H(\cdot)$ is a one-way function and that all players are PPT machines. Moreover, suppose that $\$c_b < \$\epsilon$, $\$\epsilon < \$v$, and $\gamma^{T_2} \leq \frac{\$c_b}{\$c_b + \$v}$. Then, the RAPIDASHKC protocol satisfies γ-CSP-fairness and dropout resilience.*

The formal proof of Theorem 3.1 is given in the full version [3]. Here, we outline the intuition behind the parameter constraints. Briefly, burning a large part of Bob's collateral in C_{burn} disincentivizes Bob from attempting to get both the secret and the refund. To formally achieve security against general user-miner collusion, we set the parameters with respect to the following constraints.

- $\$c_b < \$\epsilon$, and $\$\epsilon < \$v$: the former ensures that a sufficient amount is burnt should the bomb C_{burn} be triggered, and thus activating $P_{\mathsf{refund}} + C_{\mathsf{burn}}$ does not make sense for Bob; the latter ensures that Alice prefers to activate P_{default} rather than C_{burn}.
- $\$\gamma^{T_2} \leq \frac{\$c_b}{\$c_b + \$v}$ where γ is an upper bound on the fraction of mining power controlled by the coalition: If the honest Alice posts pre_s to P_{default}, this condition ensures that it is not worth it for the Bob-miner coalition to gamble and attempt to invoke both P_{refund} and C_{refund} to get Bob's deposit back. As in this case after invoking P_{refund} both pre_s and pre_b are publicly known, the coalition must mine *all* blocks within the next T_2 window to guarantee that C_{refund} is invoked. Otherwise, any non-colluding miner who mines a block during this window will trigger the bomb C_{burn}.

On Network Delay. For simplicity, we assume that the network delay δ is zero, and honest miners always include honest players' transactions in the next block. In RAPIDASHKC, T_1 is to ensure that Bob does not try to activate the refund path too early given Alice's transaction is delayed; and T_2 is to ensure that at least one non-colluding miner proposes a block among T_2 blocks with high probability. In practice, if the delay $\delta > 0$, we can choose the parameters such that T_1 is larger than δ plus the time required for Alice's transaction to be included in a block, and $\$\gamma^{T_2 - \delta} \leq \frac{\$c_b}{\$c_b + \$v}$ to account for the delay.

On Burning Coins. Burning money is adopted by major cryptocurrencies to incentivize honest behavior. For example, Ethereum's EIP1559 transaction fee mechanism burns all the base fees. While we use burning as a crucial component in our construction, we emphasize that the burning logic is only triggered if either Alice or Bob misbehaves. Our construction incentivizes players to behave honestly, so the burning logic should not be invoked in the equilibrium state.

Concrete Parameter Examples. Suppose we choose $c_b = v. Then, we need to make sure $\gamma^{T_2} \leq \frac{1}{2}$. This means that if $\gamma = 90\%$, we can set $T_2 = 7$; if $\gamma = 49.9\%$, we can set $T_2 = 1$. Asymptotically, for any $\gamma = O(1)$, T_2 is a constant. Increasing c_b helps to make T_2 smaller. For CSP fairness to hold, ϵ can be arbitrarily small. However, as we discuss later when analyzing the coalition-forming meta-game (see our full version [3]), we may want ϵ to be not too small, such that 100% coalition is not an equilibrium in the coalition-forming meta-game. In practice, we can set ϵ to be slightly smaller than v.

Comparison to He-HTLC and MAD-HTLC. The knowledge-coin exchange of the concurrent work He-HTLC is conceptually similar to ours. The difference is that in He-HTLC's path which is equivalent to our C_{burn}, player P obtains c_b (instead of our ϵ). Same as ours, their solution allows to fine-tune the collateral, i.e., there is a trade-off between the collateral size and the time that this collateral is locked for. For the example above, with $c_b = v and $\gamma = 90\%$, assuming the transaction fees are zero, we estimate the He-HTLC's equivalent of T_2 to be 11 (for us it was 7). For the example with $\gamma = 49.9\%$, we estimate their T_2 to be 2 (vs. 1 for us).

For MAD-HTLC, the collateral can be any non-zero amount (again assuming that transaction fees are zero). However, MAD-HTLC's security guarantees do not match those of He-HTLC and ours. MAD-HTLC defends only against a very specific bribery attack, and as admitted by the MAD-HTLC authors (Sec. 8 of [18]), it does not defend against general user-miner collusion where users and miners can enter into arbitrary binding contracts.

4 Atomic Swap

4.1 Naive Composition

Say Alice holds Ax_a coins on AliceChain, and wishes to trade them for Bob's Bx_b from BobChain. Consider naively composing two knowledge-coin exchange instances: First, Alice *generates* a preimage pre_s (in contrast to knowledge-coin exchange, there is no secret knowledge to be sold) uniformly at random, and publishes its hash h_s. Then, Alice deposits the prescribed amount of money into RAPIDASHKC's contract on AliceChain. Essentially, on this chain Alice acts as the secret buyer in our knowledge-coin exchange protocol. On BobChain, Bob is one who makes the deposit. On both chains, the default path P_{default} is locked via h_s. The idea is that in order to obtain Bob's money, Alice has to publish her preimage pre_s on BobChain. In doing so, Alice inadvertently reveals pre_s to Bob too, who can use it to get Alice's coins from AliceChain.

In more detail, we run one instance of RAPIDASHKC on AliceChain, and refer to its activation points as $P^A_{default}$, P^A_{refund}, C^A_{refund}, C^A_{burn}. We run another instance on BobChain, and refer to its activation points as $P^B_{default}$, P^B_{refund}, C^B_{refund}, C^B_{burn}. Alice deposits the payment Ax_a and the collateral Ac^A_a into RAPIDASHKC on AliceChain. Similarly, Bob deposits $Bx_b + Bc^B_b$ into the contract on BobChain.

Then, Alice generates $pre_s, pre_a \leftarrow \{0,1\}^\lambda$ uniformly at random, and Bob generates $pre_b \leftarrow \{0,1\}^\lambda$ uniformly at random. Here, pre_s is to facilitate the default path of the coin swap, and pre_a, pre_b are for the refund. As before, both parties reveal the corresponding hashes h_s, h_a, h_b. We use h_s to lock both $P^A_{default}$ and $P^B_{default}$, with the difference that $P^B_{default}$ can be unlocked by *Alice* sending a correct preimage, and $P^A_{default}$ can be unlocked by *Bob* sending a correct preimage. Intuitively, as Alice needs to send pre_s to $P^B_{default}$ to obtain her payment from Bob, once she has done so, everyone (in particular, Bob) will know pre_s too. Bob can then send it to $P^A_{default}$ on AliceChain to obtain his payment from Alice.

If Alice drops out, Bob posts pre_b to P^B_{refund} for a refund. If Bob drops out, Alice asks for a refund by posting pre_a to P^A_{refund}. One can hope that the intuition from the knowledge-coin exchange works here as well: Once Alice has posted pre_s to $P^B_{default}$, a Bob-miner coalition is disincentivized from posting pre_b to P^B_{refund} due to the fear of triggering the bomb (similar for Bob and Alice-miner coalition).

Vulnerability in the Naive Composition. Unfortunately, this intuition does not hold. The issue is that an Alice-miner coalition can wait for Bob to make the deposit, and instead of posting pre_s to BobChain, *first* get refunded on AliceChain. Of course, in response Bob will try to get his refund on BobChain. However, Alice-miner coalition can attempt to defer Bob's refund transaction, and *now* attempt to invoke $P^B_{default}$ by revealing pre_s. At this point, pre_s by itself is worth nothing to Bob, as pre_s in this construction is simply the means to obtain the money on each chain, and the contract on AliceChain has been emptied out already. Thus, if successful, the Alice-miner coalition gets Bob's Bx_b for free!

Alice can launch such attack by posting the following contract at the beginning: Alice will pay $\$r > \$\epsilon$ to the miner who invokes $P^B_{default}$ by using pre_s. For any miner with γ fraction of the mining power, the probability of being chosen as the block producer to invoke $P^B_{default}$ is γ. Thus, the expected utility of joining Alice's coalition, deferring Bob's refund transaction, and trying to invoke $P^B_{default}$ is $\gamma \cdot \$r$. Let $\$f$ be the maximum transaction fee a miner can get in expectation if it selects Bob's transaction. As long as $\gamma \cdot \$r > \$f$, the miner with at least γ fraction of the mining power is incentivized to join Alice's coalition.[4]

Second Attempt. To fix this, we must disincentivize Alice from refusing to post pre_s to $P^B_{default}$ at the right time, but attempting to later invoke P^A_{refund}. To

---

[4] This attack is just an example. How to censor a user's transaction in the context of HTLC is described in [18,20].

achieve this, we utilize the fact that if Alice fails to post pre_s, an honest Bob posts pre_b, and we allow the bomb $C_{\text{burn}}^{\text{A}}$ to be triggered with the pair (pre_a, pre_b).

Unfortunately, now we cannot guarantee dropout resilience for Alice: If Alice's deposit transaction takes too long to confirm, Bob will attempt to get refunded by posting pre_b to $P_{\text{refund}}^{\text{B}}$. Suppose Bob drops out at this point. In this case, whenever Alice's deposit transaction is finalized, Alice cannot get her own deposit back since if she posts pre_a to $P_{\text{refund}}^{\text{A}}$, it will trigger the bomb $C_{\text{burn}}^{\text{A}}$.

Intuitively, the key challenge is finding the right balance for how easy it is for a user to withdraw its deposit. If it is too easy, then it becomes risk-free to attack the other user. If it is too difficult, the protocol may not satisfy dropout resilience anymore. Next, we explain how we resolve the tension by introducing another hash to lock the deposits for both users.

4.2 Our Construction

To address the issues above, we introduce a "two-phase preparation" stage. Initially, $P_{\text{default}}^{\text{B}}$ and $C_{\text{burn}}^{\text{B}}$ are locked with a hash h_c of a value $pre_c \leftarrow \{0,1\}^\lambda$ generated by Bob. Bob publishes pre_c if the deposits into both contracts take effect in a timely manner. Once pre_c is published, Alice must post pre_s immediately. Now, we can distinguish between the case where the deposit transactions take too long and the case where Alice is malicious, and let Bob act accordingly:

– If the deposit transactions take too long to confirm, before posting pre_b to $P_{\text{refund}}^{\text{B}}$, Bob will post ping to $P_{\text{refund}}^{\text{A}}$ (see contract below). The ping from Bob acts as an alternative way to invoke $P_{\text{refund}}^{\text{A}}$ on the path of Alice getting her deposit back. This resolves our prior dropout resilience issue where Alice could not get her deposit back once Bob has posted pre_b, as now Alice does not need to send pre_a to $P_{\text{refund}}^{\text{A}}$ anymore. Note that it is safe for Bob to help Alice get refunded before getting refunded himself *because he has not released pre_c yet*, and thus no one else can cash out his coins in Rapidash.
– If Bob has already opened the lock with pre_c, then, should the honest Bob ever post pre_b to $P_{\text{refund}}^{\text{B}}$, it must be due to Alice's failure to post pre_a to $P_{\text{default}}^{\text{A}}$, meaning that Alice is acting dishonestly. In this case, Bob does not help Alice get her deposit back.

We now present the formal smart contracts and protocol for our atomic swap. All times are expressed in the time of the respective chain. As before, activation points of the same type are **mutually exclusive**. Moreover, the activation points can be triggered only if the contract is active, i.e. both parties have deposited.

RAPIDASH^{B}

/* Params: $(h_s, h_b, h_c, T_1^{\text{B}}, \tau^{\text{B}}, \text{\B}x_b, \text{\B}c_b^{\text{B}}, \text{\B}\epsilon^{\text{B}})$, Bob deposits $\text{\B}x_b + \text{\B}c_b^{\text{B}}$. */

$P_{\text{default}}^{\text{B}}$: On receiving z_1 from Alice and z_2 from Bob such that $H(z_1) = h_s$ and $H(z_2) = h_c$, send $\text{\B}x_b$ to Alice and $\text{\B}c_b^{\text{B}}$ to Bob.

$P_{\text{refund}}^{\text{B}}$: Time T_1^{B} or greater: On receiving z from Bob such that $H(z) = h_b$ or on receiving ping from Alice, do nothing.

$C_{\text{refund}}^{\text{B}}$: At least τ^{B} after $P_{\text{refund}}^{\text{B}}$ is activated: on receiving ping from anyone, send $\text{\B}x_b + \text{\B}c_b^{\text{B}}$ to Bob.

$C_{\text{burn}}^{\text{B}}$: On receiving (z_1, z_2, z_3) from anyone P such that $H(z_1) = h_s$, $H(z_2) = h_b$, and $H(z_3) = h_c$ send $\text{\DH}\epsilon^{\text{B}}$ to player P. All remaining coins are burnt.

Rapidash^{A}

/* Params: $(h_s, h_a, T_1^{\text{A}}, \tau^{\text{A}}, \text{\AA}x_a, \text{\AA}c_a^{\text{A}}, \text{\AA}\epsilon^{\text{A}})$, Alice deposits $\text{\AA}x_a + \text{\AA}c_a^{\text{A}}$, Bob deposits $\text{\AA}c_b^{\text{A}}$ */

$P_{\text{default}}^{\text{A}}$: On receiving z from Bob such that $H(z) = h_s$ or on receiving ping from Alice, send $\text{\AA}x_a + \text{\AA}c_b^{\text{A}}$ to Bob and $\text{\AA}c_a^{\text{A}}$ to Alice.

$P_{\text{refund}}^{\text{A}}$: Time T_1^{A} or greater: on receiving z from Alice such that $H(z) = h_a$ or on receiving ping from Bob, do nothing.

$C_{\text{refund}}^{\text{A}}$: At least τ^{A} after $P_{\text{refund}}^{\text{A}}$ is activated: on receiving ping from anyone, send $\text{\AA}x_a + \text{\AA}c_a^{\text{A}}$ to Alice and $\text{\AA}c_b^{\text{A}}$ to Bob.

$C_{\text{burn}}^{\text{A}}$: On receiving either (z_1, z_2) where $H(z_1) = h_s$ and $H(z_2) = h_a$, or (z_2, z_3) such that $H(z_2) = h_a$ and $H(z_3) = h_b$ from any P, send $\text{\AA}\epsilon^{\text{A}}$ to P. All remaining coins are burnt.

The parameters above must respect the following parameter constraints.

- **Constraints for Rapidash^{B} (on BobChain):**
  - $h_s = H(pre_s)$, $h_b = H(pre_b)$ and $h_c = H(pre_c)$.
  - $T_1^{\text{B}} > T_0^{\text{B}} > T^{\text{B}} > 0$, where T_0^{B} and T^{B} will be introduced later.
  - $\text{\DH}x_b > \text{\DH}\epsilon^{\text{B}} > \text{\DH}0$, and $\text{\DH}c_b^{\text{B}} > \text{\DH}\epsilon^{\text{B}}$
- **Constraints for Rapidash^{A} (on AliceChain):**
  - $h_s = H(pre_s)$ and $h_a = H(pre_a)$.
  - AliceChain time $T_1^{\text{A}} > $ BobChain time T_1^{B}, i.e., AliceChain block of length T_1^{A} is mined after the BobChain block of length T_1^{B}.[5]
  - $\text{\AA}\epsilon^{\text{A}} > \text{\AA}0$, $\text{\AA}c_a^{\text{A}} > \text{\AA}\epsilon^{\text{A}}$ and $\text{\AA}c_b^{\text{A}} > \text{\AA}\epsilon^{\text{A}}$.
- **Choice of timeouts:**
  - $\tau^{\text{B}} \geq 1$, $\tau^{\text{A}} \geq 1$.
  - $\gamma^{\tau^{\text{A}}} \leq \frac{\text{\AA}c_a^{\text{A}}}{\text{\AA}c_a^{\text{A}} + \text{\AA}x_a}$, $\gamma^{\tau^{\text{B}}} \leq \frac{\text{\DH}c_b^{\text{B}}}{\text{\DH}c_b^{\text{B}} + \text{\DH}x_b}$

We provide the protocol i.e., description of the behavior for the honest parties. The moment that both contracts have been posted and take effect is defined to be the start of the execution (i.e. $t = 0$). Let BobChain time 0 and AliceChain time 0 be the length of BobChain and AliceChain when the execution starts, respectively. Note that whenever parties are required to "Wait", they wait until the specified event happens, and then execute the corresponding action. When they start waiting, they also verify whether (one of) the specified events took place *already*, and execute the corresponding action if this is the case.

Atomic Swap Protocol — Alice

Preparation Phase:
1. At $t = 0$, Alice sends the deposit transaction of $\text{\AA}x_a + \text{\AA}c_a^{\text{A}}$ to Rapidash^{A};
2. Wait until one of the following happens:
   - Either Rapidash^{B} or Rapidash^{A} has not been active, and it is at least BobChain time T^{B}: Alice enters the abort phase.
   - Bob has not sent pre_c to $P_{\text{default}}^{\text{B}}$, and it is at least BobChain time T_0^{B}: Alice enters the abort phase.

---

[5] In practice, this constraint should be respected except with negligible probability despite the variance in inter-block times.

- Bob sent pre_c to P^B_{default} and it is before BobChain time T^B_0: Alice enters the execution phase.

Execution Phase:
1. Alice sends pre_s to P^B_{default}. As soon as P^B_{default} has been activated, Alice sends ping to P^A_{default}.
2. If τ^B BobChain *time* has passed since P^B_{refund} is activated, Alice sends ping to C^B_{refund}. (Note that as soon as C^B_{refund} is activated, Bob sends ping to P^A_{refund}.)
3. If τ^A AliceChain *time* has passed since activating P^A_{refund}, Alice sends ping to C^A_{refund}.

Abort Phase:
1. At BobChain time T^B_0, Alice sends ping to P^B_{refund}.
2. Wait until BobChain time T^B_1. If Bob has not sent ping to P^A_{refund}, Alice sends pre_a to P^A_{refund}.
3. If τ^A AliceChain *time* has passed since P^A_{refund} is activated, Alice sends ping to C^A_{refund}; similarly, if τ^B BobChain *time* has passed since P^B_{refund} is activated, Alice sends ping to C^B_{refunc}.

Ignore all other events.

The protocol for Bob is defined similarly, and is given in the full version [3]. In the abort phase, we require that the honest Alice and honest Bob to send ping to P^B_{refund} and P^A_{refund}, respectively, at BobChain time T^B_0 even though they would not be triggered until BobChain time T^B_1 and AliceChain time T^A_1, respectively. This gap allows the honest Alice to decide whether she should send pre_a to P^A_{refund} or not depending on Bob's behavior.

Observe that when Alice and Bob are both honest, Alice will post pre_s to P^B_{default} immediately, thus enabling Bob to learn pre_s and post it to P^A_{default} immediately after. Therefore, both players get their desired cryptocurrency and all their collateral back as soon as new block is confirmed on both chains.

Finally, we show that CSP-fairness and dropout resilience are satisfied.

Theorem 4.1 (CSP fairness and dropout resilience). *Suppose that the hash function $H(\cdot)$ is a one-way function and that all players are PPT machines. For any $\gamma \in [0, 1]$, if the parameters satisfy the constraints, then, the atomic swap protocol satisfies γ-CSP-fairness. The protocol is further dropout resilient.*

Intuition for Achieving CSP-Fairness. Intuitively, the constraint $\mathring{B}\epsilon^B < \mathring{B}x_b$ ensures that Alice, who does not have collateral in RAPIDASH^A, always prefers P^B_{default} to the bomb C^B_{burn}. The constraint $\mathring{B}c^B_b > \mathring{B}\epsilon^B$ ensures that if Bob gets Alice's $\mathring{A}x_a$ and triggers the bomb C^B_{burn}, he still loses to the honest case, and the constraint $\mathring{A}c^A_a > \mathring{A}\epsilon^A$ serves a similar purpose. The condition $\mathring{A}c^A_b > \mathring{A}\epsilon^A$ makes sure that Bob does not want to trigger the bomb C^A_{burn} even when he can get all of his deposit into RAPIDASH^A refunded. Finally, the constraint $\gamma^{\tau^B} < \frac{\mathring{B}c^B_b}{\mathring{B}c^B_b + \mathring{B}x_b}$ ensures that the window between P^B_{refund} and C^B_{refund} is sufficiently long such that once the honest Alice has posted pre_s, it is not worth it for Bob to take a gamble to trigger P^B_{refund} and C^B_{refund}. In particular, if during the τ^B window, any honest miner mines a block, then the bomb C^B_{burn} will be triggered and Bob will lose his collateral. The condition $\gamma^{\tau^A} < \frac{\text{Ḅ}c_a^A}{\text{Ḅ}c_a^A + \text{Ḅ}x_a}$ serves a similar purpose, but now for Alice and RAPIDASH^A. The formal proofs are given in the full version [3].

Concrete Parameter Examples. Suppose we choose $\text{Ḅ}c_b^B = \text{Ḅ}x_b$. Then, we should ensure $\gamma^{\tau^B} \leq 1/2$. This means that if $\gamma = 90\%$, we can set $\tau^B = 7$; if $\gamma = 49.9\%$, we can set $\tau^B = 1$. Asymptotically, for $\gamma = O(1)$, τ^B is a constant. Increasing $\text{Ḅ}c_b^B$ makes τ^B smaller. A similar calculation works for τ^A and $\text{Ḅ}c_a^A$.

4.3 Instantiation and Evaluation

Bitcoin. We now summarize the implementation of RAPIDASH^B in Bitcoin (see [3] for full version). First, Bob prepares a setup transaction tx_{stp}^B which deposits his coins into the address Adr_{stp}^B. The script associated with Adr_{stp}^B specifies activation points P_{default}^B, P_{refund}^B, and C_{burn}^B for redeeming the coins. Alice and Bob pre-sign all redeeming transactions upfront, ensuring they can later withdraw from Adr_{stp}^B. To achieve the burning of coins in C_{burn}^B, transaction $tx_{C_{\text{burn}}^B}$ is set to redeem exactly $x_b + c_b^B - \epsilon^B$ coins to an irredeemable address, leaving behind ϵ^B as a reward. This transaction is broadcast into the network, and can later be published on the blockchain by any miner provided they reveal pre_s, pre_a, and pre_c. RAPIDASH^A is similar to RAPIDASH^B, except Alice deposits $x_a + c_a^A$ and Bob deposits c_b^A using tx_{stp}^A. See Table 1 for the transaction size estimates.

Table 1. Estimates of Bitcoin transaction sizes for CSP-fair atomic swap.

Contract	Activation branch	Size (vBytes)	Fees (BTC)
RAPIDASH^B	P_{default}^B	455	0.0025
	P_{refund}^B (ping from Alice)	440	0.0022
	P_{refund}^B (Call by Bob)	448	0.0025
RAPIDASH^A	P_{default}^A (Call by Bob)	479	0.0027
	P_{default}^A (ping from Alice)	471	0.0026
	P_{refund}^A (Call by Alice)	437	0.0024
	P_{refund}^A (ping from Bob)	429	0.0024

Ethereum. We implemented our contracts in Solidity, Ethereum's smart contract language and deployed these on Goerli testnet. In Ethereum, the price of a transaction depends on its *gas* usage, which describes the cost of each operation performed by the smart contract.

Comparison of Knowledge-Coin Exchange. We compare gas cost of RAPIDASHKC with those of MAD-HTLC and He-HTLC (See Table 2 in [3]). The cost of RAPIDASHKC is very similar to the concurrent He-HTLC. The total redeem cost in the optimistic case in RAPIDASHKC is lower than MAD-HTLC's, as the latter has Alice obtain the deposit and Bob retrieve the collateral separately.

Evaluation of Atomic Swap. Our Ethereum atomic swap implementation consists of two contracts, one for RAPIDASH^B, and one for RAPIDASH^A. Table 2 details gas costs of all redeem paths. The deployment gas costs of RAPIDASH^B and RAPIDASH^A are 1,097,177 and 1,514,861 units, respectively.

Table 2. CSP-fair atomic swap, gas cost. (O) denotes an optimistic case.

Contract	Redeem path	Gas
RAPIDASH^B	Normal path (P^B_{default}), Alice	52,279
	Normal path (P^B_{default}), Bob	56,681
	Refund path ($P^B_{\text{refund}} + C^B_{\text{refund}}$), Bob	123,631
	Burn path (C^B_{burn}), Miner	42,266
RAPIDASH^A	Input, Alice	50,465
	Input, Bob	55,817
	Withdraw, Alice	38,228
	Withdraw, Bob	35,911
	(O) (P^A_{default}), Alice	54,904
	(O) (P^A_{default}), Bob	58,656
	Refund ($P^A_{\text{refund}} + C^A_{\text{refund}}$), Alice	118,379
	Refund ($P^A_{\text{refund}} + C^A_{\text{refund}}$), Bob	114,647
	Burn (C^A_{burn}), Miner	53,431

5 Conclusion and Future Work

In this work, we formalized key notions for blockchain-based fair trading and presented protocols that satisfy these notions. We leave several interesting questions for future work: Is it possible to have an atomic swap secure against user-miner collusion which requires each user to deposit collateral on at most one chain? Can we have fair exchange among more than two parties?

Acknowledgements. Hao Chung and Elaine Shi are supported by NSF awards 2212746, 2044679, 1704788, a Packard Fellowship, a generous gift from the late Nikolai Mushegian, a gift from Google, and an ACE center grant from Algorand Foundation. Elisaweta Masserova is supported by NSF Grant 1801369, the CONIX Research Center, the Defense Advanced Research Projects Agency under contract FA8750-17-1-0059, and a gift from Bosch.

References

1. Lightning network (2023). https://lightning.network/
2. Campanelli, M., Gennaro, R., Goldfeder, S., Nizzardo, L.: Zero-knowledge contingent payments revisited: attacks and payments for services. In: ACM CSS (2017)
3. Chung, H., Masserova, E., Shi, E., Thyagarajan, S.A.: Rapidash: foundations of side-contract-resilient fair exchange. Cryptology ePrint Archive arXiv:2022/1063 (2022)
4. Chung, H., Shi, E.: Foundations of transaction fee mechanism design. In: SODA (2023)
5. Chung, K.-M., Guo, Y., Lin, W.-K., Pass, R., Shi, E.: Game theoretic notions of fairness in multi-party coin toss. In: Beimel, A., Dziembowski, S. (eds.) TCC 2018. LNCS, vol. 11239, pp. 563–596. Springer, Cham (2018). https://doi.org/10.1007/978-3-030-03807-6_21
6. Ethereum: The Solidity contract-oriented programming language. https://github.com/ethereum/solidity (2022)
7. Garay, J.A., Kiayias, A., Leonardos, N.: The bitcoin backbone protocol: analysis and applications. In: Eurocrypt (2015)
8. Herlihy, M.: Atomic cross-chain swaps. In: PODC (2018)
9. Malavolta, G., Moreno-Sanchez, P., Schneidewind, C., Kate, A., Maffei, M.: Anonymous multi-hop locks for blockchain scalability and interoperability. In: NDSS (2019)
10. van der Meyden, R.: On the specification and verification of atomic swap smart contracts. In: IEEE ICBC (2019)
11. Miraz, M.H., Donald, D.C.: Atomic cross-chain swaps: development, trajectory and potential of non-monetary digital token swap facilities. In: AETiC (2019)
12. Parno, B., Howell, J., Gentry, C., Raykova, M.: Pinocchio: nearly practical verifiable computation. In: IEEE Symposium on Security and Privacy (2013)
13. Pass, R., Seeman, L., Shelat, A.: Analysis of the blockchain protocol in asynchronous networks. In: Eurocrypt (2017)
14. Pass, R., Shi, E.: Fruitchains: a fair blockchain. In: PODC (2017)
15. Pass, R., Shi, E.: Rethinking large-scale consensus. In: CSF (2017)
16. Poon, J., Dryja, T.: The bitcoin lightning network: scalable off-chain instant payments (2016)
17. Shi, E., Chung, H., Wu, K.: What can cryptography do for decentralized mechanism design? In: ITCS 2023
18. Tsabary, I., Yechieli, M., Manuskin, A., Eyal, I.: MAD-HTLC: because HTLC is crazy-cheap to attack. In: S&P (2021)
19. Wadhwa, S., Stoeter, J., Zhang, F., Nayak, K.: He-HTLC: revisiting incentives in HTLC. In: NDSS (2023)
20. Winzer, F., Herd, B., Faust, S.: Temporary censorship attacks in the presence of rational miners. In: IEEE EuroS&P Workshops (2019)
21. Wu, K., Asharov, G., Shi, E.: A complete characterization of game-theoretically fair, multi-party coin toss. In: Eurocrypt (2022)

Serial Monopoly on Blockchains with Quasi-patient Users

Paolo Penna[1](✉) and Manvir Schneider[2](✉)

[1] IOG, Zurich, Switzerland
paolo.penna@iohk.io
[2] Cardano Foundation, Zurich, Switzerland
manvir.schneider@cardanofoundation.org

Abstract. In the face of limited block size, miners (e.g., in Bitcoin) typically prioritize transactions with the highest bids, which increasingly make up a larger portion of their revenue. If the block size were to expand significantly, meeting all transaction demand due to infrastructure or protocol improvements, bids could drop to zero or to a constant minimum fee. This would diminish miners' incentives to mine, potentially affecting network security. To address this, Lavi et al. [15] study a monopolistic pricing mechanism where miners may not fill the entire block but only include transactions that pay a minimum price set by the miner. This mechanism aims to be incentive-compatible and allows miners to collect some revenue, although it may result in an unbounded loss in welfare. Nisan [19] expands this by modeling bidders as *patient*, meaning they are willing to wait without cost until block prices drop low enough for their transactions to be included, leading to wildly fluctuating prices even when demand is stable and there is no stochastic element in the model. In order to capture users' diminishing interest in having their transactions added to the ledger over time, we consider a more realistic setting with *quasi-patient* users, where only a fraction $\delta \in [0, 1]$ of pending transactions remains in the next round. This richer model encompasses both Lavi et al.'s [15] *impatient* users ($\delta = 0$) and Nisan's [19] *patient* users ($\delta = 1$) as special cases. We demonstrate that Nisan's fluctuating dynamics persist for δ close to 1, while for δ close to 0, the dynamics resemble the impatient case. For $\delta \in (0, 1)$, we establish new bounds on price dynamics, revealing unexpected effects. Unlike the fully patient case, the bounds of the dynamics for $\delta < 1$ depend on the demand curve and undergo a "transition phase". For some δ, the model mirrors the fully patient setting, and for smaller $\delta' < \delta$, it stabilizes at the highest *monopolist* price, thus collapsing to the impatient case. We provide quantitative bounds and analytical results, showing that the bounds for $\delta = 1$ are generally not tight for $\delta < 1$, and we give guarantees on the minimum ("admission") price for transactions.

Keywords: Blockchain · Transaction Fee · Monopolistic Pricing Mechanism

---

A full version of this paper can be found here: https://arxiv.org/abs/2405.17334

© International Financial Cryptography Association 2026
C. Garman and P. Moreno-Sanchez (Eds.): FC 2025, LNCS 15751, pp. 267–283, 2026.
https://doi.org/10.1007/978-3-032-07024-1_16

1 Introduction

Transaction fee mechanisms are a fundamental part of a blockchain. A block leader, in general, has full freedom to choose which transaction from the public mempool (and private mempool) to include in a block. A well designed transaction fee mechanism contributes to maximizing the social welfare, which is the total value of the chosen transactions subject to the block size constraint.[1] The most prominent proof-of-work blockchain, Bitcoin [18], employs a pay-your-bid mechanism. In particular, the higher the bid attached to a transaction, the higher the chances to be included in the next block by the miner. The user-paid bids are rewarded to the miner. Myopic rational miners will always try to maximize their revenue and will therefore choose the highest paying transactions. Since block space is scarce, this mechanism can drive prices high, especially when there is congestion and hence transaction inclusion might experience a considerable delay. On the contrary, if block space becomes large enough to meet all demand, the fees/bids would drop to 0 and miners are left with no incentive to mine and thus will compromise security.

Opposing to the pay-your-bid mechanism is the dynamic posted price mechanism, like EIP-1559. In Ethereum's EIP-1559, the transaction fee is split into base fee and a tip. The block proposer only receives the tips while the base fee is burned. Rational block proposers will therefore only select transactions that pay at least the base fee.[2] The target of EIP-1559 is to have half-full blocks. If the previous block was filled less (more) than the target, the base fee is lowered (increased) accordingly. The dynamic base fee allows to handle low and high demand phases and satisfies various good properties of transaction fee mechanisms such as incentive-compatibility properties and off-chain collusion proofness [23].[3]

A different approach to transaction fee is that of Cardano, where there is a constant minimum fee and a fixed fee per byte. The transaction selection process is a first-in-first-out (FIFO) mechanism. The transaction fees of included transactions are collected in a 'pot' and distributed at the end of an epoch (5 days) [1]. The rewards (fees) are distributed to the block producers (stake pools) proportionally to the number of proposed blocks in the epoch.[4]

---

[1] The definition social welfare may also include the value of the block producers, see Bahrani et al. [3]. However, how to derive or estimate these values, both for users and block producers is a difficult question.

[2] It may be that a block proposer has some positive intrinsic value for some transaction that pays less than the base fee, and therefore includes this transaction by paying the remaining base fee himself. Note that this is related to active block proposers, see Bahrani et al. [3].

[3] Note that also Bitcoin's fee mechanism and Ethereum's pre-EIP-1559 fee mechanism allow to handle low and high demand phases but do not satisfy various good properties of transaction fee mechanisms.

[4] For the Cardano blockchain, each stake pool, given their stake, has an expected number of blocks that it will produce during an epoch. The rewards that a stake

In the event that the (minimum) fees are not high enough to incentivice block producers (to produce blocks) and thus security is at risk, a question one could ask is whether block leaders should be allowed to set their own fees rather than a fee imposed by the protocol, and if so, whether the fee should be the same for all and how it would affect blockchain security. The study of such a monopolistic pricing mechanism is part of Nisan [19] and this paper. In the monopolist pricing mechanism, transactions willing to pay at least the price set by the monopolist are included in a block (until the block is full). Unlike in the pay-your-bid mechanism, all included transactions pay exactly the price set by the monopolist (rather than their bid). Or, in the words of Lavi et al. [15], the monopolist chooses the number of accepted transactions in the block and all transactions pay the smallest bid among the accepted transactions.

In his paper [19], Nisan assumes that block leaders set their own prices and all transaction that are not included in a block remain in the mempool forever until they are picked up eventually in a future block. On the one hand, this better captures the role and importance of the mempool in blockchain price dynamics, revealing the following surprising effect:

"[...] prices keep fluctuating wildly and this is an endogenous property of the model and happens even when demand is stable with nothing stochastic in the model." ([19])

On the other hand, the assumption above, is too strong and does not fully reflect real world behavior. In fact, partially impatient users may cancel their transaction after some time if not included in a block. The Cardano blockchain supports expiring transactions, allowing users to set an expiry time (or validity interval) for their transactions. If a transaction is not recorded in the ledger before its expiry time, it is discarded. This feature incurs no additional cost for users.[5] Therefore, we assume that only a fraction of unsupplied transactions remains in the next round, while the other fraction of unsupplied demand is removed (from the mempool).

1.1 Our Contributions

We put forward a model for monopolist pricing dynamics tailored to accommodate *quasi-patient* users (see Sect. 2 for details and formal definitions). Our model incorporates a "decay" parameter $\delta \in [0,1]$ which corresponds to the fraction of pending transactions that remain in the mempool at the next round. Thus, a

---

pools receives at the end of an epoch are scaled by a performance variable which is the fraction of the actual number of produced blocks and the expected number.

[5] On other blockchains, users cannot always cancel transactions without incurring a fee, as this could lead to denial-of-service attack vulnerabilities. Blockchains like Bitcoin and Ethereum mitigate this by allowing miners and validators to set a minimum fee increase percentage for users who wish to replace their transactions retroactively. For instance, some Bitcoin wallets support the Replace-by-Fee protocol, enabling users to replace an existing transaction with one that pays a higher fee.

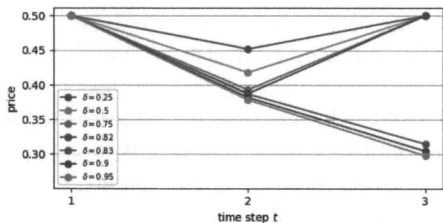 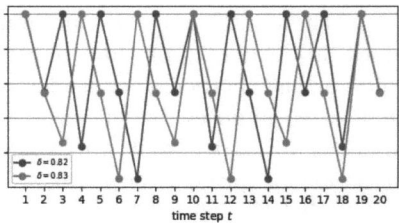

Fig. 1. Price dynamics from Example 1 for different values of δ, with 3 time steps (left) and 20 time steps (right), respectively. For δ smaller than $2\sqrt{2} - 2 \approx 0.828$ the prices jumps up after step $t = 2$. For δ above the threshold, the price decreases after step $t = 2$.

fraction $1 - \delta$ of pending transactions gets withdrawn by the users at each round. This can be motivated by users' diminishing interest in having their transactions included in a block, due to factors such as waiting costs. The case of *impatient users* in Lavi et al. [15] corresponds to $\delta = 0$, and the case of *patient users* in Nisan [19] to $\delta = 1$. Our model spans all intermediate scenarios between these two extreme cases, and it allows us to study how monopolist pricing mechanisms behave at different *patience* levels δ. In particular, we no longer assume *patient users* who are willing to wait (and pay) indefinitely long for their transactions to be included on the ledger. A simulation of few steps of the resulting dynamics is shown in Fig. 1 for several values of δ and a simple demand function. At each time step, only transactions bidding at least the price in the graph are included, and thus the following questions arise:

> *Given some daily demand function, what is the (minimum) price that users must pay to have their transactions eventually included? What is the price that users have to pay to have their transactions included immediately? Is it even possible to analytically compute these prices and how does δ affect them for arbitrary demand functions?*

In Fig. 1 (left), we observe two distinct behaviors in the price dynamics. For some values of δ, the prices jump up after step 2, while for others, the prices continue to decrease. Another interesting question arises: will the dynamics for smaller δ eventually reach the same prices as those for larger δ? For example, does the blue graph in Fig. 1 (left) eventually reach the low prices observed in the purple graph?

We provide analytical results on the monopolistic pricing dynamics for any $\delta \in (0, 1)$. Our findings highlight that monopolistic price mechanisms for *quasi-patient* users still posses good features, though with some key differences with the case of *patient* users. In Sects. 3 and 4, we analyze the dynamics for different values of δ and how it affects their behavior. In particular, we demonstrate that in regimes with a *sufficiently small fraction of expiring transactions* ($\delta < 1$ sufficiently large), the dynamics behaves qualitatively similarly to the case of *no expiring transactions* ($\delta = 1$). The analysis highlights several differences, particularly how the "structure" of the demand function Q influences the dynamics for $\delta < 1$ compared to the case $\delta = 1$.

Specifically, Theorem 2 informally states that:

- *Prices decrease or jump up to maximum price.* The price for being included in the current block is either smaller than the one at the previous block, or it is the maximum price, which is the so called monopolist price (the price that is always asked if users are *fully-impatient* and there is no pent-up demand [15]).
- *Immediate inclusion price (monopolist price).* The largest price that the monopolist ever asks (immediate transaction inclusion guaranteed) equals the monopolist price. Also for quasi-patient users the dynamics ask the monopolistic (maximum) price infinitely often, meaning that immediate inclusion is *not* guaranteed for any lower price.
- *Minimum admission price.* We call the lowest price the monopolist ever sets the *minimum admission price*, and it is bounded based on δ. If there is sufficient pent-up demand, the minimum admission price becomes low, allowing transactions to eventually be included at a cheaper price.

A direct comparison between our bounds for quasi-patient users and the case of patient users, shows the following. First, our upper bounds on the minimum admission price depend on δ. Second, the minimum admission price for $\delta < 1$ is at least the minimum admission price for $\delta = 1$ (cf. our Theorem 2 and Theorem 1 below from [19]). In Sect. 4, we prove lower bounds on the minimum admission price. In particular, Theorem 4 states the following:

- *The minimum admission price for impatient users is never tight for quasi-patient users.* That is, for every $\delta < 1$ there is a demand function for which the minimum admission price is strictly higher.
- *Collapse to the impatient case.* The change in the dynamics is not continuous in δ. For some small $\delta > 0$, the dynamics behave exactly like the case of *impatient users* ($\delta = 0$). That is, the minimum admission price coincides with the (maximum) monopolist price at all time steps.

Furthermore, the above mentioned collapse means that the positive effect of pent-up demand, which results in a minimum admission price smaller than the monopolist price, may completely be nullified for quasi-patient users. Another important difference is that, for patient users, the minimum admission price is "almost" independent of the structure of the demand function (it only depends on the block size s and on the revenue at the monopolist price). This is no longer true for quasi-patient users, where the "overall structure" of the demand function seems to play a role. Without further assumptions on the demand function, the conditions under which Theorem 2 can be applied ($\delta > \bar{\delta}_{ser}$) are essentially tight as the collapse already happens slightly below $\bar{\delta}_{ser}$ – see Theorem 5.

Proofs can be found in the extended version of this paper available online.

1.2 Related Work

Transaction fee mechanisms are analyzed from the perspective of mechanism design in Roughgarden [23]. Additionally the dynamic posted price mechanism EIP-1559 is analyzed. Follow up work on transaction fee mechanism design includes [3,5,6,8,20]. More work focusing on the dynamics of EIP-1559 (and potentially chaotic behavior) is [16,17,21,22].

Monopolistic Pricing Mechanisms. The monopolistic pricing mechanism was initially examined by Goldberg et al. [11]. Subsequently it has been analyzed within the context of blockchains by Lavi et al. [15], Yao [24] and Basu et al. [4] prior to Nisan [19] and this paper. In particular, it is motivated by its ability to maintain fee revenue when block rewards are low and blocks can be large in size. Lavi et al. [15] study the monopolistic pricing mechanism and describe the mechanism as follows: (1) Transactions specify bids (maximal fee) they are willing to pay; (2) Miners (or block leaders/monopolists) choose which subset to include in their block; (3) All transactions in the block pay the exact same fee which is equal to the smallest bid among the included transactions; (4) Miners maximize their revenue which is the product of the minimal bid and the number of included transactions. The focus of their paper is on a single shot game where users are maximally impatient in the sense that they derive utility from immediate block inclusion and no utility for inclusion in a future block. They show that truthful bidding (users bidding their true valuation) is "nearly" an equilibrium, i.e. relative gains from strategic bidding go to zero as number of transactions increase. The monopolistic pricing mechanism collects at least as much revenue from maximally impatient users as the pay-your-bid mechanism (as employed in Bitcoin). Yao [24] builds on the work of [15] and studies properties of the monopolistic pricing mechanism, in particular, incentive compatibility when users' valuations are drawn from an i.i.d. distribution. Basu et al. [4] study a setting similar to [15], where the miner has to fill the block up to a certain level to receive the reward, which consists of mean of the fees from the last B blocks, including the current constructed block (note some similarity to Cardano [1] and to Eyal et al. [7]). The model of Eyal et al. [7] assumes many miners, incentivizing them to pick the highest-value transactions, and aims to maximize social welfare. Note that the model of [15] does not aim to maximize social welfare. To see this, note that, if the monopolist chooses a subset of transactions that does not fill the block entirely, the monopolist could potentially include transactions with lower bids. However, doing so would decrease the price that all included transactions have to pay and hence would lower the monopolist's revenue.

Nisan [19] studies a monopolist pricing mechanism, in which each block leader (or proposer) is allowed to choose the price p for his block. Transactions willing to pay at least p may be included by the monopolist and all included transactions pay exactly p.[6] Rationality of block leaders implies that the block leaders will choose a price that maximizes their revenue given price and the block space filled

---
[6] In principle, this mechanism is the same as in Lavi et al. [15]. In [15] the fee to be paid by users is determined by the lowest bid p of the included transactions. There

by the chosen transactions.[7] Nisan's model involves infinitely patient users, i.e. users' valuations of transaction inclusion do not depreciate over time. Transactions stay in the mempool until eventually picked up by some block leader. Block leaders face the same demand distribution at every step in time plus the pent-up demand from the previous steps, that is, additionally to the daily demand the block leaders faces the transactions that were not picked up by previous block leaders. When optimizing given the current total demand, the block leader only optimizes for the current block (myopic block leader). Furthermore, the available block space for each block is fixed and demand is known to the block leader.

Kiayias et al. [14] study a mechanism to account for transactions with different priority/urgency In particular, the mechanism splits blocks into different tiers with each tier having its own characteristics such as fee and size. The fee and size are dynamically adjusted based on previous demand and fees. This mechanism ensures that high priority transactions can choose to be included in a tier with high priority by paying high transaction fee.

Patient blockchain users are analyzed in Huberman et al. [13], Gafni and Yaish [9]. The study of non-myopic miners includes expiring transactions [10], base-fee manipulations [2], under-cutting attacks [12].

2 Model

We extend the model of Nisan [19] for non-strategic agents with an additional parameter $\delta \in [0,1]$ which corresponds to the fraction of pending transactions remaining at next round (thus $1-\delta$ is the fraction of pending transactions withdrawn[8] by the corresponding users – see below). The dynamics is specified as follows:

- *Time* is discrete and indexed by $t = 1, 2, \ldots$,
- *Daily demand*: A demand function Q quantifies the daily demand $Q(p)$ for every price level p. Function Q is continuous and decreasing in p as $Q(p)$ is the number of newly added transactions willing to pay p or more to be included.
- *Monopolist*: A monopolist (chosen for the current round t) faces a total demand D_t consisting of daily demand and pent-up demand from previous rounds (see below). As $D_t(p)$ is the total number of transactions willing to pay at least p, the monopolist chooses a price maximizing his own revenue subject to the supply constraint s (block size = max number of transactions per block):

$$p_t = \arg\max_p p \cdot \min(s, D_t(p)) . \tag{1}$$

---

is at least one transaction with bid p (which is the lowest bidding transaction), while in Nisan [19] there need not be a transaction with bid exactly equal to p.
[7] While the other mechanism of Bitcoin and Ethereum maximize the total value of included transactions subject to the available block space (i.e. social welfare), the monopolist mechanism maximizes the block leaders revenue.
[8] Or in other words, a fraction $1-\delta$ of pending transactions expires at each time step (cf. Cardano blockchain for expiring transactions).

The corresponding supplied quantity is $q_t = D_t(p_t)$, and the monopolist's revenue (at time t) is $\text{REV}_t := p_t \cdot q_t$.

- *Pent-up demand*: Initially there is no pent-up demand from previous rounds, that is, $Z_0(p) = 0$ for all p. The pent-up demand at time $t \geq 1$ is

$$Z_t(p) := \begin{cases} D_t(p) - q_t & \text{for } p \leq p_t \\ 0 & \text{for } p > p_t \end{cases}. \qquad (2)$$

- *Total demand and δ*: Only a fraction $\delta \in [0, 1]$ of pent-up demand survives to the next round, and thus total demand is

$$D_t(p) = \delta \cdot Z_{t-1}(p) + Q(p). \qquad (3)$$

Remark 1. For $\delta = 1$ the model above boils down to the one in [19] where all transactions not included in the current round remain in the system and they are eventually included if an only if their price is above some minimum price p_{ser}. For $\delta = 0$ transactions are either immediately included or they disappear, thus implying that the dynamics above stay at the monopolist price $p_{mon} > p_{ser}$ and only transactions willing to pay this price are included.

In the sequel we shall focus on the case $\delta \in (0, 1)$ as the case $\delta = 0$ is trivial and $\delta = 1$ coincides with the model in [19].

Key Quantities. Note that by the definition of the total demand and pent-up demand we can write the total demand as follows.

Remark 2. The total demand at time t can be rewritten as

$$D_t(p) = \begin{cases} a_t \cdot Q(p) - b_t & \text{for } p \leq \min_{1 \leq \tau \leq t-1} p_\tau \\ Q(p) & \text{otherwise} \end{cases} \qquad (4)$$

where from (2) and (3) we have

$$a_t = 1 + \delta + \cdots + \delta^{t-1}, \qquad b_t = q_1 \delta^{t-1} + q_2 \delta^{t-2} + \cdots + q_{t-1} \delta. \qquad (5)$$

Note that $a_t = \frac{1-\delta^t}{1-\delta}$ for $\delta \in (0,1)$, and $a_t = t$ for $\delta = 1$.

As one of our main results (see Sect. 3) show, the price dynamics fluctuate between two prices that involve the following quantities:

Definition 1. *For any demand function Q and any supply s, the corresponding monopolist price p_{mon} and serial price p_{ser} are defined as follows:*

$$p_{mon} := \arg\max_p p \cdot \min(s, Q(p)), \qquad q_{mon} := Q(p_{mon}), \qquad (6)$$

$$p_{ser} := p_{mon} \cdot q_{mon}/s, \qquad q_{ser} := Q(p_{ser}). \qquad (7)$$

Note that the *monopolist price* p_{mon} is simply the price that maximizes the revenue of the monopolist when facing demand $Q(p)$.

Remark 3. Since $D_t(p) \geq Q(p)$ at any time $t \geq 1$, the monopolist can always obtain the revenue at the monopolist price $\text{REV}_{mon} := p_{mon} \cdot q_{mon}$ by choosing price p_{mon}. Therefore, we have $\text{REV}_t = p_t \cdot q_t \geq \text{REV}_{mon}$ for all t.

It turns out that these prices characterize tightly the dynamics for the case of *patient* users ($\delta = 1$), as shown by the next definition and theorem.

Definition 2 (Eventual Transaction Inclusion, (Minimum) Admission Price). *For a given price dynamic we consider the following definitions:*

- *A transaction with price p is eventually included if there exists Δ_p such that, for every $T \geq 1$, there exists some t with $p_t \leq p$ and $T \leq t \leq T + \Delta_p$.*
- *A price p is called admission price if all transactions paying p are eventually included.*
- *The minimum admission price p_{map} is the smallest admission price such that all transactions paying at least p_{map} are eventually included.*

Next, we state the main result from Nisan [19].

Theorem 1 (Theorem 1 in [19] restated). *For patient users ($\delta = 1$) and for any strictly decreasing demand function Q and supply s the following holds:*

1. *The dynamics stay always between p_{ser} and p_{mon}, that is, prices p_t satisfy $p_{ser} \leq p_t \leq p_{mon}$ for all $t \geq 1$. In particular, transactions paying less than p_{ser} will never be included. At each step t, the prices either decrease ($p_t < p_{t-1}$) or they jump up to the monopolist price ($p_t = p_{mon}$).*
2. *Every price larger than p_{ser} is an admission price. Therefore, p_{ser} is the minimum admission price ($p_{map} = p_{ser}$). Moreover, the dynamics pass through the monopolist price p_{mon} infinitely often.*

Transactions paying at least p_{mon} are immediately included, and this is tight as there are infinitely steps for which paying less will delay admission to a later step.

We now go back to the case of *quasi-patient* users ($\delta \in (0,1)$). In order to illustrate the dynamics and, in particular, how it differs from the case $\delta = 1$, we next revise and adapt an example in [19, Section 2.2].

Example 1. Let $Q(p) = 1 - p$ for $p \in [0,1]$, $s = 1$ and let $\delta \in (0,1)$. Then, we have the following:

($t = 1$) The initial demand is $D_1(p) = Q(p)$ and thus we maximize $pD_1(p) = p(1-p)$ which gives $p_1 = 0.5$ as maximizer and $q_1 = D_1(p_1) = 0.5$. This price p_1 is the monopolist price and the revenue is $\text{REV}_1 = \text{REV}_{mon} = p_1 q_1 = 0.25$. The pent-up demand is $Z_1(p) = D_1(p) - q_1 = \frac{1}{2} - p$ if $p < p_1$ and zero otherwise.

($t=2$) The total demand is $D_2(p) = \delta Z_1(p) + Q(p) = 1 + \delta/2 - (1+\delta)p$ if $p < p_1$ and $Q(p)$ otherwise. We maximize $pD_2(p)$ and get $p_2 = \frac{2+\delta}{4(1+\delta)}$ as maximizer and thus $q_2 = \frac{2+\delta}{4}$. Note that $p_2 < p_1$ if and only if $\delta > 0$. The revenue is $\text{REV}_2 = \frac{(2+\delta)^2}{16(1+\delta)}$. Note that $\text{REV}_2 > \text{REV}_1$ if and only if $\delta > -1$, that is, the revenue from step $t=2$ is better than the monopolist revenue. The pent-up demand is $Z_2(p) = D_2(p) - q_2 = (2+\delta)/4 - (1+\delta)p$ if $p < p_2$ and zero otherwise.

($t=3$) The total demand is $D_3(p) = \delta Z_2(p) + Q(p) = \frac{2\delta + \delta^2 + 4}{4} - (1 + \delta + \delta^2)p$ if $p < p_2$ and $Q(p)$ otherwise. Maximization yields $p_3 = \frac{2\delta + \delta^2 + 4}{8(1+\delta+\delta^2)}$. Note that $p_3 < p_2$ if and only if $\delta > 0$. Hence, $q_3 = \frac{2\delta + \delta^2 + 4}{8}$ and the revenue is $\text{REV}_3 = \frac{(2\delta+\delta^2+4)^2}{64(1+\delta+\delta^2)}$. Note that $\text{REV}_3 > \text{REV}_1$ if and only if $\delta > \delta^\star := 2\sqrt{2} - 2 \approx 0.828$. That is, if $\delta > \delta^\star$, the price dynamics do not jump and take p_3 as above. The pent-up demand is $Z_3(p) = \frac{2\delta + \delta^2 + 4}{8} - (1 + \delta + \delta^2)p$ if $p < p_3$ and zero otherwise. However, if $\delta \leq \delta^\star$, the revenue will be less than the monopolist revenue. In this case, the price dynamics would jump up to the monopolist price and take $p_3 = p_{mon} = 0.5$ and thus $q_3 = q_{mon} = 0.5$. The pent-up demand would be $Z_3(p) = D_3(p) - q_3 = Q(p) - 0.5 = 0.5 - p$ if $p < p_3$ and zero otherwise.

The price dynamics for the first 3 steps and 20 steps are depicted in Fig. 1 for different values of δ. Figure 3 shows the dynamics for a longer period of 100 steps.

3 Upper Bounds on the Minimum Admission Price

In this section, we provide a bound on the minimum price which guarantees transactions to be *eventually* included, depending on δ. The main result is summarized by the following definition and theorem (Definition 3 and Theorem 2).

Definition 3. *For any continuous decreasing demand function Q and supply s we define the following quantities:*

$$\overline{p}_{ser} := \frac{p_{ser} \cdot s}{q_{ser}}, \qquad \overline{q}_{ser} := Q(\overline{p}_{ser}), \qquad \overline{\delta}_{ser} := 1 - \frac{q_{ser} - \overline{q}_{ser}}{s}. \qquad (8)$$

Moreover, for any $\delta > \overline{\delta}_{ser}$, we let $p_{ser}^{(\delta)}$ be the price such that[9]

$$Q(p_{ser}^{(\delta)}) = q_{ser} - (1-\delta) \cdot s. \qquad (9)$$

Example 2. (Example 1 Continued). For the setting in Example 1 we observe the minimum admission prices p_{map} (over 100 steps) for every $\delta \in [0,1]$ and display it in Fig. 2.

---
[9] This price exists by continuity and monotonicity of Q, and because $Q(\overline{p}_{ser}) = \overline{q}_{ser} = q_{ser} - (1-\overline{\delta}_{ser}) \cdot s < q_{ser} - (1-\delta) \cdot s \leq q_{ser} = Q(p_{ser})$, where last inequality is due to $\delta \leq 1$.

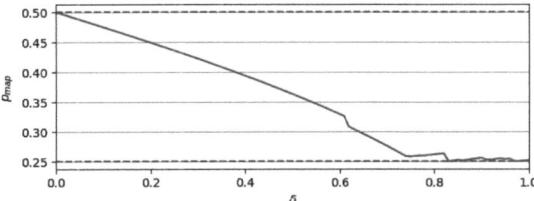

Fig. 2. Minimum admission price p_{map} (derived from 100 steps) depending on δ for daily demand $Q(p) = 1 - p$ and supply $s = 1$. Fluctuations for larger δ may be due to a lack of steps for the price dynamics to reach its minimum.

We next state the main result of this section, which highlights the main similarities and differences with the case of impatient users (see Theorem 1 above).

Theorem 2. *For any strictly decreasing demand function Q and supply s the following holds:*

1. *The minimum admission price is at least p_{ser}, and thus transactions paying less than this price will never be included. In particular, the dynamics stay always between p_{ser} and p_{mon}, that is, prices p_t satisfy $p_{ser} \leq p_t \leq p_{mon}$ for all $t \geq 1$. Moreover, at each step t, the prices either decrease ($p_t < p_{t-1}$) or they jump up to the monopolist price ($p_t = p_{mon}$).*
2. *For every $\delta > \overline{\delta}_{ser}$, the minimum admission price is at most $p_{ser}^{(\delta)}$ defined by (9) which satisfies $p_{ser} < p_{ser}^{(\delta)} < \overline{p}_{ser}$. Moreover, the dynamics pass through the monopolist price p_{mon} infinitely often.*
3. *Every price larger than p_{ser} is an admission price for a sufficiently large δ. That is, for every $p^\star > p_{ser}$, there exists $\delta_{min}(p^\star) < 1$ such that $p^\star$ is an admission price for every $\delta > \delta_{min}(p^\star)$. Moreover, the dynamics pass through the monopolist price p_{mon} infinitely often.*

Therefore, transactions paying at least p_{mon} are immediately included, and this is tight to guarantee immediate inclusion (as there are infinitely many steps for which paying less will delay admission to a later step).

Proof Idea. According to (4)–(5), the pent-up demand cannot increase arbitrarily in our setting ($\delta < 1$). We thus need to identify the pairs δ and $p^\star$ for which, at price $p^\star$, the pent-up demand becomes "sufficiently high" to induce the dynamics to take this or a smaller price. Moreover, we have to show that the dynamics cannot simply keep decreasing the prices, but must eventually jump back to the monopolist price, and then again reach $p^\star$ or a smaller price as before infinitely often. The quantities in Definition 3 can be used to identify such pairs δ and $p^\star$, which intuitively correspond to $p^\star$ being "not too small" (Item 2) or δ being "large enough" (Item 3). □

The above result allows us to compare the case of quasi-patient users ($\delta < 1$) with the case of patient users ($\delta = 1$) analyzed in Theorem 1. Item 1 in Theorem 2 says that users need to pay at least p_{ser} in order to have their transactions admitted, though this may still not be enough depending on δ. How much they have to pay in order to guarantee inclusion is addressed in Items 2 and 3. Item 2 in Theorem 2 provides an upper bound on the minimum admission price, provided δ being large enough (condition $\delta > \overline{\delta}_{ser}$). This condition on δ is necessary as implied by the results in the next section, where we prove lower bounds on the minimum admission price. Item 3 shows that the minimum admission price tends to p_{ser} from above for $\delta \to 1$. Finally, Theorem 2 implies that the price dynamic does not converge to some price $p' < p_{mon}$. This is not obvious, as in our setting the pent-up demand does not grow arbitrarily and thus, in principle, it might be possible to have a sequence of decreasing prices.

4 Lower Bounds on the Minimum Admission Price

In this section, we complement the results in the previous section, by showing that transactions below a certain price will *never* be included, depending on δ.

Recall that the monopolist aims to choose a price p maximizing the revenue $\text{REV}_t(p) := p \cdot \min(s, D_t(p))$ at the current step t. At every time step, there is always the option to choose the monopolist price p_{mon} and receive revenue REV_{mon}. We can compare $\text{REV}_t(p)$ and REV_{mon} at any t by considering the following function:

$$f_t(p) := p \cdot D_t(p) - p_{mon} q_{mon} . \tag{10}$$

Since the revenue for price p satisfies $\text{REV}_t(p) \leq p \cdot D_t(p)$, if the function above is negative for some p, it means that the revenue at p is worse than REV_{mon}, and therefore the next price p_t cannot be p. Observe that evaluating $D_t(p)$ and thus $f_t(p)$ is rather complex because of the "previous history" component involving $q_{t-1}, \ldots, q_1$ – see Eqs. (4) and (5). We next provide a simpler function to evaluate for a generic Q, which still can be used to determine "forbidden" prices for the dynamics:

$$F_t(p) := p \cdot (a_t \cdot Q(p) - (a_t - 1)q_{mon}) - p_{mon} q_{mon} , \qquad a_t = \sum_{i=0}^{t} \delta^t . \tag{11}$$

Next, we relate F_t to the dynamics.

Theorem 3. *For any p such that $F_t(p) < 0$ it cannot be $p_t = p$.*

Intuitively, this theorem states that if we show $F_t(p) < 0$ for all $p < p^*$, then the minimum admission price is at least p^*.

4.1 An Illustrative Example

We next apply the result in Theorem 3 to one of the simplest demand functions and show that, even in this case, price p_{ser} is not a tight bound for the minimum admission price.

Proposition 1. (Lower bound). *For demand function $Q(p) = 1-p$ and $s \geq \frac{1}{2}$ the price at step $t \geq 1$ is at least $p_t^\star = \dfrac{1-\delta}{2(1-\delta^t)}$ for any $\delta \in (0,1)$. Therefore, the minimum admission price is at least $p^\star = \frac{1-\delta}{2}$.*

Remark 4. According to the previous result, for $\delta = \frac{1}{2}$ the dynamics never go below $\frac{1}{4}$. That is, the minimum admission price is at least $\frac{1}{4}$ and transactions paying less than this price are never admitted. We note experimentally that this bound may not be tight, as the dynamics for $\delta = \frac{1}{2}$ never passes value ≈ 0.363 which is computed over 100 steps (see Fig. 3 showing the dynamics for different values of δ).

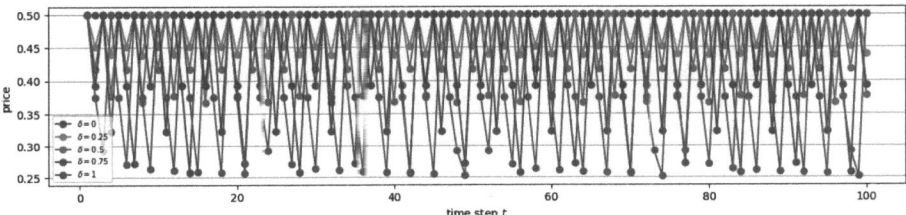

Fig. 3. The dynamics for $Q(p) = 1 - p$ and $\delta \in [0, 0.25, 0.5, 0.75, 1]$ when supply $s = 1$ (see Example 1). The smallest prices for each δ correspond to the respective minimum admission prices. Note that for a price dynamic to reach its minimum it may take more steps.

Remark 5. The minimum admission price for $\delta = 1$ goes to 0 for increasing s. Instead, for any $\delta < 1$ and any $s \geq \frac{1}{2}$, the minimum admission price is bounded away from 0, and is in fact at least $\frac{1-\delta}{2}$ as shown in the proposition above.

Remark 6. For any arbitrarily small $\delta > 0$, Proposition 1 leaves open the possibility that the minimum admission price is *strictly smaller* than $p_{mon} = \frac{1}{2}$. In the next section, we show that this is in general not the case, as there are other demand functions for which the minimum admission price *equals* the monopolist price already for $\delta > 0$.

4.2 The Admission Price Must Depend on Q

In this section, we consider the following class $\mathcal{Q}$ of daily demand functions:

$$Q_\epsilon(p) = \begin{cases} \frac{1}{2} + \epsilon - 2\epsilon p, & 0 \leq p \leq \frac{1}{2} \\ 1 - p, & \frac{1}{2} \leq p \leq 1 \end{cases} \qquad (12)$$

A function Q_ϵ of this class $\mathcal{Q}$ is depicted in Fig. 4. In particular, note that the slope of the function on the interval $[0, 0.5]$ is depending on $\epsilon \geq 0$. On the remaining interval $[0.5, 1]$ the function is just $1 - p$.

A few observations are in place.

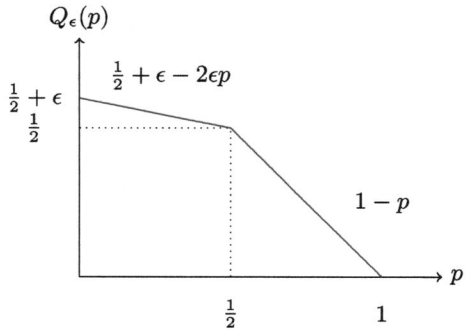

Fig. 4. Daily demand function of the class $\mathcal{Q}$.

Obs 1. Theorem 2 provides an upper bound on the minimum admission price if $\delta > \bar{\delta}_{ser}$. According to (8), this condition is equivalent to $\frac{q_{ser} - \bar{q}_{ser}}{1-\delta} > s$.[10]

Obs 2. For the type of demand function $Q_\epsilon \in \mathcal{Q}$, Theorem 2 may not apply, unless **Obs 1** is satisfied. This also depends on the value of ϵ.

Obs 3. The lower bound p_{ser} is not tight (Remark 4 deals with $\epsilon = \frac{1}{2}$).

These observations naturally suggest to obtain *lower bounds* on the minimum admission price for the class of functions above.

Example 3. Theorem 2 applies only for δ that are large enough ($\delta > \bar{\delta}_{ser}$). The necessary lower bound for δ for demand function of class $\mathcal{Q}$ is calculated below, that is, for the demand functions as in Eq. (12) and $s = 1$, we have (by Definition 3) $p_{mon} = \frac{1}{2} = q_{mon}, p_{ser} = \frac{1}{4}, q_{ser} = \frac{1+\epsilon}{2}, \bar{p}_{ser} = \frac{1}{2(1+\epsilon)}, \bar{q}_{ser} = \frac{1}{2} + \frac{\epsilon^2}{1+\epsilon}, \delta_{\min}(\bar{p}_{ser}) = 1 - \frac{\epsilon}{2} + \frac{\epsilon^2}{1+\epsilon}, p_{ser}^{(\delta)} = \frac{1}{4} + \frac{1-\delta}{\epsilon}$. Thus, for $Q(p) = 1 - p$, and $\epsilon = \frac{1}{2}$, we have $p_{ser}^{(\delta)} = \frac{1}{4} + 2(1 - \delta)$ for all $\delta > \bar{\delta}_{ser} = \delta_{\min}(\bar{p}_{ser}) = 11/12$.

Next, we state three results for the class of demand functions $\mathcal{Q}$. First, for any δ we can find a strictly decreasing demand function such that the price dynamics are stuck at p_{mon}. Second, for all demand functions $Q_\epsilon \in \mathcal{Q}$ with $\epsilon < \frac{1}{2}$, we find a δ such that the same holds. Finally, we find a lower bound on the minimum admission price for the remaining case $\epsilon \geq \frac{1}{2}$.

Theorem 4. *The following holds:*

1. *For every δ there exists a strictly decreasing $Q_\epsilon \in \mathcal{Q}$ s.t. the price dynamics stays at p_{mon}, i.e.*

$$p_t = p_{mon}, \quad \text{for all } t. \tag{13}$$

2. *Conversely, for any strictly decreasing $Q_\epsilon \in \mathcal{Q}$ with $\epsilon < \frac{1}{2}$ we find a δ such that (13) holds.*

---

[10] For $\epsilon = \frac{1}{2}$ and $s = 1$, the condition in **Obs 1** is to $\delta > 11/12 \approx 0.917$, $\frac{Q_\epsilon(p) - Q_\epsilon(p')}{1-\delta(\epsilon)} > s \iff \delta > 11/12 \approx 0.917$.

3. For every $Q_\epsilon \in \mathcal{Q}$ with $\epsilon \geq \frac{1}{2}$, the minimum admission price is at least $p^\star = \frac{1-\delta}{4\epsilon} < p_{mon}$.

The first two items of the theorem above show that the dynamics "collapse" to the monopolist price for any $\delta > 0$ for some demand function, answering negatively the question raised in Remark 6. The last item of the theorem generalizes the result in Proposition 1, as the latter corresponds to $\epsilon = 1/2$. Note that the above result for $\epsilon \to 0$ is in line with Nisan's extension to constant demand functions.

4.3 General Demand Function Q

So far we have applied the tool from Theorem 3 to specific demand functions. In this section, we instead derive a general bound. Let Q be a general non-increasing demand function. We provide a lower bound for the minimum admission price that is higher than p_{ser}.

Proposition 2. *Let Q be a general non-increasing demand function such that $Q(0) \leq s + \delta(q_{mon} - s)$. Then, the price*

$$p^\star := \frac{p_{mon} q_{mon}}{\frac{Q(0)}{1-\delta} + q_{mon} - \frac{q_{mon}}{1-\delta}}, \tag{14}$$

is a lower bound for the minimum admission price. In particular, $p^\star \geq p_{ser}$.

One example where the conditions in Proposition 2 are satisfied follows.

Example 4. For $s = \frac{Q(0)}{1-\delta}$, the condition above ($Q(0) \leq s + \delta(q_{mon}-s)$) is satisfied and $p^\star = \frac{p_{mon} q_{mon}}{s - \frac{\delta}{1-\delta} q_{mon}}$ which is larger than p_{ser}.

5 Conclusion and Future Work

Our work makes a step toward understanding how a (strategic) user can make more informed decisions about transaction fees by leveraging their belief about others' patience level, contributing to the balance between cost savings and timely inclusion. Specifically, we examined the minimum transaction fee (admission price) users must pay to guarantee that their transaction is eventually included.

We analyzed price fluctuations under a monopolistic pricing mechanism with *quasi-patient* users, whose interest in transaction inclusion diminishes over time due to costs. Our model includes impatient users [15] and patient users [19] as special cases ($\delta = 0$ and $\delta = 1$). We provide general bounds on price dynamics for $\delta \in (0,1)$, highlighting key factors affecting dynamics and the minimum admission price.

We first discuss the tightness of our bounds. Though Theorem 2 is a generic upper bound, i.e., it applies to any demand function, it is essentially tight as shown by the next result.

Theorem 5. *For any arbitrarily small $\xi > 0$, there is a demand function for which (i) the minimum admission price is strictly smaller than p_{mon} for all $\delta > \bar{\delta}_{ser}$, where $\bar{\delta}_{ser}$ is defined as in Theorem 2, and (ii) for all $\delta < \bar{\delta}_{ser} - \xi$ the minimum admission price equals to p_{mon}.*

Our work opens up interesting directions for future research. First, it might be interesting to consider restricted classes of demand functions of practical interest and provide tight bounds for *these* functions. Note that Theorem 5 may not apply, and our results suggest the need for some extension or variant of Theorems 2 and/or a stronger lower bound. Second, several extensions and variants are possible, leading to more complex dynamics. These include (i) various waiting cost functions, (ii) non-myopic monopolists maximizing revenue over multiple rounds, and (iii) strategic behavior of users and block producers. We believe some of our techniques can be adapted to handle more complex settings. In particular, dynamics where the level of patience correlates with the price could be analyzed by evaluating the counterpart of our pent-up "growth" term a_t in (5) and relating it to some "steepness" condition of the demand curve, similar to the proof of Theorems 2 and 3. Moreover, if the pent-up demand of certain complex dynamics can be "sandwiched" between two dynamics in our model, then our results could be turned into bounds for the dynamics of interest. We conjecture that more complex blockchain dynamics are qualitatively similar to ours and that this will help in obtaining useful parameter trade-offs and better design choices.

Finally, an open question remains regarding the comparison of social welfare in the case of quasi-patient users with the social welfare obtained in [19]. On one hand, Theorem 5 suggests that the dynamics collapses to the case $\delta = 0$. On the other hand, it is unclear whether this occurs for demand functions where the social welfare for $\delta = 0$ is arbitrarily bad relative to the optimum. Indeed, the proof of Theorem 5, uses demand curves with a "flat region" for which the social welfare for $\delta = 0$ is within a constant factor of that for $\delta = 1$ (the latter is the patient case in [19] for which the social welfare is at least $1/2$ of the optimum).

References

1. Cardano docs - Cardano monetary policy. https://docs.cardano.org/explore-cardano/monetary-policy/. Accessed 14 July 2024
2. Azouvi, S., Goren, G., Heimbach, L., Hicks, A.: Base fee manipulation in Ethereum's EIP-1559 transaction fee mechanism. arXiv preprint arXiv:2304.11478 (2023)
3. Bahrani, M., Garimidi, P., Roughgarden, T.: Transaction fee mechanism design in a post-MEV world. Cryptology ePrint Archive, Paper 2024/331. https://eprint.iacr.org/2024/331 (2024)
4. Basu, S., Easley, D.A., O'Hara, M., Sirer, E.G.: Towards a functional fee market for cryptocurrencies. CoRR abs/1901.06830 arXiv:1901.06830 (2019)
5. Chen, X., Simchi-Levi, D., Zhao, Z., Zhou, Y.: Bayesian mechanism design for blockchain transaction fee allocation (2024)

6. Chung, H., Shi, E.: Foundations of transaction fee mechanism design. In: Proceedings of the 2023 Annual ACM-SIAM Symposium on Discrete Algorithms (SODA), pp. 3856–3899 (2023). https://doi.org/10.1137/1.9781611977554.ch150
7. Eyal, I., Gencer, A.E., Sirer, E.G., Renesse, R.V.: Bitcoin-NG: a scalable blockchain protocol. In: 13th USENIX Symposium on Networked Systems Design and Implementation (NSDI 16), pp. 45–59. USENIX Association, Santa Clara, CA (2016). https://www.usenix.org/conference/nsdi16/technical-sessions/presentation/eyal
8. Ferreira, M.V.X., Moroz, D.J., Parkes, D.C., Stern, M.: Dynamic posted-price mechanisms for the blockchain transaction-fee market. In: AFT 2021, Proceedings of the 3rd ACM Conference on Advances in Financial Technologies, pp. 86–99. Association for Computing Machinery, New York, NY, USA (2021). https://doi.org/10.1145/3479722.3480991
9. Gafni, Y., Yaish, A.: Greedy transaction fee mechanisms for (non-) myopic miners. arXiv preprint arXiv:2210.07793 (2022)
10. Gafni, Y., Yaish, A.: Competitive revenue extraction from time-discounted transactions in the semi-myopic regime. arXiv preprint arXiv:2402.08549 (2024)
11. Goldberg, A.V., Hartline, J.D., Karlin, A.R., Saks, M., Wright, A.: Competitive auctions. Games Econ. Behav. **55**(2), 242–269 (2006)
12. Gong, T., Minaei, M., Sun, W., Kate, A.: Towards overcoming the undercutting problem. In: Eyal, I. Garay, J. (eds.) Financial Cryptography and Data Security, pp. 444–463. Springer International Publishing, Cham (2022). https://doi.org/10.1007/978-3-031-18283-9_22
13. Huberman, G., Leshno, J.D., Moallemi, C.: Monopoly without a monopolist: an economic analysis of the bitcoin payment system. Rev. Econ. Stud. **88**(6), 3011–3040 (2021). https://doi.org/10.1093/restud/rdab014
14. Kiayias, A., Koutsoupias, E., Lazos, P., Panagiotakos, G.: Tiered mechanisms for blockchain transaction fees. arXiv preprint arXiv:2304.06014 (2023)
15. Lavi, R., Sattath, O., Zohar, A.: Redesigning bitcoin's fee market. ACM Trans. Econ. Comput. **10**(1) (2022). https://doi.org/10.1145/3530799
16. Leonardos, S., Monnot, B., Reijsbergen, D., Skoulakis, E., Piliouras, G.: Dynamical analysis of the EIP-1559 Ethereum fee market. In: Proceedings of the 3rd ACM Conference on Advances in Financial Technologies, pp. 114–126 (2021)
17. Leonardos, S., Reijsbergen, D., Monnot, B., Piliouras, G.: Optimality despite chaos in fee markets. In: International Conference on Financial Cryptography and Data Security, pp. 346–362. Springer (2023). https://doi.org/10.1007/978-3-031-47751-5_20
18. Nakamoto, S.: Bitcoin: a peer-to-peer electronic cash system (2008). https://bitcoin.org/bitcoin.pdf
19. Nisan, N.: Serial monopoly on blockchains. arXiv preprint arXiv:2311.12731 (2023)
20. Pai, M., Resnick, M.: Dynamic transaction fee mechanism design (2023). https://www.mechanism.org/spec/04
21. Reijsbergen, D., Sridhar, S., Monnot, B., Leonardos, S., Skoulakis, S., Piliouras, G.: Transaction fees on a honeymoon: Ethereum's EIP-1559 one month later. In: 2021 IEEE International Conference on Blockchain (Blockchain), pp. 196–204. IEEE (2021)
22. Roughgarden, T.: Transaction fee mechanism design for the Ethereum blockchain: an economic analysis of EIP-1559. arXiv preprint arXiv:2012.00854 (2020)
23. Roughgarden, T.: Transaction fee mechanism design. ACM SIGecom Exch. **19**(1), 52–55 (2021). https://doi.org/10.1145/3476436.3476445
24. Yao, A.C.: An incentive analysis of some bitcoin fee designs. CoRR arXiv:1811.02351 (2018)

Efficient Blockchains

Pilotfish: Distributed Execution for Scalable Blockchains

Quentin Kniep[1], Lefteris Kokoris-Kogias[2,3], Alberto Sonnino[3,4], Igor Zablotchi[3(✉)], and Nuda Zhang[5]

[1] ETH Zurich, Zurich, Switzerland
qkniep@ethz.ch
[2] IST Austria, Klosterneuburg, Austria
[3] Mysten Labs, Palo Alto, USA
{lefteris,alberto,igor}@mystenlabs.com
[4] University College London (UCL), London, England
[5] University of Michigan, Ann Arbor, USA
nudzhang@umich.edu

Abstract. Scalability is a crucial requirement for modern large-scale systems, enabling elasticity and ensuring responsiveness under varying load. While cloud systems have achieved scalable architectures, blockchain systems remain constrained by the need to over-provision validator machines to handle peak load. This leads to resource inefficiency, poor cost scaling and limits on performance. To address these challenges, we introduce Pilotfish, the first scale-out transaction execution engine for blockchains. Pilotfish enables validators to scale horizontally by distributing transaction execution across multiple worker machines, allowing elasticity without compromising consistency or determinism. It integrates seamlessly with the lazy blockchain architecture, completing the missing piece of execution elasticity. To achieve this, Pilotfish tackles several key challenges: ensuring scalable and strongly consistent distributed transactions, handling partial crash recovery with lightweight replication, and maintaining concurrency with a novel versioned-queue scheduling algorithm. Our evaluation shows that Pilotfish scales linearly up to at least eight workers per validator for compute-bound workloads, while maintaining low latency. By solving scalable execution, Pilotfish brings blockchains closer to achieving end-to-end elasticity, unlocking new possibilities for efficient and adaptable blockchain systems.

1 Introduction

A crucial property required by modern large-scale computing is *scalability*,[1] which refers to a system's ability to dynamically adapt its performance as load changes, ensuring that the system remains responsive despite varying load. Scalability is fundamental because it is an essential requirement for elasticity, and thus

---

[1] Due to space constraints, many references have been omitted and deferred to the full version of our paper [7].

in turn for a good user experience (e.g., responsiveness) at a sustainable cost. Without elasticity, systems either risk being overwhelmed during peak loads, leading to poor performance and user dissatisfaction, or they incur excessive costs during low-load periods by maintaining unnecessary resources.

Over the past decades, significant effort has been devoted to developing scalable software architectures for cloud-based systems. However, the situation is starkly different for blockchain systems. Among core blockchain tasks, transaction execution is particularly challenging with respect to scalability. The current dominant approach to transaction execution in blockchain involves ensuring that validator machines are sufficiently powerful to handle peak loads. This approach is scalable up to a point, but has limitations: (1) it leads to resource inefficiency, as validators remain over-provisioned during low-load periods; (2) it has a resource ceiling, as even the most powerful single machine will eventually be insufficient if the load is high enough; (3) it has poor cost scaling, as high-end machines are expensive and limited to a few vendors.

In response to these challenges, we introduce Pilotfish, the first scale-out transaction execution engine for blockchain. The core idea of Pilotfish is to run each validator on multiple mutually trusting machines or workers, as opposed to running a single machine per validator. Each worker is only responsible for a subset of the validator's state, and only executes a subset of transactions. This approach opens the way toward elasticity, as it allows scaling each validator out and in as the load increases and decreases.

Pilotfish is designed to integrate seamlessly with the lazy blockchain architecture, which is increasingly used by modern blockchains [2]: as of the time of writing, lazy blockchains account for over $20 billion in market capitalization. Lazy blockchains separate the problems of transaction dissemination, ordering, and execution. They provide a scalable solution to two of the three core blockchain tasks: dissemination (ensuring that client transactions are available at a quorum of validators) and ordering (establishing a reliable total order over transactions, also known as consensus). However, as mentioned above, state-of-the-art lazy blockchains do not solve the *execution scalability* problem: their execution is still designed to run on a single machine.

Pilotfish must address several challenges to achieve this. First (i), it must solve the distributed transaction problem, since the validator state is sharded across multiple worker machines, and transactions may span multiple shards. This is especially challenging since blockchains need to guarantee strong consistency (serializability) and determinism, without compromising on latency or throughput. Most existing approaches to distributed transactions cannot directly be applied to our setting: (1) the two-phase commit approach guarantees strong consistency but is not scalable; (2) the relaxed consistency approach [9] is scalable but sacrifices strong consistency, which is crucial for blockchain; (3) the restricted transaction approach [3] is both scalable and strongly consistent, but sacrifices transaction generality. The most promising existing solution for our needs is that of deterministic databases [16], which balance scalability, consistency, and transaction generality. We borrow techniques from distributed databases and leverage the fact that in lazy blockchains, consensus precedes—and is decoupled from—execution, so by execution time, validators have agreed on a permanent ordering of transactions.

Secondly (ii), Pilotfish needs to tolerate workers crashing and recovering. To address this, Pilotfish maintains sufficient state among workers as *checkpoints* to allow recovering machines to catch up with the rest. A straightforward solution would be to resort to strong (and expensive) consensus-based replication techniques among workers internal to the validator [16]. However Pilotfish avoids such overhead by observing that consistency and availability of the commit sequence are already provided by the blockchain protocol. Thus, Pilotfish optimistically does lightweight, best-effort replication between workers, and relies on recovery from other validators only if optimistic replication fails.

Finally (iii), Pilotfish aims to support a simpler programming model where transactions may only partially specify their input read and write set (e.g., as required for Move). This, however, creates an additional challenge for Pilotfish, as objects that might be accessed dynamically at execution time can be located in different workers. This means that objects cannot be overwritten until all previous transactions have finished, effectively reverting to sequential execution and enforcing write-after-write dependencies. This limitation would reduce the parallelizability of the workload. Pilotfish circumvents this issue by leveraging its enforced determinism, allowing in-memory execution to be lost and safely recovered in the event of crashes. Pilotfish relies on a novel versioned-queue scheduling algorithm that allows transactions with write-after-write conflicts to execute concurrently. We couple this with our crash recovery mechanism, which only persists consistent states. As a result, upon a crash, Pilotfish simply re-executes a few transactions, but thanks to the deterministic nature of the blockchain this does not pose any inconsistency risks.

We evaluate Pilotfish by studying its latency and throughput, while varying the number of workers per validator, the computational intensity, and the degree of contention of the workload. We find that Pilotfish scales linearly to at least 8 workers per validator when the workload is compute-bound, while keeping latency under 50 ms.

Discussion. While this work focuses on a scalable protocol for distributed blockchain transactions, achieving full elasticity poses additional challenges, particularly in dynamically scaling up and down workers and repartitioning objects. These aspects, while critical to practical implementations, are well-explored in existing literature on elastic systems: dynamic workload partitioning, load-aware worker scaling, and online object migration.

2 System Model

Pilotfish implements a blockchain *validator*, composed internally of a black-box *Primary* machine, as well as a set of worker machines, simply called *workers*. The Primary is responsible for communicating with (the Primaries of) other validators in order to agree on an ordered sequence of transactions. The workers collectively execute the ordered sequence of transactions and update the validator's state accordingly.

Objects and Transactions. Pilotfish validators replicate the state of the blockchain represented as a set of *objects*. Transactions can read and write (mutate, create, and delete) objects, and reference every object by its unique identifier *oid*. A transaction is an authenticated command that references a set of objects (by their unique identifier *oid*), and an entry function into a smart contract call identifying the execution code. The transaction divides the objects it references into two disjoint sets, (i) the read set $\mathcal{R}$ referencing input objects that the transaction may only read, and (ii) the write set $\mathcal{W}$ referencing objects that the transaction may mutate. In most cases, the identifier *oid* of each object of the read and write sets can be computed using only the information provided by the transaction, without the need to execute it or access any object's data. In these cases, Pilotfish has complete knowledge of the read and write sets of the transaction. However, Pilotfish also supports dynamic accesses (Sect. 6) where the read and write set of a transaction is discovered only upon attempting to execute the transaction, adopting the execution model of Sui [1].

Network Model. We assume that the Primary and workers communicate by sending messages over the network through point-to-point connections. We assume that the network is fully connected and reliable: each message sent by a correct process (i.e., non-faulty machine) to a correct process is eventually delivered. Furthermore, we assume authenticated channels: the receiver of a message is aware of the sender's identity.

Synchrony Model. We consider the standard partially synchronous environment. Specifically, there exists an unknown Global Stabilization Time (GST) and a positive known duration δ such that message delays are bounded by δ after GST: a message sent at time τ is received by time $\max(\tau, \text{GST}) + \delta$. It has been shown that in partial synchrony, crash failures can eventually be perfectly detected, thus we assume an eventually perfect failure detector.

Threat Model. We assume that each validator is controlled by a single entity, or by a set of mutually trusting entities. This implies that the Primary and workers trust each other, and we therefore only consider crash failures for components internal to the validator (a validator as a whole may still exhibit Byzantine behavior in its interaction with other validators, but tolerating such failures is handled by the blockchain protocol, which is outside the scope of this work). For this reason, we do not require any cryptography assumptions, other than the authenticated channels.[2] For pedagogical reasons, for the first part of the paper we assume that workers cannot fail. Later in Sect. 5, we expand each logical worker to have a set of $n_e = 2f_e + 1$ replicas such that as long as for each worker

---

[2] Our network, synchrony, trust and cryptography assumptions only apply *internally* to the validator. By contrast, the outer blockchain protocol, which governs how validators interact with each other, may make entirely different assumptions on synchrony and types of failures and thus may require stronger cryptography primitives.

there are $f_e + 1$ replicas available the system remains live and safe.[3] In case this threshold is breached the validator can still synchronize with the rest of the validators of the lazy blockchain through a standard recovery procedure [2] that is out of scope.

Core Properties. The full version of our paper [7] proves that Pilotfish guarantees serializability, determinism, and liveness. Intuitively, serializability means that Pilotfish execution produces the same result as a sequential execution. Determinism means that every correct validator receiving the same sequence of transactions performs the same state transitions. Liveness means that all correct validators receiving a sequence of transactions eventually execute it.

Definition 1 (Pilotfish Serializability). *A correct validator executing the sequence of transactions* $[Tx_1, \ldots, Tx_n]$ *holds the same state as if the transactions were executed sequentially, in the given order.*

Definition 2 (Pilotfish Determinism). *No two correct validators that executed the same sequence of transactions* $[Tx_1, \ldots, Tx_n]$ *have different states.*

Definition 3 (Pilotfish Liveness). *Correct validators receiving the sequence of transactions* $[Tx_1, \ldots, Tx_n]$ *eventually execute all transactions* $Tx_1, \ldots, Tx_n$.

3 Existing Designs and Pilotfish Overview

3.1 Previous Designs

Previous designs for scaling execution in lazy blockchains fall into two categories. The first is parallel execution [1], where each validator uses a high-end server to handle increased load. This approach lacks elasticity: the cost of running a powerful validator remains high regardless of actual load, leading to inefficiency during low usage and performance ceilings due to finite server resources.

The second category employs inter-validator sharding [8], in which the blockchain state is split into shards, with a subset of the validators handling each shard in parallel. However, inter-validator sharding has limitations related to security and performance. Firstly, sharding requires a sampling process from the full validator set to subsets of validators per shard, such that each shard has more than 2/3 honest members. These systems are thus less robust to adversarial attacks. For example Omniledger [8] assumes a 25% Byzantine adversary in order to provide sufficient 34% security in all the sub-sampled shards. In the same vein, the adversary's adaptivity should be limited to once an epoch, as otherwise the adversary could target all its power in a single shard and compromise it. Finally, sharding is also challenging from a performance perspective, as transactions that span multiple shards require expensive and slow Byzantine-resilient atomic commit protocols.

---

[3] Here, f_e refers to the number of replicas that may crash per logical worker, *internally to the validator*; in particular, f_e may be different from the number of validators in the blockchain that may be Byzantine (usually denoted by f).

3.2 Intravalidator Sharding with Pilotfish

Through Pilotfish, we instead propose *intravalidator sharding*, as illustrated in Fig. 1. Each validator consists of multiple *SequencingWorkers* that collect transaction data based on the commit sequence from the Primary, similar to transaction dissemination workers in lazy blockchains like Tusk [2] and Shoal [15]. Pilotfish innovates by distributing transaction execution on several *ExecutionWorkers*. Each ExecutionWorker stores a subset of the state, executes a subset of the transactions, and contributes its memory and storage to the system.

In Pilotfish, the Primary only manages metadata (agreement on a sequence of batch digests) allowing it to scale to large volumes of batches and transactions [2]. Actual batch storage is distributed among a potentially large number of SequencingWorkers. The key insight is that transaction execution is also distributed among numerous ExecutionWorkers, enabling horizontal scaling. As workers are added, the capacity to store state and process transactions increases.

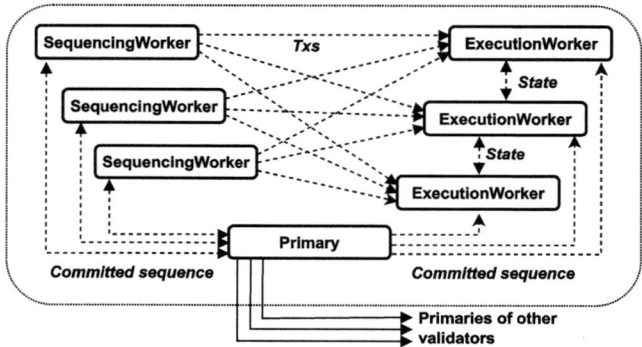

Fig. 1. Pilotfish validator's components. Each validator is composed of several SequencingWorkers to fetch and persist the client's transaction, one Primary to run Byzantine agreement on metadata, and several ExecutionWorkers to execute transactions. Each component may run on dedicated machines or be collocated with other components. Dotted arrows indicate internal messages exchanged between the components of the validator (localhost or LAN) and solid arrows indicate messages exchanged with the outside world (WAN).

Sharding Strategy. Pilotfish uses its SequencingWorkers and its ExecutionWorkers to operate two levels of sharding. (i) Pilotfish shards transaction data among its SequencingWorkers. Transactions batches (and thus clients' transactions) are assigned to SequencingWorkers deterministically based on their digest. SequencingWorker can be seen as architecturally equivalent to the worker machines used by lazy blockchains to decouple dissemination (performed by workers) from ordering (performed by the Primary). All transactions of a batch are persisted by the same SequencingWorker. Each SequencingWorker maintains a key-value store BATCHES[BatchId] → Batch mapping the batch digests BatchId to each batch handled by the SequencingWorker. (ii) Additionally, Pilotfish shards its state among its ExecutionWorkers. Each ExecutionWorker is responsible for a disjoint subset of the objects in the system (composing the state); objects are assigned to ExecutionWorkers based on their collision-resistant identifier oid. Every object in the system is handled by exactly one (logical) ExecutionWorker.

4 The Pilotfish System

Figure 2 shows the transaction life cycle in Pilotfish, from sequencing to execution. The Primary sends the committed sequence to all SequencingWorkers and ExecutionWorkers (❶). Below, we outline the core Pilotfish protocol at steps ❷, ❸, ❹, and ❺ of Fig. 2. Due to space limitations, our full algorithms are deferred to the full version of our paper [7].

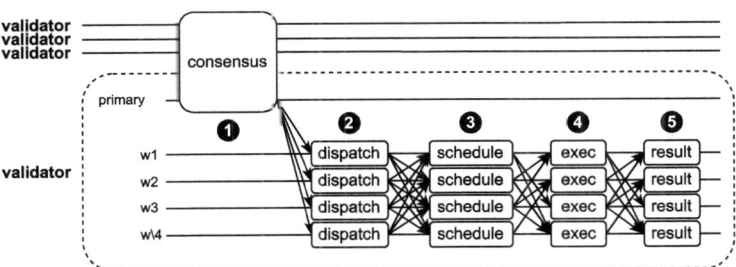

Fig. 2. Pilotfish overview. Every validator runs with 5 machines: one machine running the Primary and 4 machines running workers. Each worker machine collocates 1 SequencingWorker and 1 ExecutionWorker. The Primary runs a Byzantine agreement protocol to sequence batch digests (❶). SequencingWorkers receive the committed sequence and load the data of the corresponding transactions from their storage (❷). Each ExecutionWorkers receiving these transactions assigns a lock to each object referenced by the transaction to schedule their execution (❸). A deterministically-selected ExecutionWorker eventually receives the object's data referenced by the execution and executes it (❹). Finally, the ExecutionWorker signals all SequencingWorkers to update their state with the results of the transaction's execution (❺).

ExecutionWorkers maintain the following key-value stores:

- OBJECTS[oid] → o making all the objects handled by the ExecutionWorker accessible by their unique identifier.
- PENDING[oid] → [(op, [Tx])] mapping each object to a list of pending transactions [Tx] referencing oid in their read or write set and that are awaiting execution. The operation op indicates whether the transaction may only Read (R) the object or whether it may also write (W) it. This map is used as a

'locking' mechanism to track dependencies and determine which transactions can be executed in parallel. Entries relating to a transaction are removed from this map after its execution.
- MISSING[oid] → [Tx] mapping objects that are missing from OBJECTS to the transactions that reference them. It is used to track transactions that cannot (yet) be executed because they reference objects that are not yet available. It is cleaned after execution.

Step ❷ : Dispatch Transactions. At a high level, each SequencingWorker i observes the commit sequence and loads from storage all the batches referenced by the committed sequence that they hold in their BATCHES$_i$ store (and ignores the others). The SequencingWorker then parses each transaction of the batch (in the order specified by the batch) to determine which objects it contains. At the end of this process, SequencingWorker i composes one ProposeMessage for each ExecutionWorker j of the validator: ProposeMessage$_{i,j}$ ← (BatchId, BatchIdx, T). The message contains the batch digest BatchId, an index BatchIdx uniquely identifying the batch in the global committed sequence and a list of transactions T referencing at least one object handled by worker j. If no transactions affect worker j, the worker still receives an empty message so it can proceed.

Step ❸ : Schedule Execution. Each ExecutionWorker j awaits one ProposeMessage from each SequencingWorker. It then parses every transaction Tx included (in order) and extracts objects in Tx's read set $\mathcal{R}_j$ and write set $\mathcal{W}_j$ managed by ExecutionWorker j (and ignores the other objects that it does not handle).

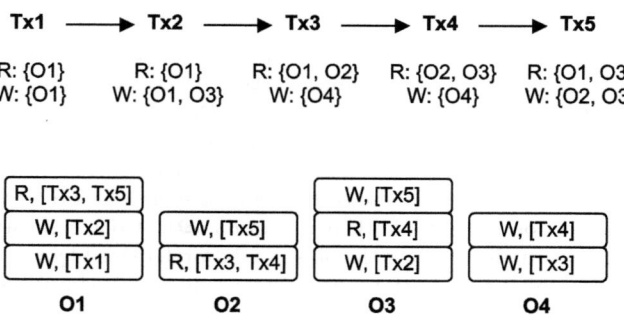

Fig. 3. Example snapshot of the PENDING queues of an ExecutionWorker. Pilotfish schedules the execution of the sequence [Tx$_1$, Tx$_2$, Tx$_3$, Tx$_4$, Tx$_5$]. The ExecutionWorker stores Tx$_1$ as (W, [Tx$_1$]) in the queue of oid_1 as it only mutates oid_1. Tx$_2$ then mutates oid_1 and writes oid_3; it is thus store in the queue of oid_1 (implicitly taking Tx$_1$ as dependency) and oid_3. Tx$_3$ schedules a read for both oid_1 and oid_2 and a write for oid_4. Tx$_4$ reads oid_2 (it can thus read oid_2 in parallel with Tx$_3$, registering (R, [Tx$_3$, Tx$_4$]) in the queue of oid_2) and oid_3, and writes oid_4. Finally Tx$_5$ reads oid_1 (it can thus read oid_1 in parallel with Tx$_3$), writes oid_2 and mutates oid_3.

Figure 3 illustrates an example snapshot of the PENDING$_j$ store of a validator. ExecutionWorkers append every object of the write set W_j to their local PENDING$_j$ indicating that Tx may mutate oid: PENDING$_j[oid]$ ← PENDING$_j[oid] \cup$ (W, Tx). The position of Tx in the PENDING$_j$ indicates that Tx can only write oid after all transactions appended before in PENDING$_j[oid]$ are executed, essentially indicating a write-after-write (or write-after-read) dependency.

ExecutionWorkers additionally register reads performed by Tx on an object id by looking at the latest entry in PENDING$_j[oid]$. If the entry is a write then they append a new entry: PENDING$_j[oid]$ ← PENDING$_j[oid] \cup$(R, Tx), indicating a read-after-write dependency. However, if the entry is a read then the transaction Tx may be executed in parallel with any other transaction Tx' also reading oid. ExecutionWorkers thus modify the latest entry of the storage to reflect this possibility by setting Tx and Tx' at the same height in the PENDING$_j$ store: PENDING$_j[oid][-1]$ ← (R, [Tx', Tx]).

A transaction Tx is ready to be executed when it reaches the head of the pending lists of all the objects it references. At this point, the ExecutionWorker loads from its OBJECTS$_j$ store all the objects data it handles: O_j ← {OBJECTS$[oid]$ s.t. $oid \in$ HANDLEDOBJECTSTx}. It then composes a ReadyMessage for the dedicated ExecutionWorker that was selected to execute Tx: ReadyMessage$_j$ ← (Tx, O_j). The message contains the transaction Tx to execute, and a list of object data (O_j) referenced by the part of the read and write set of Tx handled by ExecutionWorker j.

If an object referenced by Tx is absent from the ExecutionWorker's local OBJECTS$_j$ store, the ExecutionWorker waits until it all transactions sequenced before Tx are executed and then sends ⊥ instead of the object's data. This signals that Tx is malformed and references non-existent objects or objects that should have been created but the origin transaction failed.

Step ❹ : Execute Transactions. Upon receiving a ReadyMessage message, an ExecutionWorker waits for one ReadyMessage from all other ExecutionWorkers handling at least one object referenced by Tx. At this point, the set of ReadyMessage provides the ExecutionWorker with the objects' data behind all objects referenced by Tx (or ⊥ if missing). If all object data are available, Tx is executed; otherwise, it is aborted. Executing a transaction produces a set of objects to mutate or create O and a set of object ids to delete I: (O, I) ← $exec$(Tx, O'). The ExecutionWorker then prepares a ResultMessage for all ExecutionWorkers. For ExecutionWorkers whose objects are not affected by Tx this serves as a heartbeat message whereas for those whose objects are mutated, created or deleted by the transaction execution it informs them to update their object store OBJECTS accordingly. If Tx aborts, the worker sends a ResultMessage with empty O, I.

Step ❺ : Handle Results. When an ExecutionWorker receives a ResultMessage, it: (i) persists locally the fact that the transaction has been executed by advancing a watermark keeping track of all executed transactions; (ii) updates each object into its local OBJECTS store including deletions; and (iii) removes all occurrences of the transaction from its PENDING store. It then tries to trigger the execution of the next transactions in the queues.

5 Crash Fault Tolerance

Section 4 presents the design of Pilotfish assuming all data structures are in-memory. However, critical validator components inevitably fail over time. To handle this, Pilotfish adopts a simple replication architecture, dedicating multiple machines to each ExecutionWorker. This internal replication allows the validator to continue operating despite crash faults. Pilotfish does not replicate the Primary, which handles only lightweight operations (and holds the signing key), nor does it replicate SequencingWorkers, which perform stateless work and can be rebooted from the latest persisted sequence number. We briefly detail our replication protocol here and defer more details to our full paper [7].

5.1 Internal Replication

Figure 4 illustrates the replication strategy of Pilotfish. Each ExecutionWorker is replaced by $n_e = 2f_e + 1$ ExecutionWorkers. Pilotfish tolerates up to f_e simultaneous crash faults in a set of n_e replicated ExecutionWorkers. These replicas form a grid: each column represents replicas of a single shard; each row is a cluster containing exactly one replica from each shard. Within each cluster, workers exchange reads and maintain a consistent view of the object store.

The naïve way to achieve such reliability would be to run a black-box state machine replication engine, which is also the proposal of the state-of-the-art [16]. Pilotfish however greatly simplifies this process by leveraging (i) the Primary as a coordinator between the workers' replicas, (ii) external validators holding the blockchains state and the commit sequence, and (iii) the fact that execution is deterministic (given the commit sequence).

5.2 Normal Operation

Within each cluster, replicated ExecutionWorkers run the same core protocol as the unreplicated case. Inter-cluster communication is minimal, except for checkpoint updates. To enable recovery, each worker keeps: (1) a buffer of outgoing ReadyMessage instances (the reads it has served), which can be replayed if messages are lost, and (2) a set of checkpoints, each representing a consistent, on-disk snapshot of the local object store. Checkpoints are the only persistent state.

Garbage Collection. Once a checkpoint is deemed stable—i.e., a quorum of $f_e + 1$ replicas in every shard confirm they have persisted a checkpoint after a certain transaction index—old checkpoints and buffered messages prior to that index are garbage-collected.

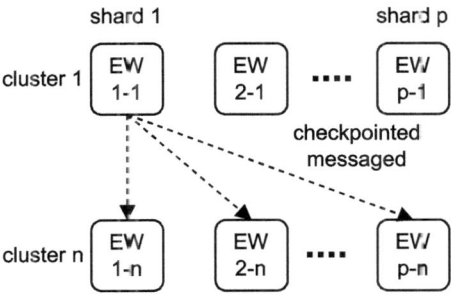

Fig. 4. Replication scheme for ExecutionWorkers. The object store is partitioned into shards, and each shard is replicated n_e-fold. Each row represents a cluster, and ExecutionWorkers within a cluster coordinate to process transactions. During normal operation, the only communication between clusters is the sending of checkpoints.

Bounding Memory Use. Even with garbage collection, differences in execution speeds of workers can prevent checkpoints from being safely garbage-collected, and thus lead to unbounded memory use. To prevent this, Pilotfish enforces a maximum of c checkpoints per worker. If a worker reaches this limit (e.g., $c = 2$), it must pause execution until it can safely discard an older checkpoint. This prevents unlimited checkpoint buildup and ensures that clusters can proceed without one shard outpacing the others indefinitely. Typically, $c = 2$ strikes a balance between performance and resource usage, letting faster clusters keep going as long as they are within one checkpoint boundary of slower ones.

5.3 Failure Recovery

Pilotfish uses two mechanisms to recover from failures (1) *reconfiguration*, a rapid process that does not reduce the system's throughput, but requires roughly synchronized clusters; and (2) *checkpoint synchronization*, a slower procedure that coordinates multiple clusters if reconfiguration fails. If both approaches fail, the system can still recover from other blockchain validators.

Recovery Through Reconfiguration. When an ExecutionWorker crashes, workers which rely on it for reads may be unable to proceed. They detect the crash and establish a new connection with a replacement replica. Typically, this requires just two round trips: one to identify a new node that can provide reads, and another to complete the handshake. Other clusters keep executing, so throughput remains unaffected as long as the failure threshold f_e is not exceeded. The full version of our paper [7] contains the full algorithm.

Recovery Through Checkpoint Synchronization. If a worker is too far behind for reconfiguration alone, it triggers a synchronization process for itself and its peers, which fetch the latest checkpoint from an up-to-date replica. Once all peers reach the same state, the worker re-establishes missing members in its cluster (via reconfiguration). This cascades recovery across clusters that depend on the slow worker, ensuring no cluster loses liveness if another shard "fast-forwards" its state.

Disaster Recovery. If an entire cluster is lost beyond the threat model of Sect. 2, the system can recover by booting a new cluster with the same peers set. This new cluster retrieves the system state from other validators, which store stable checkpoints. Though it requires wide-area network communications and is slower, this worst-case path ensures Pilotfish remains operable even with minimal replication (e.g., $f_e = 1$).

6 Dynamic Reads and Writes

In most deterministic execution engines, transactions must specify the exact data they read and write. This constraint limits developers and encourages the over-prediction of read/write sets to ensure successful execution. In distributed execution, the problem is exacerbated by the need to transmit the data between ExecutionWorkers. This means that we might need to transmit large read/write sets between computers in order to access a single item (e.g., transfer a full array to dynamically access one cell).

Pilotfish supports dynamic reads/writes but confines them to parent-child object hierarchies. A child object is an object that is owned by another object, the parent. An example parent-child relationship is that between a dynamically allocated array and its individual cells. In Pilotfish, a child object can only be accessed if the root object (the top-level object in a hierarchy of potentially numerous parents) is included in the transaction and the transaction has permission to access the root. This setup avoids overpredictions by allowing transactions to handle unexpected data accesses with minimal algorithmic changes.

One of the required modifications is to retain the reads in the queues until the transaction execution is completed. However, this leads to a loss of parallelism since we are unable to write a new version of an object until all transactions reading the previous version have finished. We resolve this false sharing situation without bloating memory usage in two ways. First, we treat every version of an object as a new object; this means that the queues in Fig. 3 are per (*oid*, Version) instead of per *oid*. Therefore, each queue consists of a single write as the initial transaction, followed by potentially several reads. This resolves the false sharing as future versions of an object initialize new queues and can proceed independently of whether the previous version is still locked because of a dynamic read operation. Unfortunately, this leads to objects potentially being written out of order, which could pollute our state and make consistent recovery from crashes impossible. For this reason, our second modification is buffering writes so that they are written to disk in order by leveraging the crash-recover algorithm in Sect. 5. Our full paper [7] provides further details on how we handle child objects, complete algorithms, and formal proofs.

Algorithm Modifications. Pilotfish handles the state of child objects like any other object: they are assigned to ExecutionWorkers that maintain their pending queues. The ExecutionWorkers schedule the execution of root objects as usual after processing a ProposeMessage by updating the queues of all the objects that the transaction directly references. This means that they update the queues of (potentially) root objects as well as the queues of (potentially currently undefined) child objects. The security of this process is ensured by following the same procedure as for object creation. Hence, the ExecutionWorker will either create these objects or garbage-collect them. Finally, when the transaction is ready for execution, either a previous transaction would have transferred ownership of child objects to the parent or the transaction would abort at execution.

On receiving a ReadyMessage, the ExecutionWorker starts execution. If it detects a new child object, it pauses and sends a UpdateProposeExec carrying an *augmented transaction* Tx+, which includes the child objects ID in its read/write sets. This UpdateProposeExec message is sent to shards handling one of the (newly discovered) child objects. This is safe because the parent is already locked, implicitly locking the child. If the transaction is not done, subsequent parent writes go to distinct queues, enabling on-demand multi-version concurrency.

Upon receiving UpdateProposeExec with Tx+, the ExecutionWorker replaces Tx in its queues with Tx+ and adds Tx+ to the queues of any newly discovered child objects. When Tx+ reaches the front of every involved queue, it re-attempts execution. Eventually, the protocol identifies every child object that the transaction dynamically accesses, and Tx+ contains their explicit ids. At this point, the transaction execution can terminate successfully.

7 Implementation

We implement a networked multi-core Pilotfish execution engine in Rust on top of the Sui blockchain. As a result, our implementation supports Sui-Move. We made this choice because Sui-Move is a simple and expressive language that is easy to reason about, provides a well-documented transaction format explicitly exposing the input read and write set, and supports dynamic reads and writes. Our implementation uses tokio for asynchronous networking across the Pilotfish workers, utilizing low-level TCP sockets for communication without relying on any RPC frameworks. While all network communications in our implementation are asynchronous, the core logic of the execution worker runs synchronously in a dedicated thread. This approach facilitates rigorous testing, mitigates race conditions, and allows for targeted profiling of this critical code path. In addition to regular unit tests, we created a command-line utility (called *orchestrator*) designed to deploy real-world clusters of Pilotfish with workers distributed across multiple machines. The orchestrator has been instrumental in pinpointing and addressing efficiency bottlenecks. We will open-source our Pilotfish implementation along with its orchestration utilities.[4]

---

[4] https://github.com/mystenlabs/sui/tree/sharded-execution.

8 Evaluation

We evaluate the performance of Pilotfish through experiments on Amazon Web Services (AWS) to show that given a sufficiently parallelizable compute-bound load, the throughput of Pilotfish linearly increases with the number of Execution-Workers without visibly impacting latency. In order to investigate the spectrum of Pilotfish, we (a) run with transactions of increasing computational load and (b) create a contented workload that is not ideal for Pilotfish as it (i) increases the amount of communication among ExecutionWorkers and (ii) might increase the queuing delays in order to unblock later transactions. We show the performance improvements of Pilotfish over the baseline execution engine of Sui.

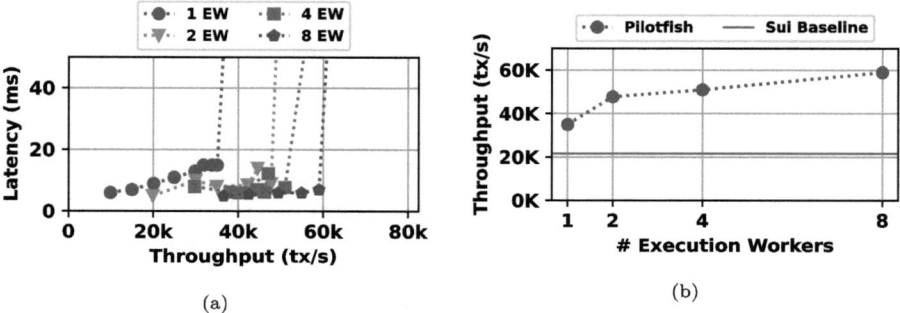

Fig. 5. Pilotfish latency vs throughput (a) and scalability (b) with simple transfers.

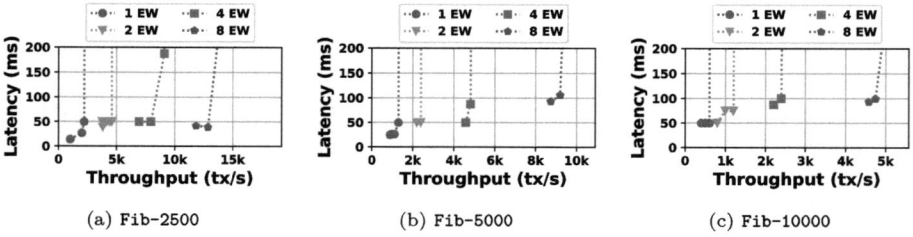

Fig. 6. Pilotfish latency vs. throughput for the heavy computation workloads.

8.1 Experimental Setup

We deploy Pilotfish on AWS, using m5d.8xlarge within a single datacenter (us-west-1). Each machine provides 10 Gbps of bandwidth, 32 virtual CPUs (16 physical cores) on a 2.5 GHz, Intel Xeon Platinum 8175, 128 GB memory, and runs Linux Ubuntu server 22.04. We select these machines because they provide decent performance, and are in the price range of 'commodity servers'.

In all graphs, each data point represents median latency/throughput over a 5-minute run. We instantiate one benchmark client collocated with each SequencingWorker submitting transactions at a fixed rate for a duration of 5 min. We experimentally increase the load of transactions sent to the systems, and record the throughput and latency of executed transactions. As a result, all plots illustrate the 'steady state' latency of all systems under low load, as well as the maximal throughput they can serve, after which latency grows quickly. We vary the types of transactions throughout the benchmark to experiment with different contention patterns. When referring to *latency*, we mean the time elapsed from when the client submits the transaction until the transaction is executed. By *throughput*, we mean the number of executed transactions over the entire duration of the run.

8.2 Simple Transfer Workload

In this workload, each transaction is a simple transfer of coins between objects. No two transactions conflict; each transaction operates on a different set of objects from the other transactions. Thus, this workload is completely parallelizable. Figure 5a shows latency vs throughput of Pilotfish on this workload with 1, 2, 4 and 8 ExecutionWorkers, and Fig. 5 shows how Pilotfish's maximum throughput scales when varying the number of ExecutionWorkers. Figure 5 includes as baseline the throughput of the Sui execution engine.[5] Since the Sui transaction manager currently relies on stable storage, whereas Pilotfish is in-memory, this baseline is a lower bound on the expected performance of our system, when using a single ExecutionWorker.

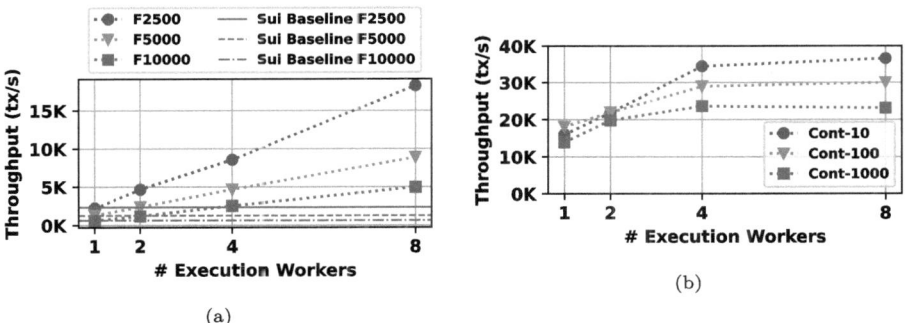

Fig. 7. (a) Pilotfish scalability with computationally heavy transactions. F{X} means that each transaction computes the X-th Fibonacci number. The horizontal lines show the single-machine throughput of the baseline on the same workloads. (b) Pilotfish scalability with condended transaction. Each transaction increments a counter. Cont-X means that for each counter we submit X increment transactions.

---

[5] We obtain the baseline by running Sui's single node benchmark with the `with-tx-manager` option.

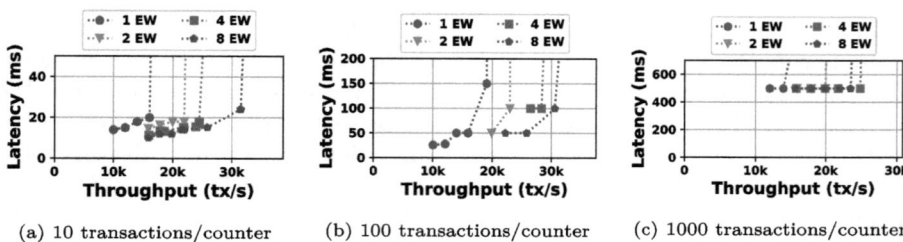

Fig. 8. Pilotfish latency vs throughput for the contended workloads. Please note the different y axis ranges between the three cases.

We observe that in all cases, Pilotfish maintains a 20ms latency envelope for this workload. Latency exhibits a linear increase as the workload grows for a single ExecutionWorker, primarily because of transaction queuing. More specifically, we see that a single machine does not have enough cores to fully exploit the parallelism of the workload, so some transactions must wait to get scheduled. This effect no longer exists for higher numbers of ExecutionWorkers, showing that more hardware has a beneficial effect on service time. Pilotfish scales up to around $60k$ tx/s. In contrast, the Sui baseline can only process around $20k$ tx/s as it cannot leverage the additional hardware. Pilotfish thus exhibits a 3× throughput improvement over the baseline. Pilotfish's scalability is not perfectly linear in this workload; in particular, it becomes less steep after 2 ExecutionWorkers. This is because the simple transfers workload is computationally light, and so the system is not compute-bound. Thus adding more resources no longer improves performance proportionally. Section 8.3 illustrates the advantages of increasing the number of ExecutionWorkers further when the workload is compute-bound.

8.3 Computationally-Heavy Workload

We study the scenario when the workload remains compute-bound even at higher numbers of ExecutionWorkers. In this workload, transactions are computationally heavy. To achieve this, each transaction merges two coins and then iteratively computes the Xth Fibonacci number, where X is a configurable parameter. We study the behavior of Pilotfish for $X \in \{2500, 5000, 10000\}$. This workload is also perfectly parallel: transactions operate on disjoint sets of coins and thus do not conflict. Figure 6 and Fig. 7a show the results: latency vs throughput and throughput scalability of Pilotfish, respectively. Figure 7a includes the behavior of Sui on the same workloads, as a baseline. As expected the performance of Pilotfish is on par with the baseline when running on a single ExecutionWorker. However, when computing resources are the bottleneck, Pilotfish scales linearly as more resources are added to the system. As a result, Pilotfish can process 20k, 10k, and 5k tx/s when setting $X = 2500$, $X = 5000$, and $X = 10000$, respectively, while maintaining the latency at around 50 ms. In contrast, the throughput of the baseline execution engine of Sui remains set to a maximum of

2,5k, 1k, and 500 tx/s (with respectively $X = 2500$, $X = 5000$, and $X = 10000$) as it is unable to take advantage of the additional hardware.

8.4 Contended Workload

We study the behavior of Pilotfish when the workload is no longer perfectly parallelizable. To achieve this, we introduce contention by making transactions operate on non-disjoint sets of objects. More concretely, in this workload each transaction increments a counter; for each counter, we generate a configurable number Y of transactions that increment it. Thus, on average, each transaction needs to wait behind $Y/2$ other transactions in its counter's queue, before being able to execute. In our experiments, $Y \in \{10, 100, 1000\}$. The results are shown in Fig. 8 and Fig. 7. Pilotfish reaches a throughput of 35k, 30k, and 22k tx/s for $Y = 10$, $Y = 100$, and $Y = 1000$ when operating with 4 ExecutionWorkers. For this workload, for technical reasons,[6] we could not include a Sui baseline.

As expected, we observe that as we increase contention, latency increases due to queueing (up to 500ms for $Y = 1000$) and throughput decreases. Nonetheless, Pilotfish is able to scale to 4 ExecutionWorkers. Similarly to the simple transfer workload (Sect. 8.2), this workload is not compute-bound, so adding compute beyond 4 ExecutionWorkers no longer improves performance proportionally.

9 Related Work

Table 1. Comparison against existing deterministic approaches

	Distributed	Crash Tolerance	Dynamic RW Set	No CC Aborts
BOHM [4]	✗	✗	✗	✓
PWV [5]	✗	✓	✗	✓
QueCC [12]	✗	✗	✗	✓
SLOG [13]	✓	✓	✗	✗
Q-Store [11]	✓	✓	✗	✓
Calvin [17]	✓	✓	✗	✓
Aria [10]	✓	✓	✓	✗
Lotus [18]	✓	✓	✓	✗
Pilotfish (this work)	✓	✓	✓	✓

---

[6] In Sui, each transaction expects object references for all input objects. Each object reference is computed based on the last transaction to modify the object. Therefore, it is difficult to pre-generate more than one valid transaction for the same object, before the experiment starts, because correct object references cannot be predicted.

Parallel Blockchain Executors. The main proposals in this area are those of Solana [14], Aptos [6], and Sui [1]. Solana [14] requires every transaction to fully specify its read and write sets, so it cannot support dynamic accesses in the same way as Pilotfish. Aptos uses the Block-STM [6] system for parallel transaction execution. Block-STM is designed with a focus on single-machine, multi-threaded performance, and it is unclear how or if its design can be extended to the scale-out, distributed deployment that Pilotfish targets. For instance, Block-STM executes transactions speculatively, and retries transactions which fail validation. This approach works well in a shared memory environment, where retries are relatively inexpensive, but it is not clear if it can be applied in a distributed environment, where retries are much more costly due to higher communication latency. Furthermore, BlockSTM focuses on a per-block execution model which requires large blocks to optimize throughput, at the expense of latency. By contrast, Pilotfish uses a streaming execution model that allows for low latency regardless of throughput. Finally, Sui [1] implicitly handles synchronization and scheduling through the tokio runtime: a tokio task is spawned for each Sui transaction; this task waits for the transaction's dependencies to be satisfied (i.e. the required object versions to be available), and then executes the transaction in parallel with other tasks. It is unclear how to directly extend this approach to multiple machines, as required by Pilotfish.

Deterministic Databases. Pilotfish is similar to deterministic database systems that employ an order-then-execute approach. Table 1 summarizes the main differences between Pilotfish and existing deterministic approaches. As Table 1 shows, Pilotfish is the first distributed, crash fault tolerant deterministic execution engine that tolerates partially unspecified read/write sets and eliminates concurrency-control-related aborts. The closest works to Pilotfish are Calvin [16], Aria [10] and Lotus [18]. Calvin [17] proposes the use of consensus to address crashes, which in our setting is overkill since the blockchain already provides sufficient determinism to recover without strong coordination. Aria and Lotus differ from Pilotfish by not establishing a total order on transactions before execution, which can lead to some transactions aborting due to conflicts; such transactions have to be retried later, increasing latency.

10 Conclusion

Pilotfish is the first blockchain execution engine allowing a blockchain validator to harness multiple machines under its control to horizontally scale execution. Pilotfish supports dynamic reads and writes, thus supporting programming models where the input read and write set is only partially specified by the transaction. Pilotfish also tolerates crash-faults internal to the validator and provably satisfies serializability, determinism, and liveness. Our implementation of Pilotfish demonstrates scalability under varying system loads, showing it outperforms the baseline Sui execution engine by up to 8x under heavy CPU loads.

Disclosure of Interests. The authors have no competing interests to declare that are relevant to the content of this article.

References

1. Blackshear, S., et al.: Sui Lutris: a blockchain combining broadcast and consensus. arXiv preprint arXiv:2310.18042 (2023)
2. Danezis, G., Kokoris-Kogias, L., Sonnino, A., Spiegelman, A.: Narwhal and Tusk: a DAG-based mempool and efficient BFT consensus. In: ACM Eurosys 2022, pp. 34–50 (2022)
3. Das, S., Agrawal, D., Abbadi, A.E.: ElasTraS: an elastic, scalable, and self-managing transactional database for the cloud. ACM Trans. Database Syst. **38**(1), 5 (2013). https://doi.org/10.1145/2445583.2445588
4. Faleiro, J.M., Abadi, D.J.: Rethinking serializable multiversion concurrency control. Proc. VLDB Endow. **8**(11), 1190–1201 (2015). https://doi.org/10.14778/2809974.2809981
5. Faleiro, J.M., Abadi, D.J., Hellerstein, J.M.: High performance transactions via early write visibility. Proc. VLDB Endow. **10**(5), 613–624 (2017). https://doi.org/10.14778/3055540.3055553
6. Gelashvili, R., et al.: Block-STM: scaling blockchain execution by turning ordering curse to a performance blessing. In: PPoPP 2023, pp. 232–244. ACM (2023). https://doi.org/10.1145/3572848.3577524
7. Kniep, Q., Kokoris-Kogias, L., Sonnino, A., Zablotchi, I., Zhang, N.: Pilotfish: elastic blockchains through distributed execution. https://arxiv.org/abs/2401.16292 (2025)
8. Kokoris-Kogias, E., Jovanovic, P., Gasser, L., Gailly, N., Syta, E., Ford, B.: OmniLedger: a secure, scale-out, decentralized ledger via sharding. In: 2018 IEEE Symposium on Security and Privacy (SP), pp. 583–598. IEEE (2018)
9. Lakshman, A., Malik, P.: Cassandra: structured storage system on a P2P network. In: PODC. ACM (2009). https://doi.org/10.1145/1582716.1582722
10. Lu, Y., Yu, X., Cao, L., Madden, S.: Aria: a fast and practical deterministic OLTP database. Proc. VLDB Endow. **13**(12), 2047–2060 (2020). https://doi.org/10.14778/3407790.3407808
11. Qadah, T., Gupta, S., Sadoghi, M.: Q-store: distributed, multi-partition transactions via queue-oriented execution and communication. In: EDBT 2020 (2020). https://doi.org/10.5441/002/edbt.2020.08
12. Qadah, T.M., Sadoghi, M.: QueCC: a queue-oriented, control-free concurrency architecture. In: Middleware, pp. 13–25. ACM (2018). https://doi.org/10.1145/3274808.3274810
13. Ren, K., Li, D., Abadi, D.J.: SLOG: serializable, low-latency, geo-replicated transactions. Proc. VLDB Endow. **12**(11), 1747–1761 (2019). https://doi.org/10.14778/3342263.3342647
14. Solana Foundation: Sealevel—parallel processing thousands of smart contracts. https://solana.com/news/sealevel---parallel-processing-thousands-of-smart-contracts (2019)
15. Spiegelman, A., Aurn, B., Gelashvili, R., Li, Z.: Shoal: Improving DAG-BFT latency and robustness. arXiv preprint arXiv:2306.03058 (2023)
16. Thomson, A., Diamond, T., Weng, S.C., Ren, K., Shao, P., Abadi, D.J.: Calvin: fast distributed transactions for partitioned database systems. In: ACM SIGMOD 2012. https://doi.org/10.1145/2213836.2213838

17. Thomson, A., Diamond, T., Weng, S.C., Ren, K., Shao, P., Abadi, D.J.: Fast distributed transactions and strongly consistent replication for OLTP database systems. ACM Trans. Database Syst. **39**(2) (2014). https://doi.org/10.1145/2556685
18. Zhou, X., Yu, X., Graefe, G., Stonebraker, M.: Lotus: scalable multi-partition transactions on single-threaded partitioned databases. Proc. VLDB Endow. **15**(11), 2939–2952 (2022). https://www.vldb.org/pvldb/vol15/p2939-zhou.pdf

ANTHEMIUS: Efficient and Modular Block Assembly for Concurrent Execution

Ray Neiheiser[1](✉) and Eleftherios Kokoris-Kogias[2]

[1] ISTA, Klosterneuburg, Austria
ray.neiheiser@proton.me
[2] Mysten Labs, Athens, Greece

Abstract. Many blockchains such as Ethereum execute all incoming transactions sequentially significantly limiting the potential throughput. A common approach to scale execution is parallel execution engines that fully utilize modern multi-core architectures. Parallel execution is then either done optimistically, by executing transactions in parallel and detecting conflicts on the fly, or guided, by requiring exhaustive client transaction hints and scheduling transactions accordingly.

However, recent studies have shown that the performance of parallel execution engines depends on the nature of the underlying workload. In fact, in some cases, only a 60% speed-up compared to sequential execution could be obtained. This is the case, as transactions that access the same resources must be executed sequentially. For example, if 10% of the transactions in a block access the same resource, the execution cannot meaningfully scale beyond 10 cores. Therefore, a single popular application can bottleneck the execution and limit the potential throughput.

In this paper, we introduce ANTHEMIUS, a block construction algorithm that optimizes parallel transaction execution throughput. We evaluate ANTHEMIUS exhaustively under a range of workloads, and show that ANTHEMIUS enables the underlying parallel execution engine to process over twice as many transactions.

Keywords: Blockchain · Parallel Execution · Smart Contracts · Distributed Ledger Technology

1 Introduction

The growing interest in blockchain and distributed ledger technology has resulted in many research advances in the field, ranging from improvements on the consensus layer [4,15] to sharding [11] and parallel transaction execution [8,14]. As most blockchains still execute transactions sequentially, parallel smart contract execution engines that take advantage of modern multi-core architectures are considered a crucial building block to scale blockchain transaction throughput [8].

Existing approaches to parallel execution can be roughly divided into two categories: optimistic and guided. Optimistic approaches, such as Block-STM [8], are designed to execute transactions in parallel, detect conflicts as they arise, and re-execute affected transactions. However, in blockchain environments characterized by highly contended workloads [14,16], conflicts arise more often, requiring more frequent re-executions of transactions.

In contrast to optimistic approaches, guided approaches strictly limit read/write access by requiring transactions to pre-declare an exhaustive list of resources (i.e., addresses) that will be accessed during execution. This allows the scheduler to identify independent transactions and execute them concurrently. Examples of this approach include FuelVM, Solana, or Sui [6,19,21]. While this avoids the re-execution overhead in settings with high contention, it puts additional load on the application developers. Furthermore, in some cases, it may not be possible to precisely predict at transaction creation time which resources will be accessed during execution, as the application state might change in the meantime. Then, an overly pessimistic approach is required, locking a wider range of resources, and potentially resulting in the sequential execution of transactions that otherwise could have been executed concurrently.

Combining both approaches, Polygon recently introduced an update [18] that extracts transaction dependencies during block creation and includes this dependency tree as metadata in the block. This approach allows to optimize scheduling during the execution phase, avoiding unnecessary re-executions and pessimistic locking [18]. Nonetheless, this approach requires executing transactions on the critical path of consensus during block creation, crippling the potential throughput. A similar approach is Chiron [14] which leverages execution hints to speed up execution on struggling validators and full nodes. Chiron guarantees safety in the presence of invalid hints by utilizing the validation step of Block-STM, which identifies conflicting resource accesses and reschedules transactions that potentially accessed shared resources in parallel for re-execution [8].

However, as outlined in [14], due to the characteristics of blockchain workloads, transaction execution remains a significant bottleneck. This is the case, as transactions that access the same resources must be executed sequentially and, as several recent studies have shown, in practice a significant portion of the transactions access the same resources, resulting in a long sequential path of transactions slowing down the system [7,14]. As such, the performance is currently limited by the workload.

Due to the nature of the problem, a single popular application can bottleneck the execution engine and cripple the throughput of the system [14]. This could be a newly launched NFT, a popularly traded token, or even the on/off-boarding of a popular layer-2 smart contract. This is further aggravated by the fact that most existing blockchains that support parallel execution currently have no pricing mechanisms to charge clients for accessing popular resources causing system bottlenecks.

Most blockchains such as Ethereum [3] prevent extensive execution times by limiting the combined execution complexity in gas of each given block. However, a single parameter is insufficient in the context of parallel execution, as it does not take transaction dependencies and potential parallelization into account.

Therefore, a novel approach is necessary to make block assembly sensitive to transaction dependencies and execution complexity, charging clients for accessing popular resources and delaying transactions that would otherwise bottleneck the execution.

In this paper, we propose ANTHEMIUS, a novel approach to construct blocks that takes both the execution complexity in gas and the distribution of resource accesses into account to construct "Good Blocks" that can be executed efficiently in parallel. We evaluate ANTHEMIUS extensively under a series of realistic workloads, showing a consistent speed-up up to 240% compared to native parallel execution. ANTHEMIUS not only vastly improves the execution performance but also prevents popular or malicious applications from bottlenecking the system, eliminating a performance attack scenario. ANTHEMIUS provides different latency paths between transactions accessing congested and not congested resources. Transactions can still be fast-tracked by paying higher transaction fees, resulting in a price that more closely reflects its resource consumption. We discuss this further in Sect. 6.

Moreover, thanks to its modular design, ANTHEMIUS can be integrated into any state-of-the-art blockchain seamlessly, without the need for a hard fork or modifications to the execution engine or consensus mechanism. ANTHEMIUS operates stateless and only requires execution hints such as the resources that will be accessed during execution. In blockchains such as Sui and Solana [19,21] these hints are already present during block construction, while in blockchains such as Aptos or Ethereum [3,5] these hints could either be simulated in a pre-execution step or generated at the full nodes.

In summary, we provide the following contributions:

- We propose ANTHEMIUS, a novel and modular block construction algorithm and approach to speed up parallel execution without security tradeoffs.
- We evaluate ANTHEMIUS integrated with both an optimistic and a guided execution engine under the Chiron benchmarks resulting in a significant speed-up in almost all settings.

In Sect. 2, we present the System Model of ANTHEMIUS, followed by a detailed overview of ANTHEMIUS in Sect. 3. Next, we describe the implementation and evaluation in Sect. 4. Related work is reviewed in Sect. 5, and potential drawbacks, along with their solutions, are discussed in Sect. 6. Finally, we conclude the paper in Sect. 7.

2 System Model

We assume a blockchain environment consisting of N server processes $p_1, p_2, .., p_N$ and I client processes $c_1, c_2, .., c_I$. Clients send signed transactions to the server processes to be included in a future block. The blockchain functions as the Public Key Infrastructure where the identifier of a client is its public key, and clients use their private keys to sign their transactions.

We assume a consensus abstraction as a blackbox, where one or more processes construct blocks of transactions and propose them to the consensus mechanism. As a result, the consensus abstraction outputs an ordered sequence of blocks $b_1, b_2, \ldots, b_n$, which is then processed by the execution engine. Additionally, we assume an execution engine abstraction as a blackbox that receives this ordered sequence of blocks from the consensus abstraction and executes them deterministically.

In the context of this work, we make no assumptions regarding the coupling between the consensus and execution layers. The interaction between consensus and execution may either follow a modular, decoupled approach, as in Sui and Aptos [5,19], or operate in a tightly coupled, sequential manner, as in Ethereum [3].

Client transactions might range from simple peer-to-peer transactions to complex application logic with the help of smart contracts. As applications might access arbitrary resources (i.e., addresses) that can not easily be deduced, we assume the existence of a system that provides hints about the resources a transaction will access during execution to the block producer. This can either be in the form of client hints as in Solana or Sui [19,21], or in the form of an optimistic pre-execution step that determines these hints locally as in Polygon [18]. However, we do not assume the list of hints to be exhaustive or correct. Transactions with incomplete or incorrect hints might trigger re-executions if the execution engine is Block-STM or a derivative [8,14], or aborted in Solana or Sui [19,21].

3 Anthemius

The primary objective of ANTHEMIUS is to redesign the block-assembly approach in blockchains that offer parallel execution to improve the overall system throughput and prevent popular applications from creating bottlenecks by factoring in transaction dependencies and execution time.

At the time of writing, most blockchains that support parallel transaction execution use a single parameter such as the computational complexity in gas, the raw block size in bytes, or the number of transactions to limit the block size [5,19,21]. However, in the context of parallel transaction execution, a single parameter does not reflect the execution complexity of a block. If all transactions in the block access the same resource, the execution time is the sum of the runtime of all transactions. In contrast, if none of the transactions access conflicting resources, the runtime depends on the number of cores.

Therefore, as a first step to begin constructing "Good Blocks", we need parameters that allow us to quantify this. We deploy two parameters to address this. First a transaction complexity parameter in Gas, similar to Ethereum, and second a concurrency parameter c describing the system's ability to execute transactions in parallel (i.e. number of cores). As a result, the total maximum capacity of each block is $c * Gas$.

In the next sections, we first discuss where ANTHEMIUS fits into existing blockchain architectures. Following that, we outline the design of the block construction algorithm that considers both parameters and constructs blocks sensitive to transaction dependencies and their execution time to speed up the parallel execution of the block.

3.1 Architecture

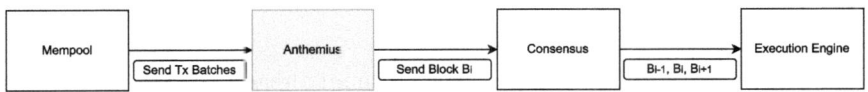

Fig. 1. ANTHEMIUS is inserted between the Mempool and Consensus

Figure 1 shows where ANTHEMIUS fits into the existing protocol stack of a blockchain. ANTHEMIUS is a modular layer that can be inserted between the consensus layer and the mempool where client transactions are stored and handled. In ANTHEMIUS, instead of fetching transactions directly from the mempool, the consensus layer fetches blocks of transactions through ANTHEMIUS. In turn, ANTHEMIUS obtains its transactions from the mempool, divides transactions into batches, and constructs the block to return to consensus. Following that, the block is proposed in consensus which outputs an ordered list of blocks to the execution engine.

ANTHEMIUS requires the read and write sets of transactions, as well as an estimation of their execution time, to assess dependencies between transactions and construct blocks that can be executed efficiently in parallel. This information is already available in blockchains such as Solana [21] and Sui [19], where transactions must declare all resource addresses they access during execution. In other blockchains, such as Ethereum [3], this information can be obtained, for example, by executing the transactions.

This design allows ANTHEMIUS to be seamlessly integrated into any existing blockchain stack with minimal architectural and system changes, and without changing the block structure. Furthermore, since ANTHEMIUS operates solely on the set of transactions, their read and write sets, and their gas footprints, it remains essentially stateless. This makes ANTHEMIUS particularly suitable for deployment in modular architectures, such as Narwhal, where only the execution layer is stateful [4].

3.2 Block Construction

An important problem that has to be tackled when constructing good blocks is the absence of information regarding the structure of the current workload. If all transactions in the mempool access the same resources, attempting to

Algorithm 1. *Batch Handler*

1: **procedure** CREATEGOODBLOCK($block, maxgas, c$)
2:     $seqlimit = \frac{maxgas}{c}$ ▷ Limit on the sequential path
3:     $resmap \leftarrow \emptyset$ ▷ Map to track transaction dependencies
4:     $skippedclients \leftarrow \emptyset$ ▷ Set to track clients with skipped transactions
5:     $numrelax \leftarrow 0$ ▷ Number of times inclusion rate was relaxed
6:     **for all** $batch \in mempool$ **do**
7:         $incrate \leftarrow$ SCHEDULE($block, batch, seqlimit, c, resmap, skippedclients$)
8:         **if** $incrate <$ TARGETINCRATE
9:             **if** $numrelax \geq$ MAXRELAXNUM $\vee (incrate = 0 \wedge batch.isfull)$
10:                 **return**
11:             $seqlimit = \frac{maxgas}{c} *$ MIN(MAXRELAXRATE, $incrate *$ TARGETINCRATE)
12:             $numrelax + +$

schedule them efficiently can further slow down an already bottlenecked system. Similarly, if the algorithm is too strict in situations where a large percentage of transactions access the same resources, the synergetic effects of executing larger batches of transactions are lost. This is the case, as, for each block, the system has to instantiate the executor and worker threads, set up the virtual machine, extract the execution results, etc.

Therefore, as a first step, we divide ANTHEMIUS into two modular elements. First, the *batch handler*, which polls batches of transactions from the mempool and hands the batches to the *batch scheduler* in a batch-by-batch fashion. Second, the *batch scheduler*, that attempts to include a given batch into the current block and provides feedback to the *batch handler* about the success rate. Subsequently, based on the feedback, the batch handler can adjust the inclusion policy to prevent too small blocks and also avoid wasting scheduling time on difficult-to-schedule workloads.

Batch Handler. The functionality of the Batch Handler is outlined in Algorithm 1. The batch handler receives a *block* to fill, the global concurrency parameter c, and the maximum gas limit. It then calculates a limit on the sequential path *seqlimit* and initiates a map to track the transaction dependencies *resmap* as well as a set of clients with skipped transactions *skippedclients*.

Next, the batch handler retrieves transaction batches from the mempool and hands them to the batch scheduler alongside the block, the limit on the gas, the number of cores, the transaction resource dependencies *resmap*, and *skippedclients* set in Line 7. The batch scheduler responds with the transaction inclusion rate *incrate*.

Depending on the workload, as mentioned, the *seqlimit* may be very strict which can result in very few transactions being included in a block. Therefore, if the inclusion rate *incrate* is smaller than some TARGETINCRATE, we relax the gas limit relative to the inclusion rate, up to some MAXRELAXRATE (Line 11).

However, if the inclusion rate was too small for several consecutive attempts (i.e. $numrelax \geq$ MAXRELAXNUM), we exit scheduling to avoid building a heavily sequential block again. Furthermore, if there was an attempt to schedule a full batch and no transaction of this batch was successfully included in the current block ($incrate = 0$) we also stop scheduling (Line 9) as this indicates that at

Algorithm 2. *Batch Scheduler - Called in Line 7 of Algorithm 1*

```
 1: procedure SCHEDULE(block, batch, seqlimit, c, resmap, skippedclients)
 2:     for all tx ∈ batch do                            ▷ Iterate over transactions
 3:         if tx.sender in skippedclients
 4:             continue                                 ▷ Skip transaction inclusion
 5:         chaincost ← 0                                ▷ Longest chain length
 6:         hotresources ← 0
 7:         for all readres ∈ tx.readset do              ▷ Iterate over readset
 8:             if readres ∈ resmap                      ▷ Find longest chain
 9:                 if resmap[readres] > chaincost       ▷ Find read with largest cost
10:                     chaincost ← resmap[readres]
11:                 if resmap[readres] > block.gas/c     ▷ Check if read exceeds limit
12:                     hotresources + +
13:         if hotresources ≥ MAXHOTR ∧ (|block| > LIM ∨ |block| < MAXLEN − LIM)
14:             skippedclients ← skippedclients ∪ tx.sender
15:             continue                                 ▷ Skip transaction inclusion
16:         if chaincost + tx.gas > seqlimit ∨ block.gas + tx.gas > seqlimit ∗ c
17:             skippedclients ← skippedclients ∪ tx.sender
18:             continue                                 ▷ Skip transaction inclusion
19:         block ← block ∪ tx                           ▷ Add tx to Block
20:         for all writeres ∈ tx.writeset do            ▷ Iterate over writeset
21:             if writeres ∉ resmap ∨ resmap[writeres] < chaincost
22:                 resmap[writeres] ← chaincost         ▷ Note new chain length
23:     return($\frac{numscheduled}{|batch|}$)
```

this point transactions are only included at a high cost to execution performance and scheduling latency. The rest of the transactions are then only included in a later block.

Batch Scheduler. Scheduling transactions with interdependencies and varying runtimes is a known NP-complete problem [2] where approximate solutions can construct near optimal schedules in polynomial time. However, polynomial runtime, particularly when executed on the critical path of consensus, may lead to a construction time that outweighs the performance gains achieved from producing "Good Blocks."

Fortunately, our first insight is that a near-optimal schedule for block construction is unnecessary. Instead, our main objective is to prevent popular resources and applications from creating a bottleneck while maximizing the parallel execution. We can achieve this by iterating over the set of resources each transaction accesses, recording the cost of the sequential path leading up to the transaction, and deciding if the transaction should be included in the current block by comparing the cost of the path with the gas per core parameter. Furthermore, we also want to delay transactions that access multiple hot resources as they make it harder to schedule subsequent transactions.

As a result, the complexity of the block construction is of $O(N \ast k)$ where N is the number of transactions and k is the average number of resource accesses per transaction.

Algorithm 2 shows how we achieve this. The algorithm starts with the call of the SCHEDULE method, which receives the block to include the transactions in, the batch of transactions to schedule, the maximum gas per core *seqlimit*, the concurrency parameter c, the map of resources and the skipped clients.

Following that, it starts iterating over all transactions in the batch (line 2). First, to maintain the order clients specified (e.g. through sequence numbers), after a client had a transaction skipped, the client is added to the *skippedclients* set and no further transaction from this client will be included in this block.(Line 4). Following that, we iterate over all reads in the transaction read-set and attempt to calculate the read with the longest path in gas leading up to this transaction (Line 7). In parallel, we count the number of *hot* reads. A hot read is a read on a resource that is accessed significantly more often than other resources.

After this, we check whether the number of hot reads exceeds a predefined threshold, MAXHOTR. If this condition is met and the transaction is not within the first or last LIM (i.e. 10%) transactions, we skip the transaction (Line 13). We delay transactions with too many hot reads as they unify several critical paths of transactions which can severely bottleneck the execution. However, we initially allow any transactions to be included up to some threshold LIM to accumulate sufficient data to assess the complexity of reads and to guarantee that transactions that access several hot resources are eventually included. Furthermore, we also allow including transactions with multiple hot reads towards the end of the block as the block is almost full already and they are less likely to cause scheduling problems at this point.

Following that, we check if the transaction cost itself is larger than the max gas per core *seqlimit* or if the current transaction exceeds the total gas limit of the block. If so, we also skip the transaction (Line 16).

Finally, we include the transaction in the block, iterate over its write set, and record the transaction path cost in the resource map *resmap* if its writes increase the critical path. This results in an algorithm that is linear to the number of transactions per block, as the map accesses are $O(1)$ and we check each transaction at most once per block.

4 Evaluation

We implemented ANTHEMIUS on top of Block-STM [8] and Chiron [14] in Rust to evaluate its performance impact on both an optimistic execution engine and a guided execution engine, covering two of the most widely adopted approaches to parallel execution in the blockchain space. The implementation is publicly available on Github[1]. As Chiron is built on top of Block-STM, this simplifies the implementation and allows for an easier comparison of the results. Furthermore, we use the parallel execution benchmarks proposed in Chiron [14].

Finally, we implemented the batch handler ($\sim$ 70 lines of code) and the batch scheduler ($\sim$ 120 lines of code) to assemble blocks and then forward these blocks to the respective execution engines.

4.1 Benchmark

The experiments were executed on a Debian GNU/Linux 12 server with two AMD EPYC 7763 64-Core Processors and 1024 GB of RAM. We generated

---
[1] https://github.com/ISTA-SPiDerS/Anthemius.

batches of transactions with different distributions of read/write-accesses and different user distributions with the help of Chiron [14] for all five proposed workloads. Namely, one peer-to-peer workload (P2PTX), two Decentralized Exchange Workloads (DEXAVG and DEXBURSTY), one NFT workload (NFT), and one mixed workload (MIXED). These workloads are derived from real-world data from Ethereum and Solana and are designed to evaluate parallel transaction execution engines under realistic levels of contention. Each workload has a unique and realistic resource access pattern, along with a varying count of read and write operations per transaction.

Each experiment was executed a total of 10 times and the results we outline in this section present the average of all 10 runs. Furthermore, in each workload, we vary the number of worker threads from 4 to 32 in increments of 4. Finally, we are interested in two key metrics: throughput, to assess the performance improvement introduced by ANTHEMIUS, and latency, to determine the average delay introduced by ANTHEMIUS.

We set the following parameters for the batch handler and batch scheduler: First, we evaluate the execution engines using blocks of up to MAXLEN = 10,000 transactions, as this block size represents a sweet spot for both engines, where the execution setup overhead (e.g., virtual machine initialization) becomes negligible. Accordingly, we configured the batch size to match the target block size, as smaller batch sizes increase block construction overhead, while larger batch sizes reduce the batch handler's flexibility to adapt to the workload's characteristics.

Next, to minimize tail latency for transactions accessing hot resources, we allow the first and last LIM = 1,000 transactions to be included freely without restrictions. Furthermore, we permit up to MAXRELAXNUM = 2 relaxations of the inclusion rate as we observed diminishing returns from additional relaxations and large scheduling costs beyond this point. We set the relaxation rate to a maximum of MAXRELAXRATE = 100, targeting an inclusion rate of TARGETINCRATE = $2\frac{maxlen}{c}$. This accounts for the higher returns from a more aggressive target inclusion rate as the concurrency potential increases. Finally, we configure MAXHOTR = 4 to avoid uniting too many critical paths of transactions, ensuring manageable contention levels.

4.2 Throughput

As ANTHEMIUS delays the inclusion of some transactions in favor of others to enhance system performance, we provide the batch handler with several batches of 10,000 transactions to saturate the system and measure the maximum throughput. Each batch is generated with the same distribution of resource accesses, both within and across batches. We then evaluate ANTHEMIUS by passing all batches to the batch handler and run ANTHEMIUS until all transactions from the first batch are successfully executed. Consequently, the evaluation for ANTHEMIUS spans multiple blocks, where the reported throughput represents the average throughput over the entire runtime and accounts for scheduling and execution time. For the baseline versions of Block-STM and Chiron, we use a single block containing 10,000 transactions that also fully saturates the system, with runtime variations dependent solely on the specific workload.

As blockchains such as Aptos or Sui decouple consensus from execution, block scheduling could be moved outside of the critical path of consensus. This can significantly reduce the overhead, as scheduling requires only a single thread and only has to be done at the proposer node. Due to this, we display two lines for ANTHEMIUS. First, one that serves as a ceiling on performance, where we assume that there is an idle thread that can be used for scheduling outside of the critical path of consensus, denoted *Decoupled ANTHEMIUS*. Second, one that serves as a floor on performance where we count the full scheduling overhead on the critical path of consensus, referred to as ANTHEMIUS.

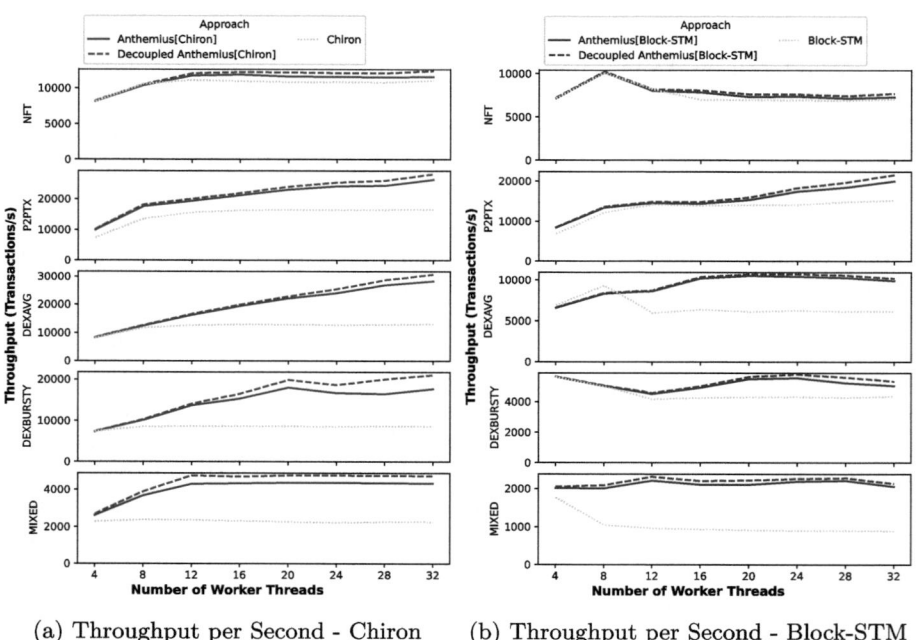

(a) Throughput per Second - Chiron (b) Throughput per Second - Block-STM

Fig. 2. Throughput per Second

The results for ANTHEMIUS with Chiron are shown in Fig. 2a, with the throughput in transactions per second on the y-axis and the number of worker threads on the x-axis. With the NFT workload, we only see a small speedup from creating good blocks. This is due to the account distribution in this workload, where transactions from users appear very frequently in several batches. Due to this, once a transaction of a given user is skipped, the following transactions also have to be skipped, resulting in long scheduling times and leaving very few transactions behind that can be included in the block. In comparison, in the peer-to-peer workload there is already a significant improvement, where with an increasing number of worker threads, we can reach almost twice the initial throughput. Following that, with increasing contention and less repetitive users, the decentralized exchange workloads reach over 240% performance boost compared to vanilla Chiron. While in the average DEX workload, the scheduling overhead is very small, with increasing contention and increasing number of worker threads we can also see an increased scheduling overhead. Finally, in the mixed workload, we also see a large performance advantage. This is also due to the much higher overall execution complexity compared to the scheduling overhead. Due to the complexity of the workload, the overhead is constant after 12 cores, but ANTHEMIUS under this workload shows over 200% performance advantage compared to vanilla Chiron.

The throughput results for ANTHEMIUS with Block-STM are shown in Fig. 2b, with the throughput in transactions per second on the y-axis and the number of worker threads on the x-axis. Compared to the results with Chiron, the results for Block-STM vary more as the high contention within each block results in a large re-execution overhead. As such, even when we build better blocks with ANTHEMIUS, the contention in the block is still so high, that Block-STM struggles to take advantage of that. We can still see the largest disadvantage in the NFT workload, due to the user distribution preventing us from building better blocks. Furthermore, we can see that in the peer-to-peer workload, once we reach 20 threads, ANTHEMIUS is starting to be able to compensate for the re-execution overhead of Block-STM and reach a speed-up of up to 25%. Similarly, for the DEX workloads, there is an initial performance drop due to the re-execution overhead, which is only compensated with more worker threads later. Finally, in the MIXED workload, ANTHEMIUS shows a constant speed up compared to vanilla Block-STM up to 200% the original performance.

4.3 Latency

As we are delaying the inclusion of some transactions that access hot resources, we expect a latency overhead increase at the tail. Similarly to the throughput evaluation, we send several batches of transactions to the batch handler. To fully assess the effect of ANTHEMIUS, we evaluate how the tail latency develops when awaiting the finished execution of up to five batches for all workloads with a fixed number of 16 cores. The results of this evaluation are shown in Fig. 3, where the yellow line indicates the 50th percentile (median), the box represents the 25th and 75th percentiles (interquartile range), and the whiskers denote the 10th and 90th percentiles.

The results mirror what we saw in the throughput evaluation where in almost all workloads and configurations where ANTHEMIUS shows a significant speedup the average transaction latency is significantly lower. Furthermore, thanks to the large throughput advantage in these settings, especially when paired with *Chiron*, ANTHEMIUS has a latency advantage for up to the 90% percentile of transactions.

On the other hand, as expected, ANTHEMIUS shows a growing tail latency with an increasing number of batches. This is expected since the congestion

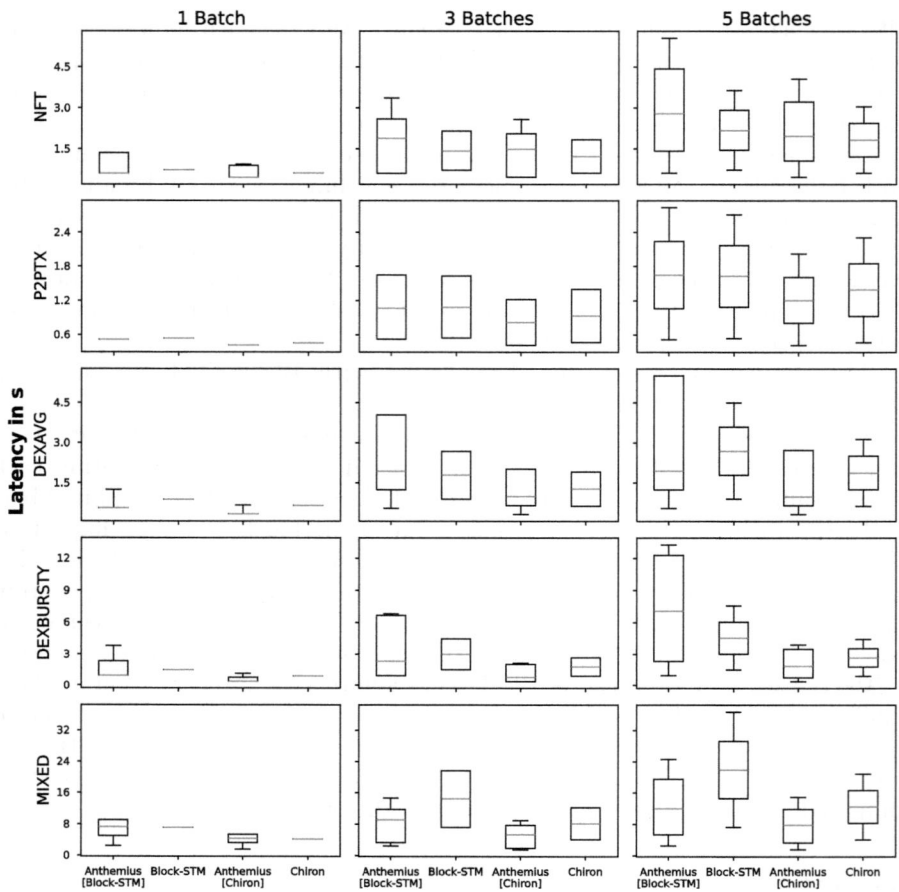

Fig. 3. Tail Latency for Chiron and Block-STM (Color figure online)

caused by the highly contended workloads results in different scheduling decisions. Nevertheless, we can see that the growing tail latency affects not only ANTHEMIUS but also the reference systems, although for certain workloads the effects of ANTHEMIUS are more prominent at the p90 percentile.

This is a tradeoff the blockchain needs to take into account based on their expected workload and tune ANTHEMIUS parameters to better match the characteristics of the transactions expected.

4.4 Summary

In this section, we evaluated the throughput improvement ANTHEMIUS can provide across different execution engines. Our findings demonstrate that while ANTHEMIUS improves throughput for both types of execution engines under several of the workloads, its impact is significantly larger when combined with guided execution engines. In this case, ANTHEMIUS provides a large throughput improvement across all but one of the workloads. The only exception is the NFT workload, where many high-frequency users appear across multiple blocks, preventing ANTHEMIUS from effectively rescheduling their transactions.

When it comes to latency, we analyzed the tail latency percentiles of delayed transactions. Our results show that for most workloads the majority of transactions (over 75%) have lower or similar latency compared to the vanilla execution, while only the slowest 25% of transactions sustain a latency overhead. This indicates that ANTHEMIUS can be a valuable addition to any blockchain with a parallel execution engine where the workload does not primarily stem from a very small set of users.

5 Related Work

To the best of our knowledge, there is no academic work proposing algorithms to construct blocks sensitive to parallel execution efficiency. While the problem is an NP-Complete scheduling problem which is explored in theoretical computer science [2], the greedy version of these algorithms still requires polynomial time which would present a large overhead and negate most of the positive effects. By relaxing the optimality requirement, instead, ANTHEMIUS achieves a linear complexity relative to the number of transactions per block.

In the database literature, there are numerous approaches to re-order transactions for reduced abort rates. Most of the work in this context reorders transactions after execution to increase the goodput. Examples of this approach are Aria [12], where an efficient algorithm reorders transactions after execution based on the read and write sets to reduce the number of aborted transactions. Similarly, Sharma et al. [17] focus on execute-order blockchains where transactions are reordered during block construction. While these approaches are efficient and can increase the goodput, none of them consider the parallel execution setting.

Eve [9] is the most similar approach to ANTHEMIUS. In Eve, transactions are organized into batches such that, with high probability, no two transactions within the same batch access the same resource. This allows the execution engine to execute the block concurrently without having to worry about concurrent accesses during execution. Although the scheduling is very efficient, this approach is unsuitable for blockchain ecosystems where we are expecting a large percentage of transactions to overlap [14] and already have execution engines that can process transactions with dependencies efficiently.

We, therefore, focus on the current state of block assembly in production blockchains. The discussion is summarized in Table 1. While Ethereum [3] does not natively support parallel execution at this moment, it constructs its blocks sensitive to the execution complexity of the smart contracts. The version of Polygon [18] with Block-STM integration supports parallel execution and takes the execution complexity into account. However, it only has a one-dimensional gas parameter and does not take dependencies into account. Aptos [5] supports parallel execution but is unaware of the execution complexity of the transactions

Table 1. Comparison of existing Block Production Approaches.

Approaches	Parallel Execution	Two-Dimensional Gas Parameter	Dependency Sensitive	Execution-Time Aware
Ethereum [3]	✗	✗	✗	✓
Polygon [18]	✓	✗	✗	✓
Aptos [5]	✓	✗	✗	✗
Solana [21]	✓	✗	✗	✓
ANTHEMIUS	✓	✓	✓	✓

at block construction time and only takes the number of transactions and byte size into account. In comparison, Finally, Solana [21] also offers parallel execution and takes the execution complexity into account. However, Solana does not take dependencies into account and only limits the combined computational complexity of transactions of a given client.

Therefore, to the best of our knowledge, ANTHEMIUS is the first work proposing a modular and practical algorithm for "Good Block" construction in the context of parallel smart contract execution.

6 Discussion

While ANTHEMIUS can achieve a performance boost of over 240%, there are tradeoffs. In this section, we discuss these tradeoffs and potential solutions.

6.1 Malicious Leader

While a correct leader can construct blocks that significantly speed up the system, the opposite is true for malicious leaders. In ANTHEMIUS the leader constructs the block sensitive to the number of cores and a gas per core measure, however, no mechanism in ANTHEMIUS enforces the leader to construct a block following this blueprint. Even though this might seem like an oversight, it is impossible to distinguish between a correct leader handling a fully sequential workload and a malicious leader deliberately constructing a sequential block.

This issue is inherent to blockchains that support parallel execution, such as Solana, Sui, or Aptos [5,19,21]. Two potential approaches could mitigate this challenge. One approach involves an expensive combination of a fair ordering protocol [10] and a pre-execution stage on the critical path of consensus such as Pompe [22]. Alternatively, leaders could be incentivized through a game-theoretic framework to construct highly parallelizable blocks, with penalties imposed for creating overly sequential ones. However, a detailed analysis of these frameworks is beyond the scope of this work and is left for future research.

Therefore, while ANTHEMIUS extends the capabilities of correct nodes to improve the system throughput and empowers them to prevent clients from bottlenecking the system, it does not alter the role a malicious validator could play in the system compared to the state of the art. In fact, due to its modular nature, individual validators on many blockchains could already plug ANTHEMIUS into their stack without requiring a hard fork.

6.2 Censorship Resistance

A common concern for leader-based protocols is censorship resistance. In ANTHEMIUS, the leader has, as part of the protocol, the power to delay some transactions to speed up the overall system. However, as the leaders in existing protocols such as Ethereum or Aptos already have this power as there is no mechanism that controls this, ANTHEMIUS would not hand the leader stronger censorship powers compared to the state of the art.

Nonetheless, protocols focused on short-term censorship resistance such as [20] might not work out of the box with ANTHEMIUS. Thus, adjustments to the protocol would be necessary, to only allow a leader to delay a given transaction up to some bounds. This presents a direct trade-off between performance and short-term censorship resistance.

Furthermore, protocols focused on fair ordering, such as [1] often require the transaction and metadata to be encrypted which strips ANTHEMIUS of the capability to use transaction meta-data to construct "Good Blocks". Nonetheless, these approaches are also generally incompatible with hint-based execution schemes as used in Chiron, Sui, or Solana.

6.3 Transaction Fees and Client Incentives

While a malicious leader can arbitrarily delay a client transaction, in ANTHEMIUS correct nodes might also delay client transactions to improve the overall system throughput. However, in some cases, a client might want their transaction to be included with higher urgency even if it accesses very hot resources, e.g. when a bidding process is approaching the time limit.

Integrating a mechanism with ANTHEMIUS that allows client transactions to be included with higher priority is fairly straightforward. Blockchains such as Bitcoin and Ethereum [3,13] already use pricing mechanisms to prioritize transaction inclusion. Therefore, a transaction with a higher fee could be transferred to the beginning of the first batch in the batch handler to guarantee its inclusion in the next block. In fact, similar to the local fee markets in Solana [21], this kind of pricing scheme, in combination with ANTHEMIUS would naturally result in a higher price for accessing hot resources, incentivizing smart contract developers to design their smart contracts with concurrency in mind and incentivizing users to avoid hot resources during system congestion times. This can help to balance the system beyond the already existing throughput advantages of ANTHEMIUS.

7 Conclusion

In this work, we presented ANTHEMIUS, a framework, and algorithm to construct highly parallelizable blocks in the context of parallel smart contract execution. We evaluated ANTHEMIUS extensively under a series of realistic workloads, demonstrating a throughput improvement of up to 240%. Furthermore, in most workloads, this approach leads to lower latency for the majority of transactions, while only delaying those that access hot resources and cause bottlenecks. Moreover, ANTHEMIUS not only improves the throughput of the underlying execution engine but also protects blockchains from being bottlenecked by popular applications. Finally, ANTHEMIUS is highly modular and can be easily integrated into any production blockchain without any security tradeoffs.

Acknowledgments. This work was supported by the Austrian Science Fund (FWF) SFB project SpyCoDe F8502 and the Vienna Science and Technology Fund (WWTF) project SCALE2 CT22-045.

References

1. Asayag, A., et al.: A fair consensus protocol for transaction ordering. In: 2018 IEEE 26th International Conference on Network Protocols (ICNP), pp. 55–65 (2018). https://doi.org/10.1109/ICNP.2018.00016
2. Baker, B.S., Coffman, E.G.: Mutual exclusion scheduling. Theor. Comput. Sci. **162**(2), 225–243 (1996). https://doi.org/10.1016/0304-3975(96)00031-X. https://www.sciencedirect.com/science/article/pii/030439759600031X
3. Buterin, V.: Ethereum Whitepaper
4. Danezis, G., Kokoris-Kogias, L., Sonnino, A., Spiegelman, A.: Narwhal and Tusk: a DAG-based mempool and efficient BFT consensus. In: Proceedings of the Seventeenth European Conference on Computer Systems, EuroSys 2022, pp. 34–50. Association for Computing Machinery, New York, NY, USA (2022). https://doi.org/10.1145/3492321.3519594
5. Aptos Foundation: Aptos Whitepaper (2023). https://aptos.dev/assets/files/Aptos-Whitepaper-47099b4b907b432f81fc0effd34f3b6a.pdf. Accessed 12 Apr 2023
6. Fuel Labs: GitHub - FuelLabs/fuel-specs: Specifications for the Fuel protocol. https://github.com/FuelLabs/fuel-specs
7. Garamvölgyi, P., Liu, Y., Zhou, D., Long, F., Wu, M.: Utilizing parallelism in smart contracts on decentralized blockchains by taming application-inherent conflicts. In: Proceedings of the 44th International Conference on Software Engineering. ACM, May 2022. https://doi.org/10.1145/3510003.3510086
8. Gelashvili, R., et al.: Block-STM: scaling blockchain execution by turning ordering curse to a performance blessing (2022). https://doi.org/10.48550/ARXIV.2203.06871
9. Kapritsos, M., Wang, Y., Quema, V., Clement, A., Alvisi, L., Dahlin, M.: All about Eve: execute-verify replication for multi-core servers. In: 10th USENIX Symposium on Operating Systems Design and Implementation (OSDI 12), pp. 237–250. USENIX Association, Hollywood, CA, October 2012. https://www.usenix.org/conference/osdi12/technical-sessions/presentation/kapritsos
10. Kelkar, M., Deb, S., Kannan, S.: Order-fair consensus in the permissionless setting. In: Proceedings of the 9th ACM on ASIA Public-Key Cryptography Workshop, APKC 2022, pp. 3–14. Association for Computing Machinery, New York, NY, USA (2022). https://doi.org/10.1145/3494105.3526239

11. Kokoris-Kogias, E., Jovanovic, P., Gasser, L., Gailly, N., Syta, E., Ford, B.: OmniLedger: a secure, scale-out, decentralized ledger via sharding. In: 2018 IEEE Symposium on Security and Privacy (SP), pp. 583–598 (2018). https://doi.org/10.1109/SP.2018.000-5
12. Lu, Y., Yu, X., Cao, L., Madden, S.: Aria: a fast and practical deterministic OLTP database. Proc. VLDB Endow. **13**(12), 2047–2060 (2020). https://doi.org/10.14778/3407790.3407808
13. Nakamoto, S.: Bitcoin: a peer-to-peer electronic cash system (2008)
14. Neiheiser, R., Babaei, A., Alexopoulos, G., Kogias, M., Kogias, E.K.: CHIRON: accelerating node synchronization without security trade-offs in distributed ledgers (2024)
15. Neiheiser, R., Matos, M., Rodrigues, L.: Kauri: scalable BFT consensus with pipelined tree-based dissemination and aggregation. In: Proceedings of the ACM SIGOPS 28th Symposium on Operating Systems Principles, SOSP 2021, pp. 35–48. Association for Computing Machinery, New York, NY, USA (2021). https://doi.org/10.1145/3477132.3483584
16. Sergey, I., Hobor, A.: A concurrent perspective on smart contracts (2017). https://doi.org/10.48550/ARXIV.1702.05511
17. Sharma, A., Schuhknecht, F.M., Agrawal, D., Dittrich, J.: Blurring the lines between blockchains and database systems: the case of hyperledger fabric. In: Proceedings of the 2019 International Conference on Management of Data, SIGMOD 2019, pp. 105–122. Association for Computing Machinery, New York, NY, USA (2019). https://doi.org/10.1145/3299869.3319883
18. Polygon Team: Innovating the Main Chain: a Polygon PoS Study in Parallelization (2022). https://polygon.technology/blog/innovating-the-main-chain-a-polygon-pos-study-in-parallelization. Accessed 05 Dec 2022
19. The MystenLabs Team: The Sui Smart Contracts Platform (2023). https://docs.sui.io/paper/sui.pdf. Accessed 15 Jan 2024
20. Xue, B., Deb, S., Kannan, S.: BigDipper: a hyperscale BFT system with short term censorship resistance (2023)
21. Yakovenko, A.: Solana: a new architecture for a high performance blockchain v0.8.13. Whitepaper (2018)
22. Zhang, Y., Setty, S., Chen, Q., Zhou, L., Alvisi, L.: Byzantine ordered consensus without byzantine oligarchy. In: 14th USENIX Symposium on Operating Systems Design and Implementation (OSDI 20), pp. 633–649 (2020)

Broadcast

Broadcast

Communication and Round Efficient Parallel Broadcast Protocols

Nibesh Shrestha[1](✉), Ittai Abraham[2], and Kartik Nayak[3]

[1] Supra Research, Rochester, USA
nibeshrestha2@gmail.com
[2] Intel Labs, Haifa, Israel
ittai.abraham@intel.com
[3] Duke University, Durham, USA
kartik@cs.duke.edu

Abstract. This work focuses on the *parallel broadcast* primitive, where each of the n parties wish to broadcast their ℓ-bit input in parallel. We consider the *authenticated* model with PKI and digital signatures that is secure against $t < n/2$ Byzantine faults under a *synchronous* network.

We show a generic reduction from parallel broadcast to a new primitive called graded parallel broadcast and a single instance of validated Byzantine agreement. Using our reduction, we obtain parallel broadcast protocols with $O(n^2\ell + \kappa n^3)$ communication (κ denotes a security parameter) and expected constant rounds. Thus, for inputs of size $\ell = \Omega(n)$ bits, our protocols are asymptotically free.

Our graded parallel broadcast uses a novel gradecast protocol with multiple grades with asymptotically optimal communication complexity of $O(n\ell + \kappa n^2)$ for inputs of size ℓ bits. We also present a multi-valued validated Byzantine agreement protocol with asymptotically optimal communication complexity of $C(n\ell + \kappa n^2)$ for inputs of size ℓ bits in expectation and expected constant rounds. Both of these primitives are of independent interest.

1 Introduction

Parallel broadcast is a primitive where all parties wish to broadcast ℓ bit messages in parallel. This is an essential building block, central to many cryptographic protocols like verifiable secret sharing (VSS), multi-party computation (MPC) [2,6,8], distributed key generation (DKG) [14] where all parties broadcast messages in parallel in the same round. For example, in MPC and DKG applications, each party broadcasts $O(1)$ VSSs in parallel to share secrets. Design of efficient protocols for parallel broadcast is therefore of paramount importance as any improvements for parallel broadcast also results in improvement of these primitives. In this work, we focus on improving the communication complexity (i.e., reducing the number of bits honest parties exchange) and the round complexity (i.e., the time required to reach a decision) of parallel broadcast in the synchronous authenticated model with PKI and digital signatures tolerating $t < n/2$ Byzantine failures under various setup assumptions.

Existing Works. Existing works on parallel broadcast typically rely on naïvely running n instances of Byzantine agreement (or Byzantine broadcast) primitives in parallel, which increases communication complexity by an undesirable factor of n [1,7,16]. Custom solutions, like the one by Tsimos et al. [32], have been proposed for parallel broadcast tolerating $t < (1 - \varepsilon)n$ (with $\varepsilon > 0$), but these protocols still suffer from high communication complexity of $O(\kappa^2 n^3 \ell)$ (where κ is a security parameter) and round complexity of $O(t \log t)$.

In this work, we focus on the parallel broadcast problem tolerating $t < n/2$ Byzantine failures and terminate in expected $O(1)$ rounds. In $t < n/2$ setting, the parallel broadcast can be obtained by using n parallel invocation of Byzantine agreement (BA) instances, albeit at the cost of increasing the communication complexity by a factor of n. Regarding termination, naïvely running n parallel instances of BA (that terminate in expected $O(1)$ rounds) terminates in expected $O(\log n)$ rounds [7], increasing the round complexity. While there are known techniques [7,21] to obtain expected constant round protocols via parallel composition of the BA protocol (each terminating in constant expected rounds), they invoke $O(n \log n)$ BA instances, resulting in high communication complexity. Additionally, we note the approach by Fitzi and Garay [18], where n parallel instances of BA are executed with a single leader election sub-protocol shared across all BA instances. Their approach saves communication when the leader election sub-protocol is expensive, but does not help when the underlying BA primitive itself is expensive. Thus, this work investigates the communication complexity and round complexity of parallel broadcast protocol when the fault tolerance is $t < n/2$. To be specific, we ask the following question:

Can we design a parallel broadcast protocol with a good communication complexity and a good round complexity while tolerating $t < n/2$ Byzantine faults?

We answer this question affirmatively by showing two parallel broadcast protocols each with $O(n^2 \ell + \kappa n^3)$ communication for inputs of size ℓ bits and termination in constant expected rounds. Thus, for inputs for size $\ell = \Omega(n)$ bits, our protocols have no asymptotic overhead. Our first protocol works in the authenticated model with PKI and digital signatures and is secure against a static adversary. Our second protocol relies on threshold setup assumption to obtain security against a (strongly rushing) adaptive adversary.

1.1 Key Technical Ideas and Results

Towards Communication and Round Efficient Parallel Broadcast. Instead of relying on n instances of Byzantine Agreement primitive, we obtain parallel broadcast using a combination of n instances of weaker primitive such as gradecast [21,31] and only one instance of (validated) Byzantine agreement protocol. Informally, in gradecast, honest parties output a grade along with their output value; the output grade can be viewed as the "confidence" of this party in the sender. In this work, we rely on a version of gradecast that supports multiple grades. To ensure an overall communication complexity of $O(n^2\ell + \kappa n^3)$ for inputs of size ℓ bits, we improve the communication complexity of gradecast (with multiple grades) to $O(n\ell + \kappa n^2)$ and the validated agreement protocol to $O(n\ell + \kappa n^2)$ in expectation. In the following, we will first describe our improvements to each of the primitives, before describing parallel broadcast (Table 1).

Table 1. Comparison of related works on MVBA with ℓ-bit input

	Net.	Res.	Communication	Latency	Adversary	Assumption
Cachin et al. [13]	async.	1/3	$O(n^2\ell) + E(O(\kappa n^2 + n^3))$	$E(O(1))$	adaptive	threshold sigs.
VABA [5]	async.	1/3	$O(n^2\ell) + E(O(\kappa n^2))$	$E(O(1))$	adaptive	threshold sigs.
DUMBO-MVBA [24]	async.	1/3	$E(O(n\ell + \kappa n^2))$	$E(O(1))$	adaptive	threshold sigs.
Shrestha et al. [31]	sync.	1/2	$E(O(n^2\ell + \kappa n^3))$	$E(O(1))$	static	PKI
This work	sync.	1/2	$E(O(n\ell + \kappa n^2))$	$E(O(1))$	adaptive	threshold sigs.

Net. refers to network model. Res. implies resilience. $E(.)$ implies "in expectation".

Gradecast with Multiple Grades. Gradecast is a relaxed version of broadcast introduced by Feldman and Micali [17] where parties output a value along with a grade. Basic versions of gradecast [21,31] have grades in the range of $\{0, 1, 2\}$. We rely on a version of gradecast that supports grades in the range $\{0, 1, 2, 3, 4\}$ (we will explain later the need for this version of gradecast). At a high level, our gradecast with multiple grades provides the following guarantees: (i) the grades of all honest parties are maximum i.e., 4 when the sender is honest, (ii) honest parties may output different grades when the sender is Byzantine; but the grades of any two honest parties differ by at most 1, (iii) when an honest party outputs a value with a grade ≥ 2, all honest parties output the same value, (iv) two honest parties may output different values with a grade of 1 when no honest party has a grade of 2. While gradecast with grades up to 4 suffices for our purpose, we generalize it to support arbitrary number of grades $\{0, 1, \ldots, g^*\}$ where g^* is the maximum supported grade.

We present a construction that tolerates $t < (1-\varepsilon)n$ Byzantine faults, achieving a communication complexity of $O(n\frac{\ell}{\varepsilon} + \kappa n^2)$. The key technique for designing a communication-efficient gradecast is for parties to multicast smaller chunks of messages using Reed-Solomon erasure codes [29] only once. They then "silently" wait to detect any conflicting messages while simultaneously increasing the grades when no conflicts are detected. We obtain the following result:

Theorem 1. *Assuming a public-key infrastructure (PKI), digital signatures and a universal structured reference string under q-SDH assumption, there exists a g^*-gradecast protocol tolerating $t < (1-\varepsilon)n$ Byzantine faults with a communication complexity of $O(n\frac{\ell}{\varepsilon} + \kappa n^2)$ for an input of size ℓ bits and a round complexity of $3g^* - 2$.*

When $\varepsilon > 0$ is a small constant, our protocol has a communication complexity of $O(n\ell + \kappa n^2)$. This communication complexity is achieved when we assume q-Strong Diffe Hellman (q-SDH) [11] setup assumption (this setup can be achieved via distributed protocols [9,12]). We can alternatively make use of Merkle tree [25] to avoid q-SDH assumption at the expense of $O(\log n)$ multiplicative increase in communication complexity.

Graded Parallel Broadcast: Composing n Instances of Gradecast with Multiple Grades and Ensuring Validated Output. Parties invoke gradecast with multiple grades, using each party as a sender to propagate their input and output an n-element grade list (GradeList). When the sender is honest, all honest parties output a common value with the highest grade. If the sender is Byzantine, honest parties may output different values with varying grades. Consequently, the GradeList of two honest parties may differ, particularly for grades corresponding to Byzantine senders.

Looking ahead, our aim is to agree on a common GradeList using a validated Byzantine agreement protocol and compute the final output vector based on the grades in the agreed GradeList to solve the parallel broadcast problem. The agreed GradeList can be the input of even a Byzantine party who may set arbitrary grades in its GradeList. In order to restrict a Byzantine party from setting arbitrary grades in its GradeList, we define the notion of *valid* GradeList and ensure the validated Byzantine agreement protocol outputs only valid GradeList. A *valid* GradeList is one that has been verified by at least one honest party. An honest party verifies a given GradeList by checking against its own GradeList and ensuring that the grades corresponding to a sender differ by at most 1. This restricts a Byzantine party to set arbitrary grades in a *valid* GradeList.

Given this notion of valid GradeList, let us see why we need a gradecast that supports grades in the range $\{0, 1, 2, 3, 4\}$ where honest parties output a common value with the highest grade of 4 when the sender is honest. Consider a Byzantine party who may set arbitrary grades in its GradeList. For its GradeList to be valid, it must set a grade of at least 3 corresponding to honest senders for its GradeList to be verified by an honest party (since gradecast ensures that the grades output by any two parties differ by at most 1). Then we can compute the final output vector (to solve parallel broadcast) by considering values that have grades at least 3 in the agreed valid GradeList. This ensures honest inputs are always included in the final output vector. Note that the Byzantine party may also set a grade of at least 3 corresponding to a Byzantine sender in its GradeList. The GradeList will be verified as long as one honest party has a grade of at least 2 corresponding to this Byzantine sender. Note that our gradecast protocol ensures that all honest parties have output the same value when an honest party sets a grade of at least 2. This ensures consistency in the final output vector.

To see why gradecast protocol that supports fewer grades does not work, let us consider a gradecast where the maximum grade is 3. We consider a GradeList of a Byzantine party who may set a grade of 2 corresponding to an honest sender (to ensure the GradeList is valid). In this version, in order to ensure honest inputs are included in the final vector, we need to output values with grades of at least 2 in the agreed GradeList. However, the Byzantine party may also set a grade of 2 corresponding to Byzantine sender for which no honest party has a grade of 2; different honest parties may have different values in this case. Thus, this violates consistency.

We formally define the process of invoking n parallel instances of gradecast with multiple grades and obtaining (possibly different) valid GradeList as *graded parallel broadcast*. We obtain the following result,

Theorem 2. *Assuming a PKI, digital signatures and a universal structured reference string under q-SDH assumption, there exists a graded parallel broadcast protocol tolerating $t < n/2$ Byzantine faults with $O(n^2\ell + \kappa n^3)$ communication for an input of size ℓ bits and constant rounds.*

Agreeing on a Common Valid GradeList Using Efficient Multi-value Validated Byzantine Agreement. We make use of a single instance of multi-valued validated Byzantine agreement (MVBA) to agree on a common GradeList. In MVBA, each party starts with a different externally valid input (possibly large) and outputs a common value; the output value can be input of any party as long as it is externally valid. To the best of our knowledge, the MVBA protocol by Shrestha et al. [31] is the only known MVBA protocol in the synchronous setting. Their protocol operates in the authenticated model with PKI and digital signatures and is secure against a static adversary tolerating $t < n/2$ faults, with $O(n^2\ell + \kappa n^3)$ communication in expectation and expected $O(1)$ rounds.

To enhance communication efficiency and ensure adaptive security, we design an MVBA protocol secure against a strongly rushing adaptive adversary, tolerating $t < n/2$ Byzantine faults. The protocol achieves expected communication complexity of $O(n\ell + \kappa n^2)$ and terminates in expected constant rounds. It assumes a threshold setup and relies on an adaptively secure threshold signature scheme [23]. Based on the communication lower bounds by Abraham et al. [3] and Fitzi et al. [19], our protocol achieves asymptotically optimal communication complexity. Specifically, we show the following result:

Theorem 3. *Assuming a PKI, digital signatures, threshold signature setup and a universal structured reference string under q-SDH assumption, there exists a multi-valued validated Byzantine agreement protocol tolerating $t < n/2$ Byzantine faults with $O(n\ell + \kappa n^2)$ communication in expectation for inputs of size ℓ bits, termination in expected $O(1)$ rounds and security against a (strongly rushing) adaptive adversary (Table 2).*

Efficient Parallel Broadcast. Finally, we obtain efficient protocols for parallel broadcast using the above primitives. In particular, we use the graded parallel broadcast and MVBA protocol to achieve parallel broadcast protocol. Specifically, we obtain the following main result:

Theorem 4. *Assuming a PKI and digital signatures, if we have a graded parallel broadcast tolerating $t < n/2$ Byzantine faults with a communication complexity of*

Table 2. Comparison of related parallel broadcast protocols

	Model	Resilience	Communication	Latency	Adversary
Nayak et al. [26]	PKI	$t < (1-\varepsilon)n$	$O(n^2\ell + \kappa n^3 + n^4)$	$O(t)$	adaptive
Tsimos et al. [32]	PKI	$t < (1-\varepsilon)n$	$\tilde{O}(\kappa^2 n^3 \ell)$	$O(t \log t)$	adaptive
Tsimos et al. [32]	trusted PKI	$t < (1-\varepsilon)n$	$\tilde{O}(\kappa^4 n^2 \ell)$	$O(\kappa \log t)$	adaptive
Abraham et al. [1]	unauthenticated	$t < n/3$	$O(n^2 \ell) + E(O(n^4 \log n))$	$E(O(1))$	static
Nayak et al. [26]+ [4]	threshold sigs.	$t < n/2$	$O(n^2 \ell) + E(O(\kappa n^3))$	$E(O(\log t))$	adaptive
This work+ [31]	PKI	$t < n/2$	$O(n^2 \ell) + E(O(\kappa n^3))$	$E(O(1))$	static
This work	threshold sigs.	$t < n/2$	$O(n^2 \ell + \kappa n^3) + E(O(\kappa n^2))$	$E(O(1))$	adaptive

Tsimos et al. [32] and Abraham et al. [1] do not assume q-SDH assumption. Tsimos et al. [32] has $\tilde{O}$ in the communication complexity which hides a $\log n$ factor unrelated to the q-SDH assumption. Without q-SDH setup assumption, our protocols would have $\log n$ multiplicative factor in the communication complexity. $E(.)$ implies "in expectation". * This is the best communication complexity as these protocols execute for a fixed number of rounds.

x and round complexity of y, and a MVBA protocol tolerating $t < n/2$ Byzantine faults with a communication complexity of a and a round complexity of b, we can have a parallel broadcast protocol tolerating $t < n/2$ Byzantine faults with a communication complexity of $x + a$ and a round complexity of $y + b$.

We obtain different results for parallel broadcast depending on the variant of the validated Byzantine agreement used. Our first parallel broadcast protocol uses the MVBA protocol of Shrestha et al. [31] which is a secure against a static adversary with $O(n^2\ell + \kappa n^3)$ communication in expectation and expected $O(1)$ rounds. Using their MVBA protocol, we obtain the following corollary:

Corollary 1. *Assuming a PKI, digital signatures, and a universal structured reference string under q-SDH assumption there exists a protocol secure against static adversary that solves parallel broadcast tolerating $t < n/2$ Byzantine faults with $O(n^2\ell) + E(O(\kappa n^3))$ communication and expected $O(1)$ rounds.*

Our second parallel broadcast protocol uses our MVBA protocol (Theorem 3). We obtain the following corollary:

Corollary 2. *Assuming a PKI, digital signatures, threshold signature setup, and a universal structured reference string under q-SDH assumption there exists a protocol that solves parallel broadcast tolerating $t < n/2$ Byzantine faults with $O(n^2\ell + \kappa n^3) + E(O(\kappa n^2))$ communication, termination in expected $O(1)$ rounds and security against a (strongly rushing) adaptive adversary.*

Observe that our second parallel broadcast has $O(n^2\ell + \kappa n^3) + E(O(\kappa n^2))$ communication. In the common case, the protocol terminates in expected constant number of rounds with total communication complexity of $O(n^2\ell + \kappa n^3)$. In the worst case, when the protocol runs for linear number of rounds, this protocol still incurs $O(n^2\ell + \kappa n^3)$ communication; thus this protocol incurs $O(n^2\ell + \kappa n^3)$ communication even in the worst-case.

On Simultaneous Termination and Sequential Composition. Our protocols cannot provide simultaneous termination. This is similar to Feldman and Micali [17] and Katz and Koo [21]. However, we can use techniques introduced in Lindell, Lysyanskaya and Rabin [22], Katz and Koo [21] and Cohen et al. [15] for sequential composition of our protocols.

Organization. The rest of the paper is organized as follows. In Sect. 2, we describe the system model and preliminaries. Section 3 introduces the multi-grade gradecast protocol. In Sect. 4, we present the graded parallel broadcast. The MVBA protocol with $O(n\ell + \kappa n^2)$ communication complexity is provided in the full version of the paper [30]. Finally, we describe our parallel broadcast protocols in Sect. 5, and discuss related work in Sect. 6.

2 Model and Preliminaries

We consider a system consisting of n parties $(P_1, \ldots, P_n)$ in a reliable, authenticated all-to-all network, where up to t parties can be Byzantine faulty. The Byzantine parties may behave arbitrarily. We consider two kinds of adversaries: (i) a static adversary, and (ii) a strongly rushing adaptive adversary. A static adversary corrupts parties before the start of the protocol execution whereas a strongly rushing adaptive adversary can adaptively decide which t parties to corrupt at any time during protocol execution. In addition, due to "strongly-rushing" nature of the adversary, the adversary is capable of corrupting a party P_h after observing message sent by party P_h in round r and remove round r messages sent by party P_h before they reach other honest parties and send round r messages after corrupting it [4]. A party that is not faulty throughout the execution is considered to be *honest* and executes the protocol as specified.

We assume a synchronous communication model. Thus, if an honest party sends a message at the beginning of some round, the recipient receives the message by the end of that round. We make use of digital signatures and a public-key infrastructure (PKI) to prevent spoofing and replays and to validate messages. Message x sent by a node P_i is digitally signed by P_i's private key and is denoted by $\langle x \rangle_i$. We use $H(x)$ to denote the invocation of hash function H on input x.

2.1 Definitions

Definition 1 (Parallel Broadcast [28]). *In a parallel broadcast protocol, each party P_i has its input value v_i and each party P_i outputs a n-element vector $\mathcal{V}_i$ of values. A parallel broadcast protocol tolerating t Byzantine failures has the following properties:*

- **Agreement.** *All honest parties must agree on the same vector of values $\mathcal{V} = [v_1, \ldots, v_n]$.*
- **Validity.** *If the input of an honest party P_j is v_j, then $\mathcal{V}_i[j] = v_j$.*
- **Termination.** *All honest parties must eventually decide on a vector $\mathcal{V}$.*

Gradecast with Multiple Grades. Gradecast with multiples grades was originally introduced by Garay et al. [20] that supports arbitrary number of grades. We present a slightly weaker definition of gradecast with multiple grades.

Definition 2 (Gradecast with multiple grades). *A protocol with a designated sender P_i holding an initial input v is a g^*-gradecast protocol tolerating t Byzantine faults if the following conditions hold:*

- *Each honest party P_j outputs a value v_j with a grade $g_j \in \{0, 1, \ldots, g^*\}$.*
- *If the sender is honest, each honest party P_j outputs v with a grade $g_j = g^*$.*
- *If two honest parties P_j and P_k output values with grades g_j and g_k respectively, then $|g_j - g_k| \leq 1$.*
- *If an honest party P_j outputs a value v with a grade $g_j > 1$, then all honest parties output value v.*

Our definition allows honest parties to output different values with a grade of 1 when no honest party outputs with a grade > 1 while the definition of Garay et al. [20] restricts honest parties to output the same value with a grade of 1.

Multi-valued Validated Byzantine Agreement. In an MVBA protocol, there is an external validity function ex-validation that every party has access to. Each honest party begins with an externally valid input v_i and must output a value upon termination. An MVBA protocol tolerating t Byzantine failures possesses the following properties:

Definition 3 (Multi-valued Validated Byzantine Agreement [5,24,31]). *A protocol solves multi-valued validated Byzantine agreement if it satisfies the following properties except with negligible probability in the security parameter κ:*

- **Agreement.** *No two honest parties decide on different values.*
- **Validity.** *If an honest party decides a value v, then ex-validation(v) = true.*
- **Quality.** *The probability of deciding a value proposed by an honest party is at least $\frac{1}{2}$.*
- **Termination.** *If all honest parties start with externally valid values, all honest parties eventually decide.*

Remark on the Quality Property. We inherit the quality property as specified in the MVBA definition from [5,24]. Our MVBA protocol, detailed in the full version [30], also satisfies this quality property. However, this property is not required for solving the parallel broadcast protocol.

2.2 Primitives

Linear Erasure and Error Correcting Codes. We use standard (n, b) Reed-Solomon (RS) codes [29]. This code encodes b data symbols into code words of

n symbols using ENC function and can decode the b elements of code words to recover the original data using DEC function. More details on ENC and DEC functions are provided in the full version [30].

In our protocol, we use the (n, b) RS codes with n set to be the number of parties in the system and b set to be the number of honest parties i.e., $b = n - t$.

Cryptographic Accumulators. A cryptographic accumulator scheme constructs an accumulation value for a set of values using Eval function and produces a witness for each value in the set using CreateWit function. Given the accumulation value and a witness, any party can verify if a value is indeed in the set using Verify function. More details on these functions are provided in the full version [30].

In this paper, we use *collision free bilinear accumulators* from Nguyen [27] as cryptographic accumulators which generates constant sized witness, but requires q-SDH assumption [11]. Alternatively, we can use Merkle trees [25] (and avoid q-SDH assumption) at the expense of $O(\log n)$ multiplicative overhead.

Normalizing the Length of Cryptographic Building Blocks. Let λ denote the security parameter, $\kappa_h = \kappa_h(\lambda)$ denote the hash size, $\kappa_s = \kappa_s(\lambda)$ denote the size of the signature size, $\kappa_a = \kappa_a(\lambda)$ denote the size of the accumulation value and witness of the accumulator. Further, let $\kappa = \max(\kappa_h, k_s, \kappa_a)$; we assume $\kappa = \Theta(\kappa_h) = \Theta(\kappa_s) = \Theta(\kappa_a) = \Theta(\lambda)$. Throughout the paper, we will use the same parameter κ to denote the hash size, signature size and accumulator size for convenience.

3 Gradecast with Multiple Grades

In this section, we present a communication optimal gradecast protocol that supports multiple grades. Our gradecast with multiple grades incurs a communication complexity of $O(n\ell + \kappa n^2)$ for input of size ℓ bits and terminates in $3g^* - 2$ rounds. It works in the authenticated model with PKI and digital signatures and achieves $t < (1 - \varepsilon)n$ resilience where $\varepsilon > 0$ is some constant.

Equivocation. Two or more messages of the same *type* but with different payload sent by a party is considered an equivocation. In order to facilitate efficient equivocation checks, the sender sends the payload along with signed hash of the payload. When an equivocation is detected, broadcasting the signed hash suffices to prove equivocation by the sender.

Deliver. As a building block, we first present a Deliver function (refer Fig. 1) used by an honest party to efficiently propagate long messages using erasure coding techniques and cryptographic accumulators. The input parameters to the function are long message m, accumulation value z corresponding to message m and the sender's signature on $(H(m), z)$. The sender is the party who originally sent message m.

Deliver(m, z, σ) :
- Partition input m into b blocks. Encode the b blocks into n code words $[s_1, \ldots, s_n]$ using ENC function. Add an index j to each code word s_j to obtain $\mathcal{D} = [(1, s_1), \ldots, (n, s_n)]$. Compute accumulation value $z_i = \text{Eval}(a_k, \mathcal{D})$. If $z \neq z_i$ or σ is not a valid signature on $(H(m), z_i)$ abort. Otherwise, compute witness w_j for each element $(j, s_j) \in \mathcal{D}$ using CreateWit function and send $\langle \text{codeword}, s_j, w_j, H(m), z \rangle_i$ and σ to party $P_j \; \forall P_j \in \mathcal{P}$.
- If party P_j receives the first valid code word $\langle \text{codeword}, s_j, w_j, H(m), z \rangle_*$ along with the sender's signature σ such that $\text{Verify}(a_k, z, w_j, (j, s_j)) = \text{true}$, forward the code word and the sender's signature σ to all the parties.
- Upon receiving b valid code words for the first accumulation value z it received, decode m using DEC function.

Fig. 1. Deliver function

We consider the invocation of the Deliver function by an honest party P_i. When the function is invoked using the above input parameters, the long message m is first partitioned into b blocks. The b blocks are then encoded into n code words $[s_1, \ldots, s_n]$ using ENC function (defined in Sect. 2). An index j is added to each code word s_j to obtain $\mathcal{D} = [(1, s_1), \ldots, (n, s_n)]$ and the accumulation value z_i is computed from $\mathcal{D}$ using Eval function. If $z \neq z_i$ or the sender signature σ is not a valid signature on $(H(m), z_i)$, party P_i aborts further operations. If party P_i did not abort, it computes the cryptographic witness w_j for each element $(j, s_j) \in \mathcal{D}$ using CreateWit (defined in Sect. 2). Then, the code word and witness pair (s_j, w_j) is sent to the node $P_j \in \mathcal{P}$ along with the sender's signature σ.

When a node P_j receives the first valid code word s_j for an accumulation value z such that the witness w_j verifies (j, s_j) (using Verify function defined in Sect. 2), it forwards the code word and witness pair (s_j, w_j) along with the sender's signature σ to all parties. Note that party P_j forwards only the first valid code word and witness pair (s_j, w_j). Thus, it is required that all honest parties forward the code word and witness pair (s_j, w_j) for long message m; otherwise all honest nodes may not receive b code words required to decode the long message m.

When a party P_i receives b valid code words corresponding to the first accumulation value z (or the first valid code word) it receives, it reconstructs m.

The Deliver function completes in 2 rounds. Our Deliver function improves on RandPiper [10] by tolerating a dishonest majority of Byzantine faults.

Set $o_i = \bot$ and $g_i = 0$. Each party P_i performs the following operations:
- **Round 1:** If party P_j is the designated sender, then it multicasts (v, z, σ) where v is the input value, z is the accumulation value of v and σ is the its signature on $(H(m), z)$.
- **Round** $2h$ ($h \in [1, g^* - 1]$): If party P_i receives (v, z, σ) for the first time, it invokes Deliver(v, z, σ).
- **Round** $2g^*$: If party P_i invoked Deliver for value v without aborting by round $2g^* - 2$ and no party P_j equivocation has been detected so far, set $o_i = v$ and $g_i = 2$. Let v_i be the first value received. If $v_i = \bot$, set $o_i = \bot$ and $g_i = 0$, else if $o_i = \bot$, set $o_i = v_i$ and $g_i = 1$.
- **Round** $2g^* + h$ ($h \in [1, g^* - 2]$): If party P_i invoked Deliver for value v by Round $2g^* - 2(h+1)$ and no party P_j equivocation has been detected so far, set $g_i = g_i + 1$. At round $3g^* - 2$, output (o_i, g_i).

Fig. 2. M-Gradecast(v, g^*) with $O(n\ell + (\kappa + w)n^2)$ **communication.**

3.1 Protocol Details

We construct a protocol M-Gradecast(v, g^*) where v is the sender's value and g^* is the maximum supported grade. The M-Gradecast(v, g^*) protocol is presented in Fig. 2. In round 1, the designated sender P_j multicasts (v, z, σ) where v is its input value, z is the accumulation value and σ is its signature on $(H(m), z)$. We note that the size of input value v can be large. In order to facilitate efficient equivocation checks, the sender P_j signs $(H(v), z)$ and sends the signature σ. Whenever an equivocation by the sender is detected, multicasting these signatures suffices to prove equivocation by the sender.

During rounds $2h$ for $h \in [1, g^* - 1]$, if party P_i receives (v, z, σ) for the first time, it invokes Deliver to propagate long message v. Note that if party P_i invoked Deliver in round 2, it does not invoke Deliver again in later rounds. Also, note that Deliver function requires 2 rounds. Rounds $2h + 1$ for $h \in [1, g^* - 1]$ accommodates steps of Deliver function invoked in rounds $2h$ for $h \in [1, g^* - 1]$. We note that although parties may invoke Deliver to propagate long message v in different rounds, they forward their code words only the first time. For example, if a party P_i invoked Deliver in round 2 and an honest party P_k received its first valid code word (s_k, w_k) in round 3 for accumulation value z, it forwards the code word to all parties in round 3. Later, if some other party (say party P_h) invokes Deliver in round 4 and party P_k receives code word (s_k, w_k) again in round 5, party P_k does not forward (s_k, w_k) again. This helps in keeping communication complexity to $O(n\ell + \kappa n^2)$.

In round $2g^*$, each party P_i sets its output value and initial grades. If party P_i invoked Deliver for value v at any prior rounds, and it did not detect any equivocation so far, it sets $o_i = v$ and $g_i = 2$. We note that an honest party decodes long messages corresponding to the first valid code word (or the first accumulation value z) they receive even though it detects equivocation as long as it receives b valid code words. We refer to this value as the first received value. Let v_i be the first value received. If $v_i = \bot$, it sets $o_i = \bot$ and $g_i = 0$. Otherwise if $o_i = \bot$, set $o_i = v_i$ and $g_i = 1$ irrespective of the equivocation i.e., if P_i did not invoke Deliver for any values but receives a value $v_i \neq \bot$, it sets $o_i = v_i$ and $g_i = 1$.

In round $2g^* + h$ for $h \in [1, g^* - 2]$, each party P_i updates their grade g_i based on when they invoked Deliver and if they have detected any equivocation.

Optimal Communication Complexity. Our M-Gradecast(v, g^*) incurs $O(n\ell + \kappa n^2)$ communication for input of ℓ bits while tolerating $t < (1 - \varepsilon)n$ Byzantine faults where $\varepsilon > 0$ is a constant. In a recent work, Shrestha et al. [31] designed a weak-gradecast protocol where grades are in the range $\{0, 1, 2\}$ with a communication complexity of $O(n\ell + \kappa n^2)$ for input of size ℓ bits in the same setting and gave a communication lower bound of $\Omega(n\ell + n^2)$ for weak-gradecast. The communication lowerbound of Shrestha et al. [31] can trivially be extended to show the optimal communication complexity of our M-Gradecast(v, g^*) protocol.

We present detailed security analysis in the full version [30].

4 Graded Parallel Broadcast

In this section, we present a new primitive that we call *Graded Parallel Broadcast* that is secure against $t < n/2$ Byzantine faults. Graded parallel broadcast is a relaxation of parallel broadcast [32] and uses gradecast with multiple grades to propagate its input. In this work, we consider an instance of gradecast with multiple grades where the grades can be in the range $\{0, 1, \ldots, 4\}$. In our construction, each party P_i uses M-Gradecast$(., 4)$ to propagate its input v_i and output an n-element list of values along with an n-element list of grades (GradeList$_i$). Looking ahead, our aim is to have each party P_i feed its output of graded parallel broadcast (i.e., GradeList$_i$) into a Byzantine consensus primitive to agree on a common GradeList$_h$. The agreed GradeList$_h$ can be a Byzantine parties' input too. However, a Byzantine party may set arbitrary grades in its GradeList corresponding to an honest sender and prevent honest input from appearing in the final output. In order to prevent this scenario, we restrict a Byzantine party from setting arbitrary grades and consider only a *valid* GradeList. A *valid* GradeList has (i) at least $n - t$ entries of grade 4, i.e., $|\{h \mid \text{GradeList}[h] = 4\}| \geq n - t$, (ii) GradeList$[i] \in \{3, 4\}$ corresponding to honest sender P_i. Note that for an honest sender P_k, each honest party P_i sets a grade GradeList$_i[k] = 4$. Thus, a valid GradeList must have at least $n - t$ entries of 4. Moreover, due to the properties of M-Gradecast$(., 4)$, the grades of two parties for the same sender can differ by at most 1. Since each honest party sets a grade of 4 for an honest sender P_k, a Byzantine party must set a grade of at least 3 corresponding to an honest sender P_k for its GradeList to be valid. In the final parallel broadcast protocol, we consider all values with grades in the range $\{3, 4\}$ corresponding to agreed GradeList.

In graded parallel broadcast, a valid GradeList is *certified*, meaning it is accompanied by a certificate consisting of at least $t + 1$ signatures (denoted as $\mathcal{AC}(\text{GradeList})$) from distinct parties.

Definition 4 (Graded Parallel Broadcast). *Each party P_i, as a sender, sends its input v_i, and each honest party P_j outputs an n-element list of values along with an n-element grade list $\mathsf{GradeList}_j$, where $\mathsf{GradeList}_j[h] \in 0,1,2,3,4$ for all $h \in [n]$. A graded parallel broadcast protocol tolerating t Byzantine failures satisfies the following properties (Fig. 3):*

- *If sender P_i is honest, then each honest party P_j sets $\mathsf{GradeList}_j[i] = 4$.*
- *A certified $\mathsf{GradeList}_k$ must have $|\{h \mid \mathsf{GradeList}_k[h] = 4\}| \geq n - t$.*
- *If the sender P_i is honest and $\mathsf{GradeList}_k$ is certified, then $\mathsf{GradeList}_k[i] \in \{3, 4\}$.*
- *If $\mathsf{GradeList}_k$ is certified and $\mathsf{GradeList}_k[i] \in \{3, 4\}$, then all honest parties have received a common value v_i.*

Each party P_i with its initial input v_i performs following operations:
- **(Round 1) Propose.** Each party P_i invokes $\mathsf{M\text{-}Gradecast}(v_i, 4)$.
- **(Round 10) Propose Grade.** Let $(o_{j,i}, g_{j,i})$ be the output of M-Gradecast of party P_i with party P_j as sender. Set $\mathsf{GradeList}_i[j] = g_{j,i}$. Multicast $\langle \text{grade-list}, \mathsf{GradeList}_i \rangle_i$.
- **(Round 11) Verify and Ack.** Upon receiving $\langle \text{grade-list}, \mathsf{GradeList}_j \rangle_j$ from party P_j, if the following conditions hold send $\langle \text{ack}, H(\mathsf{GradeList}_j) \rangle_i$ to party P_j.
  - $|\{h \mid \mathsf{GradeList}_j[h] = 4\}| \geq n - t$
  - $|\mathsf{GradeList}_j[h] - \mathsf{GradeList}_i[h]| < 2 \ \forall h \in [n]$.

Fig. 3. Graded Parallel Broadcast with $O(n^2\ell + (\kappa + w)n^3)$ communication

Protocol Details. Each party P_i uses $\mathsf{M\text{-}Gradecast}(.,4)$ to propagate its input v_i. At the end of $\mathsf{M\text{-}Gradecast}(.,4)$ invocation, each honest party P_i outputs an n element list of values along with n element list of grades, denoted by $\mathsf{GradeList}_i$, with an entry corresponding to each party as a sender.

Party P_i then multicasts its $\mathsf{GradeList}_i$ to all other parties. Party P_j then checks the validity of $\mathsf{GradeList}_i$ by checking if (i) $|\{h \mid \mathsf{GradeList}_i[h] = 4\}| \geq n-t$, and (ii) $|\mathsf{GradeList}_j[h] - \mathsf{GradeList}_i[h]| < 2 \ \forall h \in [n]$. The first check ensures that $\mathsf{GradeList}_i$ contains at least $n-t$ entries with $\mathsf{GradeList}_i[h] = 4$. Note that for an honest sender P_k, each honest party P_i outputs a value with $\mathsf{GradeList}_i[k] = 4$. Thus, a valid GradeList must have at least $n-t$ entries of 4. In addition, due to the properties of $\mathsf{M\text{-}Gradecast}(.,4)$, the grades of any two parties corresponding to a sender differs by at most 1. Thus, a valid GradeList must satisfy $|\mathsf{GradeList}_j[h] - \mathsf{GradeList}_i[h]| < 2 \ \forall h \in [n]$. This check also prevents a Byzantine party from setting too low grades corresponding to an honest sender; otherwise its GradeList would not be certified. Thus, a Byzantine party must set a grade of at least 3 corresponding to an honest sender for its GradeList to be certified.

If the checks pass, party P_j sends $\langle \text{ack}, H(\mathsf{GradeList}_i) \rangle_j$ to party P_i. A set of $t+1$ ack (ack-cert) messages for $\mathsf{GradeList}_i$ (denoted by $\mathcal{AC}(\mathsf{GradeList}_i)$) implies at least one honest party has verified $\mathsf{GradeList}_i$.

We present detailed security analysis in the full version [30].

5 Parallel Broadcast

Finally, we present two communication efficient parallel broadcast protocols tolerating $t < n/2$ Byzantine faults with a communication complexity of $O(n^2\ell + \kappa n^3)$ for input of size ℓ bits and expected $O(1)$ rounds under various setup assumptions. The first protocol is in the authenticated model with PKI and digital signatures. It is secure against a static adversary. The second protocol is secure against an adaptive adversary, but assumes threshold setup and uses adaptively-secure threshold signature scheme.

We propose parallel broadcast protocols with expected constant rounds in Fig. 4. In this protocol, each party P_i first uses graded parallel broadcast to propagate their input v_i and output a n-element list of values along with a n-element grade list GradeList$_i$ accompanied by $\mathcal{AC}$(GradeList$_i$). The tuple (GradeList$_i$, $\mathcal{AC}$(GradeList$_i$)) is then input to an MVBA protocol to agree on a common certified GradeList$_h$. The ack certificate on GradeList serves as the external validity function. Parties then output $\mathcal{V}$ with $\mathcal{V}[j] = v_j$ if GradeList$_h[j] \in \{3, 4\}$ $\forall j \in [n]$. We present two variants of this protocol based on the choice of the MVBA protocol.

- **Graded parallel broadcast.** Each party P_i invokes graded parallel broadcast protocol (refer Figure 3) with its input v_i and outputs an n element list of values along with (GradeList$_i$, $\mathcal{AC}$(GradeList$_i$)).
- **MVBA.** Each party P_i participates in MVBA with input GradeList$_i$ and $\mathcal{AC}$(GradeList$_i$). Let GradeList$_h$ be the output of the MVBA protocol.
- **Output.** Set $\mathcal{V}[j] = v_j$ if GradeList$_h[j] \in \{3, 4\}$ $\forall j \in [n]$. Output $\mathcal{V}$.

Fig. 4. Parallel broadcast with $O(n^2\ell + \kappa n^3)$ communication and expected $O(1)$ rounds

Using MVBA protocol of Shrestha et al. [31]. In Shrestha et al. [31], they gave an MVBA protocol in the authenticated model with PKI and digital signatures with security against a static adversary. Their protocol incurs $O(\kappa n^3)$ communication in expectation when $\ell = O(n)$ (i.e., the size of (GradeList, $\mathcal{AC}$(GradeList)) and terminates in expected $O(1)$ rounds. The exact round complexity of their MVBA protocol is expected 36 rounds. We refer the readers to Shrestha et al. [31] for more details. Using this MVBA protocol, gives us a parallel broadcast protocol secure against static adversary in the authenticated model with PKI and digital signatures. The resulting parallel broadcast protocol has $O(n^2\ell) + E(O(\kappa n^3))$ communication and terminates in expected constant rounds. Concretely, this protocol terminates in expected 47 rounds.

Using Our Efficient MVBA. In the second variant, we utilize our MVBA protocol, enabling a parallel broadcast protocol secure against a strongly rushing adaptive adversary. The graded parallel broadcast protocol has a communication complexity of $O(n^2\ell + \kappa n^3)$, and the MVBA protocol incurs $O(\kappa n^2)$ communication when $\ell = O(n)$ (the size of (GradeList, $\mathcal{AC}$(GradeList))). Consequently, the resulting parallel broadcast protocol achieves a total communication complexity of $O(n^2\ell + \kappa n^3) + E(O(\kappa n^2))$ and terminates in expected $O(1)$ rounds. Specifically, this protocol completes in expected 30 rounds.

We present detailed security analysis in the full version [30].

6 Related Work

The problem of parallel broadcast (aka, interactive consistency [28]) was originally introduced by Pease et al. [28]. In the same work, they present two variants of the protocol: (i) a protocol with $t < n/3$ resilience in the *plain* authenticated model without PKI (aka, the unauthenticated model), and (ii) a protocol with $t < n$ resilience in the authenticated model with authenticators. Both protocols incur exponential communication complexity and $\Theta(t)$ round complexity.

Ben-or and El-Yaniv [7] showed how to achieve expected $O(1)$ rounds for the interactive consistency problem tolerating $t < n/3$ Byzantine faults in the unauthenticated model. In their solution, they invoked $O(n \log n)$ instances of the BA protocol due to Feldman and Micali [17] in a "black-box" fashion to achieve expected $O(1)$ round parallel broadcast protocol. Their construction has a very high communication as each instance of BA protocol of Feldman and Micali [17] has $O(n^6 \log n)$ communication even for a single bit input.

Very recently, Abraham et al. [1] gave an efficient protocol in the unauthenticated model tolerating $t < n/3$ Byzantine faults and security against an adaptive adversary. Their protocol incurs $O(n^2\ell) + E(O(n^4 \log n))$ communication for input of size ℓ bits and expected $O(1)$ rounds.

Tsimos et al. [32] recently explored parallel broadcast in the authenticated model with PKI and digital signatures, tolerating $t < (1-\varepsilon)n$ Byzantine faults and ensuring security against an adaptive adversary. Their first protocol, in the authenticated model with PKI, incurs $\tilde{O}(\kappa^2 n^3)$ communication for a single-bit input and runs in $O(t \log t)$ rounds. The second protocol, under stronger setup assumptions, relies on a trusted dealer for key setup and employs *bit-specific* committee election [3] to reduce communication. It also requires parties to erase signatures after sending messages, achieving $\tilde{O}(\kappa^4 n^2)$ communication for a single-bit input and $O(\kappa \log t)$ rounds.

Concrete Round Complexity. The state-of-the-art PBC protocol by Abraham et al. [1] has an expected round complexity of 209. In comparison, our PBC protocols achieve expected 30 rounds with our MVBA and 47 rounds with the MVBA by Shrestha et al. [31] (which itself incurs 36 rounds). Tsimos et al. [32] in the PKI model require $O(t \log t)$ rounds, exceeding our protocols' exact round complexity when $t > 32$, even with a constant factor of 1. In the trusted PKI model, their protocol incurs $O(k \log t)$ rounds, and for $k = 40$ (a reasonable value), its exact round complexity is also higher than ours.

Due to space constraints, we present detailed related work in the full version [30].

Acknowledgments. We thank Adithya Bhat, Aniket Kate, Julian Loss, and the anonymous reviewers for their valuable feedback on this paper. This paper is funded in part by NSF Award #2237814.

References

1. Abraham, I., Asharov, G., Patil, S., Patra, A.: Asymptotically free broadcast in constant expected time via packed vss. In: Theory of Cryptography: 20th International Conference, TCC 2022, Chicago, IL, USA, 7–10 November 2022, Proceedings, Part I, pp. 384–414. Springer (2023). https://doi.org/10.1007/978-3-031-22318-1_14
2. Abraham, I., Asharov, G., Yanai, A.: Efficient perfectly secure computation with optimal resilience. In: Nissim, K., Waters, B. (eds.) TCC 2021. LNCS, vol. 13043, pp. 66–96. Springer, Cham (2021). https://doi.org/10.1007/978-3-030-90453-1_3
3. Abraham, I., et al.: Communication complexity of byzantine agreement, revisited. In: Proceedings of the 2019 ACM Symposium on Principles of Distributed Computing, pp. 317–326 (2019)
4. Abraham, I., Devadas, S., Dolev, D., Nayak, K., Ren, L.: Synchronous byzantine agreement with expected $O(1)$ rounds, expected $O(n^2)$ communication, and optimal resilience. In: Goldberg, I., Moore, T. (eds.) FC 2019. LNCS, vol. 11598, pp. 320–334. Springer, Cham (2019). https://doi.org/10.1007/978-3-030-32101-7_20
5. Abraham, I., Malkhi, D., Spiegelman, A.: Asymptotically optimal validated asynchronous byzantine agreement. In: Proceedings of the 2019 ACM Symposium on Principles of Distributed Computing, pp. 337–346 (2019)
6. Baum, C., Orsini, E., Scholl, P., Soria-Vazquez, E.: Efficient constant-round MPC with identifiable abort and public verifiability. In: Micciancio, D., Ristenpart, T. (eds.) CRYPTO 2020. LNCS, vol. 12171, pp. 562–592. Springer, Cham (2020). https://doi.org/10.1007/978-3-030-56880-1_20
7. Ben-Or, M., El-Yaniv, R.: Resilient-optimal interactive consistency in constant time. Distrib. Comput. **16**(4), 249–262 (2003)
8. Ben-Or, M., Goldwasser, S., Wigderson, A.: Completeness theorems for non-cryptographic fault-tolerant distributed computation. In: Providing Sound Foundations for Cryptography, pp. 351–371 (2019)
9. Ben-Sasson, E., Chiesa, A., Green, M., Tromer, E., Virza, M.: Secure sampling of public parameters for succinct zero knowledge proofs. In: 2015 IEEE Symposium on Security and Privacy, pp. 287–304. IEEE (2015)
10. Bhat, A., Shrestha, N., Luo, Z., Kate, A., Nayak, K.: Randpiper–reconfiguration-friendly random beacons with quadratic communication. In: Proceedings of the 2021 ACM SIGSAC Conference on Computer and Communications Security, pp. 3502–3524 (2021)
11. Boneh, D., Boyen, X.: Short signatures without random oracles and the SDH assumption in bilinear groups. J. Cryptol. **21**(2), 149–177 (2008)
12. Bowe, S., Gabizon, A., Miers, I.: Scalable multi-party computation for ZK-SNARK parameters in the random beacon model. In: Cryptology ePrint Archive (2017)
13. Cachin, C., Kursawe, K., Petzold, F., Shoup, V.: Secure and efficient asynchronous broadcast protocols. In: Kilian, J. (ed.) CRYPTO 2001. LNCS, vol. 2139, pp. 524–541. Springer, Heidelberg (2001). https://doi.org/10.1007/3-540-44647-8_31

14. Canetti, R., Gennaro, R., Jarecki, S., Krawczyk, H., Rabin, T.: Adaptive security for threshold cryptosystems. In: Wiener, M. (ed.) CRYPTO 1999. LNCS, vol. 1666, pp. 98–116. Springer, Heidelberg (1999). https://doi.org/10.1007/3-540-48405-1_7
15. Cohen, R., Coretti, S., Garay, J., Zikas, V.: Probabilistic termination and composability of cryptographic protocols. In: Robshaw, M., Katz, J. (eds.) CRYPTO 2016. LNCS, vol. 9816, pp. 240–269. Springer, Heidelberg (2016). https://doi.org/10.1007/978-3-662-53015-3_9
16. Dolev, D., Strong, H.R.: Authenticated algorithms for byzantine agreement. SIAM J. Comput. **12**(4), 656–666 (1983)
17. Feldman, P., Micali, S.: Optimal algorithms for byzantine agreement. In: Proceedings of the Twentieth Annual ACM Symposium on Theory of Computing, pp. 148–161 (1988)
18. Fitzi, M., Garay, J.A.: Efficient player-optimal protocols for strong and differential consensus. In: Proceedings of the Twenty-Second Annual Symposium on Principles of Distributed Computing, pp. 211–220 (2003)
19. Fitzi, M., Hirt, M.: Optimally efficient multi-valued byzantine agreement. In: Proceedings of the Twenty-Fifth Annual ACM Symposium on Principles of Distributed Computing, pp. 163–168 (2006)
20. Garay, J.A., Katz, J., Koo, C.Y., Ostrovsky, R.: Round complexity of authenticated broadcast with a dishonest majority. In: 48th Annual IEEE Symposium on Foundations of Computer Science (FOCS 2007), pp. 658–668. IEEE (2007)
21. Katz, J., Koo, C.-Y.: On expected constant-round protocols for byzantine agreement. In: Dwork, C. (ed.) CRYPTO 2006. LNCS, vol. 4117, pp. 445–462. Springer, Heidelberg (2006). https://doi.org/10.1007/11818175_27
22. Lindell, Y., Lysyanskaya, A., Rabin, T.: Sequential composition of protocols without simultaneous termination. In: Proceedings of the Twenty-First Annual Symposium on Principles of Distributed Computing, pp. 203–212 (2002)
23. Loss, J., Moran, T.: Combining asynchronous and synchronous byzantine agreement: the best of both worlds. In: Cryptology ePrint Archive (2018)
24. Lu, Y., Lu, Z., Tang, Q., Wang, G.: Dumbo-MVBA: optimal multi-valued validated asynchronous byzantine agreement, revisited. In: Proceedings of the 39th Symposium on Principles of Distributed Computing, pp. 129–138 (2020)
25. Merkle, R.C.: A digital signature based on a conventional encryption function. Pomerance, C. (eds) Advances in Cryptology — CRYPTO 1987. Conference on the Theory and Application of Cryptographic Techniques, pp. 369–378. Springer (1987). https://doi.org/10.1007/3-540-48184-2_32
26. Nayak, K., Ren, L., Shi, E., Vaidya, N.H., Xiang, Z.: Improved extension protocols for byzantine broadcast and agreement. In: 34th International Symposium on Distributed Computing (DISC 2020). Schloss Dagstuhl-Leibniz-Zentrum für Informatik (2020)
27. Nguyen, L.: Accumulators from bilinear pairings and applications. In: Menezes, A. (ed.) CT-RSA 2005. LNCS, vol. 3376, pp. 275–292. Springer, Heidelberg (2005). https://doi.org/10.1007/978-3-540-30574-3_19
28. Pease, M., Shostak, R., Lamport, L.: Reaching agreement in the presence of faults. J. ACM (JACM) **27**(2), 228–234 (1980)
29. Reed, I.S., Solomon, G.: Polynomial codes over certain finite fields. J. Soc. Ind. Appl. Math. **8**(2), 300–304 (1960)
30. Shrestha, N., Abraham, I., Nayak, K.: Communication and round efficient parallel broadcast protocols. Cryptology ePrint Archive, Paper 2023/1172 (2023)

31. Shrestha, N., Bhat, A., Kate, A., Nayak, K.: Synchronous distributed key generation without broadcasts. In: IACR Communications in Cryptology, vol. 1, no. 2 (2024)
32. Tsimos, G., Loss, J., Papamanthou, C.: Gossiping for communication-efficient broadcast. In: Dodis, Y., Shrimpton, T. (eds.) Advances in Cryptology–CRYPTO 2022: 42nd Annual International Cryptology Conference, CRYPTO 2022, Santa Barbara, CA, USA, 15–18 August 2022, Proceedings, Part III, pp. 439–469. Springer (2022). https://doi.org/10.1007/978-3-031-15982-4_15

Towards Optimal Parallel Broadcast Under a Dishonest Majority

Daniel Collins[1], Sisi Duan[2(✉)], Julian Loss[3], Charalampos Papamanthou[4], Giorgos Tsimos[5], and Haochen Wang[6(✉)]

[1] Texas A&M University, College Station, USA
[2] Tsinghua University and State Key Laboratory of Cryptography and Digital Economy Security, Beijing, China
duansisi@tsinghua.edu.cn
[3] CISPA Helmholtz Center for Information Security, Saarbrücken, Germany
[4] Yale University, New Haven, USA
charalampos.papamanthou@yale.edu
[5] University of Maryland, College Park, USA
tsimos@umd.edu
[6] Tsinghua University, Beijing, China
whc20@mails.tsinghua.edu.cn

Abstract. The parallel broadcast (PBC) problem generalizes the classic Byzantine broadcast problem to the setting where all n nodes broadcast a message and deliver $O(n)$ messages. PBC arises naturally in many settings including multi-party computation. The state-of-the-art PBC protocol, TRUSTEDPBC, is due to Tsimos, Loss, and Papamanthou (CRYPTO 2022), which is secure under an adaptive adversary assuming $f < (1-\epsilon)n$, where f is the number of Byzantine failures and $\epsilon \in (0,1)$. TRUSTEDPBC focuses on single-bit inputs and achieves $\tilde{O}(n^2\kappa^4)$ communication and $O(\kappa \log n)$ rounds.

In this work, we propose three PBC protocols for L-bit messages, for any size L, that significantly improve TRUSTEDPBC. First, we propose a new extension protocol that uses a κ-bit PBC as a black box and achieves i) communication complexity of $O(Ln^2 + n^3\kappa + \mathcal{P}(\kappa))$, where $\mathcal{P}(\kappa)$ is the communication complexity of the κ-bit PBC, and ii) round complexity same as the κ-bit PBC. By comparison, the state-of-the-art extension protocol for regular broadcast (Nayak et al., DISC 2020) incurs $O(n)$ additional rounds of communication. Next, we propose a protocol that is secure against a static adversary, for κ-bit messages with $O(n^2\kappa^{1+K} + n\kappa^3 + \kappa^4)$ communication and $O(\kappa)$ round complexity, where K is an arbitrarily small constant such that $0 < K < 1$. Finally, we propose an adaptively-secure protocol for κ-bit messages with $\tilde{O}(n^2\kappa^2 + n\kappa^3)$ communication overhead and $O(\kappa \log n)$ round complexity. Notably, our latter two protocols are $\tilde{O}(\kappa^{2-K})$ and $O(\kappa^2)$ times more communication-efficient, respectively, than the state-of-the-art protocols while achieving the same round complexity.

1 Introduction

Byzantine broadcast (BC) is a fundamental primitive for many cryptographic protocols and distributed systems. The goal of BC is to allow a designated sender to distribute its input value such that all honest nodes output the same value, even if a fraction of Byzantine nodes (including, potentially, the sender) fail arbitrarily. In spite of a large body of work studying broadcast with a single sender, in many applications such as multi-party computation (MPC) and verifiable secret sharing (VSS) broadcast is most commonly required *in parallel*, i.e., with every sender broadcasting simultaneously.

Table 1. Comparison of the PBC protocols where honest nodes broadcast messages length $\leq |m|$. ‡PBC that runs n parallel instances. ⋆The assumptions (*bulletin* board PKI, *trusted* PKI and/or structured reference string (SRS)) and the adversarial model (*static or adaptive*) depend on the underlying κ-bit PBC oracle. $\mathcal{P}(x)$ is the communication complexity of x-bit PBC, and $\mathcal{T}(\kappa)$ is the round complexity of κ-bit PBC. K is an arbitrarily small constant such that $0 < K < 1$. $\tilde{O}(f(n))$ indicates that the complexity of an algorithm is $O(f(n) \cdot \text{poly}(\log n))$ for some polynomial poly. $\mathbf{C}$ captures practical settings where $\mathbf{C} = O(n) \approx O(\kappa)$.

$|m|$	Protocol	Model	Adv.	$f <$	Communication	Rounds
1	BULLETINBC‡ [20]	bulletin	static	$(1-\epsilon)n$	$\tilde{O}(n^3\kappa^2)\ (=\tilde{O}(\mathbf{C}^5))$	$O(n)$
	FLOODBC‡ [6]	trusted	static	$(1-\epsilon)n$	$\tilde{O}(n^2\kappa^3)\ (=\tilde{O}(\mathbf{C}^5))$	$O(\kappa)$
	BULLETINPBC [20]	bulletin	adaptive	$(1-\epsilon)n$	$\tilde{O}(n^3\kappa^2)\ (=\tilde{O}(\mathbf{C}^5))$	$O(n \log n)$
	TRUSTEDPBC [20]	trusted	adaptive	$(1-\epsilon)n$	$\tilde{O}(n^2\kappa^4)\ (=\tilde{O}(\mathbf{C}^6))$	$O(\kappa \log n)$
	PBC$_1^{\text{static}}$ (§4)	trusted	static	$(1-\epsilon)n$	$O(n^2\kappa^{1+K} + n\kappa^3 + \kappa^4) = O(\mathbf{C}^4)$	$O(\kappa)$
	PBC$_1^{\text{adaptive}}$ (§5)	trusted	adaptive	$(1-\epsilon)n$	$\tilde{O}(n^2\kappa^2 + n\kappa^3) = \tilde{O}(\mathbf{C}^4)$	$O(\kappa \log n)$
L	ANS [3]	trusted	adaptive	$n/2$	$O(n^2L + n^3\kappa) = O(\mathbf{C}^2L + \mathbf{C}^4)$	$O(1)$
	NRSVX [19]	⋆	⋆	$(1-\epsilon)n$	$O(n^2L + \mathcal{P}(\kappa) + n^3\kappa + n^4)$ $(= O(\mathbf{C}^2L + \mathcal{P}(\mathbf{C}) + \mathbf{C}^4))$	$O(n)$
	TLP [20]	trusted	adaptive	$(1-\epsilon)n$	$\tilde{O}(n^2\kappa^4L)(=\tilde{O}(\mathbf{C}^6L))$	$O(\kappa \log n)$
	AC [5]	trusted	static	$n/3$	$O(n^2L + n^3\log^2 n)$ $(= O(\mathbf{C}^2L) + \tilde{O}(\mathbf{C}^3))$	$O(1)$
	PBC$_L^\star$ (§3)	SRS+⋆	⋆	$(1-\epsilon)n$	$O(n^2L + n^3\kappa + \mathcal{P}(\kappa))$ $(= O(\mathbf{C}^2L + \mathcal{P}(\mathbf{C}) + \mathbf{C}^4))$	$O(\mathcal{T}(\kappa))$
	PBC$_L^{\text{static}}$ (§3 & §4)	trusted	static	$(1-\epsilon)n$	$O(n^2L + n^3\kappa + n^2\kappa^{1+K} + n\kappa^3 + \kappa^4)$ $(= O(\mathbf{C}^2L + \mathbf{C}^4))$	$O(\kappa)$
	PBC$_L^{\text{adaptive}}$ (§3 & §5)	trusted	adaptive	$(1-\epsilon)n$	$O(n^2L + n^3\kappa) + \tilde{O}(n^2\kappa^2 + n\kappa^3)$ $(= O(\mathbf{C}^2L) + \tilde{O}(\mathbf{C}^4))$	$O(\kappa \log n)$

Motivated by this observation, Tsimos, Loss, and Papamanthou [20] gave an efficient designated parallel broadcast (PBC) protocol under dishonest majority, TRUSTEDPBC. Denoting n as the number of nodes and κ as the length of a signature, TRUSTEDPBC achieves $\tilde{O}(n^2\kappa^4)$ communication against up to $f < (1-\epsilon)n$ adaptive and malicious corruptions (for some $0 < \epsilon < 1$) under the assumption of a trusted PKI. Compared to naively running n parallel BC instances, TRUSTEDPBC improved substantially the communication with respect to n. While TRUSTEDPBC already achieves improved communication, its communication is still high, especially when n and κ are close. Additionally, TRUSTEDPBC is limited to single-bit inputs.

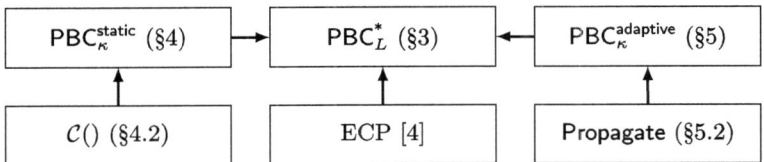

Fig. 1. Overview of our results.

Our Contributions. In this work, we study PBC with L-bit inputs in the synchronous setting assuming $f < (1-\epsilon)n$ where $0 < \epsilon < 1$. The single-bit variants of our PBC protocols simply follow, which also enjoy improved communication. We consider both the static and weakly adaptive adversarial models (adaptive for short). As summarized in Table 1 and Fig. 1, we provide three protocols with improved communication: a new extension protocol PBC_L^* that achieves both improved communication and round; a κ-bit PBC $\text{PBC}_\kappa^{\text{static}}$ in the static adversary model that achieves improved communication and round; a κ-bit PBC $\text{PBC}_\kappa^{\text{adaptive}}$ with improved communication in the adaptive adversary model. Our solutions do not trade factors of κ for factors in n and solely decrease factors in κ.

We begin with a new extension protocol for PBC, PBC_L^*, that reduces the L-bit PBC problem to a κ-bit PBC oracle. Compared to prior extension protocols, e.g., running n BC instances of the protocol of Nayak, Ren, Shi, Vaidya, and Xiang (NRSVX) [19], PBC_L^* achieves both improved communication and round complexity. The adversarial assumption of PBC_L^* depends on the underlying κ-bit PBC oracle. In particular, if the κ-bit PBC is adaptively secure, then so is PBC_L^*.

We then present $\text{PBC}_\kappa^{\text{static}}$, a κ-bit PBC protocol in the static adversarial setting. $\text{PBC}_\kappa^{\text{static}}$ can be generalized to L-bit PBC. However, using it as a κ-bit PBC in our extension protocol results in a more communication-efficient PBC. Compared to the state-of-the-art protocols BULLETINBC [20] and FLOODBC [6], $\text{PBC}_\kappa^{\text{static}}$ enjoys substantially improved communication complexity and the same or better round complexity. The core idea is to reduce the problem of PBC among n nodes to L-bit PBC among a small committee of κ nodes. Based on the most optimal constructions known so far for L-bit PBC, $\text{PBC}_\kappa^{\text{static}}$ achieves $O(n^2\kappa^{1+K} + n\kappa^3 + \kappa^4)$ communication and $O(\kappa)$ rounds for κ-bit broadcast, where K is an arbitrarily small constant such that $0 < K < 1$.

Finally, we present $\text{PBC}_\kappa^{\text{adaptive}}$, a κ-bit PBC protocol secure under an adaptive adversary. Our starting point for building PBC under an adaptive adversary is TRUSTEDPBC of Tsimos et al. [20], the most efficient 1-bit PBC protocol known so far that achieves $\tilde{O}(n^2\kappa^4)$ communication. We first construct a κ-bit PBC with $O((n^2\kappa^2 + n\kappa^3) \cdot \log^2 n)$ communication, a $O(\kappa^3)$ improvement over that of TRUSTEDPBC for κ-sized messages. Similarly to $\mathsf{PBC}_\kappa^{\mathsf{static}}$, we can use $\mathsf{PBC}_\kappa^{\mathsf{adaptive}}$ as a κ-bit PBC oracle in our extension protocol to obtain a more communication-efficient L-bit PBC.

2 Preliminaries

Model. We consider a system with n nodes $\{P_1, \cdots, P_n\}$, running over authenticated channels. Among the n nodes, f of them may become Byzantine and fail arbitrarily. We assume $f < (1-\epsilon)n$, where ϵ is a constant and $0 < \epsilon < 1$. Nodes that are not Byzantine are called *honest*. We consider a synchronous network, where there exists an upper bound on the network and message processing delay.

We consider both the static and the adaptive adversary models. In the static model, the adversary corrupts nodes prior to the start of the protocol. In the adaptive model, the adversary can choose the set of corrupted nodes at any moment during the execution of the protocol based on its current state. In this work, we focus on the weakly adaptive adversary model, where the adversary cannot perform "after-the-fact-removal" and retroactively erase the messages the node sent before they become corrupted. Additionally, we restrict the adversary by assuming *atomic sends* [7] where an honest node P_i can send to multiple nodes simultaneously, without the adversary being able to corrupt P_i in between sending to two nodes.

We assume a trusted setup unless otherwise specified, where a trusted party generates and distributes keys to the nodes prior to the protocol execution.

Normalizing Security Parameters. Let κ denote the cryptographic security parameter, i.e., the length of hashes or digital signatures. In this work, we also use λ as the statistical parameter. We may consider $\lambda = O(\kappa)$, as typically $\lambda < \kappa$. We can also say that the security parameter of the system is the maximum of λ and the cryptographic security parameter (e.g., length of digital signatures). When we discuss the concrete complexities in the main body of the paper, we differentiate λ and κ. Also note that κ and λ are independent of n and we usually assume $n \gg \kappa$ and $n \gg \lambda$. In Table 1, we provide **C** assuming $O(n) \approx O(\kappa) \approx O(\lambda)$ for the ease of understanding.

2.1 Definitions

Parallel Broadcast (PBC). In a system with n nodes $\{P_1, \cdots, P_n\}$, PBC executes n parallel BC, where each node P_i provides an input v_i and outputs an n-value vector $\boldsymbol{v}_i$. Each slot s in $\boldsymbol{v}_i$ is dedicated for the value broadcast by P_s, the output of which is denoted as $\boldsymbol{v}_i[s]$. In this work, we study PBC with both 1-bit inputs and L-bit inputs where $L > 1$.

Definition 1 (f-Secure Parallel Broadcast). *Let Π be a protocol executed by nodes $\{P_1, \cdots, P_n\}$, where each node P_i holds an input v_i and each node outputs a n-size vector $\boldsymbol{v}_i$. Π should achieve the following properties with probability $1 - \mathsf{negl}(\kappa)$ whenever at most f nodes are corrupted.*

- f-**Validity**: If P_s is honest, the output $\boldsymbol{v}_i$ at any honest node P_i satisfies $\boldsymbol{v}_i[s] = v_s$.
- f-**Consistency**: All honest nodes output the same vector $\boldsymbol{v}'$.

We will need an *external validity* property for some of our constructions defined as follows. There exists a predicate $Q()$ known by all nodes. Given a value v, every node can query $Q(v)$ to validate v. In the literature, the value v can be validated by via some additional data such as digital signatures [9]. Alternatively, v can be validated according to the local state of some nodes [1,13]. In this case, we may call the predicate a *locally validated predicate*. We use the state-based predicate in this paper.

Initialization:
- Mining probability p_{mine}.
- Let $call_i \leftarrow \bot$ for any $i \in [n]$

On input $\mathcal{F}_{mine}(\text{type}, val, i)$ from node P_i:
- If $call_i = \bot$, output $\mathbf{b} = 1$ with probability p_{mine}, or $\mathbf{b} = 0$ with probability $1 - p_{mine}$ and set $call_i = \mathbf{b}$.
- Else output $call_i$.

On input $\mathcal{F}_{mine}.\text{verify}(\text{type}, val, j)$ from node P_i:
- If $call_j = 1$, output 1, otherwise output 0.

Fig. 2. Functionality $\mathcal{F}_{mine}$ val can be $\bot$ or consists of multiple values.

- f-**External validity**: Given a predicate Q, any honest node P_i that terminates outputs a value $\boldsymbol{v}_i$ such that for each $\boldsymbol{v}_i[s] \neq \bot$, $Q(\boldsymbol{v}_i[s])$ holds by at least one honest node.

Protocol Naming Convention PBC_x^y. To differentiate the protocols we study in this paper, we use the PBC_x^y to denote a PBC protocol where each node provides an x-size input that is secure secure under y model. For example, $\text{PBC}_1^{\text{static}}$ denotes a 1-bit PBC assuming a static adversary.

2.2 Building Blocks

We review the building blocks. Due to space limitations, we provide detailed definitions and descriptions where relevant in our full paper.

Aggregate Signatures. We assume recursively combinable aggregate signatures of size $O(\kappa + S \log n)$ when signed by S nodes or $O(\kappa + n)$ using a bitmask, e.g., using BLS signatures based on pairings in the random oracle model [8] or a signature scheme and generic zero-knowledge proofs.

The $\mathcal{F}_{mine}$ oracle. We follow prior work [2,11,20] and define the $\mathcal{F}_{mine}$ ideal functionality that we use for random committee selection. $\mathcal{F}_{mine}$ is parameterised by the total number of nodes and a *mining* probability p_{mine}. $\mathcal{F}_{mine}$ provides two interfaces: $\mathcal{F}_{mine}$ and $\mathcal{F}_{mine}$.verify(), as illustrated in Fig. 2. For our static PBC, this can be implemented by nodes multicasting $O(\kappa)$-sized proofs using an SRS [2,14]. For our adaptive PBC, we assume generic zero-knowledge proofs for composing signature aggregation and $\mathcal{F}_{mine}$ proofs (or for our protocols, proving committee membership), which also can be instantiated using an SRS [14].

Erasure Codes. An (m,n) erasure coding scheme over a data block M is specified by two algorithms (encode, decode). The encode algorithm takes as input m data fragments of M, and outputs $n > m$ coded fragments. The decode algorithm takes as input any m-size subset coded fragments and outputs the original data block containing m data fragments. Namely, if $\boldsymbol{d} \leftarrow \text{encode}(M)$ and $\boldsymbol{d} = [d_1, \ldots, d_n]$, then $\text{decode}(d_{i_1}, \ldots, d_{i_m}) = M$ for any distinct $i_1, \ldots, i_m \in [1..n]$.

Erasure Coding Proof (ECP) System. The idea of ECP [4] is to allow the encoder to prove succinctly and non-interactively that an erasure-coded fragment is consistent with a commitment to the original data block. Consider an (m,n) erasure code that encodes a message M into a set of n fragments $d_1, d_2, \cdots, d_n$. An ECP system is designed to allow for efficient dispersal of these fragments. A proof contains two parts: a constant-sized commitment ϕ plus a per-node witness π_i that is around size $O(|M|/m + \kappa)$. Together, ϕ and π_i convince node P_i that d_i is the correct data fragment for the message committed to by ϕ. An ECP system consists of three algorithms:

- **setup.** The **setup** algorithm receives a security parameter κ and sets up the system parameters pp.
- **prove$_{pp}$.** The **prove$_{pp}$** algorithm takes as input a block of data M and outputs $(\phi, \boldsymbol{d}, \boldsymbol{\pi})$ where $|\boldsymbol{d}| = |\boldsymbol{\pi}| = n$. Here, ϕ is a (computationally) binding commitment to all erasure-coded fragments $\boldsymbol{d} \leftarrow \text{encode}(M)$, and each π_i is intended to serve as a proof that the corresponding d_i is the i-th data fragment with respect to the commitment ϕ.
- **verify$_{pp}$.** The **verify$_{pp}$** algorithm takes as input (ϕ, d_i, π_i) and outputs a bit. If $\text{verify}_{pp}(\phi, d_i, \pi_i) = 1$, then we say d_i is a valid fragment w.r.t. ϕ.

A secure ECP system achieves *EC-correctness* and *EC-consistency*. We use ECP-1 in this work, one of the two constructions provided in the paper. Under the trusted setup assumption (relying on a trusted setup to generate a powers-of-tau structured reference string [15] or SRS hereafter) and when the data block is of at least length $O(\kappa)$, the size of the witness has the same length as each data fragment.

Forward-Secure Public-Key Encryption (FS-PKE). A forward-secure public-key encryption scheme [10], or FS-PKE, is a probabilistic public-key cryptosystem that additionally allows the secret key to be updated such that previous keys and encrypted plaintexts cannot be derived from an updated key. It consists of algorithms **gen, enc, dec** and **upd**, the first three as in standard PKE, and the last updating the secret key into a new *epoch*. We require an appropriate IND-CCA security notion where a challenge is made in epoch j, and the adversary has access to the secret key in any epoch $i > j$. FS-PKE can be implemented using pairings with $O(\kappa \log E)$-sized keys and constant-sized ciphertexts to support E epochs [10].

3 PBC_L^*: An Extension Protocol for L-bit PBC

3.1 Technical Overview

We present a new extension protocol for L-bit PBC. PBC_L^* reduces L-bit PBC to a κ-bit PBC PBC_κ^* and uses an ECP system. We only require that the κ-bit PBC protocol is transformed into a *validated* PBC by adding a locally validated predicate to PBC_κ^*. We show that such a validated PBC can be easily achieved in our protocol (cf. Lemma 1). As described above, ECP works like an accumulator scheme for erasure coding and can be used to determine if a given fragment corresponds to the original data block. Our extension protocol achieves improved communication compared to prior extension protocols. Additionally, the round complexity remains essentially the same as the κ-bit PBC, incurring three extra rounds of communication. In contrast, the most communication-efficient extension protocol known so far (for BC rather than PBC) [19] incurs $O(n)$ rounds on top of the underlying κ-bit EC oracle.

Global Parameters:
 - M_i is the input of P_i. $\text{ExtractedSet}_i \leftarrow [\emptyset]^n$.

Phase 1:
Every node P_i performs the following:
 - $\text{ExtractedSet}_i^i \leftarrow M_i$. $(\phi_i, \mathbf{d}^i, \boldsymbol{\pi}^i) \leftarrow \mathbf{prove}_{\text{pp}}(M_i)$.
 - Send $(\textsc{Disseminate}, M_i)$ to all nodes.
 - Query PBC_κ^* with predicate Q and use ϕ_i as input.

Phase 2:
 - Upon output ϕ_j for slot j in PBC_κ^*
   - If P_i has previously received $(\textsc{Disseminate}, M_j)$ from P_j
     - $(\phi', \mathbf{d}, \boldsymbol{\pi}) \leftarrow \mathbf{prove}_{\text{pp}}(M_j)$.
     - If $\phi' = \phi_j$,
       - For $\ell = 1, 2, \cdots, n$,
         - Send $(\textsc{Send}, d_\ell, \pi_\ell)$ to P_ℓ.
 - Upon receiving $(\textsc{Send}, d_i, \pi_i)$ from P_ℓ,
   - If $\mathbf{verify}_{\text{pp}}(\phi_j, d_i, \pi_i) = 1$, fix d_i^* as d_i and send $(\textsc{Echo}, d_i^*, \pi_i)$ to all nodes.
 - Upon receiving $(\textsc{Echo}, d_\ell, \pi_\ell)$ from P_ℓ,
   - If $\mathbf{verify}_{\text{pp}}(\phi_j, d_\ell^*, \pi_\ell) = 1$, $B_j.\text{add}(d_\ell^*)$.
 - Upon $|B_j| \geq n - f$, set $M_j \leftarrow \text{decode}(B_j)$ and $\text{ExtractedSet}_i^j \leftarrow M_j$
 - Output ExtractedSet_i

Fig. 3. The PBC_L^* protocol. Q is the locally validated-predicate evaluated within PBC_κ^* defined as follows: $Q(\phi_i)$ is valid for a node P_j if, during execution, P_j has previously received M_i from P_i such that for $(\phi, \mathbf{d}, \boldsymbol{\pi}) \leftarrow \mathbf{prove}(M_i)$ it holds that $\phi_i = \phi$.

Our extension protocol is secure under an adaptive adversary, as long as PBC^*_κ is adaptively secure. The same paradigm can also be extended to obtain a communication-efficient L-bit extension protocol for (non-parallel) BC.

3.2 The Extension Protocol

The pseudocode of our extension protocol is shown in Fig. 3. Briefly speaking, each node first disseminates its input to all nodes. Then, it queries PBC^*_κ and uses the ECP commitment ϕ_i as the input. The predicate we add to PBC^*_κ ensures that if PBC^*_κ completes, at least one honest node holds M_i. Finally, after PBC^*_κ outputs some value, nodes reconstruct the data via two communication rounds.

It is worth mentioning that in our construction, we view ECP as a tailored and computation-efficient *proof* that proves the correctness of the encoding function of erasure coding. There exists more generic approach that achieves the same communication complexity as our approach, e.g., using zero knowledge proofs [12] to prove the correctness of the encoding function.

Our protocol has the following properties. Note that proofs of claims made hereafter are available in the full version of this work.

Lemma 1. *The PBC^*_κ protocol with predicate Q satisfies f-external validity.*

Theorem 1. *Assuming an SRS, the PBC^*_L protocol presented in Fig. 3 satisfies f-validity and f-consistency with probability $1 - \mathsf{negl}(\lambda)$.*

Theorem 2. *The PBC^*_L protocol achieves $O(n^2 L + n^3 \kappa + \mathcal{P}(\kappa))$ communication and the round complexity is asymptotically the same as PBC^*_κ, where $\mathcal{P}(\kappa)$ is the communication complexity of PBC^*_κ.*

4 $\mathsf{PBC}^{\mathsf{static}}_\kappa$: Efficient PBC under a Static Adversary

4.1 Technical Overview

We present $\mathsf{PBC}^{\mathsf{static}}_\kappa$, a two-layer protocol that reduces the PBC problem to best effort broadcast and a $\mathcal{C}()$ protocol among λ committee members. Although $\mathsf{PBC}^{\mathsf{static}}_\kappa$ itself can clearly be generalized to an L-bit PBC, we obtain a more efficient L-bit PBC integrating $\mathsf{PBC}^{\mathsf{static}}_\kappa$ with our extension protocol.

Our motivation is a tempting solution for committee sampling based protocols: the committee members can *reach an agreement* on some value and then convey the results to all nodes. While this is feasible for a system in the honest majority setting [2,16–18], there is no straightforward way to properly convey the results under a corrupt majority, an observation also made in prior works [11,21].

Our $\mathsf{PBC}^{\mathsf{static}}_\kappa$ protocol makes the above tempting solution work under a corrupt majority. We use a reduction from PBC to a so-called $\mathcal{C}()$ protocol, among $\lambda = O(\kappa)$ committee members. By carefully defining the security properties of $\mathcal{C}()$ and building an efficient construction from L-bit PBC among λ committee members, we ensure that if an honest committee member sees some value output by $\mathcal{C}()$ for the first time, so does any other honest committee member. Accordingly, the maximum number of interactions between an honest node and committee members is bounded by a constant. In particular, $\mathcal{C}()$ takes as input a vector of sets of 'valid' (defined below) messages, and outputs a vector of sets corresponding to the union of valid messages that were input.

Briefly speaking, our protocol roughly works as follows. Each node first disseminates its input to all nodes. Then they proceed in a constant number of rounds. In each round, every node first sends its current received values to the committees. Then, the committees query the $\mathcal{C}()$ protocol. After $\mathcal{C}()$ terminates, committee members create signatures for the values they have seen and send them to all nodes. Finally, nodes merge the signatures they receive. At the end of the protocols, for each P_s, every honest node P_i delivers some value from P_s only after P_i has received a sufficiently large number of signatures from the committee.

4.2 The $\mathcal{C}()$ Protocol

To achieve the goals mentioned above, the input of $\mathcal{C}()$ needs to be *validated* and the output needs to be *verifiable* [9]. For the protocol to be validated, the input message M must satisfy a global predicate. In our case, for M to be validated, it must consist of n vectors of valid $(r-1)$-s batches, as defined below. For the protocol to be verifiable, the output message, once sent to an honest node, should also be a valid $(r-1)$-s batches.

In our PBC protocol, each committee member P_i receives M_j from each node P_j, where $j \in [n] = \{1, 2, \cdots, n\}$ and M_j is an n-value vector in the form of $[M_j^1, \cdots, M_j^n]$. Each M_j^k is either $\bot$ or consists of up to two valid $(r-1)$-s batches. To facilitate the exposition of our protocol, we provide some definitions.

Definition 2. (Valid r-s batch). *A valid r-s batch on a message/slot pair (u, s) for (some round) $r \geq 0$ is in the form of $u||s||SIG_r$, where $u \in \{0,1\}^L$, $s \in [n]$, and SIG_r is a set of signatures that contains one signature from P_s and $\frac{3r(\epsilon-\mu)(1-\epsilon)}{\mu^2} \log \frac{1}{\delta}$ signatures on $[u,s]$ from members in the committee, where μ is a small constant such that $0 < \mu < \epsilon$ and δ is the desired failure probability.*

Definition 3 (Valid tuple for round r). *A valid tuple M_i for round $r \geq 1$ is in the form of $[M_i^1, \cdots, M_i^n]$ where each M_i^j is either $\bot$, or consists of at most two valid $(r-1)$-s batches, one for a pair (u, j) and one for a pair (u', j).*

We now specify the input and output of the $\mathcal{C}()$ protocol as follows. In some round r, the input of each node P_i for the $\mathcal{C}()$ protocol is M which consists of up to n vectors $\{M_1, \cdots, M_n\}$. Any $M_j \in M$ is sent by node P_j. Each M_j is validated if it is a valid tuple for round r. After running the $\mathcal{C}()$ protocol, each honest committee member P_i outputs an n-value vector Merged_i. Merged_i is verified if it is a valid tuple for round r. An interesting finding is that we can build $\mathcal{C}()$ from a κ-bit PBC among λ committee members.

Definition 4 (*t*-Secure $\mathcal{C}()$). *Let $\mathcal{C}()$ be a protocol executed by c nodes $\{P_1, \cdots, P_c\}$, as specified above. $\mathcal{C}()$ should satisfy the following properties for some round r with probability $1 - \mathsf{negl}(\kappa)$ whenever at most t nodes are corrupted.*

- *t-**Validity**: If an honest node P_i provides $\boldsymbol{M}$ as input, any valid tuple $M_j \in \boldsymbol{M}$ for some round r is part of Merged_k for any honest node P_k in this round.*
- *t-**Consistency**: For each slot $s \in [n]$, if an honest node P_i outputs Merged_i^s, another honest node P_j outputs Merged_j^s, $\mathsf{Merged}_i^s = \mathsf{Merged}_j^s$.*

4.3 The $\mathsf{PBC}_\kappa^{\mathsf{static}}$ Protocol

We present the workflow of $\mathsf{PBC}_\kappa^{\mathsf{static}}$ in Fig. 5. The protocol is round-based, starting from round 0 to round R where $R = \lceil \frac{(1-\epsilon+\mu)c+1}{(\epsilon-\mu)c} \rceil = O(\frac{1}{\epsilon-\mu})$, i.e., a constant number. Each round consists of three *mini-rounds*, the first and the third using a constant number of message delays, and the second being $\mathcal{C}()$ executed by the committee ($O(\lambda)$ round complexity).

We optimize the 1st mini-round and reduce the communication from $O(n^2\kappa\lambda)$ to $O(n^2\kappa\lambda^K)$, where $0 < K < 1$ via a new sampling protocol. Additionally, using ECP as a building block, we can reduce the communication of the 3rd mini-round from $O(n^2\kappa\lambda)$ to $O(n^2\kappa + n\kappa\lambda)$. We provide a detailed description of the protocol and the optimizations in the full version of this work.

Upon $\mathcal{C}(\boldsymbol{M})$
- Filter any M_j such that M_j is not a valid tuple for round r.
- For each slot $s \in [n]$:
  - $\mathsf{Aggregated}_i^s \leftarrow \cup_{j=1}^n M_j^s$.
- Provide $\mathsf{Aggregated}_i$ as input to a L-bit PBC $\mathsf{PBC}_{L,c}^*$.
- Wait until $\mathsf{PBC}_{L,c}^*$ terminates, let the output be $\boldsymbol{m}$.
- For each slot $s \in [n]$ and for each valid tuple m_j for round r that $m_j \in \boldsymbol{m}$:
  - $\mathsf{Merged}_i^s \leftarrow \cup_j m_j^s$.

Output conditions
- After $\mathsf{PBC}_{L,c}^*$ terminates, return Merged_i.

Fig. 4. The $\mathcal{C}()$ protocol.

Theorem 3. *Assuming a trusted PKI and SRS, $\mathsf{PBC}_\kappa^{\mathsf{static}}$ is an f-Secure Parallel Broadcast protocol with probability $1 - \mathsf{negl}(\lambda)$.*

Theorem 4. *Assuming a trusted PKI and SRS, the $\mathsf{PBC}_\kappa^{\mathsf{static}}$ protocol has $O(\lambda)$ round complexity and $O(n^2\kappa\lambda^K + n\kappa\lambda^2 + \kappa\lambda^3 + \lambda^4)$ communication complexity.*

> **Global Parameters:**
> - Let u_i be the input of P_i. Set $\mathsf{ExtractedSet}_i \leftarrow [\emptyset]^n$ and $\mathsf{VotedSet}_i \leftarrow [\emptyset]^n$.
>
> **Round 0:**
> - $\mathsf{ExtractedSet}_i^i \leftarrow u_i$. Send $(\textsc{Sign}, u_i, \sigma_i)$ to all where σ_i is a signature on $[u_i, i]$.
> - Upon receiving a $(\textsc{Sign}, u_j, \sigma_j)$ from P_j, add σ_j to $\mathsf{Received}_i^j$.
> - Query $b \leftarrow \mathcal{F}_{mine}(\text{static}, i)$, if $b = 1$, broadcast $(\textsc{Com}, i)$ to all nodes.
> - Upon receiving $(\textsc{Com}, j)$ s.t. $\mathcal{F}_{mine}.\text{verify}(\text{static}, j) = 1$, add P_j to committee.
>
> **Round** $r = 1, \cdots, R$: each round has three mini-rounds.
>
> **1st mini-round:** Every node P_i performs the following:
> - Send $(\textsc{Echo}, \mathsf{Received}_i)$ to all committee members
> - Upon receiving $(\textsc{Echo}, \mathsf{Received}_j)$ from P_j, $M[j] \leftarrow \mathsf{Received}_j$.
>
> **2nd mini-round:** Every committee member queries $\mathcal{C}(M)$ and obtains Merged_i.
>
> **3rd mini-round:** Set $\mathsf{Received}_i \leftarrow [\bot]^n$. For each $s \in [n]$:
> Every committee member P_i performs the following:
> - Send $(\textsc{Send}, \mathsf{Merged}_i)$ to all.
> - If a valid $(r-1)$-s batch on $[u_i^s, s]$ is included in Merged_i^s but $u_i^s \notin \mathsf{VotedSet}_i^s$:
>   - Set $\mathsf{VotedSet}_i^s \leftarrow \mathsf{VotedSet}_i^s \cup u_i^s$, create a signature for $[u_i^s, s]$ and send to all.
> - If at least two valid $(r-1)$-s batches on different pairs $[u_i^s, s]$ and $[v_i^s, s]$ are included in Merged_i^s and $u_i^s, v_i^s \notin \mathsf{VotedSet}_i^s$:
>   - Extract the first two of valid $(r-1)$-s batches and send to all.
>
> For every node P_i, upon receiving valid $(\textsc{Send}, \mathsf{Merged}_j)$
> - Merge the $(r-1)$-s batches from the $(\textsc{Send})$ messages into an n-value vector $\mathsf{Received}_i$ s.t. each $\mathsf{Received}_i^s$ contains at most two valid r-s batches.
> - If there exists u_j^s s.t. a valid r-s batch for $[u_j^s, s]$ is included in $\mathsf{Received}_j^s$ and $u_j^s \notin \mathsf{ExtractedSet}_i^s$ and $|\mathsf{ExtractedSet}_i^s| < 2$, $\mathsf{ExtractedSet}_i^s \leftarrow \mathsf{ExtractedSet}_i^s \cup u_j^s$.
>
> **Output conditions.** At the end of round R, for each slot $s \in [n]$:
> (Event 1) If $|\mathsf{ExtractedSet}_i^s| = 1$ and $\mathsf{ExtractedSet}_i^s = \{u\}$, $v_i[s] \leftarrow u$.
> (Event 2) If $|\mathsf{ExtractedSet}_i^s| = 0$ or 2, $v_i[s] \leftarrow \bot$.
> - Output v_i.

Fig. 5. The $\mathsf{PBC}_\kappa^{\text{static}}$ protocol. $R = \lceil \frac{(1-\epsilon+\mu)c+1}{(\epsilon-\mu)c} \rceil$.

5 $\mathsf{PBC}_\kappa^{\text{adaptive}}$: Efficient PBC under an Adaptive Adversary

We present our adaptively-secure PBC protocol that, for κ-sized messages, has a communication complexity of $\tilde{O}(n^2\kappa^2 + n\kappa^3)$ given $\kappa = O(\lambda)$, or in general $\tilde{O}(n^2\kappa\lambda + n^2\lambda^2 + n\kappa\lambda^2 + n\lambda^3)$. By direct application of our adaptive extension protocol PBC_L^* from §3, we obtain an L-bit protocol with a communication complexity of $O(n^2 L + n^3\kappa) + \tilde{O}(n^2\kappa^2 + n\kappa^3)$ bits.

5.1 Review of TrustedPBC

We briefly review TRUSTEDPBC [20], our starting point of $\mathsf{PBC}_\kappa^{\text{adaptive}}$. Every node P_i holds a bit b_i as input and outputs a vector of values v_i. For each bit b_j and slot j, r signatures on $[b_j, j]$ (including one from P_j) from the committee members are collectively called a valid r-batch on $[b_j, j]$. The protocol is round-based and proceeds as follows.

- In round $r = 1$, every node P_i creates a signature for $[b_i, i]$ and sends to all nodes. Each node now holds a vector of valid 1-batches, denoted as M_i, which continues to be updated throughout the protocol.
- In rounds $r = 2, \cdots, 2\kappa/\epsilon$, there are two mini-rounds in each round.
    - In the first mini-round, each node P_i executes a $\mathcal{M}$-DistinctConverge protocol, the idea being for honest nodes to disseminate their received valid r-batches to all other nodes. Their implementation of $\mathcal{M}$-DistinctConverge uses $\tilde{O}(n^2\kappa^3)$ total communication and $\lceil \log(\epsilon \cdot n) \rceil$ rounds. It is an iterative gossiping protocol, where each step a node sends each message it propagates to $O(\kappa)$ other nodes, where the number of nodes that has seen a given message doubles each round (thus converging in a logarithmic number of rounds).
    - In the second mini-round, whenever an honest committee member P_i observes a valid r-batch in M_i for the first time for slot j, it creates a digital signature for $[b_j, j]$, appends the signature to the valid r-batch, and sends to all nodes. Upon receiving a valid $(r+1)$-batch on $[b_j, j]$, each node P_i updates its M_i and adds b_j to $\mathsf{ExtractedSet}_i^s$.
- At the end of the protocol, for each slot j, if there is only one value b_j in $\mathsf{ExtractedSet}_i^j$, P_i sets $v_i[j]$ as b_j. Otherwise, P_i sets $v_i[j]$ as a canonical bit $\bot$. Finally, P_i outputs the vector v_i.

5.2 An Improved $\mathcal{M}$-DistinctConverge Protocol

Towards describing our protocol, we first formally define the aforementioned $\mathcal{M}$-DistinctConverge problem below.

Definition 5 (distinct$_k$ function). *For any set M, $\mathtt{distinct}_k(M)$ is a subset of M that contains all messages in M with distinct k-bit prefixes.*[1]

Definition 6 (t-secure $\mathcal{M}$-DistinctConverge protocol). *Let $\mathcal{M} \subseteq \{0,1\}^*$ be an efficiently recognizable set. A protocol Π executed by n nodes, where every honest node P_i initially holds input set $M_i \subseteq \mathcal{M}$ and constraint set $C_i \subseteq \mathcal{M}$, is a t-secure $\mathcal{M}$-DistinctConverge protocol if all remaining honest nodes upon termination, with probability $1 - \mathsf{negl}(\kappa)$, output a set*

$$S_i \supseteq \mathtt{distinct}_k \left(\bigcup_{P_i \in \mathcal{H}} M_i - \bigcup_{P_i \in \mathcal{H}} C_i \right),$$

when at most t nodes are corrupted and where $\mathcal{H}$ is the set of honest nodes at the beginning of the protocol.

---

[1] For example, for $M = \{01001, 01111, 11000, 10000\}$ we have that $\mathtt{distinct}_2(M) = \{01001, 11000, 10000\}$. Note that $\mathtt{distinct}_k$ is an one-to-many function, e.g., $\mathtt{distinct}_2(M)$ is also $\{01111, 11000, 10000\}$.

We build a new $\mathcal{M}$-DistinctConverge protocol (that improves the same function in TRUSTEDPBC) to reduce the overall communication from $\tilde{O}(n^2\kappa^4)$ to $\tilde{O}(n^2\kappa^3)$. The novelty is to provide a new way for nodes to disseminate the messages in each round via a more efficient *sampling* approach. We first present a Propagate sub-protocol, and define its ideal functionality in Fig. 6.

Let n be the number of nodes and $m = 10/\epsilon + \kappa$. For every node $i \in [n]$, $\mathcal{F}_{\mathsf{prop}}$ keeps a set O_i which is initialized to $\emptyset$. Let M_i be node i's input messages' set.
- On input (SendRandom, M_i) by honest node i:
    - If $|M_i| < \log n$, then for all $j \in [n]$ set $O_j = M_i$.
    - Else, for all $x \in M_i$ and for all $j \in [n]$ add (i, x) to O_j with probability m/n;
    - **return** M_i to adversary $\mathcal{A}$;
    - **return** O_i to node i.
- On input (SendDirect, $\mathbf{x}, J$) by adversary $\mathcal{A}$ (for a corrupted node i):
    - Add $(i, x[j])$ to O_j for all $j \in J$;
    - **return** O_i to adversary $\mathcal{A}$.

Fig. 6. Functionality $\mathcal{F}_{\mathsf{prop}}$.

We show the pseudocode of our Propagate protocol in Fig. 7. In Propagate, nodes send in a given round a set of messages to $O(\lambda)$ nodes. Like [20], to achieve adaptive security, message lists are encrypted and padded to the same size, preventing the adversary from learning who sent what and, e.g., blocking a single message from being propagated. [20] implement Propagate in two rounds, where in the first round nodes sample fresh public keys that are then used in the second round. To improve concrete efficiency, our protocol reduces this to one round using *forward-secure public-key encryption* [10], since the public key is fixed at initialisation and only secret keys are evolved in a one-way fashion each time Propagate is called, which suffices for security.

The challenge is then to ensure that honest nodes receive all messages with overwhelming probability while reducing communication. We use a *resampling* technique to address the issue. In particular, if any list exceeds a predetermined size (which is approximately $\kappa \times$ |size of the set of messages to be propagated|$/n$), then the node resamples the list until it does not exceed that size. In our case, we allow nodes to resample their lists $O(n)$ times in the worst case to keep the padding size to a minimum. By contrast, [20] pads lists to a predetermined maximum size in all cases, thereby incurring $O(\lambda)$ more communication than us.

Input: A set of messages M_i.
Output: A set of messages O_i.
Global Parameters:
- PK is a set of FS-PKE public keys inherited from the higher-level protocol.
- sk_i is a FS-PKE secret key inherited by the higher-level protocol.

Upon Propagate(M_i)
- If $|M_i| \leq \log n$:
  - For $\ell \in [n]$: Send (NOENC, M_i) to P_ℓ.
- Else: // {let $\Lambda_p = 2m|M_i|/n$}
  - For $j \in [n]$:
    - For $x \in M_i$:
      - Add x to list $\mathcal{L}_j$ with probability m/n.
    - If $|M_p| \leq n \log n/\lambda$ and $|\mathcal{L}_j| > \Lambda_p$, set $\mathcal{L}_j \leftarrow \bot$ and $j \leftarrow j - 1$ // {resample}
  - For $j \in [n]$:
    - Pad $\mathcal{L}_j$ to size Λ_p.
    - If (pk, j) $\in$ PK: $\mathsf{ct}_j \leftarrow \mathbf{enc}(\mathsf{pk}, e, \mathcal{L}_j)$.
    - Erase $\mathcal{L}_j$ from memory.
    - If (pk, j) $\in$ PK: Send ct_j to P_j.

Upon Δ **time after invoking Propagate**(M_i):
- For all ct_j received from P_j:
  - $\mathcal{L}_j \leftarrow \mathbf{dec}(\mathsf{pk}, e, \mathsf{sk}_e, \mathsf{ct})$.
  - If $\mathcal{L}_j \neq \bot$: Add $\mathcal{L}_j$ to O_i.
- $\mathsf{sk}_{e+1} \leftarrow \mathbf{upd}(\mathsf{pk}_i, e+1, \mathsf{sk}_e)$. and erase sk_e from memory.
- For all (NOENC, M_j) received from P_j s.t. ct_j was not received from P_j:
  - Add M_j to O_i.
- Output O_i.

Fig. 7. Our new Propagate protocol, an instantiation of the propagation process.

Lemma 2. *If M is the input set of node P in Propagate, the size of each list $\mathcal{L}_j$ is:*

$$\begin{cases} O(\log n), & \text{if } |M| < \log n \\ \leq 2m|M|/n, & \text{else,} \end{cases}$$

with probability $1 - \mathsf{negl}(\lambda)$ if $m = \Theta(\lambda)$.

Input: Sets of messages $M_i \subseteq \mathcal{M}$ and $\mathcal{C}_i \setminus \mathcal{M}$, and integer k.
Output: A set of messages S_i.

Round $r = 1, \cdots, \lceil \log(\epsilon n) \rceil$:
- $O_i \leftarrow \mathcal{F}_{\mathsf{prop}}(\mathsf{SendRandom}, \mathtt{distinct}_k(M_i - \mathcal{C}_i))$.
- For $\ell \in [n]$: Send $(\textsc{NoEnc}, M_i)$ to P_ℓ.
- $\mathsf{Local}_i \leftarrow \mathsf{Local}_i \cup O_i$.
- $\mathcal{C}_i \leftarrow \mathcal{C}_i \cup M_i$.
- $M_i \leftarrow \mathsf{Local}_i \cap \mathcal{M}$.
Output M_p.

Fig. 8. $\mathcal{M}$-DistinctCV protocol [20, Fig. 7] implementing $\mathcal{M}$-DistinctConverge.

Lemma 3. *Let s be the length in bits of each message in M for node P. Then, the communication complexity of P during* Propagate *is with prob.* $1 - \mathsf{negl}(\lambda)$:

$$\begin{cases} O(n \lcg n \cdot s), & \text{if } |M| < \log n \\ O(m \cdot |M| \cdot s), & \text{else.} \end{cases}$$

Lemma 4. *Assuming a FS-PKE scheme,* Propagate *is a secure instantiation of the F_{prop} functionality.*

Implementing $\mathcal{M}$-DistinctConverge. We use the $\mathcal{M}$-DistinctCV [20, Fig. 7] protocol in our work, besides that we now use our new Propagate protocol, which we provide pseudocode for in Fig. 8. Here, nodes input a set of messages M_i and a constraint set C_i. Running for $O(\log n)$ rounds, in each round, nodes first call Propagate with $M_i \setminus C_i$ as input, which outputs a set O_i. The output is appended to a set Local_i. M_i is then added to the constraint set, since there is no need for the caller to propagate them again, and then the set of messages M_i is set to $\mathsf{Local}_i \cap \mathcal{M}$. Ultimately, set M_i is returned.

Lemma 5. DistinctCV *is an adaptively f-secure $\mathcal{M}$-DistinctConverge protocol, for $f < (1-\epsilon)n$. The number of bits sent over all nodes is*

$$O(\sum_{l=1}^{\log \epsilon n} \cdot \sum_{i \in [n]} CC(\mathsf{Propagate}(M_i^l \setminus C_i^l))),$$

where $CC(\mathsf{Propagate}(M_i^l \setminus C_i^l))$ denotes the communication cost of node P_i calling $\mathsf{Propagate}((M_i^l \setminus C_i^l)$. *Moreover,* DistinctCV *has $O(\log n)$ round complexity.*

5.3 The $\mathsf{PBC}_\kappa^{\mathsf{adaptive}}$ Protocol

We are finally ready to present our $\mathsf{PBC}_\kappa^{\mathsf{adaptive}}$ protocol. Note that we have previously defined the notion of a valid r-s batch for our static PBC protocol in §4. We need an appropriate notion of a valid r-$batch$ as defined below.

Definition 7 ((u,j)-committee). *For each message/slot pair (u,j), the (u,j)-committee is a subset of nodes such that for each node P_i in the (u,j)-committee, whenever $\mathcal{F}_{mine}$ is queried on input $\mathcal{F}_{mine}$.verify(adaptive,u,j), $\mathcal{F}_{mine}$ outputs 1.*

Input: Each node P_i inputs κ-bit value u_i.
Output: Each node P_i outputs an n-valued vector out_i.
Global Parameters:
   - $\text{ExtractedSet}_i \leftarrow [\emptyset]^n$, $\text{VotedSet}_i \leftarrow [\emptyset]^n$, $\text{Local}_i \leftarrow \emptyset$.
   - $\text{PK} \leftarrow \emptyset$, a set of FS-PKE public keys. $\text{sk}_e \leftarrow \perp$, P_i's FS-PKE secret key.

Round 0:
   - $(\text{pk}_i, \text{sk}_i) \leftarrow \textbf{gen}\ (e = 0)$.
   - Send $(\text{SIGN}, u_i, \sigma_i)$ and $(\text{KEY}, \text{pk}_i)$ to all nodes (σ_i is a signature on $[u_i, i]$).
   - Upon receiving $(\text{SIGN}, u_j, \sigma_j)$ from P_j, add σ_j to Received_i^j.
   - Upon receiving $(\text{KEY}, \text{pk}_j, \sigma_j)$ from P_j, add (pk_j, j) to PK.

Round $r = 1, \cdots, R+1$:
   Distribute:
   - Add all received valid messages into Local_i.
   - Find all $u_j \notin \text{ExtractedSet}_i^j$ in Local_i with valid r-batches.
   - If $|\text{ExtractedSet}_i^j| \le 1$, add u_j in ExtractedSet_i^j, else disregard.
   - Find all $u_j \notin \text{ExtractedSet}_i^j$ in Local_i with valid r-batches.
   - If $r \le R$, then let C_i contain all messages that P_i has propagated exactly twice through DistinctCV_i. If for some j, $|\text{ExtractedSet}_i^j| > 1$, then C_i implicitly contains all messages of the form $[u_j, j]$.
   - $\text{Local}_i \leftarrow \mathcal{M}_r^L\text{-DistinctCV}_i(\text{Local}_i, C_i, k^*)$.

   Vote:
   If $r \le R$:
   - Find all $u_j \notin \text{ExtractedSet}_i^j$ in Local_i with valid r-batches.
   - For each such u_j s.t. $\mathcal{F}_{mine}(\text{adaptive}, u_j, i) = 1$ (and $|\text{ExtractedSet}_i^j| \le 1$):
     - Add u_j to VotedSet_i^j and ExtractedSet_i^j
     - Extend the r-batch to include the new signature.
     - Send the message with the updated batch to all nodes.

Output conditions
   - At the end of round R, return for each j for which a message is received $u_j \in \text{ExtractedSet}_i^j$ if $|\text{ExtractedSet}_i^j| = 1$, or $\perp$ else.

Fig. 9. The $\text{PBC}_\kappa^{\text{adaptive}}$ protocol.

Definition 8. *Let $\mathcal{M}_r$ denote the set of all possible valid r-batches for all $m \in \{0,1\}^\kappa$ and for all $s \in [n]$.*

Lemma 6. *Let k^* be the number of bits required to describe $s||m$, where $s \in [n]$ and $m \in \{0,1\}^{\kappa-1}$ is such that distinguishes between exactly 2 messages in $\mathcal{M}_r$) and where* distinct_{k^*} *is defined in Definition 5. Then* $|\text{distinct}_{k^*}(\mathcal{M}_r)| = 2 \cdot n$.

Definition 9 (Valid r-batch). *A valid r-batch on pair (u, j) is the element*
$$u||j||\mathsf{SIG}_r,$$
where SIG_r is a set of at least r signatures (or aggregate signature) on $[u, j]$ consisting of one signature from node P_j and at least $r - 1$ signatures from nodes in the (u, j)-committee (resp. or an aggregate signature with the contributions of P_j and at least $r - 1$ other nodes in the (u, j)-committee).

Our protocol (Fig. 9) follows the template of TRUSTEDPBC of [20], which itself follows the template of the broadcast protocol of Chan et al. [11], save for the following notable changes.

First, TRUSTEDPBC is defined only for single-bit PBC. Therefore, we generalize it for multiple nodes, the main difference coming from our use of $\mathcal{F}_{mine}$. Abstractly, there are an exponential number of possible committees, one per message/slot pair (this number is quadratic in n for TRUSTEDPBC), but since $\mathcal{F}_{mine}$ can be evaluated on-demand for a given input, this is not an issue for complexity. Also, in our protocol, we guarantee that each node will forward at most two messages from the same sender, since they are sufficient to show that the sender is dishonest. Therefore, the size of the message space does not affect the total communication, except for the message length.

Note that at the beginning of protocol execution, nodes send to all nodes their input value u_i and a signature σ_i. Recall in **Propagate** that we use FS-PKE instead of regular public-key encryption. To bootstrap keys, each node therefore sample a FS-PKE key pair and send to all nodes their public key. Recall that we use the DISTINCTCONVERGE protocol in a single round so that each honest node P_i dissembles its message and all honest nodes receive it at the end of this round; TRUSTEDPBC does not use constraint sets to this end.

Then, as shown in Fig. 9, each round r is divided into two phases. In the *distribution* phase, nodes propagate r-batches of messages associated with a given node P_j that they have not previously propagated (using DISTINCTCONVERGE), and for any such r-batches, they add the corresponding message to a set $\mathsf{ExtractedSet}_i^j$. In the *voting* phase, nodes check, for each r-batch that they have received in the distribution phase, whether they are in the committee or not for the corresponding message/slot pair using $\mathcal{F}_{mine}$. If so, and they have not previously added their signature to the r-batch, they do so. Finally, at the end of $R = O(\lambda)$ rounds, nodes output a vector of values for each node P_j, which is $\bot$ if $|\mathsf{ExtractedSet}_i^j| \neq 1$ and the message in $\mathsf{ExtractedSet}_i^j$ otherwise.

Theorem 5. *Assuming a trusted PKI and SRS, protocol $\mathsf{PBC}_\kappa^{adaptive}$ satisfies f-consistency with probability $1 - \mathsf{negl}(\kappa) - \mathsf{negl}(\lambda)$.*

Theorem 6. *Assuming a trusted PKI and SRS, protocol $\mathsf{PBC}_\kappa^{adaptive}$ satisfies f-validity with probability $1 - \mathsf{negl}(\kappa)$.*

Theorem 7. *Protocol $\mathsf{PBC}_\kappa^{adaptive}$ has $O(\kappa \log n)$ round complexity and a communication complexity of $O(\log \epsilon n(n^2 \lambda \kappa + n \lambda^2 \kappa + n \lambda^3 \log n + n^2 \lambda^2 \log n))$.*

Acknowledgments. Sisi and Haochen were supported in part by the National Key R&D Program of China under 2018YFA0704701, Beijing Natural Science Foundation under M23015, and National Natural Science Foundation of China under 92267203. Daniel and Giorgos completed part of this work while visiting CISPA, and Daniel while at EPFL, Purdue University and Georgia Institute of Technology, and was supported in part by Sunday Group, Inc. and AnalytiXIN.

References

1. Abraham, I., Asharov, G., Patra, A., Stern, G.: Perfectly secure asynchronous agreement on a core set in constant expected time. In: TCC (2024)
2. Abraham, I., et al.: Communication complexity of byzantine agreement, revisited. In: PODC (2019)
3. Abraham, I., Nayak, K., Shrestha, N.: Communication and round efficient parallel broadcast protocols. Cryptol. ePrint Arch. (2023)
4. Alhaddad, N., Duan, S., Varia, M., Zhang, H.: Succinct erasure coding proof systems. Cryptol. ePrint Arch. (2021)
5. Asharov, G., Chandramouli, A.: Perfect (parallel) broadcast in constant expected rounds via statistical vss. In: EUROCRYPT, pp. 310–339. Springer (2024)
6. Blum, E., Boyle, E., Cohen, R., Liu-Zhang, C.D.: Communication lower bounds for cryptographic broadcast protocols. In: DISC (2023)
7. Blum, E., Katz, J., Liu-Zhang, C.D., Loss, J.: Asynchronous byzantine agreement with subquadratic communication. In: TCC. Springer (2020)
8. Boneh, D., Lynn, B., Shacham, H.: Short signatures from the weil pairing. In: International Conference on the Theory and Application of Cryptology and Information Security, pp. 514–532. Springer (2001)
9. Cachin, C., Kursawe, K., Petzold, F., Shoup, V.: Secure and efficient asynchronous broadcast protocols. In: CRYPTO, pp. 524–541. Springer (2001)
10. Canetti, R., Halevi, S., Katz, J.: A forward-secure public-key encryption scheme. J. Cryptol. **20**, 265–294 (2007)
11. Chan, T.H.H., Pass, R., Shi, E.: Sublinear-round byzantine agreement under corrupt majority. In: PKC, pp. 246–265. Springer (2020)
12. Civit, P., Gilbert, S., Guerraoui, R., Komatovic, J., Monti, M., Vidigueira, M.: Every bit counts in consensus. DISC (2023)
13. Duan, S., Wang, X., Zhang, H.: Fin: Practical signature-free asynchronous common subset in constant time. In: ACM CCS (2023)
14. Groth, J.: On the size of pairing-based non-interactive arguments. In: Fischlin, M., Coron, J.-S. (eds.) EUROCRYPT 2016. LNCS, vol. 9666, pp. 305–326. Springer, Heidelberg (2016). https://doi.org/10.1007/978-3-662-49896-5_11
15. Kate, A., Zaverucha, G.M., Goldberg, I.: Constant-size commitments to polynomials and their applications. In: ASIACRYPT (2010)
16. Katz, J., Koo, C.Y.: On expected constant-round protocols for byzantine agreement. In: CRYPTO, pp. 445–462 (2006)
17. King, V., Saia, J.: Breaking the $o(n^2)$ bit barrier: scalable Byzantine agreement with an adaptive adversary. JACM **58**(4), 18 (2011)
18. King, V., Saia, J., Sanwalani, V., Vee, E.: Scalable leader election. In: SODA (2006)

19. Nayak, K., Ren, L., Shi, E., Vaidya, N.H., Xiang, Z.: Improved extension protocols for byzantine broadcast and agreement. DISC (2020)
20. Tsimos, G., Loss, J., Papamanthou, C.: Gossiping for communication-efficient broadcast. In: CRYPTO (2022)
21. Wan, J., Xiao, H., Shi, E., Devadas, S.: Expected constant round byzantine broadcast under dishonest majority. In: TCC, pp. 381–411. Springer (2020)

Encryption and Its Applications

Overlapped Bootstrapping for FHEW/TFHE and Its Application to SHA3

Deokhwa Hong[1], Youngjin Choi[1], Yongwoo Lee[1(✉)], and Young-Sik Kim[2]

[1] Inha University, Incheon, Korea
{deokhwa,yj160727}@inha.edu, yongwoo@inha.ac.kr
[2] Daegu Gyeongbuk Institute of Science and Technology, Daegu, Korea
ysk@dgist.ac.kr

Abstract. Homomorphic Encryption (HE) enables operations on encrypted data without requiring decryption, thus allowing secure handling of confidential data within smart contracts. Among the known HE schemes, FHEW and TFHE are particularly notable for use in smart contracts due to their lightweight nature and support for arbitrary logical gates. In contrast, other HE schemes often require several gigabytes of keys and are limited to supporting only addition and multiplication. As a result, many studies have been conducted on implementing smart contract functionalities over HE, broadening the potential applications of blockchain technology. However, a significant drawback of the FHEW/TFHE schemes is the need for bootstrapping after the execution of each binary gate. While bootstrapping reduces noise in the ciphertext, it also becomes a performance bottleneck due to its computational complexity.

In this work, we propose an efficient new bootstrapping method for FHEW/TFHE that takes advantage of the flexible scaling factors of encrypted data. The proposed method is particularly beneficial in circuits with consecutive XOR gates. Moreover, we implement Keccak using FHEW/TFHE, as it is one of the most important functions in smart contracts. Our experimental results demonstrate that the proposed method reduces the runtime of Keccak over HE by 42%. Additionally, the proposed method does not require additional keys or parameter sets from the key-generating party and can be adopted by the computing party without the need for any extra information.

Keywords: Homomorphic encryption · bootstrapping · cryptographic hash function

1 Introduction

Homomorphic Encryption. Homomorphic encryption (HE) is a cryptographic technique that allows operations to be performed on encrypted data without requiring decryption. Among HE schemes, those based on learning with errors (LWE) are the strongest candidates. However, one limitation of these HE schemes is the accumulation of noise in the ciphertext during operations, thus the message is usually separated from the noise by multiplying it with a large value known as the scaling factor. Despite this, noise accumulates during the evaluation of homomorphic circuits, increasing the likelihood of decryption failure. To address this, Gentry introduced the bootstrapping technique, which allows for the construction of fully homomorphic encryption (FHE) systems capable of performing an unlimited number of operations [13].

Since Gentry's breakthrough, various FHE schemes have been developed. Notable examples include the Brakerski-Gentry-Vaikuntanathan (BGV) scheme [3] and the Brakerski-Fan-Vercauteren (BFV) scheme [12], both of which are FHE schemes over integers. Another prominent scheme is CKKS [6], proposed by Cheon et al., which supports FHE over real numbers. Additionally, the FHEW/TFHE and its variants [7,8,11,16,17] provide efficient FHE for boolean (or larger) gate operations. Various libraries, such as SEAL [19], TFHE-rs [21], and OpenFHE [18], are available, facilitating the development of a wide range of FHE applications.

Applications. FHE has become a foundational cryptographic tool, and it is applied in many fields such as secure multiparty computation and private information retrieval. It is also actively being adopted privacy-preserving artificialintelligence and machine learning [5,15], as well as in symmetric key cryptosystems like AES usually for the purpose of transciphering [14,20] and cryptographic hash functions like SHA256, for example, in the Zama bounty program.

While public blockchains offer high integrity and support a wide range of applications via smart contracts, they suffer from a significant limitation: all data stored on the blockchain is publicly accessible. HE, however, allows for computation on encrypted data, enabling smart contracts to process confidential information while preserving privacy. This enhances the utility of smart contracts for handling confidential data.

For example, extensive research is being conducted on fhEVM [9], which aims to execute the Ethereum Virtual Machine (EVM), the environment for running smart contracts, using FHE. In this context, FHEW/TFHE schemes play a crucial role due to their low memory requirements and efficient handling of arbitrary boolean gate operations.

Our Contribution. In this paper, we propose a novel circuit evaluation method for the FHEW/TFHE schemes by flexibly adjusting the message scaling factor during its bootstrapping step. Our contributions are summarized as follows:

1. **Evaluation of symmetric gate with reduced failure probabilFity:** The proposed method is particularly efficient in scenarios where consecutive X(N)OR gate operations are prevalent. Such operations are commonly found in binary circuits, especially in cryptographic hash functions like Keccak, SHA3. Our technique can be applied to a wide range of algorithms and does

not require additional key generation, thus imposing no extra burden on the client. In FHEW/TFHE schemes, the first step of gate bootstrapping between two ciphertexts typically involves addition, subtraction, or multiplication by a constant, followed by functional bootstrapping with gate evaluation. Our method optimizes this process for XOR gates by replacing the initial step of subtracting two noisy ciphertexts and multiplying by a constant with a simpler addition operation. By adjusting the message scaling factor during the functional bootstrapping process, we reduce the noise introduced during these operations, thereby lowering the failure probability of XOR gate operations. Importantly, this adjustment uses only public information and does not require any additional computation.

2. **Overlapped bootstrapping:** Cheon et al. [4] highlighted the relatively high computational failure probability of FHEW/TFHE, which prevents it from achieving IND-CPA^D security (indistinguishability under chosen plaintext attack with decryption oracle). To mitigate this, parameter adjustments were made to reduce the failure probability to negligible levels. Applying our technique in this context further reduces the failure probability without sacrificing performance.

In response to these challenges, we propose a novel approach that allows multiple XOR gate operations to be performed with a single bootstrapping operation, a technique we refer to as *overlapped bootstrapping*. Empirical results show that the overlapped bootstrapping significantly reduces the runtime of circuits with consecutive XORs, especially, it reduces the runtime of Keccak256 up to 44%.

1.1 Organization

The rest of the paper is organized as follows. Section 2 presents the basics of lattice-based HE, prior FHEW/TFHE bootstrapping methods, and the Keccak algorithm. Our proposed bootstrapping method is detailed in Sect. 3. In Sect. 4, we provide implementation results and analyze runtime performance.

2 Preliminaries

The inner product between two vectors is denoted by $\langle \cdot, \cdot \rangle$, and the multiplication of two polynomials is either denoted by a dot ($\cdot$) or omitted depending on the context. Let the polynomial ring be $\mathcal{R} = \mathbb{Z}[X]/(X^N + 1)$, where $X^N + 1$ is the $2N$-th cyclotomic polynomial for some power of two N. We denote the residue ring of $\mathcal{R}$ modulo an integer Q as $\mathcal{R}_Q = \mathcal{R}/Q\mathcal{R}$. Elements in $\mathcal{R}_Q$ are represented in bold, such as $\boldsymbol{a} \in \mathcal{R}_Q$, and the i-th coefficient of the element $\boldsymbol{a}$ is denoted by a_i. Vectors are represented by $\vec{v}$, and their i-th element is written as v_i. We use $x \leftarrow \chi$ to indicate that x is sampled from the distribution χ; $x \leftarrow S$ denotes that x is uniformly sampled from a set S.

2.1 Basic (Ring-)LWE Encryption

Let q and n be positive integers. We define LWE encryption as follows:

$$\text{LWE}_{\vec{s}}(m) = (\vec{a}, b) = (\vec{a}, \langle \vec{a}, \vec{s} \rangle + m + e) \in \mathbb{Z}_q^{n+1},$$

where $m \in \mathbb{Z}_q$ is the message, $\vec{s} \leftarrow \chi_{\text{sk}}$ is the secret key, $\vec{a} \leftarrow \mathbb{Z}_q^n$ is a random vector, and $e \leftarrow \chi_e$ is the noise term. Note that χ_e is typically a discrete Gaussian distribution with variance σ^2 and zero mean, and χ_{sk} is typically chosen as $\mathcal{B} = \{0,1\}$, $\mathcal{T} = \{-1,0,1\}$, or larger secret key sets. We omit the subscript $\vec{s}$ when it is obvious. The decryption of the LWE ciphertext is defined as follows:

$$\text{LWE}^{-1}(\vec{c}, \vec{s}) = b - \langle \vec{a}, \vec{s} \rangle = m + e \approx m,$$

where $\vec{c} = (\vec{a}, b) \in \mathbb{Z}_q^{n+1}$ is the LWE ciphertext. Through this process, we can obtain a message with some errors included.

Ring-LWE (RLWE) encryption is an extension of LWE encryption to $\mathcal{R}_q$, and we define an RLWE ciphertext of message $\boldsymbol{m}$ under the secret $\boldsymbol{s}$ as follows:

$$\text{RLWE}(\boldsymbol{m}) = (\boldsymbol{a}, \boldsymbol{b}) = (\boldsymbol{a}, \boldsymbol{a} \cdot \boldsymbol{s} + \boldsymbol{m} + \boldsymbol{e}) \in \mathcal{R}_q^2,$$

where $\boldsymbol{m} \in \mathcal{R}_q$ is the message, $\boldsymbol{s} \in \mathcal{R}_q$ is the secret key, $\boldsymbol{a} \in \mathcal{R}_q$ is a polynomial with random coefficients, and $\boldsymbol{e} \in \mathcal{R}_q$ is the noise. Note that N is the degree of $\mathcal{R}_q$. Similar to LWE, we define RLWE decryption as follows:

$$\langle (\boldsymbol{a}, \boldsymbol{b}), (\boldsymbol{s}, 1) \rangle = \boldsymbol{b} - \boldsymbol{a} \cdot \boldsymbol{s} = \boldsymbol{m} + \boldsymbol{e} \approx \boldsymbol{m},$$

where $(\boldsymbol{a}, \boldsymbol{b}) \in \mathcal{R}_q^2$ is an RLWE ciphertext.

2.2 FHEW-Like Cryptosystems

FHEW and TFHE are HE schemes that support homomorphic operations on boolean gates. In FHEW/TFHE, the message is defined as $m \in \mathcal{B}$, and the LWE encryption for FHEW/TFHE is defined as follows:

$$\text{LWE}(m) = (\vec{a}, b) = (\vec{a}, \langle \vec{a}, \vec{s} \rangle + m \cdot \Delta + e) \in \mathbb{Z}_q^{n+1},$$

where $\Delta = \frac{q}{4}$ is the scaling factor used for binary messages.

FHEW-Like Bootstrapping. Ducas and Micciancio first proposed an HE scheme with bootstrapping that operates in less than a second and uses a small key size, called FHEW [11]. This bootstrapping process consists of three main functions: accumulator initialization, blind rotation, and LWE extraction. The definitions of each function are given as follows.

Accumulator Initialization. In FHEW/TFHE, the accumulator is initialized as ACC ← RLWE($\bm{h}$), where the initial polynomial $\bm{h} = \sum h_i X^i$ is determined by a mapping function $f : \mathbb{Z}_q \to \mathbb{Z}_p$. Here, p represents the plaintext modulus, and the mapping function satisfies the property $f(v + \frac{q}{2}) = -f(v)$ for all possible values $v \in \mathbb{Z}_q$. Details regarding the mapping function are elaborated upon in the blind rotation step. We initialize $h_i = f(-i)$.

Blind Rotation. The blind rotation is a core technique to refresh a high-noise ciphertext. This involves performing a homomorphic multiplication of the monomial X^u on the previously defined accumulator, where $u = -\langle \vec{a}, \vec{s} \rangle$. After this process, the constant term of the accumulator is $f(b - \langle \vec{a}, \vec{s} \rangle) = f(m+e)$, and the result is represented as an RLWE ciphertext. To refresh the noise, f is defined as the decryption function. In FHEW/TFHE, different f functions are defined for each boolean gate, and they are called mapping functions. For example, the mapping function f for the AND gate is defined as follows:

$$f(m^*) = \begin{cases} \frac{q}{8} & \text{if } \frac{3q}{8} \leq m^* < \frac{7q}{8} \\ -\frac{q}{8} & \text{if } -\frac{q}{8} \leq m^* < \frac{3q}{8} \end{cases}$$

with $\Delta = \frac{q}{4}$. The definition of the mapping function for all gate operations can be found in Table 1. Several techniques perform blind rotation using different approaches: DM [17], CGGI [7,8], and LMKCDEY [16]. The primary distinction between these techniques lies in the method used to homomorphically multiply the monomial X^u with the accumulator.

Table 1. Boolean Gate Operations and Mappings [17]. Note that in [17], the mapping ranges for the X(N)OR gate are set to $[q/8, 5q/8)$ and $[-3q/8, q/8)$. In this case, it must satisfy $|e| < \frac{q}{8}$; however, if the range is set to $[q/4, 3q/4)$ and $[-q/4, q/4)$, it only needs to satisfy $|e| < \frac{q}{4}$, making it more efficient.

Gate	Computation($\odot$)	maps to $\frac{q}{8}$	maps to $-\frac{q}{8}$
AND	$c_1 + c_2$	$[3q/8, 7q/8)$	$[-q/8, 3q/8)$
NAND	$c_1 + c_2$	$[-q/8, 3q/8)$	$[3q/8, 7q/8)$
OR	$c_1 + c_2$	$[q/8, 5q/8)$	$[-3q/8, q/8)$
NOR	$c_1 + c_2$	$[-3q/8, q/8)$	$[q/8, 5q/8)$
XOR	$2(c_1 - c_2)$	$[q/4, 3q/4)$	$[-q/4, q/4)$
XNOR	$2(c_1 - c_2)$	$[-q/4, q/4)$	$[q/4, 3q/4)$

LWE Extraction. The decrypted message, processed by homomorphic operations, is located in the constant term of the RLWE polynomial after the blind rotation. The process of extracting this into an LWE ciphertext is called LWE extraction, and it can be performed without introducing additional noise.

The function f used in the blind rotation step must satisfy $f(v+\frac{q}{2}) = -f(v)$. To meet this condition, we set the value of the function to $\frac{q}{8}$ and $-\frac{q}{8}$. After the blind rotation step and LWE extraction, to correct the scaling factor, we add $\frac{q}{8}$ to the LWE ciphertext, which is the output of LWE extraction.

RLWE' and RGSW. The blind rotation generates significant noise because it involves homomorphic multiplication. Therefore, we use variants of RLWE, called RLWE' and RGSW, which utilize gadget decomposition. Let $\boldsymbol{g} = (g_0, g_1, \ldots, g_{\ell-1}) \in \mathbb{Z}^\ell$ denote the gadget vector, and let $(d_0, \ldots, d_{\ell-1})$ be the gadget decomposition of d, where $d = \sum_{i=0}^{\ell-1} d_i g_i$ with $B = \lceil Q^{1/\ell} \rceil$ representing the gadget length, $|d_i|_\infty < B$, and B being the base of the gadget decomposition, satisfying $B^\ell \geq Q$.

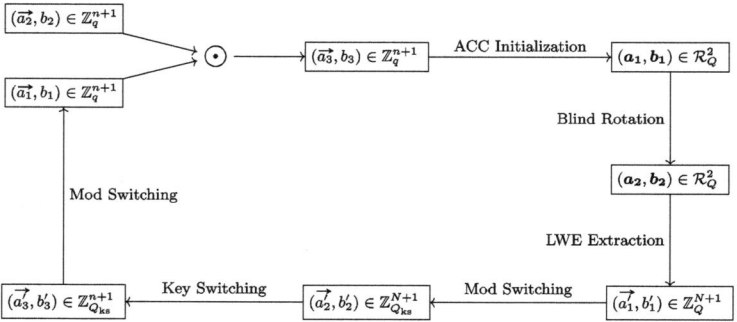

Fig. 1. This figure represents FHEW-like bootstrapping procedure. Note that this procedure is expressed in the same manner as described in [17]. In practice, after LWE extraction, performing the $\odot$ operation followed by mod switching and key switching can further reduce the noise. Here, the $\odot$ operation is a predefined operation based on the gate operation that needs to be performed. Detailed information on this can be found in Table 1.

Now we define RLWE' as follows:

$$\text{RLWE}'(\boldsymbol{m}) = (\text{RLWE}(g_0\boldsymbol{m}), \text{RLWE}(g_1\boldsymbol{m}), \cdots, \text{RLWE}(g_{\ell-1}\boldsymbol{m}));$$

and RGSW encryption of $\boldsymbol{m}$ is defined as follows:

$$\text{RGSW}(\boldsymbol{m}) = (\text{RLWE}'(-\boldsymbol{s} \cdot \boldsymbol{m}), \text{RLWE}'(\boldsymbol{m})).$$

The operations between RLWE and RGSW enable the multiplication of messages to be performed with relatively small noise [11]. We denote this operation as RLWE $\otimes$ RGSW.

Key Switching and Modulus Switching. We represent FHEW-like bootstrapping in Fig. 1. To understand the FHEW-like bootstrapping procedure, we define two new functions: **ModSwitch** and **KeySwitch**.

ModSwitch. **ModSwitch**, also known as modulus switching, is a function to switch modulus such that $\mathsf{modSwitch}: \mathbb{Z}_Q \to \mathbb{Z}_q$. We define the modulus switching function as $\mathsf{modSwitch}(x) = \lfloor \frac{q}{Q} \cdot x \rceil$, where $x \in \mathbb{Z}_q$. modSwitch is naturally extended to RLWE ciphertexts.

KeySwitch. **KeySwitch**, also known as the key switching algorithm, performs a private key change from $\mathsf{LWE}_{\vec{s}'}$ to $\mathsf{LWE}_{\vec{s}}$. To perform this algorithm, one requires a key switching key, denoted as $\mathbf{KSK}_{i,j,v}$, which is defined as $\mathbf{KSK}_{i,j,v} := \mathsf{LWE}_{\vec{s}}(vs'_i B_{\mathrm{ks}}^j)$, where $v \in [0, B_{\mathrm{ks}})$, $i \in [0, N)$, and $j \in [0, d_{\mathrm{ks}})$. As a result, let $(0, b)$ be an encryption under the secret key $\vec{s}'$. We compute $(0, b) - \sum_{i,j} \mathbf{KSK}_{i,j,a_i,j}$, after which we obtain an encryption under the secret key $\vec{s}$ with a small additional noise.

DM, CGGI, and LMKCDEY Blind Rotations. There are several differences in these methods performing blind rotation. These differences primarily concern how the monomial X^u is multiplied and the structure of the blind rotation key, brk, which is used for this multiplication with the accumulator. As a result, each technique varies in terms of computational complexity and key size.

DM Blind Rotation. The blind rotation key used in the DM method can be defined as follows:

$$\mathrm{brk}_{v,i,j} = \left\{ \mathrm{RGSW}\left(X^{vB_r^j s_i}\right) | v \in \mathbb{Z}_{B_r}, j \in [0,d), i \in [0,n) \right\},$$

where B_r is the base used in the decomposition of a_i. In other words, the blind rotation key of the DM method consists of all possible combinations of the decompositions of a_i and the secret key values s_i. The DM method updates the homomorphic accumulator ACC as ACC $\leftarrow$ ACC $\otimes$ $\mathrm{brk}_{a_i,i,j}$. It maintains the same computational complexity across different secret key distributions, including binary, ternary, and arbitrary integers.

CGGI Blind Rotation. The CGGI method uses the blind rotation key in the following form:

$$\mathrm{brk}_{j,u} = \left\{ \mathrm{RGSW}\left(x_{j,u}\right) | \vec{x_j} \in \{0,1\}^{|U|} \text{ such that } \sum_{u \in U} u \cdot x_{j,u} = s_j \right\},$$

where $U \subset \mathbb{Z}_q$. For example, we can define U for a ternary secret key as $U = 1, -1$ and $U = 1$ for a binary secret key. This blind rotation technique can be interpreted as the execution of a homomorphic CMUX operation:

$$\text{ACC} \leftarrow \text{ACC} + (X^{a_i} - 1)(\text{ACC} \otimes \text{brk}_{j,u}),$$

The CGGI method is affected by secret key distributions; it has low computational complexity when used with binary or ternary secret key distributions.

LMKCDEY Blind Rotation. The LMKCDEY blind rotation leverages automorphism to improve performance. We define the automorphism $\psi_k : \mathcal{R}_q \to \mathcal{R}_q$ as $\psi_k(m(X), \text{ak}_k) = m(X^k)$, where $\text{ak}_k = \text{RLWE}'(-s(X^k))$ is an automorphism key. Note that after applying the automorphism, key switching is required to revert the secret key from $s(X^k)$ back to s.

The keys used in blind rotation can be described as follows:

$$\left\{\text{brk}_i = \text{RGSW}(s^i) | i \in [0, n)\right\}, \{\text{ak}_{-1}, \text{ak}_j | j \in [0, w]\},$$

where w is a small integer. It has been demonstrated that this method can be performed efficiently with small constant number of automorphism keys. The blind rotation procedure can be represented as follows:

$$\text{ACC} \leftarrow \psi_{a_i}(\psi_{a_i^{-1}}(\text{ACC}, \text{ak}_{a_i^{-1}}) \otimes \text{brk}_i, \text{ak}_{a_i}).$$

2.3 SHA3 and Keccak Algorithm

SHA3 is the most recent member of the Secure Hash Algorithm family of standards by NIST in 2015. It is based on the Keccak algorithm [1], which employs a novel method called sponge construction. We briefly describe the structure of Keccak, and for more comprehensive details, we refer the readers to [1].

The Function Keccak-F. The Keccak-f function is the core permutation function of the Keccak algorithm, which serves as the foundation of SHA3. It operates on a fixed-size state and applies a sequence of invertible transformations to produce a pseudo-random permutation. To enhance understanding, key terms describing the state in detail are illustrated in Fig. 2.

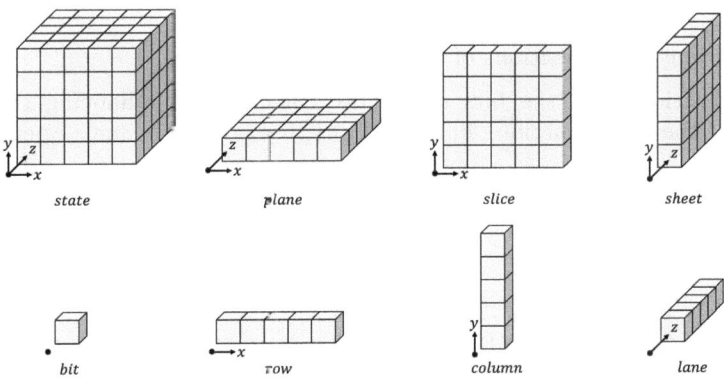

Fig. 2. This figure shows various labels that represent the state, with the x and y axes each having a size of 5×5, and the z axis having a size of 64, resulting in a total size of 1600 bits.

Let b represent the width of the state, where $b = 25 \cdot 2^l$ for some $l = 0, 1, \ldots, 6$. The state can be represented as a three-dimensional array $A[5][5][w]$, where $w = 2^l$ is the lane size. The Keccak-f permutation of b consists of $n_r = 12 + 2l$ rounds. Each round:

1. Takes an input consisting of $b = r + c$ bits, where r and c represent the *bit rate* and *capacity*, respectively.
2. Is composed of five steps: θ, ρ, π, χ, and ι.

Theta(θ) Step. The θ step aims to achieve bit diffusion across the entire state. It can be broken down into the following three steps:

– First, we compute $C[x]$ for $x = 0, 1, 2, 3, 4$:

$$C[x] = \bigoplus_{y=0}^{4} A[x, y],$$

where $A[x, y]$ refers to a w-bit lane in the state, and $\oplus$ denotes the bitwise XOR operation of two w-bit operands.
– Next, we compute $D[x]$ as follows:

$$D[x] = C[(x - 1) \bmod 5] \oplus \mathrm{rot}(C[(x + 1) \bmod 5], 1),$$

where $\mathrm{rot}(C[], 1)$ denotes a rotation of the operand by 1 bit along the z-axis.
– Finally, we apply $D[x]$ to update the array A:

$$A[x, y] = A[x, y] \oplus D[x].$$

Rho(ρ) and Pi(π) Step. The ρ and π steps work together to ensure diffusion:

- ρ: rotates each lane by a specific offset.
- π: rearranges the positions of lanes within the state.

These operations mix the bits across the entire state, enhancing the overall security of the hash function. This can be represented as a single operation:

$$B[y, (2x + 3y) \bmod 5] = \mathrm{rot}(A[x, y], r[x, y]),$$

where $x, y = 0, 1, 2, 3, 4$ and $r[x, y]$ is a predefined rotation constant for each lane.

Chi (χ) Step. The Chi step introduces non-linearity:

$$A[x, y] = B[x, y] \oplus ((\bar{B}[(x+1) \bmod 5, y]) \wedge B[(x+2) \bmod 5, y]),$$

where $\bar{B}[i, j]$ denotes the bitwise complement of the lane at address $[i, j]$, and $\wedge$ is the bitwise AND operation.

Iota(ι) Step. The ι step breaks symmetry by adding round constants:

$$A'[0, 0] = A[0, 0] \oplus \mathrm{RC}[i_r],$$

where $\mathrm{RC}[i_r]$ is the round constant for round i_r. Note that, since the round constant $\mathrm{RC}[i_r]$ is a known value, the XOR gate operation can be efficiently implemented using a NOT gate.

Sponge Construction. The Keccak hash function utilizes the sponge construction with the Keccak-f permutation. The process consists of two phases:

- **Absorbing phase:** The input message is padded and divided into r-bit blocks, which are then XORed into the first r bits of the state, interleaved with applications of Keccak-f.
- **Squeezing phase:** The first r bits of the state are output as blocks, interleaved with applications of Keccak-f, until the desired output length is reached.

The sponge construction is described as:

$$Z = \mathrm{SPONGE}[h, \mathsf{pad}, r](M, d),$$

where h is the Keccak-f permutation, pad is the padding function, r is the bitrate, M is the input message, and d is the desired output length. The padding function pad appends a 1 bit to the message M, followed by as many 0 bits as necessary, and a final 1 bit to ensure the message length is a multiple of r.

3 Overlapped Bootstrapping

In this section, we propose a variant of blind rotation that effectively optimizes circuits with consecutive XOR gate operations. The proposed method exploits the scaling factor of the message in LWE encryption, while in previous works, the scaling factor Δ is rather a fixed value ($q/4$) to determine the plaintext space. We take advantage of the fact that the mapping function f can be freely set during blind rotation without incurring additional cost.

3.1 New Blind Rotation Technique

In Table 1, we present the operations and mapping ranges that define gate operations in previous works [17,18]. The operation to perform an XOR gate is defined as $c_0 \odot c_1 = 2(c_0 - c_1)$. This operation introduces more noise because it involves multiplication by 2 after subtraction.

We observe that the output of the XOR gate operation is symmetric[1], and many algorithms, such as SHA3, are preplanned algorithms. In other words, this means that we can know in advance when the XOR gate operation will be executed.

For the symmetric gate operations, by slightly adjusting Δ to $q/2$, the original operation between input LWE ciphertexts, $c_0 \odot c_1 = 2(c_0 - c_1)$, can be modified to $c_0 + c_1$. Unfortunately, we need to revert Δ to $q/4$ for other binary gates, and most circuits utilize various gate operations. To address this, we define a mapping function f_Δ that allows for the free modification of the scaling factor, for example:

$$f_\angle(m^*) = \begin{cases} \frac{\Delta}{2} & \text{if } \frac{3q}{8} \leq m^* < \frac{7q}{8} \\ -\frac{\Delta}{2} & \text{if } -\frac{q}{8} \leq m^* < \frac{3q}{8}. \end{cases}$$

The above equation is an example of a mapping function for AND gate. For the blind rotation for any binary gates prior to X(N)OR gate, we perform blind rotation with the mapping function $f_{q/2}$ to set Δ to $q/2$. Then, before a gate other than X(N)OR, we perform blind rotation with the mapping function $f_{q/4}$ to revert Δ to $q/4$. We refer to this technique as *flexible scaling*. Note that this process does not introduce any extra computational costs, as the mapping function can be freely set by the computing party during the blind rotation process.

Noise Analysis and Failure Probability. FHEW/TFHE will fail to decrypt if the noise does not satisfy $|e| < \frac{q}{8}$ or $|e| < \frac{q}{4}$, where the condition $|e| < \frac{q}{8}$ applies to AND and OR gate, and $|e| < \frac{q}{4}$ applies to the XOR gate. We can use the complementary error function (**erfc**) to calculate the expected failure probability, which is defined as $1 - \text{erf}$, where **erf** denotes the error function. This probability can be expressed as $\textbf{erfc}\left(\frac{q/8}{\sqrt{2}\sigma_{\text{total}}}\right)$ for AND and OR gates, and $\textbf{erfc}\left(\frac{q/4}{\sqrt{2}\sigma_{\text{tot}}}\right)$ for the XOR gate. Here, σ_{tot} is the standard deviation of the noise in ciphertext after bootstrapping:

$$\sigma_{\text{tot}}^2 = 2\left(\frac{q^2}{Q_{\text{ks}}^2}\left(\frac{Q_{\text{ks}}^2}{Q^2}\sigma_{\text{ACC}}^2 + \sigma_{\text{MS}_1}^2 + \sigma_{\text{KS}}^2\right) - \sigma_{\text{MS}_2}^2\right),$$

where σ_{ACC}^2 is the noise variance of blind rotation, $\sigma_{\text{MS}_1}^2$ and $\sigma_{\text{MS}_2}^2$ are the noise variance of modulus switching, σ_{KS}^2 is the noise variance of key switching, and

---

[1] This means that if the number of ones is odd, the output is a one; otherwise, the output is zero.

Q_{ks} is the key switching modulus. For details regarding noise, we refer to [17] and [11].

For XOR gate in previous works, since the operation is defined as $2(c_0 - c_1)$ using the conventional method, the total variance is defined as follows:

$$\sigma^2_{\text{tot-XOR}} = 8 \left(\frac{q^2}{Q_{ks}^2} \left(\frac{Q_{ks}^2}{Q^2} \sigma^2_{\text{ACC}} + \sigma^2_{\text{MS}_1} + \sigma^2_{\text{KS}} \right) + \sigma^2_{\text{MS}_2} \right).$$

Since 8 is multiplied, the variance itself is large, but as long as $|e| < \frac{q}{4}$ is satisfied, the failure probability is the same as for other gate operations.

We propose to modify Δ to $q/2$, and then the $\odot$ is changed to $c_0 + c_1$, thus the noise variance is reduced to σ^2_{tot}. However, the failure condition is reduced to $|e| < \frac{q}{4}$ for X(N)OR, and thus has less failure probability.

We can delay the RLWE to LWE conversion, as suggested in [16], hereby minimizing the noise as:

$$\sigma^{*2}_{\text{tot}} = \left(\frac{q^2}{Q_{ks}^2} \left(2\frac{Q_{ks}^2}{Q^2} \sigma^2_{\text{ACC}} + \sigma^2_{\text{MS}_1} + \sigma^2_{\text{KS}} \right) + \sigma^2_{\text{MS}_2} \right).$$

Overlapped Operations and Flexible Scaling. Previously, most HE libraries, including OpenFHE, used parameters with a manageable but not particularly convenient failure probability. However, Cheon et al. demonstrated in [4] that the failure probability, **FP**, must be negligibly small, and since then, the parameters have been revised.

In the homomorphic evaluation of cryptographic hash functions like SHA3, it is crucial to minimize the failure probability, as even a single bit of failure can trigger the avalanche effect, drastically altering the final result and leading to unreliable outcomes. This is especially important when using parameters that have relatively high failure probabilities (e.g., 2^{-40}) in the past.

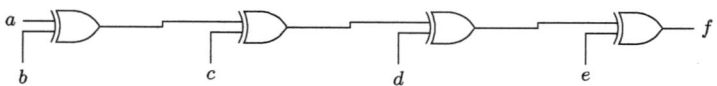

Prior : $f \longleftarrow \mathbf{FBS}(2(e - \mathbf{FBS}(2(d - \mathbf{FBS}(2(c - \mathbf{FBS}(2(a - b))))))))$ where $\Delta = \frac{q}{4}$

Overlapped : $f \longleftarrow \mathbf{FBS}(a + b + c + d + e)$ where $\Delta = \frac{q}{2}$

Fig. 3. This figure illustrates how sequential XOR gate operations are processed by the prior technique and by our proposed overlapped bootstrapping, respectively. Here, **FBS** refers to the bootstrapping function, which consumes a significant amount of computational resources. When performing four XOR gate operations, the prior technique executes the $2(c_1 - c_2)$ calculation followed by bootstrapping after each gate operation. In contrast, overlapped bootstrapping performs the calculation using $(c_1 + c_2)$, resulting in relatively less noise, allowing it to operate with only one bootstrapping.

The proposed technique reduces the failure probability of the X(N)OR gate from $\mathbf{erfc}\left(\frac{q/4}{\sqrt{2}\sigma_{\text{tot-XOR}}}\right)$ to $\mathbf{erfc}\left(\frac{q/4}{\sqrt{2}\sigma_{\text{tot}}}\right)$ (or to $\mathbf{erfc}\left(\frac{q/4}{\sqrt{2}\sigma_{\text{tot}}^*}\right)$). When the failure probability is already sufficiently low, further reduction becomes unnecessary.

Interpreting this situation from another perspective, this implies that since the failure probability has been reduced beyond what is necessary, there is no need to perform bootstrapping every time an XOR gate operation is executed. We exploit here that addition is equivalent to XOR when $\Delta = q/2$, thus functional bootstrapping is not required for gate evaluation, but only for noise reduction. The proposed technique secures more noise margin by modifying Δ, thus functional bootstrapping can be performed in a lazy manner.

In particular, when XOR gates are performed consecutively, we first set $\Delta = q/2$. Instead of performing bootstrapping after each XOR gate operation, we replace a sequence of XOR gate operations with additions and perform bootstrapping in one step. We refer to this technique as *overlapped bootstrapping*. The overlapped bootstrapping procedure is illustrated in Fig. 3. In this figure, *four nested additions followed by a single bootstrapping* with $\Delta = q/2$ replaces four individual bootstrapping operations with $\Delta = q/4$.

We apply flexible scaling in this process, although with a slight variation. Before performing an XOR gate, we adjust Δ to $q/2$. Before other gates, we use functional bootstrapping to scale $q/4$. During consecutive X(N)OR gate operations, if the noise exceeds a certain threshold, we perform functional bootstrapping with a scaling factor of $q/2$ to reduce the noise. We present a simple example of flexible scaling in Fig. 4.

The XOR gate is simply replaced by addition in overlapped bootstrapping. Hence, the variance noise introduced by the evaluation of XOR of n ciphertexts is given as follows:

$$\sigma^{*2}_{\text{tot};n} = \left(\frac{q^2}{Q_{\text{ks}}^2}\left(n\frac{Q_{\text{ks}}^2}{Q^2}\sigma_{\text{ACC}}^2 + \sigma_{\text{MS}_1}^2 + \sigma_{\text{KS}}^2\right) + \sigma_{\text{MS}_2}^2\right).$$

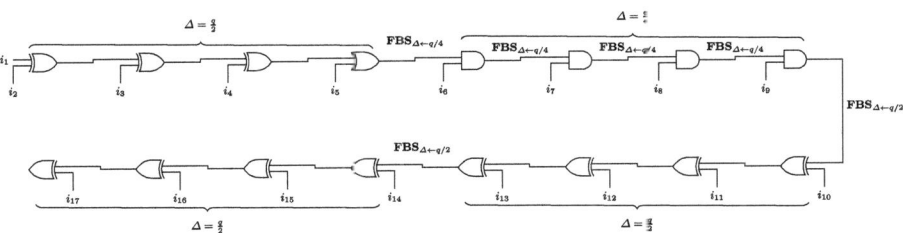

Fig. 4. This figure shows how the flexible scaling is performed. Here, where $\mathbf{FBS}_{\Delta \leftarrow \frac{q}{2}}$ (and $\mathbf{FBS}_{\Delta \leftarrow \frac{q}{4}}$) refers to bootstrapping that uses a mapping function to set Δ to $\frac{q}{2}$ (and $\frac{q}{4}$). Note that to use overlapped bootstrapping, Δ must be $\frac{q}{2}$ when performing the X(N)OR gate, and Δ must be $\frac{q}{4}$ when performing the other gates.

4 Implementation of Keccak with Overlapped Bootstrapping

In this section, we describe the implementation of the SHA3 algorithm (Keccak256, also known as SHAKE128) using FHEW/TFHE and discuss the computational speed benefits that can be achieved through overlapped bootstrapping. A detailed implementation of the SHA3 algorithm using FHEW/TFHE is provided in the full version of our paper.

Number of Nested Additions. One of the key factors that must first be determined to utilize the overlapped bootstrapping we propose is the number of additions to be performed in a nested manner. As presented in [4], the failure probability must be negligibly small for IND-CPA$^\text{D}$ security. To safely use overlapped bootstrapping, it is essential to thoroughly understand the configuration of the system being used and to appropriately determine the number of nested additions.

In the case of SHA3, boolean gate operations are performed only in the θ, χ, and ι steps. However, the round constants used in the ι step are public values, and thus, the XOR operation can be replaced by a NOT operation, reducing the number of bootstrapping operations. Therefore, the steps that need practical consideration are the θ and χ steps. The θ step can be expressed by the following equations:

$$C[i] \longleftarrow H[i] \oplus H[i+1] \oplus H[i+2] \oplus H[i+3] \oplus H[i+4], \tag{1}$$
$$D[i] \longleftarrow C[i-1] \oplus \text{rotate\_left}(C[i+1], 1),$$
$$H'[i] \longleftarrow \underbrace{H[i] \oplus D[i]}_{\mathbf{FBS}_{\Delta \leftarrow \frac{q}{4}}}. \tag{2}$$

The above process is performed independently for each lane. Assume H are fresh ciphertexts with scale $q/2$, then, if all the $\oplus$ operation is replaced with addition, the noise is maximal in (2) as variance $\sigma^{*2}_{\text{tot};11}$. Since an AND gate operation is planned to be performed in the χ step after the θ step, bootstrapping must be performed after the θ step (2) to adjust Δ to $q/4$.

Next, the χ step can be expressed by the following equations:

$$A[i] \longleftarrow H[i] \times 2, \tag{3}$$
$$H'[i] \longleftarrow A[i] \oplus \underbrace{(H[i+2] \wedge \overline{H[i+1]})}_{\mathbf{FBS}_{\Delta \leftarrow \frac{q}{2}}} \tag{4}$$
$$H \longleftarrow \mathbf{FBS}_{\Delta \leftarrow \frac{q}{2}}(H'). \tag{5}$$

Note that the reason for multiplying state H by two in (3) is that Δ has to be set to $q/2$, in order to perform the XOR gate operation in (4). The AND gate operation in (4) should be done by $\mathbf{FPS}_{\Delta \leftarrow \frac{q}{2}}$ for the next XOR; then, the noise variance is given as $\sigma^{*2}_{\text{tot};5}$. We perform $\mathbf{FBS}_{\Delta \leftarrow \frac{q}{2}}$ in (5) to reduce the noise before the next θ step, then the noise is maximal in (2) as $\sigma^{*2}_{tot;11}$, we refer this as $model_{11}$. For further reduction of runtime, $\mathbf{FBS}_{\Delta \leftarrow \frac{q}{2}}$ in (5) can also be ignored. Then, the noise in (2) is increased to $\sigma^{*2}_{tot;55}$, we call it $model_{55}$.

4.1 Implementation Results

We implemented Keccak256 and compared the cases where overlapped bootstrapping is used and not used, analyzing each step in detail. For reference, we compare performance based on cases where overlapped bootstrapping is used, particularly $model_{55}$. Note that $model_{55}$ already has a sufficiently low failure probability, so $model_{11}$ is not considered in this subsection.

Table 2. This table presents the details of **LPF_STD128**. FP represents the failure probability, with $\mathbf{FP}^*_{model_{11}}$ and $\mathbf{FP}^*_{model_{55}}$ denotes the failure probability of XOR gate with $model_{11}$ and $model_{55}$, respectively. Note that $*$ refers to the failure probability in the case where the $\odot$ operation is performed after LWE extraction.

	n	q	N	$\log_2 Q$	$\log_2 Q_{ks}$	B_g	B_{ks}	B_r	**FP**	$\mathbf{FP}^*_{model_{11}}$	$\mathbf{FP}^*_{model_{55}}$
LPF_STD128	556	2048	1024	27	15	2^7	2^6	2^6	2^{-144}	2^{-483}	2^{-140}

Our implementation[2] uses OpenFHE library v1.2.0, and the parameters were set using the **LPF_STD128** provided by the OpenFHE. Details about **LPF_STD128** can be found in Table 2. Our evaluation environment was configured with an Intel(R) Core(TM) i9-14900K processor, 64GB RAM, and Ubuntu 22.04.2 LTS. The code was compiled with clang++ 14, using the CMake flags NATIVE_SIZE=32 for ciphertext modulus less than 31 bits, and WITH_OMP=OFF, which means single thread. We use DM blind rotation method for the bootstrapping [11], but other methods like CGGI [7] and LMKCDEY [16] can also be applied.

Table 3. Step-by-step performance comparison before and after applying overlapped bootstrapping, as well as before and after replacing XOR gate operations with NOT gate operations. For the θ and χ steps, the runtime represents the average time per execution, while for the ι step, it reflects the time required for a single round function. The ρ and π steps are excluded, as they involve only bit rotations.

	θ (avg.)	χ (avg.)	ι	Total
Benchmark	194.20 s	186.37 s	123.96 s	9327.93 s
$model_{55}$	108.43 s	108.28 s	9.66×10^{-5} s	5201.04 s
(Improvements)	(44.2%)	(41.9%)	(-)	(44.2%)

---

[2] https://github.com/HONGDUCK/SHA3-with-FHE.

Runtime per Steps. The performance results for the θ and χ steps, both before and after applying overlapped bootstrapping, as well as the performance results before and after replacing the XOR gate operations with NOT gate operations in the ι step, can be found in Table 3.

It should be noted that the proof-of-concept implementation in Table 3 is relatively slow because we use the DM blind rotation method, which is known to be slower, and the experiment was conducted on a single-threaded CPU. Faster bootstrapping methods, such as CGGI and LMKCDEY [7,16], as well as faster implementations using NTRU-based HE [2], would significantly improve the runtime. The proposed technique can be easily applied to these variants of the FHEW scheme. Additionally, leveraging GPU or other hardware acceleration techniques could further enhance performance [10].

Runtime per Rounds. The runtime of the Keccak256 algorithm is proportional to the input data size. The number of rounds is determined by the input length, and this process cannot be parallelized. Therefore, the runtime of the Keccak256 can only be improved by efficiently designing each round function.

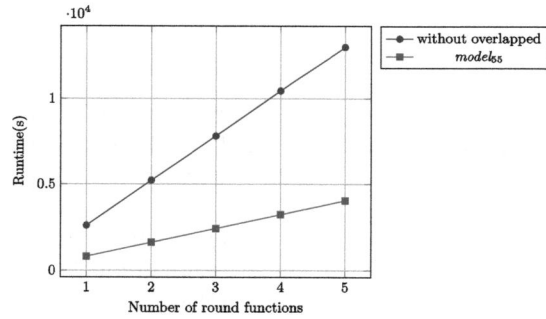

Fig. 5. This figure shows the runtime for processing large input data, with and without applying overlapped bootstrapping. A single round function consists of a total of 24 rounds, with each round performing θ, π, ρ, χ, and ι once.

Figure 5 shows the difference in runtime when processing large input data, with and without applying overlapped bootstrapping. This runtime was measured using 32 threads for multi-threading. When overlapped bootstrapping is applied, the runtime of a single round function decreases, making it more efficient than without overlapped bootstrapping when processing large input data.

5 Conclusion

Many circuits, including hash functions, rely heavily on consecutive XOR gate operations. Even for a single XOR gate, the use of flexible scaling can substantially reduce the failure probability. By leveraging this approach, both runtime and failure probability can be optimized across a wide range of applications, offering valuable strategies for compiler design in HE systems.

Future work will explore the application of flexible scaling and overlapped bootstrapping to additional key functions within smart contracts, with the goal of enhancing the efficiency of confidential data processing in blockchain environments. Another interesting direction for future research is exploring how our flexible scaling technique can be applied in batched bootstrapping.

Acknowledgements. This work was partly supported by Institute of Information & communications Technology Planning & Evaluation (IITP) grant funded by the Korean government(MSIT) (No.RS-2022-00155915, Artificial Intelligence Convergence Innovation Human Resources Development (Inha University); RS-2024-00399401, Development of Quantum-Safe Infrastructure Migration and Quantum Security Verification Technologies) and the Inha University Research Grant.

References

1. Bertoni, G., Daemen, J., Peeters, M., Van Assche, G.: Keccak. In: Johansson, T., Nguyen, P.Q. (eds.) EUROCRYPT 2013. LNCS, vol. 7881, pp. 313–314. Springer, Heidelberg (2013). https://doi.org/10.1007/978-3-642-38348-9_19
2. Bonte, C., Iliashenko, I., Park, J., Pereira, H.V.L., Smart, N.P.: Final: Faster the instantiated with NTRU and LWE. In: Advances in Cryptology – ASIACRYPT 2022, pp. 188–215 (2022)
3. Brakerski, Z., Gentry, C., Vaikuntanathan, V.: (leveled) fully homomorphic encryption without bootstrapping. In: Goldwasser, S. (ed.) Innovations in Theoretical Computer Science 2012, Cambridge, MA, USA, January 8-10, 2012, pp. 309–325 (2012). https://doi.org/10.1145/2090236.2090262
4. Cheon, J.H., Choe, H., Passelègue, A., Stehlé, D., Suvanto, E.: Attacks against the INDCPA-D security of exact fhe schemes. In: Proceedings of the 2024 ACM SIGSAC Conference on Computer and Communications Security, CCS 2024 (2024)
5. Cheon, J.H., Kang, M., Kim, T., Jung, J., Yeo, Y.: High-throughput deep convolutional neural networks on fully homomorphic encryption using channel-by-channel packing. Cryptology ePrint Archive, Paper 2023/632 (2023). https://eprint.iacr.org/2023/632
6. Cheon, J.H., Kim, A., Kim, M., Song, Y.: Homomorphic encryption for arithmetic of approximate numbers. In: Takagi, T., Peyrin, T. (eds.) ASIACRYPT 2017. LNCS, vol. 10624, pp. 409–437. Springer, Cham (2017). https://doi.org/10.1007/978-3-319-70694-8_15
7. Chillotti, I., Gama, N., Georgieva, M., Izabachène, M.: Faster packed homomorphic operations and efficient circuit bootstrapping for TFHE. In: Takagi, T., Peyrin, T. (eds.) ASIACRYPT 2017. LNCS, vol. 10624, pp. 377–408. Springer, Cham (2017). https://doi.org/10.1007/978-3-319-70694-8_14
8. Chillotti, I., Gama, N., Georgieva, M., Izabachène, M.: TFHE: Fast fully homomorphic encryption over the torus. J. Cryptol. pp. 34–91 (2020)
9. Dahl, M., et al.: fhEVM: Confidential EVM smart contracts using fully homomorphic encryption (2023). https://github.com/zama-ai/fhevm/raw/main/fhevm-whitepaper.pdf, white Paper

10. Dai, W., Sunar, B.: Cuhe: a homomorphic encryption accelerator library. In: Pasalic, E., Knudsen, L.R. (eds.) Cryptography and Information Security in the Balkans, pp. 169–186. Springer International Publishing, Cham (2016)
11. Ducas, L., Micciancio, D.: FHEW: bootstrapping homomorphic encryption in less than a second. In: Advances in Cryptology - EUROCRYPT, pp. 617–640. Springer (2015)
12. Fan, J., Vercauteren, F.: Somewhat practical fully homomorphic encryption. IACR Cryptol. ePrint Arch, p. 144 (2012)
13. Gentry, C.: Fully homomorphic encryption using ideal lattices. In: Proceedings of the Forty-first Annual ACM Symposium on Theory of Computing, pp. 169–178 (2009)
14. Gentry, C., Halevi, S., Smart, N.P.: Homomorphic evaluation of the AES circuit. In: Advances in Cryptology – CRYPTO 2012, pp. 850–867. Springer (2012)
15. Lee, J.W., et al.: Privacy-preserving machine learning with fully homomorphic encryption for deep neural network. IEEE Access **10**, 30039–30054 (2022)
16. Lee, Y., et al.: Efficient FHEW bootstrapping with small evaluation keys, and applications to threshold homomorphic encryption. In: Advances in Cryptology – EUROCRYPT 2023, pp. 227–256. Springer (2023)
17. Micciancio, D., Polyakov, Y.: Bootstrapping in FHEW-like cryptosystems. In: WAHC'21, pp. 17–28 (2021)
18. OpenFHE: Open-Source Fully Homomorphic Encryption Library. https://github.com/openfheorg/openfhe-development (2022)
19. Microsoft SEAL (release 4.1). https://github.com/Microsoft/SEAL (2023). Microsoft Research, Redmond, WA
20. Trama, D., Clet, P., Boudguiga, A., Sirdey, R.: A homomorphic AES evaluation in less than 30 seconds by means of TFHE. In: Proceedings of the 11th Workshop on Encrypted Computing & Applied Homomorphic Cryptography, pp. 79–90 (2023)
21. Zama: TFHE-rs: A Pure Rust Implementation of the TFHE Scheme for Boolean and Integer Arithmetics Over Encrypted Data (2022). https://github.com/zama-ai/tfhe-rs

Lixom: Protecting Encryption Keys with Execute-Only Memory

Tristan Hornetz[✉], Lukas Gerlach, and Michael Schwarz

CISPA Helmholtz Center for Information Security, Saarbrücken, Germany
{tristan.hornetz,lukas.gerlach,michael.schwarz}@cispa.de

Abstract. The confidentiality of cryptographic secrets is crucial for the security of modern computing systems. However, ensuring confidentiality is difficult in the presence of privileged attackers or transient-execution vulnerabilities such as Meltdown or Spectre. While Trusted Execution Environments (TEEs) provide robust protection, they suffer from limited hardware availability, performance overhead, and the need for substantial system redesign, making them impractical for many deployments.

In this paper, we present Lixom, a lightweight and generic technique to prevent data leakage of cryptographic secrets on x86 processors. Lixom achieves its confidentiality guarantees by storing secrets in code instead of data and preventing access to them with execute-only memory (XOM). In virtual machines, Lixom protects secrets from a compromised guest kernel, providing security guarantees akin to TEEs. Additionally, Lixom protects against Spectre, Meltdown, and Foreshadow attacks without performance overhead for algorithms such as AES. In 3 case studies, we show that Lixom improves the security of applications like disk encryption or digital rights management in real-world applications.

1 Introduction

Cryptographic secrets are high-value targets that require special protection from attackers. However, protecting cryptographic secrets is incredibly challenging if attackers have native privileged code execution, i.e., root attackers, or can exploit transient-execution attacks [9], such as Spectre [20] or Meltdown [25]. Existing hardware mechanisms, such as Trusted Execution Environments (TEEs) or Trusted Platform Modules (TPMs), can protect secrets against many such attacks [10], but they are not universally available. Moreover, even TEEs are susceptible to microarchitectural attacks breaking confidentiality [5,11,24,29,46,52]. Additionally, many systems still use hardware vulnerable to powerful and virtually unfixable transient-execution attacks such as Meltdown [25] or Foreshadow [46] that leak data across security domains.

This paper presents Lixom, a generic protection mechanism that prevents the disclosure of cryptographic secrets by leveraging *Execute-only memory (XOM)* on x86. The core idea of Lixom is to embed secret data directly into code, such as encoding secrets as immediate values in mov instructions, rather than storing them in data sections. XOM then prevents any direct disclosure or modification of these secrets while permitting their regular usage by executing the protected code. This provides leakage resistance and helps with policy enforcement, as secrets are only usable within the scope of what the protected code allows.

Lixom considers a powerful threat model: We show that it can protect secrets from attackers that have fully compromised the kernel of a VM guest, a level of protection previously only possible with a TEE. We achieve this by utilizing Intel's hypervisor-controlled *Extended Page Tables (EPT)* [18] to enforce XOM. Furthermore, we introduce two novel techniques: *Page locking*, which allows guests to securely relinquish read access to sensitive code, and *register clearing*, which prevents a malicious guest kernel from disclosing a program's register state. Together, these measures can defend against many attacks, including transient-execution attacks. The reason is one observation we make in this paper: Most transient-execution attacks only leak data, not code. We demonstrate this fact for transient-execution attacks, such as Meltdown [25] or Foreshadow [46].

For native, non-virtualized environments, we additionally present Lixom-Light, which uses *Memory Protection Keys (MPK)* instead of EPT to enforce XOM [18]. This hardware mechanism is widely available and well-supported in the Linux kernel. Lixom-Light provides strong disclosure protection against transient-execution attacks and is practical to deploy on existing software stacks.

We evaluate Lixom with 3 case studies in which we protect cryptographic algorithms and analyze the security benefits and performance overhead of Lixom. Our case studies involve the secure handling of password hashes and key protection for AES and HMAC. Furthermore, we integrate these implementations into an OpenSSL provider module, making them available to established programs and tools, such as the nginx web server. As Lixom involves hypervisor-based components, we create a customized version of the Xen hypervisor and a set of libraries that make EPT available to guests securely. Our results show that Lixom provides strong disclosure protection without affecting the throughput of AES and outperforming OpenSSL by up to 6%, making Lixom an ideal hardening mechanism for applications like disk encryption or digital rights management.

Contributions. In summary, the contributions of this paper are:
1. We propose and design Lixom, a technique to protect cryptographic secrets with execute-only memory. Lixom works without hardware changes.
2. We create implementations for cryptographic algorithms that use Lixom, demonstrating their practicability.
3. We show that Lixom is resistant against various attack vectors, including transient-execution attacks, and can defend against privileged attackers.
4. We perform an extensive performance analysis to show the low runtime overhead of Lixom.

Availability. Lixom is available at https://github.com/cispa/Lixom.

2 Background

In the following, we introduce the necessary background to understand the remainder of this paper.

2.1 Memory Protection Keys

Execute-only memory (XOM) permits instruction fetches but can neither be read nor written. Although simple in principle, the x86 page tables do not support XOM, which means that programs must use alternative mechanisms to create XOM mappings [18]. One method for XOM are Memory Protection Keys (MPK), which are widely supported on recent hardware [18]. This feature allows tagging page table entries with a 4-bit protection key, with each possible value associated with a configurable set of access restrictions. Programs can then modify these restrictions in the special 32-bit *PKRU* register. Notably, this does not require supervisor-mode privileges, making it trivial to turn off their restrictions. It is, therefore, challenging to use them for security purposes, with early works containing various vulnerabilities [17,45,47]. Nevertheless, MPK sees use in certain sandboxing techniques [17,45,47] and as a Spectre mitigation [19], demonstrating that this feature can provide security benefits if used correctly.

2.2 Hardware-Assisted Virtualization and EPT

Virtualization allows the execution of multiple *guest* operating systems on a single *host* machine. The *hypervisor* occupies the highest privilege domain and governs hardware resources and communication between guests. Modern CPUs support virtualization in hardware, e.g., as Intel's *virtual-machine extensions (VMX)* [1,18]. VMX introduces a mode of operation for guests named *VMX non-root operation*, which, from a guest perspective, is indistinguishable from native execution. However, privileged instructions, interrupts, or accesses to protected memory regions can trigger *VM exits*, which transfer control from the guest to the hypervisor. Another addition of VMX is *Second Layer Address Translation (SLAT)*. With SLAT, guest-managed page tables translate virtual addresses to so-called *guest-physical addresses*. These addresses undergo a second translation step with the hypervisor-managed *Extended Page Tables (EPT)*, resulting in a hardware-backed physical address. Notably, however, EPT entries follow a different format than the regular page tables on x86, allowing for the creation of XOM. EPT-enforced XOM provides security guarantees that are far stronger than MPK. Moreover, since the hypervisor manages EPT entries, not even guest kernels can modify them, minimizing the attack surface. This approach to XOM was pioneered by Readactor [12], which protects diversified code with EPT to prevent code-reuse attacks. Other works utilizing EPT-enforced XOM include KHide [14] and ExOShim [7]. Unfortunately, EPT is exclusive to Intel CPUs, making approaches involving it incompatible with AMD. While AMD's Reverse Map Table (RMP) provides a similar mechanism to enforce XOM [1], this is far less widely supported, and not considered in the remainder of this paper.

3 Design of Lixom

This section presents the design of Lixom and Lixom-Light. Section 3.1 provides an overview, Sect. 3.2 defines the threat model, and Sect. 3.3 introduces the challenges we have to solve.

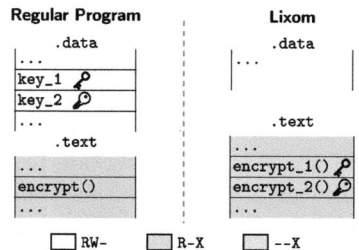
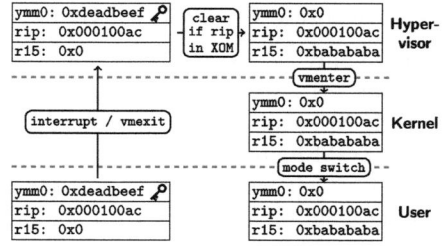

Fig. 1. Key storage in memory with Lixom.

Fig. 2. Illustration of the register clearing process. *r15* is the signal register.

3.1 Overview

The main idea of Lixom is to move secrets, such as cryptographic key material, to code protected by XOM, as shown in Fig. 1. This conversion can be as simple as having a mov instruction with an immediate value as the source operand. The hardware then prevents reading the secret both architecturally and transiently (e.g., via Meltdown). As Lixom relies on EPT-enforced XOM for the highest security guarantees, it also requires a method for securely allocating and deallocating such pages in the guest. We support two operations guests can invoke: *lock* and *unlock*. *lock* transforms regular memory pages into XOM, preventing read and write accesses. *unlock* transforms XOM pages into regular memory, but only after clearing them. This way, guests can dynamically allocate XOM without compromising secrets. We refer to this concept as *page locking*. However, while the main idea is intuitive, implementing it requires solving several challenges discussed in Sect. 3.3 and ultimately solved with Lixom.

3.2 Threat Model

For Lixom, we assume an attacker who fully compromised the kernel of a VM guest. They can remap, read, and overwrite memory, execute arbitrary code in the victim's context, and interrupt the victim at any time. The attacker can mount Spectre and other microarchitectural attacks. Fault injection attacks, e.g., Rowhammer [38], are out of scope. For Lixom-Light, the attack runs without kernel privileges and aims to disclose secrets from another security domain. We assume that the isolation is not compromised architecturally level. However, attackers can execute arbitrary code in their own unprivileged process.

3.3 Challenges

While the basic idea of Lixom is intuitive, we must address several challenges to ensure robust guarantees for the protection of cryptographic secrets.

Memory-Less Cryptography. Most implementations of cryptographic algorithms store key-dependent data in regular memory accessible to a privileged attacker. Hence, code protected with Lixom must use *memory-less cryptography*, keeping secrets and intermediary results in the registers at all times. While the capacity of the general-purpose register is generally too small to hold key material and perform meaningful computation simultaneously, the vector registers provide significantly more storage space. AVX2 provides registers with 512 bytes of confidential "memory", ample for many cryptographic algorithms. Previous works established this approach to protect encryption keys against cold-boot attacks [30]. If more memory is required, secrets are encrypted with AES-NI before saving them to memory. The AES-NI key is stored in code alongside other protected secrets [13,15]. Additionally, we expect programs to authenticate such backups, for example with schemes like AES-GCM. Confidentiality and integrity are strictly required, as the attacker has full control over non-XOM memory.

Defending Against Interrupts. XOM guarantees protection for secrets in memory. However, at some point, confidential information must enter the register state for processing. If a privileged attacker interrupts the program at such times, they can disclose any secrets that are currently in use. We call code sections where secrets are in the registers *critical zones* (not to be confused with critical sections in concurrent programming). While it is possible to restrict how the guest can interrupt a program, non-maskable interrupts (NMIs) cannot be turned off or deferred. Should an NMI occur by chance at the wrong time, it could compromise encryption keys. With Lixom, we do not attempt to prevent interrupts. Instead, we leverage that VMX permits hypervisors to handle interrupts before transferring control back to the guest. This allows us to perform *register clearing*, where the hypervisor partially overwrites the register state when handling interrupts occurring during the execution of an XOM page. In practice, Lixom only overwrites the processor's vector registers and two general-purpose registers, making it easy to recover from clearing events, as the instruction pointer and most general-purpose registers remain unaffected. At the same time, programs can store and process key material in the vector registers. One of the 2 overwritten general-purpose registers transfers data from immediate values in code to the vector registers. The other register serves as a *signal register*, which the hypervisor fills with a magic value during register clearing. By checking the value in the signal register at regular intervals, the program can determine whether register clearing took place and initiate recovery procedures when needed. Figure 2 illustrates register clearing and how different privilege levels perceive the program's register state during a clearing event.

Defending Against Control-Flow Hijacking. Even with the aforementioned measures in place, there remains a potent attack vector against programs in XOM. An attacker may hijack control flow in a critical zone and redirect it to a disclosure primitive. The easiest way to achieve this is by manipulating code pointers in memory, such as return or function pointers. Spectre attacks, which *speculatively* redirect control flow, also pose a significant risk. The solution we propose to this problem is the complete elimination of indirect branches in critical zones. As shown in previous work [4,44], this elimination can be done automatically. This way, there are no code pointers to manipulate, and speculative branch target injection with Spectre is no longer possible. Furthermore, while Spectre can still manipulate direct conditional branches, the branch targets are under the programmer's control. Thus, it is possible to ensure that speculative control flow cannot exit the critical zone without going through designated 'exit points' that erase any secrets from the register state. Without gadgets in the critical zone, Spectre attacks are prevented.

Apart from pointer manipulation and Spectre, there is a second way in which a privileged attacker could hijack control flow: Although they cannot access the XOM pages directly, they can map them to an arbitrary location in a process's virtual address space. Therefore, if a program crosses a code page boundary in a critical zone, the next page can be any page chosen by the guest kernel. The kernel can thus disclose the register state by inserting gadget code there. Unfortunately, this limits the maximum size of a critical zone to a single code page. More complex programs may require 2 MB pages instead of 4 kB pages.

Finally, an attacker may manipulate control flow by priming the registers with chosen values and jumping to arbitrary addresses in critical zones. This is usually not a problem, as a critical zone typically starts with the secret being loaded into the register state. If the start is not executed, the secrets are not in the registers and, hence, cannot be leaked. However, in cases where the program loads additional secrets later, leakage must be avoided with defensive programming measures, such as assertions on the current state.

3.4 Lixom-Light

Lixom-Light employs all programming rules of Lixom, but uses MPK instead of EPT to enforce XOM. It does not rely on virtualization and hence uses neither page locking nor register clearing. Since it does not rely on EPT, it is compatible with both Intel and AMD.

In contrast to Lixom, Lixom-Light only considers attackers with code execution in a different privilege domain. If isolation is not compromised on an architectural level, this attacker must resort to transient execution attacks, which exploit flaws in the microarchitecture. We argue that in this scenario, we can safely rely on MPK. To disable its XOM protection, the attacker must execute code architecturally, which is not the case, e.g., with Spectre attacks. Furthermore, the `wrpkru` instruction, which is the only way to modify PKRU, serializes memory accesses similarly to memory fences [18]. Therefore, Spectre attackers may execute a `wrpkru` gadget but cannot leak code afterward. Lixom-Light hence provides robust disclosure protection against Spectre. In Sect. 6.2, we show that Lixom-Light also resists attacks like Meltdown and RIDL [35], making it a practical defense against several classes of transient execution attacks.

4 Implementation

We develop a proof-of-concept implementation of Lixom via a series of patches for the Xen hypervisor (Sect. 4.1), a Linux kernel module named *modxom* (Sect. 4.2), and a user-mode library called *libxom* (Sect. 4.3).

4.1 Xen Hypervisor Patches

We extend the Xen hypervisor to support page locking and register clearing.

Page Locking. Our patches add a *vmcall* interface for locking 4 KB memory pages into XOM. Guests can then enable register clearing for individual XOM pages. Furthermore, our patches add a *sub-page XOM* mechanism, which allows guests to manage XOM on a 128 B granularity. This makes Lixom more memory efficient since programs would otherwise have to lock an entire 4 kB for every individual secret, thus wasting memory if the protected code is smaller. Setting up a memory range for sub-page XOM zeroes it, and immediately locks it into XOM without initialization. However, guests can invoke the hypervisor to populate uninitialized sub-pages with data, with the hypervisor ensuring that a sub-page can only be written to when still uninitialized. Once the data is in place, it is therefore unreadable and immutable, as with regular XOM. Unlocking uses the regular page-granularity *unlock* function, freeing all sub-pages at once. This way, we can support page locking for memory ranges smaller than 4 kB.

Register Clearing. We enforce the register clearing mechanism in Xen's VM exit handler. Whenever an interrupt or a fault occurs, we check whether the currently executed code page is among the previously marked XOM pages and modify the guest's register state accordingly. To reliably catch every interrupt, our patches also disable the virtual interrupt controller (vAPIC) of VMX by default, as it typically delivers interrupts directly to the guest kernel rather than the hypervisor. While enabling the vAPIC is technically still possible, we strongly discourage it, as this may undermine the security of register clearing.

4.2 Kernel Module

modxom, Lixom's kernel module, serves two functions: Firstly, it provides an interface to issue hypervisor operations from user-space, as user-mode programs cannot issue hypercalls directly. Secondly, *modxom* prevents the Linux kernel from attempting to read from XOM pages, which could lead to irrecoverable error conditions, i.e., when swapping out or reusing pages. To effectively address these issues, modxom implements a separate in-kernel memory allocator and restricts the hypervisor operations to memory allocated with this mechanism. User-mode programs can access this allocator through the *mmap* system call, and issue operations with *write* calls to a special file in Linux's /proc filesystem. Through this approach, modxom reliably ensures that every XOM page is pinned to memory, thereby preventing it from being swapped out. Additionally, modxom's handler for the *close* system call is invoked whenever a process closes its handle to the /proc file, which occurs when the process terminates or crashes. Therefore, we can reliably unlock every XOM page that is still in use at this point, preventing Linux from reusing locked XOM pages.

4.3 User Space Library

Finally, we present a shared user-mode library that simplifies the management of XOM by abstracting modxom's interface. Additionally, the user-space library can emulate the Xen hypervisor's XOM behavior with MPK if the hardware supports it. This way, programs setting up a Lixom environment do not need to distinguish between Lixom-Light and Lixom, with any code for Lixom also working for Lixom-Light. We use this mechanism for our case studies so that all experiments for both Lixom-Light and Lixom can use the same code.

5 Case Studies

In this section, we present 3 case studies in which we implement programs that utilize Lixom to protect cryptographic secrets. Section 6 evaluates the performance of these implementations.

5.1 Case Study 1: Message Authentication with HMAC

We show that it is possible to perform message authentication with HMAC-SHA256 purely in XOM using Lixom. Although widely supported hardware extensions exist for SHA-256, they are only partially usable as the SHA extensions only cover certain primitive operations. Therefore, the bulk of SHA-256 must be implemented using more conventional techniques. These techniques involve control-flow structures that are challenging to create using only direct branches. Our case study, therefore, provides insights into the performance of Lixom for more involved algorithms.

An implementation challenge of SHA-256 is that it uses round constants, manipulation of which may undermine the algorithm's security guarantees. To prevent attackers from changing these round constants, we store them in code as immediate values. As with the key, each round constant requires a small code segment moving it to the correct register. Although these segments are not large individually, they alone consume 720 bytes of the available 4 kB memory page.

Another challenge is that the hash state, which updates with each message block, is lost after register clearing and cannot be easily recovered. Therefore, we utilize authenticated encryption with AES-128-GCM to confidentially store the hash state in memory at regular intervals. When interrupted, the hash function then restores its internal state from the latest checkpoint instead of starting from scratch. This enables the authentication of messages of arbitrary size, even with heavy CPU contention from other processes. The encryption key is generated randomly and inserted into the program simultaneously with the HMAC key.

5.2 Case Study 2: Encryption with AES

Our second application for Lixom protects AES encryption keys. The AES-NI instruction set extensions allow for implementing AES with little to no control flow structures. Furthermore, most AES-NI instructions work on vector register operands, making it easy to derive round keys and perform encryptions without writing key material to memory. For most modes of operation, gracefully handling register clearing events is relatively straightforward, as the program can check the signal register after encrypting a message block. When the registers are cleared, we simply need to re-derive the round keys, and can continue at the block that was last processed. The current block offset is not confidential and is thus stored in a register that is unaffected by register clearing.

For this paper, we provide two Lixom-compliant implementations of AES-128-CTR: One utilizing the 128-bit AES-NI extensions and one using the 256-bit VAES extensions. Both implementations can also serve as the GCTR function for AES-128-GCM, allowing for authenticated encryption with Lixom. Our case study does not pre-compute the round keys, as loading them from immediates takes roughly 330 bytes of code under Lixom's rules, whereas key expansion with AES-NI takes as little as 211 bytes. An implementation with pre-computed round keys may exhibit slightly better runtime performance at a higher memory cost per encryption key.

5.3 Case Study 3: Protecting Password Hashes

One of the more straightforward application scenarios for Lixom is to provide leakage resistance to password hashes, which are popular targets for Spectre attacks [42,49]. Following the programming rules from Sect. 3 in this scenario is trivial, as the correct hash is subject only to simple equality checks. If implemented with conditional move instructions, this does not require any branches. Therefore, once the protected code is fully initialized, there is no longer any attack surface for Spectre. Note that this specific application does not benefit from Lixom's resistance against privileged attackers, as the guest kernel can trivially disclose the correct hash when a user authenticates with the correct password. Attackers may also use the protected code as an oracle for dictionary attacks, albeit at a relatively low test rate compared to the GPU-powered methods available when the hash is known directly. Nevertheless, we argue that Lixom's low cost in this scenario justifies its use as a hardening technique.

6 Evaluation of Lixom

In this section, we evaluate the performance and attack resistance of Lixom.

6.1 Performance

Our performance study of Lixom investigates 3 aspects: Encryption throughput, setup costs, and application performance. We analyze the former two aspects with custom benchmarks and employ the nginx benchmark of the Phoronix test suite [22] to gauge Lixom's impact on real-world applications. All tests utilize a custom-built OpenSSL provider library, making the case-study implementations

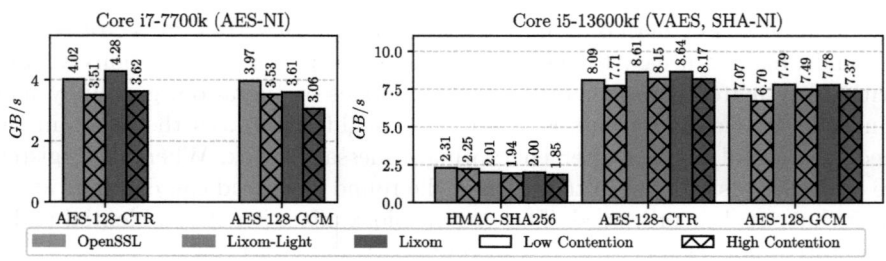

Fig. 3. Throughput of our Lixom implementations ($n = 128$, $\frac{SE}{\mu} < 0.7\,\%$, 256 MB per sample, single thread). Cross-hatching indicates that the test was conducted with high contention for CPU time, causing frequent interrupts.

from Sect. 5 available to any program using OpenSSL without requiring code changes. This way, the nginx benchmark utilizes the Lixom-compliant AES-128-GCM implementation for its TLS connections. In summary, the only significant overhead of Lixom occurs when setting up an encryption context. However, some of our implementations outperform OpenSSL in throughput, meaning that Lixom may not incur any overhead, depending on the application.

Test Environment. Unless otherwise stated, we test Lixom on a 2-core HVM guest of our modified Xen hypervisor based on Xen v4.18.1. The guest runs Debian 12 with Linux v6.1.0. Tests involving OpenSSL use OpenSSL v3.0.11.

Data Throughput. The first benchmark series measures the data throughput of our Lixom-compliant implementations under various conditions and hardware configurations. Furthermore, it aims to quantify to which extent frequent interrupts degrade the performance of Lixom, since the protected code must run recovery procedures after register clearing. We run two threads parallel to the benchmark to increase the interrupt frequency, one with high CPU usage and one spinning the *sync* system call. On the test VM with two virtual cores, this fully utilizes the available CPU resources, while the frequent system calls require many context switches. Note that the benchmarks for Lixom-Light and Lixom execute the same code, only with a different XOM-enforcement method and the addition of register clearing for Lixom.

Figure 3 shows the results. All AES implementations except for AES-128-GCM on the Core i7 7700K slightly outperform OpenSSL. Monitoring the performance counters reveals this is primarily due to execution stalls when loading the plain text. On the Core i5 13600KF, for instance, the OpenSSL AES-128-CTR benchmark executes 80.4 % more stall cycles on average, and 161 % more stall cycles with a concurrently pending L3 cache miss. Contrarily, our HMAC implementation's throughput is 13.4 % lower than OpenSSL's. This is expected, as the code requires changes to eliminate indirect branches, load round constants from the code, and backup internal state.

While Lixom-Light is faster than Lixom on average, the overhead is low. The most significant difference occurs in the high-contention HMAC-SHA256 bench-

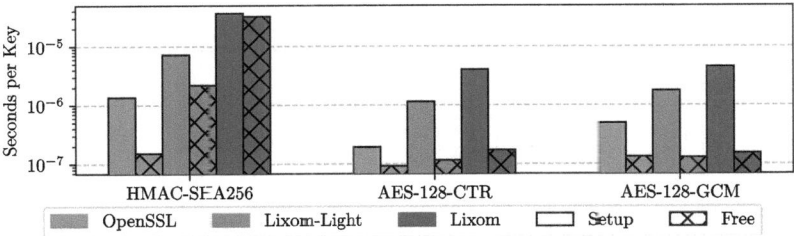

Fig. 4. Mean time required for allocating and freeing encryption contexts ($n = 2^{14}$, Intel Core i5 13600kf). Less is better.

mark, where Lixom-Light's throughput is 4.9 % higher than Lixom's. This, too, is expected, as Lixom loses its progress up to the last checkpoint when interrupted, whereas Lixom-Light does not. However, there is virtually no overhead with the AES benchmarks. For AES-128-CTR, Lixom's average throughput is even 0.3 % higher than Lixom-Light's. We conclude that register clearing has a minor impact on performance if the protected code section has appropriate recovery mechanisms. Note, however, that an algorithm more complex than HMAC or AES may require more involved recovery procedures, increasing performance degradation from register clearing.

Setup Costs. Another source of overhead are setup and teardown costs. Lixom requires creating and freeing a separate executable memory segment for every secret we use, meaning we need to modify the NX bit in the page tables. In contrast to standard memory allocations, this always requires a system call. For Lixom, creating and freeing XOM requires a hypercall on top of this. Figure 4 shows the overhead of the setup. Both Lixom-Light and Lixom have setup overheads that are higher than an unprotected OpenSSL version. However, using sub-page granularity XOM eliminates most of the freeing costs for AES. This way, system- and hypercalls are only necessary when all 128 B sub-pages in an XOM region are freed. For the AES benchmarks, we allocate and free the sub-page XOM ranges in 16 kB chunks, so we only need a hypercall after freeing all encryption contexts in this range. Our HMAC implementation does not use this mechanism, hence the significantly higher freeing costs. These results indicate that Lixom is better suited for applications with few, rarely changing encryption keys. Note that our results are an upper bound for Lixom's setup costs. There is still room for optimization.

Application Performance. Finally, we investigate the performance impact of Lixom on the popular nginx web server using the Phoronix test suite [22]. Its nginx benchmark measures the number of requests nginx can handle per second while using our AES-128-GCM implementation for TLS connections. We use this benchmark because nginx is a worst-case scenario given Lixom's cost profile in the previous experiments. Encryption keys are frequently exchanged, meaning that nginx should be among the applications most affected by the high setup costs. We expect other real-world applications to be less affected. For comparison,

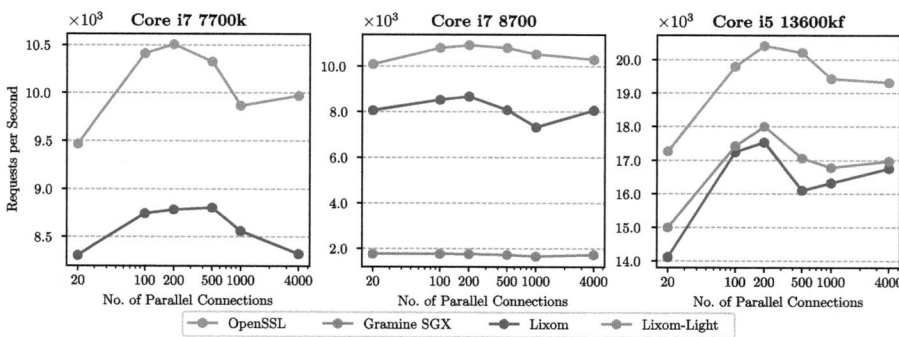

Fig. 5. Results from the Phoronix nginx benchmark v.3.0.1, which measures the number of HTTPS requests processed per second with parallel connections.

we also perform a benchmark with Gramine-SGX v1.7 [43], which allows running nginx inside an SGX enclave. For this SGX benchmark only, we use KVM (Linux v6.1.0) as the hypervisor, as Xen does not fully support SGX. This benchmark is performed on a Core i7 8700, as neither of the other processors supports SGX Launch Control, which Gramine-SGX requires.

Figure 5 illustrates our results. As expected, Lixom reduces nginx's performance, with Lixom incurring a higher overhead than Lixom-Light. However, this overhead is significantly smaller than in the setup benchmark. Lixom-Light reduces the amount of requests per second by roughly 13 % on average across all configurations, and Lixom reduces them by roughly 18 %. Also, Lixom is significantly faster than Gramine-SGX, which reduces them by 83 %. This demonstrates that despite Lixom's high setup costs, the effect on real-world software is not as significant as in a raw benchmark, even in a worst-case scenario.

6.2 Attack Resistance

This section shows that Lixom mitigates many architectural and microarchitectural attacks, including transient execution attacks such as Spectre [20] and Meltdown [25]. We also discuss interrupt-based attacks [36] and DMA attacks.

Spectre-Like Attacks. We experimentally verify that XOM prohibits direct read access even under speculation and thus prevents attackers with Spectre read primitives from disclosing secrets in memory. The attack surface is, therefore, restricted to program sections where secrets are in the registers. Our programming rules effectively prevent the successful exploitation of these sections. Spectre-BTB [20] and Spectre-RSB [26] are impossible, and direct branches only target code within the protected code section. Furthermore, disclosure gadgets outside this section cannot be used since the program can only leave this section through exit points that erase secrets. If the protected code segments are free of exploitable Spectre gadgets, we can guarantee resistance against Spectre.

Other Transient Execution Attacks. Meltdown-type attacks exploit lazy exception handling in combination with out-of-order execution [9]. Such attacks have targeted various microarchitectural buffers, including the L1 data cache [25, 46], store buffer [8], load ports [35], and line-fill buffer [37]. However, none of these buffers hold any secret information in the context of Lixom. The programming rules prohibit storing secrets in memory, and loading secrets from memory uses instruction fetches, which affect none of these buffers directly. The only buffer in the core's memory subsystem that may hold instructions is the L2 cache, which, to our knowledge, is unaffected by any such attack. Therefore, attacks like Meltdown [25] and Foreshadow [48] do not threaten Lixom's confidentiality, even on affected processors. We experimentally verify this with an Intel Core i7 7700K processor. However, Lixom cannot protect secrets against attacks that target the vector registers, such as ZenBleed [31], Downfall [28], and RFDS [2]. These attacks are mitigated using microcode updates, making Lixom secure on these affected CPUs if the newest microcode is applied.

Side Channel Attacks. Side channels are a well-known threat to the confidentiality of cryptographic operations. As with any implementation of a cryptographic algorithm, we expect code for Lixom to be free from key-dependent control flow and other key-dependent memory access patterns. Such programming techniques prevent timing and cache-based side channels [32].

Interrupt-Based Attacks. Information gathering through interrupts is one of the most potent attack vectors against XOM. Naturally, this affects key material stored in the registers, which a privileged attacker can disclose with a well-timed interrupt. We argue that Lixom's register clearing fully prevents the leakage of cryptographic secrets through malicious interrupts. However, an attacker can still infer instruction semantics by observing changes in unprotected registers. Previous work demonstrates the practicability of similar code-recovery attacks [36]. We stress that the goal of Lixom is to protect cryptographic secrets, not to prevent code disclosure.

DMA Attacks. Attacks leveraging peripheral devices with Direct Memory Access (DMA) bypass the processor's MMU and, thus, the page table configuration entirely. However, we can mitigate DMA attacks using an IOMMU, such as Intel's VT-d [18]. Our implementation of Lixom already considers this, preventing DMA peripherals from accessing XOM regions.

7 Discussion

7.1 Deployment and Potential Applications

Lixom is generic and applicable to a wide range of use cases. Therefore, the most practical means of deploying Lixom is in the form of a cryptographic library next to a set of hypervisor patches. While users can also integrate Lixom-compliant cryptography into projects directly, this necessitates assembly programming. Future work may explore the code generation for Lixom with a compiler pass.

Digital Rights Management (DRM) systems enforcing the copyright associated with remotely distributed media is another use case for Lixom. DRM systems encrypt media before delivery and only allow decryption in a restricted environment to prevent leakage of the encryption key. Modern DRM systems such as Google's Widevine rely on a TEE for this purpose [33]. However, many consumer-level x86 processors are not equipped with a TEE, forcing DRM systems to utilize obfuscation-based software-only mechanisms instead [33].

We argue that Lixom can improve upon pure obfuscation. With a TPM, it is possible to remotely attest the hypervisor's integrity to media distributors. If keys are exchanged with the hypervisor and then made available to guests with Lixom, its use is governed by a trusted component without reducing performance. This is generic and does not require the entire DRM system to be implemented in the hypervisor. Furthermore, since operating systems like Windows already use virtualization for security [27], we expect that this is easy to integrate.

Furthermore, Lixom can also efficiently allocate and manage EPT-enforced XOM for other purposes. While the primary functionality of Lixom is to hide cryptographic secrets, we envision our implementation's potential for further research involving XOM. We make our code publicly available, hoping it will facilitate future developments in this field. For example, it may help implement a leakage-resistant diversity scheme akin to Readactor [12].

7.2 Related Work

Other Ways to Create Execute-only Memory. While Lixom relies on explicit hardware support for XOM, other ways to enforce execute-only permissions exist. For instance, Sparks and Butler propose ShadowWalker [40], a technique to hide kernel rootkits via a *split TLB*. The instruction TLB's state differs from that of the data TLB through a special page fault handler, which yields different address translations depending on the type of access. However, shared higher-level TLBs make a split TLB unreliable on recent hardware [41]. Execute-no-Read (XnR) [3] uses a custom page-fault handler to keep only a sliding window of the most recently used code pages readable. Kwon et al. propose uXOM [21], which leverages *unprivileged memory instructions* on ARM Cortex-M. Such instructions always perform unprivileged memory accesses, regardless of the program's actual privileges. Hence, a privileged program with only unprivileged memory instructions can execute privileged code but not read it. Finally, approaches like LR^2 [6] and kR^X [34] require only the standard $W \oplus X$ policy to enforce XOM, using range checks and software-based load address masking.

Microarchitectural Defense Mechanisms. T-SGX [39] defends against controlled-channel attacks on SGX using Intel TSX. T-SGX assumes a TEE-specific attack model in which the enclave is trusted, but the operating system is not. Most closely related to our work, Guan et al. [16] protect encryption keys by performing AES encryptions inside a TSX transaction. However, this approach is limited by the TSX transaction length.

Memory-Less Encryption. Programs for Lixom must rely on memory-less encryption, where any key-dependent information remains in the registers. This concept was pioneered by TRESOR [30], which stores AES keys in the debug registers to defend against cold boot attacks. Later works, such as PRIME [13], Copker [15] and Mimosa [23] demonstrate the practicability of memory-less encryption for RSA. Yang et al. propose a memory-less implementation of ECDH key exchange algorithm with curve SECT163K1 [50].

Cryptographic Secrets in Protected Code. As part of uXOM, Kwon et al. proposed embedding encryption keys into XOM on ARM Cortex-M [21]. uXOM's threat model does not include transient execution or a malicious kernel, and the approach, therefore, lacks Lixom's defense measures. Yang et al. propose the PLCrypto library [51]. PLCrypto leverages the programming model of industrial Programmable Logic Controllers, where only data is remotely accessible. Hence, it stores cryptographic secrets in code to prevent manipulation.

8 Conclusion

This paper presented Lixom, a novel and generic technique for protecting cryptographic secrets with execute-only memory. Lixom-Light defends against transient execution attacks, and Lixom additionally protects secrets from the kernel of a VM guest. We implemented 3 case studies for Lixom, showing its applicability to password checking, AES encryption, and message authentication. Our performance studies showed that Lixom works with real-world software and can achieve a better throughput for AES than OpenSSL. Lixom can serve as a low-cost hardening technique in many applications using AES, and its unique properties are particularly well-suited for DRM systems.

Acknowledgment. We would like to thank our anonymous shepherd, and our anonymous reviewers for their insightful and constructive feedback.

References

1. AMD64 Architecture Programmer's Manual (2024)
2. INTEL-SA-00898: 2024.1 IPU - Intel Atom Processor Advisory (2024). https://www.intel.com/content/www/us/en/security-center/advisory/intel-sa-00898.html. Accessed 03 Aug 2024
3. Backes, M., Holz, T., Kollenda, B., Koppe, P., Nürnberger, S., Pewny, J.: You can run but you can't read: preventing disclosure exploits in executable code. In: ACM SIGSAC CCS (2014)
4. Bauer, M., Hetterich, L., Schwarz, M., Rossow, C.: Switchpoline: a software mitigation for Spectre-BTB and Spectre-BHB on ARMv8. In: AsiaCCS (2024)
5. Borrello, P., Kogler, A., Schwarzl, M., Lipp, M., Gruss, D., Schwarz, M.: ÆPIC leak: architecturally leaking uninitialized data from the microarchitecture. In: USENIX Security (2022)

6. Braden, K., Davi, L., Liebchen, C., Sadeghi, A.R., Crane, S., Franz, M., Larsen, P.: Leakage-resilient layout randomization for mobile devices. In: NDSS, vol. 16 (2016)
7. Brookes, S., Denz, R., Osterloh, M., Taylor, S.: Exoshim: preventing memory disclosure using execute-only kernel code. Int. J. Inf. Comput. Secur. (2022)
8. Canella, C., et al.: Fallout: leaking data on meltdown-resistant CPUs. In: CCS (2019)
9. Canella, C., et al.: A systematic evaluation of transient execution attacks and defenses. In: USENIX Security (2019)
10. Chakraborty, D., Schwarz, M., Bugiel, S.: TALUS: reinforcing TEE confidentiality with cryptographic coprocessors. In: FC (2023)
11. Chen, G., Chen, S., Xiao, Y., Zhang, Y., Lin, Z., Lai, T.H.: SgxPectre attacks: stealing intel secrets from SGX enclaves via speculative execution. In: EuroS&P (2019)
12. Crane, S., et al.: Readactor: practical code randomization resilient to memory disclosure. In: IEEE SP (2015)
13. Garmany, B., Müller, T.: Prime: private RSA infrastructure for memory-less encryption. In: ACSAC (2013). https://doi.org/10.1145/2523649.2523656
14. Gionta, J., Enck, W., Larsen, P.: Preventing kernel code-reuse attacks through disclosure resistant code diversification. In: IEEE CNS (2016)
15. Guan, L., Lin, J., Luo, B., Jing, J.: Copker: computing with private keys without ram. In: NDSS (2014)
16. Guan, L., Lin, J., Luo, B., Jing, J., Wang, J.: Protecting private keys against memory disclosure attacks using hardware transactional memory. In: S&P (2015)
17. Hedayati, M., et al.: Hodor: intra-process isolation for high-throughput data plane libraries. In: USENIX ATC (2019)
18. Intel: Intel 64 and IA-32 Architectures Software Developer's Manual Combined Volumes: 1, 2A, 2B, 2C, 2D, 3A, 3B, 3C, 3D and 4 (2024)
19. Jenkins, I.R., Anantharaman, P., Shapiro, R., Brady, J.P., Bratus, S., Smith, S.W.: Ghostbusting: mitigating spectre with intraprocess memory isolation. In: Proceedings of the 7th Symposium on Hot Topics in the Science of Security (2020)
20. Kocher, P., et al.: Spectre attacks: exploiting speculative execution. In: S&P (2019)
21. Kwon, D., Shin, J., Kim, G., Lee, B., Cho, Y., Paek, Y.: uXOM: efficient eXecute-only memory on ARM cortex-M. In: USENIX Security (2019)
22. Larabel, M., Tippett, M.: Phoronix test suite. Phoronix Media (2011). https://www.phoronix-test-suite.com/. Accessed 03 Aug 2024
23. Li, C., et al.: Mimosa: protecting private keys against memory disclosure attacks using hardware transactional memory. IEEE Trans. Dependable Secure Comput. (2021). https://doi.org/10.1109/TDSC.2019.2897666
24. Li, M., Zhang, Y., Lin, Z.: CrossLine: breaking "security-by-crash" based memory isolation in AMD SEV. In: SIGSAC (2021)
25. Lipp, M., et al.: Meltdown: reading kernel memory from user space. In: USENIX Security (2018)
26. Maisuradze, G., Rossow, C.: ret2spec: speculative execution using return stack buffers. In: CCS (2018)
27. Microsoft: Virtualization-based security (VBS) (2021). https://docs.microsoft.com/en-us/windows-hardware/design/device-experiences/oem-vbs
28. Moghimi, D.: Downfall: exploiting speculative data gathering. In: USENIX Security (2023)
29. Morbitzer, M., Huber, M., Horsch, J., Wessel, S.: Severed: subverting AMD's virtual machine encryption. In: EuroSec (2018)

30. Müller, T., Freiling, F.C., Dewald, A.: TRESOR runs encryption securely outside RAM. In: USENIX Security (2011)
31. Ormandy, T.: Zenbleed (2023). https://lock.cmpxchg8b.com/zenbleed.html
32. Osvik, D.A., Shamir, A., Tromer, E.: Cache attacks and countermeasures: the case of AES. In: CT-RSA (2006)
33. Patat, G., Sabt, M., Fouque, F.A.: Exploring widevine for fun and profit. In: 2022 IEEE Security and Privacy Workshops (SPW). IEEE (2022)
34. Pomonis, M., Petsios, T., Keromytis, A.D., Polychronakis, M., Kemerlis, V.P.: kR^X: comprehensive kernel protection against just-in-time code reuse. In: EuroSys (2017)
35. van Schaik, S., et al.: RIDL: rogue in-flight data load. In: S&P (2019)
36. Schink, M., Obermaier, J.: Taking a look into Execute-Only memory. In: USENIX WOOT (2019)
37. Schwarz, M., et al.: ZombieLoad: cross-privilege-boundary data sampling. In: CCS (2019)
38. Seaborn, M., Dullien, T.: Exploiting the dram rowhammer bug to gain kernel privileges. Black Hat (2015)
39. Shih, M.W., Lee, S., Kim, T., Peinado, M.: T-SGX: eradicating controlled-channel attacks against enclave programs. In: NDSS (2017)
40. Sparks, S., Butler, J.: Shadow walker: raising the bar for rootkit detection. Black Hat Japan (2005)
41. Torrey, J.: More shadow walker: TLB-splitting on modern x86. Blackhat USA (2014)
42. Trujillo, D., Wikner, J., Razavi, K.: Inception: exposing new attack surfaces with training in transient execution. In: USENIX Security (2023)
43. Tsai, C.C., Porter, D.E., Vij, M.: Graphene-SGX: a practical library OS for unmodified applications on SGX. In: 2017 USENIX Annual Technical Conference (USENIX ATC 2017) (2017)
44. Turner, P.: Retpoline: a software construct for preventing branch-target-injection (2018). https://support.google.com/faqs/answer/7625886
45. Vahldiek-Oberwagner, A., Elnikety, E., Duarte, N.O., Sammler, M., Druschel, P., Garg, D.: ERIM: secure, efficient in-process isolation with protection keys (MPK). In: USENIX Security (2019)
46. Van Bulck, J., et al.: Foreshadow: extracting the keys to the intel sgx kingdom with transient out-of-order execution. In: USENIX Security (2018)
47. Voulimeneas, A., Vinck, J., Mechelinck, R., Volckaert, S.: You shall not (by) pass! practical, secure, and fast PKU-based sandboxing. In: EuroSys (2022)
48. Weisse, O., et al.: Foreshadow-NG: Breaking the Virtual Memory Abstraction with Transient Out-of-Order Execution (2018)
49. Wikner, J., Razavi, K.: Retbleed: arbitrary speculative code execution with return instructions. In: USENIX Security (2022)
50. Yang, Y., Guan, Z., Liu, Z., Chen, Z.: Protecting elliptic curve cryptography against memory disclosure attacks. In: Hui, L.C.K., Qing, S.H., Shi, E., Yiu, S.M. (eds.) Information and Communications Security. Springer, Cham (2015)
51. Yang, Z., Bao, Z., Jin, C., Liu, Z., Zhou, J.: Plcrypto: a symmetric cryptographic library for programmable logic controllers. IACR Transactions on Symmetric Cryptology (2021)
52. Zhang, R., et al.: CacheWarp: software-based fault injection using selective state reset. In: USENIX Security (2024)

Leveraging Homomorphic Encryption for Maximal Extractable Value (MEV) Mitigation: Blind Arbitrage on Decentralised Exchanges

Jonathan Passerat-Palmbach[1,2](✉)

[1] Flashbots, London, UK
jonathan@flashbots.net
[2] Imperial College London, London, UK

Abstract. This paper presents a novel exploration of Fully Homomorphic Encryption (FHE) applied to the problem of Maximal Extractable Value (MEV) in blockchain transactions, explicitly focusing on arbitrage scenarios. Building upon previous work by Flashbots, we adapt their secret-sharing-based protocol to FHE to reduce data transmission overhead. We introduce a protocol that enables searchers to blindly backrun a user transaction, executing specific conditions and arithmetic operations on the transaction content using FHE. Our protocol leverages the TFHE scheme to handle the data extraction, constraint verification and arithmetic calculation on 128-bit unsigned integers representing the tokens stored on the UniswapV2 Decentralised Exchange (DEX). Despite significant runtime constraints, our work provides a solid foundation for future research, identifying key areas for improvement and expansion. This study represents a significant advancement in applying FHE to blockchain transactions, stimulating further collaboration within the FHE community to address open challenges and bring privacy-preserving protocols for MEV mitigation closer to real-world deployment.

Keywords: MEV · Arbitrage · Fully Homomorphic Encryption

1 Introduction

Blockchains function by creating blocks containing user-generated transactions, typically in a sequential order proposed by block producers. However, this order manipulation capability has spurred the emergence of Maximal Extractable Value (MEV) [8]. MEV entails extracting value beyond regular block rewards and transaction fees by controlling transaction sequencing. According to Flashbots' transparency dashboard[1], close to $750M worth of value has been extracted over the past year alone. Essentially a form of economic rent, MEV is usually

---
[1] https://transparency.flashbots.net/.

© International Financial Cryptography Association 2026
C. Garman and P. Moreno-Sanchez (Eds.): FC 2025, LNCS 15751, pp. 402–418, 2026.
https://doi.org/10.1007/978-3-032-07024-1_23

a value transfer from average to elaborate users. The incentives it creates span beyond poor user experience and lead to increased gas prices, transaction delays, fairness and security concerns, impeding the progress of new applications on the whole network [15].

The actors ultimately extracting MEV are block producers like miners or validators, courtesy of the blockchain's consensus mechanism. Tactics to extract MEV, include front-running (prioritising personal transactions), sandwich attacks (strategically positioning personal transactions around others), and order manipulation (re-arranging transactions for personal gain). Some MEV-related activities, like arbitrage (taking advantage of a price imbalance for the same asset across multiple markets) and liquidations (selling off collateral to cover outstanding loans when their value falls below a certain threshold), are viewed more positively as providing a service to the network in return for a profit [14].

Addressing MEV involves diverse approaches, from altering consensus mechanisms to developing user protection tools. Some approaches try to prevent all forms of MEV extraction by hiding the transaction data using traditional encryption until they have been included in a committed block [17,18]. This approach prevents advanced block building constructs and extraction strategies dependent on analysing the effects a pending (set of) transaction(s) will have on chain.

While consensus on a definitive solution remains elusive, in the rest of this work, we will focus on arbitrage as a form of MEV and try to facilitate such extraction under the condition that the user transaction creating the opportunity does not incur a financial penalty. Specifically, we examine MEV extraction scenarios called backrunning, where additional transactions are inserted after the user's original transaction, excluding front-running as a possibility.

1.1 Contributions

This paper proposes a novel approach leveraging Fully Homomorphic Encryption (FHE) to overcome these limitations. Using the tfhe-rs Rust library [19], which implements the TFHE (Torus Fully Homomorphic Encryption) [5] scheme, we present an alternative protocol targeting a specific Decentralised Exchange (DEX), UniswapV2 [1] Unlike other recent proposals[2] powered by the so-called fhEVM [6], which aim to provide private smart contract blockchains, our goal is not to offer long-term confidential storage but to enable off-chain interactions between users and MEV searchers while ensuring pre-trade privacy.

In the following sections, we present our method and results, demonstrating the feasibility of using FHE for MEV extraction while acknowledging significant performance overhead for practical deployment (Sect. 3). We then evaluate the protocol, highlighting its limitations and identifying key performance bottlenecks (Sect. 4). In response to these challenges, we propose three algorithmic modifications to improve the efficiency of encrypted computation (Sect. 5).

---

[2] https://www.fhenix.io, https://www.inco.org.

2 Background: Arbitrage on UniswapV2

Uniswap V2 [1] is the most commonly used decentralised exchange (DEX) on the Ethereum public blockchain. Its design is inspired by the Automated Market Maker (AMM) concept that maintains a constant k relation between the quantity of each of the two crypto-tokens in the reserve of a pool. Each pool represents a trading pair and has its k value. The pool is ruled by the equation $k = x*y$ which determines the price of each token with respect to the other. Users interact with these pools by swapping a certain amount of a first token A for the corresponding amount of paired token B based on the current price in the pool. Since each Ethereum transaction executes atomically, the price of each asset in the pool is immediately updated for all the other users once the swap completes; the on-chain state now reflects the new values for the token reserves.

The price quoted by the Uniswap v2 DEX is only valid for this specific pair on the DEX, and the same pair often trades at different prices on different exchanges. Traders can exploit this momentary price discrepancy by buying one token of the pair on a first exchange and selling the other back on a second exchange, pocketing the price difference as a profit. This manoeuvre is called arbitrage and is widely considered to positively affect end users since it rebalances prices across all exchanges. Arbitrage is a form of MEV that we want to enable as many traders as possible to participate in. The intuition behind this philosophy is that more arbitrageurs in the network will be more efficient at solving price differences across markets and thus provide an overall better experience to end users.

To exploit arbitrage opportunities successfully, arbitrageurs need guarantees that the price they have identified as an opportunity on an exchange will remain the same while they purchase the other asset in the pair to trigger the first hop in the simplified arbitrage scenario described above. The only way to obtain this guarantee on a DEX is to ensure the trader's transaction initiating the arbitrage is executed right after the user's which triggered the price change. Transactions are executed in the order in which they appear in a block. We denote the action of deliberately trying to insert one's transaction after another in the same block as backrunning. For simplicity in defining our encrypted backrunning protocol, we leave out the other case when a searcher can have price certainty: the top of the next block.

To summarise, this work proposes a solution for traders to blindly backrun a user transaction performing a token swap on the UniswapV2 DEX, without seeing its data in cleartext while still being able to execute certain conditions and arithmetic operations on the content of the transaction using FHE.

3 A Confidential Backrunning Protocol

Arbitrage through backrunning is a critical mechanism for exploiting price discrepancies across blockchain markets, yet competition in public mempools has driven up transaction fees and introduced risks for users. To address these issues, we propose a confidential backrunning protocol that enables secure arbitrage on encrypted transactions. This protocol protects users who create arbitrage opportunities by ensuring pre-trade privacy and mitigating the execution costs associated with backrunning.

In our design, users submit fully encrypted transactions into an FHE-enabled backrunning protocol. Searchers securely input constraints and parameters to guide their strategy, with encrypted outputs passed to a trusted block builder for decryption and blockchain insertion. Importantly, the protocol ensures that searchers cannot directly observe transaction details.

The searcher does not obtain any observable output from the computation: the resulting backrunning transaction contains either a profitable transaction or an invalid one that will be rejected by the block builder. This guarantees user privacy while enabling the searcher to execute a backrunning strategy blindly, in line with a set of predefined preferences.

3.1 Threat Model

The scenario we consider is represented in Fig. 1. There are three distinct parties: 1) a **User** who provides their transaction data but requires strong pre-trade privacy guarantees; 2) **Searcher** who aims to exploit an arbitrage opportunity by producing a bundle comprising the user's transaction immediately followed by a backrunning transaction that capitalises on the price discrepancy introduced by the user's operation. The searcher blindly applies a predefined algorithmic strategy to the encrypted data and has control over input parameters such as a minimum profit threshold; 3) a **Block Builder** who inserts the resulting bundle, along with other externally sourced transactions and bundles, into a candidate block without modifying its contents. The builder acts as a trusted entity, decrypting the resulting bundle securely.

This work focuses on interactions between the user and the searcher, while the block builder's role remains limited to decryption and block insertion. The trust assumption for the block builder ensures that they act as a passive participant, securely decrypting and handling the transactions without interfering in the backrunning process. The parties operate under the honest-but-curious security model, where the searcher follows the protocol but may attempt to extract additional information from intermediate states. In this setting, the searcher cannot directly observe the transaction details due to encryption but could manipulate their inputs or execute modified strategies to extract sensitive information. To mitigate such risks, zero-knowledge proofs (ZKPs) of well-formed ciphertexts could be employed to validate the correctness of the user's encrypted transaction, as demonstrated in prior literature [13]. Additionally, the correctness of the encrypted computation itself could be verified using emerging verifiable FHE techniques [3]. However, these methods introduce substantial overhead with the current state of the art, making them less practical for immediate deployment.

For this study, we assume the use of a secret key shared between the user and the block builder, a reasonable assumption given that Ethereum builders are increasingly operating within Trusted Execution Environments (TEEs), as

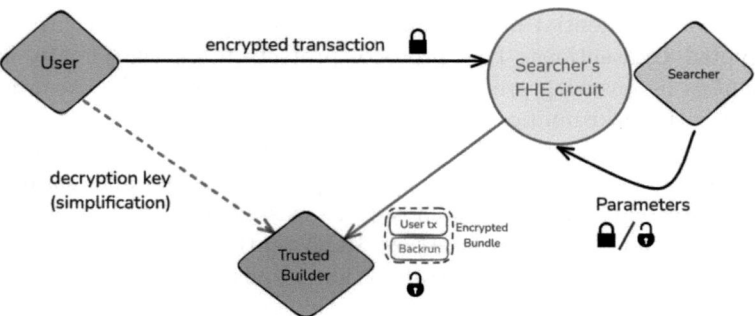

Fig. 1. High-level overview of the parties involved in the confidential backrunning protocol. The user encrypts their Ethereum transaction and propagates it to a searcher's infrastructure equipped with the FHE backrunning program. The searcher runs the FHE program on their preferences and the user's encrypted transaction to generate an encrypted backrunning transaction. Together with the user's encrypted transaction, this forms a bundle of encrypted transactions transferred to a trusted block builder for decryption and inclusion in a block. The current design assumes shared private keys, but future iterations could replace this with a public-key infrastructure managed via threshold decryption [7].

demonstrated by Flashbots' implementation of block building inside SGX [9,10]. Notably, our protocol introduces no additional requirements for the searcher, who runs the FHE computation without the need for a TEE. Both the user and the searcher can independently verify the block builder's use of a TEE through remote attestation before securely sharing their respective ciphertexts with the builder, maintaining trust without compromising decentralisation.

The cryptographic parameters provided by TFHE-rs ensure at least 128 bits of security, as verified by the Lattice Estimator[3]. The builder generates the secret key securely and shares it with the user over a remotely attested trusted channel before the protocol begins.

While this assumption simplifies implementation, it has limitations in real-world deployments. Specifically, it assumes a trusted channel for key sharing and does not account for scenarios involving multiple, potentially untrusted builders. Future iterations of the protocol aim to address these limitations by adopting a public-key cryptographic model. In particular, we propose transitioning to a threshold decryption setup, as outlined in [11], where a distributed network of parties collaboratively manages the private key. This approach enhances resilience against builder compromise and aligns with a permissionless deployment model.

---

[3] https://github.com/malb/lattice-estimator.

3.2 FHE Parsing of User Transactions

The FHE program begins by parsing the encrypted user transaction, serialized in Recursive-Length Prefix (RLP[4]) format. This process is critical because it ensures that the data matches specific acceptance criteria established by the searcher in their strategy. The searcher typically focuses on transactions involving particular token pools, with this focus being encoded in the search strategy's parameters.

During this initial phase, the protocol evaluates aspects such as gas price, gas limit, and token pool addresses, ensuring that transactions do not incur prohibitive execution costs for the searcher. The FHE-enabled logic systematically reads bytes from the input transaction, comparing them with the predefined values from the searcher program. An encrypted boolean, 'match', tracks whether all conditions are met. If any condition fails, 'match' is set to 'false', signaling that the transaction does not meet the searcher's criteria.

In the event of a failed condition, the protocol outputs an empty transaction (filled with zeroes). This approach accommodates FHE's limitations, notably the inability to handle branching logic directly.

3.3 Arithmetic Calculations for Profit Optimization

Once the transaction is validated, the next step involves calculating the optimal amount of tokens to buy for a profitable backrun. This calculation relies on the Uniswap V2 pricing formula, adapted to the FHE setting.

Uniswap V2 Pricing Function. In Uniswap V2, token prices are determined using a constant product formula. The price of a token is the ratio of reserves in the liquidity pool, adjusted for a 0.3% fee. For arbitrage, searchers aim to exploit price differences between decentralized exchanges like Uniswap and centralized exchanges such as Binance. To backrun a trade, the searcher needs to calculate the number of tokens to buy at the updated pool price, which is determined by the pending user transaction.

In our protocol, the searcher inputs three constants into the strategy: 'FEE' (the trading fee in Uniswap V2), 'PRICE' (the maximum price they are willing to pay for the asset), and 'PREC' (precision for on-chain calculations). The pool reserves, 'X' and 'Y', depend on the encrypted user transaction and are required to compute the updated price after the pending swap.

The optimal amount Eq. 1 used in this work and obtained from [16] is as follows:

$$\text{amount} = \frac{\sqrt{\text{PREC} \cdot X \cdot (\text{FEE}^2 \cdot \text{PREC} \cdot X + 4 \cdot \text{PRICE} \cdot Y \cdot (1 - \text{FEE}))} + \text{PREC} \cdot X \cdot (\text{FEE} - 2)}{2 \cdot \text{PREC} \cdot (1 - \text{FEE})} \quad (1)$$

---

[4] RLP is the format used to serialise Ethereum transactions - https://ethereum.org/en/developers/docs/data-structures-and-encoding/rlp/.

This equation calculates the optimal token amount for the searcher to purchase based on the new state of the pool's reserves 'X' and 'Y' after the user's transaction.

FHE Challenges: Square Roots and Divisions. The main technical challenge in applying this equation under FHE lies in two costly operations: division by a scalar and calculating the square root of an encrypted number. These operations are computational bottlenecks, particularly the square root calculation, which we approximate using the Newton-Raphson method, limiting precision to five iterations. Each iteration involves additional homomorphic divisions, significantly increasing computation time. In recent benchmarks using the tfhe-rs library[5], this square root approximation required approximately 20 s on an AWS *hpc7a.96xlarge* server equipped with an AMD EPYC 9R14 CPU running at 2.60 GHz, highlighting the performance costs of FHE in such scenarios.

3.4 Data Types and Precision Considerations

Uniswap V2 uses 112-bit unsigned integers to represent token reserves, while our FHE protocol handles these values as 128-bit unsigned integers to ensure compatibility with homomorphic encryption libraries like tfhe-rs. Moreover, the calculations use 256-bit integers internally to avoid overflow during encrypted multiplications and other operations. These larger data types help manage the inherent complexity of FHE while preserving numerical accuracy during the backrun.

To handle fractions (which are unsupported by the Ethereum Virtual Machine), Uniswap relies on a fixed-precision representation over 224-bit values equally split between integer and fractional parts. Our FHE implementation similarly adopts this strategy, using 256-bit unsigned integers to ensure safe computations across the backrun.

4 Evaluation of the Confidential Backrunning Solution

4.1 RLP Data Extraction

In this first set of experiments, we evaluate the performance of different configurations of a single backrun by focusing on the RLP data extraction part. We report performances of the encrypted workload where the strategy's constants are represented using 128-bit cleartext unsigned integers in the setting where the workload runs on the searcher's machine, as well as their homomorphic equivalent, to understand the possibility of running the protocol on a third party's machine.

Please note that we do not report the key generation and encryption steps separately in the results table as they are negligible (a few seconds) in light of the

---

[5] https://docs.zama.ai/tfhe-rs/0.6-3/get-started/benchmarks.

core workload's runtime. They could also take place as part of a preprocessing phase where users and searchers would encrypt once, and this already minimal time would be amortised over many executions.

All results reported in Table 1 were obtained using a 128-core Intel Xeon Platinum 8375C CPU running at 2.90 GHz with AVX2 instructions enabled.

Not surprisingly, the amount calculation phase dominates the RLP extraction by two orders of magnitude due to the series of homomorphic divisions it has to perform as part of Eq. 1 to approximate the square root using Newton's method. The present setting is particularly challenging since it is not trivial to initialise the square root approximation algorithm with a reasonable initial estimate without computing even more encrypted operations. Indeed, the square root entirely depends on the user transaction, which can significantly impact the new reserves' amounts in the equation. This performance discrepancy highlights the gap in computational efficiency that will need to be bridged to support any input data for protocols running in the EVM.

Table 1. Runtime comparison for different configurations of the confidential backrun protocol averaged over 5 runs. The first two rows depict the runtime and memory utilization during the RLP extraction phase, contrasting settings with searcher constants in cleartext (*Clear*) or encrypted. The third row showcases the runtime and memory consumption when enabling AVX512 instructions. The last two rows present the same breakdown for the amount calculation phase. Note: Key generation and encryption impacts are considered negligible compared to the reported metrics, and as such are included as part of the overall runtime.

Phase	Runtime (seconds)	Memory (kB)
RLP (Clear)	36.706 ($\pm$0.193)	331,992
RLP (Encrypted)	38.782 ($\pm$0.336)	334,000
RLP (Clear + AVX512)	31.787 ($\pm$0.921)	337,100
Amount	1024.928 ($\pm$0.925)	432,116
Amount (AVX512)	846.409 ($\pm$3.134)	462,146

4.2 SIMD Optimisation: AVX2 Vs AVX512

Another significant aspect of our analysis focused on the impact of SIMD (Single Instruction, Multiple Data) instruction sets on the execution speed of the FHE algorithm. The TFHE scheme relies on a fast bootstrapping operation implemented via external products that can be accelerated using Fast Fourier Transforms (FFTs).

Our investigation included the AVX2 and AVX512 instruction sets. Notably, the AVX512 instruction set demonstrated substantial performance improvements over the AVX2, providing a speed-up of approximately 20%. However, AVX512 instructions are less widely available in customer-grade CPUs and would require running the workload on high-end servers. This strong hardware requirement reinforces our flexible design goal of being able to run the protocol on the searcher's machine or a third party's.

4.3 Key and Ciphertexts Size

Fully Homomorphic Encryption (FHE), notably TFHE, faces ciphertext expansion, causing data transfers significantly larger than plaintext versions. However, the data payload of Ethereum transactions is relatively small, curbing transfer demands to the encrypted data payload only, compared to MPC requirements for the protocol itself, even under weaker security models. The server key currently consumes around 105 MB, while the ciphertexts for the transaction and strategy contain 47 MB and 20 MB of data, respectively.

5 Methodological Enhancements for FHE Performance

5.1 Reducing Security to 80 Bits

In the realm of fully homomorphic encryption (FHE), a fundamental trade-off exists between the level of security and the computational performance. Traditionally, the security parameter for FHE schemes has been set to 128 bits, providing robust protection against brute-force attacks and ensuring long-term security. However, some applications make for a compelling case to lower the security parameter to 80 bits or less when long-term confidentiality is not required.

This is typically the case in our current work, for which we can leverage the inherently public nature of Ethereum transactions. Once included in a block, transactions become part of the public ledger, and their contents are openly accessible to all parties. Consequently, the need for long-term confidentiality of the encrypted data diminishes, as the sensitive information will inevitably be revealed upon block inclusion.

As such, we experiment with the performance benefits of lower security parameters when encrypting user transactions for our confidential backrun protocol. Reducing the security parameter to 80 bits still provides substantial protection against brute-force attacks and remains more than enough in the context of short-term data confidentiality.

It is important to note that the reduction in security parameters does not compromise the integrity or correctness of the FHE scheme itself. While 80-bit encryption has been studied and can reuse existing publicly available parameter sets carefully chosen for tools such as Zama's Concrete [4], there is no guarantee we can venture lower down the security level and still guarantee correctness. Indeed, generated parameters need to balance security properties with the probability of correctly decrypting the result of a computation. This type of decryption error is completely silent and, as a result, would not be detected. In the context of the backrunning application, the searcher would miss potential opportunities without knowing whether this is due to his choice of parameters or an unfortunate decryption error that tampered with the result and changed the outcome of the computation. As such, we experiment with lower security settings while remaining overly conservative about the level of security we still guarantee.

Here, we select 80-bit security parameters from the publicly available set made available along with Concrete's open source code. Our algorithm uses the standard encoding of 2-bit precision to store the message and 2-bit precision for the carry. This leads us to select a set of parameters in the 4-bit precision table and a log2 of 2-norm = 3. Table 2 presents the new runtimes for the 80-bit security parameters. All other parameters remain identical to the original 128-bit parameter set.

Table 2. Runtime comparison for different configurations of the confidential backrun protocol using lower 80-bit security. The speed-up column is calculated as a ratio of the Cleartext 128-bit alternative.

Phase	Runtime (seconds)	Speed-up over 128-bit
RLP (Cleartext)	22.607 (±0.143)	1.62
RLP (Cleartext + AVX512)	19.277 (±0.098)	1.90
Amount	619.325 (±0.429)	1.65
Amount (AVX512)	504.351 (±10.25)	2.03

We observe a 62–65% speedup over the original settings for both phases of the algorithm. When coupled with the AVX512 instructions, the workload's runtime is about twice as fast as the original 128-bit setting. Considering the very short time our application needs to guarantee the confidentiality of its input data, we could lower the security level even further. However, this requires careful investigation to generate a correct set of parameters that will preserve the correctness of the encrypted calculation.

5.2 Circuit-Level Optimisation Through Levelled Operation Grouping

Another promising optimisation technique for enhancing the performance of FHE schemes is circuit-level optimisations, specifically the grouping of levelled operations. This approach aims to minimise unnecessary Programmable Bootstrapping (PBS) operations, which can significantly improve the overall computational efficiency of the FHE scheme.

The TFHE scheme [5] exposes two types of operations: levelled operations and operations implemented via Programmable Bootstrapping (PBS). Levelled operations, like additions of ciphertexts with scalars, are typically less computationally intensive and can be performed without bootstrapping. On the other hand, operations like multiplications or divisions require PBS to maintain the noise level within acceptable bounds and implement their functionality. This means that contrary to levelled operations, evaluating PBS-based operations will require performing a bootstrapping, which, while fast in TFHE relative to other schemes, remains a performance bottleneck at the application scope.

A second observation we need to make is that TFHE does not have native support for integers beyond 8 bits of precision. When it comes to handling non-natively supported big integers, one approach that TFHE offers is to decompose a large integer using a radix representation in blocks of the same size, each containing an LWE ciphertext encoding a plaintext of low precision (usually 4 bits) [4]. This plaintext space is further split into bits for the actual message and bits available to store carries resulting from arithmetic operations. These carries need to be propagated from one block to the next to ensure the correctness of arithmetic operations under the radix representation for large integers. TFHE propagates carries through PBS calls, one to extract the message and a second for the carry itself, resulting in fresh LWE ciphertexts where needed in the chain of radix blocks. Depending on the arithmetic operations performed, carries may or may not need to be propagated. Thus, optimally handling when carry should be propagated can be a source of performance gain, avoiding superfluous calls to the costly PBS operation.

On top of the complex management of carries, an algorithm's logic might naturally present intertwined levelled operations and operations that can only be done via PBS, such as encrypted comparisons. PBS-based operations expect carries to be cleaned before running; hence, a ciphertext might still be able to support further levelled arithmetic computation but will see unnecessary PBS invocations to support a comparison.

The security parameters discussed in the previous section also control the number of levelled operations that can be performed without the need for bootstrapping or propagating carries through radix blocks. By strategically grouping levelled operations together, we can reduce the number of PBS operations required, thereby improving the overall performance of the FHE scheme. By lowering the number of PBS invocations that would otherwise be induced by unnecessary carry cleansing, we are effectively trading code readability for performance.

Figure 2 shows the example of a function extracted from the protocol's RLP decoding phase. The function `right_shift_equal_block` will be called multiple times in a row with different input parameters. By doing so, the subtraction on the last line will be followed by a PBS call corresponding to the first line of the function's next call in the actual FHE circuit. This process will break the series of levelled operations and force two extra PBS calls to propagate the carries through the radix blocks.

```
1  fn right_shift_equal_block(in_tx_cipher, ...) {
2     let shifted: FheUint =
3        in_tx_cipher >> right_shift_const;
4     let eq = shifted.eq(eq_const);
5     let enc_is_match = in_match_ctxt & eq;
6     let rse: FheUint = in_tx_cipher - sub_const;
7     (res, enc_is_match)
8  }
```

Fig. 2. Example of intertwined levelled and PBS-based operations.

However, carefully observing the code snippet in Fig. 2 reveals a pattern that allows rewriting the same function differently. The subtraction is independent of the other operations and, as such, does not need to be computed right after the PBS-based operations. Our solution consists of collecting the input parameters for all the different operations in each call to the function before processing them out of order after the final instance of this repeated pattern. Thanks to this approach, we can compute all the subtractions back to back, thus minimising the number of PBS calls across the sequence of calls to the `right_shift_equal_block` function without changing its result.

The process of grouping levelled operations can be perceived as a circuit- or graph-level optimisation, where the algorithm is represented as a computational graph, and levelled operations are strategically merged together to minimise the number of PBS operations required. This optimisation technique requires a deep understanding of the underlying FHE scheme and its internals, such as the radix representation and carry propagation mechanisms.

By minimising the number of PBS operations, the overall execution time of the FHE computation can be significantly reduced. In our backrun context, this approach is particularly efficient in the RLP decoding phase of the algorithm, where subtractions often follow comparisons as part of the program's logic. However, these operations do not need to be computed in this order and can be re-arranged to benefit from this optimisation technique. Our experiments confirmed that we process 8 fewer PBS calls in the deferred execution version over 4 consecutive calls to the `right_shift_equal_block` function, saving 2 * 4 superfluous carry propagation steps.

It is important to note that this optimisation technique is generic and can be applied to a wide range of FHE-enabled applications. Furthermore, while it requires a deep understanding of the underlying FHE scheme, better tooling and compiler-level support could automate this optimisation process. With proper tooling, graph-level optimisation through levelled operation grouping could be systematically applied without requiring developer intervention at the code level.

5.3 Efficient Amount Calculations Using Uniswap V3 Arithmetic

In this section, we present a method for calculating the output amount of a Uniswap V2 trade using the arithmetic principles of Uniswap V3. Our approach centers on the key observation that Uniswap V3's internal state is built around the square root of the product of reserves and price. This representation leads to a more computationally efficient arithmetic model, which eliminates the need for costly square root approximations. This feature is even more prevalent when speeding up calculations in cryptographic environments, since we have previously identified the square root approximation function as the bottleneck of the V2 pool simulation method in the FHE context.

Uniswap v3 was initially designed to optimize liquidity deployment through concentrated liquidity, where liquidity providers (LPs) selectively contribute to price ranges, maximizing capital efficiency. Each of these virtual liquidity pools within Uniswap v3 behaves similarly to a standard Uniswap v2 pool, meaning we can apply the same arithmetics to a v2 pool if we construct an initial state consistent with v3 expectations.

Unlike Uniswap v2, Uniswap v3 does not directly store the reserves (x and y) of the two trading assets. Instead, it stores the square root of the product of reserves ($\sqrt{x \cdot y}$), known as the liquidity, and the square root of the current price. The key innovation here is that once a v3 pool is initialized with the square root of the current price, subsequent price updates can be performed using only integer multiplications and divisions. This approach avoids recalculating the square root—previously a performance bottleneck in FHE contexts—thus improving both the speed and accuracy of our trade simulations.

Additionally, the liquidity parameter remains constant for any given price-range in a V3 pool, hence for a whole V2 pool. We can pre-calculate this value from public blockchain data and inject it as a constant in price calculations. This results in lighter computational requirements: for price updates following a swap, we require one encrypted multiplication, one scalar multiplication, and one encrypted division; for the searcher to obtain the input amount to bid to receive the maximum number of tokens at a target price, one scalar multiplication, one encrypted multiplication, and one encrypted division; and for the corresponding output amount, just one scalar multiplication with an optional division.

The searcher in our system can specify the next target price and provide the pool's liquidity, reducing the FHE circuit's input size and complexity. Notably, unlike Uniswap v2 simulations that require computing the user's exact trade output, in this protocol only the updated price matters, so the searcher does not need to compute the exact amount of assets received by the user. This optimization fits naturally within the RLP decoding phase of our framework, allowing the searcher to only specify liquidity values for the targeted pools, thus minimizing the input data required by the FHE algorithm.

The impact of the new calculation method's performance is presented in Table 3, which demonstrates a drastic reduction in the number of operations required to simulate the user's transaction and calculate the optimal price and amount for the searcher. To provide a clearer picture of where these improvements originate, we chose to present the breakdown of operations individually along with their respective runtime costs for 128-bit and 256-bit unsigned integers. This breakdown allows us to isolate and emphasize the specific reductions in computational overhead that would have been harder to observe at the whole application level. Profiling a complex FHE library like tfhe-rs is challenging, as its execution engine is highly optimized and involves intricate processing pipelines, making it difficult to extract fine-grained operation-level details from typical profiling tools.

By categorizing the operations and presenting them separately, we can more effectively highlight the improvements achieved through the use of UniswapV3-style arithmetics—most notably, the elimination of the square root approximation, which was a major bottleneck in the UniswapV2-based approach, and results in a nearly 12X overhead decrease in the new version.

Table 3. Detailed comparison of the arithmetic operations performed in the two versions of our FHE backrunning program: one using UniswapV2's traditional reserve-based pricing function and the other employing UniswapV3-style arithmetic, which updates the square root of the price in a virtual pool. The operations are classified into four types: Ciphertext-scalar multiplication, Ciphertext-scalar division, Ciphertext-ciphertext multiplication, and Ciphertext-ciphertext division. Each operation is evaluated for both 128-bit and 256-bit unsigned integer variants. The total runtime for each type is calculated using Zama's per-operation benchmarks from the tfhe-rs v0.6.3 library. The results illustrate significant differences in computational overhead, demonstrating that UniswapV3's arithmetic reduces the cost of encrypted computations by nearly 12X, primarily due to the elimination of the square root approximation.

		128-bit unsigned integers				256-bit unsigned integers			
		Scalar Multiplication	Ciphertext Multiplication	Scalar Division	Ciphertext Division	Ciphertext Multiplication	Ciphertext Division	Total	Total
UniV2	Number of Operations	6	1	2	2	2	9	22	22
	Contribution To Runtime	2.226	0.961	1.498	41.2	6.4	484.2	536.485	536.485
UniV3	Number of Operations	3	2	1	2	0	0	8	8
	Contribution To Runtime	1.113	1.922	0.749	41.2	0	0	44.984	44.984

5.4 Performance and Comparison with the MPC Version

The backrunning protocol based on Multi-Party Computation (MPC), as proposed in [16], demonstrates significant computational and communication overheads that limit its practicality. Under the most stringent MPC security model (MASCOT protocol [12]), the protocol requires approximately 22.5 h of computation and 33.7 PB of data transfer spread over 9.6 million communication rounds for a single transaction. In the semi-honest security model [2], the runtime is reduced to 4 min, but still requires an overwhelming 6 GB of data transfer over 3.5 million communication rounds.

While the MPC version demonstrates the feasibility of confidential MEV extraction, its extreme communication demands make it impractical, especially in high-frequency scenarios. These limitations are even more problematic in the context of high-frequency MEV extraction scenarios, where reduction of communication costs will be sought via co-location at the expense of geographic decentralisation. It is also important to view the MPC protocol as a proof of concept and not a definitive representation of MPC performance in all MEV contexts.

In comparison, our FHE-based protocol eliminates the need for communication rounds during the encrypted computation phase, significantly reducing network dependence. This architectural advantage not only addresses bandwidth constraints but also avoids incentives for co-location, preserving the level of decentralisation of the unencrypted protocol. However, the computational overhead introduced by homomorphic operations remains a significant challenge that will be a focus for future work.

Our FHE protocol operates under a semi-honest model, and its most optimised configuration (leveraging UniswapV3-style arithmetic, 80-bit security, and a 128-core server) produces a backrunning transaction in 5.59 min. The associated data transfers include 47 MB for the encrypted user transaction, 20 MB for the searcher's strategy, and another 47 MB for the resulting encrypted backrun transaction, totalling approximately 114 MB.

This comparison highlights the trade-offs: while the FHE protocol achieves a substantial reduction of 53X in communication requirements and aligns better with real-world deployment constraints as this exchange happens over a single round of communications.

6 Conclusion

In this work, we have explored the application of Fully Homomorphic Encryption (FHE) to the problem of Maximal Extractable Value (MEV) in blockchain transactions. We have focused on the specific case of arbitrage, where a transaction swapping two tokens on a given market can create a price discrepancy in another market. Our approach builds upon previous work by Flashbots, adapting their secret-sharing-based protocol with FHE to reduce the overhead in data transmission.

We have presented a protocol that allows traders to blindly backrun a user transaction, executing certain conditions and arithmetic operations on the content of the transaction using FHE to mimic what is known as searcher's strategy. This protocol uses the tfhe-rs Rust library and targets the UniswapV2 Decentralised Exchange (DEX).

We introduced three improvements to accelerate the performance of our FHE algorithm. Combining the reduced security parameter approach discussed in the previous section with circuit-level optimisation through levelled operation grouping can achieve significant performance gains in FHE schemes. These optimisations are generic to any FHE program and can be adopted in addition to the new mode of calculation inspired from Uniswap V3.

Our evaluation has shown that while the protocol is feasible, it faces significant runtime constraints. We have identified several areas for future research, including handling multiple input transactions, overcoming ECDSA signature challenges, and extending the protocol to other forms of MEV and other DEXs.

In conclusion, this work represents a significant step forward in applying FHE to blockchain transactions. While many challenges remain, our work provides a solid foundation for future research at the interface of MEV and encrypted computing. Our findings will stimulate further collaboration within the FHE community to address the open challenges and bring privacy-preserving protocols for MEV mitigation closer to real-world deployment.

References

1. Adams, H., Zinsmeister, N., Robinson, D.: Uniswap V2 core. Technical report, March 2020
2. Araki, T., Furukawa, J., Lindell, Y., Nof, A., Ohara, K.: High-throughput semi-honest secure three-party computation with an honest majority. In: Proceedings of the 2016 ACM SIGSAC Conference on Computer and Communications Security, CCS 2016, pp. 805–817. Association for Computing Machinery, New York, NY, USA (2016). https://doi.org/10.1145/2976749.2978331
3. Aranha, D.F., Costache, A., Guimarães, A., Soria-Vazquez, E.: HELIOPOLIS: verifiable computation over homomorphically encrypted data from interactive oracle proofs is practical. In: Chung K.M., Sasaki, Y. (eds.) Advances in Cryptology – ASIACRYPT 2024. LNCS, vol. 15488, pp. 302–334. Springer, Singapore (2025). https://doi.org/10.1007/978-981-96-0935-2_10
4. Bergerat, L., et al.: Parameter optimization and larger precision for (T)FHE. J. Cryptol. **36**(3), 28 (2023)
5. Chillotti, I., Gama, N., Georgieva, M., Izabachène, M.: TFHE: fast fully homomorphic encryption over the torus. J. Cryptol. **33**(1), 34–91 (2020)
6. Dahl, M., et al.: Confidential EVM smart contracts using fully homomorphic encryption. Technical report, Zama (2023)
7. Dahl, M., et al.: Noah's ark: efficient threshold-FHE using noise flooding. In: Proceedings of the 11th Workshop on Encrypted Computing & Applied Homomorphic Cryptography, pp. 35–46. ACM, Copenhagen, Denmark, November 2023. https://doi.org/10.1145/3605759.3625259
8. Daian, P., et al.: Flash boys 2.0: frontrunning in decentralized exchanges, miner extractable value, and consensus instability. In: 2020 IEEE Symposium on Security and Privacy (SP), pp. 910–927. IEEE (2020)
9. Flashbots: Introducing BuilderNet (2024). https://buildernet.org/blog/introducing-buildernet
10. Hager, C., Paape, F.: Block building inside SGX (2023). https://writings.flashbots.net/block-building-inside-sgx
11. Joye, M.: TFHE public-key encryption revisited. Cryptology ePrint Archive, Paper 2023/603 (2023). https://eprint.iacr.org/2023/603

12. Keller, M., Orsini, E., Scholl, P.: MASCOT: faster malicious arithmetic secure computation with oblivious transfer. In: Proceedings of the 2016 ACM SIGSAC Conference on Computer and Communications Security, CCS 2016, pp. 830–842. Association for Computing Machinery, New York, NY, USA (2016). https://doi.org/10.1145/2976749.2978357
13. Libert, B.: Vector commitments with proofs of smallness: short range proofs and more (2023/800) (2023). https://eprint.iacr.org/2023/800
14. McLaughlin, R., Kruegel, C., Vigna, G.: A large scale study of the Ethereum arbitrage ecosystem. In: Proceedings of the 32nd USENIX Conference on Security Symposium, SEC 2023. USENIX Association (2023)
15. Qin, K., Zhou, L., Gervais, A.: Quantifying blockchain extractable value: how dark is the forest? In: 2022 IEEE Symposium on Security and Privacy (SP), pp. 198–214 (2022). https://doi.org/10.1109/SP46214.2022.9833734
16. Annessi, R.: Backrunning private transactions using multi-party computation (2023). https://writings.flashbots.net/backrunning-private-txs-MPC
17. Rondelet, A., Kilbourn, Q.: Mempool privacy: an economic perspective (2023)
18. Shutter: Introducing shutter network - Combating front running and malicious MEV using threshold cryptography (2021). https://blog.shutter.network
19. Zama: TFHE-RS: a pure rust implementation of the TFHE scheme for Boolean and integer arithmetics over encrypted data (2022)

Author Index

A
Abraham, Ittai 327
Adams, Austin 93
AravindaKrishnan Thyagarajan, Sri 249
Aumayr, Lukas 73
Avarikioti, Zeta 73

B
Bonneau, Joseph 197

C
C. Moallemi, Ciamac 56
Campanelli, Matteo 219
Chiang, James Hsin-Yu 126
Choi, Youngjin 367
Chung, Hao 249
Cohney, Shaanan 197
Collins, Daniel 345
Crapis, Davide 56

D
Damgård, Ivan 126
Dao, Quang 163
Duan, Sisi 345

F
Fabiański, Grzegorz 3
Fisch, Ben 180

G
Garay, Juan 233
Gerlach, Lukas 385
Gong, Tiantian 109

H
H. Deng, Robert 39
Hall-Andersen, Mathias 219
Hishon-Rezaizadeh, Ismael 144
Hong, Deokhwa 367
Hornetz, Tristan 385

K
Kamp, Simon Holmgaard 219
Kate, Aniket 109
Kim, Young-Sik 367
Kniep, Quentin 287
Kokoris-Kogias, Eleftherios 307
Kokoris-Kogias, Lefteris 287
Kwan, Carl 163

L
Lai, Junzuo 39
Lazzaretti, Arthur 144
Lee, Yongwoo 367
Li, Ming 39
Li, Yingjiu 39
Li, Yuxian 39
Litos, Orfeas Stefanos Thyfronitis 3
Liu, Zeyu 109
Livshits, Benjamin 180
Loss, Julian 345
Lu, Yun 233

M
Masserova, Elisaweta 249
Moallemi, Ciamac C. 93

N
Nayak, Kartik 327
Neiheiser, Ray 307

O
Orlandi, Claudio 126

P
Pancholi, Mahak 126
Papamanthou, Charalampos 144, 345
Passerat-Palmbach, Jonathan 402
Penna, Paolo 267
Prat, Julien 233

R
Reynolds, Sara 93
Robinson, Dan 93

S
S. M. Chow, Sherman 21
Salem, Iosif 73
Schmid, Stefan 73
Schneider, Manvir 267
Schwarz, Michael 385
Shi, Elaine 249
Shrestha, Nibesh 327
Simkin, Mark 126
Sonnino, Alberto 287
Stefański, Rafał 3

T
Tang, Shuyang 21
Testa, Brady 233

Thaler, Justin 163
Tsimos, Giorgos 345

W
Wang, Faxing 197
Wang, Haochen 345
Wang, Shouqiao 56
Wang, Wenhao 180
Weng, Jian 39
Weng, Jiasi 39

Y
Yaish, Aviv 180
Yeo, Michelle 73

Z
Zablotchi, Igor 287
Zhang, Fan 180
Zhang, Nuda 287
Zhou, Lulu 180
Zikas, Vassilis 233

MIX
Papier aus verantwortungsvollen Quellen
Paper from responsible sources
FSC® C105338

If you have any concerns about our products,
you can contact us on
ProductSafety@springernature.com

In case Publisher is established outside the EU,
the EU authorized representative is:
**Springer Nature Customer Service Center GmbH
Europaplatz 3, 69115 Heidelberg, Germany**

Printed by Libri Plureos GmbH
in Hamburg, Germany